Gulliver's Travels and Other Writings

SELECTED NEW RIVERSIDE EDITIONS

Series Editor for the British Volumes
Alan Richardson

Sense and Sensibility, Jane Austen
Edited by Beth Lau

Wuthering Heights, Emily Brontë
Edited by Diane Long Hoeveler

Fictions of Empire: Heart of Darkness, Joseph Conrad;
The Man Who Would Be King, Rudyard Kipling; and
The Beach of Falesá, Robert Louis Stevenson
Edited by John Kucich

Two Irish National Tales: Castle Rackrent, Maria Edgeworth, and
The Wild Irish Girl, Sydney Owenson (Lady Morgan)
Edited by James M. Smith

The Mill on the Floss, George Eliot
Edited by Nancy Henry

Early Black British Writing, Olaudah Equiano, Mary Prince and Others
Edited by Alan Richardson and Debbie Lee

Making Humans: Frankenstein, Mary Shelley, and
The Island of Doctor Moreau, H. G. Wells
Edited by Judith Wilt

Three Oriental Tales: History of Nourjahad, Frances Sheridan;
Vathek, William Beckford; and *The Giaour,* Lord Byron
Edited by Alan Richardson

Three Vampire Tales: Dracula, Bram Stoker;
Carmilla, Sheridan Le Fanu; and *The Vampyre,* John Polidori
Edited by Anne Williams

Gulliver's Travels and Other Writings, Jonathan Swift
Edited by Clement Hawes

The Picture of Dorian Gray, Oscar Wilde
Edited by Richard Kaye

Romantic Natural Histories, William Wordsworth,
Charles Darwin and Others
Edited by Ashton Nichols

For a complete listing of our American and British New Riverside Editions, visit our website at **http://college.hmco.com.**

NEW RIVERSIDE EDITIONS
Series Editor for the British Volumes
Alan Richardson, Boston College

JONATHAN SWIFT

Gulliver's Travels and Other Writings

Complete Text with Introduction
Historical Context • Critical Essays

Edited by

Clement Hawes
PENN STATE UNIVERSITY

With "A Note on the Texts" by Robert J. Griffin

Houghton Mifflin Company
BOSTON • NEW YORK

Sponsoring Editor: Michael Gillespie
Associate Editor: Bruce Cantley
Editorial Assistant: Lisa Minter
Associate Project Editor: Lindsay Frost
Editorial Assistant: Teresa Huang
Production/Design Assistant: Bethany Schlegel
Manufacturing Manager: Florence Cadran
Marketing Manager: Cindy Graff Cohen
Marketing Assistant: Sarah Donelson

Cover image: Shipwreck in a Lagoon at Bora-Bora Island © The Purcell Team/CORBIS.

Credits appear on page 550, which is a continuation of the copyright page.

Printed in the U.S.A.

Library of Congress Control Number:
ISBN: 0-618-08491-6
3 4 5 6 7 8 9-MV-10 09 08 07

CONTENTS

ABOUT THIS SERIES

Alan Richardson

The Riverside imprint, stamped on a book's spine or printed on its title page, carries a special aura for anyone who loves and values books. As well it might: by the middle of the nineteenth century, Houghton Mifflin had already established the Riverside Edition as an important presence in American publishing. The Riverside series of British poets brought trustworthy editions of Milton and Wordsworth, Spenser and Pope, and (then) lesser-known writers like Herbert, Vaughan, and Keats to a growing nation of readers. There was both a Riverside Shakespeare and a Riverside Chaucer by the century's end, titles that would be revived and recreated as the authoritative editions of the late twentieth century. Riverside Editions of writers like Emerson, Hawthorne, Longfellow, and Thoreau helped establish the first canon of American literature. Early in the twentieth century, the Cambridge editions published by Houghton Mifflin at the Riverside Press made the complete works of dozens of British and American poets widely available in single-volume editions that can still be found in libraries and homes throughout the United States and beyond.

The Riverside Editions of the 1950s and 1960s brought attractive, affordable, and carefully edited versions of a range of British and American titles into the thriving new market for serious paperback literature. Prepared by leading scholars and critics of the time, the Riversides rapidly became known for their lively introductions, reliable texts, and lucid annotation. Though aimed primarily at the college market, the series was also created (as one editor put) with the "general reader's private library" in mind. These were paperbacks to hold onto and read again, and many a "private" library was seeded with the colorful spines of Riverside Editions kept long after graduation.

Houghton Mifflin's New Riverside Editions now bring the combination of high editorial values and wide popular appeal long associated with the Riverside imprint into line with the changing needs and desires of twenty-first-century students and general readers. Inaugurated in 2000 with the first set of American titles under the general editorship of Paul Lauter, the New Riversides reflect both the changing canons of literature in English and the greater emphases on historical and cultural context that have helped a new generation of critics to extend and reenliven literary studies. The series not only is concerned with keeping the classic works of British and American literature alive, but also grows out of the excitement that a broader range of literary texts and cultural reference points has brought to the classroom. Works by formerly marginalized authors, including women writers and writers of color, will find a place in the series along with titles from the traditional canons that a succession of Riverside imprints helped establish beginning a century and a half ago. New Riverside titles will reflect the recent surge of interest in the connections among literary activity, historical change, and social and political issues, including slavery, abolition, and the construction of "race"; gender relations and the history of sexuality; the rise of the British Empire and of nationalism on both sides of the Atlantic; and changing conceptions of nature and of human beings.

The New Riverside Editions respond to recent changes in literary studies not only in the range of titles but also in the design of individual volumes. Issues and debates crucial to a book's author and original audience find voice in selections from contemporary writings of many kinds as well as in early reactions and reviews. Some volumes will place contemporary writers into dialogue, as with the pairing of Irish national tales by Maria Edgeworth and Sydney Owenson or of vampire stories by Bram Stoker and Sheridan Le Fanu. Other volumes provide alternative ways of constructing literary tradition, juxtaposing Mary Shelley's *Frankenstein* with H. G. Wells's *Island of Dr. Moreau,* or Byron's *The Giaour,* an "Eastern Tale" in verse, with Frances Sheridan's *Nourjahad* and William Beckford's *Vathek,* its most important predecessors in Orientalist prose fiction. Chronologies, selections from major criticism, notes on textual history, and bibliographies will allow readers to go beyond the text and explore a given writer or issue in greater depth. Seasoned critics will find fresh new contexts and juxtapositions, and general readers will find intriguing new material to read alongside familiar titles in an attractive format.

Houghton Mifflin's New Riverside Editions maintain the values of reliability and readability that have marked the Riverside name for well over a century. Each volume also provides something new—often unexpected—and each in a distinctive way. Freed from the predictable monotony and rigidity of a set template, editors can build their volumes around the special opportunities presented by a given title or set of related works. We hope that the resulting blend of innovative scholarship, creative format, and high production values will help the Riverside imprint continue to thrive well into the new century.

Gulliver's Travels and Other Writings

GULLIVER'S TRAVELS: COLONIAL MODERNITY SATIRIZED

Clement Hawes

> *. . . a crew of pirates are driven by a storm they know not whither, at length a boy discovers land from the topmast, they go on shore to rob and plunder, they see an harmless people, are entertained with kindness, they give the country a new name, they take formal possession of it for the king, they set up a rotten plank or a stone for a memorial, they murder two or three dozen of the natives, bring away a couple more by force for a sample, return home, and get their pardon. Here commences a new dominion acquired with a title by* divine right. *Ships are sent with the first opportunity, the natives driven out or destroyed, their princes tortured to discover their gold, a free license given to all acts of inhumanity and lust, the earth reeking with the blood of its inhabitants: and this execrable crew of butchers employed in so pious an expedition, is a modern colony sent to convert and civilize an idolatrous and barbarous people.*
>
> — Gulliver's Travels, *p. 278*

The chief vocation of a satirist—to expose the outlandishness of home—necessitates a form of mental traveling. No better literary device than a travel narrative could be found to ring every possible change on our greatest satirist's greatest theme: detachment from the familiar. Critical and imaginative distance begins with attempts to think otherwise. Actual geographical circulation often opens up for comparisons, sometimes shocking, the variety of human social systems: legal, political, linguistic, cultural. Real travel, by the same token, can reveal startling zones of inequality within the same political system. Merely by crossing the Irish Channel, the Anglo-Irishman Jonathan Swift felt that he became a "slave," that is, a person denied any form of political representation (Kelly, 1976, 848). Indeed, in 1723 he claimed in a letter to John Gay to dislike even hearing news from Britain because such tidings only made his habitual condition of "scurvy sleep" harder to maintain (McLoughlin, 1999, pp. 80–81). Satire often involves a degree of discomfort in just this sense: the disruption of a habitual sleepwalking. Celebrated for his "savage indignation," Swift is the most brilliantly acid satirist around—an ironist capable of mocking even the absurdity and impotence of his own reformist rage. Among the many familiar things that *Gulliver's Travels* renders strange, few have a wider resonance than the process described in the epigraph above: the colonial making of modernity.

We know Swift as a shocking writer, an unflinching elaborator of black humor. Swift has attracted some very high-caliber commentary that circles around his capacity to think the "unthinkable." Unmistakably "Swiftian" topics include dung-hurling yahoos and boiled infants. Satire at its best, as in the case of Swift's rude awakenings, is inspired by historical particulars. We can see this in Swift's signature theme of flaying: the removal of human flesh from a cadaver, as was newly visible in the anatomy theaters popularized by eighteenth-century surgical research. The narrator of Swift's *A Tale of a Tub* (1704) remarks, in his chatty way, that "Last week I saw a Woman *flay'd,* and you will hardly believe how it altered her Person for the worse" (p. 173). Few scenes in all of literature, moreover, can match the nonchalant terror involved in the building of Gulliver's next-to-last nautical vessel: a canoe that he coolly fashions from the hide and tallow of his fellow yahoos (p. 266–67). Human anatomical dissections were an emblematic aspect of the Enlightenment's modern ambience, and Gulliver, after all, is a trained physician. Swift's grotesque elaborations on this emerging medical practice illustrate a great deal about the ambivalent significance of the eighteenth-century moment for understanding his satire.

Yet the uncountable number of editions and translations of *Gulliver's Travels* also confirms a different case: the shuddering laughs that Swift provokes are universal. His satirical jests are, to be precise, both universal and historically embedded, for the satire in *Gulliver's Travels* has resounded around the globe in part because of the way it speaks to a specific, and oppressive, development in global history. *Gulliver's Travels* satirizes a specifically "modern" mode of power that would eventually engulf—in ways no more thinkable than flaying—most of the world. Swift's satire, registering the deepest conflicts of a moment just beginning to preen itself as "modern," achieves universality precisely *through* its historical topicality. *Gulliver's Travels* satirizes the vices of arrogance, greed, lying, sycophancy, and cruelty by way of their particular expression in an emerging technical and scientific enterprise that "anatomized" human populations on an entirely new scale. The real bite of *Gulliver's Travels* lies in its satirical engagement with the intensifying sophistication and scale of this colonial project: an escalation manifest in the various forms of technical expertise that enabled, for example, routine circumnavigations of the globe. As a satire of the eighteenth-century project of modernity—a project that *Gulliver's Travels* reveals to be colonial at its core—Swift's satire is best understood both as rooted in its eighteenth-century moment and as universally resonant. The chief aim of *Gulliver's Travels and Other Writings* is to mediate between the eighteenth-century particulars of Swift's existence—his "Irish landscape" (Fabricant)—and the larger resonance of his literary achievement.

The grotesque modernity predicted by the adventures of Lemuel Gulliver has, quite simply, come to pass. We inhabit the aftermath of a harsh process by which one continent aggrandized itself at the expense of all others. Great Britain emerged, after its eighteenth-century duel with France, as the leader of this pack of European powers. The conflict between Britain and Ireland provides the slant by which Swift engages with the colonial genealogy of global modernity. Many of the topical references in *Gulliver's Travels,* as sketched out in the footnotes to this edition, question the legitimacy of a commercial modernity exposed as aggressively expansionist. My annotations to these allusions negotiate between specific references (which Swift's contemporaries often recognized) and their general resonance (which Swift, writing for posterity as well, certainly intended). This Irish–British conflict, however topical, has a universal resonance precisely because the core of the modernity we continue to inhabit is colonial. Swift's satire on modernity belongs to world literature in part because of the violence with which the entire world has subsequently been—unevenly and incompletely—modernized. *Gulliver's Travels* offers a rival account of "modern progress" that challenges its claims to universal beneficence, highlights its colonial violence, and subverts its legitimacy with allegations of lying and criminality. We ought not to be surprised to find Mohandas K. Gandhi—the leader of an anticolonial struggle that set the stage for decolonization around the world—praising Swift's satire almost two centuries after its publication. Writing from South Africa in 1911, Gandhi, himself an ardent critic of modernity, describes the *Travels* as containing "so effective a condemnation, in an ironic vein, of modern civilization that the book deserves to be read again and again" (Gandhi, vol. 11, letter 63, 77).

Gulliver's Travels and Other Writings seeks to illuminate Swift's famous masterwork as a satire of just such a colonial modernity. Swift's responses, in pamphlets, poems, and personal letters, to Ireland's colonial conflict with Britain are included here to situate *Gulliver's Travels* in this broader context. Swift's decision "to dignify Irish politics," in the words of Irvin Ehrenpreis (vol. 3, p. 5), belongs to a way of seeing—a testing of humanity—that also informs *Gulliver's Travels. Gulliver's Travels and Other Writings* proceeds from the assumption that the colonial antagonisms in Ireland are precisely the lens through which we can appreciate the universal achievement of *Gulliver's Travels:* its biting satire on the questionable colonial pedigree of modernity.

An Irish Book?

The compilers of standard anthologies have often presented us with a rather Anglicized Swift. The full import of even the most familiar texts by Swift has been diluted by a habitual filtering out, as merely occasional, of his Irish writings. A recontextualizing of *Gulliver's Travels* through the lens of Ireland thus serves to reveal how Jonathan Swift exploited his position on the cusp between English culture and Irish location to confront the arrogance of the splendid and glowering metropole across the Irish Channel. In the course of his travels, the English Gulliver evokes a great many questions of identification and representation. In some of the book's most unforgettable scenes, he discursively "represents" England both to the king of Brobdingnag and to the master Houyhnhnm, with humiliating results for the judgment on "Englishness" as such. The nation most boastful of its sharp breaks with the past, most keen to legitimate itself on the basis of "progress," comes in for the most caustic satire in *Gulliver's Travels.*

The themes of *Gulliver's Travels* are of a piece, more than is sometimes acknowledged, with a phase of Swift's career that begins in 1720. Often described as an Irishman against his will, Swift in 1714 permanently assumed the post he had landed the previous year as dean of St. Patrick's Cathedral in Dublin. Resolved at first not to meddle in Irish politics, he viewed himself, nearing age 47, as undergoing a mode of exile. During this year his formerly powerful friends in London, whose political agenda he had cogently advocated as a highly placed columnist, had suffered a catastrophic reversal. In quick succession, the Tory ministry collapsed, Queen

Anne died, George I assumed the crown, and the feuding Tory leaders, Oxford and Bolingbroke, were subjected to political impeachments, the latter fleeing to Calais.

Swift describes this biographical moment in his "Verses on the Death of Dr. Swift." The voice projected by Swift into the poem's frame story belongs to an unnamed figure who—having outlived the Irish dean—rakes over the details of his career to some friends gathered at a club:

> "With horror, grief, despair the Dean
> Beheld the dire destructive scene:
> His friends in exile, or the Tower,
> Himself within the frown of power;
> 5 Pursu'd by base envenom'd pens,
> Far to the land of slaves and fens;
> A servile race in folly nurs'd,
> Who truckle most, when treated worst."
>
> (p. 365)

Far from sentimentalizing Ireland, Swift much preferred to cultivate his stylized ritual of cursing it. By 1720, nevertheless, his politics had begun to shift. He began to write anonymous and pseudonymous pamphlets challenging the latest manifestations of British arrogance toward Irish public affairs. His rebellion likewise challenged the complicity of his own community and class, the Anglo-Irish, who usually swallowed subordination to Britain as the price for their own privileges as Anglicans in Ireland vis-à-vis the disenfranchised Catholic majority. The Irish pamphlets included in this edition display Swift's constitutional arguments for Ireland's legislative independence and in favor of economic self-reliance. These insurgent views angered Sir Robert Walpole—satirized in *Gulliver's Travels* as the Lilliputian treasurer Flimnap—the power behind Britain's attempt to force Wood's halfpence on Ireland. Throughout most of Swift's later career, Walpole occupied the seat of political power in Britain: a prime target because he was the prime minister of an entrenched regime that Swift despised. Among the correspondence included in this volume is Swift's account of a futile meeting with Walpole: a letter, meant for Walpole's eyes, during which he again asserts Irish interests (p. 379–81). Like "Britishness," "Irishness" had to be laboriously created, and Swift belongs to the eighteenth-century phase of that making. In his *Life of Swift,* Samuel Johnson credits Swift with having been the first to teach the Irish "to know their own interest, their weight and their strength" (Johnson, vol. 3, 50).

The colonial process in Ireland, as elsewhere, did not produce the simple clarity of single combat between the poles of colonizer and "native." The ambiguities of a borderline figure such as Swift belie easy polarizations.

Ambiguities of national identification in a number of places echo the conflicted response of the hyphenated group most ambiguously caught in between Ireland and England: the Anglo-Irish. This group produced egregiously oppressive legislation and was quite often more ferociously anti-Catholic than was the government in Britain. Yet the Anglo-Irish also produced the early stirring of a certain Irish nationalism. Given that Swift is Anglo-Irish—an Anglican clergyman during the eighteenth-century Anglican ascendancy—his constitutional patriotism fits uneasily within the framework of the sectarian Catholic nationalism that was consolidated in Ireland by the early nineteenth century. Though Swift continues to be suspected of harboring Jacobite sympathies, an "Irish Swift" is of course not the same thing as a Catholic or a "Green" Swift.

Anglo-Irish patriotism arguably finds its richest exponent in Jonathan Swift. Swift's campaign against Wood's halfpence, through his *Drapier's Letters,* challenged the subordination of Ireland to the British Parliament. Eventually (in his fourth *Drapier's Letter*) Swift provoked the British government, through the office of its viceroy in Ireland, John Cartaret, to offer £300 for the discovery of the author of the *Drapier's Letters,* known in print only as M. B. Drapier. Of this lord-lieutenant of Ireland—Swift's friend, awkwardly enough—he later wrote the following lines of verse:

> He comes to drain a beggar's purse;
> He comes to tye our Chains on faster
> And show us England is our Master.
>
> (p. 351)

Although Swift's printer suffered legal harassment for the fourth *Drapier's Letter,* the bounty for unmasking its author went unclaimed. The political skirmish ended with a victory for the much celebrated "Drapier": a mythic folk hero constructed by a pamphleteer who had mastered the modern art of shaping public opinion. The widely successful tactic of boycotting British-sponsored coins—the brass halfpence minted by William Wood—created an early chapter in the history of Irish nationalism.

The Irish contents of this volume serve as well to demonstrate that Swift's contradictory relation to "Irishness" is a general problem: an epitome of the messily disjointed invention of national cultures as such. Swift is a renowned "Hibernian patriot," even sometimes adorning Irish currency; yet he also stands accused in some quarters as merely another colonizer, at best a "colonial nationalist" who spoke to and for a Protestant conception of the nation. Eighteenth-century Anglo-Irish nationalism was in general a more complex phenomenon than a term such as *colonial nationalism* would allow. This latter term—reducing the history of Ireland to the singular struggle between colonizer and colonized, Protestant and Catholic—in effect privileges as the one legitimate voice of Ireland the Catholic sectarian nationalism that finally produced the Irish Free State in 1922. As such, the term brushes aside a wide variety of nationalisms (civic, economic, universalist, romantic, linguistic, and cultural) that have been passionately articulated in Ireland, each of which potentially cuts across these binaries (Kearney). The reputation of Swift in Ireland is itself an index of the divisive conflicts that characterize much of Irish history (Mahony). The aim of this volume, then, is not simply to counter the tradition of an English Swift with an Irish Swift. I hope, rather, to present, through Swift's Irish engagements in *Gulliver's Travels,* along with a selection of his other writings, his critique of the project of colonial modernity as a whole.

The *Drapier's Letters* campaign unfolded exactly during the years in which Swift was writing *Gulliver's Travels.* A fablelike version of Dublin's triumph in fending off the unwanted halfpence—the successful insurrection of Lindalino against the Flying Island—appears as an episode in book 3, the last book written of the four (pp. 177–78). *Gulliver's Travels,* though written in a more ambitious mode than Swift's Irish pamphlets, shares with them the turbulent spawning ground of the early 1720s: the zenith of Swift's activism and the basis for much of his satiric perspective. As we undertake to reread the cultural archive with a greater awareness of the traces left on it by colonial antagonisms, we may begin to appreciate the full extent to which the Irish context for *Gulliver's Travels* reveals it as modern: a book born out of the struggle, even within Swift himself, between England and Ireland. *Gulliver's Travels* is ultimately a book that advances the project of decolonizing modernity.

The Colonial Making of Modernity

England had experienced in 1649 the first bourgeois revolution. The subsequent events of 1688–90, putting the Protestant religion ahead of monarchical succession, had consolidated a constitutional settlement in which Parliament was paramount. In this, as well as in many other respects, England can be seen as the first modern society (Beier; Stone). The Dutch prince William of Orange was hailed as a Protestant Moses, arrived to deliver Europe from Catholic domination. The Protestant triumphalism of this moment can be glimpsed in a bit of doggerel produced in 1690 by Charles Montagu to describe William III's conquering force in Ireland:

> As when the swelling Ocean burst his Bounds,
> And, foaming, overwhelms the neighb'ring Grounds,
> The roaring Deluge, rushing headlong on,
> Sweeps Cities in its Course, and bears whole Forests down.
>
> (Montagu, 7)

England's "financial revolution" of the 1690s enabled William III to establish new relations between politics and commerce. Adopting and sophisticating Dutch financial institutions, the English almost simultaneously nationalized the public debt (1693) and founded the Bank of England (1694) to manage it (Braudel, vol. 2, 525–82; Dickson). By reorganizing its fiscal institutions, the English government increased its control over the minting of money, the legitimation of legal tender, and the availability of both money and credit. Whence a remarkable "lead," as P. J. Cain and A. G. Hopkins put it, "in the area of finance and commercial services": a lead that set the country apart from its rivals (64). As a means of financing war, moreover, deficit financing was vastly more efficient and lucrative than raising taxes. William III soon plunged the nation into the War of the Grand Alliance (1689–97). The War of Spanish Succession (1701–13), finally brought to an end by Queen Anne, quickly followed. A "military–fiscal state" began to emerge: a strong government capable "of greatly increasing the funds at its disposal, of sustaining warfare for long periods, and of maintaining political unity" (Cain and Hopkins, 71).

After the Act of Union in 1707 produced Great Britain—a union of England and Scotland that pointedly excluded Ireland—the latter began to be described legally as a "dependent kingdom." The Declaratory Act of 1720 (reprinted in this volume) casually marginalized the Irish Parliament. Though the latter had spoken for Protestant interests only, the Declaratory Act marked the end of any pretense, for some fifty years, that anyone in Ireland had rights to proper channels of political representation. To be sure, Ireland was not formally designated as a colony, as happened to wide swathes of the world during the nineteenth century. Some leading historians argue that the position of the Irish was relatively "normal" for the time, far more like than unlike, say, the condition of the peasantry under the *ancien régime* in France and elsewhere in Europe (Connolly, 25–26). Such ambiguities—the "kingdom-or-colony" question—deserve acknowledgment. Responsibility to the historical archive nevertheless demands that we acknowledge the unevenly shared history of Ireland and Britain. Like Nicholas Canny, I conclude that Ireland's historical trajectory moves between kingdom and colony. It goes without saying that no sectarian vindictiveness or easy polarities follow from such a conclusion.

The different impact of such innovations in Britain (the first modern nation) and in Ireland (its oldest colony) can be seen in Swift's writings after 1720. The fiscal mediations of colonial greed could be unhealthy even for the metropolitan center. The infamous South Sea Bubble of 1720 served to create unease throughout England about the volatility attending the state's dual role as fiscal administrator and political authority. *Trust, credit, interest:* Swift achieves a powerful critical distance from the familiar ambiguities that surface, in a commercializing society, around the institutional force of these words. As Nigel Dodd points out, "trust in money's abstract properties is, by extension, trust in those agencies responsible for monetary administration" (27). The South Sea Company, established in 1711, had been the brainchild of Swift's patron Robert Harley, the earl of Oxford. The company was conceived as a Tory alternative to the Bank of England, and among its early investors was Jonathan Swift. Driven into retirement by the Whigs, Harley was not in power when subsequent legal and financial machinations (Sunderland's South Sea Act of 1720) produced a doomed speculative scheme depending on the perpetual rise of South Sea stock. Colluding with government officials, the company exploited golden dreams of colonial wealth with a complex scheme of financial hocus-pocus involving privatization of the national debt. During 1720, as the company's directors artificially inflated the price of its stock, eager speculators borrowed to buy still more. By meeting this demand with inadequately secured loans, the company fed a manic spiral of greed and folly. All this climaxed in a sensational "bubble" that spread far beyond London. Toward the end of 1720 the bubble burst with nationwide casualties. Public confidence in the "paper wings" of national credit and paper currency took a severe drubbing (Carswell). In his poem "The Bubble," Swift describes the typical investor about to pay the price of his grandiose dreams:

> Thus the deluded bankrupt raves,
> Puts all upon a desperate bet;
> Then plunges in the Southern waves,
> Dipped over head and ears—in debt.
> (p. 333).

The superior liquidity of paper credit suddenly seemed a symptom of insubstantiality and corruption (Pocock, 496–97). For Swift, the very notion of a solid status quo had been revealed as a fantasy (Brantlinger, 71). "The Bubble," describing damage to key British financial institutions, reflects sardonically upon a project in which Swift had himself participated. "I had my self been a sort of projector," as Gulliver says (p. 183), "in my younger days."

England's precocious process of self-modernization, however bumpy, played out very differently in Ireland. The invasion of Ireland by Oliver Cromwell's army in 1649 had set in motion a massive transfer of land from Catholics to Protestants. In 1733, Swift, whose paternal grandfather had supported Charles I during the Cromwellian invasion, describes as follows the arrival in Ireland of Cromwellian modernity:

> The Catholicks of Ireland, in the great Rebellion, lost their Estates for fighting in Defence of their King. The Schismaticks, who cut off the Father's Head, forced the Son to fly for his life, and overturned the whole ancient Frame of Government, Religious and Civil; obtained Grants of those very Estates which the Catholicks lost in Defence of the ancient Constitution, many of which Estates are at this Day possessed by the Posterity of those Schismaticks: And thus they gained by the *Rebellion*, what the Catholicks lost by their *Loyalty*. (Davis, vol. 12, 288)[1]

According to Swift, moreover, the supposedly stabilizing moment of the Glorious Revolution—a watershed of the British Enlightenment—likewise eventuated in catastrophe for Ireland. Celebrated as "bloodless" in England, the decisive defeat of James II (a Catholic) by the Dutch William of Orange (a Protestant) required a series of major battles and sieges in Ireland, culminating in the bloody Battle of Boyne (1690). Swift's view is remote from a triumphal celebration of "King Billy" as a modern Moses:

> Forty years are now passed since the Revolution, when the contention of the British empire was, most unfortunately for us, and altogether against the usual course of such mighty changes in government, decided in the least important nation, but with such ravages and ruin executed on both sides, as to leave the kingdom a desert, which, in some sort, is still continues. (Davis, vol. 12, 132)

Though Swift does voice support for the constitutional contract established in 1689 by the Bill of Rights, he never forgets that those rights instantly evaporated when he entered Ireland.

Though the Treaty of Limerick (October 1689) had refrained from vindictive measures toward Irish Catholics in Ireland, the honorable terms of the treaty began to erode in the 1690s as the Penal Laws took shape. By 1704, under Queen Anne, the system was in place: an apartheid-like contrivance that required the registration of Catholic priests; that required of Catholic priests an oath abjuring allegiance to James II; that rewarded "priest hunters" with a bounty for detecting those who did not register; that denied Catholics access to education at home or abroad; and that denied Catholics access to all official posts. One law, maintaining an Anglican supremacy in horseflesh, denied any "papist" the right to own a horse valued at five pounds or more. Above all, the Penal Laws prohibited Catholics from inheriting land. The net result was to continue the massive transfer of

---

[1] Swift's pamphlet, though intended to block the repeal of the Test Act for Protestant Dissenters, musters arguments that demonstrate that the claims of Irish Catholics are at least as valid as those of the Presbyterians.

land from Catholic to Protestant hands. W.E.H. Lecky describes the distinctive character of this legislation as follows:

> It was directed not against the few, but against the many. It was not the persecution of a sect, but the degradation of a nation. It was the instrument employed by a conquering race, supported by a neighboring Power, to crush to the dust the people among whom they were planted. (vol. 1, 169–70)

Aimed above all at the Catholic gentry (through property rights and access to education), the Penal Laws established what became known several generations later as the Protestant Ascendancy. The economic violence unleashed against Catholics—some of whom, it ought to be noted, were the "Old English" who had arrived prior to the Reformation—was harsh, and sometimes extended to the island as a whole.

The fiscal issues so conspicuous in *Gulliver's Travels* could sometimes trump all others in the early eighteenth century. Swift's works, like the satires of the 1690s analyzed by Robert Markley, must be read both "as a contribution to, and a protest against, the practices of political economy" (111). Since the Navigation Acts, beginning in 1650, England's restrictive trade laws had been designed to produce a favorable balance of trade. This implementation of mercantile theory tended in Ireland to strangle local manufactures in certain sectors. The passage of such laws also implied a broader jurisdictional claim: that the English Parliament ruled over the Irish nation. The effects of the Woollen Act (1699) were visible daily to Swift, whose own neighborhood thronged with unemployed Irish weavers. Hence Swift's first published Irish pamphlet: "A Proposal for the Universal Use of Irish Manufacture" (1720), which broadcasts (as an overheard observation) the sentiment that "Ireland *would never be happy 'till a Law were made for* burning *every Thing that came from* England, *except their* People *and their* Coals . . ." (p. 283). Such outbursts surface every so often in Swift's writings, marking his responses to a systemic dilemma: the constant bleeding of wealth from Ireland to the colonial metropole.

The colonial skirmish known as the Wood's halfpence controversy (1722–25) illustrates the way that the fiscal might of one nation could be used to undermine that of another. Britain's inept attempt to impose, without consultation, a dubious coin on Ireland's monetary system pitted established political muscle against a disorganized mass of suspicions in Ireland. Those suspicions revolved around the cheapening of Irish currency that might result when a base coinage, made from brass, depreciated in relation to coins made of gold and silver. These suspicious sentiments Swift, writing as the Drapier, a Dublin tradesman, successfully mobilized as *Irish* national defiance and mistrust. The first *Drapier's Letter*, which

Anonymous, *Wood's Halfpence*, 1724. In the detail shown here, devils—under the lash of Englishmen—pull a cart-load of Wood's coinage: an emblem of the ruinous hyperinflation predicted for Ireland by Swift and his allies.

THE PIERPONT MORGAN LIBRARY, NEW YORK. PEEL COL. VOL. 2, F.9V, #30.

plays with statistics and scale, its depiction of an overwhelming flood of brass, seems to anticipate Gulliver's misadventures with physical size in Brobdingnag (Schmidt, 253). The Drapier envisions the awful logistical consequences of hyperinflation: that William Wood's privately minted halfpence will have so little value that merely using it for ordinary transactions will require teams of horses pulling carts full of the coin. Such a deluge of worthless coinage, illustrated in the detail of a 1724 Dublin print reproduced on the opposite page, seems hallucinatory: not unlike public credit itself, which translated the collective force of private fantasies about the future into the newly quantifiable political fact of public trust. As the Drapier, Swift might be said to have fleetingly anticipated a decolonized modernity. The *Drapier's Letters,* precisely to expose the double standards of British modernity, make pointed arguments about the consent of the governed.

The constant play with scale in *Gulliver's Travels* serves as an apt metaphor for the boundary-crossing required to do justice to the scope of Swift's satire. The unit of analysis it demands, neither Britain nor Ireland alone, is ultimately that of the globe. Gulliver's third voyage provides a convenient illustration of an important contrast in historical periods: the early eighteenth-century awareness that power was operating on a new scale. Commenting on the fondness of European mathematicians for intervening in public affairs, Gulliver speculates that such people suppose "that because the smallest circle hath as many degrees as the largest, therefore the regulation and management of the world require no more abilities than the handling and turning of a globe" (p. 169). Globalization, as this joke suggests, has a history that leads inexorably back to the moment when new sciences of wealth and society emerged hand in hand with the international activities of, for example, the Swedish, Dutch, English, and French East India Companies (Rothschild). Improvements in cartography provoked fantasies of world ascendance.

Gulliver's Travels as a Critique of Colonial Modernity

Many of the most powerful moments in *Gulliver's Travels* develop lacerating satire against the self-legitimating rhetoric of a specifically colonial modernity. In the broadest terms, this rhetoric revolves around the notion that history chronicles a grand pageant of "progress": a Whiggish narrative tracing the cumulative growth of scientific knowledge marching hand in hand with the growth of political liberty "at home." This "grand narrative" (now known as the Whig version of history) was not really consolidated until the nineteenth century (Butterfield, 109–32). The long tradition of Whiggish historiography in Britain—dividing the past into the friends and enemies of a single definition of "progress"—has often chosen to emphasize events visible only within a narrow circumference: the boundaries of the nation-state. Swift's position on the threshold of modernity enables his satirical critique to assert more cosmopolitan norms. From his Irish vantage point in the 1720s, Swift is proportionately more skeptical about claims to "progress."

Gulliver's Travels registers newly sophisticated methods of finance, new refinements in map making, and newly quantitative modes of governance, all in the context of a perfectly traditional arrogance and greed. A brilliant example of this involves the Lilluputian's ethnological speculation about Gulliver's pocket watch, which they conclude is his "oracle" (p. 63). At a single glance, this merely mocks cultural misunderstandings, and so mocks ethnological myopia. When one considers how the watch, even as it marks time, conditions Gulliver to obey it as a secular idol, the estranging satire on a "modern" refinement strikes home. Indeed, Gulliver's pocket watch condenses many eighteenth-century themes surrounding the "modern" ability to quantify time more precisely, an ability built into the very form of the travel journal (Sherman, 159–84). The book as a whole, interlaced as it is with straight-faced "data" and cartography, is an object lesson in "modern" misrepresentation: how to lie, in other words, with maps and dates and statistics.

Gulliver's Travels produces a scathing account of the dedication of human rationality to lethally irrational goals. The eighteenth century in England had begun with a sense that warfare had changed in scope and severity. Public borrowing enabled great improvements in the logistics of warfare. The hawkish tone of this moment can be captured in an early passage from Daniel Defoe's *An Essay upon Projects:* "The Art of War, which I take to be the highest Perfection of Human Knowledge, is a sufficient Proof of what I say [about the superiority of "Modern" knowledge], especially in conducting Armies, and in offensive Engines. . . ." After he catalogues new weapons and tactics at some length, Defoe concludes with the following example: "our new-invented Child of Hell, the Machine [probably a hollow-shot mortar] which carries Thunder, Lightning, and Earthquakes in its Bowels, and tears up the most impregnable Fortifications" (34). For Swift, the figure who links the public purse to the sword is John Churchill, duke of Marlborough, the preeminent general of his age. In *The Conduct of the Allies* (1711), a verbal torpedo that hastened Marlborough's political downfall, Swift depicts him as profiteering from the public trough, at the expense of future generations, on the behalf of unreliable Dutch allies. Allusions throughout *Gulliver's Travels* continue to gibe at such profiteering from professional carnage. The Lilliputian character Skyresh Bolgolam, glancing at Marlborough, imposes the dishonorable obligation on Gulliver to serve as a sort of one-man mercenary army against Blefuscu (p. 70).

The cliché that Swift was a gloomy reactionary who hated science needs to be qualified in light of the complicity of early science with the colonial project. Moreover, the claim that science produces a linear accumulation of verifiable knowledge cannot be the final word in a larger conversation about human progress. No more salient counterexample could be found than the evolution of military technology, definitively attacked in book 4, when Gulliver enumerates "the arts of war" to the horror-struck master Houyhnhnm (p. 239). Gulliver's offer of the recipe for gunpowder to the king of Brobdingnag (pp. 145–46), indifferent to human suffering as it is, likewise deflates any misplaced pride in the possession of superior ordnance. Swift's eighteenth-century critique of modern knowledge serves to remind us that scientists have never been inhibited by the equivalent of the oath that binds doctors, above all, to do no harm. Ominous escalations in the killing leverage provided by military technology severely strain any optimistic vision of the broader march of human progress.

No more prestigious mediator of the modern exists than science. Specifically "modern" knowledge in eighteenth-century England, however, was not infrequently knowledge of Ireland. The land confiscation inaugurated by Cromwell required improved maps and other new forms of demographic knowledge. Enter Sir William Petty: a physician trained, like Gulliver, at the Dutch University of Leiden, where medical training involved witnessing the dissection of cadavers in an anatomy theater (Roberts). Along with John Graunt, Petty invented political economy, a new quantitative science of wealth and statistics, using Ireland as his "political animal" for dissection (Coughlin, 215; Rusnock, 49–68). He likewise supervised the Down Survey (1654–59), which ultimately eventuated in the *Hiberniae Delineatio* (1685), the first general atlas of Ireland. (See the map reprinted on the opposite page.) Petty provided the political basis for the Protestant redistribution of confiscated Irish land. It is some measure of the historical erasure involved that Petty claimed, in the course of his cartographic exertions, that Ireland was a *tabula rasa*—a blank page, waiting in its pristine purity to be first named, inscribed, and conceptually partitioned by him. In subjecting post-Cromwellian Ireland to his formidable demographic, cartographic, and statistical abilities, moreover, Petty recurs more than once, as Patricia Coughlin points out, to the metaphor of *anatomy:* a cool analogy between his analytical and quantitative method, that is, and the medical dissection of "cheap and common animals (215)." Petty's "anatomies" of Ireland's population in the later seventeenth century, as surveyor general of the kingdom of Ireland, illustrate the historical link in Ireland between cartography and successive waves of land confiscation.

William Petty, *A General Mapp of Ireland.* From Hiberniae Delineatio, 1685. Petty's atlas emphasized a hierarchy of scales and administrative boundaries: the parish, the county, and the barony. He synthesized the national map shown here by piecing together many smaller regional maps.

THE BEINECKE RARE BOOK AND MANUSCRIPT LIBRARY, YALE UNIVERSITY.

Petty specialized in the numerical representation of populations ("political arithmetic"); he encouraged a centralization of governmental record keeping; and he began to theorize wealth in terms of domestic production (Poovey, 120–38). Simon Schama neatly sums up Petty's role as "the chief scientist of dispossession" (vol. 1, 236). After the Cromwellian invasion of 1649, Ireland was thus the first place to bear the full brunt of a specifically colonial modernity: the sophisticated techniques of domination available to a commercially advanced imperial power. And so it was, albeit earlier than James Morris seems to think, "that it was around the name of Ireland that the moral problems of imperialism first assembled" (478).

The eighteenth-century name for science was natural history, and the latter routinely included early attempts at ethnography. The legitimacy of eighteenth-century ethnography was bound up with the political and ethical legitimacy of the colonial project. To be sure, the recording of charged encounters under uneven conditions did not always produce something so monolithic as negative stereotypes. Those unquestionably exist, of course, and hostile English views of the "savage Irish" are well documented. The Hottentots (Khoikhoi peoples in southern Africa) are the special objects of a relentless exercise in this vein (Merians). John Ovington describes Hottentots in 1696 as somewhere between the human and the bestial. The data-gathering exercise, however, is often less predictable. When the English did not have the upper hand—as was decidedly the case in Ovington's racy account of Mughal India in the 1690s—the resulting cross-cultural encounter strikes a contemporary reader as more balanced and engaged. One notes in a similar vein that mountain-sized Gulliver is clueless about his transgression in urinating on the queen's palace in Lilliput (pp. 81–82), but tiny Gulliver is exquisitely sensitive in Brobdingnag to the impropriety of planting his backside on a chair made from woven fibers of the queen's hair (p. 137). Compelled to negotiate, with the accountability attendant upon that position, one cannot afford to be patronizing, openly hostile, or ignorant. Absent that countervailing pressure, written accounts of cross-cultural encounters tend to drift into the orbit of the stronger power.

Swift's paternalistic views about civic virtue are often viewed as backward. In one of his aphorisms, he offers the following political rationale for placing legal limits on economic maximizing by individuals: "when bounds are set to Mens Desires, after they have acquired as much as the Laws will permit them, their private Interest is at an End; and they have nothing to do, but to take care of the Publick" (Davis, vol. 1, 243). Warren Montag diagnoses in Swift an illiberal rejection of actually existing British society, and especially of its increasing individualism. If Swift assumes social stratification within a given society as inevitable, however, the egalitarianism he rejects is far from innocent. He rejects the views of those, in Montag's words, "who would posit a hierarchy of nations, according to which some are destined to command and others are to serve, in favor of what appears to be a doctrine of the juridical equality of all nations" (138). The international angle of Swift's critique illustrates an insight expressed in 1944 by Herbert Butterfield: "that the real alternative to whig history in recent times—the real tory alternative to the organization of English history on the basis of the growth of liberty—was the story of British expansion overseas" (81). It was, of course, overseas that the most brutal contradictions of modernity emerged: the double standards of law and morality that stripped indigenous peoples of certain protections available "at home." To characterize as merely reactionary a figure who grasps the negativity of this global history seems inadequate. Although *Gulliver's Travels* mocks scientific utopias, it strongly asserts the potential value, in this world, of making two ears of corn grow where only one grew before (p. 147). Swift indeed epitomizes a double-edged type: a "Tory Anarchist," to paraphrase Edward Said (54). To this formulation, Declan Kiberd adds, "the protesting nostalgist" and "the dynamic traditionalist" (105). The list of Janus-faced epithets has been completed by Ann Cline Kelly, who emphasizes Swift's deliberate self-construction in such terms as the following: "an unchristian priest, a vulgar gentleman, an elite populist, a misanthropic philanthropist, a serious trifler, a Grubstreet Apollo, a pro-Irish Englishman" (2002, 7–8). The global scale of Swift's satire reframes both the political context of his work and the terminology needed to describe him. His satire, rather than lashing out at "progress" as such, critiques its colonial genealogy.

Travel Writing

The form in which Lemuel Gulliver presents his writings to the world further serves Swift's satire on the project of colonial modernity. Swift's satires do not begin as "foreign" denunciations: they slowly emerge in an insider's idiom, building toward an unfamiliar perspective on things supposedly known. It is no accident that his satire of the colonial enterprise impersonates the genre of travel writing as the ideal vehicle for its scathing ironies. The asymmetry of colonial power makes the genre of eighteenth-century travel literature, with its standard excursions into natural history and anthropology, a prime vessel of colonial ideology. The assumptions of colonial ethnography had emerged because a society with an increasingly global reach had the technical means to represent more locally bound ones, as cooperative or resistant, without being compelled to engage seriously with itself as seen by others. Gulliver is a highly unusual traveler simply in imagining that the people of Brobdingnag may some day complain upon reading his account of them in translation (p. 129). *Gulliver's Travels* as a whole constantly disrupts the illusory comforts of a gaze that is not returned.

Though travel writing is an ancient genre, the merging of the genre with early science—with a protocol of observation and data gathering—developed no earlier than the very late seventeenth century. The Royal Society in fact generated a detailed set of guidelines for the production of systematically informative travel narratives. Narratives such as William Dampier's *New Voyage Round the World* (1697) described and sought to justify newly globalized relations of knowledge and power. The competition among European powers to expand their maritime trading monopolies, moreover, produced a slew of such narratives by eighteenth-century sailor–narrators: not only Dampier and Woodes Rogers, but also Lionel Wafer, John Narbrough, George Shelvocke, William Funnell, and William Betagh. These navigators followed in each other's paths; corrected each other's errors in navigation; hailed their own discoveries; acted out personal rivalries; and analyzed each other's conduct in great detail. Indeed, Daniel Defoe's fictitious *New Voyage Round the World,* which appeared one year before *Gulliver's Travels,* registers in its opening paragraph a jaded sense that global circumnavigation had become a tedious affair:

> It has for some ages been thought so wonderful a thing to sail the tour or circle of the globe, that when a man has done this mighty feat he presently thinks it deserves to be recorded, like Sir Francis Drake's. So, as soon as men have acted the sailor, they come ashore, and write books of their voyage, not only to make a great noise of what they have done themselves, but, pretending to show the way to others to come after them, they set up for teachers and chart-makers to posterity. (1)

The moment was right for a satirical riposte against the genre.

The tales of the eighteenth-century voyagers were proudly distinct, so they thought, from the fabulous exaggerations of a book such as the fourteenth-century *Travels of Sir John Mandeville.* To be sure, rumors of Patagonian giants stubbornly persisted throughout much of the century (Wallis). Given the eighteenth-century's "sharp rise in the threshold of belief" (Lamb, 82), however, a closer commitment to the probable was the norm. Opting for a plain prose style, Enlightenment narrators purported to offer a voyage into useful substance (Stafford). The potential bad faith of this eighteenth-century genre, then, lies elsewhere: in its implicit restrictions on the horizons of moral and political concern. The voyager-narrators were mostly propagandists for an expansionist agenda. They identified practical problems—the hazards of Spanish, Dutch, and native hostility, tropical fevers, faulty maps, and so on—mainly to demonstrate that solutions existed. Insofar as this travel writing involved the written and graphic representations of "natives," it often foreclosed their reality through a shallowness of engagement that was finally more pernicious than deliberate falsehood. The objectifying stance common among eighteenth-century voyagers subsumed fellow human beings, by way of a "science of man," into a colonial archive of collected facts.

The voyaging narrators tended to bury their readers in an avalanche of tediously logged details, manifesting an unresolved "dithering," as Philip Edwards puts it, "between the demands of science and the claims of the general reader" (7). Along the way, a good deal of valuable knowledge was produced: of indigenous pharmacology, of weather patterns, of ocean currents, of coastlines, of waterspouts, of foreign plants, of enormous edible turtles. A discourse can be factual, so far as it goes, and yet profoundly implicated in the misdirection of attention and the foreclosure of certain questions. As satirists have always known, there are a great many things that people have a vested interest in not knowing. Much of what is "unknown" cannot be chalked up to mere innocent ignorance. "Sanctioned ignorance"—the luxury of being unaccountable—often marks the insulating effects of domination on groups who dominate (Spivak, 291). The eighteenth-century British public's appetite for travel narratives illustrates a hunger to experience exotica without reflecting too deeply. Like war, the colonial project blurred the line between what was permitted and what was forbidden. The right of an explorer to name and thereby possess "discoveries" was seldom remarked. The neutral idiom of much voyage literature serves to disconnect unequal exchanges from bothersome empathy or guilt. *Gulliver's Travels* refuses the touristic comforts of the travelogue genre.

An acquaintance with a few such voyage narratives serves to chasten one's confidence in the reliability of their narrators. The nuggets of knowledge found in the voyage literature are mingled with considerable fool's gold: self-serving lies, exaggerations, plagiarisms, inaccurate maps, and extensive ghostwriting. The name *Gulliver,* as has been widely observed, sounds enough like *gullible* to mock the overly credulous. *Gulliver's Travels* is both the tallest of tall tales and the most literal-minded exercise in flat-footed reportage. Gulliver is that doggedly sincere narrator who insists on telling us the whole truth, after all, about the public hygiene problem his bodily functions posed for the Lilliputians (p. 58).

Gulliver's Travels appeared at a moment when the loudly claimed eyewitness veracity of voyage-narrators was growing stale. Gulliver's unfailing veracity is attested by the fictitious Cousin Sympson in the book's prefatory matter. At least two likely sources exist for the name adopted here by Swift for the risky business of negotiating with his publisher. Swift could have borrowed the name Sympson from the pseudonym of another supposed voyager of the day, the putative author of *A New Voyage to the East-Indies* (1715). This plagiarized work bears the name of Captain William Symson. Swift might also have learned of a sailor–narrator named Richard Simson, who sailed to the South Sea in 1689 with Captain John Strong aboard the *Welfare* and wrote an unpublished manuscript, to which subsequent travelers alluded.[2] In any case, Gulliver's complaints to "Cousin Sympson" about interpolations, cuts, garbled dates, and misspellings in the 1726 edition of his book—in a highly typical Swiftian paradox—continue to function as awkward evidence in scholarly attempts to reconstruct the actual textual history of *Gulliver's Travels.* No wonder that the final chapter of book 4 comes adorned with a quotation from Virgil alluding to the episode of the Trojan horse (p. 327): the most celebrated stratagem, whether it ever happened or not, in military lore.

Lying—a crucial theme of *Gulliver's Travels*—is far more complex, as Swift well knows, than merely "saying the thing which is *not*" (Rodino, 1066). In 1706, George Psalmanazar—the French impostor who had posed as a native son of Japanese-ruled Formosa—confessed to the fraudulence of *An Historical and Geographical Description of Formosa, An Island Subject to the Emperor of Japan* (1704). Psalmanazar, mentioned by name in *A Modest Proposal* (p. 327), had invented a Formosa complete with a spurious bible, a spurious map, a spurious grammar and alphabet, and a spurious practice of ritual child sacrifice on a staggering scale. The question of "travel liars" (Adams) only begins to open up for critical examination a genre that thrives on ethnic impersonation and ventriloquism. Audiences have escapist yearnings that make them susceptible to particular illusions; travelers have cultural and political agendas that render their views myopic; narrators can scarcely escape the logic that produces exotic adventures as their most valuable commodity; and printers feel the pressure of government surveillance. Even as he critiques a certain sort of bad faith, Swift himself, as a potential object of government harassment, adopts ruses, legal camouflage, and satirical strategies of indirect allusion. Gulliver's trip to Japan—the single "real" country described in a sequence of otherwise fantastic kingdoms—may be a sardonic salute to Psalmanazar: the impostor who "invented" an actually existing country in the Far East.

Swift's Gulliver goes abroad, as does Daniel Defoe's Robinson Crusoe, because such real-life British voyagers as Captains William Dampier and

---

[2] I have an essay in progress, "Cousins Sympson and Simson: Gulliverian Intertextuality," on the significance of this manuscript.

Woodes Rogers were creating a vastly popular new genre of quasi-scientific travel writing. Dampier's *New Voyage Round the World* was a striking literary success for an author whose origins were modest and whose maritime career was, to say the least, checkered. Rogers's *Cruising Voyage Round the World* (1712) introduced the world to Alexander Selkirk, the hermit of Juan Fernandez. Rogers's description of Selkirk, castaway for some four solitary years on an island in the Juan Fernandez cluster, famously inspired Defoe's fiction of *Robinson Crusoe.* Such voyager-narrators as Rogers and Dampier provided their readers with a vicarious experience of encounters with strange new worlds. Beyond Ireland, beyond the Atlantic colonies along the eastern coast of America, there loomed a vast new frontier. Many of the eighteenth-century voyaging narratives were focused on the South Sea because the latter was viewed as the royal road to the most vulnerable flank of the waning Spanish empire. A botched attempt in 1695–99 to found a Scottish colony on Darien (the Isthmus of Panama) had nevertheless concentrated public attention in England and Scotland on the advantages of having an opening to the Pacific Ocean. Hence a predictable set of geographical references, powerfully invested with elements of romance specific to navigational prowess (Lamb, 41–43). The Dutch colony on the Cape of Good Hope, situated between the Atlantic and the Indian Oceans, was a crucial African way station for South Sea explorers (a clue, along with Madagascar, as to the general vicinity of Gulliver's fourth voyage). The poorly mapped region of Australia (New Holland) and Tasmania (Van Dieman's Land) loomed large in this geography. (Lilliput, the site of Gulliver's first voyage, is somewhere near Van Dieman's Land.) Across the vast Pacific Ocean lay the weakly fortified western coast of the Spanish Indies: Florida, Mexico, Cuba, Peru, Chile, and even California. (Brobdingnag, site of Gulliver's second voyage, is a Californian peninsula.). Dutch control of the East Indies impeded British voyages to the Pacific from that side, and the alternative routes required either trekking by land across the Isthmus of Panama or sailing through the Strait of Magellan.

Gulliver, the narrator with whom the reader is invited to identify, is simultaneously the subject and object of Swift's satire. As he progresses through his four major voyages, Gulliver moves inexorably toward a rejection of the mentality that permeates Defoe's fictitious *New Voyage Round the World* (1725), the title of which deliberately echoes Dampier's book of 1697. The anonymous narrator promises that a sailor who adheres to his South Sea itinerary "shall never fail to discover new worlds, new nations, and new inexhaustible funds of wealth and commerce, such as never were yet known to the merchants of Europe" (156). Whether Defoe fully believes in "inexhaustible wealth" or not, his narrative functions as part of his sustained propaganda campaign for extending the tentacles of British exploration into the South Sea. A perspective legitimizing colonial expansion likewise informs that far greater literary achievement, *Robinson Crusoe.* Hence a potent contrast: the two greatest travel fictions of the early eighteenth century, *Robinson Crusoe* (1719) and *Gulliver's Travels* (1726), manifest sharply opposed attitudes toward the colonial enterprise. The illustrations paired in the following two pages capture this contrast. The first, by Clément-Pierre Marillier (engraved by Remi-Henri-Joseph Delvaux), shows the Amerindian character Friday groveling at the foot of a proudly upright Robinson Crusoe. The second, by J. J. Grandville—countering the assumptions of superiority built into the first—depicts Gulliver himself obsequiously kissing the loftily extended hoof of the master Houyhnhnm. As I argue more fully in an essay included in this volume, Gulliver the Englishman himself becomes in the course of his voyages the object of colonial assaults upon his identity.

The Misanthropic Spectrum

Reading *Gulliver's Travels* as a satire on colonial modernity, both in substance and in form, also provides a way of nuancing another familiar topic in studies of Jonathan Swift: the author's supposed misanthropy. Book 4 of *Gulliver's Travels,* in particular, has been described as a libel on humanity. *Gulliver's Travels* does satirize the human race, and no one would argue that Swift is confident of our abilities, as a very cussed species, to live together without lethal manifestations of greed and pride. "Drown the world," so writes Swift to Pope in his scriptural idiom, invoking a second flood in Noah's tradition (Williams, vol. 3, 117). Swift cultivates in his letters a pose of wishing merely to vex the world. At the same time, however, *Gulliver's Travels* targets, as an egregious example of pride, Gulliver's own misanthropy at the end of book 4. Gulliver's shocking self-righteousness at the end of his final voyage, deranging all conventions of homecoming and reunion, makes the purgatorial moralist himself an object of ridicule. Claude Rawson has been especially persuasive on Swift's tendency to implicate himself in such second-order impulses: violent recoils from disgusting violence. No self-congratulatory escape from complicity is allowed to go unchallenged, not even the satirist's, for Swift's impulse is to expose a universal culpability as regards an attraction to violent "solutions." Beyond the question of individual purity and complicity, however—and yet less cosmic than "humanity" as such—lie the true targets of Swift's satire: the behavior of collective entities such as organized faiths, kingdoms, dynasties, and—above all—nations. *Gulliver's Travels* reserves its harshest satire

Marillier-Delvaux, *Friday Groveling at Crusoe's Foot.* From Charles Garnier, *Voyages Imaginaires, Romanesques, Merveilleux,* Volume 1, 1787.

J. J. Grandville, *Gulliver Kissing the Houyhnhnm's Hoof,* 1838.
THE BEINECKE RARE BOOK AND MANUSCRIPT LIBRARY, YALE UNIVERSITY.

for the appalling violence sanctioned by national interests, often commercial: the trading of blood for money.

As numerous examples attest, the violence that Swift satirizes in *Gulliver's Travels,* seen in a colonial framework, is not after all so blandly generic. His effort to delegitimate violence in the name of the nation comes into sharper focus when we consider the pirate-infested nature of the reigns of Queen Anne and George I. Several historians describe the interval between 1695 and 1725—the generation just before *Gulliver's Travels*—as the Golden Age of Piracy. The rivalry among European powers for the lead in colonizing the Americas and East Indies was in this age heavily influenced by privateers. Indeed, no more perturbing symbol for the illicit shadiness of national violence could be found than piracy (Fuchs, 48–49).

The category of "privateer" gave many a captain a license to rob under the cloak of patriotism. Looting and plundering the Spanish main—a violence not effectively controlled by the state—could usually be licensed, or retroactively pardoned, as an act of war. This dithering attempt to channel pirates in the right direction was inherently unstable, reflecting criminality back on the governments that sometimes promoted substate violence and sometimes sought to quell it (Thomson, 22–54). Piratical violence exposed deep continuities between buccaneering and colonizing ventures in places such as Panama and the Caribbean. Buccaneers operating in the West Indies were the first to cross the Isthmus of Panama into the South Seas (Lamb, 50). Consider the exemplary career of Henry Morgan, who sometimes sailed with a fleet of fifty ships under his command. Alexander Exquemelin's *Buccaneers of America,* first published in English in 1684, recounts with quizzical incomprehension a typical episode of Captain Morgan's biography: the burning and sacking of the city of Panamá in 1671 by Morgan's crew. Exquemelin grimly notes that "the fire increased so fast that before night the greatest part of the city was in a flame" (223). Morgan, who slaughtered Panamanian "Indians" with equal nonchalance, was rewarded for his atrocities on the Spanish main with the office of lieutenant governor of Jamaica. Pirates, mutinies, burning cities, scuffles with "natives": these scurvy facts of the sea-roving life perturbed moral and legal categories. Piracy is thus Swift's delegitimating metaphor for, in the words of Gulliver, the founding of a *modern* colony.

William Dampier (1652–1715)—dubbed Cousin Dampier by Gulliver—is in all respects the most important of such privateering voyagers, and he remains representative as well in the extent of his involvement in buccaneering activities. Dampier, the most famous voyager–narrator of his time, was a buccaneer, ethnographer, mapmaker, botanist, and meteorologist. His best-selling *New Voyage Round the World* includes impressive maps, drawings of Australian flora, and accounts of the manners of peoples he encountered. For obvious reasons, Dampier is fairly circumspect about the illicit aspects of his sea-raiding adventures, highlighting instead the motive of scientific curiosity. Dampier's acquisition and selling of the "Painted Prince" illustrates how casually relations of mutuality between human subjects got warped in the zone of colonial encounters. Jeoly or Job, nicknamed the Painted Prince due to his elaborate tattoos, was a South Sea islander displayed for profit around England as a "sight" until he died of smallpox. In his terse account of these events, which I have included in this volume, Dampier the freak-monger simply fails to imagine a reader who might identify with Jeoly.

Dampier's observations gained him considerable legitimacy as a man of science. His associates included several fellows of the Royal Society, and *A New Voyage Round the World* is dedicated to its president, Charles Montagu. The following entry from John Evelyn's diary (6 August 1698) illustrates the way Dampier straddles the worlds of science and piracy:

> I dined with [Samuel] Pepys, where was Captain Dampier, who had been a famous buccaneer, had brought hither the painted Prince Job [Jeoly], and printed a relation of his very strange adventure and his observations. He was now going abroad again by the King's encouragement, who furnished a ship of 290 tons. He seemed a more modest man than one would imagine by the relation of the crew he had assorted with. He brought a map of his observation of the course of the winds in the South Sea, and assured us that the maps hitherto extant were all false as to the Pacific Sea, which he makes on the south of the line [equator], that on the north end running by the coast of Peru being extremely tempestuous. (vol. 2, 343)

The portrait of Dampier by William Murray in the National Portrait Gallery in London bears the legend "Captain William Dampier: Pirate and Hydrographer."

The continuities between piracy proper and colonial predations constitute a crucial seam in the weave of colonial discourse. Elizabethan "sea-dogs" such as Sir Francis Drake, Sir John Hawkins, and Sir Walter Raleigh won knighthoods at home for raids on the ports and treasure ships of the Spanish empire. Dampier, following in Captain Morgan's path, was involved in 1680 with a second sacking of Panamá. Such figures expose a loose thread: a point at which the legitimacy of the colonial project threatens to unravel. Buccaneers were involved not only in the obvious violence of the colonial project, imposed by weapons, but in its subtler violence as well: protocols of mapping, collection, and ethnography. Swift counters the new scale of colonial predation with a satire exposing the global making of Great Britain as glorified piracy.

The "unthinkability" of Swift lies precisely in the way he brings together the familiar (modern forms of knowledge) and the violently exploitative (colonialism). In "A Modest Proposal" (1729), the butchery of pirates escalates into the refined cannibalism of modern demographers. Swift's so-called misanthropy often entails a reversal of the demographic gaze: a diagnosis that implicates the map makers and statisticians at the top of the colonial food chain (Flynn, 174–75). The surface appearance of rationality is no guarantee against an aggressivity that pervades the unmistakably combined—if also brutally uneven and discrepant—development of both Britain and Ireland within a common system. Swift's achievement in "A Modest Proposal," an estrangement of the voice of reason, depends precisely on the way it exposes the instrumental use of rationality for murderous purposes. The irony for which "A Modest Proposal" is famous depends upon the application of a highly rational and statistically based discourse about population to the "problem" of children starving in the dependency of Ireland. The statistical features of this discourse parody the work on political economy done by Petty, a sample of which is included in this volume. The absurdist humor of "A Modest Proposal," which inhabits, perfects, and thus explodes the logic of such "biopolitics," reclaims for Britain a cannibalism that never really was beyond the pale. Couched in a familiar discourse of public-spirited mercantile rhetoric, the proposed cannibalism induces the disorienting discovery, for Swift's reading public in Ireland and Britain, that they are not insulated within the comfortable automatism of their own routines—not securely *inside* their own clothes and dining habits, their own houses and minds and digestive systems. Swift's satire entails the uncanny recognition of a disowned and disavowed brutality. In such mental traveling lies a principled refusal to claim innocence: a renunciation of any claim to speak from "outside" the violence of the international system of Britain's first empire.

When *Gulliver's Travels* is read through its engagement with colonial modernity, its famous "gelding episode" in book 4 does not read, as has sometimes been supposed, as Swift's endorsement of the Houyhnhnms' program of exterminating the human brutes. Gelding, to the horror of the Houyhnhnms, is what human beings often do to horses. When the Houyhnhnms in their turn apply this logic to the "yahoo question," Swift glances ironically at their smug mingling of rationality with total war. Their assembly, moreover, rehearses questions that were in fact in the air of early eighteenth-century London and Dublin. To provide a significant context for book 4 of *Gulliver's Travels,* I have chosen to publish in this edition an anonymous pamphlet that illustrates how chilling the public discourse of the time could be: *Reasons Humbly offer'd to both Houses of Parliament, For a Law to Enact the Castration or, Gelding of Popish Ecclesiastics* (Dublin, 1710). I would certainly not wish to make the dubious claim that such a document as *Reasons Humbly offer'd* can be said to "represent" Protestant opinion in Ireland at the time. The unhappy fact nevertheless remains, as Marcus Tanner reminds us, that a similar scheme to squeeze Catholic clergy out of Ireland did occupy the Protestant elite in both Ireland and England for a time just prior to Swift's emergence as an Irish pamphleteer:

> In 1719, the Irish Parliament even mused over a draconian proposal to hound priests out of the kingdom by branding their cheeks, while the Irish Privy Council suggested castration The heads of a bill were sent

over to England for approval but ran into opposition in the English Privy Council and no more was heard of it (164).

Perhaps *Reasons Humbly offer'd* played some role in these cheery debates. Among its arguments, in any case, we find the following case for the relative leniency of its proposal: "[Castration] can no ways be reckon'd cruel, since it may be done without hazard of Life, as common experience shews both in Man and Beast, and by consequence less to be complain'd of, than those Laws which condemn [Catholic priests] to the Gallows" (p. 406). The "rational" weighing of two absurdly vicious alternatives illustrates much of what inspired Swift's attacks on instrumental reason, whether in Lilliput or Houyhnhnm-land. According to the internal chronology of *Gulliver's Travels,* moreover, *Reasons Humbly offer'd* was reprinted just before Gulliver's fourth voyage (1710–15). Though *Gulliver's Travels* provides ironic signposts, such cues are very hard to find in *Reasons Humbly offer'd.* This contrast confirms that Swift's satire—almost always double-edged—cuts against the Houyhnhnms' arrogant debate about whether to exterminate, or merely to castrate, the wretched yahoos.

The discussion of Swift's supposed "misanthropy" has too often conflated, in Eurocentric fashion, his particular targets with the world at large. The satirical targets of the *Travels* in fact comprise concentric circles of increasing intensity and specificity. The colonial project, according to Swift's analysis, *magnifies* the already dismal faults of humankind. For this reason, Europe is named as a special haven for liars (p. 42). The vanguard of commercial colonizers from northwest Europe—the maritime traders of the Dutch East India Company—are more harshly satirized than other Europeans, especially in book 3. At the very center of the target sits a complacently battening Britain, the object of Swift's most lacerating satire. One should not forget that Swift suggests in *Gulliver's Travels* that the yahoos, like the Anglo-Irish, are of *English* descent (p. 279). This detail has often been overlooked in the rush to insist that Swift, that misanthropist, targets the entire human race as a degenerate species. So he does: but the English remain, after all, at the center of the bull's-eye.

The contents of this volume as a whole seek to disclose a recalibrated view of Swift's relation to particular battles and universal dilemmas. By virtue of colonial history, his "Irish" moments often have a universal resonance. Swift's supposedly universal misanthropy, for the same reason, subdivides into a graded spectrum of indignant responses. He directs his greatest wrath at the abuse of power between nations, focusing in particular throughout *Gulliver's Travels* on colonial arrogance. Swift's presentation of the complacent Houyhnhnms is not so different from the beguiling voice who proposes the solution of cannibalism in "A Modest Proposal."

Our knowledge of Swift's activist career in Ireland serves, for us, to nuance his perilous approach to the unthinkable. *Why not* eat children? Economic violence by remote control, in this view, is little better, and Swift shocks us with that recognition.

Ways of Seeing Gulliver

Swift's critiques of colonial modernity are the more powerful for emerging from within the proverbial belly of the whale. He achieves this critical detachment above all through the manipulation of scale. In *Gulliver's Travels,* Swift hits upon a happy intersection of three related themes: visual scale, modernity, and empire. Certain objects repeat through the different voyages—ropes, meals, books, grass, animals, clothing, body parts and functions, dolls ("babies")—so that we may gauge their size relative to Gulliver. The book often alludes to optical instruments such as telescopes, mirrors, and spectacles; it shocks with grotesque microscopic close-ups; and it explores political threats of punitive blinding. Hence the metaphorical resonance of visual perception. A broader horizon reframes—and may render strange—objects originally perceived more narrowly. The texture of human complexions, whether grainy or fine, is shown to be relative to one's vantage point. And so different ways of seeing, in the cultural and ideological sense, are made to clash in *Gulliver's Travels.*

It is no coincidence that so visual a book has attracted a great many distinguished illustrators. The best of these, such as J. J. Grandville, have inflected the task of illustration with their own visual imagination. Grandville's eggs—cracked, vulnerable, and yet still scary (p. 75)—extend Swift's satire. That satire on the wars between Lilliput and Blefuscu depicts what we might call the "history of sectarian difference": the way, that is, that a random practice—the suddenly reversed habit of an emperor who cut his finger while cracking an egg at its larger end—gets promoted into a sacred tradition for which people are willing to die, and to kill, by the thousands. From this tiny difference—the little versus the big end—flow objectified identities: Big-Endians and Little-Endians. From these oppositional identifications, each the inverted mirror image of the other, flow endless casualties. Personifying the eggs, Grandville further emphasizes the spirit of petty aggression captured in this famous passage from the *Travels.* The Lilliputians and Blefuscudians, defined by their breakfast habits, become eggs in his drawing. Fragile and mutilated as they may be, moreover, Grandville's fighting eggs look ready to fight on. This edition, by including several unusual and striking illustrations of the *Travels,* seeks to convey a bit of its generative appeal to visual artists. From 1726 onward

(Welcher), visual spinoffs from *Gulliver's Travels* have exploited the transgressive potential of clashing scales.

What Swift mocks is violence, on a modern scale, unleashed in the name of traditions—Protestants versus Catholics. No wonder that Voltaire, that distinguished basher of organized Christian violence, found much to admire in *Gulliver's Travels.* Yet Swift's critique is not against religion as mere mystification. "We have just enough religion," Swift mused elsewhere, "to make us *hate,* but not enough to make us *love* one another" (Davis, vol. 1, 241). Christians are not nearly Christian enough. And there may be a sense in which the writings of Swift demonstrate that the "moderns," for all their invocations of reason, are likewise not modern enough. The egg-wars fable does not mock innovation as such. To break one's egg in the most convenient way is fine. Though Swift draws on the critical thought of earlier figures such as Sir Thomas More, François Rabelais, and Michel de Montaigne, he is himself neither premodern nor even simply antimodern. Swift accepts, more than is sometimes acknowledged, that modernity constitutes the political space in which human affairs must be negotiated. Newly precise "anatomies," of bodies and bodies politic, can be used for or against human beings. Above all, Swift's satire envisions, through Gulliver's scruples about claiming foreign lands for the British Crown, a higher rationality than the world has yet seen: distributive justice *between nations.* In thus repudiating the colonial highjacking of modernity, Jonathan Swift looks forward to a decolonized modernity yet to come.

A NOTE ON THE TEXTS

Robert J. Griffin

The textual history of *Gulliver's Travels* is vexed because Benjamin Motte, the publisher of the first edition of 1726, together with Andrew Tooke, his editor and silent partner, took liberties with Swift's manuscript, either removing passages altogether, toning them down, or replacing them with versions considered to be more acceptable. For instance, since Motte published a conservative list of books that included works on law, he was understandably sensitive about the satire on lawyers in part 5, chapter 5. Motte's other changes to the text took the sting out of some of the political satire. The trial and execution of the printer John Matthews only seven years earlier, in 1719, served as a powerful cautionary example. Remarks by Swift and his friends in letters reveal that the possibility of legal retaliation was in their minds as well, which perhaps accounts for the series of measures Swift took at first to keep his identity hidden from Motte himself: he corresponded with Motte under the name Richard Sympson, and once the manuscript had been delivered, left England and returned to Dublin.

Faced with the (to use Swift's word) "mangled" state of the first edition, scholars have naturally focused on the status, and the extent, of the corrections subsequently made to the 1726 text, both in the partially corrected Motte edition of 1727 and the more fully corrected Dublin edition by George Faulkner of 1735. The authority for the corrections derives from two sources: (1) a letter Charles Ford sent to Motte with a list of requested changes, and (2) alterations recorded in Ford's interleaved copy of the first edition, most of which are thought to have been made by comparison with a copy of the original manuscript. Scholars have also speculated, however, that certain passages copied out by Ford might actually be authorial revisions rather than restorations. In any case, Faulkner was able to examine Ford's copy and take notes while preparing his edition.

Perhaps the most significant of the passages restored in the Faulkner edition are: (1) the "Tribnia" allegory of the Atterbury plot in book 3, chapter 6 (p. 194); (2) the satire on lawyers in book 4, chapter 5 (pp. 240–41), together with the final sentence of the penultimate paragraph and the final paragraph of the passage on judges, and other figures (p. 240); (3) the cutting of Motte's obsequious passage on Queen Anne and the insertion of a bridging sentence in book 4, chapter 6 (p. 246); and (4) the restoration of the attack on the nobility and the House of Lords in book 4, chapter 6 (pp. 246–47 and last two paragraphs of the chapter).

For the purposes of the present edition, however, it is pertinent to call attention to passages that, although sometimes reprinted in modern editions (depending on editorial policy), *do not* appear in the Faulkner edition. For example, since we have evidence that Swift at least partially oversaw the production of Faulkner's edition of his works, it needs to be more widely recognized that, in the process of restoring the satiric bite to passages softened by Motte, either Swift or Faulkner himself may have acquiesced in the removal of a passage that even Motte had dared to print. I am referring specifically to Gulliver's speculation in the last chapter of the book that the original Yahoos may have been English. Defending himself against the charge that he failed to seize the lands he visited in the name of the Crown, Gulliver is nonetheless ready to depose that no European had visited Houyhnhnmland before him. At this point, Motte's text reads: "I mean, if the inhabitants ought to be believed; unless a dispute may arise about the two yahoos, said to have been seen many ages ago on a mountain in Houyhnhnmland, from whence the opinion is, that the race of those brutes hath descended; and these, for any thing I know, may have been English, which indeed I was apt to suspect from the lineaments of their own posterity's countenances, although much defaced. But, how far that will go to make out a title, I leave to the learned in colony-law."

Faulkner's edition of 1735, however, omits everything after "if the inhabitants ought to be believed." Lucius Hubbard wrote in 1922, "Swift's words are too strong for an English ear, even two hundred years away. Possibly, however, Swift relented in this instance, and consented to expunge this brutal slur on his countrymen" (124). Harold Williams notes the special acidity of this satirical pedigree in his 1926 edition: "Although Ford passes over this passage without remark, later editors felt the brutal slight upon their countrymen to be intolerable" (489).

For whatever reason, Faulkner also cut another passage that had appeared in the first edition. In book 4, chapter 11, Pedro de Mendez corroborates Gulliver's "veracity" by observing that a Dutch skipper had told him he had seen a horse driving before him creatures that resemble Gulliver's description of the yahoos when stopping on an island to the south of New Holland, but he had not believed him until hearing Gulliver's account (p. 272).

Faulkner also declines to print two more passages, which do not appear in the first edition either but are given as corrections in Ford's interleaved copy. The first one is the famous Lindalino rebellion episode which allegorizes Dublin's resistance to the capital, book 3, chapter 3 (pp. 177–78). Angus Ross comments that "even Faulkner left out five paragraphs at the end of book 3, chapter 3, as being too dangerous politically" (18); these paragraphs waited until 1899 to appear in print. Treadwell speculates that Swift wrote the Lindalino episode subsequent to the publication of the first edition, but it may also be the case that Motte, like Faulkner, simply refused to publish it. The second passage is brief—no more than a few words—but it is highly charged. In book 4, chapter 5, Gulliver explains the practice of hiring out mercenaries: "There are likewise a kind of Princes in Europe . . . such are those in many Northern Parts of Europe" (p. 238). Ford's version inserts: "in Germany and other Northern Parts of Europe." No doubt because the Hanovers still ruled England, as Hubbard observed, "Even Faulkner, in 1735, did not dare print Ford's substitute" (115).

The present edition includes all of these passages and thus reprints Louis Landa's Riverside edition (1960), with the addition of the Pedro de Mendez corroboration in chapter 4, book 11, not included by Landa (p. 272).

Landa's edition of 1960 is also the source for the versions used here of "A Modest Proposal" and "To the Shopkeepers, Tradesmen, Farmers, and Common People of Ireland," better known as the *Drapier's First Letter;* and for "Verses on the Death of Dr. Swift, D.S.P.D." The other Irish pamphlets are reprinted from the standard edition of Swift's prose works by Herbert Davis (1965–68). The remaining poems are from Harold Williams's *Swift's Poems,* (2nd ed., 1958), and the letters by Swift, with one exception, are taken from Harold Williams's *The Correspondence of Jonathan Swift* (1963). That exception is Swift's letter of August 6, 1735, to Mary Pendarves [Delany], which was first published by Richard Frushell in *Philological Quarterly.*

William Dampier's account of dung-hurling monkeys on the Isle of Triste first appeared in his *Voyages and Descriptions* (London, 1699). This volume also contained his well-known *Discourse on Winds*—a respected contribution to hydrography—and his map of the South Sea reprinted on p. 390. Like all of his writings, Dampier's account of Campeachy was reprinted many times thereafter, and the paragraph about nasty monkeys included here is taken from *Mr. Dampier's Voyages to the Bay of Campeachy,* in volume 2 of a four-volume compilation entitled *A Collection of Voyages* (1729). The remaining selections from Dampier's *New Voyage*

Round the World, first published in 1697, are taken from the 1965 Dover edition of that work. The selections from Sir William Petty's *Political Anatomy of Ireland,* first published in 1691, are taken from the 1969 edition of that work by the Irish University Press. The text of the Declaratory Act of 1720 comes from *The Statutes at large from Magna Charta, to the end of the eleventh Parliament of Great Britain, anno 1761* (Anno sexto Georgii I. c.5).

Reasons Humbly offer'd, the anti-Catholic "gelding" pamphlet, is here reprinted for the first time since the early eighteenth century. Though this pamphlet was briefly and mistakenly attributed to Daniel Defoe in the twentieth century, its eighteenth-century author remains anonymous. The first version of the pamphlet was printed by A. Baldwin in London in 1700. The Dublin version of 1710, reprinted in this volume, has been very slightly adapted to its later moment and Irish location. This volume reprints the copy in the Trinity College Dublin library.

Part One

GULLIVER'S TRAVELS AND OTHER WRITINGS

TRAVELS

INTO SEVERAL

Remote NATIONS

OF THE

WORLD.

In FOUR PARTS.

By *LEMUEL GULLIVER*,
Firſt a SURGEON, and then a CAP-
TAIN of ſeveral SHIPS.

VOL. I.

LONDON:

Printed for BENJ. MOTTE, *at the*
Middle Temple-Gate *in* Fleet-ſtreet.
MDCCXXVI.

Title page of the first edition, 1726.

A Letter from Capt. Gulliver to His Cousin Sympson.

I hope you will be ready to own publicly, whenever you shall be called to it, that by your great and frequent urgency you prevailed on me to publish a very loose and uncorrect account of my travels; with direction to hire some young gentlemen of either university to put them in order, and correct the style, as my cousin Dampier did by my advice, in his book called *A Voyage round the World.* But I do not remember I gave you power to consent, that any thing should be omitted, and much less that any thing should be inserted: therefore, as to the latter, I do here renounce every thing of that kind; particularly a paragraph about her Majesty the late Queen Anne, of most pious and glorious memory; although I did reverence and esteem her more than any of human species. But you, or your interpolator, ought to have considered, that as it was not my inclination, so was it not decent to praise any animal of our composition before my master Houyhnhnm: and besides, the fact was altogether false; for to my knowledge, being in England during some part of her Majesty's reign, she did govern by a chief minister; nay, even by two successively; the first whereof was the Lord of Godolphin, and the second the Lord of Oxford, so that you have made me *say the thing that was not.* Likewise, in the account of the Academy of Projectors, and several passages of my discourse to my master Houyhnhnm, you have either omitted some material circumstances, or minced or changed them in such a manner, that I do hardly know mine own work. When I formerly hinted to you something of this in a letter, you were pleased to answer, that you were

---

Based on *Gulliver's Travels and Other Writings*, ed. Louis Landa (Boston: Houghton Mifflin, 1960). (Like that edition, this one is "blended": while occasionally restoring a passage cut from the 1726 London edition, it follows the 1735 Dublin edition.)

Cousin Sympson. The fictive author of the brief preface that follows this letter. Sympson is the supposed intermediary operating between Captain Gulliver and Benjamin Motte, the actual publisher in London of *Gulliver's Travels* in 1726. Swift used this pseudonym throughout his dealings with Motte. This letter first appears in the 1735 edition of *Gulliver's Travels,* published in Dublin by George Faulkner. See p. 32.

Cousin Dampier. Along with the eighteenth-century mapmaker Herman Moll, one of the few real people mentioned by name in *Gulliver's Travels.* William Dampier (1652–1715), the most famous voyager-narrator of his time, was a pirate, ethnographer, mapmaker, botanist, and meteorologist. See pp. 26–28.

Lord of Oxford. Robert Harley (1661–1724), the leading Tory minister during the reign of Queen Anne and the person most associated with the rise of the political press in England. Harley assembled an intricate opinion-molding apparatus for which Swift served as the foremost writer from 1710 until 1714 (Downie, 1979). See also the note on Lord Munodi, p. 180.

afraid of giving offence; that people in power were very watchful over the press, and apt not only to interpret, but to punish every thing which looked like an *innuendo* (as I think you called it). But pray, how could that which I spoke so many years ago, and at above five thousand leagues distance, in another reign, be applied to any of the yahoos who now are said to govern the herd; especially at a time when I little thought on or feared the unhappiness of living under them? Have not I the most reason to complain, when I see these very yahoos carried by Houyhnhnms in a vehicle, as if these were brutes, and those the rational creatures? And, indeed, to avoid so monstrous and detestable a sight was one principal motive of my retirement hither.

Thus much I thought proper to tell you in relation to your self, and to the trust I reposed in you.

I do in the next place complain of my own great want of judgment, in being prevailed upon by the intreaties and false reasonings of you and some others, very much against mine own opinion, to suffer my travels to be published. Pray bring to your mind how often I desired you to consider, when you insisted on the motive of public good, that the yahoos were a species of animals utterly incapable of amendment by precepts or examples, and so it hath proved; for instead of seeing a full stop put to all abuses and corruptions, at least in this little island, as I had reason to expect: behold, after above six months' warning, I cannot learn that my book hath produced one single effect according to mine intentions: I desired you would let me know by a letter, when party and faction were extinguished; judges learned and upright; pleaders honest and modest, with some tincture of common sense; and Smithfield blazing with pyramids of law-books; the young nobility's education entirely changed; the physicians banished; the female yahoos abounding in virtue, honour, truth and good sense; courts and levees of great ministers thoroughly weeded and swept; wit, merit and learning rewarded; all disgracers of the press in prose and verse condemned to eat nothing but their own cotton, and quench their thirst with their own ink. These, and a thousand other reformations, I firmly counted upon by your encouragement; as indeed they were plainly deducible from the precepts delivered in my book. And, it must be owned, that seven months were a sufficient time to correct every vice and folly to which yahoos are subject, if their natures had been capable of the least disposition to virtue or wisdom; yet so far have you been from answering mine expectation in any of your letters, that on the contrary you are loading our carrier every week with libels, and keys, and reflections,

---

Libels, and keys. Public interest in *Gulliver's Travels* was piqued by the parlor game of decoding its satirical targets. Soon after the first publication of *Gulliver's Travels* in 1726, a wave of "decyphering" guides began to appear, many of them churned out by the unscrupulous publisher Edmund Curll. The decoding game still continues.

and memoirs, and second parts; wherein I see myself accused of reflecting upon great states-folk; of degrading human nature (for so they have still the confidence to style it), and of abusing the female sex. I find likewise, that the writers of those bundles are not agreed among themselves; for some of them will not allow me to be author of mine own travels; and others make me author of books to which I am wholly a stranger.

I find likewise that your printer hath been so careless as to confound the times, and mistake the dates of my several voyages and returns, neither assigning the true year, or the true month, or day of the month; and I hear the original manuscript is all destroyed since the publication of my book. Neither have I any copy left; however, I have sent you some corrections, which you may insert if ever there should be a second edition: and yet I cannot stand to them, but shall leave that matter to my judicious and candid readers, to adjust it as they please.

I hear some of our sea-yahoos find fault with my sea-language, as not proper in many parts, nor now in use. I cannot help it. In my first voyages, while I was young, I was instructed by the oldest mariners, and learned to speak as they did. But I have since found that the sea-yahoos are apt, like the land ones, to become new-fangled in their words; which the latter change every year, insomuch as I remember upon each return to mine own country, their old dialect was so altered that I could hardly understand the new. And I observe, when any yahoo comes from London out of curiosity to visit me at mine own house, we neither of us are able to deliver our conceptions in a manner intelligible to the other.

If the censure of yahoos could any way affect me, I should have great reason to complain that some of them are so bold as to think my book of travels a mere fiction out of mine own brain; and have gone so far as to drop hints that the Houyhnhnms and yahoos have no more existence than the inhabitants of Utopia.

Indeed I must confess, that as to the people of Lilliput, Brobdingrag (for so the word should have been spelt, and not erroneously "Brobdingnag") and Laputa, I have never yet heard of any yahoo so presumptuous as to dispute their being, or the facts I have related concerning them; because the truth immediately strikes every reader with conviction. And is there less probability in my account of the Houyhnhnms or yahoos, when it is manifest as to the latter, there are so many thousands even in this city, who only differ from their brother brutes in Houyhnhnmland, because they use

---

Inhabitants of Utopia. Sir Thomas More published his *Utopia* in 1516. The book's title means "Nowhere." The imaginary voyage described in *Utopia* enables More to criticize actually existing sixteenth-century England by imagining a society that provided universal education and refused to foster inequalities of wealth. See Real, 2001.

a sort of a jabber, and do not go naked? I wrote for their amendment, and not their approbation. The united praise of the whole race would be of less consequence to me than the neighing of those two degenerate Houyhnhnms I keep in my stable; because from these, degenerate as they are, I still improve in some virtues, without any mixture of vice.

Do these miserable animals presume to think that I am so far degenerated as to defend my veracity? Yahoo as I am, it is well known through all Houyhnhnmland, that by the instructions and example of my illustrious master, I was able in the compass of two years (although I confess with the utmost difficulty) to remove that infernal habit of lying, shuffling, deceiving, and equivocating, so deeply rooted in the very souls of all my species, especially the Europeans.

I have other complaints to make upon this vexatious occasion; but I forbear troubling myself or you any further. I must freely confess, that since my last return some corruptions of my yahoo nature have revived in me by conversing with a few of your species, and particularly those of mine own family, by an unavoidable necessity; else I should never have attempted so absurd a project as that of reforming the yahoo race in this kingdom; but I have now done with all such visionary schemes for ever.

April 2, 1727

The Publisher to the Reader

The author of these *Travels,* Mr. Lemuel Gulliver, is my ancient and intimate friend; there is likewise some relation between us by the mother's side. About three years ago Mr. Gulliver, growing weary of the concourse of curious people coming to him at his house in Redriff, made a small purchase of land, with a convenient house, near Newark in Nottinghamshire, his native country; where he now lives retired, yet in good esteem among his neighbours.

Although Mr. Gulliver was born in Nottinghamshire, where his father dwelt, yet I have heard him say, his family came from Oxfordshire; to confirm which, I have observed in the churchyard at Banbury, in that county, several tombs and monuments of the Gullivers.

Before he quitted Redriff, he left the custody of the following papers in my hands, with the liberty to dispose of them as I should think fit. I have carefully perused them three times: the style is very plain and

---

Especially the Europeans. Although *Gulliver's Travels* satirizes the entire human race, the book singles out—as an especially appropriate eighteenth-century target—European arrogance in its relations with the peoples of other continents.

simple; and the only fault I find is, that the author, after the manner of travellers, is a little too circumstantial. There is an air of truth apparent through the whole; and indeed, the author was so distinguished for his veracity, that it became a sort of proverb among his neighbours at Redriff, when any one affirmed a thing, to say, it was as true as if Mr. Gulliver had spoke it.

By the advice of several worthy persons, to whom, with the author's permission, I communicated these papers, I now venture to send them into the world, hoping they may be at least, for some time, a better entertainment to our young noblemen than the common scribbles of politics and party.

This volume would have been at least twice as large, if I had not made bold to strike out innumerable passages relating to the winds and tides, as well as to the variations and bearings in the several voyages; together with the minute descriptions of the management of the ship in storms, in the style of sailors: likewise the account of the longitudes and latitudes; wherein I have reason to apprehend that Mr. Gulliver may be a little dissatisfied: but I was resolved to fit the work as much as possible to the general capacity of readers. However, if my own ignorance in sea-affairs shall have led me to commit some mistakes, I alone am answerable for them: and if any traveler hath a curiosity to see the whole work at large, as it came from the hand of the author, I will be ready to gratify him.

As for any further particulars relating to the author, the reader will receive satisfaction from the first pages of the book.

Richard Sympson.

The Contents

Part I

[*A Voyage to Lilliput*]

Winds and tides. Dampier's main claim to scientific fame was his *Discourse of the Trade-Winds, Breezes, Storms, Seasons of the Year, Tides and Currents of the* Torrid Zone *throughout the World* (1699). The map on p. 390 accompanied this treatise.

Chap. II. *The Emperor of Lilliput, attended by several of the nobility, come to see the author in his confinement. The Emperor's person and habit described. Learned men appointed to teach the author their language. He gains favour by his mild disposition. His pockets are searched, and his sword and pistols taken from him.*

Chap. III. *The author diverts the Emperor and his nobility of both sexes, in a very uncommon manner. The diversions of the court of Lilliput described. The author hath his liberty granted him upon certain conditions.*

Chap. IV. *Mildendo, the metropolis of Lilliput, described, together with the Emperor's palace. A conversation between the author and a principal secretary, concerning the affairs of that empire. The author's offers to serve the Emperor in his wars.*

Chap. V. *The author, by an extraordinary stratagem, prevents an invasion. A high title of honour is conferred upon him. Ambassadors arrive from the Emperor of Blefuscu and sue for peace. The Empress's apartment on fire by an accident. The author instrumental in saving the rest of the palace.*

Chap. VI. *Of the inhabitants of Lilliput, their learning, laws and customs, the manner of educating their children. The author's way of living in that country. His vindication of a great lady.*

Chap. VII. *The author, being informed of a design to accuse him of high treason, makes his escape to Blefuscu. His reception there.*

Chap. VIII. *The author, by a lucky accident, finds means to leave Blefuscu, and after some difficulties returns safe to his native country.*

Part II

[*A Voyage to Brobdingnag*]

Chap. I. *A great storm described, the long-boat sent to fetch water, the author goes with it to discover the country. He is left on shore, is seized by one of the natives, and carried to a farmer's house. His reception there, with several accidents that happened there. A description of the inhabitants.*

Chap. II. *A description of the farmer's daughter. The author carried to a market-town, and then to the metropolis. The particulars of his journey.*

Chap. III. *The author sent for to court. The Queen buys him of his master the farmer, and presents him to the King. He disputes with his Majesty's great scholars. An apartment at court provided for the author. He is in high favour with the Queen. He stands up for the honour of his own country. His quarrels with the Queen's dwarf.*

Chap. IV. *The country described. A proposal for correcting modern maps. The King's palace, and some account of the metropolis. The author's way of travelling. The chief temple described.*

Chap. V. *Several adventures that happened to the author. The execution of a criminal. The author shows his skill in navigation.*

Chap. VI. *Several contrivances of the author to please the King and Queen. He shows his skill in music. The King enquires into the state of Europe, which the author relates to him. The King's observations thereon.*

Chap. VII. *The author's love of his country. He makes a proposal of much advantage to the King, which is rejected. The learning of that country very imperfect and confined. Their laws, and military affairs, and parties in the State.*

Chap. VIII. *The King and Queen make a progress to the frontiers. The author attends them. The manner in which he leaves the country very particularly related. He returns to England.*

Part III

[*A Voyage to Laputa, Balnibarbi, Glubbdubdrib, Luggnagg, and Japan*]

Chap. I. *The author sets out on his third voyage; is taken by pirates. The malice of a Dutchman. His arrival at an island. He is received into Laputa.*

Chap. II. *The humours and dispositions of the Laputans described. An account of their learning. Of the King and his court. The author's reception there. The inhabitants subject to fears and disquietudes. An account of the women.*

Chap. III. *A phænomenon solved by modern philosophy and astronomy. The Laputans' great improvements in the latter. The King's method of suppressing insurrections.*

Chap. IV. *The author leaves Laputa, is conveyed to Balnibarbi, arrives at the metropolis. A description of the metropolis and the country adjoining. The author hospitably received by a great lord. His conversation with that lord.*

Chap. V. *The author permitted to see the Grand Academy of Lagado. The Academy largely described. The arts wherein the professors employ themselves.*

Chap. VI. *A further account of the Academy. The author proposes some improvements, which are honourably received.*

Chap. VII. *The author leaves Lagado, arrives at Maldonada. No ship ready. He takes a short voyage to Glubbdubdrib. His reception by the Governor.*

Chap. VIII. *A further account of Glubbdubdrib. Ancient and modern history corrected.*

Chap. IX. *The author's return to Maldonada. Sails to the kingdom of Luggnagg. The author confined. He is sent for to court. The manner of his admittance. The King's great lenity to his subjects.*

Chap. X. *The Luggnaggians commended. A particular description of the struldbruggs, with many conversations between the author and some eminent persons upon that subject.*

Chap. XI. *The author leaves Luggnagg, and sails to Japan. From thence he returns in a Dutch ship to Amsterdam, and from Amsterdam to England.*

Part IV

[*A Voyage to the Country of the Houyhnhnms*]

Chap. I. *The author sets out as captain of a ship. His men conspire against him, confine him a long time to his cabin. Set him on shore in an unknown land. He travels up in the country. The yahoos, a strange sort of animal, described. The author meets two Houyhnhnms.*

Chap. II. *The author conducted by a Houyhnhnm to his house. The house described. The author's reception. The food of the Houyhnhnms. The author in distress for want of meat, is at last relieved. His manner of feeding in this country.*

Chap. III. *The author studious to learn the language, the Houyhnhnm his master assists in teaching him. The language described. Several Houyhnhnms of quality come out of curiosity to see the author. He gives his master a short account of his voyage.*

Chap. IV. *The Houyhnhnms' notion of truth and falsehood. The author's discourse disapproved by his master. The author gives a more particular account of himself, and the accidents of his voyage.*

Chap. V. *The author at his master's command informs him of the state of England. The causes of war among the princes of Europe. The author begins to explain the English constitution.*

Chap. VI. *A continuation of the state of England under Queen Anne. The character of a first minister in the courts of Europe.*

Chap. VII. *The author's great love of his native country. His master's observations upon the constitution and administration of England, as described by the author, with parallel cases and comparisons. His master's observations upon human nature.*

Chap. VIII. *The author relates several particulars of the yahoos. The great virtues of the Houyhnhnms. The education and exercises of their youth. Their general assembly.*

Chap. IX. *A grand debate at the general assembly of the Houyhnhnms, and how it was determined. The learning of the Houyhnhnms. Their buildings. Their manner of burials. The defectiveness of their language.*

Chap. X. *The author's œconomy and happy life among the Houyhnhnms. His great improvement in virtue, by conversing with them. Their conversations. The author has notice given him by his master that he must depart from the country. He falls into a swoon for grief, but submits. He contrives and finishes a canoe, by the help of a fellow-servant, and puts to sea at a venture.*

Chap. XI. *The author's dangerous voyage. He arrives at New Holland, hoping to settle there. Is wounded with an arrow by one of the natives. Is seized and carried by force into a Portuguese ship. The great civilities of the captain. The author arrives at England.*

Chap. XII. *The author's veracity. His design in publishing this work. His censure of those travellers who swerve from the truth. The author clears himself from any sinister ends in writing. An objection answered. The method of planting colonies. His native country commended. The right of the crown to those countries described by the author is justified. The difficulty of conquering them. The author takes his last leave of the reader, proposeth his manner of living for the future, gives good advice, and concludes.*

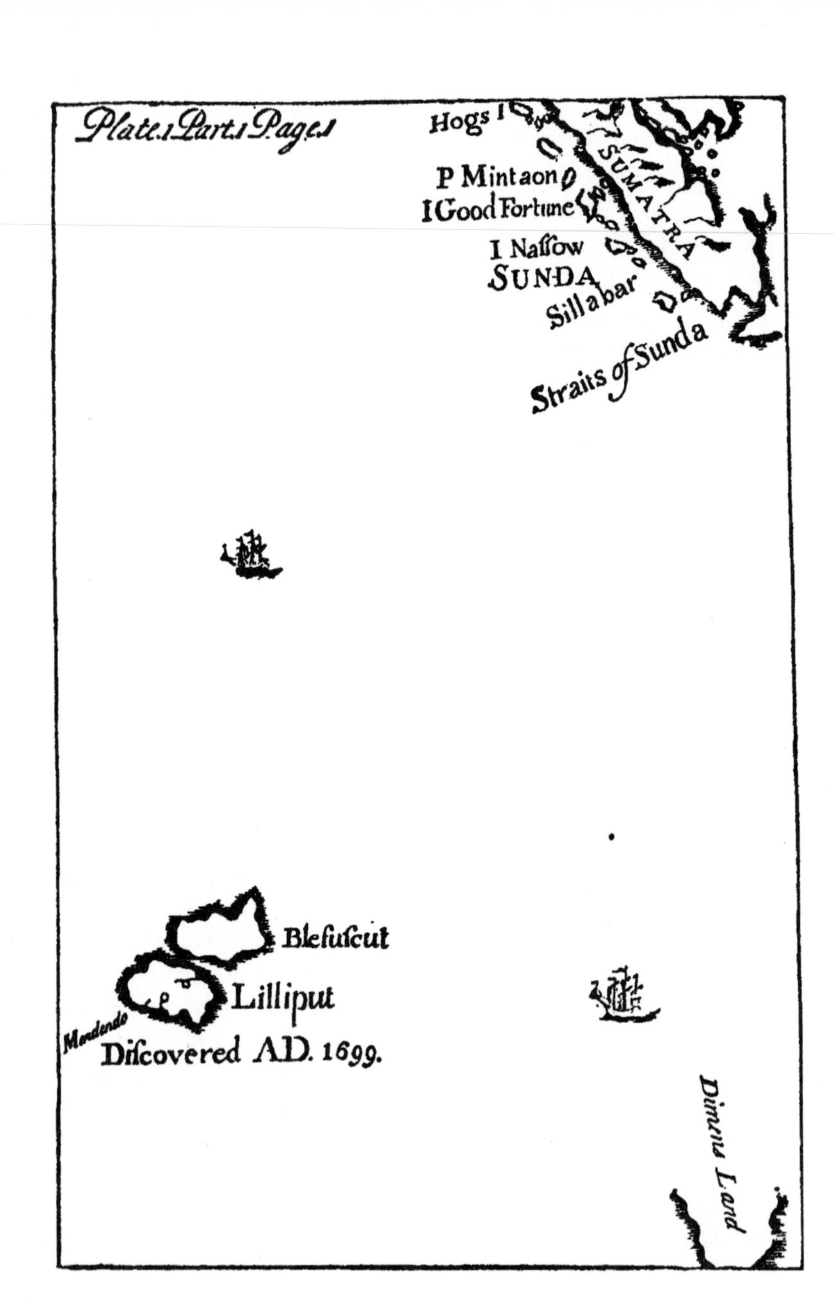
Plate.1 Part.1 Page.1
Hogs I
P Mintaon
I Good Fortune
SUMATRA
I Nassow
SUNDA
Sillabar
Straits of Sunda
Blefuscu
Lilliput
Discovered AD. 1699.
Dimens Land

Travels

Part I

A Voyage to Lilliput

CHAPTER I

The author gives some account of himself and family; his first inducements to travel. He is shipwrecked, and swims for his life, gets safe on shore in the country of Lilliput, is made a prisoner, and carried up the country.

My father had a small estate in Nottinghamshire; I was the third of five sons. He sent me to Emanuel College in Cambridge, at fourteen years old, where I resided three years, and applied my self close to my studies: but the charge of maintaining me (although I had a very scanty allowance) being too great for a narrow fortune, I was bound apprentice to Mr. James Bates, an eminent surgeon in London, with whom I continued four years; and my father now and then sending me small sums of money, I laid them out in learning navigation, and other parts of the mathematics, useful to those who intend to travel, as I always believed it would be some time or other my fortune to do. When I left Mr. Bates, I went down to my father; where, by the assistance of him and my uncle John, and some other relations I got forty pounds, and a promise of thirty pounds a year to maintain me at

---

Emanuel College. Founded in 1584 at Cambridge University; known in Gulliver's era as a stronghold of Puritan sentiment. Gulliver's scriptural first name, *Lemuel* (Hebrew for "devoted to God"), may likewise suggest an atmosphere of nonconformity such as that surrounding the dissenting author of *Robinson Crusoe,* Daniel Defoe. See Wagner, 62–63.

Navigation. Herman Moll's *Atlas Geographus: or, A Compleat System of Geography, Ancient and Modern* (London: 1711–17) introduces the topic of geography with an extended discussion of geometry, arithmetic, and trigonometry.

Leyden: there I studied physic two years and seven months, knowing it would be useful in long voyages.

Soon after my return from Leyden, I was recommended, by my good master Mr. Bates, to be surgeon to the *Swallow*, Captain Abraham Pannell commander; with whom I continued three years and a half, making a voyage or two into the Levant, and some other parts. When I came back, I resolved to settle in London, to which Mr. Bates, my master, encouraged me, and by him I was recommended to several patients. I took part of a small house in the Old Jury; and being advised to alter my condition, I married Mrs. Mary Burton, second daughter to Mr. Edmond Burton hosier in Newgate Street, with whom I received four hundred pounds for a portion.

But, my good master Bates dying in two years after, and I having few friends, my business began to fail; for my conscience would not suffer me to imitate the bad practice of too many among my brethren. Having therefore consulted with my wife, and some of my acquaintance, I determined to go again to sea. I was surgeon successively in two ships, and made several voyages, for six years, to the East and West Indies, by which I got some addition to my fortune. My hours of leisure I spent in reading the best authors ancient and modern, being always provided with a good number of books; and when I was ashore, in observing the manners and dispositions of the people, as well as learning their language, wherein I had a great facility by the strength of my memory.

Leyden. The site of a prestigious medical school that drew students from all over Europe. The training at this Dutch university emphasized a major cultural phenomenon of the Enlightenment: the public dissection of human cadavers in anatomy theaters.

Physic. medicine. Along with law and theology, one of three learned professions at this time. Academically trained physicians were satirically equated with undertakers, not without reason, and they were forced to compete against a lively array of quacks, folk healers, and astrologers.

The Levant. The Near East, especially Syria and Lebanon.

The Old Jury. *Gulliver's Travels,* like *Robinson Crusoe,* opens with a pointed emphasis on the middling status of its narrator. The neighborhood of the Old Jury, near London's financial district, suits this picture. William Dampier died in the Old Jury in 1715.

***Mrs.* Mary Burton.** The term *Mrs.* signals respectability rather than marital status.

East and West Indies. Due to the geographical disorientation of Christopher Columbus—he believed he had found a westward route to the Spice Islands in Southeast Asia—the new world (of the Caribbean) was confounded with the old one (of the lands of the Great Khan). The contagious force of this blunder is reflected in the all-encompassing term *Indian,* subsequently applied by Europeans to indigenous peoples around the globe.

The last of these voyages not proving very fortunate, I grew weary of the sea, and intended to stay at home with my wife and family. I removed from the Old Jury to Fetter Lane, and from thence to Wapping, hoping to get business among the sailors; but it would not turn to account. After three years' expectation that things would mend, I accepted an advantageous offer from Captain William Prichard, master of the *Antelope*, who was making a voyage to the South Sea. We set sail from Bristol May 4th, 1699, and our voyage at first was very prosperous.

It would not be proper, for some reasons, to trouble the reader with the particulars of our adventures in those seas: let it suffice to inform him, that in our passage from thence to the East Indies we were driven by a violent storm to the northwest of Van Diemen's Land. By an observation, we found ourselves in the latitude of 30 degrees 2 minutes south. Twelve of our crew were dead by immoderate labour, and ill food, the rest were in a very weak condition. On the fifth of November, which was the beginning of summer in those parts, the weather being very hazy, the seamen spied a rock, within half a cable's length of the ship; but the wind was so strong, that we were driven directly upon it, and immediately split. Six of the crew, of whom I was one, having let down the boat into the sea, made a shift to get clear of the ship, and the rock. We rowed by my computation about three leagues, till we were able to work no longer, being already spent with labour while we were in the ship. We therefore trusted ourselves to the mercy of the waves, and in about half an hour the boat was overset by a sudden flurry from the north. What became of my companions in the boat, as well as of those who escaped on the rock, or were left in the vessel, I cannot tell; but

---

The Antelope. Dampier met the *Antelope* of London, bound for the East Indies, on June 3, 1699, off the Cape of Good Hope. See Bonner, 167.

South Sea. "Discovered" by Vasco Nuñez de Balboa in 1513. By the early eighteenth century, the South Sea—the western rim of the Spanish American empire—was increasingly the object of British colonial aspirations. The published works of such South Sea voyagers as Dampier, Lionel Wafer, Woodes Rogers, John Narbrough, George Shelvocke, and William Betagh fueled dreams of inexhaustible colonial wealth.

Van Diemen's Land. An island off the southeastern shore of Australia, now named *Tasmania* (after its so-called discoverer, the Dutch explorer Abel Janszoon Tasman). Tasman's voyage proved that Australia is an island rather than part of a fabled southern continent extending toward the pole. An English translation of Tasman's journal from this voyage appeared in 1694.

Fifth of November. A highly charged date for a shipwreck. November 5 was the anniversary of the landing of William of Orange at Torbay, famously forwarded by a "Protestant wind." At William's insistence, moreover, the traditional prayer of deliverance from the Gunpowder Plot was subsequently amended to incorporate thanksgivings that his own arrival had providentially delivered the church and nation (Cruickshanks, 40–41).

conclude they were all lost. For my own part, I swam as fortune directed me, and was pushed forward by wind and tide. I often let my legs drop, and could feel no bottom: but when I was almost gone and able to struggle no longer, I found myself within my depth; and by this time the storm was much abated. The declivity was so small, that I walked near a mile before I got to the shore, which I conjectured was about eight o'clock in the evening. I then advanced forward near half a mile, but could not discover any sign of houses or inhabitants; at least I was in so weak a condition, that I did not observe them. I was extremely tired, and with that, and the heat of the weather, and about half a pint of brandy that I drank as I left the ship, I found myself much inclined to sleep. I lay down on the grass, which was very short and soft, where I slept sounder than ever I remember to have done in my life, and, as I reckoned, above nine hours; for when I awaked, it was just daylight. I attempted to rise, but was not able to stir: for as I happened to lie on my back, I found my arms and legs were strongly fastened on each side to the ground; and my hair, which was long and thick, tied down in the same manner. I likewise felt several slender ligatures across my body, from my armpits to my thighs. I could only look upwards, the sun began to grow hot, and the light offended my eyes. I heard a confused noise about me, but, in the posture I lay, could see nothing except the sky. In a little time I felt something alive moving on my left leg, which advancing gently forward over my breast, came almost up to my chin; when, bending my eyes downwards as much as I could, I perceived it to be a human creature not six inches high, with a bow and arrow in his hands, and a quiver at his back. In the mean time, I felt at least forty more of the same kind (as I conjectured) following the first. I was in the utmost astonishment, and roared so loud, that they all ran back in a fright; and some of them, as I was afterwards told, were hurt with the falls they got by leaping from my sides upon the ground. However, they soon returned, and one of them, who ventured so far as to get a full sight of my face, lifting up his hands and eyes by way of admiration, cried out in a shrill, but distinct voice, *Hekinah degul:* the others repeated the same words several times, but I then knew not what they meant. I lay all this while, as the reader may believe, in great uneasiness: at length, struggling to get loose, I had the fortune to break the strings and wrench out the pegs that fastened my left arm to the ground; for, by lifting it up to my face, I discovered the methods they had taken to bind me; and, at the same time, with a violent pull, which gave me excessive pain, I a little loosened the strings that tied down my hair on the left side, so that I was just able to turn my head about two inches. But the creatures ran off a second time, before I could seize them; whereupon there was a great shout in a very shrill accent, and after it ceased, I heard one of them cry aloud, *Tolgo phonac;* when in an instant I felt above an hundred arrows discharged on my left hand, which pricked me like so many needles; and besides they shot another flight into the air, as we do bombs in Europe, whereof many, I suppose, fell on my body (though I felt them not) and some on my face, which I immediately covered with my left hand. When this shower of arrows was over, I fell a groaning with grief and pain, and then striving again to get loose, they discharged another volley larger than the first, and some of them attempted with spears to stick me in the sides; but, by good luck, I had on me a buff jerkin, which they could not pierce. I thought it the most prudent method to lie still, and my design was to continue so till night, when, my left hand being already loose, I could easily free myself: and as for the inhabitants, I had reason to believe I might be a match for the greatest armies they could bring against me, if they were all of the same size with him that I saw. But fortune disposed otherwise of me. When the people observed I was quiet, they discharged no more arrows: but by the noise increasing, I knew their numbers were greater; and about four yards from me, over-against my right ear, I heard a knocking for above an hour, like people at work; when, turning my head that way, as well as the pegs and strings would permit me, I saw a stage erected about a foot and a half from the ground, capable of holding four of the inhabitants, with two or three ladders to mount it: from whence one of them, who seemed to be a person of quality, made me a long speech, whereof I understood not one syllable. But I should have mentioned, that before the principal person began his oration, he cried out three times, *Langro dehul san:* (these words and the former were afterwards repeated and explained to me). Whereupon immediately about fifty of the inhabitants came, and cut the strings that fastened the left side of my head, which gave me the liberty of turning it to the right, and of observing the person and gesture of him who was to speak. He appeared to be of a middle age, and taller than any of the other three who attended him, whereof one was a page who held up his train, and seemed to be some-what longer than my middle finger; the other two stood one on each side to support him. He acted every part of an orator, and I could observe many periods of threatenings, and others of promises, pity and kindness. I answered in a few words, but in the most submissive manner, lifting up my left hand and both eyes to the sun, as calling him for a witness; and being almost famished with hunger, having not eaten a morsel for some hours before I left the ship, I found the demands of nature so strong upon me, that I could not forbear showing my impatience (perhaps against the strict rules of decency) by putting my finger frequently on my mouth, to signify that I wanted food. The *Hurgo* (for so they call a great lord, as I afterwards learnt) understood me very well. He descended from the stage, and commanded that several ladders should be applied to my sides, on which above an hundred of the inhabitants mounted, and walked towards my mouth, laden with baskets full of meat, which had been provided and sent thither by the King's orders upon the first intelligence he received of me. I observed there was the flesh of several animals, but could not distinguish them by the taste. There were shoulders, legs and loins shaped like those of mutton, and very well dressed, but smaller than the wings of a lark. I eat them by two or three at a mouthful, and took three loaves at a time, about the bigness of musket bullets. They supplied me as fast as they could, showing a thousand marks of wonder and astonishment at my bulk and appetite. I then made another sign that I wanted drink. They found by my eating that a small quantity would not suffice me, and being a most ingenious people, they slung up with great dexterity one of their largest hogsheads, then rolled it towards my hand, and beat out the top; I drank it off at a draught, which I might well do, for it hardly held half a pint, and tasted like a small wine of Burgundy, but much more delicious. They brought me a second hogshead, which I drank in the same manner, and made signs for more, but they had none to give me. When I had performed these wonders, they shouted for joy, and danced upon my breast, repeating several times as they did at first, *Hekinah degul.* They made me a sign that I should throw down the two hogsheads, but first warned the people below to stand out of the way, crying aloud, *Borach mivola,* and when they saw the vessels in the air, there was an universal shout of *Hekinah degul.* I confess I was often tempted, while they were passing backwards and forwards on my body, to seize forty or fifty of the first that came in my reach, and dash them against the ground. But the remembrance of what I had felt, which probably might not be the worst they could do, and the promise of honour I made them, for so I interpreted my submissive behavior, soon drove out those imaginations. Besides, I now considered my self as bound by the laws of hospitality to a people who had treated me with so much expense and magnificence. However, in my thoughts I could not sufficiently wonder at the intrepidity of these diminutive mortals, who durst venture to mount and walk on my body, while one of my hands was at liberty, without trembling at the very sight of so prodigious a creature as I must appear to them. After some time, when they observed that I made no more demands for meat, there appeared before me a person of high rank from his Imperial Majesty. His Excellency, having mounted on the small of my right leg, advanced forwards up to my face, with about a dozen of his retinue. And producing his credentials under the Signet Royal, which he applied close to my eyes, spoke about ten minutes, without any signs of anger, but with a kind of determinate resolution; often pointing forwards, which, as I afterwards found, was towards the capital city, about half a mile distant, whither it was agreed by his Majesty in council that I must be conveyed. I answered in few words, but to no purpose, and made a sign with my hand that was loose, putting it to the other (but over his Excellency's head, for fear of hurting him or his train) and then to my own head and body, to signify that I desired my liberty. It appeared that he understood me well enough, for he shook his head by way of disapprobation, and held his hand in a posture to show that I must be carried as a prisoner. However, he made other signs to let me understand that I should have meat and drink enough, and very good treatment. Whereupon I once more thought of attempting to break my bonds, but again, when I felt the smart of their arrows upon my face and hands, which were all in blisters, and many of the darts still sticking in them, and observing likewise that the number of my enemies encreased, I gave tokens to let them know that they might do with me what they pleased. Upon this the *Hurgo* and his train withdrew with much civility and cheerful countenances. Soon after I heard a general shout, with frequent repetitions of the words, *Peplom selan,* and I felt great numbers of the people on my left side relaxing the cords to such a degree, that I was able to turn upon my right, and to ease myself with making water; which I very plentifully did, to the great astonishment of the people, who conjecturing by my motions what I was going to do, immediately opened to the right and left on that side to avoid the torrent which fell with such noise and violence from me. But before this, they had daubed my face and both my hands with a sort of ointment very pleasant to the smell, which in a few minutes removed all the smart of their arrows. These circumstances, added to the refreshment I had received by their victuals and drink, which were very nourishing, disposed me to sleep. I slept about eight hours, as I was afterwards assured; and it was no wonder, for the physicians, by the Emperor's order, had mingled a sleeping potion in the hogsheads of wine.

It seems that upon the first moment I was discovered sleeping on the ground after my landing, the Emperor had early notice of it by an express, and determined in council that I should be tied in the manner I have related (which was done in the night while I slept), that plenty of meat and drink should be sent me, and a machine prepared to carry me to the capital city.

This resolution perhaps may appear very bold and dangerous, and I am confident would not be imitated by any prince in Europe on the like occasion; however, in my opinion, it was extremely prudent as well as generous. For supposing these people had endeavoured to kill me with their spears and arrows while I was asleep, I should certainly have awaked with the first sense of smart, which might so far have roused my rage and strength, as to enable me to break the strings wherewith I was tied; after which, as they were not able to make resistance, so they could expect no mercy.

These people are most excellent mathematicians, and arrived to a great perfection in mechanics by the countenance and encouragement of the Emperor, who is a renowned patron of learning. This prince hath several machines fixed on wheels for the carriage of trees and other great weights. He often builds his largest men of war, whereof some are nine foot long, in the woods where the timber grows, and has them carried on these engines three or four hundred yards to the sea. Five hundred carpenters and engineers were immediately set at work to prepare the greatest engine they had. It was a frame of wood raised three inches from the ground, about seven foot long and four wide, moving upon twenty-two wheels. The shout I heard was upon the arrival of this engine, which it seems set out in four hours after my landing. It was brought parallel to me as I lay. But the principal difficulty was to raise and place me in this vehicle. Eighty poles, each of one foot high, were erected for this purpose, and very strong cords of the bigness of packthread were fastened by hooks to many bandages, which the workmen had girt round my neck, my hands, my body, and my legs. Nine hundred of the strongest men were employed to draw up these cords by many pulleys fastened on the poles, and thus, in less than three hours, I was raised and slung into the engine, and there tied fast. All this I was told, for while the whole operation was performing, I lay in a profound sleep, by the force of that soporiferous medicine infused into my liquor. Fifteen hundred of the Emperor's largest horses, each about four inches and a half high, were employed to draw me towards the metropolis, which, as I said, was half a mile distant.

About four hours after we began our journey, I awaked by a very ridiculous accident; for, the carriage being stopped a while to adjust something that was out of order, two or three of the young natives had the curiosity to see how I looked when I was asleep; they climbed up into the engine, and advancing very softly to my face, one of them, an officer in the guards, put the sharp end of his half-pike a good way up into my left nostril, which tickled my nose like a straw, and made me sneeze violently: whereupon they stole off unperceived, and it was three weeks before I knew the cause of my awaking so suddenly. We made a long march the remaining part of the day, and rested at night with five hundred guards on each side of me, half with torches, and half with bows and arrows, ready to shoot me if I should offer to stir. The next morning at sunrise we continued our march, and arrived within two hundred yards of the city gates about noon. The Emperor and all his court came out to meet us, but his great officers would by no means suffer his Majesty to endanger his person by mounting on my body.

At the place where the carriage stopped, there stood an ancient temple, esteemed to be the largest in the whole kingdom, which having been polluted some years before by an unnatural murder, was, according to the zeal of those people, looked on as profane, and therefore had been applied to common use, and all the ornaments and furniture carried away. In this edifice it was determined I should lodge. The great gate fronting to the north was about four foot high, and almost two foot wide, through which I could easily creep. On each side of the gate was a small window not above six inches from the ground: into that on the left side, the King's smiths conveyed fourscore and eleven chains, like those that hang to a lady's watch in Europe, and almost as large, which were locked to my left leg with six and thirty padlocks. Over against this temple, on the other side of the great highway, at twenty foot distance, there was a turret at least five foot high. Here the Emperor ascended with many principal lords of his court, to have an opportunity of viewing me, as I was told, for I could not see them. It was reckoned that above an hundred thousand inhabitants came out of the town upon the same errand; and in spite of my guards, I believe there could not be fewer than ten thousand, at several times, who mounted upon my body by the help of ladders. But a proclamation was soon issued to forbid it upon pain of death. When the workmen found it was impossible for me to break loose, they cut all the strings that bound me; whereupon I rose up with as melancholy a disposition as ever I had in my life. But the noise and astonishment of the people at seeing me rise and walk are not to be expressed. The chains that held my left leg were about two yards long, and gave me not only the liberty of walking backwards and forwards in a semicircle; but, being fixed within four inches of the gate, allowed me to creep in, and lie at my full length in the temple.

CHAPTER II

The Emperor of Lilliput, attended by several of the nobility, comes to see the author in his confinement. The Emperor's person and habit described. Learned men appointed to teach the author their language. He gains favour by his mild disposition. His pockets are searched, and his sword and pistols taken from him.

When I found myself on my feet, I looked about me, and must confess I never beheld a more entertaining prospect. The country round appeared like a continued garden, and the inclosed fields, which were generally forty foot square, resembled so many beds of flowers. These fields were intermingled with woods of half a stang, and the tallest trees, as I could judge, appeared to be seven foot high. I viewed the town on my left hand, which looked like the painted scene of a city in a theatre.

I had been for some hours extremely pressed by the necessities of nature; which was no wonder, it being almost two days since I had last disburthened myself. I was under great difficulties between urgency and shame. The best expedient I could think on, was to creep into my house, which I accordingly did; and shutting the gate after me, I went as far as the length of my chain would suffer, and discharged my body of that uneasy load. But this was the only time I was ever guilty of so uncleanly an action; for which I cannot but hope the candid reader will give some allowance, after he hath maturely and impartially considered my case, and the distress I was in. From this time my constant practice was, as soon as I rose, to perform that business in open air, at the full extent of my chain, and due care was taken every morning before company came, that the offensive matter should be carried off in wheelbarrows by two servants appointed for that purpose. I would not have dwelt so long upon a circumstance, that perhaps at first sight may appear not very momentous, if I had not thought it necessary to justify my character in point of cleanliness to the world; which I am told some of my maligners have been pleased, upon this and other occasions, to call in question.

When this adventure was at an end, I came back out of my house, having occasion for fresh air. The Emperor was already descended from the tower, and advancing on horseback towards me, which had like to have cost him dear; for the beast, although very well trained, yet wholly unused to such a sight, which appeared as if a mountain moved before him, reared up on his hinder feet: but that prince, who is an excellent horseman, kept his seat, until his attendants ran in, and held the bridle, while his Majesty had time to dismount. When he alighted, he surveyed me round with great admiration, but kept beyond the length of my chains. He ordered his cooks and butlers, who were already prepared, to give me victuals and drink, which they pushed forward in a sort of vehicles upon wheels until I could reach them. I took these vehicles, and soon emptied them all; twenty of them were filled with meat, and ten with liquor; each of the former afforded me two or three good mouthfuls, and I emptied the liquor of ten vessels, which was contained in earthen vials, into one vehicle, drinking it off at a draught, and so I did with the rest. The Empress, and young princes of the blood, of both sexes, attended by many ladies, sat at some distance

---

Stang. Square rod; a quarter of an acre.

in their chairs; but upon the accident that happened to the Emperor's horse, they alighted, and came near his person, which I am now going to describe. He is taller, by almost the breadth of my nail, than any of his court, which alone is enough to strike an awe into the beholders. His features are strong and masculine, with an Austrian lip and arched nose, his complexion olive, his countenance erect, his body and limbs well proportioned, all his motions graceful, and his deportment majestic. He was then past his prime, being twenty-eight years and three quarters old, of which he had reigned about seven, in great felicity, and generally victorious. For the better convenience of beholding him, I lay on my side, so that my face was parallel to his, and he stood but three yards off: however, I have had him since many times in my hand, and therefore cannot be deceived in the description. His dress was very plain and simple, and the fashion of it between the Asiatic and the European; but he had on his head a light helmet of gold, adorned with jewels, and a plume on the crest. He held his sword drawn in his hand, to defend himself, if I should happen to break loose; it was almost three inches long, the hilt and scabbard were gold enriched with diamonds. His voice was shrill, but very clear and articulate, and I could distinctly hear it when I stood up. The ladies and courtiers were all most magnificently clad, so that the spot they stood upon seemed to resemble a petticoat spread on the ground, embroidered with figures of gold and silver. His Imperial Majesty spoke often to me, and I returned answers, but neither of us could understand a syllable. There were several of his priests and lawyers present (as I conjectured by their habits) who were commanded to address themselves to me, and I spoke to them in as many languages as I had the least smattering of, which were High and Low Dutch, Latin, French, Spanish, Italian, and Lingua Franca; but all to no purpose. After about two hours the court retired, and I was left with a strong guard, to prevent the impertinence, and probably the malice of the rabble, who were very impatient to crowd about me as near as they durst, and some of them had the impudence to shoot their arrows at me as I sat on the ground by the door of my house, whereof one very narrowly missed my left eye. But the colonel ordered six of the ringleaders to be seized, and thought no punishment so proper as to deliver them bound into my hands, which some of his soldiers accordingly did, pushing them forwards with the butt-ends of their pikes into my reach; I took them all in my right hand, put five of them into my coat-pocket, and as to the sixth,

---

Austrian lip and arched nose. Hapsburg features. The War of the Spanish Succession had its immediate origins in dynastic wrangling between the Hapsburgs in Austria and the Bourbons in France, both Catholic dynasties. Austria was part of England's coalition against France.

I made a countenance as if I would eat him alive. The poor man squalled terribly, and the colonel and his officers were in much pain, especially when they saw me take out my penknife: but I soon put them out of fear; for, looking mildly, and immediately cutting the strings he was bound with, I set him gently on the ground, and away he ran; I treated the rest in the same manner, taking them one by one out of my pocket, and I observed both the soldiers and people were highly obliged at this mark of my clemency, which was represented very much to my advantage at court.

Towards night I got with some difficulty into my house, where I lay on the ground, and continued to do so about a fortnight; during which time the Emperor gave orders to have a bed prepared for me. Six hundred beds of the common measure were brought in carriages, and worked up in my house; an hundred and fifty of their beds sewn together made up the breadth and length, and these were four double, which however kept me but very indifferently from the hardness of the floor, that was of smooth stone. By the same computation they provided me with sheets, blankets, and coverlets, tolerable enough for one who had been so long enured to hardships as I.

As the news of my arrival spread through the kingdom, it brought prodigious numbers of rich, idle, and curious people to see me; so that the villages were almost emptied, and great neglect of tillage and household affairs must have ensued, if his Imperial Majesty had not provided by several proclamations and orders of state against this inconveniency. He directed that those who had already beheld me should return home, and not presume to come within fifty yards of my house without licence from court: whereby the secretaries of state got considerable fees.

In the mean time, the Emperor held frequent councils to debate what course should be taken with me; and I was afterwards assured by a particular friend, a person of great quality, who was as much in the secret as any, that the court was under many difficulties concerning me. They apprehended my breaking loose, that my diet would be very expensive, and might cause a famine. Sometimes they determined to starve me, or at least to shoot me in the face and hands with poisoned arrows, which would soon dispatch me: but again they considered, that the stench of so large a carcase might produce a plague in the metropolis, and probably spread through the whole kingdom. In the midst of these consultations, several officers of the army went to the door of the great council-chamber; and two of them being admitted, gave an account of my behaviour to the six criminals above-mentioned, which made so favourable an impression in the breast of his Majesty and the whole board in my behalf, that an imperial commission was issued out, obliging all the villages nine hundred yards round the city to deliver in every morning six beeves, forty sheep, and other victuals for my sustenance; together with a proportionable quantity of bread, and wine, and other liquors: for the due payment of which his Majesty gave assignments upon his treasury. For this prince lives chiefly upon his own demesnes, seldom except upon great occasions raising any subsidies upon his subjects, who are bound to attend him in his wars at their own expense. An establishment was also made of six hundred persons to be my domestics, who had board-wages allowed for their maintenance, and tents built for them very conveniently on each side of my door. It was likewise ordered, that three hundred tailors should make me a suit of clothes after the fashion of the country: that six of his Majesty's greatest scholars should be employed to instruct me in their language: and, lastly, that the Emperor's horses, and those of the nobility and troops of guards, should be exercised in my sight, to accustom themselves to me. All these orders were duly put in execution, and in about three weeks I made a great progress in learning their language; during which time the Emperor frequently honoured me with his visits, and was pleased to assist my masters in teaching me. We began already to converse together in some sort; and the first words I learnt were to express my desire that he would please to give me my liberty, which I every day repeated on my knees. His answer, as I could apprehend was, that this must be a work of time, not to be thought on without the advice of his council, and that first I must *lumos kelmin pesso desmar lon emposo;* that is, swear a peace with him and his kingdom. However, that I should be used with all kindness, and he advised me to acquire, by my patience, and discreet behaviour, the good opinion of himself and his subjects. He desired I would not take it ill, if he gave orders to certain proper officers to search me; for probably I might carry about me several weapons, which must needs be dangerous things, if they answered the bulk of so prodigious a person. I said, his Majesty should be satisfied, for I was ready to strip myself, and turn up my pockets before him. This I delivered part in words, and part in signs. He replied, that by the laws of the kingdom I must be searched by two of his officers; that he knew this could not be done without my consent and assistance; that he had so good an opinion of my generosity and justice, as to trust their persons in my hands: that whatever they took from me should be returned when I left the country, or paid for at the rate which I would set upon them. I took up the two officers in my hands, put them first into my coat-pockets, and then into every other

---

Their own expense. The Lilliputians have not begun to harness national credit for deficit financing. Gulliver, though intermittently useful, is of course also a serious drain on Lilliput's resources. See Brantlinger, 65–68.

pocket about me, except my two fobs, and another secret pocket which I had no mind should be searched, wherein I had some little necessaries of no consequence to any but myself. In one of my fobs there was a silver watch, and in the other a small quantity of gold in a purse. These gentlemen, having pen, ink and paper about them, made an exact inventory of every thing they saw; and when they had done, desired I would set them down, that they might deliver it to the Emperor. This inventory I afterwards translated into English, and is word for word as follows.

Imprimis, In the right coat-pocket of the Great Man-Mountain (for so I interpret the words *Quinbus Flestrin*) after the strictest search, we found only one great piece of coarse cloth, large enough to be a foot-cloth for your Majesty's chief room of state. In the left pocket, we saw a huge silver chest, with a cover of the same metal, which we the searchers were not able to lift. We desired it should be opened, and one of us, stepping into it, found himself up to the mid leg in a sort of dust, some part whereof, flying up to our faces, set us both a sneezing for several times together. In his right waistcoat-pocket, we found a prodigious bundle of white thin substances, folded one over another, about the bigness of three men, tied with a strong cable, and marked with black figures; which we humbly conceive to be writings, every letter almost half as large as the palm of our hands. In the left, there was a sort of engine, from the back of which were extended twenty long poles, resembling the palisados before your Majesty's court; wherewith we conjecture the Man-Mountain combs his head, for we did not always trouble him with questions, because we found it a great difficulty to make him understand us. In the large pocket on the right side of his middle cover (so I translate the word *ranfu-lo,* by which they meant my breeches) we saw a hollow pillar of iron, about the length of a man, fastened to a strong piece of timber, larger than the pillar; and upon one side of the pillar were huge pieces of iron sticking out, cut into strange figures, which we know not what to make of. In the left pocket, another engine of the same kind. In the smaller pocket on the right side, were several round flat pieces of white and red metal, of different bulk; some of the white, which seemed to be silver, were so large and heavy, that my comrade and I could hardly lift them. In the left pocket were two black pillars irregularly shaped: we could not, without difficulty, reach the top of them as we stood at the bottom of his pocket. One of them was covered, and seemed all of a piece: but at the upper end of the other, there appeared a white round substance, about twice the bigness of our heads. Within each of these was inclosed a prodigious plate of steel; which, by our orders, we obliged him to show us, because we apprehended they might be dangerous engines. He took them out of their cases, and told us, that in his own country his practice was to shave his beard with one of these, and to cut his meat with the other. There were two pockets which we could not enter: these he called his fobs; they were two large slits cut into the top of his middle cover, but squeezed close by the pressure of his belly. Out of the right fob hung a great silver chain, with a wonderful kind of engine at the bottom. We directed him to draw out whatever was at the end of that chain; which appeared to be a globe, half silver, and half of some transparent metal: for on the transparent side we saw certain strange figures circularly drawn, and thought we could touch them, until we found our fingers stopped with that lucid substance. He put this engine to our ears, which made an incessant noise like that of a watermill. And we conjecture it is either some unknown animal, or the god that he worships: but we are more inclined to the latter opinion, because he assured us (if we understood him right, for he expressed himself very imperfectly), that he seldom did any thing without consulting it. He called it his oracle, and said it pointed out the time for every action of his life. From the left fob he took out a net almost large enough for a fisherman, but contrived to open and shut like a purse, and served him for the same use: we found therein several massy pieces of yellow metal, which, if they be of real gold, must be of immense value.

Having thus, in obedience to your Majesty's commands, diligently searched all his pockets, we observed a girdle about his waist made of the hide of some prodigious animal; from which, on the left side, hung a sword of the length of five men, and on the right, a bag or pouch divided into two cells, each cell capable of holding three of your Majesty's subjects. In one of these cells were several globes or balls of a most ponderous metal, about the bigness of our heads, and required a strong hand to lift them: the other cell contained a heap of certain black grains, but of no great bulk or weight, for we could hold above fifty of them in the palms of our hands.

This is an exact inventory of what we found about the body of the Man-Mountain, who used us with great civility, and due respect to your Majesty's commission. Signed and sealed on the fourth day of the eighty-ninth moon of your Majesty's auspicious reign.

Clefren Frelock, Marsi Frelock

When this inventory was read over to the Emperor, he directed me to deliver up the several particulars. He first called for my scimitar, which I took out, scabbard and all. In the mean time he ordered three thousand of his choicest troops (who then attended him) to surround me at a distance, with their bows and arrows just ready to discharge: but I did not observe it, for my eyes were wholly fixed upon his Majesty. He then desired me to draw my scimitar, which, although it had got some rust by the seawater, was in most parts exceeding bright. I did so, and immediately all the troops gave a shout between terror and surprise; for the sun shone clear, and the reflection dazzled their eyes as I waved the scimitar to and fro in my hand. His Majesty, who is a most magnanimous prince, was less daunted than I could expect; he ordered me to return it into the scabbard, and cast it on the ground as gently as I could, about six foot from the end of my chain. The next thing he demanded was one of the hollow iron pillars, by which he meant my pocket-pistols. I drew it out, and at his desire, as well as I could, expressed to him the use of it; and charging it only with powder, which by the closeness of my pouch happened to escape wetting in the sea (an inconvenience that all prudent mariners take special care to provide against), I first cautioned the Emperor not to be afraid, and then I let it off in the air. The astonishment here was much greater than at the sight of my scimitar. Hundreds fell down as if they had been struck dead; and even the Emperor, although he stood his ground, could not recover himself in some time. I delivered up both my pistols in the same manner as I had done my scimitar, and then my pouch of powder and bullets; begging him that the former might be kept from the fire, for it would kindle with the smallest spark, and blow up his imperial palace into the air. I likewise delivered up my watch, which the Emperor was very curious to see, and commanded two of his tallest yeomen of the guards to bear it on a pole upon their shoulders, as draymen in England do a barrel of ale. He was amazed at the continual noise it made, and the motion of the minute-hand, which he could easily discern; for their sight is much more acute than ours: he asked the opinions of his learned men about him, which were various and remote, as the reader may well imagine without my repeating; although indeed I could not very perfectly understand them. I then gave up my silver and copper money, my purse with nine large pieces of gold, and some smaller ones; my knife and razor, my comb and silver snuff-box, my handkerchief and journal book. My scimitar, pistols, and pouch, were conveyed in carriages to his Majesty's stores; but the rest of my goods were returned me.

I had, as I before observed, one private pocket which escaped their search, wherein there was a pair of spectacles (which I sometimes use for the weakness of my eyes), a pocket perspective, and several other little conveniences; which, being of no consequence to the Emperor, I did not think my self bound in honour to discover, and I apprehended they might be lost or spoiled if I ventured them out of my possession.

CHAPTER III

The author diverts the Emperor and his nobility of both sexes in a very uncommon manner. The diversions of the court of Lilliput described. The author hath his liberty granted him upon certain conditions.

My gentleness and good behaviour had gained so far on the Emperor and his court, and indeed upon the army and people in general, that I began to conceive hopes of getting my liberty in a short time. I took all possible methods to cultivate this favourable disposition. The natives came by degrees to be less apprehensive of any danger from me. I would sometimes lie down, and let five or six of them dance on my hand. And at last the boys and girls would venture to come and play at hide and seek in my hair. I had now made a good progress in understanding and speaking their language. The Emperor had a mind one day to entertain me with several of the country shows, wherein they exceed all nations I have known, both for dexterity and magnificence. I was diverted with none so much as that of the ropedancers, performed upon a slender white thread, extended about two foot, and twelve inches from the ground. Upon which I shall desire liberty, with the reader's patience, to enlarge a little.

This diversion is only practised by those persons who are candidates for great employments, and high favour, at court. They are trained in this art from their youth, and are not always of noble birth, or liberal education. When a great office is vacant either by death or disgrace (which often happens) five or six of those candidates petition the Emperor to entertain his Majesty and the court with a dance on the rope, and whoever jumps the highest without falling, succeeds in the office. Very often the chief ministers themselves are commanded to show their skill, and to convince the Emperor that they have not lost their faculty. Flimnap, the Treasurer, is

---

Flimnap, the Treasurer. Glancing at Sir Robert Walpole (1676–1745), who was both Swift's arch enemy and the most agile British politician of the age. Walpole was the *de facto* prime minister from 1721 to 1742. A staunch Whig, he rose to power by containing the damage wrought by the South Sea Bubble (see pp. 8–9 and note, p. 183), and by shielding several of the best-connected culprits from political retribution. Walpole used bribery and patronage to maintain the effective political machine that drove the Tory ministry out of power following the death of Queen Anne in 1714. Walpole was likewise behind Britain's attempt to impose Wood's halfpence on Ireland. Walpole's reign—perhaps peaceful in relative terms—nevertheless featured wars against Spain (1718–20 and again in 1727); naval battles in the Baltic Sea against Sweden (1715–17); and the First Maroon War in Jamaica (1730–39). See Bowen.

allowed to cut a caper on the strait rope, at least an inch higher than any other lord in the whole empire. I have seen him do the summerset several times together upon a trencher fixed on the rope, which is no thicker than a common packthread in England. My friend Reldresal, Principal Secretary for Private Affairs, is, in my opinion, if I am not partial, the second after the Treasurer; the rest of the great officers are much upon a par.

These diversions are often attended with fatal accidents, whereof great numbers are on record. I my self have seen two or three candidates break a limb. But the danger is much greater when the ministers themselves are commanded to show their dexterity; for by contending to excel themselves and their fellows, they strain so far, that there is hardly one of them who hath not received a fall, and some of them two or three. I was assured that a year or two before my arrival, Flimnap would have infallibly broke his neck, if one of the King's cushions, that accidentally lay on the ground, had not weakened the force of his fall.

There is likewise another diversion, which is only shown before the Emperor and Empress, and first minister, upon particular occasions. The Emperor lays on a table three fine silken threads of six inches long. One is blue, the other red, and the third green. These threads are proposed as prizes for those persons whom the Emperor hath a mind to distinguish by a peculiar mark of his favour. The ceremony is performed in his Majesty's great chamber of state, where the candidates are to undergo a trial of dexterity very different from the former, and such as I have not observed the least resemblance of in any other country of the old or the new world. The Emperor holds a stick in his hands, both ends parallel to the horizon, while the candidates, advancing one by one, sometimes leap over the stick, sometimes creep under it backwards and forwards several times, according as the stick is advanced or depressed. Sometimes the Emperor holds one end of the stick, and his first minister the other; sometimes the minister has it entirely to himself. Whoever performs his part with most agility, and holds out the longest in leaping and creeping, is rewarded with the blue-coloured silk; the red is given to the next, and the green to the third, which they all wear girt twice round about the middle; and you see few great persons about this court who are not adorned with one of these girdles.

The horses of the army, and those of the royal stables, having been daily led before me, were no longer shy, but would come up to my very feet without starting. The riders would leap them over my hand as I held it on the ground, and one of the Emperor's huntsmen, upon a large courser, took

---

Reldresal. Probably based on Lord Cartaret. He was friendly with Swift, as Landa points out (504), but nevertheless—in his official capacity as lord lieutenant of Ireland—offered a reward in 1724 for the discovery of the author of the *Drapier's Letters.*

my foot, shoe and all; which was indeed a prodigious leap. I had the good fortune to divert the Emperor one day after a very extraordinary manner. I desired he would order several sticks of two foot high, and the thickness of an ordinary cane, to be brought me; whereupon his Majesty commanded the master of his woods to give directions accordingly, and the next morning six woodmen arrived with as many carriages, drawn by eight horses to each. I took nine of these sticks, and fixing them firmly in the ground in a quadrangular figure, two foot and a half square, I took four other sticks, and tied them parallel at each corner, about two foot from the ground; then I fastened my handkerchief to the nine sticks that stood erect, and extended it on all sides till it was as tight as the top of a drum; and the four parallel sticks, rising about five inches higher than the handkerchief, served as ledges on each side. When I had finished my work, I desired the Emperor to let a troop of his best horse, twenty-four in number, come and exercise upon this plain. His Majesty approved of the proposal, and I took them up one by one in my hands, ready mounted and armed, with the proper officers to exercise them. As soon as they got into order, they divided into two parties, performed mock skirmishes, discharged blunt arrows, drew their swords, fled and pursued, attacked and retired, and in short discovered the best military discipline I ever beheld. The parallel sticks secured them and their horses from falling over the stage; and the Emperor was so much delighted, that he ordered this entertainment to be repeated several days, and once was pleased to be lifted up, and give the word of command; and, with great difficulty, persuaded even the Empress her self to let me hold her in her close chair within two yards of the stage, from whence she was able to take a full view of the whole performance. It was my good fortune that no ill accident happened in these entertainments, only once a fiery horse that belonged to one of the captains pawing with his hoof struck a hole in my handkerchief, and his foot slipping, he overthrew his rider and himself: but I immediately relieved them both, for covering the hole with one hand, I set down the troop with the other, in the same manner as I took them up. The horse that fell was strained in the left shoulder, but the rider got no hurt, and I repaired my handkerchief as well as I could; however, I would not trust to the strength of it any more in such dangerous enterprises.

About two or three days before I was set at liberty, as I was entertaining the court with these kinds of feats, there arrived an express to inform his Majesty that some of his subjects, riding near the place where I was first taken up, had seen a great black substance lying on the ground, very oddly shaped, extending its edges round as wide as his Majesty's bedchamber, and rising up in the middle as high as a man; that it was no living creature, as they at first apprehended, for it lay on the grass without motion, and some of them had walked round it several times; that by mounting upon each others' shoulders, they had got to the top, which was flat and even, and stamping upon it they found it was hollow within; that they humbly conceived it might be something belonging to the Man-Mountain, and if his Majesty pleased, they would undertake to bring it with only five horses. I presently knew what they meant, and was glad at heart to receive this intelligence. It seems upon my first reaching the shore after our shipwreck, I was in such confusion, that before I came to the place where I went to sleep, my hat, which I had fastened with a string to my head while I was rowing, and had stuck on all the time I was swimming, fell off after I came to land; the string, as I conjecture, breaking by some accident which I never observed, but thought my hat had been lost at sea. I entreated his Imperial Majesty to give orders it might be brought to me as soon as possible, describing to him the use and the nature of it: and the next day the waggoners arrived with it, but not in a very good condition; they had bored two holes in the brim, within an inch and half of the edge, and fastened two hooks in the holes; these hooks were tied by a long cord to the harness, and thus my hat was dragged along for above half an English mile: but the ground in that country being extremely smooth and level, it received less damage than I expected.

Two days after this adventure, the Emperor having ordered that part of his army which quarters in and about his metropolis to be in a readiness, took a fancy of diverting himself in a very singular manner. He desired I would stand like a colossus, with my legs as far asunder as I conveniently could. He then commanded his general (who was an old experienced leader, and a great patron of mine) to draw up the troops in close order, and march them under me, the foot by twenty-four in a breast, and the horse by sixteen, with drums beating, colours flying, and pikes advanced. This body consisted of three thousand foot, and a thousand horse. His Majesty gave orders, upon pain of death, that every soldier in his march should observe the strictest decency with regard to my person; which, however, could not prevent some of the younger officers from turning up their eyes as they passed under me. And, to confess the truth, my breeches were at that time in so ill a condition, that they afforded some opportunities for laughter and admiration.

I had sent so many memorials and petitions for my liberty, that his Majesty at length mentioned the matter, first in the cabinet, and then in a

---

Colossus. Gulliver's feat mimics one of the seven wonders of the ancient world: the gigantic statue that straddled the harbor of ancient Rhodes.

full council; where it was opposed by none, except Skyresh Bolgolam, who was pleased, without any provocation, to be my mortal enemy. But it was carried against him by the whole board, and confirmed by the Emperor. That minister was *Galbet,* or Admiral of the Realm, very much in his master's confidence, and a person well versed in affairs, but of a morose and sour complexion. However, he was at length persuaded to comply; but prevailed that the articles and conditions upon which I should be set free, and to which I must swear, should be drawn up by himself. These articles were brought to me by Skyresh Bolgolam in person, attended by two under-secretaries, and several persons of distinction. After they were read, I was demanded to swear to the performance of them; first in the manner of my own country, and afterwards in the method prescribed by their laws; which was to hold my right foot in my left hand, to place the middle finger of my right hand on the crown of my head, and my thumb on the tip of my right ear. But because the reader may perhaps be curious to have some idea of the style and manner of expression peculiar to that people, as well as to know the articles upon which I recovered my liberty, I have made a translation of the whole instrument word for word, as near as I was able, which I here offer to the public.

> Golbasto Momaren Evlame Gurdilo Shefin Mully Ully Gue, most mighty Emperor of Lilliput, delight and terror of the universe, whose dominions extend five thousand blustrugs (about twelve miles in circumference) to the extremities of the globe; monarch of all monarchs, taller than the sons of men; whose feet press down to the center, and whose head strikes against the sun: at whose nod the princes of the earth shake their knees; pleasant as the spring, comfortable as the summer, fruitful as autumn, dreadful as winter. His most sublime Majesty proposeth to the Man-Mountain, lately arrived at our celestial dominions, the following articles, which by a solemn oath he shall be obliged to perform.

Skyresh Bolgolam. *Bolgolam* is a near anagram for Marlborough (John Churchill, first duke of Marlborough). Having defected in 1688 from a high position in the military forces of James II, Marlborough became a dominant figure during the reign of Queen Anne. During the War of Spanish Succession, he commanded the allied British and Dutch forces from 1702–11, winning a decisive victory over Louis XIV in the battle of Blenheim. Marlborough eventually came under charges of profiteering from military contracts. Swift's writings contributed powerfully to the successful campaign to topple this Whig icon from his position as captain general, which he had attempted to secure for life.

Morose and sour complexion. Refers to the ancient "humor" theory, which correlated temperament and complexion with various blends of the four humors: the sanguine, the bilious, the phlegmatic, and the choleric. This venerable theory persisted among scientists well into the eighteenth century. See Glacken.

First, The Man-Mountain shall not depart from our dominions, without our licence under our great seal.

Secondly, He shall not presume to come into our metropolis, without our express order; at which time the inhabitants shall have two hours warning to keep within their doors.

Thirdly, The said Man-Mountain shall confine his walks to our principal high roads, and not offer to walk or lie down in a meadow or field of corn.

Fourthly, As he walks the said roads, he shall take the utmost care not to trample upon the bodies of any of our loving subjects, their horses, or carriages, nor take any of our said subjects into his hands, without their own consent.

Fifthly, If an express require extraordinary dispatch, the Man-Mountain shall be obliged to carry in his pocket the messenger and horse a six days' journey once in every moon, and return the said messenger back (if so required) safe to our Imperial Presence.

Sixthly, He shall be our ally against our enemies in the island of Blefuscu, and do his utmost to destroy their fleet, which is now preparing to invade us.

Seventhly, That the said Man-Mountain shall, at his times of leisure, be aiding and assisting to our workmen, in helping to raise certain great stones, towards covering the wall of the principal park, and other our royal buildings.

Eighthly, That the said Man-Mountain shall, in two moons' time, deliver in an exact survey of the circumference of our dominions by a computation of his own paces round the coast.

Lastly, That upon his solemn oath to observe all the above articles, the said Man-Mountain shall have a daily allowance of meat and drink sufficient for the support of 1728 of our subjects, with free access to our Royal Person, and other marks of our favour. Given at our palace at Belfaborac the twelfth day of the ninety-first moon of our reign.

I swore and subscribed to these articles with great cheerfulness and content, although some of them were not so honourable as I could have wished; which proceeded wholly from the malice of Skyresh Bolgolam the High Admiral: whereupon my chains were immediately unlocked, and I was at full liberty; the Emperor himself in person did me the honour to be by at the whole ceremony. I made my acknowledgements by prostrating myself at his

---

Blefuscu. Catholic France, with which Protestant England had been at war during the War of Spanish Succession.

By a computation of his own paces round the coast. The Lilliputians expect Gulliver to work as a surveyor, starting—as was usual—with their coastline. In 1700, Dampier surveyed the coast of New Britain (now part of New Guinea) as a hydrographer employed by the English government.

Majesty's feet: but he commanded me to rise; and after many gracious expressions, which, to avoid the censure of vanity, I shall not repeat, he added, that he hoped I should prove a useful servant, and well deserve all the favours he had already conferred upon me, or might do for the future.

The reader may please to observe, that in the last article for the recovery of my liberty, the Emperor stipulates to allow me a quantity of meat and drink sufficient for the support of 1728 Lilliputians. Some time after, asking a friend at court how they came to fix on that determinate number, he told me, that his Majesty's mathematicians, having taken the height of my body by the help of a quadrant, and finding it to exceed theirs in the proportion of twelve to one, they concluded from the similarity of their bodies, that mine must contain at least 1728 of theirs, and consequently would require as much food as was necessary to support that number of Lilliputians. By which the reader may conceive an idea of the ingenuity of that people, as well as the prudent and exact economy of so great a prince.

CHAPTER IV

Mildendo, the metropolis of Lilliput, described, together with the Emperor's palace. A conversation between the author and a principal secretary, concerning the affairs of that empire; the author's offers to serve the Emperor in his wars.

The first request I made after I had obtained my liberty, was, that I might have licence to see Mildendo, the metropolis; which the Emperor easily granted me, but with a special charge to do no hurt, either to the inhabitants, or their houses. The people had notice by proclamation of my design to visit the town. The wall which encompassed it is two foot and an half high, and at least eleven inches broad, so that a coach and horses may be driven very safely round it; and it is flanked with strong towers at ten foot distance. I stepped over the great western gate, and passed very gently, and sideling through the two principal streets, only in my short waistcoat, for fear of damaging the roofs and eaves of the houses with the skirts of my coat. I walked with the utmost circumspection, to avoid treading on any stragglers, who might remain in the streets, although the orders were very strict, that all people should keep in their houses, at their own peril. The garret windows and tops of houses were so crowded with spectators, that I thought in all my travels I had not seen a more populous place. The city is an exact square, each side of the wall being five hundred foot long. The two great streets, which run cross and divide it into four quarters, are five foot wide. The lanes and alleys, which I could not enter, but only viewed them as I passed, are from twelve to eighteen inches. The town is capable of holding five hundred thousand souls. The houses are from three to five stories. The shops and markets well provided.

The Emperor's palace is in the center of the city, where the two great streets meet. It is inclosed by a wall of two foot high, and twenty foot distant from the buildings. I had his Majesty's permission to step over this wall; and the space being so wide between that and the palace, I could easily view it on every side. The outward court is a square of forty foot, and includes two other courts: in the inmost are the royal apartments, which I was very desirous to see, but found it extremely difficult; for the great gates, from one square into another, were but eighteen inches high, and seven inches wide. Now the buildings of the outer court were at least five foot high, and it was impossible for me to stride over them, without infinite damage to the pile, although the walls were strongly built of hewn stone, and four inches thick. At the same time the Emperor had a great desire that I should see the magnificence of his palace; but this I was not able to do till three days after, which I spent in cutting down with my knife some of the largest trees in the royal park, about an hundred yards distant from the city. Of these trees I made two stools, each about three foot high, and strong enough to bear my weight. The people having received notice a second time, I went again through the city to the palace, with my two stools in my hands. When I came to the side of the outer court, I stood upon one stool, and took the other in my hand: this I lifted over the roof, and gently set it down on the space between the first and second court, which was eight foot wide. I then stepped over the buildings very conveniently from one stool to the other, and drew up the first after me with a hooked stick. By this contrivance I got into the inmost court; and lying down upon my side, I applied my face to the windows of the middle stories, which were left open on purpose, and discovered the most splendid apartments that can be imagined. There I saw the Empress, and the young princes in their several lodgings, with their chief attendants about them. Her Imperial Majesty was pleased to smile very graciously upon me, and gave me out of the window her hand to kiss.

But I shall not anticipate the reader with farther descriptions of this kind, because I reserve them for a greater work, which is now almost ready for the press, containing a general description of this empire, from its first erection, through a long series of princes, with a particular account of their wars and politics, laws, learning, and religion; their plants and animals, their peculiar manners and customs, with other matters very curious and useful; my chief design at present being only to relate such events and transactions as happened to the public, or to myself, during a residence of about nine months in that empire.

One morning, about a fortnight after I had obtained my liberty, Reldresal, Principal Secretary (as they style him) of Private Affairs, came to my house, attended only by one servant. He ordered his coach to wait at a distance, and desired I would give him an hour's audience; which I readily consented to, on account of his quality, and personal merits, as well as of the many good offices he had done me during my solicitations at court. I offered to lie down, that he might the more conveniently reach my ear; but he chose rather to let me hold him in my hand during our conversation. He began with compliments on my liberty, said he might pretend to some merit in it; but, however, added, that if it had not been for the present situation of things at court, perhaps I might not have obtained it so soon. For, said he, as flourishing a condition as we appear to be in to foreigners, we labour under two mighty evils; a violent faction at home, and the danger of an invasion by a most potent enemy from abroad. As to the first, you are to understand, that for above seventy moons past, there have been two struggling parties in the empire, under the names of *Tramecksan* and *Slamecksan,* from the high and low heels on their shoes, by which they distinguish themselves. It is alleged indeed, that the high heels are most agreeable to our ancient constitution: but however this be, his Majesty hath determined to make use of only low heels in the administration of the government and all offices in the gift of the crown, as you cannot but observe; and particularly, that his Majesty's imperial heels are lower at least by a *drurr* than any of his court; (*drurr* is a measure about the fourteenth part

---

Tramecksan and Slamecksan. Tory and Whig. The parliamentary political parties—a novel phenomenon often castigated as "factionalism"—that emerged in England in the wake of the Exclusion Crisis of the 1680s. A fierce contest ensued over the legitimacy of new financial institutions. Tories, though not opposed to trade, were inclined to lodge the capacity for virtuous public policy in real estate: the stability and autonomy that attended ownership of land. They opposed their agrarian notion of civic virtue—the paternalistic ethic of country squires—to the urban drive to entangle public affairs with private commercial speculation. Whigs were aligned with more mobile forms of property: above all, city financiers inaugurating a military-fiscal state through the transformation of public credit. By instituting the national debt, the Whigs created a revolutionary means of financing war. Whigs favored—and Tories opposed—a standing professional army. When George I succeeded to the throne in 1715, the Whigs gained long-term ascendancy in Parliament and the cabinet. See Pocock, 423–61 and Hill, 29–90.

High heels. Party affiliation also played out conflicts around confessional distinctions among Protestants. Whigs tended to be Low Church; friendly at home to Nonconformist dissenters—Quakers, Baptists, and Presbyterians—and to an alliance with the Dutch abroad. Tories tended to be High Church: staunch defenders of the established power of the Church of England. They tended to be somewhat less hostile to Catholic nations abroad and were presumed—in the balance of power between parliament and monarch—to favor a strong monarchy.

of an inch). The animosities between these two parties run so high, that they will neither eat nor drink, nor talk with each other. We compute the *Tramecksan,* or High-Heels, to exceed us in number; but the power is wholly on our side. We apprehend his Imperial Highness, the heir to the crown, to have some tendency towards the High-Heels; at least we can plainly discover one of his heels higher than the other, which gives him a hobble in his gait. Now, in the midst of these intestine disquiets, we are threatened with an invasion from the island of Blefuscu, which is the other great empire of the universe, almost as large and powerful as this of his Majesty. For as to what we have heard you affirm, that there are other kingdoms and states in the world, inhabited by human creatures as large as yourself, our philosophers are in much doubt, and would rather conjecture that you dropped from the moon, or one of the stars; because it is certain, that an hundred mortals of your bulk would, in a short time, destroy all the fruits and cattle of his Majesty's dominions. Besides, our histories of six thousand moons make no mention of any other regions, than the two great empires of Lilliput and Blefuscu. Which two mighty powers have, as I was going to tell you, been engaged in a most obstinate war for six and thirty moons past. It began upon the following occasion. It is allowed on all hands, that the primitive way of breaking eggs before we eat them, was upon the larger end: but his present Majesty's grandfather, while he was a boy, going to eat an egg, and breaking it according to the ancient practice, happened to cut one of his fingers. Whereupon the Emperor his father published an edict, commanding all his subjects, upon great penalties, to break the smaller end of their eggs. The people so highly resented this law, that our histories tell us there have been six rebellions raised on that account; wherein one emperor lost his life, and another his crown. These civil commotions were constantly fomented by the monarchs of Blefuscu; and when they were quelled, the exiles always fled for refuge to that empire. It is computed, that eleven thousand persons have, at several times, suf-

---

Occasion. Gulliver refers in the passage that follows to the continent-wide hostilities between Roman Catholics (Big-Endians) and Protestants (Little-Endians). These were hostilities for which Ireland served as an especially unlucky theater. This account blends various linked conflicts: (a) that between Henry VIII in England and papal authority in Rome—the origin of the Anglican Church (1531–34); (b) that within England between Anglicans and Puritans, which led to the execution of Charles I (1649); (c) that within England between Catholics and Protestants that led to the "Glorious Revolution" deposing James II (1688); and (d) that between Protestant England and Catholic France (1701–13). Though celebrated as "bloodless" in England, the Glorious Revolution of 1688–90 devastated parts of Ireland. And though William III was invited to enter England peacefully, he invaded Ireland with a force of some 36,000 troops.

J. J. Grandville, *Egg Wars*, 1838.

THE BEINECKE RARE BOOK AND MANUSCRIPT LIBRARY, YALE UNIVERSITY.

fered death, rather than submit to break their eggs at the smaller end. Many hundred large volumes have been published upon this controversy: but the books of the Big-Endians have been long forbidden, and the whole party rendered incapable by law of holding employments. During the course of these troubles, the emperors of Blefuscu did frequently expostulate by their ambassadors, accusing us of making a schism in religion, by offending against a fundamental doctrine of our great prophet Lustrog, in the fifty-fourth chapter of the *Brundecral* (which is their Alcoran). This, however, is thought to be a mere strain upon the text: for the words are these; That all true believers shall break their eggs at the convenient end: and which is the convenient end, seems, in my humble opinion, to be left to every man's conscience, or at least in the power of the chief magistrate to determine. Now the Big-Endian exiles have found so much credit in the Emperor of Blefuscu's court, and so much private assistance and encouragement from their party here at home, that a bloody war hath been carried on between the two empires for six and thirty moons with various success; during which time we have lost forty capital ships, and a much greater number of smaller vessels, together with thirty thousand of our best seamen and soldiers; and the damage received by the enemy is reckoned to be somewhat greater than ours. However, they have now equipped a numerous fleet, and are just preparing to make a descent upon us; and his Imperial Majesty, placing great confidence in your valour and strength, hath commanded me to lay this account of his affairs before you.

I desired the Secretary to present my humble duty to the Emperor, and to let him know, that I thought it would not become me, who was a foreigner, to interfere with parties; but I was ready, with the hazard of my life, to defend his person and state against all invaders.

Whole party rendered incapable by law of holding employments. Swift strongly opposed the repeal of an equivalent law in Ireland, the Sacramental Test Act, which served to exclude from public office anyone who was not committed to the Anglican Church. Those Whigs who clamored to repeal the Test Act, however, argued not on behalf of excluded Catholics, but rather of dissenting Protestants (many of whom were Ulster Presbyterians). Swift, who viewed such a repeal as a step on the way to disestablishment of the Church of Ireland, broke with the Whigs over the Test Act issue.

Alcoran. Koran.

CHAPTER V

The author by an extraordinary stratagem prevents an invasion. A high title of honour is conferred upon him. Ambassadors arrive from the Emperor of Blefuscu, and sue for peace. The Empress's apartment on fire by an accident; the author instrumental in saving the rest of the palace.

The empire of Blefuscu is an island situated to the north-northeast side of Lilliput, from whence it is parted only by a channel of eight hundred yards wide. I had not yet seen it, and upon this notice of an intended invasion, I avoided appearing on that side of the coast, for fear of being discovered by some of the enemy's ships, who had received no intelligence of me, all intercourse between the two empires having been strictly forbidden during the war, upon pain of death, and an embargo laid by our Emperor upon all vessels whatsoever. I communicated to his Majesty a project I had formed of seizing the enemy's whole fleet; which, as our scouts assured us, lay at anchor in the harbour ready to sail with the first fair wind. I consulted the most experienced seamen upon the depth of the channel, which they had often plumbed, who told me, that in the middle at high water it was seventy *glumgluffs* deep, which is about six foot of European measure; and the rest of it fifty *glumgluffs* at most. I walked to the northeast coast over against Blefuscu; where, lying down behind a hillock, I took out my small pocket perspective-glass, and viewed the enemy's fleet at anchor, consisting of about fifty men of war, and a great number of transports: I then came back to my house, and gave order (for which I had a warrant) for a great quantity of the strongest cable and bars of iron. The cable was about as thick as packthread, and the bars of the length and size of a knitting-needle. I trebled the cable to make it stronger, and for the same reason I twisted three of the iron bars together, bending the extremities into a hook. Having thus fixed fifty hooks to as many cables, I went back to the northeast coast, and putting off my coat, shoes, and stockings, walked into the sea in my leathern jerkin, about half an hour before high water. I waded with what haste I could, and swam in the middle about thirty yards until I felt ground; I arrived at the fleet in less than half an hour. The enemy was so frighted when they saw me, that they leaped out of their ships, and swam to shore, where there could not be fewer than thirty thousand souls. I then took my tackling, and fastening a hook to the hole at the prow of each, I tied all the cords together at the end. While I was thus employed, the enemy discharged several thousand arrows, many of which stuck in my hands and face; and besides the excessive smart, gave me much disturbance in my work. My greatest apprehension was for my eyes, which I should have infallibly lost, if I had not suddenly thought of an expedient. I kept among other little necessaries a pair of spectacles[28] in a private pocket, which, as I observed before, had escaped the Emperor's searchers. These I took out and fastened as strongly as I could upon my nose, and thus armed went on boldly with my work in spite of the enemy's arrows, many of which struck against the glasses of my spectacles, but without any other effect, further than a little to discompose them. I had now fastened all the hooks, and taking the knot in my hand, began to pull; but not a ship would stir, for they were all too fast held by their anchors, so that the boldest part of my enterprise remained. I therefore let go the cord, and leaving the hooks fixed to the ships, I resolutely cut with my knife the cables that fastened the anchors, receiving above two hundred shots in my face and hands; then I took up the knotted end of the cables to which my hooks were tied, and with great ease drew fifty of the enemy's largest men-of-war after me.

The Blefuscudians, who had not the least imagination of what I intended, were at first confounded with astonishment. They had seen me cut the cables, and thought my design was only to let the ships run adrift, or fall foul on each other: but when they perceived the whole fleet, moving in order, and saw me pulling at the end, they set up such a scream of grief and despair, that it is almost impossible to describe or conceive. When I had got out of danger, I stopped a while to pick out the arrows that stuck in my hands and face, and rubbed on some of the same ointment that was given me at my first arrival, as I have formerly mentioned. I then took off my spectacles, and waiting about an hour until the tide was a little fallen, I waded through the middle with my cargo, and arrived safe at the royal port of Lilliput.

The Emperor and his whole court stood on the shore expecting the issue of this great adventure. They saw the ships move forward in a large half-moon, but could not discern me, who was up to my breast in water. When I advanced to the middle of the channel, they were yet more in pain, because I was under water to my neck. The Emperor concluded me to be drowned, and that the enemy's fleet was approaching in a hostile manner: but he was soon eased of his fears, for, the channel growing shallower every step I made, I came in a short time within hearing, and holding up the end of the cable by which the fleet was fastened, I cried out in a loud voice, Long live the most puissant Emperor of Lilliput! This great prince received me at

---

Pair of spectacles. Gulliver may be English literature's first "bespectacled hero" (Rogers, 1978, 179).

my landing with all possible encomiums, and created me a *Nardac* upon the spot, which is the highest title of honour among them.

His Majesty desired I would take some other opportunity of bringing all the rest of his enemy's ships into his ports. And so unmeasureable is the ambition of princes, that he seemed to think of nothing less than reducing the whole empire of Blefuscu into a province, and governing it by a viceroy; of destroying the Big-Endian exiles, and compelling that people to break the smaller end of their eggs, by which he would remain sole monarch of the whole world. But I endeavoured to divert him from this design, by many arguments drawn from the topics of policy as well as justice: and I plainly protested, that I would never be an instrument of bringing a free and brave people into slavery. And when the matter was debated in council, the wisest part of the ministry were of my opinion.

This open bold declaration of mine was so opposite to the schemes and politics of his Imperial Majesty, that he could never forgive me; he mentioned it in a very artful manner at council, where I was told that some of the wisest appeared, at least, by their silence, to be of my opinion; but others, who were my secret enemies, could not forbear some expressions, which by a side-wind reflected on me. And from this time began an intrigue between his Majesty and a junta of ministers maliciously bent against me, which broke out in less than two months, and had like to have ended in my utter destruction. Of so little weight are the greatest services to princes, when put into the balance with a refusal to gratify their passions.

About three weeks after this exploit, there arrived a solemn embassy from Blefuscu, with humble offers of a peace; which was soon concluded upon conditions very advantageous to our Emperor, wherewith I shall not trouble the reader. There were six ambassadors, with a train of about five hundred persons, and their entry was very magnificent, suitable to the grandeur of their master, and the importance of their business. When their treaty was finished, wherein I did them several good offices by the credit I now had, or at least appeared to have at court, their Excellencies, who were privately told how much I had been their friend, made me a visit in form.

Reducing the whole empire of Blefuscu into a province, and governing it by a viceroy. Most obviously, a mockery of the desire for total victory over France. It is a project not unlike British rule over the "dependent kingdom" of Ireland.

Offers of a peace. Perhaps an echo of the Treaty of Utrecht (1713): an agreement with France that ended the War of Spanish Succession while relegating Holland, Britain's erstwhile ally, to the sidelines. Numerous critics have linked the political transgression involved—Bolingbroke's secret negotiation of a separate peace with France—to Gulliver's unorthodox means of putting out the fire in the Lilliputian queen's palace. François Rabelais's Gargantua, who drowns more than a quarter million Parisians in a urinary tidal wave, provides a literary precedent for Gulliver's feat.

They began with many compliments upon my valour and generosity, invited me to that kingdom in the Emperor their master's name, and desired me to show them some proofs of my prodigious strength, of which they had heard so many wonders; wherein I readily obliged them, but shall not interrupt the reader with the particulars.

When I had for some time entertained their Excellencies to their infinite satisfaction and surprise, I desired they would do me the honour to present my most humble respects to the Emperor their master, the renown of whose virtues had so justly filled the whole world with admiration, and whose royal person I resolved to attend before I returned to my own country: accordingly, the next time I had the honour to see our Emperor, I desired his general licence to wait on the Blefuscudian monarch, which he was pleased to grant me, as I could plainly perceive, in a very cold manner; but could not guess the reason, till I had a whisper from a certain person, that Flimnap and Bolgolam had represented my intercourse with those ambassadors as a mark of disaffection, from which I am sure my heart was wholly free. And this was the first time I began to conceive some imperfect idea of courts and ministers.

It is to be observed, that these ambassadors spoke to me by an interpreter, the languages of both empires differing as much from each other as any two in Europe, and each nation priding itself upon the antiquity, beauty, and energy of their own tongues, with an avowed contempt for that of their neighbour; yet our Emperor, standing upon the advantage he had got by the seizure of their fleet, obliged them to deliver their credentials, and make their speech, in the Lilliputian tongue. And it must be confessed, that from the great intercourse of trade and commerce between both realms, from the continual reception of exiles, which is mutual among them, and from the custom in each empire to send their young nobility and richer gentry to the other, in order to polish themselves, by seeing the world, and understanding men and manners, there are few persons of distinction, or merchants, or seamen, who dwell in the maritime parts, but what can hold conversation in both tongues; as I found some weeks after, when I went to pay my respects to the Emperor of Blefuscu, which in the midst of great misfortunes, through the malice of my enemies, proved a very happy adventure to me, as I shall relate in its proper place.

Mark of disaffection. Swift wrote as follows to Alexander Pope on September 3, 1735: "I heartily wish you were what they call disaffected, as I, who detest abominate & abhor every Creature who hath a dram of Power in either Kingdom" (i.e., Ireland and Britain). See *Correspondence,* vol. 4, p. 383. Swift's disenchantment with Walpole and the Hanovers does not mean that he was a Jacobite. See Downie, 1984, 345. To be "looked on as not well affected," as the first paragraph of *A Short View of the State of Ireland* makes clear (p. 315), was to be suspected of disloyalty.

The reader may remember, that when I signed those articles upon which I recovered my liberty, there were some which I disliked upon account of their being too servile, neither could any thing but an extreme necessity have forced me to submit. But being now a *Nardac,* of the highest rank in that empire, such offices were looked upon as below my dignity, and the Emperor (to do him justice) never once mentioned them to me. However, it was not long before I had an opportunity of doing his Majesty, at least as I then thought, a most signal service. I was alarmed at midnight with the cries of many hundred people at my door; by which being suddenly awaked, I was in some kind of terror. I heard the word *burglum* repeated incessantly: several of the Emperor's court, making their way through the crowd, intreated me to come immediately to the palace, where her Imperial Majesty's apartment was on fire, by the carelessness of a maid of honour, who fell asleep while she was reading a romance. I got up in an instant; and orders being given to clear the way before me, and it being likewise a moonshine night, I made a shift to get to the palace without trampling on any of the people. I found they had already applied ladders to the walls of the apartment, and were well provided with buckets, but the water was at some distance. These buckets were about the size of a large thimble, and the poor people supplied me with them as fast as they could; but the flame was so violent that they did little good. I might easily have stifled it with my coat, which I unfortunately left behind me for haste, and came away only in my leathern jerkin. The case seemed wholly desperate and deplorable, and this magnificent palace would have infallibly been burnt down to the ground, if, by a presence of mind, unusual to me, I had not suddenly thought of an expedient. I had the evening before drank plentifully of a most delicious wine, called *glimigrim* (the Blefuscudians call it *flunec,* but ours is esteemed the better sort), which is very diuretic. By the luckiest chance in the world, I had not discharged myself of any part of it. The heat I had contracted by coming very near the flames, and by my labouring to quench them, made the wine begin to operate by urine; which I voided in such a quantity, and applied so well to the proper places, that in three minutes the fire was wholly extinguished, and the rest of that noble pile, which had cost so many ages in erecting, preserved from destruction.

It was now daylight, and I returned to my house, without waiting to congratulate with the Emperor; because, although I had done a very eminent piece of service, yet I could not tell how his Majesty might resent the manner by which I had performed it: for, by the fundamental laws of the realm, it is capital in any person, of what quality soever, to make water within the precincts of the palace. But I was a little comforted by a message from his Majesty, that he would give orders to the Grand Justi-

J. J. Grandville, *Gulliver Extinguishing the Fire,* 1838.
THE BEINECKE RARE BOOK AND MANUSCRIPT LIBRARY, YALE UNIVERSITY.

ciary for passing my pardon in form; which, however, I could not obtain. And I was privately assured, that the Empress, conceiving the greatest abhorrence of what I had done, removed to the most distant side of the court, firmly resolved that those buildings should never be repaired for her use; and, in the presence of her chief confidents, could not forbear vowing revenge.

CHAPTER VI

Of the inhabitants of Lilliput; their learning, laws, and customs, the manner of educating their children. The author's way of living in that country. His vindication of a great lady.

Although I intend to leave the description of this empire to a particular treatise, yet in the mean time I am content to gratify the curious reader with some general ideas. As the common size of the natives is somewhat under six inches, so there is an exact proportion in all other animals, as well as plants and trees: for instance, the tallest horses and oxen are between four and five inches in height, the sheep an inch and a half, more or less; their geese about the bigness of a sparrow, and so the several gradations downwards, till you come to the smallest, which, to my sight, were almost invisible; but nature hath adapted the eyes of the Lilliputians to all objects proper for their view: they see with great exactness, but at no great distance. And to show the sharpness of their sight towards objects that are near, I have been much pleased with observing a cook pulling a lark, which was not so large as a common fly; and a young girl threading an invisible needle with invisible silk. Their tallest trees are about seven foot high; I mean some of those in the great royal park, the tops whereof I could but just reach with my fist clenched. The other vegetables are in the same proportion; but this I leave to the reader's imagination.

I shall say but little at present of their learning, which for many ages hath flourished in all its branches among them: but their manner of writing is very peculiar, being neither from the left to the right, like the Europeans; nor from the right to the left, like the Arabians; nor from up to down, like the Chinese; nor from down to up, like the Cascagians, but aslant from one corner of the paper to the other, like ladies in England.

They bury their dead with their heads directly downwards, because they hold an opinion that in eleven thousand moons they are all to rise again, in which period the earth (which they conceive to be flat) will turn upside down, and by this means they shall, at their resurrection, be found ready standing on their feet. The learned among them confess the absurdity of this doctrine, but the practice still continues, in compliance to the vulgar.

Like ladies in England. This passage on Lilliputian handwriting combines several possible sources, including the plagiarized narrative ascribed to William Symson, *A Voyage to the East-Indies* (1715); John Ovington's *A Voyage to Suratt* (1696); and Sir William Temple's "Of Heroick Virtue" (1690). The "Cascagians" are a figment of Swift's imagination. See p. 382.

There are some laws and customs in this empire very peculiar, and if they were not so directly contrary to those of my own dear country, I should be tempted to say a little in their justification. It is only to be wished, that they were as well executed. The first I shall mention relates to informers. All crimes against the state are punished here with the utmost severity; but if the person accused make his innocence plainly to appear upon his trial, the accuser is immediately put to an ignominious death; and out of his goods or lands, the innocent person is quadruply recompensed for the loss of his time, for the danger he underwent, for the hardship of his imprisonment, and for all the charges he hath been at in making his defence. Or, if that fund be deficient, it is largely supplied by the crown. The Emperor doth also confer on him some public mark of his favour, and proclamation is made of his innocence through the whole city.

They look upon fraud as a greater crime than theft, and therefore seldom fail to punish it with death; for they allege, that care and vigilance, with a very common understanding, may preserve a man's goods from thieves, but honesty hath no fence against superior cunning: and since it is necessary that there should be a perpetual intercourse of buying and selling, and dealing upon credit, where fraud is permitted and connived at, or hath no law to punish it, the honest dealer is always undone, and the knave gets the advantage. I remember when I was once interceding with the King for a criminal who had wronged his master of a great sum of money, which he had received by order, and ran away with; and happening to tell his Majesty, by way of extenuation, that it was only a breach of trust; the Emperor thought it monstrous in me to offer, as a defence, the greatest aggravation of the crime: and truly I had little to say in return, farther than the common answer, that different nations had different customs; for, I confess, I was heartily ashamed.

Although we usually call reward and punishment the two hinges upon which all government turns, yet I could never observe this maxim to be put in practice by any nation except that of Lilliput. Whoever can there bring sufficient proof that he hath strictly observed the laws of his country for seventy-three moons, hath a claim to certain privileges, according to his quality and condition of life, with a proportionable sum of money out of a fund appropriated for that use: he likewise acquires the title of *Snilpall,* or *Legal,* which is added to his name, but doth not descend to his posterity. And these people thought it a prodigious defect of policy among us, when I told them that our laws were enforced only by penalties without any mention of reward. It is upon this account that the image of Justice, in their courts of judicature, is formed with six eyes, two before, as many behind, and on each side one, to signify circumspection; with a bag of gold open in her right hand, and a sword sheathed in her left, to show she is more disposed to reward than to punish.

In choosing persons for all employments, they have more regard to good morals than to great abilities; for, since government is necessary to mankind, they believe that the common size of human understandings is fitted to some station or other, and that Providence never intended to make the management of public affairs a mystery, to be comprehended only by a few persons of sublime genius, of which there seldom are three born in an age: but they suppose truth, justice, temperance, and the like, to be in every man's power; the practice of which virtues, assisted by experience and a good intention, would qualify any man for the service of his country, except where a course of study is required. But they thought the want of moral virtues was so far from being supplied by superior endowments of the minds, that employments could never be put into such dangerous hands as those of persons so qualified; and at least, that the mistakes committed by ignorance in a virtuous disposition would never be of such fatal consequence to the public weal, as the practices of a man whose inclinations led him to be corrupt, and had great abilities to manage, to multiply, and defend his corruptions.

In like manner, the disbelief of a divine Providence renders a man uncapable of holding any public station; for since kings avow themselves to be the deputies of Providence, the Lilliputians think nothing can be more absurd than for a prince to employ such men as disown the authority under which he acts.

In relating these and the following laws, I would only be understood to mean the original institutions, and not the most scandalous corruptions into which these people are fallen by the degenerate nature of man. For as to that infamous practice of acquiring great employments by dancing on the ropes, or badges of favour and distinction by leaping over sticks, and creeping under them, the reader is to observe, that they were first introduced by the grandfather of the Emperor now reigning, and grew to the present height by the gradual increase of party and faction.

Ingratitude is among them a capital crime, as we read it to have been in some other countries; for they reason thus, that whoever makes ill returns to his benefactor, must needs be a common enemy to the rest of mankind, from whom he hath received no obligation, and therefore such a man is not fit to live.

Their notions relating to the duties of parents and children differ extremely from ours. For, since the conjunction of male and female is founded upon the great law of nature, in order to propagate and continue the species, the Lilliputians will needs have it, that men and women are joined together like other animals, by the motives of concupiscence; and that their tenderness towards their young proceeds from the like natural principle: for which reason they will never allow, that a child is under any obligation to his father for begetting him, or to his mother for bringing him into the world; which, considering the miseries of human life, was neither a benefit in itself, nor intended so by his parents, whose thoughts in their love-encounters were otherwise employed. Upon these, and the like reasonings, their opinion is, that parents are the last of all others to be trusted with the education of their own children: and therefore they have in every town public nurseries, where all parents, except cottagers and labourers, are obliged to send their infants of both sexes to be reared and educated when they come to the age of twenty moons, at which time they are supposed to have some rudiments of docility. These schools are of several kinds, suited to different qualities, and to both sexes. They have certain professors well skilled in preparing children for such a condition of life as befits the rank of their parents, and their own capacities as well as inclinations. I shall first say something of the male nurseries, and then of the female.

The nurseries for males of noble or eminent birth are provided with grave and learned professors, and their several deputies. The clothes and food of the children are plain and simple. They are bred up in the principles of honour, justice, courage, modesty, clemency, religion, and love of their country; they are always employed in some business, except in the times of eating and sleeping, which are very short, and two hours for diversions, consisting of bodily exercises. They are dressed by men until four years of age, and then are obliged to dress themselves, although their quality be ever so great; and the women attendants, who are aged proportionably to ours at fifty, perform only the most menial offices. They are never suffered to converse with servants, but go together in small or greater numbers to take their diversions, and always in the presence of a professor, or one of his deputies; whereby they avoid those early bad impressions of folly and vice to which our children are subject. Their parents are suffered to see them only twice a year; the visit is not to last above an hour. They are allowed to kiss the child at meeting and parting; but a professor, who always stands by on those occasions, will not suffer them to whisper, or use any fondling expressions, or bring any presents of toys, sweetmeats, and the like.

The pension from each family for the education and entertainment of a child, upon failure of due payment, is levied by the Emperor's officers.

Concupiscence. Lust.

The nurseries for children of ordinary gentlemen, merchants, traders, and handicrafts, are managed proportionably after the same manner; only those designed for trades are put out apprentices at seven years old, whereas those of persons of quality continue in their nurseries till fifteen, which answers to one and twenty with us: but the confinement is gradually lessened for the last three years.

In the female nurseries, the young girls of quality are educated much like the males, only they are dressed by orderly servants of their own sex, but always in the presence of a professor or deputy, until they come to dress themselves, which is at five years old. And if it be found that these nurses ever presume to entertain the girls with frightful or foolish stories, or the common follies practiced by chambermaids among us, they are publicly whipped thrice about the city, imprisoned for a year, and banished for life to the most desolate parts of the country. Thus the young ladies there are as much ashamed of being cowards and fools as the men, and despise all personal ornaments beyond decency and cleanliness: neither did I perceive any difference in their education, made by their difference of sex, only that the exercises of the females were not altogether so robust, and that some rules were given them relating to domestic life, and a smaller compass of learning was enjoined them: for their maxim is, that among people of quality, a wife should be always a reasonable and agreeable companion, because she cannot always be young. When the girls are twelve years old, which among them is the marriageable age, their parents or guardians take them home, with great expressions of gratitude to the professors, and seldom without tears of the young lady and her companions.

In the nurseries of females of the meaner sort, the children are instructed in all kinds of works proper for their sex, and their several degrees: those intended for apprentices are dismissed at seven years old, the rest are kept to eleven.

The meaner families who have children at these nurseries are obliged, besides their annual pension, which is as low as possible, to return to the steward of the nursery a small monthly share of their gettings, to be a portion for the child; and therefore all parents are limited in their expenses by the law. For the Lilliputians think nothing can be more unjust, than that people, in subservience to their own appetites, should bring children into the world, and leave the burthen of supporting them on the public. As to persons of quality, they give security to appropriate a certain sum for each child, suitable to their condition; and these funds are always managed with good husbandry, and the most exact justice.

The cottagers and labourers keep their children at home, their business being only to till and cultivate the earth, and therefore their education is of little consequence to the public; but the old and diseased among them are supported by hospitals: for begging is a trade unknown in this empire.

And here it may perhaps divert the curious reader, to give some account of my domestic, and my manner of living in this country, during a residence of nine months and thirteen days. Having a head mechanically turned, and being likewise forced by necessity, I had made for myself a table and chair convenient enough, out of the largest trees in the royal park. Two hundred sempstresses were employed to make me shirts, and linen for my bed and table, all of the strongest and coarsest kind they could get; which, however, they were forced to quilt together in several folds, for the thickest was some degrees finer than lawn. Their linen is usually three inches wide, and three foot make a piece. The sempstresses took my measure as I lay on the ground, one standing at my neck, and another at my midleg, with a strong cord extended, that each held by the end, while the third measured the length of the cord with a rule of an inch long. Then they measured my right thumb, and desired no more; for by a mathematical computation, that twice round the thumb is once round the wrist, and so on to the neck and the waist, and by the help of my old shirt, which I displayed on the ground before them for a pattern, they fitted me exactly. Three hundred tailors were employed in the same manner to make me clothes; but they had another contrivance for taking my measure. I kneeled down, and they raised a ladder from the ground to my neck; upon this ladder one of them mounted, and let fall a plumb-line from my collar to the floor, which just answered the length of my coat; but my waist and arms I measured myself. When my clothes were finished, which was done in my house (for the largest of theirs would not have been able to hold them) they looked like the patchwork made by the ladies in England, only that mine were all of a colour.

I had three hundred cooks to dress my victuals, in little convenient huts built about my house, where they and their families lived, and prepared me two dishes apiece. I took up twenty waiters in my hand, and placed them on the table; an hundred more attended below on the ground, some with dishes of meat, and some with barrels of wine, and other liquors, slung on their shoulders; all which the waiters above drew up as I wanted, in a very ingenious manner, by certain cords, as we draw the bucket up a well in Europe. A dish of their meat was a good mouthful, and a barrel of their liquor a reasonable draught. Their mutton yields to ours, but their beef is

---

Hospitals. Charity homes. Swift was deeply agitated by the problem of widespread begging in Ireland.

Domestic. Household.

excellent. I have had a sirloin so large, that I have been forced to make three bits of it; but this is rare. My servants were astonished to see me eat it bones and all, as in our country we do the leg of a lark. Their geese and turkeys I usually eat at a mouthful, and I must confess they far exceed ours. Of their smaller fowl I could take up twenty or thirty at the end of my knife.

One day his Imperial Majesty, being informed of my way of living, desired that himself and his royal consort, with the young princes of the blood of both sexes, might have the happiness (as he was pleased to call it) of dining with me. They came accordingly, and I placed them upon chairs of state on my table, just over-against me, with their guards about them. Flimnap the Lord High Treasurer attended there likewise, with his white staff; and I observed he often looked on me with a sour countenance, which I would not seem to regard, but eat more than usual, in honour to my dear country, as well as to fill the court with admiration. I have some private reasons to believe, that this visit from his Majesty gave Flimnap an opportunity of doing me ill offices to his master. That minister had always been my secret enemy, although he outwardly caressed me more than was usual to the moroseness of his nature. He represented to the Emperor the low condition of his treasury; that he was forced to take up money at great discount; that exchequer bills would not circulate under nine per cent below par; that I had cost his Majesty above a million and a half of *sprugs* (their greatest gold coin, about the bigness of a spangle); and upon the whole, that it would be advisable in the Emperor to take the first fair occasion of dismissing me.

I am here obliged to vindicate the reputation of an excellent lady, who was an innocent sufferer upon my account. The Treasurer took a fancy to be jealous of his wife, from the malice of some evil tongues, who informed him that her Grace had taken a violent affection for my person, and the court-scandal ran for some time, that she once came privately to my lodging. This I solemnly declare to be a most infamous falsehood, without any grounds, farther than that her Grace was pleased to treat me with all innocent marks of freedom and friendship. I own she came often to my house, but always publicly, nor ever without three more in the coach, who were usually her sister and young daughter, and some particular acquaintance; but this was common to many other ladies of the court. And I still appeal to my servants round, whether they at any time saw a coach at my door without knowing what persons were in it. On those occasions, when a servant had given me notice, my custom was to go immediately to the door; and, after paying my respects, to take up the coach and two horses very

---

White staff. The symbol of office of the lord high treasurer (Fox, 77).

carefully in my hands (for if there were six horses, the postillion always unharnessed four) and place them on a table, where I had fixed a moveable rim quite round, of five inches high, to prevent accidents. And I have often had four coaches and horses at once on my table full of company, while I sat in my chair leaning my face towards them; and when I was engaged with one set, the coachmen would gently drive the others round my table. I have passed many an afternoon very agreeably in these conversations. But I defy the Treasurer, or his two informers (I will name them, and let them make their best of it) Clustril and Drunlo, to prove that any person ever came to me *incognito,* except the Secretary Reldresal, who was sent by express command of his Imperial Majesty, as I have before related. I should not have dwelt so long upon this particular, if it had not been a point wherein the reputation of a great lady is so nearly concerned, to say nothing of my own; although I had the honour to be a *Nardac,* which the Treasurer himself is not; for all the world knows he is only a *Clumglum,* a title inferior by one degree, as that of a marquis is to a duke in England, yet I allow he preceded me in right of his post. These false informations, which I afterwards came to the knowledge of, by an accident not proper to mention, made the Treasurer show his lady for some time an ill countenance, and me a worse; for although he was at last undeceived and reconciled to her, yet I lost all credit with him, and found my interest decline very fast with the Emperor himself, who was indeed too much governed by that favourite.

CHAPTER VII

The author, being informed of a design to accuse him of high treason, makes his escape to Blefuscu. His reception there.

Before I proceed to give an account of my leaving this kingdom, it may be proper to inform the reader of a private intrigue which had been for two months forming against me.

I had been hitherto all my life a stranger to courts, for which I was unqualified by the meanness of my condition. I had indeed heard and read enough of the dispositions of great princes and ministers; but never expected to have found such terrible effects of them in so remote a country, governed, as I thought, by very different maxims from those in Europe.

When I was just preparing to pay my attendance on the Emperor of Blefuscu, a considerable person at court (to whom I had been very serviceable at a time when he lay under the highest displeasure of his Imperial Majesty) came to my house very privately at night in a close chair, and without sending his name, desired admittance: the chairmen were dismissed; I put the chair, with his Lordship in it, into my coat-pocket; and giving orders to a trusty servant to say I was indisposed and gone to sleep, I fastened the door of my house, placed the chair on the table, according to my usual custom, and sat down by it. After the common salutations were over, observing his Lordship's countenance full of concern, and enquiring into the reason, he desired I would hear him with patience in a matter that highly concerned my honour and my life. His speech was to the following effect, for I took notes of it as soon as he left me.

You are to know, said he, that several committees of council have been lately called in the most private manner on your account: and it is but two days since his Majesty came to a full resolution.

You are very sensible that Skyresh Bolgolam (*Galbet,* or High Admiral) hath been your mortal enemy almost ever since your arrival. His original reasons I know not, but his hatred is much encreased since your great success against Blefuscu, by which his glory, as Admiral, is obscured. This lord, in conjunction with Flimnap the High Treasurer, whose enmity against you is notorious on account of his lady, Limtoc the General, Lalcon the Chamberlain, and Balmuff the Grand Justiciary, have prepared articles of impeachment against you, for treason, and other capital crimes.

This preface made me so impatient, being conscious of my own merits and innocence, that I was going to interrupt; when he entreated me to be silent, and thus proceeded.

Out of gratitude for the favours you have done me, I procured information of the whole proceedings, and a copy of the articles, wherein I venture my head for your service.

Articles of Impeachment against Quinbus Flestrin (the Man-Mountain)

ARTICLE I

Whereas, by a statute made in the reign of his Imperial Majesty Calin Deffar Plune, it is enacted, that whoever shall make water within the precincts of the royal palace shall be liable to the pains and penalties of high treason: notwithstanding, the said Quinbus Flestrin, in open breach of the said law, under colour of extinguishing the fire kindled in the apartment of his Majesty's most dear imperial consort, did maliciously, traitorously, and devilishly, by discharge of his urine, put out the said fire kindled in the said apartment, lying and being within the precincts of the said royal palace, against the statute in that case provided, etc., against the duty, etc.

ARTICLE II

That the said Quinbus Flestrin, having brought the imperial fleet of Blefuscu into the royal port, and being afterwards commanded by his Imperial Majesty to seize all the other ships of the said empire of Blefuscu, and reduce that empire to a province, to be governed by a viceroy from hence, and to destroy and put to death not only all the Big-Endian exiles, but likewise all the people of that empire who would not immediately forsake the Big-Endian heresy: he, the said Flestrin, like a false traitor against his most Auspicious, Serene, Imperial Majesty, did petition to be excused from the said service, upon pretence of unwillingness to force the consciences, or destroy the liberties and lives of an innocent people.

ARTICLE III

That, whereas certain ambassadors arrived from the court of Blefuscu to sue for peace in his Majesty's court: he the said Flestrin did, like a false traitor, aid, abet, comfort, and divert the said ambassadors, although he knew them to be servants to a prince who was lately an open enemy to his Imperial Majesty, and in open war against his said Majesty.

ARTICLE IV

That the said Quinbus Flestrin, contrary to the duty of a faithful subject, is now preparing to make a voyage to the court and empire of Blefuscu, for which he hath received only verbal licence from his Imperial Majesty; and under colour of the said licence, doth falsely and traitorously intend to take the said voyage, and thereby to aid, comfort, and abet the Emperor of Blefuscu, so late an enemy, and in open war with his Imperial Majesty aforesaid.

There are some other articles, but these are the most important, of which I have read you an abstract.

In the several debates upon this impeachment, it must be confessed that his Majesty gave many marks of his great lenity, often urging the services you had done him, and endeavouring to extenuate your crimes. The Treasurer and Admiral insisted that you should be put to the most painful and ignominious death, by setting fire on your house at night, and the General was to attend with twenty thousand men armed with poisoned arrows to shoot you on the face and hands. Some of your servants were to have private orders to strew a poisonous juice on your shirts and sheets, which would soon make you tear your own flesh, and die in the utmost torture. The General came into the same opinion, so that for a long time there was

---

Forsake the Big-Endian heresy. Catholicism. The passage parodies the violence of Protestant overkill.

a majority against you. But his Majesty resolving, if possible, to spare your life, at last brought off the Chamberlain.

Upon this incident, Reldresal, Principal Secretary for Private Affairs, who always approved himself your true friend, was commanded by the Emperor to deliver his opinion, which he accordingly did; and therein justified the good thoughts you have of him. He allowed your crimes to be great, but that still there was room for mercy, the most commendable virtue in a prince, and for which his Majesty was so justly celebrated. He said the friendship between you and him was so well known to the world, that perhaps the most honourable board might think him partial: however, in obedience to the command he had received, he would freely offer his sentiments. That if his Majesty, in consideration of your services, and pursuant to his own merciful disposition, would please to spare your life, and only give order to put out both your eyes, he humbly conceived, that by this expedient justice might in some measure be satisfied, and all the world would applaud the lenity of the Emperor, as well as the fair and generous proceedings of those who have the honour to be his counsellors. That the loss of your eyes would be no impediment to your bodily strength, by which you might still be useful to his Majesty. That blindness is an addition to courage, by concealing dangers from us; that the fear you had for your eyes was the greatest difficulty in bringing over the enemy's fleet, and it would be sufficient for you to see by the eyes of the ministers, since the greatest princes do no more.

This proposal was received with the utmost disapprobation by the whole board. Bolgolam, the Admiral, could not preserve his temper; but rising up in fury, said, he wondered how the Secretary durst presume to give his opinion for preserving the life of a traitor: that the services you had performed were, by all true reasons of state, the great aggravation of your crimes; that you, who were able to extinguish the fire by discharge of urine in her Majesty's apartment (which he mentioned with horror), might, at another time, raise an inundation by the same means, to drown the whole palace; and the same strength which enabled you to bring over the enemy's fleet might serve, upon the first discontent, to carry it back: that he had good reasons to think you were a Big-Endian in your heart; and as treason begins in the heart before it appears in overt acts, so he accused you as a traitor on that account, and therefore insisted you should be put to death.

True friend. Reldresal's awkward position in devising the punishment of Gulliver seems to resemble the painful role of Swift's friend, Lord Cartaret, who was lord lieutenant of Ireland during the *Drapier's Letters* campaign. Cartaret offered a bounty of £300 to encourage someone in Ireland to betray the Drapier's identity. See Swift's poem in this volume, "A Libel on the Reverend Dr. Delany and His Excellency John, Lord Cartaret."

The Treasurer was of the same opinion; he showed to what straits his Majesty's revenue was reduced by the charge of maintaining you, which would soon grow insupportable: that the Secretary's expedient of putting out your eyes was so far from being a remedy against this evil, that it would probably increase it, as it is manifest from the common practice of blinding some kind of fowl, after which they fed the faster, and grew sooner fat: that his sacred Majesty, and the council, who are your judges, were in their own consciences fully convinced of your guilt, which was a sufficient argument to condemn you to death, without the formal proofs required by the strict letter of the law.

But his Imperial Majesty, fully determined against capital punishment, was graciously pleased to say, that since the council thought the loss of your eyes too easy a censure, some other may be inflicted hereafter. And your friend the Secretary humbly desiring to be heard again, in answer to what the Treasurer had objected concerning the great charge his Majesty was at in maintaining you, said, that his Excellency, who had the sole disposal of the Emperor's revenue, might easily provide against this evil, by gradually lessening your establishment; by which, for want of sufficient food, you would grow weak and faint, and lose your appetite, and consequently decay and consume in a few months; neither would the stench of your carcass be then so dangerous, when it should become more than half diminished; and immediately upon your death, five or six thousand of his Majesty's subjects might, in two or three days, cut your flesh from your bones, take it away by cart-loads, and bury it in distant parts to prevent infection, leaving the skeleton as a monument of admiration to posterity.

Thus by the great friendship of the Secretary, the whole affair was compromised. It was strictly enjoined, that the project of starving you by degrees should be kept a secret, but the sentence of putting out your eyes was entered on the books; none dissenting except Bolgolam the Admiral, who being a creature of the Empress, was perpetually instigated by her Majesty to insist upon your death, she having borne perpetual malice against you, on account of that infamous and illegal method you took to extinguish the fire in her apartment.

In three days your friend the Secretary will be directed to come to your house, and read before you the articles of impeachment; and then to signify the great lenity and favour of his Majesty and council, whereby you are

---

Monument of admiration to posterity. Human anatomical specimens ("Humana") featuring wonders and curiosities were among the many important collections of Sir Hans Sloane, secretary and eventual president of the Royal Society. One such is described as follows: "The monstrous large femur & leg bones of a man giant found in a coffin under the foundations in St. Martin's Lane." See MacGregor, 71.

only condemned to the loss of your eyes, which his Majesty doth not question you will gratefully and humbly submit to; and twenty of his Majesty's surgeons will attend, in order to see the operation well performed, by discharging very sharp-pointed arrows into the balls of your eyes, as you lie on the ground.

I leave to your prudence what measures you will take; and to avoid suspicion, I must immediately return in as private a manner as I came.

His Lordship did so, and I remained alone, under many doubts and perplexities of mind.

It was a custom introduced by this prince and his ministry (very different, as I have been assured, from the practices of former times) that after the court had decreed any cruel execution, either to gratify the monarch's resentment, or the malice of a favourite, the Emperor always made a speech to his whole council, expressing his great lenity and tenderness, as qualities known and confessed by all the world. This speech was immediately published through the kingdom; nor did any thing terrify the people so much as those encomiums on his Majesty's mercy; because it was observed, that the more these praises were enlarged and insisted on, the more inhuman was the punishment, and the sufferer more innocent. Yet as to myself, I must confess, having never been designed for a courtier either by my birth or education. I was so ill a judge of things, that I could not discover the lenity and favour of this sentence, but conceived it (perhaps erroneously) rather to be rigorous than gentle. I sometimes thought of standing my trial, for although I could not deny the facts alleged in the several articles, yet I hoped they would admit of some extenuations. But having in my life perused many state trials, which I ever observed to terminate as the judges thought fit to direct, I durst not rely on so dangerous a decision, in so critical a juncture, and against such powerful enemies. Once I was strongly bent upon resistance, for while I had liberty, the whole strength of that empire could hardly subdue me, and I might easily with stones pelt the metropolis to pieces; but I soon rejected that project with horror, by remembering the oath I had made to the Emperor, the favours I received from him, and the high title of *Nardac* he conferred upon me. Neither had I so soon learned the gratitude of courtiers, to persuade myself that his Majesty's present severities acquitted me of all past obligations.

At last I fixed upon a resolution, for which it is probable I may incur some censure, and not unjustly; for I confess I owe the preserving my eyes, and consequently my liberty, to my own great rashness and want of experience: because if I had then known the nature of princes and ministers, which I have since observed in many other courts, and their methods of treating criminals less obnoxious than myself, I should with great alacrity and readiness have submitted to so easy a punishment. But hurried on by the precipitancy of youth, and having his Imperial Majesty's licence to pay my attendance upon the Emperor of Blefuscu, I took this opportunity, before the three days were elapsed, to send a letter to my friend the Secretary, signifying my resolution of setting out that morning for Blefuscu pursuant to the leave I had got; and without waiting for an answer, I went to that side of the island where our fleet lay. I seized a large man of war, tied a cable to the prow, and, lifting up the anchors, I stripped myself, put my clothes (together with my coverlet, which I carried under my arm) into the vessel, and drawing it after me between wading and swimming, arrived at the royal port of Blefuscu, where the people had long expected me; they lent me two guides to direct me to the capital city, which is of the same name. I held them in my hands until I came within two hundred yards of the gate, and desired them to signify my arrival to one of the secretaries, and let him know, I there waited his Majesty's commands. I had an answer in about an hour, that his Majesty, attended by the royal family, and great officers of the court, was coming out to receive me. I advanced a hundred yards. The Emperor, and his train, alighted from their horses, the Empress and ladies from their coaches, and I did not perceive they were in any fright or concern. I lay on the ground to kiss his Majesty's and the Empress's hand. I told his Majesty that I was come according to my promise, and with the licence of the Emperor my master, to have the honour of seeing so mighty a monarch, and to offer him any service in my power, consistent with my duty to my own prince; not mentioning a word of my disgrace, because I had hitherto no regular information of it, and might suppose myself wholly ignorant of any such design; neither could I reasonably conceive that the Emperor would discover the secret while I was out of his power: wherein, however, it soon appeared I was deceived.

I shall not trouble the reader with the particular account of my reception at this court, which was suitable to the generosity of so great a prince; nor of the difficulties I was in for want of a house and bed, being forced to lie on the ground, wrapped up in my coverlet.

CHAPTER VIII

The author, by a lucky accident, finds means to leave Blefuscu; and, after some difficulties, returns safe to his native country.

Three days after my arrival, walking out of curiosity to the northeast coast of the island, I observed, about half a league off, in the sea, somewhat that looked like a boat overturned. I pulled off my shoes and stockings, and wading two or three hundred yards, I found the object to approach nearer by force of the tide, and then plainly saw it to be a real boat, which I supposed might, by some tempest, have been driven from a ship; whereupon I returned immediately towards the city, and desired his Imperial Majesty to lend me twenty of the tallest vessels he had left after the loss of his fleet, and three thousand seamen under the command of his Vice-Admiral. This fleet sailed round, while I went back the shortest way to the coast where I first discovered the boat; I found the tide had driven it still nearer. The seamen were all provided with cordage, which I had beforehand twisted to a sufficient strength. When the ships came up, I stripped myself, and waded till I came within an hundred yards of the boat, after which I was forced to swim till I got up to it. The seamen threw me the end of the cord, which I fastened to a hole in the fore-part of the boat, and the other end to a man of war: but I found all my labour to little purpose; for being out of my depth, I was not able to work. In this necessity, I was forced to swim behind, and push the boat forwards as often as I could, with one of my hands; and the tide favouring me, I advanced so far, that I could just hold up my chin and feel the ground. I rested two or three minutes, and then gave the boat another shove, and so on till the sea was no higher than my armpits; and now the most laborious part being over, I took out my other cables, which were stowed in one of the ships, and fastening them first to the boat, and then to nine of the vessels which attended me; the wind being favourable the seamen towed, and I shoved till we arrived within forty yards of the shore, and waiting till the tide was out, I got dry to the boat, and by the assistance of two thousand men, with ropes and engines, I made a shift to turn it on its bottom, and found it was but little damaged.

I shall not trouble the reader with the difficulties I was under by the help of certain paddles, which cost me ten days making, to get my boat to the royal port of Blefuscu, where a mighty concourse of people appeared upon my arrival, full of wonder at the sight of so prodigious a vessel. I told the Emperor that my good fortune had thrown this boat in my way, to carry me to some place from whence I might return into my native country, and begged his Majesty's orders for getting materials to fit it up, together with his licence to depart; which, after some kind expostulations, he was pleased to grant.

I did very much wonder, in all this time, not to have heard of any express relating to me from our Emperor to the court of Blefuscu. But I was afterwards given privately to understand, that his Imperial Majesty, never imagining I had the least notice of his designs, believed I was only gone to Blefuscu in performance of my promise, according to the licence he had given me, which was well known at our court, and would return in a few days when that ceremony was ended. But he was at last in pain at my long absence; and after consulting with the Treasurer, and the rest of that cabal, a person of quality was dispatched with the copy of the articles against me. This envoy had instructions to represent to the monarch of Blefuscu the great lenity of his master, who was content to punish me no further than with the loss of my eyes; that I had fled from justice, and if I did not return in two hours, I should be deprived of my title of *Nardac*, and declared a traitor. The envoy further added, that in order to maintain the peace and amity between both empires, his master expected, that his brother of Blefuscu would give orders to have me sent back to Lilliput, bound hand and foot, to be punished as a traitor.

The Emperor of Blefuscu, having taken three days to consult, returned an answer consisting of many civilities and excuses. He said, that as for sending me bound, his brother knew it was impossible; that although I had deprived him of his fleet, yet he owed great obligations to me for many good offices I had done him in making the peace. That however both their Majesties would soon be made easy; for I had found a prodigious vessel on the shore, able to carry me on the sea, which he had given order to fit up with my own assistance and direction, and he hoped in a few weeks both empires would be freed from so insupportable an incumbrance.

With this answer the envoy returned to Lilliput, and the monarch of Blefuscu related to me all that had passed, offering me at the same time (but under the strictest confidence) his gracious protection if I would continue in his service; wherein although I believed him sincere, yet I resolved never more to put any confidence in princes or ministers, where I could possibly avoid it; and therefore, with all due acknowledgements for his favourable intentions, I humbly begged to be excused. I told him, that since fortune, whether good or evil, had thrown a vessel in my way, I was resolved to venture myself in the ocean, rather than be an occasion of difference between two such mighty monarchs. Neither did I find the Emperor at all displeased; and I discovered by a certain accident, that he was very glad of my resolution, and so were most of his ministers.

These considerations moved me to hasten my departure somewhat sooner than I intended; to which the court, impatient to have me gone, very readily contributed. Five hundred workmen were employed to make two sails to my boat, according to my directions, by quilting thirteen fold of their strongest linen together. I was at the pains of making ropes and cables, by twisting ten, twenty or thirty of the thickest and strongest of theirs. A great stone that I happened to find, after a long search by the seashore, served me for an anchor. I had the tallow of three hundred cows for greasing my boat, and other uses. I was at incredible pains in cutting down some of the largest timber trees for oars and masts, wherein I was, however, much assisted by his Majesty's ship-carpenters, who helped me in smoothing them, after I had done the rough work.

In about a month, when all was prepared, I sent to receive his Majesty's commands, and to take my leave. The Emperor and royal family came out of the palace; I lay down on my face to kiss his hand, which he very graciously gave me: so did the Empress, and young princes of the blood. His Majesty presented me with fifty purses of two hundred *sprugs* apiece, together with his picture at full length, which I put immediately into one of my gloves, to keep it from being hurt. The ceremonies at my departure were too many to trouble the reader with at this time.

I stored the boat with the carcasses of an hundred oxen, and three hundred sheep, with bread and drink proportionable, and as much meat ready dressed as four hundred cooks could provide. I took with me six cows and two bulls alive, with as many ewes and rams, intending to carry them into my own country, and propagate the breed. And to feed them on board, I had a good bundle of hay, and a bag of corn. I would gladly have taken a dozen of the natives, but this was a thing the Emperor would by no means permit; and besides a diligent search into my pockets, his Majesty engaged my honour not to carry away any of his subjects, although with their own consent and desire.

Having thus prepared all things as well as I was able, I set sail on the twenty-fourth day of September, 1701, at six in the morning; and when I had gone about four leagues to the northward. the wind being at southeast, at six in the evening, I descried a small island about half a league to the northwest. I advanced forward, and cast anchor on the lee-side of the island, which seemed to be uninhabited. I then took some refreshment, and went to my rest. I slept well, and as I conjecture at least six hours, for I found the day broke in two hours after I awaked. It was a clear night. I eat my breakfast before the sun was up; and heaving anchor, the wind being favourable, I steered the same course that I had done the day before, wherein I was directed by my pocket-compass. My intention was to reach, if possible, one of those islands which I had reason to believe lay to the northeast of Van Diemen's Land. I discovered nothing all that

---

A dozen of the natives. Following the precedent of Columbus, the practice of returning with a sampling of "natives"—with or without their consent—became common among subsequent European explorers. In *A New Voyage Round the World* (1697), William Dampier recounts how he acquired a half share in Prince Jeoly—an elaborately tattooed native of Meangis in the Philippines—and brought him to England. Jeoly's unnamed mother, whom Dampier also took aboard, died at Bencoolen in Sumatra. See pp. 392–397.

day; but upon the next, about three in the afternoon, when I had by my computation made twenty-four leagues from Blefuscu, I descried a sail steering to the southeast; my course was due east. I hailed her, but could get no answer; yet I found I gained upon her, for the wind slackened. I made all the sail I could, and in half an hour she spied me, then hung out her ancient, and discharged a gun. It is not easy to express the joy I was in upon the unexpected hope of once more seeing my beloved country, and the dear pledges I had left in it. The ship slackened her sails, and I came up with her between five and six in the evening, September 26; but my heart leapt within me to see her English colours. I put my cows and sheep into my coat-pockets, and got on board with all my little cargo of provisions. The vessel was an English merchantman, returning from Japan by the North and South Seas, the captain, Mr. John Biddel of Deptford, a very civil man, and an excellent sailor. We were now in the latitude of 30 degrees south; there were about fifty men in the ship; and here I met an old comrade of mine, one Peter Williams, who gave me a good character to the captain. This gentleman treated me with kindness, and desired I would let him know what place I came from last, and whither I was bound; which I did in few words, but he thought I was raving, and that the dangers I underwent had disturbed my head; whereupon I took my black cattle and sheep out of my pocket, which, after great astonishment, clearly convinced him of my veracity. I then showed him the gold given me by the Emperor of Blefuscu, together with his Majesty's picture at full length, and some other rarities of that country. I gave him two purses of two hundred *sprugs* each, and promised, when we arrived in England, to make him a present of a cow and a sheep big with young.

I shall not trouble the reader with a particular account of this voyage, which was very prosperous for the most part. We arrived in the Downs on the 13th of April, 1702. I had only one misfortune, that the rats on board carried away one of my sheep; I found her bones in a hole, picked clean from the flesh. The rest of my cattle I got safe on shore, and set them a grazing in a bowling-green at Greenwich, where the fineness of the grass made them feed very heartily, though I had always feared the contrary; neither could I possibly have preserved them in so long a voyage, if the captain had

---

Ancient. Naval flag (ensign): a signal between ships at a distance.

Dear pledges. Gulliver's wife and children. Possibly an allusion to the following words of Francis Bacon: "He that hath wife and children hath given hostages to fortune. . . ."

North and South Seas. Now the Pacific Ocean. The South Sea was so named due to its position south of the Isthmus of Darien (now Panama).

Downs. The English channel off the coast of Kent.

not allowed me some of his best biscuit, which, rubbed to powder, and mingled with water, was their constant food. The short time I continued in England, I made a considerable profit by showing my cattle to many persons of quality, and others: and before I began my second voyage, I sold them for six hundred pounds. Since my last return, I find the breed is considerably increased, especially the sheep; which I hope will prove much to the advantage of the woollen manufacture, by the fineness of the fleeces.

I stayed but two months with my wife and family; for my insatiable desire of seeing foreign countries would suffer me to continue no longer. I left fifteen hundred pounds with my wife, and fixed her in a good house at Redriff. My remaining stock I carried with me, part in money, and part in goods, in hopes to improve my fortunes. My eldest uncle John had left me an estate in land, near Epping, of about thirty pounds a year; and I had a long lease of the Black Bull in Fetter Lane, which yielded me as much more: so that I was not in any danger of leaving my family upon the parish. My son Johnny, named so after his uncle, was at the grammar school, and a towardly child. My daughter Betty (who is now well married, and has children) was then at her needlework. I took leave of my wife, and boy and girl with tears on both sides, and went on board the *Adventure*, a merchant-ship of three hundred tons, bound for Surat, Captain John Nicholas of Liverpool, commander. But my account of this voyage must be referred to the second part of my *Travels*.

THE END OF THE FIRST PART.

Advantage of the woollen manufacture. Swift was no friend to the British wool industry, so this is an ironic touch. Ireland had been prohibited by law since 1699 from exporting goods that would compete with England's woollen industries. In his *Proposal for the Universal Use of Irish Manufacture* (1720), included herein, Swift had responded by urging an Irish boycott of all English goods.

Upon the parish. Financially dependent on parish charity.

Surat. A port city and major center of international trade on the west coast of India, not far from Bombay. By permission of the Mughal emperors, the East India Company had possessed a walled factory in Surat since the early seventeenth century. During the 1690s, the Emperor Aurangzeb (1618–1707) compelled the English in Surat to pay restitution after the English pirate Henry Every brutally attacked two richly laden ships bearing Muslims home to Surat from the pilgrimage to Mecca. Every is the model for Defoe's title character in *The Life, Adventures, and Pyracies of the Famous Captain Singleton* (1720). Every—also known as John Avery or Long Ben Avery—was never captured.

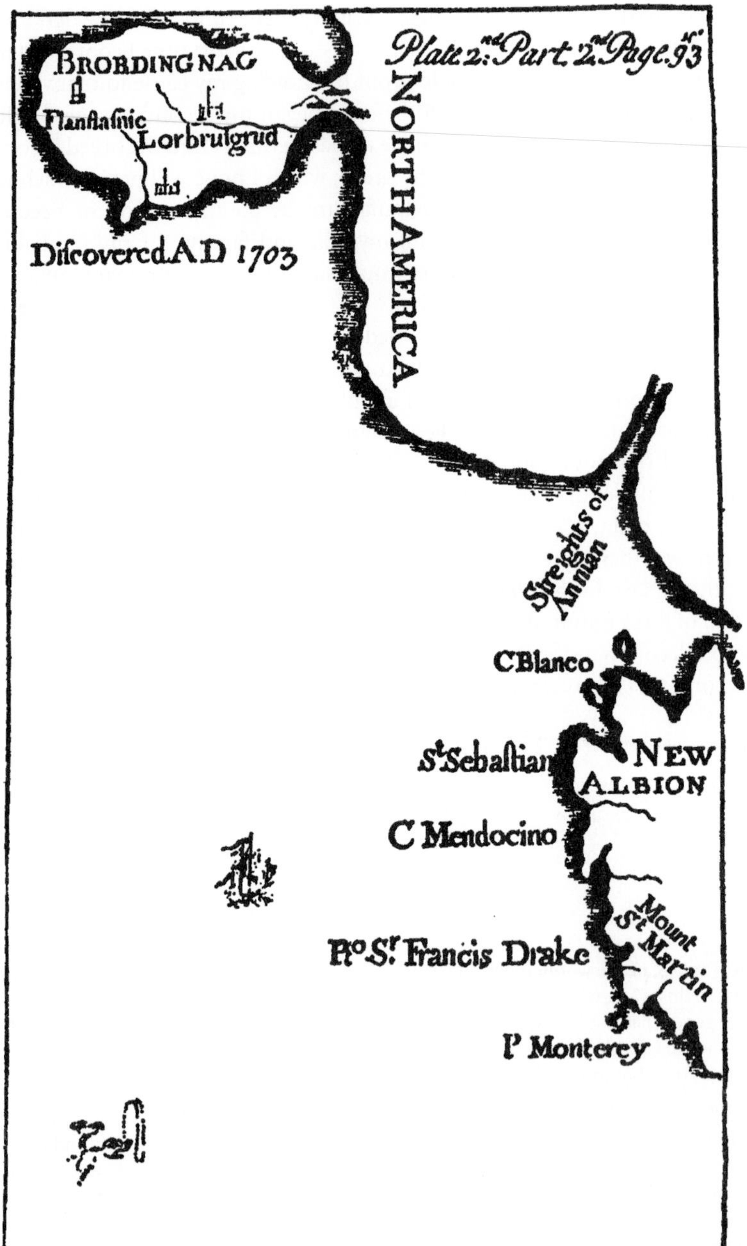

Plate. 2.nd Part. 2.nd Page. 93

BROBDINGNAG

Flanflasnic

Lorbrulgrud

Discovered A.D 1703

NORTH AMERICA

Streights of Annian

C Blanco

St Sebastian

NEW ALBION

C Mendocino

Po Sr Francis Drake

Mount St Martin

P Monterey

Travels

Part II

Voyage to Brobdingnag

CHAPTER I

A great storm described. The longboat sent to fetch water, the author goes with it to discover the country. He is left on shore, is seized by one of the natives, and carried to a farmer's house. His reception there, with several accidents that happened there. A description of the inhabitants.

Having been condemned by nature and fortune to an active and restless life, in two months after my return I again left my native country, and took shipping in the Downs on the 20th day of June, 1702, in the *Adventure,* Capt. John Nicholas, a Cornish man, commander, bound for Surat. We had a very prosperous gale till we arrived at the Cape of Good Hope, where we landed for fresh water, but discovering a leak we unshipped our goods, and wintered there; for the captain falling sick of an ague, we could not leave the Cape till the end of March. We then set sail, and had a good voyage till we passed the Straits of Madagascar; but having got northward of that island, and to about five degrees south latitude, the winds, which in those seas are observed to blow a constant equal gale between the north and west from the beginning of December to the beginning of May, on the 19th of April began to blow with much greater violence, and more westerly than usual, continuing so for twenty days together, during which time we were driven a little to the east

---

Cape of Good Hope. Near the southern tip of Africa. The Dutch had established a colony there in 1652. The shortest sea route to India, as Asimov points out, was around Africa; and the cape colony was a convenient way station.

of the Molucca Islands, and about three degrees northward of the Line, as our captain found by an observation he took the 2nd of May, at which time the wind ceased, and it was a perfect calm, whereat I was not a little rejoiced. But he, being a man well experienced in the navigation of those seas, bid us all prepare against a storm, which accordingly happened the day following: for a southern wind, called the southern monsoon, began to set in.

Finding it was like to overblow, we took in our spritsail, and stood by to hand the foresail; but making foul weather, we looked the guns were all fast, and handed the missen. The ship lay very broad off, so we thought it better spooning before the sea, than trying or hulling. We reefed the foresail and set him, we hauled aft the fore-sheet; the helm was hard a weather. The ship wore bravely. We belayed the fore-downhaul; but the sail was split, and we hauled down the yard, and got the sail into the ship, and unbound all the things clear of it. It was a very fierce storm; the sea broke strange and dangerous. We hauled off upon the lanyard of the whipstaff, and helped the man at helm. We would not get down our topmast, but let all stand, because she scudded before the sea very well, and we knew that the topmast being aloft, the ship was the wholesomer, and made better way through the sea, seeing we had searoom. When the storm was over, we set foresail and mainsail, and brought the ship to. Then we set the missen, main-topsail and the fore-topsail. Our course was east-northeast, the wind was at southwest. We got the starboard tacks aboard, we cast off our weather-braces and lifts; we set in the lee braces, and hauled forward by the weather bowlings, and hauled them tight, and belayed them, and hauled over the missen tack to windward, and kept her full and by as near as she would lie.

During this storm, which was followed by a strong wind west-southwest, we were carried by my computation about five hundred leagues

---

Molucca Islands. Indonesian islands controlled by the Dutch. The military skirmishes leading to this result involved conflicts over trading routes between the Dutch East India Company and its rivals—private trading companies—rather than sovereign states as such. In these battles, as so often elsewhere, indigenous inhabitants were pressed into service as mercenaries.

Line. Equator.

Overblow. Nautical shoptalk for going too fast. The paragraph spoofs nautical jargon.

Guns were all fast. Privateers aside, guns might come into play when traders had disputes with indigenous officials on the ground in Asia or Africa, where trading posts were generally fortified. The routine arming of private merchant vessels illustrates a much larger issue for Gulliver's time: the pervasive use of violence by substate actors such as the East India Company. Such private corporations, though chartered by the state, demonstrated the state's inability to achieve an effective monopoly on violence. See Thomson, 21–42.

to the east, so that the oldest sailor on board could not tell in what part of the world we were. Our provisions held out well, our ship was staunch, and our crew all in good health; but we lay in the utmost distress for water. We thought it best to hold on the same course rather than turn more northerly, which might have brought us to the northwest parts of Great Tartary, and into the frozen sea.

On the 16th day of June, 1703, a boy on the topmast discovered land. On the 17th we came in full view of a great island or continent (for we knew not whether) on the south side whereof was a small neck of land jutting out into the sea, and a creek too shallow to hold a ship of above one hundred tons. We cast anchor within a league of this creek, and our captain sent a dozen of his men well armed in the longboat, with vessels for water if any could be found. I desired his leave to go with them, that I might see the country, and make what discoveries I could. When we came to land we saw no river or spring, nor any sign of inhabitants. Our men therefore wandered on the shore to find out some fresh water near the sea, and I walked alone about a mile on the other side, where I observed the country all barren and rocky. I now began to be weary, and seeing nothing to entertain my curiosity, I returned gently down towards the creek; and the sea being full in my view, I saw our men already got into the boat, and rowing for life to the ship. I was going to hollow after them, although it had been to little purpose, when I observed a huge creature walking after them in the sea, as fast as he could: he waded not much deeper than his knees, and took prodigious strides: but our men had the start of him half a league, and the sea thereabouts being full of sharp pointed rocks, the monster was not able to overtake the boat. This I was afterwards told, for I durst not stay to see the issue of that adventure; but ran as fast as I could the way I first went; and then climbed up a steep hill which gave me some prospect of the country. I found it fully cultivated; but that which first surprised me was the length of the grass, which in those grounds that seemed to be kept for hay was above twenty foot high.

I fell into a high road, for so I took it to be, although it served to the inhabitants only as a footpath through a field of barley. Here I walked on for some time, but could see little on either side, it being now near harvest, and the corn rising at least forty foot. I was an hour walking to the end of this field, which was fenced in with a hedge of at least one hundred and twenty foot high, and the trees so lofty that I could make no computation of their altitude. There was a stile to pass from this field into the next. It had

---

Frozen sea. The Arctic Ocean. As Asimov points out, there was no knowledge regarding the juncture of the Pacific and the Arctic Oceans at the time *Gulliver's Travels* was published.

four steps, and a stone to cross over when you came to the uppermost. It was impossible for me to climb this stile, because every step was six foot high, and the upper stone above twenty. I was endeavouring to find some gap in the hedge, when I discovered one of the inhabitants in the next field advancing towards the stile, of the same size with him whom I saw in the sea pursuing our boat. He appeared as tall as an ordinary spire-steeple, and took about ten yards at every stride, as near as I could guess. I was struck with the utmost fear and astonishment, and ran to hide my self in the corn, from whence I saw him at the top of the stile, looking back into the next field on the right hand, and heard him call in a voice many degrees louder than a speaking-trumpet; but the noise was so high in the air, that at first I certainly thought it was thunder. Whereupon seven monsters like himself came towards him with reaping-hooks in their hands, each hook about the largeness of six scythes. These people were not so well clad as the first, whose servants or labourers they seemed to be. For, upon some words he spoke, they went to reap the corn in the field where I lay. I kept from them at as great a distance as I could, but was forced to move with extreme difficulty, for the stalks of the corn were sometimes not above a foot distant, so that I could hardly squeeze my body betwixt them. However, I made a shift to go forward till I came to a part of the field where the corn had been laid by the rain and wind. Here it was impossible for me to advance a step: for the stalks were so interwoven that I could not creep through, and the beards of the fallen ears so strong and pointed that they pierced through my clothes into my flesh. At the same time I heard the reapers not above an hundred yards behind me. Being quite dispirited with toil, and wholly overcome by grief and despair, I lay down between two ridges, and heartily wished I might there end my days. I bemoaned my desolate widow, and fatherless children. I lamented my own folly and wilfulness in attempting a second voyage against the advice of all my friends and relations. In this terrible agitation of mind I could not forbear thinking of Lilliput, whose inhabitants looked upon me as the greatest prodigy that ever appeared in the world: where I was able to draw an imperial fleet in my hand, and perform those other actions which will be recorded for ever in the chronicles of that empire, while posterity shall hardly believe them, although attested by millions. I reflected what a mortification it must prove to me to appear as inconsiderable in this nation as one single Lilliputian would be among us. But this I conceived was to be the least of my misfortunes: for, as human creatures are observed to be more savage and cruel in proportion to their bulk, what could I expect but to be a morsel in the mouth of the first among these enormous barbarians who should happen to seize me? Undoubtedly philosophers are in the right when they tell us, that nothing is great or little otherwise than by comparison. It might have pleased fortune to let the Lilliputians find some nation, where the people were as diminutive with respect to them, as they were to me. And who knows but that even this prodigious race of mortals might be equally overmatched in some distant part of the world, whereof we have yet no discovery?

Scared and confounded as I was, I could not forbear going on with these reflections, when one of the reapers, approaching within ten yards of the ridge where I lay, made me apprehend that with the next step I should be squashed to death under his foot, or cut in two with his reaping hook. And therefore, when he was again about to move, I screamed as loud as fear could make me. Whereupon the huge creature trod short, and looking round about under him for some time, at last espied me as I lay on the ground. He considered a while with the caution of one who endeavours to lay hold on a small dangerous animal in such a manner that it shall not be able either to scratch or to bite him, as I my self have sometimes done with a weasel in England. At length he ventured to take me up behind by the middle between his forefinger and thumb, and brought me within three yards of his eyes, that he might behold my shape more perfectly. I guessed his meaning, and my good fortune gave me so much presence of mind, that I resolved not to struggle in the least as he held me in the air above sixty foot from the ground, although he grievously pinched my sides, for fear I should slip through his fingers. All I ventured was to raise my eyes towards the sun, and place my hands together in a supplicating posture, and to speak some words in an humble melancholy tone, suitable to the condition I then was in. For I apprehended every moment that he would dash me against the ground, as we usually do any little hateful animal which we have a mind to destroy. But my good star would have it, that he appeared pleased with my voice and gestures, and began to look upon me as a curiosity, much wondering to hear me pronounce articulate words, although he could not understand them. In the mean time I was not able to forbear groaning and shedding tears, and turning my head towards my sides; letting him know, as well as I could, how cruelly I was hurt by the pressure of his thumb and finger. He seemed to apprehend my meaning; for, lifting up the lappet of his coat, he put me gently into it, and immediately ran along with me to his master, who was a substantial farmer, and the same person I had first seen in the field.

The farmer, having (as I supposed by their talk) received such an account of me as his servant could give him, took a piece of a small straw, about the size of a walking staff, and therewith lifted up the lappets of my coat; which it seems he thought to be some kind of covering that nature had given me. He blew my hairs aside to take a better view of my face. He called his hinds about him, and asked them (as I afterwards learned) whether they had ever seen in the fields any little creature that resembled me. He then placed me softly on the ground upon all four, but I got immediately up, and walked slowly backwards and forwards, to let those people see I had no intent to run away. They all sat down in a circle about me, the better to observe my motions. I pulled off my hat, and made a low bow towards the farmer. I fell on my knees, and lifted up my hands and eyes, and spoke several words as loud as I could: I took a purse of gold out of my pocket, and humbly presented it to him. He received it on the palm of his hand, then applied it close to his eye, to see what it was, and afterwards turned it several times with the point of a pin (which he took out of his sleeve), but could make nothing of it. Whereupon I made a sign that he should place his hand on the ground. I then took the purse, and opening it, poured all the gold into his palm. There were six Spanish pieces of four pistoles each, beside twenty or thirty smaller coins. I saw him wet the tip of his little finger upon his tongue, and take up one of my largest pieces, and then another, but he seemed to be wholly ignorant what they were. He made me a sign to put them again into my purse, and the purse again into my pocket, which after offering to him several times, I thought it best to do.

The farmer by this time was convinced I must be a rational creature. He spoke often to me, but the sound of his voice pierced my ears like that of a watermill, yet his words were articulate enough. I answered as loud as I could, in several languages, and he often laid his ear within two yards of me, but all in vain, for we were wholly unintelligible to each other. He then sent his servants to their work, and taking his handkerchief out of his pocket, he doubled and spread it on his left hand, which he placed flat on the ground, with the palm upwards, making me a sign to step into it, as I could easily do, for it was not above a foot in thickness. I thought it my part to obey, and for fear of falling, laid my self at full length upon the handkerchief, with the remainder of which he lapped me up to the head for further security, and in this manner carried me home to his house. There he called his wife, and showed me to her; but she screamed and ran back as women in England do at the sight of a toad or a spider. However, when she had a while seen my behaviour, and how well I observed the signs her husband made, she was soon reconciled, and by degrees grew extremely tender of me.

It was about twelve at noon, and a servant brought in dinner. It was only one substantial dish of meat (fit for the plain condition of an husbandman) in a dish of about four and twenty foot diameter. The company were the farmer and his wife, three children, and an old grandmother: when they were sat down, the farmer placed me at some distance from him on the table, which was thirty foot high from the floor. I was in a terrible fright, and kept as far as I could from the edge for fear of falling. The wife minced a bit of meat, then crumbled some bread on a trencher, and placed it before me. I made her a low bow, took out my knife and fork, and fell to eat, which gave them exceeding delight. The mistress sent her maid for a small dram cup, which held about two gallons, and filled it with drink; I took up the vessel with much difficulty in both hands, and in a most respectful manner drank to her ladyship's health, expressing the words as loud as I could in English, which made the company laugh so heartily, that I was almost deafened with the noise. This liquor tasted like a small cider, and was not unpleasant. Then the master made me a sign to come to his trencher side; but as I walked on the table, being in great surprise all the time, as the indulgent reader will easily conceive and excuse, I happened to stumble against a crust, and fell flat on my face, but received no hurt. I got up immediately, and observing the good people to be in much concern, I took my hat (which I held under my arm out of good manners) and waving it over my head, made three huzzas to show I had got no mischief by the fall. But advancing forwards toward my master (as I shall henceforth call him) his youngest son who sat next him, an arch boy of about ten years old, took me up by the legs, and held me so high in the air, that I trembled every limb; but his father snatched me from him, and at the same time gave him such a box on the left ear, as would have felled an European troop of horse to the earth, ordering him to be taken from the table. But being afraid the boy might owe me a spite, and well remembering how mischievous all children among us naturally are to sparrows, rabbits, young kittens, and puppy dogs, I fell on my knees, and pointing to the boy, made my master understand, as well as I could, that I desired his son might be pardoned. The father complied, and the lad took his seat again; whereupon I went to him and kissed his hand, which my master took, and made him stroke me gently with it.

In the midst of dinner, my mistress's favourite cat leapt into her lap. I heard a noise behind me like that of a dozen stocking-weavers at work; and turning my head I found it proceeded from the purring of this animal, who seemed to be three times larger than an ox, as I computed by the view of her head, and one of her paws, while her mistress was feeding and stroking her. The fierceness of this creature's countenance altogether discomposed me; although I stood at the further end of the table, above fifty foot off, and although my mistress held her fast for fear she might give a spring, and seize me in her talons. But it happened there was no danger; for the cat took not the least notice of me when my master placed me within three yards of her. And as I have been always told, and found true by experience in my travels, that flying, or discovering fear before a fierce animal, is a certain way to make it pursue or attack you, so I resolved in this dangerous juncture to show no manner of concern. I walked with intrepidity five or six times before the very head of the cat, and came within half a yard of her; whereupon she drew her self back, as if she were more afraid of me: I had less apprehension concerning the dogs, whereof three or four came into the room, as it is usual in farmers' houses; one of which was a mastiff equal in bulk to four elephants, and a greyhound somewhat taller than the mastiff, but not so large.

When dinner was almost done, the nurse came in with a child of a year old in her arms, who immediately spied me, and began a squall that you might have heard from London Bridge to Chelsea, after the usual oratory of infants, to get me for a plaything. The mother out of pure indulgence took me up, and put me towards the child, who presently seized me by the middle, and got my head in his mouth, where I roared so loud that the urchin was frighted, and let me drop, and I should infallibly have broke my neck if the mother had not held her apron under me. The nurse to quiet her babe made use of a rattle, which was a kind of hollow vessel filled with great stones, and fastened by a cable to the child's waist: but all in vain, so that she was forced to apply the last remedy by giving it suck. I must confess no object ever disgusted me so much as the sight of her monstrous breast, which I cannot tell what to compare with, so as to give the curious reader an idea of its bulk, shape and colour. It stood prominent six foot, and could not be less than sixteen in circumference. The nipple was about half the bigness of my head, and the hue both of that and the dug so varified with spots, pimples and freckles, that nothing could appear more nauseous: for I had a near sight of her, she sitting down the more conveniently to give suck, and I standing on the table. This made me reflect upon the fair skins of our English ladies, who appear so beautiful to us, only because they are of our own size, and their defects not to be seen but through a magnifying glass, where we find by experiment that the smoothest and whitest skins look rough and coarse, and ill coloured.

I remember when I was at Lilliput, the complexions of those diminutive people appeared to me the fairest in the world; and talking upon this subject with a person of learning there, who was an intimate friend of mine, he said that my face appeared much fairer and smoother when he looked on me from the ground, than it did upon a nearer view when I took him up in my hand, and brought him close, which he confessed was at first a very shocking sight. He said he could discover great holes in my skin, that the stumps of my beard were ten times stronger than the bristles of a boar, and my complexion made up of several colours altogether disagreeable: although I must beg leave to say for my self, that I am as fair as most of my sex and country, and very little sunburnt by all my travels. On the other side, discoursing of the ladies in that emperor's court, he used to tell me, one had freckles, another too wide a mouth, a third too large a nose, nothing of which I was able to distinguish. I confess this reflection was obvious enough; which however I could not forbear, lest the reader might think those vast creatures were actually deformed: for I must do them justice to say they are a comely race of people; and particularly the features of my master's countenance, although he were but a farmer, when I beheld him from the height of sixty foot, appeared very well proportioned.

When dinner was done, my master went out to his labourers, and, as I could discover by his voice and gesture, gave his wife a strict charge to take care of me. I was very much tired and disposed to sleep, which my mistress perceiving, she put me on her own bed, and covered me with a clean white handkerchief, but larger and coarser than the mainsail of a man of war.

I slept about two hours, and dreamed I was at home with my wife and children, which aggravated my sorrows when I awaked and found my self alone in a vast room, between two and three hundred foot wide, and above two hundred high, lying in a bed twenty yards wide. My mistress was gone about her household affairs, and had locked me in. The bed was eight yards from the floor. Some natural necessities required me to get down; I durst not presume to call, and if I had, it would have been in vain with such a voice as mine at so great a distance from the room where I lay to the kitchen where the family kept. While I was under these circumstances two rats crept up the curtains, and ran smelling backwards and forwards on the bed. One of them came up almost to my face, whereupon I rose in a fright, and drew out my hanger to defend my self. These horrible animals had the boldness to attack me on both sides, and one of them held his fore-feet at my collar; but I had the good fortune to rip up his belly before he could do me any mischief. He fell down at my feet, and the other, seeing the fate of his comrade, made his escape, but not without one good wound on the back, which I gave him as he fled, and made the blood run trickling from him. After this exploit, I walked gently to and fro on the bed, to recover my breath and loss of spirits. These creatures were of the size of a large mastiff, but infinitely more nimble and fierce, so that if I had taken off my belt before I went to sleep, I must have infallibly been torn to pieces and devoured. I measured the tail of the dead rat, and found it to be two yards long wanting an inch; but it went against my stomach to drag the carcass off the bed, where it lay still bleeding; I observed it had yet some life, but with a strong slash cross the neck I thoroughly dispatched it.

Soon after my mistress came into the room, who seeing me all bloody, ran and took me up in her hand. I pointed to the dead rat, smiling and making other signs to show I was not hurt, whereat she was extremely rejoiced, calling the maid to take up the dead rat with a pair of tongs, and throw it out of the window. Then she set me on a table, where I showed her my hanger all bloody, and wiping it on the lappet of my coat, returned it to the scabbard. I was pressed to do more than one thing which another could not do for me, and therefore endeavoured to make my mistress understand that I desired to be set down on the floor; which after she had done, my bashfulness would not suffer me to express my self farther than by pointing to the door, and bowing several times. The good woman with much difficulty at last perceived what I would be at, and taking me up again in her hand, walked into the garden, where she set me down. I went on one side about two hundred yards, and beckoning to her not to look or to follow me, I hid myself between two leaves of sorrel, and there discharged the necessities of nature.

I hope the gentle reader will excuse me for dwelling on these and the like particulars, which, however insignificant they may appear to grovelling vulgar minds, yet will certainly help a philosopher to enlarge his thoughts and imagination, and apply them to the benefit of public as well as private life, which was my sole design in presenting this and other accounts of my travels to the world; wherein I have been chiefly studious of truth, without affecting any ornaments of learning or of style. But the whole scene of this voyage made so strong an impression on my mind, and is so deeply fixed in my memory, that in committing it to paper I did not omit one material circumstance: however, upon a strict review, I blotted out several passages of less moment which were in my first copy, for fear of being censured as tedious and trifling, whereof travellers are often, perhaps not without justice, accused.

CHAPTER II

A description of the farmer's daughter. The author carried to a market-town, and then to the metropolis. The particulars of his journey.

My mistress had a daughter of nine years old, a child of forward parts for her age, very dextrous at her needle, and skilful in dressing her baby. Her mother and she contrived to fit up the baby's cradle for me against night:

Baby. Doll.

the cradle was put into a small drawer of a cabinet, and the drawer placed upon a hanging shelf for fear of the rats. This was my bed all the time I stayed with those people, although made more convenient by degrees, as I began to learn their language, and make my wants known. This young girl was so handy, that after I had once or twice pulled off my clothes before her, she was able to dress and undress me, although I never gave her that trouble when she would let me do either my self. She made me seven shirts, and some other linen, of as fine cloth as could be got, which indeed was coarser than sackcloth; and these she constantly washed for me with her own hands. She was likewise my school-mistress to teach me the language: when I pointed to any thing, she told me the name of it in her own tongue, so that in a few days I was able to call for whatever I had a mind to. She was very good natured, and not above forty foot high, being little for her age. She gave me the name of *Grildrig,* which the family took up, and afterwards the whole kingdom. The word imports what the Latins call *nanunculus,* the Italians *homunceletino,* and the English *mannikin.* To her I chiefly owe my preservation in that country: we never parted while I was there; I called her my *glumdalclitch,* or "little nurse": and I should be guilty of great ingratitude if I omitted this honourable mention of her care and affection towards me, which I heartily wish it lay in my power to requite as she deserves, instead of being the innocent but unhappy instrument of her disgrace, as I have too much reason to fear.

It now began to be known and talked of in the neighborhood, that my master had found a strange animal in the field, about the bigness of a *splacknuck,* but exactly shaped in every part like a human creature; which it likewise imitated in all its actions; seemed to speak in a little language of its own, had already learned several words of theirs, went erect upon two legs, was tame and gentle, would come when it was called, do whatever it was bid, had the finest limbs in the world, and a complexion fairer than a nobleman's daughter of three years old. Another farmer who lived hard by, and was a particular friend of my master, came on a visit on purpose to enquire into the truth of this story. I was immediately produced, and placed upon a table, where I walked as I was commanded, drew my hanger, put it up again, made my reverence to my master's guest, asked him in his own language how he did, and told him he was welcome, just as my little nurse had instructed me. This man, who was old and dim-sighted, put on his spectacles to behold me better, at which I could not forbear laughing very heartily, for his eyes appeared like the full moon shining into a chamber at two windows. Our people, who discovered the cause of my mirth, bore me company in laughing, at which the old fellow was fool enough to be angry and out of countenance. He had the character of a great miser, and to my misfortune he well deserved it, by the cursed advice he gave my master to show me as a sight upon a market-day in the next town, which was half an hour's riding, about two and twenty miles from our house. I guessed there was some mischief contriving, when I observed my master and his friend whispering long together, sometimes pointing at me; and my fears made me fancy that I overheard and understood some of their words. But the next morning Glumdalclitch my little nurse told me the whole matter, which she had cunningly picked out from her mother. The poor girl laid me on her bosom, and fell a weeping with shame and grief. She apprehended some mischief would happen to me from rude vulgar folks, who might squeeze me to death, or break one of my limbs by taking me in their hands. She had also observed how modest I was in my nature, how nicely I regarded my honour, and what an indignity I should conceive it to be exposed for money as a public spectacle to the meanest of the people. She said, her papa and mamma had promised that Grildrig should be hers, but now she found they meant to serve her as they did last year, when they pretended to give her a lamb, and yet, as soon as it was fat, sold it to a butcher. For my own part, I may truly affirm that I was less concerned than my nurse. I had a strong hope, which never left me, that I should one day recover my liberty; and as to the ignominy of being carried about for a monster, I considered my self to be a perfect stranger in the country, and that such a misfortune could never be charged upon me as a reproach if ever I should return to England; since the King of Great Britain himself, in my condition, must have undergone the same distress.

My master, pursuant to the advice of my friend, carried me in a box the next market-day to the neighbouring town, and took along with him his little daughter my nurse upon a pillion behind him. The box was close on every side, with a little door for me to go in and out, and a few gimlet-holes to let in air. The girl had been so careful to put the quilt of her baby's bed into it, for me to lie down on. However, I was terribly shaken and discomposed in this journey, although it were but of half an hour. For the horse went about forty foot at every step, and trotted so high, that the agitation was equal to the rising and falling of a ship in a great storm, but much more frequent: our journey was somewhat further than from London to St. Albans. My master alighted at an inn which he used to frequent; and after

---

Monster. A freak. William Dampier had hoped to reap profits from displaying Jeoly, a tattooed man from the Philippines, upon their return to England, but was forced to sell his share. The "Painted Prince" was nevertheless, in Dampier's words, "carried about to be shown for a Sight." See p. 397.

consulting a while with the inn-keeper, and making some necessary preparations, he hired the *Grultrud*, or crier, to give notice through the town of a strange creature to be seen at the Sign of the Green Eagle, not so big as a *splacknuck* (an animal in that country very finely shaped, about six foot long) and in every part of the body resembling an human creature, could speak several words, and perform an hundred diverting tricks.

I was placed upon a table in the largest room of the inn, which might be near three hundred foot square. My little nurse stood on a low stool close to the table, to take care of me, and direct what I should do. My master, to avoid a crowd, would suffer only thirty people at a time to see me. I walked about on the table as the girl commanded; she asked me questions as far as she knew my understanding of the language reached, and I answered them as loud as I could. I turned about several times to the company, paid my humble respects, said they were welcome, and used some other speeches I had been taught. I took up a thimble filled with liquor, which Glumdalclitch had given me for a cup, and drank their health. I drew out my hanger, and flourished with it after the manner of fencers in England. My nurse gave me part of a straw, which I exercised as a pike, having learned the art in my youth. I was that day shown to twelve sets of company, and as often forced to go over again with the same fopperies, till I was half dead with weariness and vexation. For those who had seen me made such wonderful reports, that the people were ready to break down the doors to come in. My master for his own interest would not suffer any one to touch me except my nurse; and, to prevent danger, benches were set round the table at such a distance as put me out of every body's reach. However, an unlucky school-boy aimed a hazel nut directly at my head, which very narrowly missed me; otherwise, it came with so much violence that it would have infallibly knocked out my brains, for it was almost as large as a small pumpion: but I had the satisfaction to see the young rogue well beaten, and turned out of the room.

My master gave public notice, that he would show me again the next market-day, and in the mean time he prepared a more convenient vehicle for me, which he had reason enough to do; for I was so tired with my first journey, and with entertaining company for eight hours together, that I could hardly stand upon my legs, or speak a word. It was at least three days before I recovered my strength; and that I might have no rest at home, all the neighbouring gentlemen from an hundred miles round, hearing of my fame, came to see me at my master's own house. There could not be fewer than thirty persons with their wives and children (for the country is very populous); and my master demanded the rate of a full room whenever he showed me at home, although it were only to a single family. So that for some time I had but little ease every day of the week (except Wednesday, which is their Sabbath) although I were not carried to the town.

My master, finding how profitable I was like to be, resolved to carry me to the most considerable cities of the kingdom. Having therefore provided himself with all things necessary for a long journey, and settled his affairs at home, he took leave of his wife, and upon the 17th of August, 1703, about two months after my arrival, we set out for the metropolis, situated near the middle of that empire, and about three thousand miles distance from our house: my master made his daughter Glumdalclitch ride behind him. She carried me on her lap in a box tied about her waist. The girl had lined it on all sides with the softest cloth she could get, well quilted underneath, furnished it with her baby's bed, provided me with linen and other necessaries, and made every thing as convenient as she could. We had no other company but a boy of the house, who rode after us with the luggage.

My master's design was to show me in all the towns by the way, and to step out of the road for fifty or an hundred miles, to any village or person of quality's house where he might expect custom. We made easy journeys of not above seven or eight-score miles a day: for Glumdalclitch, on purpose to spare me, complained she was tired with the trotting of the horse. She often took me out of my box at my own desire, to give me air, and show me the country, but always held me fast by leading-strings. We passed over five or six rivers many degrees broader and deeper than the Nile or the Ganges; and there was hardly a rivulet so small as the Thames at London Bridge. We were ten weeks in our journeys, and I was shown in eighteen large towns, besides many villages and private families.

On the 26th day of October, we arrived at the metropolis, called in their language *Lorbrulgrud,* or *Pride of the Universe.* My master took a lodging in the principal street of the city, not far from the royal palace, and put out bills in the usual form, containing an exact description of my person and parts. He hired a large room between three and four hundred foot wide. He provided a table sixty foot in diameter, upon which I was to act my part, and palisadoed it round three feet from the edge, and as many high, to prevent my falling over. I was shown ten times a day to the wonder and satisfaction of all people. I could now speak the language tolerably well, and perfectly understood every word that was spoken to me. Besides, I had

---

Which is their Sabbath. Possibly a contrast between the Julian and Gregorian Calendars, which divided Britain from much of Europe. The two calendars differed by eleven days at the time of the voyage to Brobdingnag, placing Julian Sunday on Gregorian Wednesday. Britain converted to the Gregorian calendar in 1752. See Fitzgerald, 95–96.

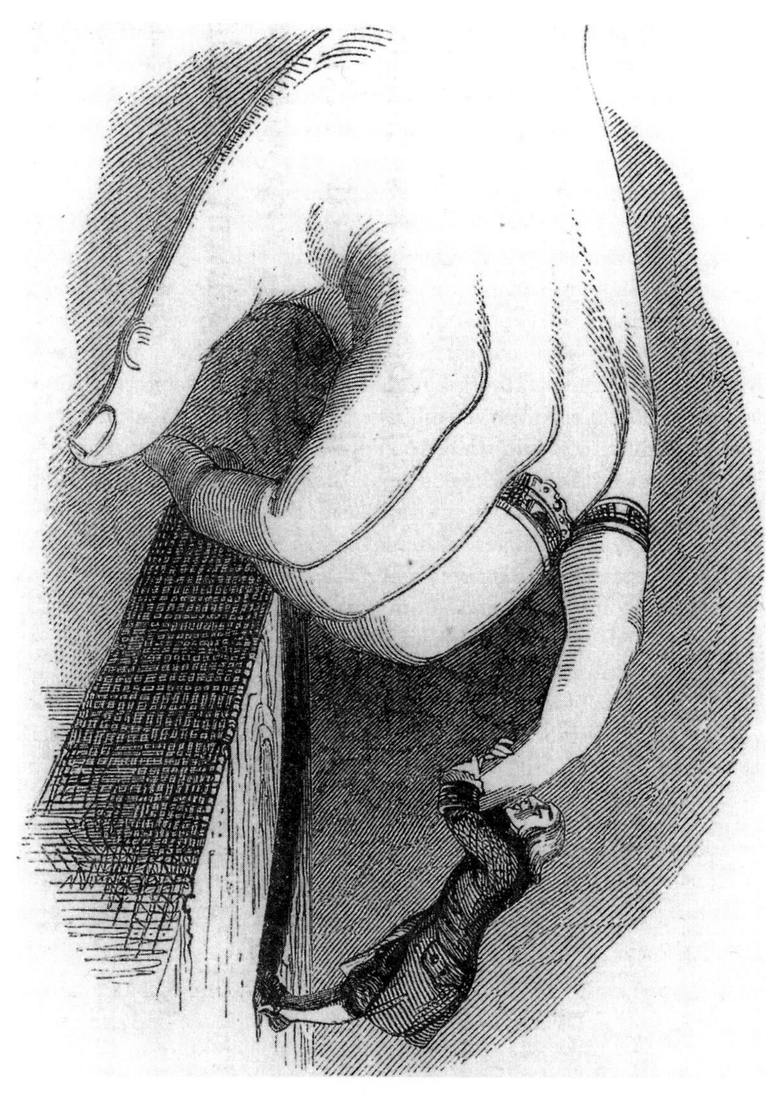

J. J. Grandville, *Gulliver Kissing the Brobdingnagian Finger,* 1838.
THE BEINECKE RARE BOOK AND MANUSCRIPT LIBRARY, YALE UNIVERSITY.

learnt their alphabet, and could make a shift to explain a sentence here and there; for Glumdalclitch had been my instructor while we were at home, and at leisure hours during our journey. She carried a little book in her pocket, not much larger than a Sanson's *Atlas;* it was a common treatise for the use of young girls, giving a short account of their religion; out of this she taught me my letters, and interpreted the words.

CHAPTER III

The author sent for to court. The Queen buys him of his master the farmer, and presents him to the King. He disputes with his Majesty's great scholars. An apartment at court provided for the author. He is in high favour with the Queen. He stands up for the honour of his own country. His quarrels with the Queen's dwarf.

The frequent labours I underwent every day made in a few weeks a very considerable change in my health: the more my master got by me, the more unsatiable he grew. I had quite lost my stomach, and was almost reduced to a skeleton. The farmer observed it, and concluding I soon must die, resolved to make as good a hand of me as he could. While he was thus reasoning and resolving with himself, a *slardral,* or gentleman usher, came from court, commanding my master to bring me immediately thither for the diversion of the Queen and her ladies. Some of the latter had already been to see me, and reported strange things of my beauty, behaviour, and good sense. Her Majesty and those who attended her were beyond measure delighted with my demeanor. I fell on my knees, and begged the honour of kissing her imperial foot; but this gracious princess held out her little finger towards me (after I was set on a table) which I embraced in both my arms, and put the tip of it, with the utmost respect, to my lip. She made me some general questions about my country and my travels, which I answered as distinctly and in as few words as I could. She asked whether I would be content to live at court. I bowed down to the board of the table, and humbly answered that I was my master's slave, but if I were at my own disposal, I should be proud to devote my life to her Majesty's service. She then asked my master whether he were willing to sell me at a good price.

Sanson's *Atlas.* The Sanson mapmaking firm in France, founded by Nicholas Sanson (1600–67), produced a four-volume "pocket atlas" (*L'Amerique en Plusiers Cartes,* 1657) in a format measuring about seven by ten inches.

He, who apprehended I could not live a month, was ready enough to part with me, and demanded a thousand pieces of gold, which were ordered him on the spot, each piece being about the bigness of eight hundred moidores; but, allowing for the proportion of all things between that country and Europe, and the high price of gold among them, was hardly so great a sum as a thousand guineas would be in England. I then said to the Queen, since I was now her Majesty's most humble creature and vassal, I must beg the favour, that Glumdalclitch, who had always tended me with so much care and kindness, and understood to do it so well, might be admitted into her service, and continue to be my nurse and instructor. Her Majesty agreed to my petition, and easily got the farmer's consent, who was glad enough to have his daughter preferred at court: and the poor girl herself was not able to hide her joy: my late master withdrew, bidding me farewell, and saying he had left me in a good service; to which I replied not a word, only making him a slight bow.

The Queen observed my coldness, and when the farmer was gone out of the apartment, asked me the reason. I made bold to tell her Majesty that I owed no other obligation to my late master, than his not dashing out the brains of a poor harmless creature found by chance in his field; which obligation was amply recompensed by the gain he had made in showing me through half the kingdom, and the price he had now sold me for. That the life I had since led was laborious enough to kill an animal of ten times my strength. That my health was much impaired by the continual drudgery of entertaining the rabble every hour of the day, and that if my master had not thought my life in danger, her Majesty perhaps would not have got so cheap a bargain. But as I was out of all fear of being ill treated under the protection of so great and good an empress, the Ornament of Nature, the Darling of the World, the Delight of her Subjects, the Phoenix of the Creation; so, I hoped, my late master's apprehensions would appear to be groundless, for I already found my spirits to revive by the influence of her most august presence.

This was the sum of my speech, delivered with great improprieties and hesitation; the latter part was altogether framed in the style peculiar to that people, whereof I learned some phrases from Glumdalclitch, while she was carrying me to court.

The Queen, giving great allowance for my defectiveness in speaking, was however surprised at so much wit and good sense in so diminutive an animal. She took me in her own hand, and carried me to the King, who was then retired to his cabinet. His Majesty, a prince of much gravity, and austere countenance, not well observing my shape at first view, asked the Queen after a cold manner, how long it was since she grew fond of a *splacknuck;* for such it seems he took me to be, as I lay upon my breast in her Majesty's right hand. But this princess, who hath an infinite deal of wit and humour, set me gently on my feet upon the scrutore, and commanded me to give his Majesty an account of my self, which I did in a very few words; and Glumdalclitch, who attended at the cabinet door, and could not endure I should be out of her sight, being admitted, confirmed all that had passed from my arrival at her father's house.

The King, although he be as learned a person as any in his dominions, had been educated in the study of philosophy, and particularly mathematics; yet when he observed my shape exactly, and saw me walk erect, before I began to speak, conceived I might be a piece of clock-work (which is in that country arrived to a very great perfection), contrived by some ingenious artist. But, when he heard my voice, and found what I delivered to be regular and rational, he could not conceal his astonishment. He was by no means satisfied with the relation I gave him of the manner I came into his kingdom, but thought it a story concerted between Glumdalclitch and her father, who had taught me a set of words to make me sell at a higher price. Upon this imagination he put several other questions to me, and still received rational answers, no otherwise defective than by a foreign accent, and an imperfect knowledge in the language, with some rustic phrases which I had learned at the farmer's house, and did not suit the polite style of a court.

His Majesty sent for three great scholars who were then in their weekly waiting (according to the custom in that country). These gentlemen, after they had a while examined my shape with much nicety, were of different opinions concerning me. They all agreed that I could not be produced according to the regular laws of nature, because I was not framed with a capacity of preserving my life, either by swiftness, or climbing of trees, or digging holes in the earth. They observed by my teeth, which they viewed with great exactness, that I was a carnivorous animal; yet most quadrupeds being an overmatch for me, and field mice, with some others, too nimble, they could not imagine how I should be able to support my self, unless I fed upon snails and other insects, which they offered by many learned arguments to evince that I could not possibly do. One of them seemed to think that I might be an embryo, or abortive birth. But this opinion was rejected by the other two, who observed my limbs to be perfect and

---

A piece of clock-work. Mechanized dolls devised by clock makers and other skilled craftsmen were commonly displayed in the courts of Gulliver's time. Clocks and clockwork toys were an especially popular currency in European dealings with the Chinese imperial court. In his *De l'Homme* (1664), moreover, René Descartes—drawing in part on such automata—had described the human body itself in mechanistic terms.

finished, and that I had lived several years, as it was manifested from my beard, the stumps whereof they plainly discovered through a magnifying-glass. They would not allow me to be a dwarf, because my littleness was beyond all degrees of comparison; for the Queen's favourite dwarf, the smallest ever known in that kingdom, was near thirty foot high. After much debate, they concluded unanimously that I was only *relplum scalcath,* which is interpreted literally, *lusus naturæ;* a determination exactly agreeable to the modern philosophy of Europe, whose professors, disdaining the old evasion of occult causes, whereby the followers of Aristotle endeavour in vain to disguise their ignorance, have invented this wonderful solution of all difficulties to the unspeakable advancement of human knowledge.

After this decisive conclusion, I entreated to be heard a word or two. I applied myself to the King, and assured his Majesty that I came from a country which abounded with several millions of both sexes, and of my own stature; where the animals, trees, and houses were all in proportion, and where by consequence I might be as able to defend my self, and to find sustenance, as any of his Majesty's subjects could do here; which I took for a full answer to those gentlemen's arguments. To this they only replied with a smile of contempt, saying, that the farmer had instructed me very well in my lesson. The King, who had a much better understanding, dismissing his learned men, sent for the farmer, who by good fortune was not yet gone out of town; having therefore first examined him privately, and then confronted him with me and the young girl, his Majesty began to think that what we told him might possibly be true. He desired the Queen to order that a particular care should be taken of me, and was of opinion, that Glumdalclitch should still continue in her office of tending me, because he observed we had a great affection for each other. A convenient apartment was provided for her at court; she had a sort of governess appointed to take care of her education, a maid to dress her, and two other servants for menial offices; but the care of me was wholly appropriated to her self. The Queen commanded her own cabinet-maker to contrive a box that might serve me for a bed-chamber, after the model that Glumdalclitch and I should agree upon. This man was a most ingenious artist, and according to my directions, in three weeks finished for me a wooden chamber of sixteen

---

Lusus naturae. Sport of nature. In his attempt to classify the sciences, Francis Bacon had suggested subdividing natural history into "creatures, marvels, and arts" (*De Augmentis,* 1623). Bacon's second category constituted a science of marvelous monsters—teratology—dedicated to exploring exceptions to categories deemed natural. The great eighteenth-century collector Sir Hans Sloane counted various freakish curios among his numerous human specimens, including six sets of conjoined twins.

foot square, and twelve high, with sash-windows, a door, and two closets, like a London bed-chamber. The board that made the ceiling was to be lifted up and down by two hinges, to put in a bed ready furnished by her Majesty's upholsterer, which Glumdalclitch took out every day to air, made it with her own hands, and letting it down at night, locked up the roof over me. A nice workman, who was famous for little curiosities, undertook to make me two chairs, with backs and frames, of a substance not unlike ivory, and two tables, with a cabinet to put my things in. The room was quilted on all sides, as well as the floor and the ceiling, to prevent any accident from the carelessness of those who carried me, and to break the force of a jolt when I went in a coach. I desired a lock for my door to prevent rats and mice from coming in: the smith after several attempts made the smallest that was ever seen among them, for I have known a larger at the gate of a gentleman's house in England. I made a shift to keep the key in a pocket of my own, fearing Glumdalclitch might lose it. The Queen likewise ordered the thinnest silks that could be gotten, to make me clothes, not much thicker than an English blanket, very cumbersome till I was accustomed to them. They were after the fashion of the kingdom, partly resembling the Persian, and partly the Chinese, and are a very grave decent habit.

The Queen became so fond of my company, that she could not dine without me. I had a table placed upon the same at which her Majesty eat, just at her left elbow, and a chair to sit on. Glumdalclitch stood upon a stool on the floor, near my table, to assist and take care of me. I had an entire set of silver dishes and plates, and other necessaries, which, in proportion to those of the Queen, were not much bigger than what I have seen in a London toy-shop, for the furniture of a baby-house: these my little nurse kept in her pocket, in a silver box, and gave me at meals as I wanted them, always cleaning them her self. No person dined with the Queen but the two princesses royal, the elder sixteen years old, and the younger at that time thirteen and a month. Her Majesty used to put a bit of meat upon one of my dishes, out of which I carved for my self; and her diversion was to see me eat in miniature. For the Queen (who had indeed but a weak stomach) took up at one mouthful as much as a dozen English farmers could eat at a meal, which to me was for some time a very nauseous sight. She would craunch the wing of a lark, bones and all, between her teeth, although it were nine times as large as that of a full-grown turkey; and put a bit of bread in her mouth, as big as two twelve-penny loaves. She drank out of a golden cup, above a hogshead at a draught. Her knives were twice as long as a scythe set straight upon the handle. The spoons, forks, and other instruments were all in the same proportion. I remember when Glumdalclitch carried me out of curiosity to see some of the tables at court, where ten or a dozen of these enormous knives and forks were lifted up together, I thought I had never till then beheld so terrible a sight.

It is the custom that every Wednesday (which, as I have before observed, was their Sabbath) the King and Queen, with the royal issue of both sexes, dine together in the apartment of his Majesty, to whom I was now become a favourite; and at these times my little chair and table were placed at his left hand before one of the salt-cellars. This prince took a pleasure in conversing with me, enquiring into the manners, religion, laws, government, and learning of Europe, wherein I gave him the best account I was able. His apprehension was so clear, and his judgment so exact, that he made very wise reflections and observations upon all I said. But I confess, that after I had been a little too copious in talking of my own beloved country, of our trade, and wars by sea and land, of our schisms in religion, and parties in the state, the prejudices of his education prevailed so far, that he could not forbear taking me up in his right hand, and stroking me gently with the other, after an hearty fit of laughing, asked me whether I were a Whig or a Tory. Then turning to his first minister, who waited behind him with a white staff, near as tall as the main-mast of the *Royal Sovereign*, he observed how contemptible a thing was human grandeur, which could be mimicked by such diminutive insects as I: And yet, said he, I dare engage, those creatures have their titles and distinctions of honour, they contrive little nests and burrows, that they call houses and cities; they make a figure in dress and equipage; they love, they fight, they dispute, they cheat, they betray. And thus he continued on, while my colour came and went several times, with indignation to hear our noble country, the mistress of arts and arms, the scourge of France, the arbitress of Europe, the seat of virtue, piety, honour and truth, the pride and envy of the world, so contemptuously treated.

But, as I was not in a condition to resent injuries, so, upon mature thoughts, I began to doubt whether I were injured or no. For, after having been accustomed several months to the sight and converse of this people,

---

A Whig or a Tory. Swift had been a prominent columnist for the Tory ministry between 1710 and 1714. Much of the satire in *Gulliver's Travels*—especially the attack on public financing of war through the use of national credit—has a Tory flavor. Swift nevertheless preferred to call himself an "Old Whig," an adherent, that is, to the original principles that served to legitimate the exclusion of James II from the throne. *The Drapier's Letters* highlight Swift's "Whiggish" emphasis on the consent of the governed. His libertarian opposition to absolutism is consistent.

and observed every object upon which I cast my eyes to be of proportionable magnitude, the horror I had first conceived from their bulk and aspect was so far worn off, that if I had then beheld a company of English lords and ladies in their finery and birthday clothes, acting their several parts in the most courtly manner of strutting, and bowing, and prating, to say the truth, I should have been strongly tempted to laugh as much at them as this king and his grandees did at me. Neither indeed could I forbear smiling at my self, when the Queen used to place me upon her hand towards a looking-glass, by which both our persons appeared before me in full view together; and there could nothing be more ridiculous than the comparison: so that I really began to imagine my self dwindled many degrees below my usual size.

Nothing angered and mortified me so much as the Queen's dwarf, who being of the lowest stature that was ever in that country (for I verily think he was not full thirty foot high) became so insolent at seeing a creature so much beneath him, that he would always affect to swagger and look big as he passed by me in the Queen's antechamber, while I was standing on some table talking with the lords or ladies of the court, and he seldom failed of a smart word or two upon my littleness; against which I could only revenge my self by calling him brother, challenging him to wrestle, and such repartees as are usual in the mouths of court pages. One day at dinner this malicious little cub was so nettled with something I had said to him, that raising himself upon the frame of her Majesty's chair, he took me up by the middle, as I was sitting down, not thinking any harm, and let me drop into a large silver bowl of cream, and then ran away as fast as he could. I fell over head and ears, and if I had not been a good swimmer, it might have gone very hard with me; for Glumdalclitch in that instant happened to be at the other end of the room, and the Queen was in such a fright that she wanted presence of mind to assist me. But my little nurse ran to my relief, and took me out, after I had swallowed above a quart of cream. I was put to bed; however I received no other damage than the loss of a suit of clothes, which was utterly spoiled. The dwarf was soundly whipped, and as a further punishment, forced to drink up the bowl of cream into which he had thrown me; neither was he ever restored to favour: for, soon after, the Queen bestowed him to a lady of high quality, so that I saw him no more, to my very great satisfaction; for I could not tell to what extremities such a malicious urchin might have carried his resentment.

He had before served me a scurvy trick, which set the Queen a laughing, although at the same time she were heartily vexed, and would have immediately cashiered him, if I had not been so generous as to intercede. Her Majesty had taken a marrow-bone upon her plate, and after knocking out the marrow, placed the bone again in the dish erect as it stood before; the dwarf watching his opportunity, while Glumdalclitch was gone to the side-board, mounted the stool she stood on to take care of me at meals, took me up in both hands, and squeezing my legs together, wedged them into the marrow-bone above my waist, where I stuck for some time, and made a very ridiculous figure. I believe it was near a minute before any one knew what was become of me, for I thought it below me to cry out. But, as princes seldom get their meat hot, my legs were not scalded, only my stockings and breeches in a sad condition. The dwarf at my entreaty had no other punishment than a sound whipping.

I was frequently rallied by the Queen upon account of my fearfulness, and she used to ask me whether the people of my country were as great cowards as my self. The occasion was this. The kingdom is much pestered with flies in summer, and these odious insects, each of them as big as a Dunstable lark, hardly gave me any rest while I sat at dinner, with their continual humming and buzzing about my ears. They would sometimes alight upon my victuals, and leave their loathsome excrement or spawn behind, which to me was very visible, although not to the natives of that country, whose large optics were not so acute as mine in viewing smaller objects. Sometimes they would fix upon my nose or forehead, where they stung me to the quick, smelling very offensively, and I could easily trace that viscous matter, which our naturalists tell us enables those creatures to walk with their feet upwards upon a ceiling. I had much ado to defend my self against these detestable animals, and could not forbear starting when they came on my face. It was the common practice of the dwarf to catch a number of these insects in his hand as schoolboys do among us, and let them out suddenly under my nose on purpose to frighten me, and divert the Queen. My remedy was to cut them in pieces with my knife as they flew in the air, wherein my dexterity was much admired.

I remember one morning when Glumdalclitch had set me in my box upon a window, as she usually did in fair days to give me air (for I durst not venture to let the box be hung on a nail out of the window, as we do with cages in England) after I had lifted up one of my sashes, and sat down at my table to eat a piece of sweet cake for my breakfast, above twenty wasps, allured by the smell, came flying into the room, humming louder than the drones of as many bagpipes. Some of them seized my cake, and carried it piecemeal away, others flew about my head and face, confounding me with the noise, and putting me in the utmost terror of their stings. However I had the courage to rise and draw my hanger, and attack them in the air. I dispatched four of them, but the rest got away, and I presently shut my window. These insects were as large as partridges: I took out their stings, found them an inch and a half long, and as sharp as needles. I carefully preserved them all, and having since shown them with some other curiosities in several parts of Europe, upon my return to England I gave three of them to Gresham College, and kept the fourth for my self.

CHAPTER IV

The country described. A proposal for correcting modern maps. The King's palace, and some account of the metropolis. The author's way of travelling. The chief temple described.

I now intend to give the reader a short description of this country, as far as I travelled in it, which was not above two thousand miles round Lorbrulgrud the metropolis. For the Queen, whom I always attended, never went further when she accompanied the King in his progresses, and there stayed till his Majesty returned from viewing his frontiers. The whole extent of this prince's dominions reacheth about six thousand miles in length, and from three to five in breadth. From whence I cannot but conclude that our geographers of Europe are in a great error, by supposing nothing but sea between Japan and California; for it was ever my opinion, that there must be a balance of earth to counterpoise the great continent of Tartary; and therefore they ought to correct their maps and charts, by joining this vast tract of land to the northwest parts of America, wherein I shall be ready to lend them my assistance.

The kingdom is a peninsula, terminated to the northeast by a ridge of mountains thirty miles high, which are altogether impassable by reason of the volcanoes upon the tops. Neither do the most learned know what sort

---

Gresham College. As DeMaria points out, this was the home of the Royal Society and its museum of natural rarities. Such museums mark an institutional convergence—through the notion of systematic collection and display—of eighteenth-century natural history and the colonial project. The Royal Society also generated a detailed set of guidelines for the production of systematically informative travel narratives. Sir Hans Sloane (1660–1753), who collected buccaneer narratives along with books, coins, insects, fossils, and botanical and zoological specimens, would in 1753 bequeath one of the great founding collections for the British Museum in London. Many of the shells in his collection came from Dampier's circumnavigation of the globe. See de Beer, 112.

Altogether impassable by reason of the volcanoes upon the tops. The geographical seclusion of Brobdingnag may suggest the isolationist policy by which Chinese rulers strictly limited interaction with the outside world during this period.

of mortals inhabit beyond these mountains, or whether they be inhabited at all. On the three other sides it is bounded by the ocean. There is not one seaport in the whole kingdom, and those parts of the coasts into which the rivers issue are so full of pointed rocks, and the sea generally so rough, that there is no venturing with the smallest of their boats, so that these people are wholly excluded from any commerce with the rest of the world. But the large rivers are full of vessels, and abound with excellent fish, for they seldom get any from the sea, because the sea-fish are of the same size with those in Europe, and consequently not worth catching; whereby it is manifest, that nature in the production of plants and animals of so extraordinary a bulk is wholly confined to this continent, of which I leave the reasons to be determined by philosophers. However, now and then they take a whale that happens to be dashed against the rocks, which the common people feed on heartily. These whales I have known so large that a man could hardly carry one upon his shoulders; and sometimes for curiosity they are brought in hampers to Lorbrulgrud: I saw one of them in a dish at the King's table, which passed for a rarity, but I did not observe he was fond of it; for I think indeed the bigness disgusted him, although I have seen one somewhat larger in Greenland.

The country is well inhabited, for it contains fifty-one cities, near an hundred walled towns, and a great number of villages. To satisfy my curious reader, it may be sufficient to describe Lorbrulgrud. This city stands upon almost two equal parts on each side the river that passes through. It contains above eighty thousand houses, and about six hundred thousand inhabitants. It is in length three *glonglungs* (which make about fifty-four English miles) and two and a half in breadth, as I measured it my self in the royal map made by the King's order, which was laid on the ground on purpose for me, and extended an hundred feet; I paced the diameter and circumference several times barefoot, and computing by the scale, measured it pretty exactly.

The King's palace is no regular edifice, but an heap of buildings about seven miles round: the chief rooms are generally two hundred and forty foot high, and broad and long in proportion. A coach was allowed to Glumdalclitch and me, wherein her governess frequently took her out to see the town, or go among the shops; and I was always of the party, carried in my box; although the girl at my own desire would often take me out, and hold me in her hand, that I might more conveniently view the houses and the people as we passed along the streets. I reckoned our coach to be about a square of Westminster Hall, but not altogether so high; however, I cannot be very exact. One day the governess ordered our coachman to stop at several shops, where the beggars, watching their opportunity, crowded to the sides of the coach, and gave me the most horrible spectacles that ever an European eye beheld. There was a woman with a cancer in her breast, swelled to a monstrous size, full of holes, in two or three of which I could have easily crept, and covered my whole body. There was a fellow with a wen in his neck, larger than five woolpacks, and another with a couple of wooden legs, each about twenty foot high. But the most hateful sight of all was the lice crawling on their clothes. I could see distinctly the limbs of these vermin with my naked eye, much better than those of an European louse through a microscope, and their snouts with which they rooted like swine. They were the first I had ever beheld, and I should have been curious enough to dissect one of them, if I had proper instruments (which I unluckily left behind me in the ship) although indeed the sight was so nauseous, that it perfectly turned my stomach.

Beside the large box in which I was usually carried, the Queen ordered a smaller one to be made for me, of about twelve foot square, and ten high, for the convenience of travelling, because the other was somewhat too large for Glumdalclitch's lap, and cumbersome in the coach; it was made by the same artist, whom I directed in the whole contrivance. This travelling closet was an exact square with a window in the middle of three of the squares, and each window was latticed with iron wire on the outside, to prevent accidents in long journeys. On the fourth side, which had no window, two strong staples were fixed, through which the person that carried me, when I had a mind to be on horseback, put in a leathern belt, and buckled it about his waist. This was always the office of some grave trusty servant in whom I could confide, whether I attended the King and Queen in their progresses, or were disposed to see the gardens, or pay a visit to some great lady or minister of state in the court, when Glumdalclitch happened to be out of order: for I soon began to be known and esteemed among the greatest officers, I suppose more upon account of their Majesties' favour than any merit of my own. In journeys, when I was weary of the coach, a servant on horseback would buckle my box, and place it on a cushion before him; and there I had a full prospect of the country on three sides from my three windows. I had in this closet a field-bed and a hammock hung from the ceiling, two chairs and a table, neatly screwed to the floor, to prevent being tossed about by the agitation of the horse or the coach. And having been long used to sea-voyages, those motions, although sometimes very violent, did not much discompose me.

Whenever I had a mind to see the town, it was always in my travelling-closet, which Glumdalclitch held in her lap in a kind of open sedan, after the fashion of the country, borne by four men, and attended by two others in the Queen's livery. The people, who had often heard of me, were very curious to crowd about the sedan, and the girl was complaisant enough to make the bearers stop, and to take me in her hand that I might be more conveniently seen.

I was very desirous to see the chief temple, and particularly the tower belonging to it, which is reckoned the highest in the kingdom. Accordingly one day my nurse carried me thither, but I may truly say I came back disappointed; for the height is not above three thousand foot, reckoning from the ground to the highest pinnacle top; which, allowing for the difference between the size of those people and us in Europe, is no great matter for admiration, nor at all equal in proportion (if I rightly remember) to Salisbury steeple. But, not to detract from a nation to which during my life I shall acknowledge my self extremely obliged, it must be allowed that whatever this famous tower wants in height is amply made up in beauty and strength. For the walls are near an hundred foot thick, built of hewn stone, whereof each is about forty foot square, and adorned on all sides with statues of gods and emperors cut in marble larger than the life, placed in their several niches. I measured a little finger which had fallen down from one of these statues, and lay unperceived among some rubbish, and found it exactly four foot and an inch in length. Glumdalclitch wrapped it up in a handkerchief, and carried it home in her pocket to keep among other trinkets, of which the girl was very fond, as children at her age usually are.

The King's kitchen is indeed a noble building, vaulted at top, and about six hundred foot high. The great oven is not so wide by ten paces as the cupola at St. Paul's: for I measured the latter on purpose after my return. But if I should describe the kitchen-grate, the prodigious pots and kettles, the joints of meat turning on the spits, with many other particulars, perhaps I should be hardly believed; at least a severe critic would be apt to think I enlarged a little, as travellers are often suspected to do. To avoid which censure, I fear I have run too much into the other extreme; and that if this treatise should happen to be translated into the language of Brobdingnag (which is the general name of that kingdom) and transmitted thither, the King and his people would have reason to complain that I had done them an injury by a false and diminutive representation.

His Majesty seldom keeps above six hundred horses in his stables: they are generally from fifty-four to sixty foot high. But, when he goes abroad on solemn days, he is attended for state by a militia guard of five hundred horse, which indeed I thought was the most splendid sight that could be ever beheld, till I saw part of his army in battalia, whereof I shall find another occasion to speak.

CHAPTER V

Several adventures that happened to the author. The execution of a criminal. The author shows his skill in navigation.

I should have lived happy enough in that country, if my littleness had not exposed me to several ridiculous and troublesome accidents, some of which I shall venture to relate. Glumdalclitch often carried me into the gardens of the court in my smaller box, and would sometimes take me out of it and hold me in her hand, or set me down to walk. I remember, before the dwarf left the Queen, he followed us one day into those gardens, and my nurse having set me down, he and I being close together, near some dwarf apple-trees, I must needs show my wit by a silly allusion between him and the trees, which happens to hold in their language as it doth in ours. Whereupon the malicious rogue, watching his opportunity, when I was walking under one of them, shook it directly over my head, by which a dozen apples, each of them near as large as a Bristol barrel, came tumbling about my ears; one of them hit me on the back as I chanced to stoop, and knocked me down flat on my face, but I received no other hurt, and the dwarf was pardoned at my desire, because I had given the provocation.

Another day Glumdalclitch left me on a smooth grass-plot to divert my self while she walked at some distance with her governess. In the mean time there suddenly fell such a violent shower of hail, that I was immediately by the force of it struck to the ground: and when I was down, the hailstones gave me such cruel bangs all over the body, as if I had been pelted with tennis-balls; however I made a shift to creep on all four, and shelter my self by lying flat on my face on the lee-side of a border of lemon thyme, but so bruised from head to foot that I could not go abroad in ten days. Neither is this at all to be wondered at, because nature in that country observing the same proportion through all her operations, a hailstone is near eighteen hundred times as large as one in Europe, which I can assert upon experience, having been so curious to weigh and measure them.

But a more dangerous accident happened to me in the same garden, when my little nurse, believing she had put me in a secure place, which I often entreated her to do, that I might enjoy my own thoughts, and having left my box at home to avoid the trouble of carrying it, went to another part of the gardens with her governess and some ladies of her acquaintance. While she was absent and out of hearing, a small white spaniel belonging to one of the chief gardeners, having got by accident into the garden, happened to range near the place where I lay. The dog, following the scent, came directly up, and taking me in his mouth ran straight to his master, wagging his tail, and set me gently on the ground. By good fortune he had been so well taught, that I was carried between his teeth without the least hurt, or even tearing my clothes. But the poor gardener, who knew me well, and had a great kindness for me, was in a terrible fright. He gently took me up in both his hands, and asked me how I did; but I was so amazed and out of breath, that I could not speak a word. In a few minutes I came to my self, and he carried me safe to my little nurse, who by this time had returned to the place where she left me, and was in cruel agonies when I did not appear, nor answer when she called: she severely reprimanded the gardener on account of his dog. But the thing was hushed up, and never known at court; for the girl was afraid of the Queen's anger, and truly as to my self, I thought it would not be for my reputation that such a story should go about.

This accident absolutely determined Glumdalclitch never to trust me abroad for the future out of her sight. I had been long afraid of this resolution, and therefore concealed from her some little unlucky adventures that happened in those times when I was left by my self. Once a kite hovering over the garden made a stoop at me, and if I had not resolutely drawn my hanger, and run under a thick espalier, he would have certainly carried me away in his talons. Another time walking to the top of a fresh mole-hill, I fell to my neck in the hole through which that animal had cast up the earth, and coined some lie not worth remembering, to excuse my self for spoiling my clothes. I likewise broke my right shin against the shell of a snail, which I happened to stumble over, as I was walking alone, and thinking on poor England.

I cannot tell whether I were more pleased or mortified to observe in those solitary walks, that the smaller birds did not appear to be at all afraid of me, but would hop about within a yard distance, looking for worms and other food with as much indifference and security as if no creature at all were near them. I remember a thrush had the confidence to snatch out of my hand with his bill a piece of cake that Glumdalclitch had just given me for my breakfast. When I attempted to catch any of these birds, they would boldly turn against me, endeavouring to pick my fingers, which I durst not venture within their reach; and then they would hop back unconcerned to hunt for worms or snails, as they did before. But one day I took a thick cudgel, and threw it with all my strength so luckily at a linnet, that I knocked him down, and seizing him by the neck with both my hands, ran with him in triumph to my nurse. However, the bird, who had only been stunned, recovering himself, gave me so many boxes with his wings on both sides of my head and body, although I held him at arm's length, and was out of the reach of his claws, that I was twenty times thinking to let him go. But I was soon relieved by one of our servants, who wrung off the bird's neck, and I had him next day for dinner by the Queen's command. This linnet, as near as I can remember, seemed to be somewhat larger than an English swan.

The maids of honour often invited Glumdalclitch to their apartments, and desired she would bring me along with her, on purpose to have the pleasure of seeing and touching me. They would often strip me naked from top to toe, and lay me at full length in their bosoms; wherewith I was much disgusted; because, to say the truth, a very offensive smell came from their skins; which I do not mention or intend to the disadvantage of those excellent ladies, for whom I have all manner of respect; but I conceive that my sense was more acute in proportion to my littleness, and that those illustrious persons were no more disagreeable to their lovers, or to each other, than people of the same quality are with us in England. And, after all, I found their natural smell was much more supportable than when they used perfumes, under which I immediately swooned away. I cannot forget that an intimate friend of mine in Lilliput took the freedom, in a warm day, when I had used a good deal of exercise, to complain of a strong smell about me, although I am as little faulty that way as most of my sex: but I suppose his faculty of smelling was as nice with regard to me, as mine was to that of this people. Upon this point, I cannot forbear doing justice to the Queen my mistress, and Glumdalclitch my nurse, whose persons were as sweet as those of any lady in England.

That which gave me most uneasiness among these maids of honour, when my nurse carried me to visit them, was to see them use me without any manner of ceremony, like a creature who had no sort of consequence. For they would strip themselves to the skin, and put on their smocks in my presence, while I was placed on their toilet directly before their naked bodies, which, I am sure, to me was very far from being a tempting sight, or from giving me any other emotions than those of horror and disgust. Their skins appeared so coarse and uneven, so variously coloured, when I saw them near, with a mole here and there as broad as a trencher, and hairs hanging from it thicker than pack-threads; to say nothing further concerning the rest of their persons. Neither did they at all scruple while I was by to discharge what they had drunk, to the quantity of at least two hogsheads, in a vessel that held above three tuns. The handsomest among these maids of honour, a pleasant frolicsome girl of sixteen, would sometimes set me astride upon one of her nipples, with many other tricks, wherein the reader will excuse me for not being over particular. But I was so much displeased, that I entreated Glumdalclitch to contrive some excuse for not seeing that young lady any more.

Many other tricks, wherein the reader will excuse me for not being over particular. Gulliver refers to his exploitation as a sexual toy.

One day a young gentleman, who was nephew to my nurse's governess, came and pressed them both to see an execution. It was of a man who had murdered one of that gentleman's intimate acquaintance. Glumdalclitch was prevailed on to be of the company, very much against her inclination, for she was naturally tender-hearted: and as for my self, although I abhorred such kind of spectacles, yet my curiosity tempted me to see something that I thought must be extraordinary. The malefactor was fixed in a chair upon a scaffold erected for the purpose, and his head cut off at one blow with a sword of about forty foot long. The veins and arteries spouted up such a prodigious quantity of blood, and so high in the air, that the great *jet d'eau* at Versailles was not equal for the time it lasted; and the head, when it fell on the scaffold floor, gave such a bounce as made me start, although I was at least an English mile distant.

The Queen, who often used to hear me talk of my sea-voyages, and took all occasions to divert me when I was melancholy, asked me whether I understood how to handle a sail or an oar, and whether a little exercise of rowing might not be convenient for my health. I answered that I understood both very well. For although my proper employment had been to be surgeon or doctor to the ship, yet often, upon a pinch, I was forced to work like a common mariner. But I could not see how this could be done in their country, where the smallest wherry was equal to a first rate man of war among us, and such a boat as I could manage would never live in any of their rivers: her Majesty said, if I would contrive a boat, her own joiner should make it, and she would provide a place for me to sail in. The fellow was an ingenious workman, and by my instructions in ten days finished a pleasure-boat with all its tackling, able conveniently to hold eight Europeans. When it was finished, the Queen was so delighted, that she ran with it in her lap to the King, who ordered it to be put in a cistern full of water, with me in it, by way of trial, where I could not manage my two sculls or little oars for want of room. But the Queen had before contrived another project. She ordered the joiner to make a wooden trough of three hundred foot long, fifty broad, and eight deep; which being well pitched to prevent leaking, was placed on the floor along the wall, in an outer room of the palace. It had a cock near the bottom to let out the water when it began to grow stale, and two servants could easily fill it in half an hour. Here I often used to row for my diversion, as well as that of the Queen and her ladies, who thought themselves agreeably entertained with my skill and agility. Sometimes I would put up my sail, and then my business was only to steer, while the ladies gave me a gale with their fans; and when they were weary, some of the pages would blow my sail forward with their breath, while

I showed my art by steering starboard or larboard as I pleased. When I had done, Glumdalclitch always carried back my boat into her closet, and hung it on a nail to dry.

In this exercise I once met an accident which had like to have cost me my life. For, one of the pages having put my boat into the trough, the governess who attended Glumdalclitch very officiously lifted me up to place me in the boat, but I happened to slip through her fingers, and should have infallibly fallen down forty foot upon the floor if, by the luckiest chance in the world, I had not been stopped by a corking-pin that stuck in the good gentlewoman's stomacher; the head of the pin passed between my shirt and the waistband of my breeches, and thus I was held by the middle in the air till Glumdalclitch ran to my relief.

Another time, one of the servants, whose office it was to fill my trough every third day with fresh water, was so careless to let a huge frog (not perceiving it) slip out of his pail. The frog lay concealed till I was put into my boat, but then seeing a resting place, climbed up, and made it lean so much on one side, that I was forced to balance it with all my weight on the other, to prevent overturning. When the frog was got in, it hopped at once half the length of the boat, and then over my head, backwards and forwards, daubing my face and clothes with its odious slime. The largeness of its features made it appear the most deformed animal that can be conceived. However, I desired Glumdalclitch to let me deal with it alone. I banged it a good while with one of my sculls, and at last forced it to leap out of the boat.

But the greatest danger I ever underwent in that kingdom was from a monkey, who belonged to one of the clerks of the kitchen. Glumdalclitch had locked me up in her closet, while she went somewhere upon business or a visit. The weather being very warm, the closet window was left open, as well as the windows and the door of my bigger box, in which I usually lived, because of its largeness and conveniency. As I sat quietly meditating at my table, I heard something bounce in at the closet window, and skip about from one side to the other; whereat, although I were much alarmed, yet I ventured to look out, but not stirring from my seat; and then I saw this frolicsome animal, frisking and leaping up and down till at last he came to my box, which he seemed to view with great pleasure and curiosity, peeping in at the door and every window. I retreated to the farther corner of my room, or box, but the monkey, looking in at every side, put me into such a fright, that I wanted presence of mind to conceal my self under the bed, as I might easily have done. After

---

Stomacher. Decorative cloth worn over the bosom and stomach (Fox, 122).

some time spent in peeping, grinning, and chattering, he at last espied me, and reaching one of his paws in at the door, as a cat does when she plays with a mouse, although I often shifted place to avoid him, he at length seized the lappet of my coat (which being made of that country silk, was very thick and strong) and dragged me out. He took me up in his right forefoot, and held me as a nurse does a child she is going to suckle, just as I have seen the same sort of creature do with a kitten in Europe: and when I offered to struggle, he squeezed me so hard, that I thought it more prudent to submit. I have good reason to believe that he took me for a young one of his own species, by his often stroking my face very gently with his other paw. In these diversions he was interrupted by a noise at the closet door, as if some body were opening it; whereupon he suddenly leaped up to the window at which he had come in, and thence upon the leads and gutters, walking upon three legs, and holding me in the fourth, till he clambered up to a roof that was next to ours. I heard Glumdalclitch give a shriek at the moment he was carrying me out. The poor girl was almost distracted: that quarter of the palace was all in an uproar; the servants ran for ladders; the monkey was seen by hundreds in the court sitting upon the ridge of a building, holding me like a baby in one of his fore-paws, and feeding me with the other, by cramming into my mouth some victuals he had squeezed out of the bag on one side of his chaps, and patting me when I would not eat; whereat many of the rabble below could not forbear laughing; neither do I think they justly ought to be blamed, for without question the sight was ridiculous enough to every body but my self. Some of the people threw up stones, hoping to drive the monkey down; but this was strictly forbidden, or else very probably my brains had been dashed out.

The ladders were now applied, and mounted by several men, which the monkey observing, and finding himself almost encompassed, not being able to make speed enough with his three legs, let me drop on a ridge tile, and made his escape. Here I sat for some time five hundred yards from the ground, expecting every moment to be blown down by the wind, or to fall by my own giddiness, and come tumbling over and over from the ridge to the eaves. But an honest lad, one of my nurse's footmen, climbed up, and putting me into his breeches pocket, brought me down safe.

I was almost choked with the filthy stuff the monkey had crammed down my throat; but my dear little nurse picked it out of my mouth with a small needle, and then I fell a vomiting, which gave me great relief. Yet I was so weak and bruised in the sides with the squeezes given me by this odious animal, that I was forced to keep my bed a fortnight. The King, Queen and all the court sent every day to enquire after my health, and her Majesty made me several visits during my sickness. The monkey was killed, and an order made that no such animal should be kept about the palace.

When I attended the King after my recovery, to return him thanks for his favours, he was pleased to rally me a good deal upon this adventure. He asked me what my thoughts and speculations were while I lay in the monkey's paw, how I liked the victuals he gave me, his manner of feeding, and whether the fresh air on the roof had sharpened my stomach. He desired to know what I would have done upon such an occasion in my own country. I told his Majesty, that in Europe we had no monkeys, except such as were brought for curiosities from other places, and so small, that I could deal with a dozen of them together, if they presumed to attack me. And as for that monstrous animal with whom I was so lately engaged (it was indeed as large as an elephant), if my fears had suffered me to think so far as to make use of my hanger (looking fiercely and clapping my hand upon the hilt as I spoke) when he poked his paw into my chamber, perhaps I should have given him such a wound as would have made him glad to withdraw it with more haste than he put it in. This I delivered in a firm tone, like a person who was jealous lest his courage should be called in question. However, my speech produced nothing else besides a loud laughter, which all the respect due to his Majesty from those about him could not make them contain. This made me reflect how vain an attempt it is for a man to endeavour doing himself honour among those who are out of all degree of equality or comparison with him. And yet I have seen the moral of my own behaviour very frequent in England since my return, where a little contemptible varlet, without the least title to birth, person, wit, or common sense, shall presume to look with importance, and put himself upon a foot with the greatest persons of the kingdom.

I was every day furnishing the court with some ridiculous story; and Glumdalclitch, although she loved me to excess, yet was arch enough to inform the Queen whenever I committed any folly that she thought would be diverting to her Majesty. The girl, who had been out of order, was carried by her governess to take the air about an hour's distance, or thirty miles from town. They alighted out of the coach near a small footpath in a field, and Glumdalclitch setting down my travelling box, I went out of it to walk. There was a cow-dung in the path, and I must needs try my activity by attempting to leap over it. I took a run, but unfortunately jumped short, and found my self just in the middle up to my knees. I waded through with some difficulty, and one of the footmen wiped me as clean as he could with his handkerchief; for I was filthily bemired, and my nurse confined me to my box till we returned home; where the Queen was soon informed of what had passed, and the footmen spread it about the court, so that all the mirth, for some days, was at my expense.

CHAPTER VI

Several contrivances of the author to please the King and Queen. He shows his skill in music. The King enquires into the state of Europe, which the author relates to him. The King's observations thereon.

I used to attend the King's levee once or twice a week, and had often seen him under the barber's hand, which indeed was at first very terrible to behold. For the razor was almost twice as long as an ordinary scythe. His Majesty according to the custom of the country was only shaved twice a week. I once prevailed on the barber to give me some of the suds or lather, out of which I picked forty or fifty of the strongest stumps of hair. I then took a piece of fine wood, and cut it like the back of a comb, making several holes in it at equal distance with as small a needle as I could get from Glumdalclitch. I fixed in the stumps so artificially, scraping and sloping them with my knife towards the points, that I made a very tolerable comb; which was a seasonable supply, my own being so much broken in the teeth, that it was almost useless: neither did I know any artist in that country so nice and exact, as would undertake to make me another.

And this puts me in mind of an amusement wherein I spent many of my leisure hours. I desired the Queen's woman to save for me the combings of her Majesty's hair, whereof in time I got a good quantity, and consulting with my friend the cabinet-maker, who had received general orders to do little jobs for me, I directed him to make two chair-frames, no larger than those I had in my box, and then to bore little holes with a fine awl round those parts where I designed the backs and seats; through these holes I wove the strongest hairs I could pick out, just after the manner of cane-chairs in England. When they were finished, I made a present of them to her Majesty, who kept them in her cabinet, and used to show them for curiosities, as indeed they were the wonder of every one who beheld them. The Queen would have had me sit upon one of these chairs, but I absolutely refused to obey her, protesting I would rather die a thousand deaths than place a dishonourable part of my body on those precious hairs that once adorned her Majesty's head. Of these hairs (as I had always a mechanical genius) I likewise made a neat little purse about five foot long, with her Majesty's name deciphered in gold letters, which I gave to Glumdalclitch, by the Queen's consent. To say the truth, it was more for show than use, being not of strength to bear the weight of the larger coins, and therefore she kept nothing in it, but some little toys that girls are fond of.

The King, who delighted in music, had frequent concerts at court, to which I was sometimes carried, and set in my box on a table to hear them:

but the noise was so great, that I could hardly distinguish the tunes. I am confident that all the drums and trumpets of a royal army, beating and sounding together just at your ears, could not equal it. My practice was to have my box removed from the places where the performers sat, as far as I could, then to shut the doors and windows of it, and draw the window curtains; after which I found their music not disagreeable.

I had learned in my youth to play a little upon the spinet. Glumdalclitch kept one in her chamber, and a master attended twice a week to teach her: I call it a spinet, because it somewhat resembled that instrument, and was played upon in the same manner. A fancy came into my head that I would entertain the King and Queen with an English tune upon this instrument. But this appeared extremely difficult: for the spinet was near sixty foot long, each key being almost a foot wide, so that, with my arms extended, I could not reach to above five keys, and to press them down required a good smart stroke with my fist, which would be too great a labour, and to no purpose. The method I contrived was this. I prepared two round sticks about the bigness of common cudgels; they were thicker at one end than the other, and I covered the thicker ends with a piece of a mouse's skin, that by rapping on them I might neither damage the tops of the keys, nor interrupt the sound. Before the spinet a bench was placed about four foot below the keys, and I was put upon the bench. I ran sideling upon it that way and this, as fast as I could, banging the proper keys with my two sticks, and made a shift to play a jig to the great satisfaction of both their Majesties: but it was the most violent exercise I ever underwent, and yet I could not strike above sixteen keys, nor, consequently, play the bass and treble together, as other artists do; which was a great disadvantage to my performance.

The King, who, as I before observed, was a prince of excellent understanding, would frequently order that I should be brought in my box, and set upon the table in his closet. He would then command me to bring one of my chairs out of the box, and sit down within three yards distance upon the top of the cabinet, which brought me almost to a level with his face. In this manner I had several conversations with him. I one day took the freedom to tell his Majesty, that the contempt he discovered towards Europe, and the rest of the world, did not seem answerable to those excellent qualities of mind he was master of. That reason did not extend it self with the bulk of the body: on the contrary, we observed in our country that the tallest persons were usually least provided with it. That among other animals, bees and ants had the reputation of more industry, art and sagacity than many of the larger kinds. And that, as inconsiderable as he took me to be, I hoped I might live to do his Majesty some signal service. The King heard me with attention, and began to conceive a much better opinion of me than he had ever before. He desired I would give him as exact an account of the government of England as I possibly could; because, as fond as princes commonly are of their own customs (for so he conjectured of other monarchs by my former discourses), he should be glad to hear of any thing that might deserve imitation.

Imagine with thy self, courteous reader, how often I then wished for the tongue of Demosthenes or Cicero, that might have enabled me to celebrate the praise of my own dear native country in a style equal to its merits and felicity.

I began my discourse by informing his Majesty that our dominions consisted of two islands, which composed three mighty kingdoms under one sovereign, besides our plantations in America. I dwelt long upon the fertility of our soil, and the temperature of our climate. I then spoke at large upon the constitution of an English parliament, partly made up of an illustrious body called the House of Peers, persons of the noblest blood, and of the most ancient and ample patrimonies. I described that extraordinary care always taken of their education in arts and arms, to qualify them for being counsellors born to the king and kingdom, to have a share in the legislature, to be members of the highest court of judicature from whence there could be no appeal; and to be champions always ready for the defence of their prince and country by their valour, conduct and fidelity. That these were the ornament and bulwark of the kingdom, worthy followers of their most renowned ancestors, whose honour had been the reward of their virtue, from which their posterity were never once known to degenerate. To these were joined several holy persons, as part of that assembly, under the title of bishops, whose peculiar business it is to take care of religion, and of

---

Two islands. Britain and Ireland.

Three mighty kingdoms under one sovereign. England, Scotland, and Ireland. Swift reasserts the constitutional basis of his civic nationalism: the *legislative* independence of Ireland. The Irish Parliament had been rendered impotent by the Declaratory Act of 1720, ending any pretense that Ireland was not ruled directly from Westminster. Scotland experienced a different trajectory. The Act of Union in 1707, while excluding Ireland from "Great Britain," provided for a certain degree of Scottish representation in the British parliament. Gulliver's visit to Brobdingnag occurs in 1703, four years prior to the Act of Union. Swift's pamphlet *The Injured Lady*, published only after his death, laments Ireland's exclusion from the union. In "Verses said to be written on the Union," he compares the "ship of state" resulting from the union to "A Vessel with a double Keel."

Plantations in America. Along with Ireland, these American colonies constituted the totality of Britain's relatively modest First Empire. This Atlantic empire extended from what is now Canada (Nova Scotia and Newfoundland), across the mid-Atlantic seaboard, and south to the Caribbean. The Second Empire, emerging from the conquest of Bengal (complete by 1765), the loss of the American colonies (1783), and increased state regulation of the East India Company (1784), was self-consciously eastward and global. By 1829 the boast was made that the sun never set on the British Empire.

those who instruct the people therein. These were searched and sought out through the whole nation, by the prince and wisest counsellors, among such of the priesthood as were most deservedly distinguished by the sanctity of their lives, and the depth of their erudition; who were indeed the spiritual fathers of the clergy and the people.

That the other part of the parliament consisted of an assembly called the House of Commons, who were all principal gentlemen, freely picked and culled out by the people themselves, for their great abilities, and love of their country, to represent the wisdom of the whole nation. And these two bodies make up the most august assembly in Europe, to whom, in conjunction with the prince, the whole legislature is committed.

I then descended to the courts of justice, over which the judges, those venerable sages and interpreters of the law, presided, for determining the disputed rights and properties of men, as well as for the punishment of vice, and protection of innocence. I mentioned the prudent management of our treasury, the valour and achievements of our forces by sea and land. I computed the number of our people, by reckoning how many millions there might be of each religious sect, or political party among us. I did not omit even our sports and pastimes, or any other particular which I thought might redound to the honour of my country. And I finished all with a brief historical account of affairs and events in England for about an hundred years past.

This conversation was not ended under five audiences, each of several hours, and the King heard the whole with great attention, frequently taking notes of what I spoke, as well as memorandums of what questions he intended to ask me.

When I had put an end to these long discourses, his Majesty in a sixth audience, consulting his notes, proposed many doubts, queries, and objections, upon every article. He asked, what methods were used to cultivate the minds and bodies of our young nobility, and in what kind of business they commonly spent the first and teachable part of their lives. What course was taken to supply that assembly when any noble family became extinct. What qualifications were necessary in those who are to be created new lords: whether the humour of the prince, a sum of money to a court-lady, or a prime minister, or a design of strengthening a party opposite to the public interest, ever happened to be motives in those advancements. What share of knowledge these lords had in the laws of

---

Prime minister. This term often carried overtones of excessive power. *Prime minister* was not an official title until the following century.

their country, and how they came by it, so as to enable them to decide the properties of their fellow-subjects in the last resort. Whether they were always so free from avarice, partialities, or want, that a bribe, or some other sinister view, could have no place among them. Whether those holy lords I spoke of were constantly promoted to that rank upon account of their knowledge in religious matters, and the sanctity of their lives; had never been compliers with the times while they were common priests, or slavish prostitute chaplains to some nobleman, whose opinions they continued servilely to follow after they were admitted into that assembly.

He then desired to know what arts were practised in electing those whom I called commoners. Whether a stranger with a strong purse might not influence the vulgar voters to choose him before their own landlords, or the most considerable gentleman in the neighbourhood. How it came to pass, that people were so violently bent upon getting into this assembly, which I allowed to be a great trouble and expense, often to the ruin of their families, without any salary or pension: because this appeared such an exalted strain of virtue and public spirit, that his Majesty seemed to doubt it might possibly not be always sincere: and he desired to know whether such zealous gentlemen could have any views of refunding themselves for the charges and trouble they were at, by sacrificing the public good to the designs of a weak and vicious prince in conjunction with a corrupted ministry. He multiplied his questions, and sifted me thoroughly upon every part of this head, proposing numberless enquiries and objections, which I think it not prudent or convenient to repeat.

Upon what I said in relation to our courts of justice, his Majesty desired to be satisfied in several points: and this I was the better able to do, having been formerly almost ruined by a long suit in chancery, which was decreed for me with costs. He asked, what time was usually spent in determining between right and wrong, and what degree of expense. Whether advocates and orators had liberty to plead in causes manifestly known to be unjust, vexatious, or oppressive. Whether party in religion or politics were observed to be of any weight in the scale of justice. Whether those pleading orators were persons educated in the general knowledge of equity, or only in provincial, national, and other local customs. Whether they or their judges had any part in penning those laws which they assumed the liberty of interpreting and glossing upon at their pleasure. Whether they had ever at different times pleaded for and against the same cause, and cited precedents to prove contrary opinions. Whether they were a rich or a poor corporation. Whether they received any pecuniary reward for pleading or delivering their opinions. And particularly whether they were ever admitted as members in the lower senate.

He fell next upon the management of our treasury; and said, he thought my memory had failed me, because I computed our taxes at about five or six millions a year, and when I came to mention the issues, he found they sometimes amounted to more than double, for the notes he had taken were very particular in this point, because he hoped, as he told me, that the knowledge of our conduct might be useful to him, and he could not be deceived in his calculations. But, if what I told him were true, he was still at a loss how a kingdom could run out of its estate like a private person. He asked me, who were our creditors; and where we found money to pay them. He wondered to hear me talk of such chargeable and extensive wars; that certainly we must be a quarrelsome people, or live among very bad neighbours, and that our generals must needs be richer than our kings. He asked what business we had out of our own islands, unless upon the score of trade or treaty, or to defend the coasts with our fleet. Above all, he was amazed to hear me talk of a mercenary standing army in the midst of peace, and among a free people. He said if we were governed by our own consent in the persons of our representatives, he could not imagine of whom we were afraid, or against whom we were to fight, and would hear

---

double. In *Examiner* 13 (November 2, 1710) Swift excoriates Britain's deficit spending on behalf of the War of Spanish Succession. He depicts the national debt—as opposed to the traditional royal one—as the result of a war prolonged for the private profit of generals and colonels who had a financial stake in the relevant military enterprises. The newly nationalized debt was funded through government bonds and interest on it was to be paid for by taxes on land and excise duties. See Dickson, 39–57.

Generals . . . richer than our kings. Swift insinuates in *Examiner* 27 (February 8, 1710) that the duke of Marlborough is now the richest person in the commonwealth. In *The Conduct of the Allies* (1711), Swift scathingly characterizes the true motive of the war as "aggrandizing a particular family, and in short a War of the *General* . . . and not of the *Prince* or *People* . . ." (Davis, vol. 6, 41). Marlborough was dismissed in 1711 by the Tory ministry for whom Swift had been pamphleteering.

Out of our own islands. A moral critique of colonial expansion.

A mercenary standing army. Control over the army had been a central political issue since the Restoration in 1660. Professional armies were associated by Swift both with the repression of civil liberties at home and with the militarization of civilian society. In *Examiner* 20 (December 21, 1710)—a warning that the British military is usurping civil power—Swift associates the tyrannies of Caesar and Cromwell with military government. At this time, moreover, foreign mercenaries—often supplied from Germany—made up a substantial portion of the major European armies. The demands of an international market in war had, in effect, produced a vast traffic in military manpower. See also pp. 238, 373 below.

my opinion, whether a private man's house might not better be defended by himself, his children, and family, than by a half a dozen rascals picked up at a venture in the streets, for small wages, who might get an hundred times more by cutting their throats.

He laughed at my odd kind of arithmetic (as he was pleased to call it) in reckoning the numbers of our people by a computation drawn from the several sects among us in religion and politics. He said, he knew no reason, why those who entertain opinions prejudicial to the public should be obliged to change, or should not be obliged to conceal them. And as it was tyranny in any government to require the first, so it was weakness not to enforce the second: for a man may be allowed to keep poisons in his closets, but not to vend them about as cordials.

He observed, that among the diversions of our nobility and gentry I had mentioned gaming. He desired to know at what age this entertainment was usually taken up, and when it was laid down. How much of their time it employed; whether it ever went so high as to affect their fortunes. Whether mean vicious people by their dexterity in that art might not arrive at great riches, and sometimes keep our very nobles in dependence, as well as habituate them to vile companions, wholly take them from the improvement of their minds, and force them, by the losses they received, to learn and practice that infamous dexterity upon others.

He was perfectly astonished with the historical account I gave him of our affairs during the last century, protesting it was only an heap of conspiracies, rebellions, murders, massacres, revolutions, banishments, the very worst effects that avarice, faction, hypocrisy, perfidiousness, cruelty, rage, madness, hatred, envy, lust, malice, and ambition could produce.

His Majesty in another audience was at the pains to recapitulate the sum of all I had spoken, compared the questions he made with the answers I had given; then taking me into his hands, and stroking me gently, delivered himself in these words, which I shall never forget, nor the manner he spoke them in: My little friend Grildrig, you have made a most admirable panegyric upon your country. You have clearly proved that ignorance, idleness and vice are the proper ingredients for qualifying a legislator. That laws are best explained, interpreted, and applied by those whose interest and abilities lie in perverting, confounding, and eluding them. I observe among you some lines of an institution, which in its original might have been tolerable,

---

My odd kind of arithmetic. The emerging science of political economy, purporting to quantify national prosperity with statistics. *Political Arithmetic* was published in 1690, three years after the death of its author, Sir William Petty, a fellow of the Royal Society. See pp. 15–17, 397–99.

but these half erased, and the rest wholly blurred and blotted by corruptions. It doth not appear from all you have said, how any one perfection is required towards the procurement of any one station among you, much less that men are ennobled on account of their virtue, that priests are advanced for their piety or learning, soldiers for their conduct or valour, judges for their integrity, senators for the love of their country, or counsellors for their wisdom. As for yourself, continued the King, who have spent the greatest part of your life in travelling, I am well disposed to hope you may hitherto have escaped many vices of your country. But, by what I have gathered from your own relation, and the answers I have with much pains wringed and extorted from you, I cannot but conclude the bulk of your natives to be the most pernicious race of little odious vermin that nature ever suffered to crawl upon the surface of the earth.

CHAPTER VII

The author's love of his country. He makes a proposal of much advantage to the King, which is rejected. The King's great ignorance in politics. The learning of that country very imperfect and confined. Their laws, and military affairs, and parties in the state.

Nothing but an extreme love of truth could have hindered me from concealing this part of my story. It was in vain to discover my resentments, which were always turned into ridicule; and I was forced to rest with patience while my noble and most beloved country was so injuriously treated. I am heartily sorry as any of my readers can possibly be, that such an occasion was given: but this prince happened to be so curious and inquisitive upon every particular, that it could not consist either with gratitude or good manners to refuse giving him what satisfaction I was able. Yet thus much I may be allowed to say in my own vindication, that I artfully eluded many of his questions, and gave to every point a more favourable turn by many degrees than the strictness of truth would allow. For I have always borne that laudable partiality to my own country, which Dionysius Halicarnassensis with so much justice recommends to an historian. I would hide the frailties and deformities of my political mother, and place her virtues and beauties in the most advantageous light. This was my sincere endeavour in those many discourses I had with that mighty monarch, although it unfortunately failed of success.

But great allowances should be given to a king who lives wholly secluded from the rest of the world, and must therefore be altogether unacquainted with the manners and customs that most prevail in other nations: the want of which knowledge will ever produce many prejudices, and a certain narrowness of thinking, from which we and the politer countries of Europe are wholly exempted. And it would be hard indeed, if so remote a prince's notions of virtue and vice were to be offered as a standard for all mankind.

To confirm what I have now said, and further to show the miserable effects of a confined education, I shall here insert a passage which will hardly obtain belief. In hopes to ingratiate my self farther into his Majesty's favour, I told him of an invention discovered between three and four hundred years ago, to make a certain powder, into an heap of which the smallest spark of fire falling, would kindle the whole in a moment, although it were as big as a mountain, and make it all fly up in the air together, with a noise and agitation greater than thunder. That a proper quantity of this powder rammed into an hollow tube of brass or iron, according to its bigness, would drive a ball of iron or lead with such violence and speed as nothing was able to sustain its force. That the largest balls, thus discharged, would not only destroy whole ranks of an army at once, but batter the strongest walls to the ground, sink down ships, with a thousand men in each, to the bottom of the sea; and when linked together by a chain, would cut through masts and rigging, divide hundreds of bodies in the middle, and lay all waste before them. That we often put this powder into large hollow balls of iron, and discharged them by an engine into some city we were besieging, which would rip up the pavement, tear the houses to pieces, burst and throw splinters on every side, dashing out the brains of all who came near. That I knew the ingredients very well, which were cheap, and common; I understood the manner of compounding them, and could direct his workmen how to make those tubes

---

A certain powder. By Gulliver's time, the "gunpowder revolution" had been underway for about three centuries in Europe and the Ottoman Empire, making artillery and small arms the usual arbiter of eighteenth-century siege warfare. Leading thinkers of Swift's era, moreover—from Francis Bacon (in *New Atlantis*) to Defoe (in "An Essay upon Projects")—celebrate the advantages of gunpowder and related innovations in military technology. The Chinese had invented the powder in question as early as the ninth century. They did develop numerous military applications for it (including guns and multistage rockets), as well as peaceful ones. That they did so without promoting a gunpowder revolution at home, however, reflects their subordination of the military services to civilian control (Needham).

of a size proportionable to all other things in his Majesty's kingdom, and the largest need not be above two hundred foot long; twenty or thirty of which tubes, charged with the proper quantity of powder and balls, would batter down the walls of the strongest town in his dominions in a few hours, or destroy the whole metropolis, if ever it should pretend to dispute his absolute commands. This I humbly offered to his Majesty as a small tribute of acknowledgment in return of so many marks that I had received of his royal favour and protection.

The King was struck with horror at the description I had given of those terrible engines, and the proposal I had made. He was amazed how so impotent and groveling an insect as I (these were his expressions) could entertain such inhuman ideas, and in so familiar a manner as to appear wholly unmoved at all the scenes of blood and desolation, which I had painted as the common effects of those destructive machines, whereof he said, some evil genius, enemy to mankind, must have been the first contriver. As for himself, he protested, that although few things delighted him so much as new discoveries in art or in nature, yet he would rather lose half his kingdom than be privy to such a secret, which he commanded me, as I valued my life, never to mention any more.

A strange effect of narrow principles and short views! that a prince possessed of every quality which procures veneration, love, and esteem; of strong parts, great wisdom and profound learning, endued with admirable talents for government, and almost adored by his subjects, should from a nice unnecessary scruple, whereof in Europe we can have no conception, let slip an opportunity put into his hands, that would have made him absolute master of the lives, the liberties, and the fortunes of his people. Neither do I say this with the least intention to detract from the many virtues of that excellent king, whose character I am sensible will on this account be very much lessened in the opinion of an English reader: but I take this defect among them to have risen from their ignorance, by not having hitherto reduced politics into a science, as the more acute wits of Europe have done. For I remember very well, in a discourse one day with the King, when I happened to say there were several thousand books among us written upon the art of government, it gave him (directly contrary to my intention) a very mean opinion of our understandings. He professed both to abominate and despise all mystery, refinement, and intrigue, either in a prince or a minister. He could not tell what I meant by secrets of state, where an enemy or some rival nation were not in the case. He confined the knowledge of governing within very narrow bounds; to common sense and reason, to justice and lenity, to the speedy determination of civil and criminal causes; with some other obvious topics which are not worth considering. And he gave it for his opinion, that whoever could make two ears of corn, or two blades of grass to grow upon a spot of ground where only one grew before, would deserve better of mankind, and do more essential service to his country, than the whole race of politicians put together.

The learning of this people is very defective, consisting only in morality, history, poetry, and mathematics, wherein they must be allowed to excel. But the last of these is wholly applied to what may be useful in life, to the improvement of agriculture and all mechanical arts; so that among us it would be little esteemed. And as to ideas, entities, abstractions and transcendentals, I could never drive the least conception into their heads.

No law of that country must exceed in words the number of letters in their alphabet, which consists only of two and twenty. But indeed, few of them extend even to that length. They are expressed in the most plain and simple terms, wherein those people are not mercurial enough to discover above one interpretation. And to write a comment upon any law is a capital crime. As to the decision of civil causes, or proceedings against criminals, their precedents are so few, that they have little reason to boast of any extraordinary skill in either.

They have had the art of printing, as well as the Chinese, time out of mind. But their libraries are not very large; for that of the King's, which is reckoned the largest, doth not amount to above a thousand volumes, placed in a gallery of twelve hundred foot long, from whence I had liberty to borrow what books I pleased. The Queen's joiner had contrived in one of Glumdalclitch's rooms a kind of wooden machine five and twenty foot high, formed like a standing ladder; the steps were each fifty foot long. It was indeed a moveable pair of stairs, the lowest end placed at ten foot distance from the wall of the chamber. The book I had a mind to read was put up leaning against the wall. I first mounted to the upper step of the ladder, and turning my face towards the book, began at the top of the page, and so walking to the right and left about eight or ten paces, according to the length of the lines, till I had gotten a little below the level of my eyes, and then descending gradually till I came to the bottom: after which I mounted again, and began the other page in the same manner, and so turned over the leaf, which I could easily do with both my hands, for it was as thick and stiff as a pasteboard, and in the largest folios not above eighteen or twenty foot long.

Their style is clear, masculine, and smooth, but not florid, for they avoid nothing more than multiplying unnecessary words, or using various expressions. I have perused many of their books, especially those in history and morality. Among the latter I was much diverted with a little old treatise, which always lay in Glumdalclitch's bedchamber, and belonged to her governess, a grave elderly gentlewoman, who dealt in writings of morality and devotion. The book treats of the weakness of human kind, and is in little esteem except among women and the vulgar. However, I was curious to see what an author of that country could say upon such a subject. This writer went through all the usual topics of European moralists, showing how diminutive, contemptible, and helpless an animal was man in his own nature; how unable to defend himself from the inclemencies of the air, or the fury of wild beasts. How much he was excelled by one creature in strength, by another in speed, by a third in foresight, by a fourth in industry. He added, that nature was degenerated in these latter declining ages of the world, and could now produce only small abortive births in comparison of those in ancient times. He said it was very reasonable to think, not only that the species of men were originally much larger, but also that there must have been giants in former ages, which, as it is asserted by history and tradition, so it hath been confirmed by huge bones and skulls casually dug up in several parts of the kingdom, far exceeding the common dwindled race of man in our days. He argued, that the very laws of nature absolutely required we should have been made, in the beginning, of a size more large and robust, not so liable to destruction from every little accident of a tile falling from an house, or a stone cast from the hand of a boy, or of being drowned in a little brook. From this way of reasoning the author drew several moral applications useful in the conduct of life, but needless here to repeat. For my own part, I could not avoid reflecting how universally this talent was spread of drawing lectures in morality, or indeed rather matter of discontent and repining, from the quarrels we raise with nature. And, I believe, upon a strict enquiry those quarrels might be shown as ill-grounded among us as they are among that people.

As to their military affairs, they boast that the King's army consists of an hundred and seventy-six thousand foot, and thirty-two thousand horse, if that may be called an army which is made up of tradesmen in the several

---

Little old treatise. The sentiments of this imaginary text as regards the "decay-of-nature" theme—a congenial defense of the Ancients over the Moderns—are not without precedent in actual voyage literature. In his *Voyage to Surratt* (1699), John Ovington reports that the Hindus on the island of Elephanta, a small Portuguese possession near Bombay, believed that the large statues that they venerated represented "the first Race of Mortals which, according to the Account of their Chronicles, were all Gyants, but dwindled by degrees into lesser proportions, and at length, thro' the degeneracy of Manners, which caused an Universal Decay of Humane Nature, they shrank into these small proportions in which they appear now in the World" (161–62). Swift might have encountered Ovington's book in the library of Archbishop Narcissus Marsh, adjacent to St. Patrick's Cathedral.

cities, and farmers in the country, whose commanders are only the nobility and gentry without pay or reward. They are indeed perfect enough in their exercises, and under very good discipline, wherein I saw no great merit; for how should it be otherwise, where every farmer is under the command of his own landlord, and every citizen under that of the principal men in his own city, chosen after the manner of Venice by ballot?

I have often seen the militia of Lorbrulgrud drawn out to exercise in a great field near the city, of twenty miles square. They were in all not above twenty-five thousand foot, and six thousand horse; but it was impossible for me to compute their number, considering the space of ground they took up. A cavalier mounted on a large steed might be about ninety foot high. I have seen this whole body of horse upon the word of command draw their swords at once, and brandish them in the air. Imagination can figure nothing so grand, so surprising and so astonishing. It looked as if ten thousand flashes of lightning were darting at the same time from every quarter of the sky.

I was curious to know how this prince, to whose dominions there is no access from any other country, came to think of armies, or to teach his people the practice of military discipline. But I was soon informed, both by conversation, and reading their histories. For in the course of many ages they have been troubled with the same disease to which the whole race of mankind is subject; the nobility often contending for power, the people for liberty, and the King for absolute dominion. All which, however happily tempered by the laws of that kingdom, have been sometimes violated by each of the three parties, and have more than once occasioned civil wars, the last whereof was happily put an end to by this prince's grandfather in a general composition; and the militia then settled with common consent hath been ever since kept in the strictest duty.

CHAPTER VIII

The King and Queen make a progress to the frontiers. The author attends them. The manner in which he leaves the country very particularly related. He returns to England.

I had always a strong impulse that I should sometime recover my liberty, although it was impossible to conjecture by what means, or to form any

---

Without pay or reward. The Brobdingnagians have a citizen-based militia rather than a standing professional army.

project with the least hope of succeeding. The ship in which I sailed was the first ever known to be driven within sight of that coast, and the King had given strict orders, that if at any time another appeared, it should be taken ashore, and with all its crew and passengers brought in a tumbril to Lorbrulgrud. He was strongly bent to get me a woman of my own size, by whom I might propagate the breed: but I think I should rather have died than undergone the disgrace of leaving a posterity to be kept in cages like tame canary birds, and perhaps in time sold about the kingdom to persons of quality for curiosities. I was indeed treated with much kindness; I was the favourite of a great king and queen, and the delight of the whole court, but it was upon such a foot as ill became the dignity of human kind. I could never forget those domestic pledges I had left behind me. I wanted to be among people with whom I could converse upon even terms, and walk about the streets and fields without fear of being trod to death like a frog or young puppy. But my deliverance came sooner than I expected, and in a manner not very common: the whole story and circumstances of which I shall faithfully relate.

I had now been two years in this country; and about the beginning of the third, Glumdalclitch and I attended the King and Queen in a progress to the south coast of the kingdom. I was carried as usual in my travelling-box, which, as I have already described, was a very convenient closet of twelve foot wide. I had ordered a hammock to be fixed by silken ropes from the four corners at the top, to break the jolts, when a servant carried me before him on horseback, as I sometimes desired, and would often sleep in my hammock while we were upon the road. On the roof of my closet, just over the middle of the hammock, I ordered the joiner to cut out a hole of a foot square to give me air in hot weather as I slept, which hole I shut at pleasure with a board that drew backwards and forwards through a groove.

When we came to our journey's end, the King thought proper to pass a few days at a palace he hath near Flanflasnic, a city within eighteen English miles of the seaside. Glumdalclitch and I were much fatigued; I had gotten a small cold, but the poor girl was so ill as to be confined to her chamber. I longed to see the ocean, which must be the only scene of my escape, if ever it should happen. I pretended to be worse than I really was, and desired leave to take the fresh air of the sea, with a page whom I was very fond of, and who had sometimes been trusted with me. I shall never forget with what unwillingness Glumdalclitch consented, nor the strict charge she gave the page to be careful of me, bursting at the same time into a flood of tears, as if she had some foreboding of what was to happen. The boy took me out in my box about half an hour's walk from the palace towards the rocks on the seashore. I ordered him to set me down, and lifting up one of my sashes, cast many a wistful melancholy look towards the sea. I found my self not very well, and told the page that I had a mind to take a nap in my hammock, which I hoped would do me good. I got in, and the boy shut the window close down to keep out the cold. I soon fell asleep, and all I can conjecture is, that while I slept, the page, thinking no danger could happen, went among the rocks to look for birds' eggs, having before observed him from my window searching about, and picking up one or two in the clefts. Be that as it will, I found my self suddenly awaked with a violent pull upon the ring which was fastened at the top of my box for the conveniency of carriage. I felt the box raised very high in the air, and then borne forward with prodigious speed. The first jolt had like to have shaken me out of my hammock, but afterwards the motion was easy enough. I called out several times as loud as I could raise my voice, but all to no purpose. I looked towards my windows, and could see nothing but the clouds and sky. I heard a noise just over my head like the clapping of wings, and then began to perceive the woful condition I was in; that some eagle had got the ring of my box in his beak, with an intent to let it fall on a rock like a tortoise in a shell, and then pick out my body and devour it. For the sagacity and smell of this bird enable him to discover his quarry at a great distance, although better concealed than I could be within a two-inch board.

In a little time I observed the noise and flutter of wings to encrease very fast, and my box was tossed up and down like a signpost in a windy day. I heard several bangs or buffets, as I thought, given to the eagle (for such I am certain it must have been that held the ring of my box in his beak) and then all on a sudden felt my self falling perpendicularly down for above a minute, but with such incredible swiftness that I almost lost my breath. My fall was stopped by a terrible squash, that sounded louder to my ears than the cataract of Niagara; after which I was quite in the dark for another minute, and then my box began to rise so high that I could see light from the tops of my windows. I now perceived that I was fallen into the sea. My box, by the weight of my body, the goods that were in, and the broad plates of iron fixed for strength at the four corners of the top and bottom, floated about five foot deep in water. I did then, and do now suppose that the eagle which flew away with my box was pursued by two or three others, and forced to let me drop while he was defending himself against the rest, who hoped to share in the prey. The plates of iron fastened at the bottom of the box (for those were the strongest) preserved the balance while it fell, and hindered it from being broken on the surface of the water. Every joint of it was well grooved, and the door did not move on hinges, but up and down like a sash, which kept my closet so tight that very little water came in. I got with much difficulty out of my hammock, having first ventured to draw back the slip-board on the roof already mentioned, contrived on purpose to let in air, for want of which I found my self almost stifled.

How often did I then wish my self with my dear Glumdalclitch, from whom one single hour had so far divided me! And I may say with truth, that in the midst of my own misfortune I could not forbear lamenting my poor nurse, the grief she would suffer for my loss, the displeasure of the Queen, and the ruin of her fortune. Perhaps many travellers have not been under greater difficulties and distress than I was at this juncture, expecting every moment to see my box dashed in pieces, or at least overset by the first violent blast, or a rising wave. A breach in one single pane of glass would have been immediate death: nor could any thing have preserved the windows but the strong lattice wires placed on the outside against accidents in travelling. I saw the water ooze in at several crannies, although the leaks were not considerable, and I endeavoured to stop them as well as I could. I was not able to lift up the roof of my closet, which otherwise I certainly should have done, and sat on the top of it, where I might at least preserve my self from being shut up, as I may call it, in the hold. Or, if I escaped these dangers for a day or two, what could I expect but a miserable death of cold and hunger! I was four hours under these circumstances, expecting and indeed wishing every moment to be my last.

I have already told the reader, that there were two strong staples fixed upon the side of my box which had no window, and into which the servant who used to carry me on horseback would put a leathern belt, and buckle it about his waist. Being in this disconsolate state, I heard or at least thought I heard some kind of grating noise on that side of my box where the staples were fixed, and soon after I began to fancy that the box was pulled or towed along in the sea; for I now and then felt a sort of tugging which made the waves rise near the tops of my windows, leaving me almost in the dark. This gave me some faint hopes of relief, although I was not able to imagine how it could be brought about. I ventured to unscrew one of my chairs, which were always fastened to the floor; and having made a hard shift to screw it down again directly under the slipping-board that I had lately opened, I mounted on the chair, and putting my mouth as near as I could to the hole, I called for help in a loud voice, and in all the languages I understood. I then fastened my handkerchief to a stick I usually carried, and thrusting it up the hole, waved it several times in the air, that if any boat or ship were near, the seamen might conjecture some unhappy mortal to be shut up in the box.

I found no effect from all I could do, but plainly perceived my closet to be moved along; and in the space of an hour, or better, that side of the box where the staples were, and had no window, struck against something that was hard. I apprehended it to be a rock, and found my self tossed more than ever. I plainly heard a noise upon the cover of my closet, like that of a cable, and the grating of it as it passed through the ring. I then found my self hoisted up by degrees at least three foot higher than I was before. Whereupon I again thrust up my stick and handkerchief, calling for help till I was almost hoarse. In return to which, I heard a great shout repeated three times, giving me such transports of joy as are not to be conceived but by those who feel them. I now heard a trampling over my head, and somebody calling through the hole with a loud voice in the English tongue, If there be any body below let them speak. I answered, I was an Englishman, drawn by ill fortune into the greatest calamity that ever any creature underwent, and begged, by all that was moving, to be delivered out of the dungeon I was in. The voice replied, I was safe, for my box was fastened to their ship; and the carpenter should immediately come, and saw an hole in the cover, large enough to pull me out. I answered, that was needless, and would take up too much time, for there was no more to be done, but let one of the crew put his finger into the ring, and take the box out of the sea into the ship, and so into the captain's cabin. Some of them upon hearing me talk so wildly thought I was mad; others laughed; for indeed it never came into my head that I was now got among people of my own stature and strength. The carpenter came, and in a few minutes sawed a passage about four foot square, then let down a small ladder, upon which I mounted, and from thence was taken into the ship in a very weak condition.

The sailors were all in amazement, and asked me a thousand questions, which I had no inclination to answer. I was equally confounded at the sight of so many pigmies, for such I took them to be, after having so long accustomed my eyes to the monstrous objects I had left. But the captain, Mr. Thomas Wilcocks, an honest worthy Shropshire man, observing I was ready to faint, took me into his cabin, gave me a cordial to comfort me, and made me turn in upon his own bed, advising me to take a little rest, of which I had great need. Before I went to sleep I gave him to understand that I had some valuable furniture in my box, too good to be lost; a fine hammock, an handsome fieldbed, two chairs, a table and a cabinet: that my closet was hung on all sides, or rather quilted, with silk and cotton: that if he would let one of the crew bring my closet into his cabin, I would open it there before him, and show him my goods. The captain, hearing me utter these absurdities, concluded I was raving: however (I suppose to pacify me), he promised to give order as I desired, and going upon deck sent some of his men down into my closet, from whence (as I afterwards found) they drew up all my goods, and stripped off the quilting; but the chairs, cabinet and bedstead, being screwed to the floor, were much damaged by the ignorance of the seamen, who tore them up by force. Then they knocked off some of the boards for the use of the ship, and when they had got all they had a mind for, let the hulk drop into the sea, which, by reason of many breaches made in the bottom and sides, sunk to rights. And indeed I was glad not to have been a spectator of the havoc they made; because I am confident it would have sensibly touched me, by bringing former passages into my mind, which I had rather forget.

I slept some hours, but perpetually disturbed with dreams of the place I had left, and the dangers I had escaped. However, upon waking I found my self much recovered. It was now about eight o'clock at night, and the captain ordered supper immediately, thinking I had already fasted too long. He entertained me with great kindness, observing me not to look wildly, or talk inconsistently; and when we were left alone, desired I would give him a relation of my travels, and by what accident I came to be set adrift in that monstrous wooden chest. He said, that about twelve o'clock at noon, as he was looking through his glass, he spied it at a distance, and thought it was a sail, which he had a mind to make, being not much out of his course, in hopes of buying some biscuit, his own beginning to fall short. That upon coming nearer, and finding his error, he sent out his longboat to discover what I was; that his men came back in a fright, swearing they had seen a swimming house. That he laughed at their folly, and went himself in the boat, ordering his men to take a strong cable along with them. That the weather being calm, he rowed round me several times, observed my windows, and the wire lattices that defended them. That he discovered two staples upon one side, which was all of boards, without any passage for light. He then commanded his men to row up to that side, and fastening a cable to one of the staples, ordered his men to tow my chest (as he called it) towards the ship. When it was there, he gave directions to fasten another cable to the ring fixed in the cover, and to raise up my chest with pulleys, which all the sailors were not able to do above two or three foot. He said, they saw my stick and handkerchief thrust out of the hole, and concluded that some unhappy man must be shut up in the cavity. I asked whether he or the crew had seen any prodigious birds in the air about the time he first discovered me. To which he answered, that discoursing this matter with the sailors while I was asleep, one of them said he had observed three eagles flying towards the north, but remarked nothing of their being larger than the usual size, which I suppose must be imputed to the great height they were at: and he could not guess the reason of my question. I then asked the captain how far he reckoned we might be from land; he said, by the best computation he could make, we were at least an hundred leagues. I assured him, that he must be mistaken by almost half, for I had not left the country from whence I came above two hours before I dropped into the sea. Whereupon he began again to think that my brain was disturbed, of which he gave me a hint, and advised me to go to bed in a cabin he had provided. I assured him I was well refreshed with his good entertainment and company, and as much in my senses as ever I was in my life. He then grew serious, and desired to ask me freely whether I were not troubled in mind by the consciousness of some enormous crime, for which I was punished at the command of some prince, by exposing me in that chest, as great criminals in other countries have been forced to sea in a leaky vessel without provisions: for although he should be sorry to have taken so ill a man into his ship, yet he would engage his word to set me safe on shore in the first port where we arrived. He added, that his suspicions were much increased by some very absurd speeches I had delivered at first to the sailors, and afterwards to himself, in relation to my closet or chest, as well as by my odd looks and behaviour while I was at supper.

I begged his patience to hear me tell my story, which I faithfully did from the last time I left England to the moment he first discovered me. And, as truth always forceth its way into rational minds, so this honest worthy gentleman, who had some tincture of learning, and very good sense, was immediately convinced of my candor and veracity. But further to confirm all I had said, I entreated him to give order that my cabinet should be brought, of which I kept the key in my pocket (for he had already informed me how the seamen disposed of my closet); I opened it in his presence, and showed him the small collection of rarities I made in the country from whence I had been so strangely delivered. There was the comb I had contrived out of the stumps of the King's beard, and another of the same materials, but fixed into a paring of her Majesty's thumb-nail, which served for the back. There was a collection of needles and pins from a foot to half a yard long. Four wasp-stings, like joiners' tacks: some combings of the Queen's hair: a gold ring which one day she made me a present of in a most obliging manner, taking it from her little finger, and throwing it over my head like a collar. I desired the captain would please to accept this ring in return of his civilities, which he absolutely refused. I showed him a corn that I had cut off with my own hand from a maid of honour's toe; it was about the bigness of a Kentish pippin, and grown so hard, that when I returned to England, I got it hollowed into a cup and set in silver. Lastly, I desired him to see the breeches I had then on, which were made of a mouse's skin.

I could force nothing on him but a footman's tooth, which I observed him to examine with great curiosity, and found he had a fancy for it. He received it with abundance of thanks, more than such a trifle could deserve. It was drawn by an unskilful surgeon in a mistake from one of Glumdalclitch's men, who was afflicted with the toothache, but it was as sound as any in his head. I got it cleaned, and put it into my cabinet. It was about a foot long, and four inches in diameter.

The captain was very well satisfied with this plain relation I had given him; and said, he hoped, when we returned to England I would oblige the world by putting it in paper, and making it public. My answer was, that I thought we were already overstocked with books of travels: that nothing could now pass which was not extraordinary, wherein I doubted some authors less consulted truth than their own vanity or interest, or the diversion of ignorant readers. That my story could contain little besides common events, without those ornamental descriptions of strange plants, trees, birds, and other animals, or of the barbarous customs and idolatry of savage people, with which most writers abound. However, I thanked him for his good opinion, and promised to take the matter into my thoughts.

He said he wondered at one thing very much, which was to hear me speak so loud, asking me whether the King or Queen of that country were thick of hearing. I told him it was what I had been used to for above two years past, and that I admired as much at the voices of him and his men, who seemed to me only to whisper, and yet I could hear them well enough. But when I spoke in that country, it was like a man talking in the street to another looking out from the top of a steeple, unless when I was placed on a table, or held in any person's hand. I told him I had likewise observed another thing, that when I first got into the ship, and the sailors stood all about me, I thought they were the most little contemptible creatures I had ever beheld. For, indeed, while I was in that prince's country, I could never endure to look in a glass after my eyes had been accustomed to such prodigious objects, because the comparison gave me so despicable a conceit of my self. The captain said, that while we were at supper, he observed me to look at every thing with a sort of wonder, and that I often seemed hardly able to contain my laughter, which he knew not well how to take, but imputed it to some disorder in my brain. I answered, it was very true, and I wondered how I could forbear, when I saw his dishes of the size of a silver threepence, a leg of pork hardly a mouthful, a cup not so big as a nutshell: and so I went on, describing the rest of his household-stuff and provisions after the same manner. For although the Queen had ordered a little equipage of all things necessary for me while I was in her service, yet my ideas were wholly taken up with what I saw on every side of me, and I winked at my own littleness as people do at their own faults. The captain understood my raillery very well, and merrily replied with the old English proverb, that he doubted my eyes were bigger than my belly, for he did not observe my stomach so good, although I had fasted all day; and continu-

---

Barbarous customs and idolatry of savage people. The point here is not merely that travel writers lie—a truism—but that they slant their depictions of foreign peoples so as to justify aggression against them. See p. 42 for Gulliver's assertion that Europeans are especially prone to compulsive mendacity.

ing in his mirth, protested he would have gladly given an hundred pounds to have seen my closet in the eagle's bill, and afterwards in its fall from so great an height into the sea; which would certainly have been a most astonishing object, worthy to have the description of it transmitted to future ages: and the comparison of Phaeton was so obvious, that he could not forbear applying it, although I did not much admire the conceit.

The captain, having been at Tonquin, was in his return to England driven northeastward to the latitude of 44 degrees, and of longitude 143. But meeting a trade wind two days after I came on board him, we sailed southward a long time, and coasting New Holland kept our course west-southwest, and then south-southwest till we doubled the Cape of Good Hope. Our voyage was very prosperous, but I shall not trouble the reader with a journal of it. The captain called in at one or two ports and sent in his longboat for provisions and fresh water, but I never went out of the ship till we came into the Downs, which was on the 3d day of June, 1706, about nine months after my escape. I offered to leave my goods in security for payment of my freight; but the captain protested he would not receive one farthing. We took kind leave of each other, and I made him promise he would come to see me at my house in Redriff. I hired a horse and guide for five shillings, which I borrowed of the captain.

As I was on the road, observing the littleness of the houses, the trees, the cattle and the people, I began to think my self in Lilliput. I was afraid of trampling on every traveller I met, and often called aloud to have them stand out of the way, so that I had like to have gotten one or two broken heads for my impertinence.

When I came to my own house, for which I was forced to enquire, one of the servants opening the door, I bent down to go in (like a goose under a gate) for fear of striking my head. My wife ran out to embrace me, but I stooped lower than her knees, thinking she could otherwise never be able to reach my mouth. My daughter kneeled to ask me blessing, but I could not see her till she arose, having been so long used to stand with my head and eyes erect to above sixty foot; and then I went to take her up with one hand, by the waist. I looked down upon the servants and one or two friends who were in the house, as if they had been pigmies, and I a giant. I told my wife she had been too thrifty, for I found she had starved herself and her daughter to nothing. In short, I behaved my self so unaccountably, that they were all of the captain's opinion when he first saw me, and concluded

---

New Holland. Now Australia. Dampier published *A Voyage to New Holland* in 1703 and *A Continuation of a Voyage to New Holland* in 1709: accounts of a disastrous voyage under his command.

I had lost my wits. This I mention as an instance of the great power of habit and prejudice.

In a little time I and my family and friends came to a right understanding: but my wife protested I should never go to sea any more; although my evil destiny so ordered that she had not power to hinder me, as the reader may know hereafter. In the mean time I here conclude the second part of my unfortunate voyages.

THE END OF THE SECOND PART.

Parts Unknown

C Patience
LAND OF
St James Bay
Robbin I
IESSO
Salmon B
Canal
Companys
Land
Stats I
Straits of the Vries
Laputa
BALNIBARBI
Lagado
Dicovered A.D 1701
Sea of Corea
Sande I
Tou Pt
Red Pt
Bosho Pt
Barnevelts
JAPON
Tonsa I
Bungo I
South I
I Tanaxima
Stalo
Glangurn
Maldoneda
LUGGNAGG
Traldragdub
Clumegnig
I Durti
Glubdubdrib
Tinal

Travels

Part III

A Voyage to Laputa, Balnibarbi, Glubbdubdrib, Luggnagg, and Japan

CHAPTER I

The author sets out on his third voyage. Is taken by pirates. The malice of a Dutchman. His arrival at an island. He is received into Laputa.

I had not been at home above ten days, when Captain William Robinson, a Cornish man, commander of the *Hope-well,* a stout ship of three hundred tons, came to my house. I had formerly been surgeon of another ship where he was master, and a fourth part owner, in a voyage to the Levant; he had always treated me more like a brother than an inferior officer, and hearing of my arrival made me a visit, as I apprehended, only out of friendship, for nothing passed more than what is usual after long absence. But repeating his visits often, expressing his joy to find me in good health, asking whether I were now settled for life, adding that he intended a voyage to the East Indies, in two months, at last plainly invited me, although with some apologies, to be surgeon of the ship; that I should have another surgeon under me besides our two mates; that my salary should be double to the usual pay; and that having experienced my knowledge in sea-affairs to be at least equal to his, he would enter into any engagement to follow my advice, as much as if I had share in the command.

Surgeon of the ship. Like their professional brethren, the barbers, surgeons were trained to wield sharp tools. More than one sailor-surgeon subsequently turned author. Lionel Wafer (1660–1705), whose buccaneering career intersected several times with Dampier's, provides a prominent example. In 1699 Wafer published *A New Voyage and Description of the Isthmus of America,* describing a stay of some four months among the "Darien Indians" or Cuna. Swift owned this book. See Sherbo, 114–17.

He said so many other obliging things, and I knew him to be so honest a man, that I could not reject his proposal; the thirst I had of seeing the world, notwithstanding my past misfortunes, continuing as violent as ever. The only difficulty that remained was to persuade my wife, whose consent however I at last obtained, by the prospect of advantage she proposed to her children.

We set out the 5th day of August, 1706, and arrived at Fort St. George the 11th of April, 1707. We stayed there three weeks to refresh our crew, many of whom were sick. From thence we went to Tonquin, where the captain resolved to continue some time, because many of the goods he intended to buy were not ready, nor could he expect to be dispatched in several months. Therefore in hopes to defray some of the charges he must be at, he bought a sloop, loaded it with several sorts of goods, wherewith the Tonquinese usually trade to the neighbouring islands, and putting fourteen men on board, whereof three were of the country, he appointed me master of the sloop, and gave me power to traffic while he transacted his affairs at Tonquin.

We had not sailed above three days, when, a great storm arising, we were driven five days to the north-northeast, and then to the east, after which we had fair weather, but still with a pretty strong gale from the west. Upon the tenth day we were chased by two pirates, who soon overtook us; for my sloop was so deep loaden, that she sailed very slow, neither were we in a condition to defend our selves.

We were boarded about the same time by both the pirates, who entered furiously at the head of their men, but finding us all prostrate upon our faces (for so I gave order), they pinioned us with strong ropes, and setting a guard upon us, went to search the sloop.

I observed among them a Dutchman, who seemed to be of some authority, although he was not commander of either ship. He knew us by our countenances to be Englishmen, and jabbering to us in his own language, swore we should be tied back to back, and thrown into the sea. I

Fort St. George. Now Madras or Chennai; the headquarters in southern India of the East India Company since 1639–40. Dampier was there in 1690 on a trading voyage.

Dutchman. The Dutch pirate's role on the Japanese ship reflects the particular role of the Dutch as intermediaries between Japan and the rest of the world. Swift seldom misses a chance to lash the Dutch as a land of mercenary Calvinists. The seventeenth-century Dutch—trading imperialists who displaced the Portuguese empire in Indonesia—had pioneered in making *commercial strength* the basis for a new strategy of imperial expansion (Israel, 934–46).

spoke Dutch tolerably well; I told him who we were, and begged him in consideration of our being Christians and Protestants, of neighbouring countries, in strict alliance, that he would move the captains to take some pity on us. This inflamed his rage, he repeated his threatenings, and turning to his companions, spoke with great vehemence, in the Japanese language, as I suppose, often using the word *Christianos.*

The largest of the two pirate ships was commanded by a Japanese captain, who spoke a little Dutch, but very imperfectly. He came up to me, and after several questions, which I answered in great humility, he said we should not die. I made the captain a very low bow, and then turning to the Dutchman, said, I was sorry to find more mercy in a heathen, than in a brother Christian. But I had soon reason to repent those foolish words; for that malicious reprobate, having often endeavoured in vain to persuade both the captains that I might be thrown into the sea (which they would not yield to after the promise made me, that I should not die), however prevailed so far as to have a punishment inflicted on me, worse in all human appearance than death it self. My men were sent by an equal division into both the pirate ships, and my sloop new manned. As to my self, it was determined that I should be set adrift in a small canoe, with paddles and a sail, and four days' provisions, which last the Japanese captain was so kind to double out of his own stores, and would permit no man to search me. I got down into the canoe, while the Dutchman, standing upon the deck, loaded me with all the curses and injurious terms his language could afford.

About an hour before we saw the pirates, I had taken an observation, and found we were in the latitude of 46 N. and of longitude 183. When I was at some distance from the pirates, I discovered by my pocket-glass several islands to the southeast. I set up my sail, the wind being fair, with a design to reach the nearest of those islands, which I made a shift to do in about three hours. It was all rocky; however I got many birds' eggs, and striking fire I kindled some heath and dry seaweed, by which I roasted my eggs. I eat no other supper, being resolved to spare my provisions as much as I could.

Countries, in strict alliance. The Grand Alliance (in the war with France). Swift had argued against this alliance in *The Conduct of the Allies* (1711). In the poem "Peace and Dunkirk," he writes, "We spent our money and our blood, / To make the Dutchman proud and great."

Latitude of 46 N. and of longitude 183. As Asimov points out, the method of counting longitude was not yet fixed in Swift's time. Gulliver, counting eastward from Greenwich, has gone past the 180-degree line.

I passed the night under the shelter of a rock, strowing some heath under me, and slept pretty well.

The next day I sailed to another island, and thence to a third and fourth, sometimes using my sail, and sometimes my paddles. But not to trouble the reader with a particular account of my distresses, let it suffice that on the 5th day I arrived at the last island in my sight, which lay south-southeast to the former.

This island was at a greater distance than I expected, and I did not reach it in less than five hours. I encompassed it almost round before I could find a convenient place to land in, which was a small creek, about three times the wideness of my canoe. I found the island to be all rocky, only a little intermingled with tufts of grass, and sweet-smelling herbs. I took out my small provisions, and after having refreshed myself, I secured the remainder in a cave, whereof there were great numbers. I gathered plenty of eggs upon the rocks, and got a quantity of dry seaweed, and parched grass, which I designed to kindle the next day, and roast my eggs as well as I could. (For I had about me my flint, steel, match, and burning-glass.) I lay all night in the cave where I had lodged my provisions. My bed was the same dry grass and seaweed which I intended for fuel. I slept very little, for the disquiets of my mind prevailed over my weariness, and kept me awake. I considered how impossible it was to preserve my life in so desolate a place, and how miserable my end must be. Yet I found my self so listless and desponding, that I had not the heart to rise, and before I could get spirits enough to creep out of my cave, the day was far advanced. I walked a while among the rocks; the sky was perfectly clear, and the sun so hot, that I was forced to turn my face from it: when all on a sudden it became obscured, as I thought, in a manner very different from what happens by the interposition of a cloud. I turned back, and perceived a vast opaque body between me and the sun, moving forwards towards the island: it seemed to be about two miles high, and hid the sun six or seven minutes, but I did not observe the air to be much colder, or the sky more darkened, than if I had stood under the shade of a mountain. As it approached nearer over the place where I was, it appeared to be a firm substance, the bottom flat, smooth, and shining very bright from the reflection of the sea below. I stood upon a height about two hundred yards from the shore, and saw this vast body descending almost to a parallel with me, at less than an English mile distance. I took out my pocket-perspective, and could plainly discover numbers of people moving up and down the sides of it, which appeared to be sloping, but what those people were doing I was not able to distinguish.

The natural love of life gave me some inward motions of joy, and I was ready to entertain a hope, that this adventure might some way or other help to deliver me from the desolate place and condition I was in. But at the same time the reader can hardly conceive my astonishment, to behold an island in the air, inhabited by men, who were able (as it should seem) to raise, or sink, or put it into a progressive motion, as they pleased. But not being at that time in a disposition to philosophize upon this phenomenon, I rather chose to observe what course the island would take, because it seemed for a while to stand still. Yet soon after it advanced nearer, and I could see the sides of it, encompassed with several gradations of galleries, and stairs, at certain intervals, to descend from one to the other. In the lowest gallery, I beheld some people fishing with long angling rods, and others looking on. I waved my cap (for my hat was long since worn out) and my handkerchief towards the island; and upon its nearer approach, I called and shouted with the utmost strength of my voice; and then looking circumspectly, I beheld a crowd gathered to that side which was most in my view. I found by their pointing towards me and to each other, that they plainly discovered me, although they made no return to my shouting. But I could see four or five men running in great haste up the stairs to the top of the island, who then disappeared. I happened rightly to conjecture, that these were sent for orders to some person in authority upon this occasion.

The number of people increased, and in less than half an hour the island was moved and raised in such a manner, that the lowest gallery appeared in a parallel of less than an hundred yards' distance from the height where I stood. I then put my self into the most supplicating postures, and spoke in the humblest accent, but received no answer. Those who stood nearest over-against me seemed to be persons of distinction, as I supposed by their habit. They conferred earnestly with each other, looking often upon me. At length one of them called out in a clear, polite, smooth dialect, not unlike in sound to the Italian; and therefore I returned an answer in that language, hoping at least that the cadence might be more agreeable to his ears. Although neither of us understood the other, yet my meaning was easily known, for the people saw the distress I was in.

They made signs for me to come down from the rock, and go towards the shore, which I accordingly did; and the flying island being raised to a convenient height, the verge directly over me, a chain was let down from the lowest gallery, with a seat fastened to the bottom, to which I fixed my self, and was drawn up by pulleys.

CHAPTER II

The humours and dispositions of the Laputans described. An account of their learning. Of the King and his court. The author's reception there. The inhabitants subject to fears and disquietudes. An account of the women.

At my alighting I was surrounded by a crowd of people, but those who stood nearest seemed to be of better quality. They beheld me with all the marks and circumstances of wonder, neither indeed was I much in their debt, having never till then seen a race of mortals so singular in their shapes, habits, and countenances. Their heads were all reclined either to the right, or the left; one of their eyes turned inward, and the other directly up to the zenith. Their outward garments were adorned with the figures of suns, moons, and stars, interwoven with those of fiddles, flutes, harps, trumpets, guitars, harpsichords, and many more instruments of music, unknown to us in Europe. I observed here and there many in the habits of servants, with a blown bladder fastened like a flail to the end of a short stick, which they carried in their hands. In each bladder was a small quantity of dried pease or little pebbles (as I was afterwards informed). With these bladders they now and then flapped the mouths and ears of those who stood near them, of which practice I could not then conceive the meaning; it seems, the minds of these people are so taken up with intense speculations, that they neither can speak, nor attend to the discourses of others, without being roused by some external taction upon the organs of speech and hearing; for which reason those persons who are able to afford it always keep a flapper (the original is *climenole*) in their family, as one of their domestics, nor ever walk abroad or make visits without him. And the business of this officer is, when two or more persons are in company, gently to strike with his bladder the mouth of him who is to speak, and the right ear of him or them to whom the speaker addresseth himself. This flapper is likewise employed diligently to attend his master in his walks, and upon occasion to give him a soft flap on his eyes, because he is always so wrapped up in cogitation, that he is in manifest danger of falling down every precipice, and bouncing his head against every post, and in the streets, of jostling others or being jostled himself into the kennel.

It was necessary to give the reader this information, without which he would be at the same loss with me, to understand the proceedings of these people, as they conducted me up the stairs, to the top of the island, and from thence to the royal palace. While we were ascending, they forgot several times what they were about, and left me to my self, till their memories were again roused by their flappers; for they appeared altogether unmoved by the sight of my foreign habit and countenance, and by the shouts of the vulgar, whose thoughts and minds were more disengaged.

At last we entered the palace, and proceeded into the chamber of presence, where I saw the King seated on his throne, attended on each side by persons of prime quality. Before the throne was a large table filled with globes and spheres, and mathematical instruments of all kinds. His Majesty took not the least notice of us, although our entrance was not without sufficient noise, by the concourse of all persons belonging to the court. But he was then deep in a problem, and we attended at least an hour before he could solve it. There stood by him, on each side, a young page, with flaps in their hands, and when they saw he was at leisure, one of them gently struck his mouth, and the other his right ear, at which he started like one awaked on the sudden, and looking towards me, and the company I was in, recollected the occasion of our coming, whereof he had been informed before. He spoke some words, whereupon immediately a young man with a flap came up to my side, and flapped me gently on the right ear; but I made signs as well as I could, that I had no occasion for such an instrument; which as I afterwards found gave his Majesty and the whole court a very mean opinion of my understanding. The King, as far as I could conjecture, asked me several questions, and I addressed my self to him in all the languages I had. When it was found that I could neither understand nor be understood, I was conducted by his order to an apartment in his palace (this prince being distinguished above all his predecessors for his hospitality to strangers), where two servants were appointed to attend me. My dinner was brought, and four persons of quality, whom I remembered to have seen very near the King's person, did me the honour to dine with me. We had two courses, of three dishes each. In the first course there was a shoulder of mutton, cut into an equilateral triangle, a piece of beef into a rhomboides, and a pudding into a cycloid. The second course was two ducks, trussed up into the form of fiddles; sausages and puddings resembling flutes and hautboys, and a breast of veal in the shape of a harp. The servants cut our bread into cones, cylinders, parallelograms, and several other mathematical figures.

While we were at dinner, I made bold to ask the names of several things in their language, and those noble persons, by the assistance of their flappers, delighted to give me answers, hoping to raise my admiration of their great abilities, if I could be brought to converse with them. I was soon able to call for bread and drink, or whatever else I wanted.

Hautboys. Oboes.

After dinner my company withdrew, and a person was sent to me by the King's order, attended by a flapper. He brought with him pen, ink, and paper, and three or four books, giving me to understand by signs, that he was sent to teach me the language. We sat together four hours, in which time I wrote down a great number of words in columns, with the translations over against them. I likewise made a shift to learn several short sentences. For my tutor would order one of my servants to fetch something, to turn about, to make a bow, to sit, or stand, or walk and the like. Then I took down the sentence in writing. He showed me also in one of his books the figures of the sun, moon, and stars, the zodiac, the tropics, and polar circles, together with the denominations of many figures of planes and solids. He gave me the names and descriptions of all the musical instruments, and the general terms of art in playing on each of them. After he had left me, I placed all my words with their interpretations in alphabetical order. And thus in a few days, by the help of a very faithful memory, I got some insight into their language.

The word which I interpret the *Flying* or *Floating Island* is in the original *Laputa,* whereof I could never learn the true etymology. *Lap* in the old obsolete language signifieth *high,* and *untuh* a *governor,* from which they say by corruption was derived *Laputa,* from *Lapuntuh.* But I do not approve of this derivation, which seems to be a little strained. I ventured to offer to the learned among them a conjecture of my own, that *Laputa* was *quasi Lap outed; Lap* signifying properly the dancing of the sunbeams in the sea, and *outed* a wing, which however I shall not obtrude, but submit to the judicious reader.

Those to whom the King had entrusted me, observing how ill I was clad, ordered a tailor to come next morning, and take my measure for a suit of clothes. This operator did his office after a different manner from those of his trade in Europe. He first took my altitude by a quadrant, and then, with rule and compasses, described the dimensions and outlines of my whole body, all which he entered upon paper, and in six days brought my clothes very ill made, and quite out of shape, by happening to mistake a figure in the calculation. But my comfort was, that I observed such accidents very frequent and little regarded.

Laputa. Though Gulliver overlooks it, *Laputa* is most obviously Spanish for "the whore." The name thus insinuates a comparison of the British metropole to the biblical "Whore of Babylon," a reversal of standard Protestant invective. See pp. 400, 405, and 415.

Submit to the judicious reader. In "A Discourse to Prove the Antiquity of the English Tongue" (Davis, vol. 4, 1–21), Swift parodies the speculative etymologies—in effect, unconscious puns—beloved of antiquarians, absurdly deriving Greek, Latin, and Hebrew words from spurious English "origins."

During my confinement for want of clothes, and by an indisposition that held me some days longer, I much enlarged my dictionary; and when I went next to court, was able to understand many things the King spoke, and to return him some kind of answers. His Majesty had given orders that the island should move northeast and by east, to the vertical point over Lagado, the metropolis of the whole kingdom below upon the firm earth. It was about ninety leagues distant, and our voyage lasted four days and an half. I was not in the least sensible of the progressive motion made in the air by the island. On the second morning about eleven o'clock, the King himself in person, attended by his nobility, courtiers, and officers, having prepared all their musical instruments, played on them for three hours without intermission, so that I was quite stunned with the noise, neither could I possibly guess the meaning till my tutor informed me. He said that the people of their island had their ears adapted to hear the music of the spheres, which always played at certain periods, and the court was now prepared to bear their part in what ever instrument they most excelled.

In our journey towards Lagado, the capital city, his Majesty ordered that the island should stop over certain towns and villages, from whence he might receive the petitions of his subjects. And to this purpose several packthreads were let down with small weights at the bottom. On these packthreads the people strung their petitions, which mounted up directly like the scraps of paper fastened by schoolboys at the end of the string that holds their kite. Sometimes we received wine and victuals from below, which were drawn up by pulleys.

The knowledge I had in mathematics gave me great assistance in acquiring their phraseology, which depended much upon that science and music; and in the latter I was not unskilled. Their ideas are perpetually conversant in lines and figures. If they would, for example, praise the beauty of a woman or any other animal, they describe it by rhombs, circles, parallelograms, ellipses, and other geometrical terms, or else by words of art drawn from music, needless here to repeat. I observed in the King's kitchen all sorts of mathematical and musical instruments, after the figures of which they cut up the joints that were served to his Majesty's table.

Their houses are very ill built, the walls bevil, without one right angle in any apartment, and this defect ariseth from the contempt they bear for practical geometry, which they despise as vulgar and mechanic, those instructions they give being too refined for the intellectuals of their work-

---

Stunned with the noise. Perhaps a sardonic glance at George I's only notable cultural interest: his patronage of music. George Frederick Handel (1685–1759) belongs to this milieu.

Intellectuals. Minds.

men, which occasions perpetual mistakes. And although they are dextrous enough upon a piece of paper in the management of the rule, the pencil, and the divider, yet in the common actions and behaviour of life I have not seen a more clumsy, awkward, and unhandy people, nor so slow and perplexed in their conceptions upon all other subjects, except those of mathematics and music. They are very bad reasoners, and vehemently given to opposition, unless when they happen to be of the right opinion, which is seldom their case. Imagination, fancy, and invention, they are wholly strangers to, nor have any words in their language by which those ideas can be expressed; the whole compass of their thoughts and mind being shut up within the two forementioned sciences.

Most of them, and especially those who deal in the astronomical part, have great faith in judicial astrology, although they are ashamed to own it publicly. But what I chiefly admired, and thought altogether unaccountable, was the strong disposition I observed in them towards news and politics, perpetually enquiring into public affairs, giving their judgments in matters of state, and passionately disputing every inch of a party opinion. I have indeed observed the same disposition among most of the mathematicians I have known in Europe, although I could never discover the least analogy between the two sciences; unless those people suppose, that because the smallest circle hath as many degrees as the largest, therefore the regulation and management of the world require no more abilities than the handling and turning of a globe. But I rather take this quality to spring from a very common infirmity of human nature, inclining us to be more curious and conceited in matters where we have least concern, and for which we are least adapted either by study or nature.

These people are under continual disquietudes, never enjoying a minute's peace of mind; and their disturbances proceed from causes which very little affect the rest of mortals. Their apprehensions arise from several changes they dread in the celestial bodies. For instance; that the earth, by

---

Judicial astrology. The divinatory art concerned with making judgments and predictions about human affairs based on a decoding of celestial events. Often contrasted with "natural astrology," seen as having anticipated empirical astronomy (Geneva, 9).

The same disposition among most of the mathematicians I have known in Europe. A gibe at Sir Isaac Newton, who served as master of the mint during the controversy in Ireland over Wood's halfpence (1722–25). Newton earned Swift's ire both by legitimating the quality of Wood's halfpence and by advising British administrations against establishing an Irish mint. Though he attacked popular astrology in print, Newton was involved with private alchemical pursuits based on ancient hermetic doctrines, some of which involved astrological calculations. See White, 131–62, and Curry, 142–47.

the continual approaches of the sun towards it, must in course of time be absorbed or swallowed up. That the face of the sun will by degrees be encrusted with its own effluvia, and give no more light to the world. That the earth very narrowly escaped a brush from the tail of the last comet, which would have infallibly reduced it to ashes; and that the next, which they have calculated for one and thirty years hence, will probably destroy us. For, if in its perihelion it should approach within a certain degree of the sun (as by their calculations they have reason to dread), it will conceive a degree of heat ten thousand times more intense than that of red-hot glowing iron; and in its absence from the sun, carry a blazing tail ten hundred thousand and fourteen miles long; through which if the earth should pass at the distance of one hundred thousand miles from the nucleus or main body of the comet, it must in its passage be set on fire, and reduced to ashes. That the sun daily spending its rays without any nutriment to supply them, will at last be wholly consumed and annihilated; which must be attended with the destruction of this earth, and of all the planets that receive their light from it.

They are so perpetually alarmed with the apprehensions of these and the like impending dangers, that they can neither sleep quietly in their beds, nor have any relish for the common pleasures or amusements of life. When they meet an acquaintance in the morning, the first question is about the sun's health, how he looked at his setting and rising, and what hopes they have to avoid the stroke of the approaching comet. This conversation they are apt to run into with the same temper that boys discover in delighting to hear terrible stories of sprites and hobgoblins, which they greedily listen to, and dare not go to bed for fear.

The women of the island have abundance of vivacity; they contemn their husbands, and are exceedingly fond of strangers, whereof there is always a considerable number from the continent below, attending at court, either upon affairs of the several towns and corporations, or their own particular occasions, but are much despised, because they want the same endowments. Among these the ladies choose their gallants: but the vexation is, that they act with too much ease and security, for the husband is always so rapt in speculation, that the mistress and lover may proceed to the greatest familiarities before his face, if he be but provided with paper and implements, and without his flapper at his side.

The wives and daughters lament their confinement to the island, although I think it the most delicious spot of ground in the world; and although they live here in the greatest plenty and magnificence, and are allowed to do whatever they please, they long to see the world, and take the diversions of the metropolis, which they are not allowed to do without a particular licence from the King; and this is not easy to be obtained because the people of quality have found by frequent experience how hard it is to persuade their women to return from below. I was told that a great court lady, who had several children, is married to the prime minister, the richest subject in the kingdom, a very graceful person, extremely fond of her, and lives in the finest palace of the island, went down to Lagado, on the pretence of health, there hid her self for several months, till the King sent a warrant to search for her, and she was found in an obscure eating house all in rags, having pawned her clothes to maintain an old deformed footman, who beat her every day, and in whose company she was taken much against her will. And although her husband received her with all possible kindness, and without the least reproach, she soon after contrived to steal down again with all her jewels, to the same gallant, and hath not been heard of since.

This may perhaps pass with the reader rather for an European or English story, than for one of a country so remote. But he may please to consider, that the caprices of womankind are not limited by any climate or nation, and that they are much more uniform than can be easily imagined.

In about a month's time I had made a tolerable proficiency in their language, and was able to answer most of the King's questions, when I had the honour to attend him. His Majesty discovered not the least curiosity to enquire into the laws, government, history, religion, or manners of the countries where I had been, but confined his questions to the state of mathematics, and received the account I gave him with great contempt and indifference, though often roused by his flapper on each side.

The prime minister. Glancing at Walpole's marriage, openly unfaithful on both sides.

The caprices of womankind are not limited by any climate or nation. Gulliver's complacent joke must be set against his own imperfections as regards home life. His anti-domestic pattern in this regard resembles that of the perpetually roving Dampier, whose wife Judith would have seen little of him between 1679 and 1691. The links between exploration and masculinity have been analyzed in Phillips.

CHAPTER III

A phenomenon solved by modern philosophy and astronomy. The Laputians' great improvements in the latter. The King's method of suppressing insurrections.

I desired leave of this prince to see the curiosities of the island, which he was graciously pleased to grant, and ordered my tutor to attend me. I chiefly wanted to know to what cause in art or in nature it owed its several motions, whereof I will now give a philosophical account to the reader.

The Flying or Floating Island is exactly circular, its diameter 7,837 yards, or about four miles and an half, and consequently contains ten thousand acres. It is three hundred yards thick. The bottom or under surface, which appears to those who view it from below, is one even regular plate of adamant, shooting up to the height of about two hundred yards. Above it lie the several minerals in their usual order, and over all is a coat of rich mould ten or twelve foot deep. The declivity of the upper surface, from the circumference to the center, is the natural cause why all the dews and rains which fall upon the island are conveyed in small rivulets towards the middle, where they are emptied into four large basons, each of about half a mile in circuit, and two hundred yards distant from the center. From these basons the water is continually exhaled by the sun in the day time, which effectually prevents their overflowing. Besides, as it is in the power of the monarch to raise the island above the region of clouds and vapours, he can prevent the falling of dews and rains when ever he pleases. For the highest clouds cannot rise above two miles, as naturalists agree, at least they were never known to do so in that country.

At the center of the island there is a chasm about fifty yards in diameter, from whence the astronomers descend into a large dome, which is therefore called *Flandona Gagnole*, or the *Astronomer's Cave*, situated at the depth of an hundred yards beneath the upper surface of the adamant. In this cave are twenty lamps continually burning, which from the reflection of the adamant cast a strong light into every part. The place is stored with great variety of sextants, quadrants, telescopes, astrolabes, and other astronomical instruments. But the greatest curiosity, upon which the fate of the island depends, is a loadstone of a prodigious size, in shape resembling a weaver's shuttle. It is in length six yards, and in the thickest part at least three yards

---

Resembling a weaver's shuttle. This analogy links the Flying Island's lodestone—its power—to the British linen and woollen manufactures, protected by legal monopoly against competition from Ireland and elsewhere. The lodestone also evokes a principal technology of navigation, the magnetized needle of the compass.

over. This magnet is sustained by a very strong axle of adamant passing through its middle, upon which it plays, and is poised so exactly that the weakest hand can turn it. It is hooped round with an hollow cylinder of adamant, four foot deep, as many thick, and twelve yards in diameter, placed horizontally, and supported by eight adamantine feet, each six yards high. In the middle of the concave side there is a groove twelve inches deep, in which the extremities of the axle are lodged, and turned round as there is occasion.

The stone cannot be moved from its place by any force, because the hoop and its feet are one continued piece with that body of adamant which constitutes the bottom of the island.

By means of this loadstone, the island is made to rise and fall, and move from one place to another. For, with respect to that part of the earth over which the monarch presides, the stone is endued at one of its sides with an attractive power, and at the other with a repulsive. Upon placing the magnet erect with its attracting end towards the earth, the island descends; but when the repelling extremity points downwards, the island mounts directly upwards. When the position of the stone is oblique, the motion of the island is so too. For in this magnet the forces always act in lines parallel to its direction.

By this oblique motion the island is conveyed to different parts of the monarch's dominions. To explain the manner of its progress, let *A B* represent a line drawn cross the dominions of Balnibarbi, let the line *c d* represent the loadstone, of which let *d* be the repelling end, and *c* the attracting end, the island being over *C;* let the stone be placed in the position *c d* with its repelling end downwards; then the island will be driven upwards obliquely towards *D.* When it is arrived at *D,* let the stone be turned upon its axle till its attracting end points towards *E,* and then the island will be carried obliquely towards *E;* where if the stone be again turned upon its axle till it stands in the position *E F,* with its repelling point downwards, the island will rise obliquely towards *F,* where by directing the attracting end towards *G,* the island may be carried to *G,* and from *G* to *H,* by turning the stone, so as to make its repelling extremity point directly downwards. And thus by changing the situation of the stone as often as there is occasion, the island is made to rise and fall by turns in an oblique direction, and by those alternate risings and fallings (the obliquity being not considerable) is conveyed from one part of the dominions to the other.

But it must be observed, that this island cannot move beyond the extent of the dominions below, nor can it rise above the height of four miles. For which the astronomers (who have written large systems concerning the stone) assign the following reason: that the magnetic virtue does not extend beyond the distance of four miles, and that the mineral which acts upon the stone in the bowels of the earth, and in the sea about six leagues

Plate 4. Part 3. *Page 218.*

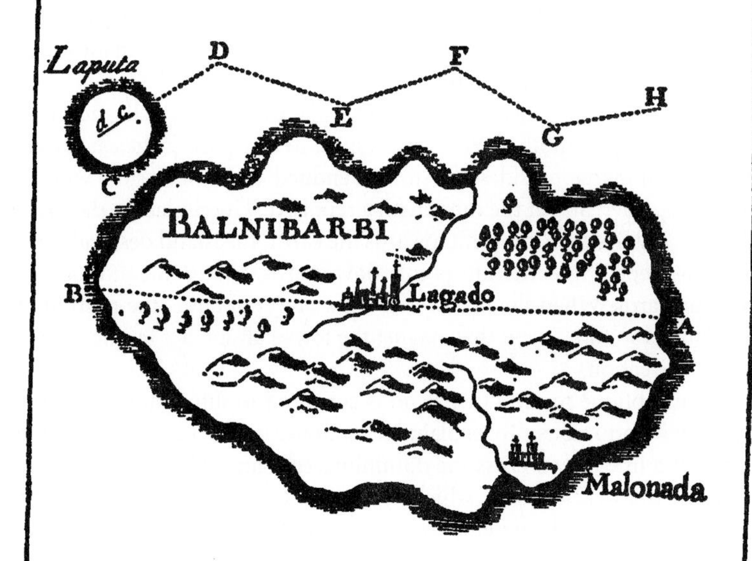

distant from the shore, is not diffused through the whole globe, but terminated with the limits of the King's dominions; and it was easy, from the great advantage of such a superior situation, for a prince to bring under his obedience whatever country lay within the attraction of that magnet.

When the stone is put parallel to the plane of the horizon, the island standeth still; for in that case, the extremities of it, being at equal distance from the earth, act with equal force, the one in drawing downwards, the other in pushing upwards, and consequently no motion can ensue.

This loadstone is under the care of certain astronomers, who from time to time give it such positions as the monarch directs. They spend the greatest part of their lives in observing the celestial bodies, which they do by the assistance of glasses far excelling ours in goodness. For although their largest telescopes do not exceed three feet, they magnify much more than those of a hundred with us, and at the same time show the stars with greater clearness. For this advantage hath enabled them to extend their discoveries much farther than our astronomers in Europe. They have made a catalogue of ten thousand fixed stars, whereas the largest of ours do not contain above one third part of that number. They have likewise discovered two lesser stars, or "satellites," which revolve about Mars, whereof the innermost is distant from the center of the primary planet exactly three of his diameters, and the outermost five; the former revolves in the space of ten hours, and the latter in twenty-one and an half; so that the squares of their periodical times are very near in the same proportion with the cubes of their distance from the center of Mars, which evidently shows them to be governed by the same law of gravitation, that influences the other heavenly bodies.

They have observed ninety-three different comets, and settled their periods with great exactness. If this be true (and they affirm it with great confidence) it is much to be wished that their observations were made public, whereby the theory of comets, which at present is very lame and defective, might be brought to the same perfection with other parts of astronomy.

The King would be the most absolute prince in the universe, if he could but prevail on a ministry to join with him; but these having their estates

---

Glasses. Telescopes.

Satellites. Widely remarked as a prediction of the two moons of Mars (Phobos and Deimos), confirmed only in 1877. Swift's striking guess may hark back to a curious episode in the annals of early modern science. Scientists of the seventeenth and eighteenth centuries often concealed their discoveries in anagrams, a practice that, while protecting their monopoly on esoteric information, opened up the possibility of misreadings. Johannes Kepler rearranged a Latin anagram devised by Galileo so as to decode a message never intended by the latter: "Hail, twin companionship, children of Mars" (Geneva, 33).

below on the continent, and considering that the office of a favourite hath a very uncertain tenure, would never consent to the enslaving their country.

If any town should engage in rebellion or mutiny, fall into violent factions, or refuse to pay the usual tribute, the King hath two methods of reducing them to obedience. The first and the mildest course is by keeping the island hovering over such a town, and the lands about it, whereby he can deprive them of the benefit of the sun and the rain, and consequently afflict the inhabitants with dearth and diseases. And if the crime deserve it they are at the same time pelted from above with great stones, against which they have no defence but by creeping into cellars or caves, while the roofs of their houses are beaten to pieces. But if they still continue obstinate, or offer to raise insurrections, he proceeds to the last remedy, by letting the island drop directly upon their heads, which makes a universal destruction both of houses and men. However, this is an extremity to which the prince is seldom driven, neither indeed is he willing to put it in execution, nor dare his ministers advise him to an action which, as it would render them odious to the people, so it would be a great damage to their own estates, that lie all below, for the island is the King's demesne.

But there is still indeed a more weighty reason, why the kings of this country have been always averse from executing so terrible an action, unless upon the utmost necessity. For if the town intended to be destroyed should have in it any tall rocks, as it generally falls out in the larger cities, a situation probably chosen at first with a view to prevent such a catastrophe; or if it abound in high spires or pillars of stone, a sudden fall might endanger the bottom or under surface of the island, which although it consist, as I have said, of one entire adamant two hundred yards thick, might happen to crack by too great a shock, or burst by approaching too near the fires from the houses below, as the backs both of iron and stone will often do in our chimneys. Of all this the people are well apprised, and understand how far to carry their obstinacy, where their liberty or property is concerned. And the King, when he is highest provoked, and most determined to press a city to rubbish, orders the island to descend with great

---

Having their Estates below on the continent. Absentee landlords are a favorite target of Swiftian wrath. Insulated by distance from the necessity of confronting their Irish tenants face to face, they were notorious for "racking" that much more ruthlessly.

Deprive them of the benefit of the sun and the rain. Often taken to represent England's legal strangulation of Irish trade through the Navigation Acts, the Woollen Act, and so on.

Great damage to their own estates. An especially pointed jab at the political irresponsibility of absentee landlords.

Tall rocks. A reference to the successful resistance of Ireland to English arrogance in the *Drapier's Letters* campaign. May suggest the spire of St. Patrick's Cathedral.

gentleness, out of a pretence of tenderness to his people, but indeed for fear of breaking the adamantine bottom; in which case it is the opinion of all their philosophers, that the loadstone could no longer hold it up, and the whole mass would fall to the ground.

About three years before my arrival among them, while the King was in his progress over his dominions, there happened an extraordinary accident which had like to have put a period to the fate of that monarchy, at least as it is now instituted. Lindalino, the second city in the kingdom, was the first his Majesty visited in his progress. Three days after his departure, the inhabitants, who had often complained of great oppressions, shut the town gates, seized on the governor, and with incredible speed and labour erected four large towers, one at every corner of the city (which is an exact square), equal in height to a strong pointed rock that stands directly in the center of the city. Upon the top of each tower, as well as upon the rock, they fixed a great loadstone, and in case their design should fail, they had provided a vast quantity of the most combustible fuel, hoping to burst therewith the adamantine bottom of the island, if the loadstone project should miscarry.

It was eight months before the King had perfect notice that the Lindalinians were in rebellion. He then commanded that the island should be wafted over the city. The people were unanimous, and had laid in store of provisions, and a great river runs through the middle of the town. The King hovered over them several days to deprive them of the sun and the rain. He ordered many packthreads to be let down, yet not a person offered to send up a petition, but instead thereof, very bold demands, the redress of all their grievances, great immunities, the choice of their own governor, and other the like exorbitances. Upon which his Majesty commanded all the inhabitants of the island to cast great stones from the lower gallery into the town; but the citizens had provided against this mischief by conveying their persons and effects into the four towers, and other strong buildings, and vaults underground.

The King being now determined to reduce this proud people, ordered that the island should descend gently within forty yards of the top of the towers and rock. This was accordingly done; but the officers employed in that work found the descent much speedier than usual, and by turning the loadstone could not without great difficulty keep it in a firm position, but found the island inclining to fall. They sent the King immediate intelligence of this astonishing event and begged his Majesty's permission to raise

---

Three years before my arrival. The following passage allegorically recounts Ireland's successful resistance to Britain during the *Drapier's Letters* campaign.

Lindalino. A play on *Dublin* (that is, double-*Lin*).

Combustible fuel. The *Drapier's Letters.*

the island higher; the King consented, a general council was called, and the officers of the loadstone ordered to attend. One of the oldest and expertest among them obtained leave to try an experiment. He took a strong line of an hundred yards, and the island being raised over the town above the attracting power they had felt, he fastened a piece of adamant to the end of his line which had in it a mixture of iron mineral, of the same nature with that whereof the bottom or lower surface of the island is composed, and from the lower gallery let it down slowly towards the top of the towers. The adamant was not descended four yards, before the officer felt it drawn so strongly downwards, that he could hardly pull it back. He then threw down several small pieces of adamant, and observed that they were all violently attracted by the top of the tower. The same experiment was made on the other three towers, and on the rock with the same effect.

This incident broke entirely the King's measures and (to dwell no longer on other circumstances) he was forced to give the town their own conditions.

I was assured by a great minister, that if the island had descended so near the town as not to be able to raise it self, the citizens were determined to fix it for ever, to kill the King and all his servants, and entirely change the government.

By a fundamental law of this realm, neither the King nor either of his two elder sons are permitted to leave the island, nor the Queen, till she is past child-bearing.

CHAPTER IV

The author leaves Laputa, is conveyed to Balnibarbi, arrives at the metropolis. A description of the metropolis and the country adjoining. The author hospitably received by a great lord. His conversation with that lord.

Although I cannot say that I was ill treated in this island, yet I must confess I thought my self too much neglected, not without some degree of contempt. For neither prince nor people appeared to be curious in any part of knowledge, except mathematics and music, wherein I was far their inferior, and upon that account very little regarded.

Forced to give the town their own conditions. The patent for Wood's halfpence was withdrawn in August, 1725, a triumph for Swift.

Kill the King. See Griffin, "A Note on the Texts," p. 34; see also p. 308.

On the other side, after having seen all the curiosities of the island, I was very desirous to leave it, being heartily weary of those people. They were indeed excellent in two sciences for which I have great esteem, and wherein I am not unversed, but at the same time so abstracted and involved in speculation that I never met with such disagreeable companions. I conversed only with women, tradesmen, flappers, and court-pages, during two months of my abode there, by which at last I rendered my self extremely contemptible, yet these were the only people from whom I could ever receive a reasonable answer.

I had obtained by hard study a good degree of knowledge in their language; I was weary of being confined to an island where I received so little countenance, and resolved to leave it with the first opportunity.

There was a great lord at court, nearly related to the King, and for that reason alone used with respect. He was universally reckoned the most ignorant and stupid person among them. He had performed many eminent services for the crown, had great natural and acquired parts, adorned with integrity and honour, but so ill an ear for music, that his detractors reported he had been often known to beat time in the wrong place; neither could his tutors without extreme difficulty teach him to demonstrate the most easy proposition in the mathematics. He was pleased to show me many marks of favour, often did me the honour of a visit, desired to be informed in the affairs of Europe, the laws and customs, the manners and learning of the several countries where I had travelled. He listened to me with great attention, and made very wise observations on all I spoke. He had two flappers attending him for state, but never made use of them except at court, and in visits of ceremony, and would always command them to withdraw when we were alone together.

I intreated this illustrious person to intercede in my behalf with his Majesty for leave to depart, which he accordingly did, as he was pleased to tell me, with regret: for indeed he had made me several offers very advantageous, which however I refused with expressions of the highest acknowledgement.

On the 16th day of February, I took leave of his Majesty and the court. The King made me a present to the value of about two hundred pounds English, and my protector his kinsman as much more, together with a letter of recommendation to a friend of his in Lagado, the metropolis; the island being then hovering over a mountain about two miles from it, I was let down from the lowest gallery, in the same manner as I had been taken up.

The continent, as far as it is subject to the monarch of the Flying Island, passes under the general name of Balnibarbi, and the metropolis, as I said before, is called Lagado. I felt some little satisfaction in finding my self on firm ground. I walked to the city without any concern, being clad like one of the natives, and sufficiently instructed to converse with them. I soon found out the person's house to whom I was recommended, presented my letter from his friend the grandee in the island, and was received with much kindness. This great lord, whose name was Munodi, ordered me an apartment in his own house, where I continued during my stay, and was entertained in a most hospitable manner.

The next morning after my arrival he took me in his chariot to see the town, which is about half the bigness of London, but the houses very strangely built, and most of them out of repair. The people in the streets walked fast, looked wild, their eyes fixed, and were generally in rags. We passed through one of the town gates, and went about three miles into the country, where I saw many labourers working with several sorts of tools in the ground, but was not able to conjecture what they were about, neither did I observe any expectation either of corn or grass, although the soil appeared to be excellent. I could not forbear admiring at these odd appearances both in town and country, and I made bold to desire my conductor, that he would be pleased to explain to me what could be meant by so many busy heads, hands, and faces, both in the streets and the fields, because I did not discover any good effects they produced; but on the contrary, I never knew a soil so unhappily cultivated, houses so ill contrived and so ruinous, or a people whose countenances and habit expressed so much misery and want.

This Lord Munodi was a person of the first rank, and had been some years Governor of Lagado, but by a cabal of ministers was discharged for insufficiency. However, the King treated him with tenderness, as a well-meaning man, but of a low contemptible understanding.

When I gave that free censure of the country and its inhabitants, he made no further answer than by telling me that I had not been long enough among them to form a judgment, and that the different nations of the world had different customs, with other common topics to the same purpose. But when we returned to his palace, he asked me how I liked the building, what absurdities I observed, and what quarrel I had with the dress and looks of his domestics. This he might safely do, because every thing about him was magnificent, regular, and polite. I answered that his Excellency's prudence, quality, and fortune had exempted him from those

---

Whose name was Munodi. Suggests a contraction of *Mundum odi* ("I hate the world": the traditional metaphysical stance toward transient worldy things). Munodi is a paternalistic Tory squire, possibly based on Robert Harley, the earl of Oxford, who survived impeachment by the ascendant Whigs in 1714.

defects which folly and beggary had produced in others. He said if I would go with him to his country house, about twenty miles distant, where his estate lay, there would be more leisure for this kind of conversation. I told his Excellency that I was entirely at his disposal, and accordingly we set out next morning.

During our journey, he made me observe the several methods used by farmers in managing their lands, which to me were wholly unaccountable, for, except in some very few places, I could not discover one ear of corn or blade of grass. But in three hours travelling the scene was wholly altered; we came into a most beautiful country; farmers' houses at small distances, neatly built, the fields enclosed, containing vineyards, corn-grounds and meadows. Neither do I remember to have seen a more delightful prospect. His Excellency observed my countenance to clear up; he told me with a sigh, that there his estate began, and would continue the same till we should come to his house. That his countrymen ridiculed and despised him for managing his affairs no better, and for setting so ill an example to the kingdom, which however was followed by very few, such as were old and wilful, and weak like himself.

We came at length to the house, which was indeed a noble structure, built according to the best rules of ancient architecture. The fountains, gardens, walks, avenues, and groves were all disposed with exact judgment and taste. I gave due praises to every thing I saw, whereof his Excellency took not the least notice till after supper, when, there being no third companion, he told me with a very melancholy air, that he doubted he must throw down his houses in town and country, to rebuild them after the present mode, destroy all his plantations, and cast others into such a form as modern usage required, and give the same directions to all his tenants, unless he would submit to incur the censure of pride, singularity, affectation, ignorance, caprice, and perhaps encrease his Majesty's displeasure.

That the admiration I appeared to be under would cease or diminish when he had informed me of some particulars, which probably I never heard of at court, the people there being too much taken up in their own speculations to have regard to what passed here below.

The sum of his discourse was to this effect. That about forty years ago, certain persons went up to Laputa either upon business or diversion, and after five months continuance came back with a very little smattering in mathematics, but full of volatile spirits acquired in that airy region. That these persons upon their return began to dislike the management of every thing below, and fell into schemes of putting all arts, sciences, languages, and mechanics upon a new foot. To this end they procured a royal patent for erecting an academy of PROJECTORS in Lagado; and the humour prevailed so strongly among the people, that there is not a town of any consequence in the kingdom without such an academy. In these colleges the professors contrive new rules and methods of agriculture and building, and new instruments and tools for all trades and manufactures, whereby, as they undertake, one man shall do the work of ten; a palace may be built in a week, of materials so durable as to last for ever without repairing. All the fruits of the earth shall come to maturity at whatever season we think fit to choose, and increase an hundred fold more than they do at present, with innumerable other happy proposals. The only inconvenience is, that none of these projects are yet brought to perfection, and in the mean time the whole country lies miserably waste, the houses in ruins, and the people without food or clothes. By all which, instead of being discouraged, they are fifty times more violently bent upon prosecuting their schemes, driven equally on by hope and despair; that as for himself, being not of an enterprising spirit, he was content to go on in the old forms, to live in the houses his ancestors had built, and act as they did in every part of life without innovation. That some few other persons of quality and gentry had done the same, but were looked on with an eye of contempt and ill will, as enemies to art, ignorant, and ill commonwealth's-men, preferring their own ease and sloth before the general improvement of their country.

His Lordship added, that he would not by any further particulars prevent the pleasure I should certainly take in viewing the Grand Academy, whither he was resolved I should go. He only desired me to observe a ruined building upon the side of a mountain about three miles distant, of which he gave me this account. That he had a very convenient mill within half a mile of his house, turned by a current from a large river, and sufficient for his own family as well as a great number of his tenants. That about seven years ago a club of those projectors came to him with proposals to destroy this mill, and build another on the side of that mountain, on the long ridge whereof a long canal must be cut for a repository of water,

---

Academy of PROJECTORS: A parody, by way of the tour-of-the-madhouse genre, of the Royal Society, whose "Philosophical Transactions" Swift mined almost verbatim for the strange, cruel, and futile experiments described above. In 1699, the *Journal Book of the Royal Society* reported, for example, that "cow's piss drank to about a pint, will either purge or vomit with great ease" (White, 285). Swift's satire inverts the triumphs of the research establishment called "Solomon's House," described in Francis Bacon's *New Atlantis* (1627), where scientific mastery over nature yields "the enlarging of the bounds of human empire, to the effecting of all things possible." Bacon's utopian scientific society, marked by an elaborate division of intellectual and technical labor, served as the model for the Royal Society, founded in 1660.

to be conveyed up by pipes and engines to supply the mill: because the wind and air upon a height agitated the water, and thereby made it fitter for motion: and because the water descending down a declivity would turn the mill with half the current of a river whose course is more upon a level. He said, that being then not very well with the court, and pressed by many of his friends, he complied with the proposal; and after employing an hundred men for two years, the work miscarried, the projectors went off, laying the blame entirely upon him, railing at him ever since, and putting others upon the same experiment, with equal assurance of success, as well as equal disappointment.

In a few days we came back to town, and his Excellency, considering the bad character he had in the Academy, would not go with me himself, but recommended me to a friend of his to bear me company thither. My Lord was pleased to represent me as a great admirer of projects, and a person of much curiosity and easy belief, which indeed was not without truth, for I had my self been a sort of projector in my younger days.

CHAPTER V

The author permitted to see the Grand Academy of Lagado. The Academy largely described. The arts wherein the professors employ themselves.

This academy is not an entire single building, but a continuation of several houses on both sides of a street, which growing waste was purchased and applied to that use.

I was received very kindly by the Warden, and went for many days to the Academy. Every room hath in it one or more projectors, and I believe I could not be in fewer than five hundred rooms.

The first man I saw was of a meagre aspect, with sooty hands and face, his hair and beard long, ragged and singed in several places. His clothes, shirt, and skin were all of the same colour. He had been eight years upon a project for extracting sunbeams out of cucumbers, which were to be put into vials hermetically sealed, and let out to warm the air in raw inclement summers. He told me, he did not doubt in eight years more that he should

---

The work miscarried. A fable about the self-levitating economics of the South Sea Bubble of 1720. Swift intends to link this sort of commercial "project" to the research projects under way in the Academy of Lagado. See introduction, pp. 8–9, and also pp. 332–39.

be able to supply the Governor's gardens with sunshine at a reasonable rate; but he complained that his stock was low, and entreated me to give him something as an encouragement to ingenuity, especially since this had been a very dear season for cucumbers. I made him a small present, for my Lord had furnished me with money on purpose, because he knew their practice of begging from all who go to see them.

I went into another chamber, but was ready to hasten back, being almost overcome with a horrible stink. My conductor pressed me forward, conjuring me in a whisper to give no offence, which would be highly resented, and therefore I durst not so much as stop my nose. The projector of this cell was the most ancient student of the Academy. His face and beard were of a pale yellow; his hands and clothes daubed over with filth. When I was presented to him, he gave me a very close embrace (a compliment I could well have excused). His employment from his first coming into the Academy was an operation to reduce human excrement to its original food, by separating the several parts, removing the tincture which it receives from the gall, making the odour exhale, and scumming off the saliva. He had a weekly allowance from the society of a vessel filled with human ordure, about the bigness of a Bristol barrel.

I saw another at work to calcine ice into gunpowder, who likewise showed me a treatise he had written concerning the malleability of fire, which he intended to publish.

There was a most ingenious architect who had contrived a new method for building houses, by beginning at the roof and working downwards to the foundation, which he justified to me by the like practice of those two prudent insects, the bee and the spider.

There was a man born blind, who had several apprentices in his own condition: their employment was to mix colours for painters, which their master taught them to distinguish by feeling and smelling. It was indeed my misfortune to find them at that time not very perfect in their lessons, and the professor himself happened to be generally mistaken; this artist is much encouraged and esteemed by the whole fraternity.

In another apartment I was highly pleased with a projector, who had found a device of plowing the ground with hogs, to save the charges of plows, cattle, and labour. The method is this: in an acre of ground you bury, at six inches distance, and eight deep, a quantity of acorns, dates, chestnuts, and other mast or vegetables whereof these animals are fondest: then you drive six hundred or more of them into the field, where in a few days they will root up the whole ground in search of their food, and make it fit for sowing, at the same time manuring it with their dung; it is true upon experiment they found the charge and trouble very great, and they had little or no crop. However, it is not doubted that this invention may be capable of great improvement.

I went into another room, where the walls and ceiling were all hung round with cobwebs, except a narrow passage for the artist to go in and out. At my entrance he called aloud to me not to disturb his webs. He lamented the fatal mistake the world had been so long in of using silk-worms, while we had such plenty of domestic insects, who infinitely excelled the former, because they understood how to weave as well as spin. And he proposed farther, that by employing spiders the charge of dyeing silks would be wholly saved, whereof I was fully convinced when he showed me a vast number of flies most beautifully coloured, wherewith he fed his spiders, assuring us that the webs would take a tincture from them; and as he had them of all hues, he hoped to fit every body's fancy, as soon as he could find proper food for the flies, of certain gums, oils, and other glutinous matter, to give a strength and consistence to the threads.

There was an astronomer who had undertaken to place a sundial upon the great weathercock on the town-house, by adjusting the annual and diurnal motions of the earth and sun, so as to answer and coincide with all accidental turnings by the wind.

I was complaining of a small fit of the colic, upon which my conductor led me into a room, where a great physician resided, who was famous for curing that disease by contrary operations from the same instrument. He had a large pair of bellows with a long slender muzzle of ivory. This he conveyed eight inches up the anus, and drawing in the wind, he affirmed he could make the guts as lank as a dried bladder. But when the disease was more stubborn and violent, he let in the muzzle while the bellows were full of wind, which he discharged into the body of the patient, then withdrew the instrument to replenish it, clapping his thumb strongly against the orifice of the fundament; and this being repeated three or four times, the adventitious wind would rush out, bringing the noxious along with it (like water put into a pump) and the patient recovers. I saw him try both experiments upon a dog, but could not discern any effect from the former. After the latter, the animal was ready to burst, and made so violent a discharge, as was very offensive to me and my companions. The dog died on the spot, and we left the doctor endeavouring to recover him by the same operation.

I visited many other apartments, but shall not trouble my reader with all the curiosities I observed, being studious of brevity.

I had hitherto seen only one side of the Academy, the other being appropriated to the advancers of speculative learning, of whom I shall say something when I have mentioned one illustrious person more, who is called among them "the universal artist." He told us he had been thirty years employing his thoughts for the improvement of human life. He had two large rooms full of wonderful curiosities, and fifty men at work. Some were condensing air into a dry tangible substance, by extracting the nitre, and letting the aqueous or fluid particles percolate; others softening marble for pillows and pincushions; others petrifying the hoofs of a living horse to preserve them from foundering. The artist himself was at that time busy upon two great designs; the first, to sow land with chaff, wherein he affirmed the true seminal virtue to be contained, as he demonstrated by several experiments which I was not skilful enough to comprehend. The other was, by a certain composition of gums, minerals, and vegetables outwardly applied to prevent the growth of wool upon two young lambs; and he hoped in a reasonable time to propagate the breed of naked sheep all over the kingdom.

We crossed a walk to the other part of the Academy, where, as I have already said, the projectors in speculative learning resided.

The first professor I saw was in a very large room, with forty pupils about him. After salutation, observing me to look earnestly upon a frame, which took up the greatest part of both the length and breadth of the room, he said perhaps I might wonder to see him employed in a project for improving speculative knowledge by practical and mechanical operations. But the world would soon be sensible of its usefulness, and he flattered himself that a more noble, exalted thought never sprang in any other man's head. Every one knows how laborious the usual method is of attaining to arts and sciences; whereas by his contrivance the most ignorant person at a reasonable charge, and with a little bodily labour, may write books in philosophy, poetry, politics, law, mathematics and theology, without the least assistance from genius or study. He then led me to the frame, about the sides whereof all his pupils stood in ranks. It was twenty foot square, placed in the middle of the room. The superficies was composed of several bits of wood, about the bigness of a die, but some larger than others. They were all linked together by slender wires. These bits of wood were covered on every square with papers pasted on them, and on these papers were written all the words of their language in their several moods, tenses, and declensions, but without any order. The professor then desired me to observe, for he was going to set his engine at work. The pupils at his command took each of them hold of an iron handle, whereof there were forty fixed round the edges of the frame, and giving them a sudden turn, the whole disposition of the words was entirely changed. He then commanded six and thirty of the lads to read the several lines softly as they appeared upon the frame; and where they found three or four words together that might make part of a sentence, they dictated to the four remaining boys who were scribes. This work was repeated three or four times, and at every turn the engine

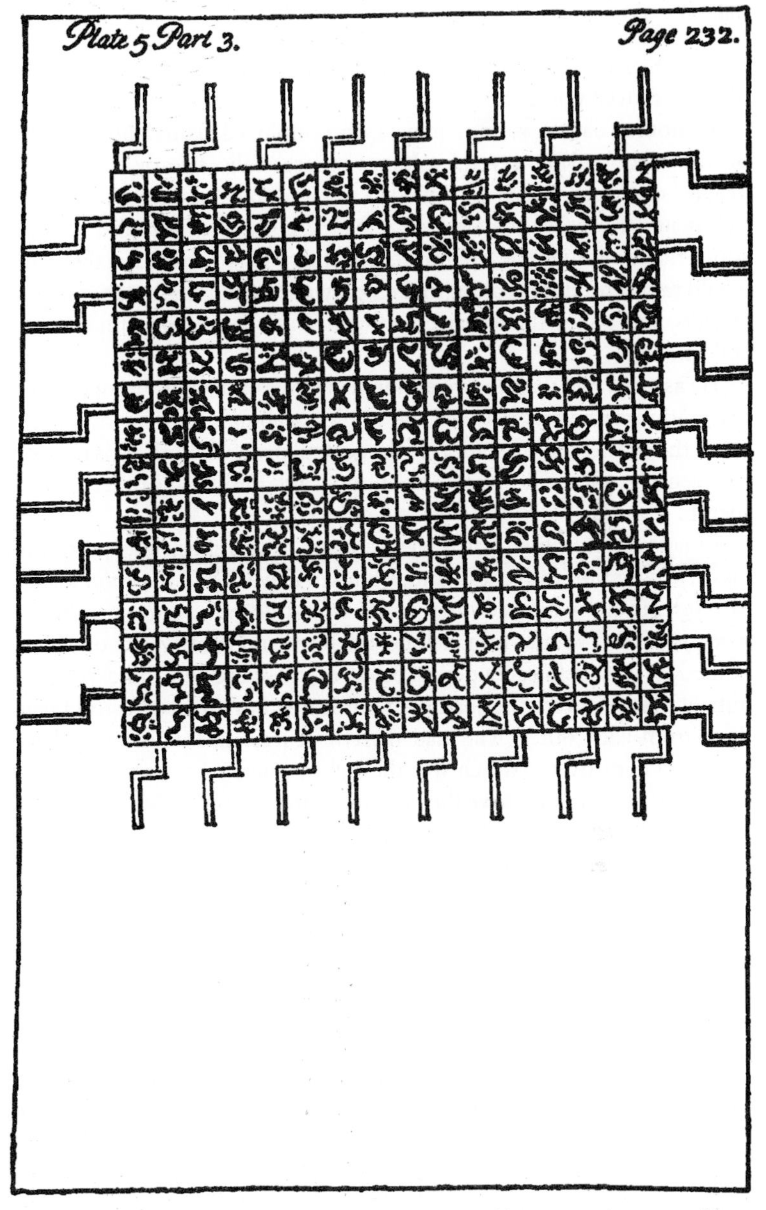

The "Writing Machine" in Lagado plays on a sense of language as structured by elements that can be combined with, or without, human intention. Perhaps the earliest inventor of such "robo-poetics" was the thirteenth-century Spanish theologian Ramon Lull, who devised such a combinatory machine in his *Ars Magna.* The possibility of random or mechanized writing has been lionized in the twentieth century by avant-garde writers such as William S. Burroughs in his "cut up" phase.

was so contrived, that the words shifted into new places, as the square bits of wood moved upside down.

Six hours a day the young students were employed in this labour, and the professor showed me several volumes in large folio already collected, of broken sentences, which he intended to piece together, and out of those rich materials to give the world a complete body of all arts and sciences; which however might be still improved, and much expedited, if the public would raise a fund for making and employing five hundred such frames in Lagado, and oblige the managers to contribute in common their several collections.

He assured me, that this invention had employed all his thoughts from his youth, that he had emptied the whole vocabulary into his frame, and made the strictest computation of the general proportion there is in books between the numbers of particles, nouns, and verbs, and other parts of speech.

I made my humblest acknowledgements to this illustrious person for his great communicativeness, and promised if ever I had the good fortune to return to my native country, that I would do him justice, as the sole inventor of this wonderful machine; the form and contrivance of which I desired leave to delineate upon paper as in the figure here annexed. I told him, although it were the custom of our learned in Europe to steal inventions from each other, who had thereby at least this advantage, that it became a controversy which was the right owner, yet I would take such caution, that he should have the honour entire without a rival.

We next went to the school of languages, where three professors sat in consultation upon improving that of their own country.

The first project was to shorten discourse by cutting poly-syllables into one, and leaving out verbs and participles, because in reality all things imaginable are but nouns.

Steal inventions from each other. Leibniz and Newton, now acknowledged to have invented the calculus independently, notoriously wrangled over who was first to devise this immensely influential contribution. Swift may also be thinking of the famous eighteenth-century contest for devising a method of determining longitude at sea, sponsored beginning in 1714 (with the enormous prize of £20,000) by the British Parliament. Competing "solutions" proliferated rapidly. See note, p. 209, and Swift's letter to John Wheldon, p. 384.

Improving that of their own country. The Royal Society, motivated by the dream of wholly literal communication, had appointed a committee in 1662 to push an agenda of linguistic purification. As Rivero points out, the passage may also parody early Enlightenment fantasies about Chinese written characters (as so many silent pictures not linked to a system of phonetic sounds), as purveyed by, for example, Sir William Temple's "Of Heroick Virtue."

The other was a scheme for entirely abolishing all words whatsoever; and this was urged as a great advantage in point of health as well as brevity. For it is plain, that every word we speak is in some degree a diminution of our lungs by corrosion, and consequently contributes to the shortening of our lives. An expedient was therefore offered, that since words are only names for *things*, it would be more convenient for all men to carry about them such *things* as were necessary to express the particular business they are to discourse on. And this invention would certainly have taken place, to the great ease as well as health of the subject, if the women in conjunction with the vulgar and illiterate had not threatened to raise a rebellion, unless they might be allowed the liberty to speak with their tongues, after the manner of their forefathers; such constant irreconcilable enemies to science are the common people. However, many of the most learned and wise adhere to the new scheme of expressing themselves by *things*, which hath only this inconvenience attending it, that if a man's business be very great, and of various kinds, he must be obliged in proportion to carry a greater bundle of *things* upon his back, unless he can afford one or two strong servants to attend him. I have often beheld two of those sages almost sinking under the weight of their packs, like pedlars among us; who when they met in the streets would lay down their loads, open their sacks and hold conversation for an hour together; then put up their implements, help each other to resume their burthens, and take their leave.

But for short conversations a man may carry implements in his pockets and under his arms, enough to supply him, and in his house he cannot be at a loss; therefore the room where company meet who practise this art is full of all *things* ready at hand, requisite to furnish matter for this kind of artificial converse.

Another great advantage proposed by this invention was that it would serve as an universal language to be understood in all civilised nations, whose goods and utensils are generally of the same kind, or nearly resembling, so that their uses might easily be comprehended. And thus ambassadors would be qualified to treat with foreign princes or ministers of state to whose tongues they were utter strangers.

I was at the mathematical school, where the master taught his pupils after a method scarce imaginable to us in Europe. The proposition and demonstration were fairly written on a thin wafer, with ink composed of a cephalic tincture. This the student was to swallow upon a fasting stomach, and for three days following eat nothing but bread and water. As the wafer digested, the tincture mounted to his brain, bearing the proposition along

---

Cephalic tincture. Medicine for the head (Fox, 177).

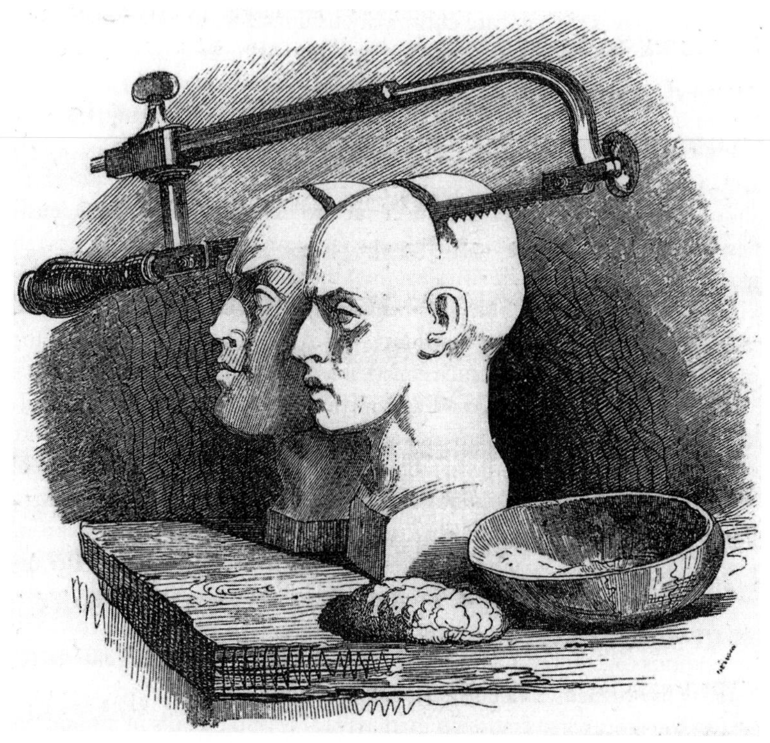

J. J. Grandville, *Cranial Surgery and Brain Exchange*, 1838.
THE BEINECKE RARE BOOK AND MANUSCRIPT LIBRARY, YALE UNIVERSITY.

with it. But the success hath not hitherto been answerable, partly by some error in the *quantum* or composition, and partly by the perverseness of lads, to whom this bolus is so nauseous that they generally steal aside, and discharge it upwards before it can operate; neither have they been yet persuaded to use so long an abstinence as the prescription requires.

CHAPTER VI

A further account of the Academy. The author proposes some improvements which are honourably received.

In the school of political projectors I was but ill entertained, the professors appearing in my judgment wholly out of their senses, which is a scene that never fails to make me melancholy. These unhappy people were proposing schemes for persuading monarchs to choose favourites upon the score of their wisdom, capacity and virtue; of teaching ministers to consult the public good; of rewarding merit, great abilities and eminent services; of instructing princes to know their true interest by placing it on the same foundation with that of their people: of choosing for employments persons qualified to exercise them; with many other wild impossible chimæras, that never entered before into the heart of man to conceive, and confirmed in me the old observation, that there is nothing so extravagant and irrational which some philosophers have not maintained for truth.

But, however, I shall so far do justice to this part of the Academy, as to acknowledge that all of them were not so visionary. There was a most ingenious doctor who seemed to be perfectly versed in the whole nature and system of government. This illustrious person had very usefully employed his studies in finding out effectual remedies for all diseases and corruptions to which the several kinds of public administration are subject by the vices or infirmities of those who govern, as well as by the licentiousness of those who are to obey. For instance: whereas all writers and reasoners have agreed, that there is a strict universal resemblance between the natural and the political body; can there be any thing more evident, than that the health of both must be preserved, and the diseases cured, by the same prescriptions? It is allowed that senates and great councils are often troubled with redundant, ebullient, and other peccant humours, with many diseases of the head, and more of the heart; with strong convulsions, with grievous contractions of the nerves and sinews in both hands, but especially the right; with spleen, flatus, vertigos and deliriums; with scrofulous tumours full of fœtid purulent matter; with sour frothy ructations, with canine appetites and crudeness of digestion, besides many others needless to mention. This doctor therefore proposed, that upon the meeting of a senate, certain physicians should attend at the three first days of their sitting, and, at the close of each day's debate, feel the pulses of every senator; after which, having maturely considered, and consulted upon the nature of the several maladies, and the methods of cure, they should on the fourth day return to the senate house, attended by their apothecaries stored with proper medicines, and before the members sat, administer to each of them lenitives, aperitives, abstersives, corrosives, restringents, palliatives, laxatives, cephalalgics, icterics, apophlegmatics, acoustics, as their several cases required; and according as these medicines should operate, repeat, alter, or omit them at the next meeting.

This project could not be of any great expense to the public, and might, in my poor opinion, be of much use for the dispatch of business in those countries where senates have any share in the legislative power, beget unanimity, shorten debates, open a few mouths which are now closed, and close many more which are now open; curb the petulancy of the young, and correct the positiveness of the old; rouse the stupid, and damp the pert.

Again, because it is a general complaint that the favourites of princes are troubled with short and weak memories, the same doctor proposed, that whoever attended a first minister, after having told his business with the utmost brevity, and in the plainest words, should at his departure give the said minister a tweak by the nose, or a kick in the belly, or tread on his corns, or lug him thrice by both ears, or run a pin into his breech, or pinch his arm black and blue, to prevent forgetfulness: and at every levee day repeat the same operation, till the business were done or absolutely refused.

He likewise directed, that every senator in the great council of a nation, after he had delivered his opinion, and argued in the defence of it, should be obliged to give his vote directly contrary; because if that were done, the result would infallibly terminate in the good of the public.

When parties in a state are violent, he offered a wonderful contrivance to reconcile them. The method is this. You take an hundred leaders of each party, you dispose them into couples of such whose heads are nearest of a size; then let two nice operators saw off the occiput of each couple at the same time, in such a manner that the brain may be equally divided. Let the occiputs thus cut off be interchanged, applying each to the head of his opposite party-man. It seems indeed to be a work that requireth some exactness, but the professor assured us, that if it were dextrously performed the cure would be infallible. For he argued thus; that the two half brains being left to debate the matter between themselves within the space of one skull, would soon come to a good understanding, and produce that moderation, as well as regularity of thinking, so much to be wished for in the heads of those who imagine they came into the world only to watch and govern its motion. and as to the difference of brains in quantity or quality, among those who are directors in faction, the doctor assured us from his own knowledge, that it was a perfect trifle.

I heard a very warm debate between two professors, about the most commodious and effectual ways and means of raising money without grieving the subject. The first affirmed the justest method would be to lay a certain tax upon vices and folly, and the sum fixed upon every man to be rated after the fairest manner by a jury of his neighbours. The second was of an opinion directly contrary, to tax those qualities of body and mind for which men chiefly value themselves, the rate to be more or less according to the degrees of excelling, the decision whereof should be left entirely to their own breast. The highest tax was upon men who are the greatest favourites of the other sex, and the assessments according to the number and natures of the favours they have received; for which they are allowed to be their own vouchers. Wit, valour, and politeness were likewise proposed to be largely taxed, and collected in the same manner, by every person's giving his own word for the quantum of what he possessed. But as to honour, justice, wisdom and learning, they should not be taxed at all, because they are qualifications of so singular a kind, that no man will either allow them in his neighbour, or value them in himself.

The women were proposed to be taxed according to their beauty and skill in dressing, wherein they had the same privilege with the men, to be determined by their own judgment. But constancy, chastity, good sense, and good nature were not rated, because they would not bear the charge of collecting.

To keep senators in the interest of the crown, it was proposed that the members should raffle for employments, every man first taking an oath, and giving security that he would vote for the court, whether he won or no, after which the losers had in their turn the liberty of raffling upon the next vacancy. Thus hope and expectation would be kept alive, none would complain of broken promises, but impute their disappointments wholly to Fortune, whose shoulders are broader and stronger than those of a ministry.

Another professor showed me a large paper of instructions for discovering plots and conspiracies against the government. He advised great statesmen to examine into the diet of all suspected persons; their times of eating; upon which side they lay in bed; with which hand they wiped their posteriors; to take a strict view of their excrements, and from the colour, the odour, the taste, the consistence, the crudeness or maturity of digestion, form a judgment of their thoughts and designs. Because men are never so serious, thoughtful, and intent, as when they are at stool, which he found by frequent experiment: for in such conjunctures, when he used merely as a trial to consider which was the best way of murdering the King, his ordure would have a tincture of green, but quite different when he thought only of raising an insurrection or burning the metropolis.

The whole discourse was written with great acuteness, containing many observations both curious and useful for politicians, but as I conceived not altogether complete. This I ventured to tell the author, and offered if he pleased to supply him with some additions. He received my proposition with more compliance than is usual among writers, especially those of the projecting species, professing he would be glad to receive farther information.

I told him, that in the kingdom of Tribnia, by the natives called Langden, where I had long sojourned, the bulk of the people consisted wholly of discoverers, witnesses, informers, accusers, prosecutors, evidences, swearers, together with their several subservient and subaltern instruments, all under the colours, the conduct, and pay of ministers and their deputies. The plots in that kingdom are usually the workmanship of those persons who desire to raise their own characters of profound politicians, to restore new vigour to a crazy administration, to stifle or divert general discontents, to fill their coffers with forfeitures, and raise or sink the opinion of public credit, as either shall best answer their private advantage. It is first agreed and settled among them what suspected persons shall be accused of a plot: then effectual care is taken to secure all their letters and other papers, and put the owners in chains. These papers are delivered to a set of artists, very dextrous in finding out the mysterious meanings of words, syllables, and letters. For instance, they can decipher a close-stool to signify a privy-council, a flock of geese a senate, a lame dog an invader, a codshead a _____, the plague a standing army, a buzzard a prime minister, the gout a high priest, a gibbet a secretary of state, a chamberpot a committee of grandees, a sieve a court lady, a broom a revolution, a mousetrap an employment, a bottomless pit the treasury, a sink a court, a cap and bells a favourite, a broken reed a court of justice, an empty tun a general, a running sore the administration.

When this method fails, they have two others more effectual, which the learned among them call acrostics and anagrams. First they can decipher all initial letters into political meanings. Thus N shall signify a plot, B a regiment of horse, L a fleet at sea. Or secondly by transposing the letters of the alphabet in any suspected paper, they can lay open the deepest designs of a discontented party. So, for example, if I should say in a letter to a friend, Our brother Tom has just got the piles, a man of skill in this art would discover how the same letters which compose that sentence may be analysed into the following words: Resist—a plot is brought home—the tour. And this is the anagrammatic method.

Opinion of public credit. Registered, as DeMaria points out, most importantly in the price of treasury bonds. A source of anxiety in the wake of the South Sea Bubble, which demonstrated that the entire system depended on public confidence in the credit-worthiness of the state.

The anagrammatic method. This passage—describing encoded writing in a world of secret plots—evokes the atmosphere of Jacobite intrigue surrounding figures such as Swift's associate Bolingbroke toward the end of Queen Anne's reign. Cryptography in such contexts was a tool of high politics, and Francis Atterbury was tried in 1721 on the basis of supposedly deciphered messages. Swift, a lover of word games and puns, also uses many anagram-like transpositions in the "little language" devised in the *Journal to Stella* to express particular intimacy with Esther Johnson.

The professor made me great acknowledgments for communicating these observations, and promised to make honourable mention of me in his treatise.

I saw nothing in this country that could invite me to a longer continuance, and began to think of returning home to England.

CHAPTER VII

The author leaves Lagado, arrives at Maldonada. No ship ready. He takes a short voyage to Glubbdubdrib. His reception by the Governor.

The continent of which this kingdom is a part extends itself, as I have reason to believe, eastward to that unknown tract of America, westward of California and north to the Pacific Ocean, which is not above an hundred and fifty miles from Lagado, where there is a good port and much commerce with the great island of Luggnagg, situated to the northwest about 29 degrees north latitude, and 140 longitude. This island of Luggnagg stands southeastwards of Japan, about an hundred leagues disstant. There is a strict alliance between the Japanese Emperor and the King of Luggnagg, which affords frequent opportunities of sailing from one island to the other. I determined therefore to direct my course this way in order to my return to Europe. I hired two mules with a guide to show me the way, and carry my small baggage. I took leave of my noble protector, who had shown me so much favour, and made me a generous present at my departure.

My journey was without any accident or adventure worth relating. When I arrived at the port of Maldonada (for so it is called) there was no ship in the harbour bound for Luggnagg, nor like to be in some time. The town is about as large as Portsmouth. I soon fell into some acquaintance, and was very hospitably received. A gentleman of distinction said to me, that since the ships bound for Luggnagg could not be ready in less than a month, it might be no disagreeable amusement for me to take a trip to the little island of Glubbdubdrib, about five leagues off to the southwest. He offered himself and a friend to accompany me, and that I should be provided with a small convenient barque for the voyage.

Glubbdubdrib, as nearly as I can interpret the word, signifies The Island of *Sorcerers* or *Magicians.* It is about one third as large as the Isle of Wight, and extremely fruitful: it is governed by the head of a certain tribe, who are all magicians. This tribe marries only among each other, and the eldest in succession is prince or governor. He hath a noble palace and a park of about three thousand acres, surrounded by a wall of hewn stone twenty foot high. In this park are several smaller inclosures for cattle, corn, and gardening.

The Governor and his family are served and attended by domestics of a kind somewhat unusual. By his skill in necromancy, he hath power of calling whom he pleaseth from the dead, and commanding their service for twenty-four hours, but no longer; nor can he call the same persons up again in less than three months, except upon very extraordinary occasions.

When we arrived at the island, which was about eleven in the morning, one of the gentlemen who accompanied me went to the Governor, and desired admittance for a stranger, who came on purpose to have the honour of attending on his Highness. This was immediately granted, and we all three entered the gate of the palace between two rows of guards, armed and dressed after a very antic manner, and something in their countenances that made my flesh creep with a horror I cannot express. We passed through several apartments between servants of the same sort, ranked on each side as before, till we came to the chamber of presence, where, after three profound obeisances, and a few general questions, we were permitted to sit on three stools near the lowest step of his Highness's throne. He understood the language of Balnibarbi, although it were different from that of his island. He desired me to give him some account of my travels; and to let me see that I should be treated without ceremony, he dismissed all his attendants with a turn of his finger, at which to my great astonishment they vanished in an instant, like visions in a dream, when we awake on a sudden. I could not recover my self in some time, till the Governor assured me that I should receive no hurt; and observing my two companions to be under no concern, who had been often entertained in the same manner, I began to take courage, and relate to his Highness a short history of my several adventures, yet not without some hesitation, and frequently looking behind me to the place where I had seen those domestic spectres. I had the honour to dine with the Governor, where a new set of ghosts served up the meat, and waited at table. I now observed my self to be less terrified than I had been in the morning. I stayed till sunset, but humbly desired his Highness to excuse me for not accepting his invitation of lodging in the palace. My two friends and I lay at a private house in the town adjoining, which is the capital of this little island; and the next morning we returned to pay our duty to the Governor, as he was pleased to command us.

After this manner we continued in the island for ten days, most part of every day with the Governor, and at night in our lodging. I soon grew so familiarized to the sight of spirits, that after the third or fourth time they gave me no emotion at all; or if I had any apprehensions left, my curiosity prevailed over them. For his Highness the Governor ordered me to call up whatever persons I would choose to name, and in whatever numbers among all the dead from the beginning of the world to the present time, and command them to answer any questions I should think fit to ask; with this condition, that my questions must be confined within the compass of the times they lived in. And one thing I might depend upon, that they would certainly tell me truth, for lying was a talent of no use in the lower world.

I made my humble acknowledgements to his Highness for so great a favour. We were in a chamber, from whence there was a fair prospect into the park. And because my first inclination was to be entertained with scenes of pomp and magnificence, I desired to see Alexander the Great, at the head of his army just after the battle of Arbela, which upon a motion of the Governor's finger immediately appeared in a large field under the window, where we stood. Alexander was called up into the room: it was with great difficulty that I understood his Greek, and had but little of my own. He assured me upon his honour that he was not poisoned, but died of a fever by excessive drinking.

Next I saw Hannibal passing the Alps, who told me he had not a drop of vinegar in his camp.

I saw Cæsar and Pompey at the head of their troops, just ready to engage. I saw the former in his last great triumph. I desired that the Senate of Rome might appear before me in one large chamber, and a modern representative in counterview in another. The first seemed to be an assembly of heroes and demigods; the other a knot of pedlars, pickpockets, highwaymen and bullies.

The Governor at my request gave the sign for Cæsar and Brutus to advance towards us. I was struck with a profound veneration at the sight of Brutus, and could easily discover the most consummate virtue, the

---

Alexander the Great. 356–23 B.C. The mightiest conqueror of ancient times. The bloody "greatness" of such figures was frequently scrutinized with bemusement by Swift and his fellow Scriblerians Alexander Pope and John Gay.

Brutus. Marcus Junius Brutus (85–42 B.C.) led the conspiracy that succeeded in assassinating Julius Caesar on March 15, 44 B.C. Swift, who admired Brutus for sacrificing private friendship to the struggle against tyranny, may have adopted his initials in fabricating his pseudonym, M. B. Drapier. See Bertelsen.

greatest intrepidity and firmness of mind, the truest love of his country and general benevolence for mankind in every lineament of his countenance. I observed with much pleasure that these two persons were in good intelligence with each other, and Cæsar freely confessed to me, that the greatest actions of his own life were not equal by many degrees to the glory of taking it away. I had the honour to have much conversation with Brutus; and was told, that his ancestor Junius, Socrates, Epaminondas, Cato the younger, Sir Thomas More and himself were perpetually together: a *sextumvirate* to which all the ages of the world cannot add a seventh.

It would be tedious to trouble the reader with relating what vast numbers of illustrious persons were called up, to gratify that insatiable desire I had to see the world in every period of antiquity placed before me. I chiefly fed my eyes with beholding the destroyers of tyrants and usurpers, and the restorers of liberty to oppressed and injured nations. But it is impossible to express the satisfaction I received in my own mind, after such a manner as to make it a suitable entertainment to the reader.

CHAPTER VIII

A further account of Glubbdubdrib. Ancient and modern history corrected.

Having a desire to see those ancients who were most renowned for wit and learning, I set apart one day on purpose. I proposed that Homer and Aristotle might appear at the head of all their commentators; but these were so numerous that some hundreds were forced to attend in the court and outward rooms of the palace. I knew and could distinguish those two heroes at first sight, not only from the crowd, but from each other. Homer was the taller and comelier person of the two, walked very erect for one of his age, and his eyes were the most quick and piercing I ever beheld. Aristotle

---

Sir Thomas More. A Catholic hero and saint. Sir Thomas More (1478–1535), as Asimov observes, was the sole modern that Swift allowed to enter this company of hallowed ancients. More adhered to his faith, refusing to acknowledge Henry VIII as the head of the English church, and was duly beheaded for his principles. Swift referred to More as the "only Man of Virtue that England ever produced." More wrote *Utopia* (1516), mentioned on p. 41.

stooped much, and made use of a staff. His visage was meager, his hair lank and thin, and his voice hollow. I soon discovered that both of them were perfect strangers to the rest of the company, and had never seen or heard of them before. And I had a whisper from a ghost, who shall be nameless, that these commentators always kept in the most distant quarters from their principals in the lower world, through a consciousness of shame and guilt, because they had so horribly misrepresented the meaning of those authors to posterity. I introduced Didymus and Eustathius to Homer, and prevailed on him to treat them better than perhaps they deserved, for he soon found they wanted a genius to enter into the spirit of a poet. But Aristotle was out of all patience with the account I gave him of Scotus and Ramus, as I presented them to him, and he asked them whether the rest of the tribe were as great dunces as themselves.

I then desired the Governor to call up Descartes and Gassendi, with whom I prevailed to explain their systems to Aristotle. This great philosopher freely acknowledged his own mistakes in natural philosophy, because he proceeded in many things upon conjecture, as all men must do; and he found that Gassendi, who had made the doctrine of Epicurus as palatable as he could, and the *vortices* of Descartes, were equally exploded. He predicted the same fate to *attraction*, whereof the present learned are such zealous asserters. He said, that new systems of nature were but new fashions, which would vary in every age; and even those who pretend to demonstrate them from mathematical principles would flourish but a short period of time, and be out of vogue when that was determined.

I spent five days in conversing with many others of the ancient learned. I saw most of the first Roman emperors. I prevailed on the Governor to call up Eliogabalus's cooks to dress us a dinner, but they could not show us much of their skill, for want of materials. A helot of Agesilaus made us a dish of Spartan broth, but I was not able to get down a second spoonful.

The two gentlemen who conducted me to the island were pressed by their private affairs to return in three days, which I employed in seeing some of the modern dead who had made the greatest figure for two or three hundred years past in our own and other countries of Europe; and having been always a great admirer of old illustrious families, I desired the Governor would call up a dozen or two of kings with their ancestors in order for eight or nine generations. But my disappointment was grievous and unexpected. For instead of a long train with royal diadems, I saw in one family,

---

As great dunces. Aristotle makes a pun on Duns Scotus, from whose name the word *dunce* is derived. Scotus was a medieval scholastic philosopher.

two fiddlers, three spruce courtiers, and an Italian prelate. In another, a barber, an abbot, and two cardinals. I have too great a veneration for crowned heads to dwell any longer on so nice a subject. But as to counts, marquesses, dukes, earls, and the like, I was not so scrupulous. And I confess it was not without some pleasure that I found my self able to trace the particular features, by which certain families are distinguished, up to their originals. I could plainly discover from whence one family derives a long chin, why a second hath abounded with knaves for two generations, and fools for two more; why a third happened to be crack-brained, and a fourth to be sharpers. Whence it came what Polydore Virgil says of a certain great house, *Nec vir fortis, nec fœmina casta.* How cruelty, falsehood, and cowardice grew to be characteristics by which certain families are distinguished as much as by their coat of arms. Who first brought the pox into a noble house, which hath lineally descended in scrofulous tumours to their posterity. Neither could I wonder at all this, when I saw such an interruption of lineages by pages, lackeys, valets, coachmen, gamesters, fiddlers, players, captains, and pickpockets.

I was chiefly disgusted with modern history. For having strictly examined all the persons of greatest name in the courts of princes for an hundred years past, I found how the world had been misled by prostitute writers, to ascribe the greatest exploits in war to cowards, the wisest counsel to fools, sincerity to flatterers, Roman virtue to betrayers of their country, piety to atheists, chastity to sodomites, truth to informers. How many innocent and excellent persons had been condemned to death or banishment, by the practising of great ministers upon the corruption of judges, and the malice of factions. How many villains had been exalted to the highest places of trust, power, dignity, and profit: how great a share in the motions and events of courts, councils, and senates might be challenged by bawds, whores, pimps, parasites, and buffoons: how low an opinion I had of human wisdom and integrity, when I was truly informed of the springs and motives of great enterprises and revolutions in the world, and of the contemptible accidents to which they owed their success.

Here I discovered the roguery and ignorance of those who pretend to write *anecdotes,* or secret history, who send so many kings to their graves with a cup of poison; will repeat the discourse between a prince and chief

---

Secret history. A historiographical genre of breathless anecdotes purporting to give an "insider's story." Probably glancing here at Bishop Gilbert Burnett's *History of My Own Time* (1723), a scandal-mongering book attacking the Stuarts by a propagandist for William III. Swift called him "the most partial of all writers that ever pretended to impartiality."

minister, where no witness was by; unlock the thoughts and cabinets of ambassadors and secretaries of state, and have the perpetual misfortune to be mistaken. Here I discovered the true causes of many great events that have surprised the world, how a whore can govern the back-stairs, the back-stairs a council, and the council a senate. A general confessed in my presence, that he got a victory purely by the force of cowardice and ill conduct: and an admiral that for want of proper intelligence, he beat the enemy to whom he intended to betray the fleet. Three kings protested to me, that in their whole reigns they did never once prefer any person of merit, unless by mistake or treachery of some minister in whom they confided: neither would they do it if they were to live again; and they showed with great strength of reason, that the royal throne could not be supported without corruption, because that positive, confident, restive temper, which virtue infused into man, was a perpetual clog to public business.

I had the curiosity to enquire in a particular manner, by what method great numbers had procured to themselves high titles of honour, and prodigious estates; and I confined my enquiry to a very modern period: however, without grating upon present times, because I would be sure to give no offence even to foreigners (for I hope the reader need not be told that I do not in the least intend my own country in what I say upon this occasion) a great number of persons concerned were called up, and upon a very slight examination, discovered such a scene of infamy, that I cannot reflect upon it without some seriousness. Perjury, oppression, subornation, fraud, pandarism, and the like infirmities, were amongst the most excusable arts they had to mention, and for these I gave, as it was reasonable, due allowance. But when some confessed they owed their greatness and wealth to sodomy or incest, others to the prostituting of their own wives and daughters; others to the betraying their country or their prince; some to poisoning, more to the perverting of justice in order to destroy the innocent: I hope I may be pardoned if these discoveries inclined me a little to abate of that profound veneration which I am naturally apt to pay to persons of high rank, who ought to be treated with the utmost respect due to their sublime dignity, by us their inferiors.

I had often read of some great services done to princes and states, and desired to see the persons by whom those services were performed. Upon enquiry I was told that their names were to be found on no record, except a few of them whom history hath represented as the vilest rogues and traitors. As to the rest, I had never once heard of them. They all appeared with dejected looks, and in the meanest habit, most of them telling me they died in poverty and disgrace, and the rest on a scaffold or a gibbet.

Among others there was one person whose case appeared a little singular. He had a youth about eighteen years old standing by his side. He told me he had for many years been commander of a ship, and in the sea fight at Actium had the good fortune to break through the enemy's great line of battle, sink three of their capital ships, and take a fourth, which was the sole cause of Antony's flight, and of the victory that ensued; that the youth standing by him, his only son, was killed in the action. He added, that upon the confidence of some merit, the war being at an end, he went to Rome, and solicited at the court of Augustus to be preferred to a greater ship, whose commander had been killed; but without any regard to his pretensions, it was given to a boy who had never seen the sea, the son of a Libertina, who waited on one of the Emperor's mistresses. Returning back to his own vessel, he was charged with neglect of duty, and the ship given to a favourite page of Publicola the Vice-Admiral; whereupon he retired to a poor farm, at a great distance from Rome, and there ended his life. I was so curious to know the truth of this story, that I desired Agrippa might be called, who was admiral in that fight. He appeared and confirmed the whole account, but with much more advantage to the captain, whose modesty had extenuated or concealed a great part of his merit.

I was surprised to find corruption grown so high and so quick in that empire, by the force of luxury so lately introduced, which made me less wonder at many parallel cases in other countries, where vices of all kinds have reigned so much longer, and where the whole praise as well as pillage hath been engrossed by the chief commander, who perhaps had the least title to either.

As every person called up made exactly the same appearance he had done in the world, it gave me melancholy reflections to observe how much the race of human kind was degenerate among us, within these hundred years past. How the pox under all its consequences and denominations had altered every lineament of an English countenance, shortened the size of bodies, unbraced the nerves, relaxed the sinews and muscles, introduced a sallow complexion, and rendered the flesh loose and rancid.

I descended so low as to desire that some English yeomen of the old stamp might be summoned to appear, once so famous for the simplicity of

---

Court of Augustus. Despite platitudes about the "Augustan Age," this unflattering story is specifically *anti*-Augustan. Swift's classicism was republican, and he admired neither Roman nor British imperialism. See Erskine-Hill, 57.

Chief commander. Glancing again at Marlborough, roasted by Swift in *Examiner* 16 and elsewhere. Though Marlborough had died in 1722, Blenheim Palace remained as a monument both to military glory and its considerable material rewards.

English yeomen of the old stamp. For a civic republican, the repositories of national virtue.

their manners, diet and dress, for justice in their dealings, for their true spirit of liberty, for their valour and love of their country. Neither could I be wholly unmoved after comparing the living with the dead, when I considered how all these pure native virtues were prostituted for a piece of money by their grandchildren, who in selling their votes, and managing at elections, have acquired every vice and corruption that can possibly be learned in a court.

CHAPTER IX

The author's return to Maldonada. Sails to the kingdom of Luggnagg. The author confined. He is sent for to court. The manner of his admittance. The King's great lenity to his subjects.

The day of our departure being come, I took leave of his Highness the Governor of Glubbdubdrib, and returned with my two companions to Maldonada, where after a fortnight's waiting, a ship was ready to sail for Luggnagg. The two gentlemen and some others were so generous and kind as to furnish me with provisions, and see me on board. I was a month in this voyage. We had one violent storm, and were under a necessity of steering westward to get into the trade wind, which holds for above sixty leagues. On the 21st of April, 1709, we sailed in the river of Clumegnig, which is a seaport town, at the southeast point of Luggnagg. We cast anchor within a league of the town, and made a signal for a pilot. Two of them came on board in less than half an hour, by whom we were guided between certain shoals and rocks, which are very dangerous in the passage, to a large basin, where a fleet may ride in safety within a cable's length of the town wall.

Some of our sailors, whether out of treachery or inadvertence, had informed the pilots that I was a stranger and a great traveller, whereof these gave notice to a custom-house officer, by whom I was examined very strictly upon my landing. This officer spoke to me in the language of Balnibarbi, which by the force of much commerce is generally understood in that town, especially by seamen, and those employed in the customs. I gave him a short account of some particulars, and made my story as plausible and consistent as I could; but I thought it necessary to disguise my country, and call my self a Hollander, because my intentions were for Japan, and

I knew the Dutch were the only Europeans permitted to enter into that kingdom. I therefore told the officer, that having been shipwrecked on the coast of Balnibarbi, and cast on a rock, I was received up into Laputa, or the Flying Island (of which he had often heard) and was now endeavouring to get to Japan, from whence I might find a convenience of returning to my own country. The officer said I must be confined till he could receive orders from court, for which he would write immediately, and hoped to receive an answer in a fortnight. I was carried to a convenient lodging, with a sentry placed at the door; however I had the liberty of a large garden, and was treated with humanity enough, being maintained all the time at the King's charge. I was visited by several persons, chiefly out of curiosity, because it was reported I came from countries very remote of which they had never heard.

I hired a young man who came in the same ship to be an interpreter; he was a native of Luggnagg, but had lived some years at Maldonada, and was a perfect master of both languages. By his assistance I was able to hold a conversation with those that came to visit me; but this consisted only of their questions, and my answers.

The dispatch came from court about the time we expected. It contained a warrant for conducting me and my retinue to Traldragdubh or Trildrogdrib, for it is pronounced both ways as near as I can remember, by a party of ten horse. All my retinue was that poor lad for an interpreter, whom I persuaded into my service. At my humble request, we had each of us a mule to ride on. A messenger was dispatched half a day's journey before us, to give the King notice of my approach, and to desire that his Majesty would please to appoint a day and hour, when it would be his gracious pleasure that I might have the honour to "lick the dust before his footstool." This is the court style, and I found it to be more than matter of form. For upon my admittance two days after my arrival, I was commanded to crawl up on my belly, and lick the floor as I advanced; but on account of my being a stranger, care was taken to have it so clean that the

---

Dutch were the only Europeans permitted to enter into that kingdom. In 1637 Japan had begun to persecute Portuguese missionaries and their Japanese converts. In their attempt to ferret out hidden Christians, Japanese officials imposed an annual desecration ritual on those under suspicion: the *Fumie,* a ceremonial trampling of bronze plaques bearing Christian icons. For two centuries thereafter, Japan closed its ports and remained self-secluded. The single exception to this policy of isolation was the periodic access permitted to Dutch East India traders on the island of Deshima in the harbor of Nagasaki (Jansen, 75–85).

Lick the dust before his footstool. Oriental potentates were often described as exacting extreme forms of deference. This may also be an image of Irish Protestants kowtowing to the hardline Protestant myth of William III as the liberator of Ireland. *Lough Neagh,* a lake in Ulster province, may have suggested *Luggnagg.* See Gardener, 35–39.

dust was not offensive. However, this was a peculiar grace, not allowed to any but persons of the highest rank, when they desire an admittance. Nay, sometimes the floor is strewed with dust on purpose, when the person to be admitted happens to have powerful enemies at court. And I have seen a great lord with his mouth so crammed, that when he had crept to the proper distance from the throne, he was not able to speak a word. Neither is there any remedy, because it is capital for those who receive an audience to spit or wipe their mouths in his Majesty's presence. There is indeed another custom, which I cannot altogether approve of. When the King hath a mind to put any of his nobles to death in a gentle indulgent manner, he commands to have the floor strowed with a certain brown powder, of a deadly composition, which being licked up infallibly kills him in twenty-four hours. But in justice to this prince's great clemency, and the care he hath of his subjects' lives (wherein it were much to be wished that the monarchs of Europe would imitate him) it must be mentioned for his honour, that strict orders are given to have the infected parts of the floor well washed after every such execution, which if his domestics neglect, they are in danger of incurring his royal displeasure. I my self heard him give directions, that one of his pages should be whipped, whose turn it was to give notice about washing the floor after an execution, but maliciously had omitted it, by which neglect a young lord of great hopes coming to an audience, was unfortunately poisoned, although the King at that time had no design against his life. But this good prince was so gracious as to forgive the page his whipping, upon promise that he would do so no more, without special orders.

To return from this digression; when I had crept within four yards of the throne, I raised my self gently upon my knees, and then striking my forehead seven times against the ground, I pronounced the following words, as they had been taught me the night before, *Ickpling gloffthrobb squutserumm blhiop mlashnalt, zwin tnodbalkguffh slhiophad gurdlubh asht.* This is the compliment established by the laws of the land for all persons admitted to the King's presence. It may be rendered into English thus: May your Cœlestial Majesty outlive the sun, eleven moons and an half. To this the King returned some answer, which although I could not understand, yet I replied as I had been directed: *Fluft drin yalerick dwuldum prastrad mirplush,* which properly signifies, My tongue is in the mouth of my friend, and by this expression was meant that I desired leave to bring my interpreter; whereupon the young man already mentioned was accordingly introduced, by whose intervention I answered as many questions as his Majesty could put in above an hour. I spoke in the Balnibarbian tongue, and my interpreter delivered my meaning in that of Luggnagg.

The King was much delighted with my company, and ordered his *Bliff-marklub* or high chamberlain to appoint a lodging in the court for me and my interpreter, with a daily allowance for my table, and a large purse of gold for my common expenses.

I stayed three months in this country out of perfect obedience to his Majesty, who was pleased highly to favour me, and made me very honourable offers. But I thought it more consistent with prudence and justice to pass the remainder of my days with my wife and family.

CHAPTER X

The Luggnaggians commended. A particular description of the struldbruggs, with many conversations between the author and some eminent persons upon that subject.

The Luggnaggians are a polite and generous people, and although they are not without some share of that pride which is peculiar to all eastern countries, yet they show themselves courteous to strangers, especially such who are countenanced by the court. I had many acquaintance among persons of the best fashion, and being always attended by my interpreter, the conversation we had was not disagreeable.

One day in much good company I was asked by a person of quality, whether I had seen any of their *struldbruggs* or *immortals.* I said I had not, and desired he would explain to me what he meant by such an appellation applied to a mortal creature. He told me, that sometimes, although very rarely, a child happened to be born in a family with a red circular spot in the forehead, directly over the left eyebrow, which was an infallible mark that it should never die. The spot, as he described it, was about the compass of a silver three pence, but in the course of time grew larger, and changed its colour; for at twelve years old it became green, so continued till five and twenty, then turned to a deep blue; at five and forty it grew coal black, and as large as an English shilling, but never admitted any farther alteration. He said these births were so rare, that he did not believe there could be above eleven hundred *struldbruggs* of both sexes in the whole kingdom, of which he computed about fifty in the metropolis, and among the rest a young girl born about three years ago. That these productions were not peculiar to any family, but a mere effect of chance, and the children of the *struldbruggs* themselves were equally mortal with the rest of the people.

I freely own my self to have been struck with inexpressible delight upon hearing this account: and the person who gave it me happening to understand the Balnibarbian language, which I spoke very well, I could not forbear breaking out into expressions perhaps a little too extravagant. I cried out as in a rapture: Happy nation where every child hath at least a chance for being immortal! Happy people who enjoy so many living examples of ancient virtue, and have masters ready to instruct them in the wisdom of all former ages! But happiest beyond all comparison are those excellent *struldbruggs*, who being born exempt from that universal calamity of human nature, have their minds free and disengaged, without the weight and depression of spirits caused by the continual apprehension of death. I discovered my admiration that I had not observed any of these illustrious persons at court, the black spot on the forehead being so remarkable a distinction, that I could not have easily overlooked it and it was impossible that his Majesty, a most judicious prince, should not provide himself with a good number of such wise and able counsellors. Yet perhaps the virtue of those reverend sages was too strict for the corrupt and libertine manners of a court. And we often find by experience that young men are too opinionative and volatile to be guided by the sober dictates of their seniors. However, since the King was pleased to allow me access to his royal person, I was resolved upon the very first occasion to deliver my opinion to him on this matter freely, and at large by the help of my interpreter; and whether he would please to take my advice or no, yet in one thing I was determined, that his Majesty having frequently offered me an establishment in this country, I would with great thankfulness accept the favour, and pass my life here in the conversation of those superior beings the *struldbruggs*, if they would please to admit me.

The gentleman to whom I addressed my discourse, because (as I have already observed) he spoke the language of Balnibarbi, said to me with a sort of a smile, which usually ariseth from pity to the ignorant, that he was glad of any occasion to keep me among them, and desired my permission to explain to the company what I had spoke. He did so, and they talked together for some time in their own language, whereof I understood not a syllable, neither could I observe by their countenances what impression my discourse had made on them. After a short silence the same person told me, that his friends and mine (so he thought fit to express himself) were very much pleased with the judicious remarks I had made on the great happiness and advantages of immortal life, and they were desirous to know in a particular manner, what scheme of living I should have formed to my self, if it had fallen to my lot to have been born a *struldbrugg*.

I answered, it was easy to be eloquent on so copious and delightful a subject, especially to me who have been often apt to amuse my self with visions of what I should do if I were a king, a general, or a great lord; and upon this very case I had frequently run over the whole system how I should employ my self and pass the time if I were sure to live for ever.

That if it had been my good fortune to come into the world a *struldbrugg,* as soon as I could discover my own happiness by understanding the difference between life and death, I would first resolve by all arts and methods whatsoever to procure my self riches. In the pursuit of which by thrift and management, I might reasonably expect in about two hundred years to be the wealthiest man in the kingdom. In the second place, I would from my earliest youth apply myself to the study of arts and sciences, by which I should arrive in time to excel all others in learning. Lastly, I would carefully record every action and event of consequence that happened in the public, impartially draw the characters of the several successions of princes, and great ministers of state, with my own observations on every point. I would exactly set down the several changes in customs, languages, fashions of dress, diet and diversions. By all which acquirements, I should be a living treasury of knowledge and wisdom, and certainly become the oracle of the nation.

I would never marry after threescore, but live in an hospitable manner, yet still on the saving side. I would entertain myself in forming and directing the minds of hopeful young men, by convincing them from my own remembrance, experience and observation, fortified by numerous examples, of the usefulness of virtue in public and private life. But my choice and constant companions should be a set of my own immortal brotherhood, among whom I would elect a dozen from the most ancient down to my own contemporaries. Where any of these wanted fortunes, I would provide them with convenient lodges round my own estate, and have some of them always at my table, only mingling a few of the most valuable among you mortals, whom length of time would harden me to lose with little or no reluctance, and treat your posterity after the same manner, just as a man diverts himself with the annual succession of pinks and tulips in his garden, without regretting the loss of those which withered the preceding year.

These *struldbruggs* and I would mutually communicate our observations and memorials through the course of time, remark the several gradations by which corruption steals into the world, and oppose it in every step, by giving perpetual warning and instruction to mankind; which, added to the strong influence of our own example, would probably prevent that continual degeneracy of human nature so justly complained of in all ages.

Add to all this, the pleasure of seeing the various revolutions of states and empires, the changes in the lower and upper world, ancient cities in ruins, and obscure villages become the seats of kings. Famous rivers lessening into shallow brooks, the ocean leaving one coast dry, and overwhelming another; the discovery of many countries yet unknown. Barbarity overrunning the politest nations, and the most barbarous becoming civilized. I should then see the discovery of the longitude, the perpetual motion, the universal medicine, and many other great inventions brought to the utmost perfection.

What wonderful discoveries should we make in astronomy, by outliving and confirming our own predictions, by observing the progress and returns of comets, with the changes of motion in the sun, moon and stars.

I enlarged upon many other topics which the natural desire of endless life and sublunary happiness could easily furnish me with. When I had ended, and the sum of my discourse had been interpreted as before to the rest of the company, there was a good deal of talk among them in the language of the country, not without some laughter at my expense. At last the same gentleman who had been my interpreter said, he was desired by the rest to set me right in a few mistakes, which I had fallen into through the common imbecility of human nature, and upon that allowance was less answerable for them. That this breed of *struldbruggs* was peculiar to their country, for there were no such people either in Balnibarbi or Japan, where he had the honour to be ambassador from his Majesty, and found the natives in both those kingdoms very hard to believe that the fact was possible, and it appeared from my astonishment when he first mentioned the matter to me, that I received it as a thing wholly new, and scarcely to be credited. That in the two kingdoms above mentioned, where during his residence he had conversed very much, he observed long life to be the universal desire and wish of mankind. That whoever had one foot in the grave was sure to hold back the other as strongly as he could. That the oldest had still hopes of living one day longer, and looked on death as the greatest evil, from which nature always prompted him to retreat; only in this island of Luggnagg the appetite for living was not so eager, from the continual example of the *struldbruggs* before their eyes.

That the system of living contrived by me was unreasonable and unjust, because it supposed a perpetuity of youth, health, and vigour, which no

---

Longitude . . . perfection. To determine longitude at sea was considered impossible in the earlier eighteenth century. For a popular account of how John Harrison (1693–1776), a master clock maker, spent a lifetime solving this problem, see Sobel. Harrison's breakthrough, marine chronometer H4, was finished in 1759. H4, about the size of a very large pocketwatch, can be seen at the National Maritime Museum in Greenwich.

man could be so foolish to hope, however extravagant he might be in his wishes. That the question therefore was not whether a man would choose to be always in the prime of youth, attended with prosperity and health, but how he would pass a perpetual life under all the usual disadvantages which old age brings along with it. For although few men will avow their desires of being immortal upon such hard conditions, yet in the two kingdoms before-mentioned of Balnibarbi and Japan, he observed that every man desired to put off death for some time longer, let it approach ever so late, and he rarely heard of any man who died willingly, except he were incited by the extremity of grief or torture. And he appealed to me whether in those countries I had travelled, as well as my own, I had not observed the same general disposition.

After this preface he gave me a particular account of the *struldbruggs* among them. He said they commonly acted like mortals, till about thirty years old, after which by degrees they grew melancholy and dejected, increasing in both till they came to fourscore. This he learned from their own confession; for otherwise there not being above two or three of that species born in an age, they were too few to form a general observation by. When they came to fourscore years, which is reckoned the extremity of living in this country, they had not only all the follies and infirmities of other old men, but many more which arose from the dreadful prospect of never dying. They were not only opinionative, peevish, covetous, morose, vain, talkative, but uncapable of friendship, and dead to all natural affection, which never descended below their grandchildren. Envy and impotent desires are their prevailing passions. But those objects against which their envy seems principally directed, are the vices of the younger sort, and the deaths of the old. By reflecting on the former, they find themselves cut off from all possibility of pleasure; and whenever they see a funeral, they lament and repine that others are gone to an harbour of rest, to which they themselves never can hope to arrive. They have no remembrance of any thing but what they learned and observed in their youth and middle age, and even that is very imperfect. And for the truth or particulars of any fact, it is safer to depend on common traditions than upon their best recollections. The least miserable among them appear to be those who turn to dotage and entirely lose their memories; these meet with more pity and assistance, because they want many bad qualities which abound in others.

If a *struldbrugg* happen to marry one of his own kind, the marriage is dissolved of course by the courtesy of the kingdom, as soon as the younger of the two comes to be fourscore. For the law thinks it a reasonable indulgence, that those who are condemned without any fault of their own to a perpetual continuance in the world, should not have their misery doubled by the load of a wife.

As soon as they have completed the term of eighty years, they are looked on as dead in law; their heirs immediately succeed to their estates, only a small pittance is reserved for their support, and the poor ones are maintained at the public charge. After that period they are held incapable of any employment of trust or profit; they cannot purchase lands or take leases, neither are they allowed to be witnesses in any cause, either civil or criminal, not even for the decision of meers and bounds.

At ninety they lose their teeth and hair, they have at that age no distinction of taste, but eat and drink whatever they can get, without relish or appetite. The diseases they were subject to still continue without encreasing or diminishing. In talking they forget the common appellation of things, and the names of persons, even of those who are their nearest friends and relations. For the same reason they never can amuse themselves with reading, because their memory will not serve to carry them from the beginning of a sentence to the end; and by this defect they are deprived of the only entertainment whereof they might otherwise be capable.

The language of this country being always upon the flux, the *struldbruggs* of one age do not understand those of another, neither are they able after two hundred years to hold any conversation (farther than by a few general words) with their neighbours the mortals, and thus they lie under the disadvantage of living like foreigners in their own country.

This was the account given me of the *struldbruggs,* as near as I can remember. I afterwards saw five or six of different ages, the youngest not above two hundred years old, who were brought to me at several times by some of my friends; but although they were told that I was a great traveller, and had seen all the world, they had not the least curiosity to ask me a question; only desired I would give them *slumskudask,* or a token of remembrance, which is a modest way of begging, to avoid the law that strictly forbids it, because they are provided for by the public, although indeed with a very scanty allowance.

They are despised and hated by all sorts of people; when one of them is born, it is reckoned ominous, and their birth is recorded very particularly; so that you may know their age by consulting the registry, which however hath not been kept above a thousand years past, or at least hath been destroyed by time or public disturbances. But the usual way of computing how old they are, is by asking them what kings or great persons they can remember, and then consulting history, for infallibly the last prince in their mind did not begin his reign after they were fourscore years old.

They were the most mortifying sight I ever beheld, and the women more horrible than the men. Besides the usual deformities in extreme old age, they acquired an additional ghastliness in proportion to their number of years, which is not to be described, and among half a dozen I soon distinguished which was the eldest, although there was not above a century or two between them.

The reader will easily believe, that from what I had heard and seen, my keen appetite for perpetuity of life was much abated. I grew heartily ashamed of the pleasing visions I had formed, and thought no tyrant could invent a death into which I would not run with pleasure from such a life. The King heard of all that had passed between me and my friends upon this occasion, and rallied me very pleasantly, wishing I would send a couple of *struldbruggs* to my own country, to arm our people against the fear of death; but this it seems is forbidden by the fundamental laws of the kingdom, or else I should have been well content with the trouble and expense of transporting them.

I could not but agree that the laws of this kingdom, relating to the *struldbruggs,* were founded upon the strongest reasons, and such as any other country would be under the necessity of enacting in the like circumstances. Otherwise, as avarice is the necessary consequent of old age, those immortals would in time become proprietors of the whole nation, and engross the civil power, which, for want of abilities to manage, must end in the ruin of the public.

CHAPTER XI

The author leaves Luggnagg and sails to Japan. From thence he returns in a Dutch ship to Amsterdam, and from Amsterdam to England.

I thought this account of the *struldbruggs* might be some entertainment to the reader, because it seems to be a little out of the common way, at least, I do not remember to have met the like in any book of travels that hath come to my hands: and if I am deceived, my excuse must be, that it is necessary for travellers who describe the same country very often to agree in dwelling on the same particulars, without deserving the censure of having borrowed or transcribed from those who wrote before them.

There is indeed a perpetual commerce between this kingdom and the great empire of Japan, and it is very probable that the Japanese authors may have given some account of the *struldbruggs;* but my stay in Japan was so short, and I was so entirely a stranger to the language, that I was not qualified to make any enquiries. But I hope the Dutch upon this notice will be curious and able enough to supply my defects.

His Majesty having often pressed me to accept some employment in his court, and finding me absolutely determined to return to my native country, was pleased to give me his licence to depart, and honoured me with a letter of recommendation under his own hand to the Emperor of Japan. He likewise presented me with four hundred forty-four large pieces of gold (this nation delighting in even numbers) and a red diamond which I sold in England for eleven hundred pounds.

On the 6th day of May, 1709, I took a solemn leave of his Majesty, and all my friends. This prince was so gracious as to order a guard to conduct me to Glanguenstald, which is a royal port to the southwest part of the island. In six days I found a vessel ready to carry me to Japan, and spent fifteen days in the voyage. We landed at a small port-town called Xamoschi, situated on the southeast part of Japan; the town lies on the western part where there is a narrow strait, leading northward into a long arm of the sea, upon the northwest part of which Yedo, the metropolis stands. At landing I showed the custom-house officers my letter from the King of Luggnagg to his Imperial Majesty. They knew the seal perfectly well; it was as broad as the palm of my hand. The impression was, *a king lifting up a lame beggar from the earth.* The magistrates of the town, hearing of my letter, received me as a public minister; they provided me with carriages and servants, and bore my charges to Yedo, where I was admitted to an audience, and delivered my letter, which was opened with great ceremony, and explained to the Emperor by an interpreter, who gave me notice of his Majesty's order, that I should signify my request, and whatever it were, it should be granted for the sake of his royal brother of Luggnagg. This interpreter was a person employed to transact affairs with the Hollanders; he soon conjectured by my countenance that I was an European, and therefore repeated his Majesty's commands in Low Dutch, which he spoke perfectly well. I answered (as I had before determined) that I was a Dutch merchant, ship-wrecked in a very remote country, from whence I travelled by sea and land to Luggnagg, and then took shipping for Japan, where I knew my countrymen often traded, and with some of these I hoped to get an opportunity of returning into Europe: I therefore most humbly

---

Xamoschi. A syllabic scrambling of Shimosa or Ximosa, shown in this location on maps of Japan by Sanson and Moll. See Shimada, 33.

Yedo. Tokyo.

Low Dutch. Dutch, as opposed to what was called High Dutch, or German (Fox, 201).

entreated his royal favour to give order, that I should be conducted in safety to Nangasac: to this I added another petition, that for the sake of my patron the King of Luggnagg, his Majesty would condescend to excuse my performing the ceremony imposed on my countrymen of *trampling upon the crucifix,* because I had been thrown into his kingdom by my misfortunes, without any intention of trading. When this latter petition was interpreted to the Emperor, he seemed a little surprised, and said he believed I was the first of my countrymen who ever made any scruple in this point, and that he began to doubt whether I was a real Hollander or no; but rather suspected I must be a Christian. However, for the reasons I had offered, but chiefly to gratify the King of Luggnagg, by an uncommon mark of his favour, he would comply with the singularity of my humour; but the affair must be managed with dexterity, and his officers should be commanded to let me pass as it were by forgetfulness. For he assured me, that if the secret should be discovered by my countrymen, the Dutch, they would cut my throat in the voyage. I returned my thanks by the interpreter for so unusual a favour, and some troops being at that time on their march to Nangasac, the commanding officer had orders to convey me safe thither, with particular instructions about the business of the crucifix.

On the 9th day of June, 1709, I arrived at Nangasac, after a very long and troublesome journey. I soon fell into company of some Dutch sailors belonging to the *Amboyna* of Amsterdam, a stout ship of 450 tons. I had lived long in Holland, pursuing my studies at Leyden, and I spoke Dutch well. The seamen soon knew from whence I came last; they were curious to enquire into my voyages and course of life. I made up a story as short and probable as I could, but concealed the greatest part. I knew many persons in Holland, I was able to invent names for my parents, whom I pretended to be obscure people in the province of Gelderland. I would have given the

---

Nangasac. Nagasaki.

Whether I was a real Hollander or no. The willingness of the Dutch to disclaim Christianity for reasons of commerce with Japan became the occasion of gibes across Europe. Such gibes were especially prevalent in England during the Anglo-Dutch wars of the later seventeenth century. See Kiernan, 18; and Jansen, 80–85.

Amboyna. Now Ambon, Indonesia. The nutmeg island of Amboina was "discovered" in 1511 by the Portuguese and subsequently conquered by them. In 1605 the Dutch seized Amboina from the Portuguese, inaugurating their powerful empire in the East Indies. For the English, however, the name evoked the events of 1623, when the Dutch governor of Amboina ordered the massacre of a band of English and Japanese traders. John Dryden's tragedy *Amboyna* (1672), which depicts this atrocity, reflects English hostility toward their Dutch trading rivals during the Anglo-Dutch wars of this period.

captain (one Theodorus Vangrult) what he pleased to ask for my voyage to Holland; but understanding I was a surgeon, he was contented to take half the usual rate, on condition that I would serve him in the way of my calling. Before we took shipping, I was often asked by some of the crew, whether I had performed the ceremony above-mentioned. I evaded the question by general answers, that I had satisfied the Emperor and court in all particulars. However, a malicious rogue of a skipper went to an officer, and pointing to me, told him, I had not yet *trampled on the crucifix* but the other, who had received instructions to let me pass, gave the rascal twenty strokes on the shoulders with a bamboo, after which I was no more troubled with such questions.

Nothing happened worth mentioning in this voyage. We sailed with a fair wind to the Cape of Good Hope, where we stayed only to take in fresh water. On the 6th of April we arrived safely at Amsterdam, having lost only three men by sickness in the voyage, and a fourth who fell from the foremast into the sea, not far from the coast of Guinea. From Amsterdam I soon after set sail for England in a small vessel belonging to that city.

On the 10th of April, 1710, we put in at the Downs. I landed the next morning, and saw once more my native country after an absence of five years and six months complete. I went straight to Redriff, where I arrived the same day at two in the afternoon, and found my wife and family in good health.

THE END OF THE THIRD PART.

Amsterdam. Amsterdam was both the center of European finance and a vital *entrepôt:* a port mainly devoted to the storage and redistribution of traded goods on the way to other destinations. Though they did export cheese and tulips, the Dutch were strongest commercially as middlemen.

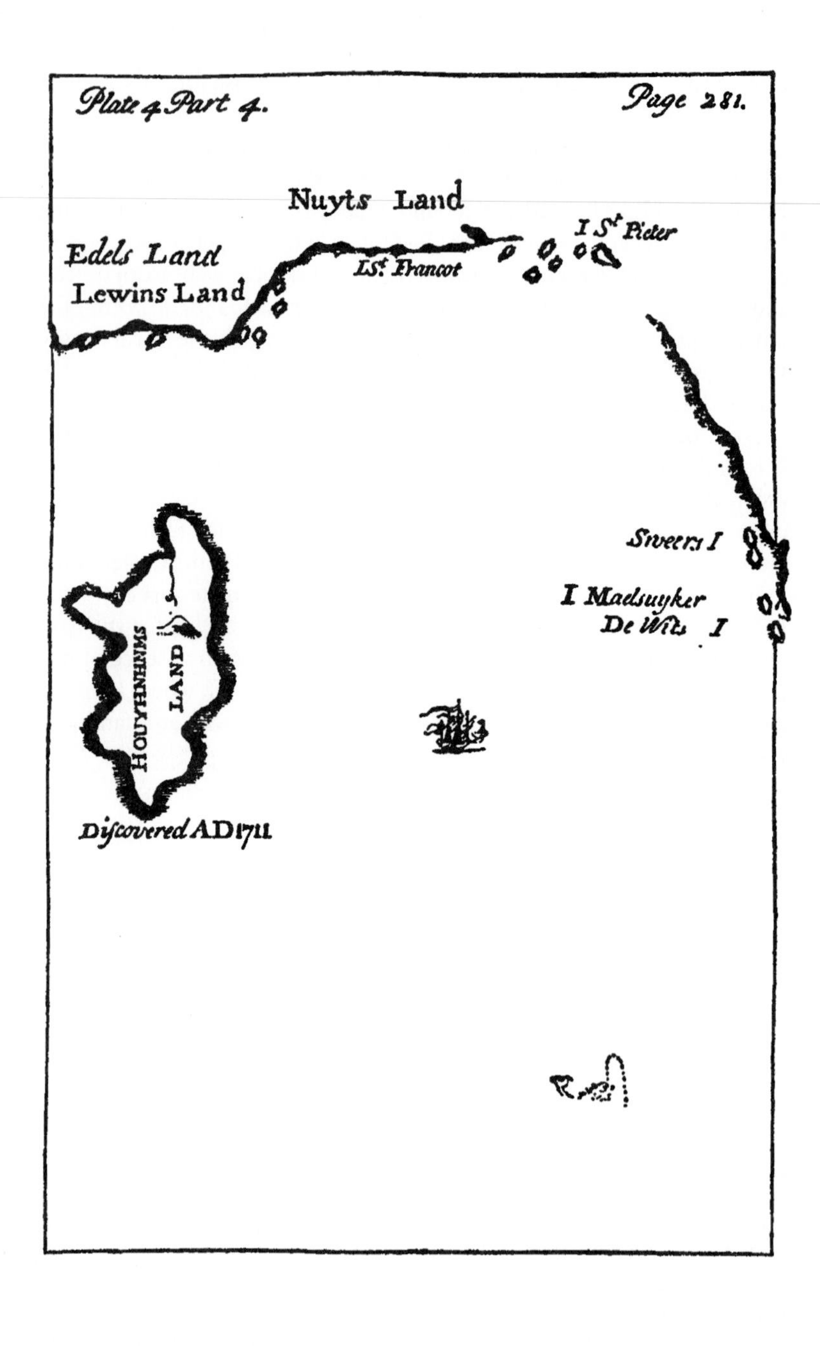
Plate 4 Part 4.
Page 281.
Nuyts Land
Edels Land
Lewins Land
I S.t Francot
I S.t Pieter
Sweers I
I Maelsuyker
De Wits I
HOUYHNHNMS LAND
Discovered AD1711

Travels

Part IV

A Voyage to the Country of the Houyhnhnms

CHAPTER I

The author sets out as captain of a ship. His men conspire against him, confine him a long time to his cabin, set him on shore in an unknown land. He travels up in the country. The yahoos, a strange sort of animal, described. The author meets two Houyhnhnms.

I continued at home with my wife and children about five months in a very happy condition, if I could have learned the lesson of knowing when I was well. I left my poor wife big with child, and accepted an advantageous offer made me to be captain of the *Adventure*, a stout merchantman of 350 tons: for I understood navigation well, and being grown weary of a surgeon's employment at sea, which however I could exercise upon occasion, I took a skilful young man of that calling, one Robert Purefoy, into my ship. We set sail from Portsmouth upon the 7th day of September, 1710; on the 14th, we met with Captain Pocock of Bristol, at Tenariff, who was going to the bay of Campechy, to cut logwood. On the 16th, he was parted from us by a storm; I heard since my return that his ship foundered, and none escaped, but one cabin-boy. He was an honest man, and a good sailor, but a little too positive in his own opinions, which was the cause of his destruction, as it

---

Adventure. The name of a ship used by the American pirate Captain Kidd, tried in London during 1701 and subsequently hanged. The name was common.

Captain Pocock of Bristol. As Bonner suggests (165), probably glancing at Dampier.

Logwood. Also known as Campeachy wood. A tree, valuable as the source of a dye and an astringent, found in Central America and the West Indies. Dampier was engaged in cutting logwood along the eastern shore of the Bay of Campeachy between 1675 and 1678 and later published his adventures there in *Voyages to Campeachy* (1699). For the link between logwood-cutters and pirates, see Cordingly, 147–51.

hath been of several others. For if he had followed my advice, he might at this time have been safe at home with his family as well as myself.

I had several men died in my ship of calentures, so that I was forced to get recruits out of Barbadoes, and the Leeward Islands, where I touched by the direction of the merchants who employed me, which I had soon too much cause to repent; for I found afterwards that most of them had been buccaneers. I had fifty hands on board, and my orders were, that I should trade with the Indians in the South Sea, and make what discoveries I could. These rogues whom I had picked up debauched my other men, and they all formed a conspiracy to seize the ship and secure me; which they did one morning, rushing into my cabin, and binding me hand and foot, threatening to throw me overboard, if I offered to stir. I told them, I was their prisoner, and would submit. This they made me swear to do, and then unbound me, only fastening one of my legs with a chain near my bed, and placed a sentry at my door with his piece charged, who was commanded to shoot me dead if I attempted my liberty. They sent me down victuals and drink, and took the government of the ship to themselves. Their design was to turn pirates, and plunder the Spaniards, which they could not do till they got more men. But first they resolved to sell the goods in the ship, and then go to Madagascar for recruits, several among them having died since my confinement. They sailed many weeks, and traded with the Indians, but I knew not what course they took, being kept close prisoner in my cabin, and expecting nothing less than to be murdered, as they often threatened me.

Upon the 9th day of May, 1711, one James Welch came down to my cabin; and said he had orders from the captain to set me ashore. I expostulated with him, but in vain; neither would he so much as tell me who their new captain was. They forced me into the long-boat, letting me put on my best suit of clothes, which were as good as new, and a small bundle of linen, but no arms except my hanger; and they were so civil as not to search my pockets, into which I conveyed what money I had, with some other little necessaries. They rowed about a league, and then set me down

---

Barbadoes. A sugar colony possessed since 1626 by the English.

Madagascar. Colonized by North American and European pirates after 1693, this island off the southeast coast of Africa evolved into a "pirate commonwealth." Madagascar piracy was alternately suppressed and condoned according to the vagaries of policy shifts in Britain. During the War of the Spanish Succession, Madagascar pirates were authorized to prey on French and Spanish shipping. The government later employed Woodes Rogers—a poacher turned gamekeeper—to break up pirate monopolies in Madagascar and the Bahamas. See Cordingly, 146–48.

on a strand. I desired them to tell me what country it was. They all swore, they knew no more than myself, but said, that the captain (as they called him) was resolved, after they had sold the lading, to get rid of me in the first place where they discovered land. They pushed off immediately, advising me to make haste, for fear of being overtaken by the tide, and bade me farewell.

In this desolate condition I advanced forward, and soon got upon firm ground, where I sat down on a bank to rest myself, and consider what I had best to do. When I was a little refreshed I went up into the country, resolving to deliver myself to the first savages I should meet, and purchase my life from them by some bracelets, glass rings, and other toys, which sailors usually provide themselves with in those voyages, and whereof I had some about me: the land was divided by long rows of trees, not regularly planted, but naturally growing; there was great plenty of grass, and several fields of oats. I walked very circumspectly for fear of being surprised, or suddenly shot with an arrow from behind or on either side. I fell into a beaten road, where I saw many tracks of human feet, and some of cows, but most of horses. At last I beheld several animals in a field, and one or two of the same kind sitting in trees. Their shape was very singular, and deformed, which a little discomposed me, so that I lay down behind a thicket to observe them better. Some of them coming forward near the place where I lay, gave me an opportunity of distinctly marking their form. Their heads and breasts were covered with a thick hair, some frizzled and others lank; they had beards like goats, and a long ridge of hair down their backs, and the foreparts of their legs and feet, but the rest of their bodies were bare, so that I might see their skins, which were of a brown buff colour. They had no tails, nor any hair at all on their buttocks, except about the anus; which, I presume, nature had placed there to defend them as they sat on the ground; for this posture they used, as well as lying down, and often stood on their hind feet. They climbed high trees, as nimbly as a squirrel, for they had strong extended claws before and behind, terminating in sharp points, and hooked. They would often spring, and bound, and leap with prodigious agility. The females were not so large as the males; they had long lank hair on their heads, and only a sort of down on the rest of their bodies, except about the anus, and pudenda. Their dugs hung between their fore-feet, and often reached almost to the ground as they walked. The hair of both sexes was of several colours, brown, red, black, and yellow. Upon the whole, I never beheld in all my travels so disagreeable an animal, or one against which I naturally conceived so strong antipathy. So that thinking I had seen enough, full of contempt and aversion, I got up and pursued the beaten road, hoping it might direct me to the cabin of some Indian. I had not gone far when I met one of these creatures full in my way, and coming up directly to me. The ugly monster, when he saw me, distorted several ways every feature of his visage, and stared as at an object he had never seen before; then approaching nearer, lifted up his forepaw, whether out of curiosity or mischief, I could not tell. But I drew my hanger, and gave him a good blow with the flat side of it, for I durst not strike him with the edge, fearing the inhabitants might be provoked against me, if they should come to know that I had killed or maimed any of their cattle. When the beast felt the smart, he drew back, and roared so loud, that a herd of at least forty came flocking about me from the next field, howling and making odious faces; but I ran to the body of a tree, and leaning my back against it, kept them off, by waving my hanger. Several of this cursed brood getting hold of the branches behind leaped up into the tree, from whence they began to discharge their excrements on my head: however, I escaped pretty well, by sticking close to the stem of a tree, but was almost stifled with the filth, which fell about me on every side.

In the midst of this distress, I observed them all to run away on a sudden as fast as they could, at which I ventured to leave the tree, and pursue the road, wondering what it was that could put them into this fright. But looking on my left hand, I saw a horse walking softly in the field, which my persecutors having sooner discovered, was the cause of their flight. The horse started a little when he came near me, but soon recovering himself, looked full in my face with manifest tokens of wonder: he viewed my hands and feet, walking round me several times. I would have pursued my journey, but he placed himself directly in the way, yet looking with a very mild aspect, never offering the least violence. We stood gazing at each other for some time; at last I took the boldness to reach my hand towards his neck, with a design to stroke it, using the common style and whistle of jockeys when they are going to handle a strange horse. But this animal, seeming to receive my civilities with disdain, shook his head, and bent his brows, softly raising up his left forefoot to remove my hand. Then he neighed three or four times, but in so different a cadence, that I almost began to think he was speaking to himself in some language of his own.

While he and I were thus employed, another horse came up; who applying himself to the first in a very formal manner, they gently struck each other's right hoof before, neighing several times by turns, and varying the sound, which seemed to be almost articulate. They went some paces off, as if it were to confer together, walking side by side, backward and forward, like persons deliberating upon some affair of weight, but often turning their eyes towards me, as it were to watch that I might not escape. I was amazed to see such actions and behaviour in brute beasts, and concluded with myself, that if the inhabitants of this country were endued with a proportionable degree of reason, they must needs be the wisest people

I. S. Müller, *Gulliver Under a Tree Besieged by Yahoos,* from Hawkesworth Edition, 1755.

THE BEINECKE RARE BOOK AND MANUSCRIPT LIBRARY, YALE UNIVERSITY.

upon earth. This thought gave me so much comfort, that I resolved to go forward until I could discover some house or village, or meet with any of the natives, leaving the two horses to discourse together as they pleased. But the first, who was a dapple grey, observing me to steal off, neighed after me in so expressive a tone, that I fancied myself to understand what he meant; whereupon I turned back, and came near him, to expect his farther commands. But concealing my fear as much as I could, for I began to be in some pain, how this adventure might terminate; and the reader will easily believe I did not much like my present situation.

The two horses came up close to me, looking with great earnestness upon my face and hands. The grey steed rubbed my hat all round with his right fore-hoof, and discomposed it so much, that I was forced to adjust it better, by taking it off, and settling it again; whereat both he and his companion (who was a brown bay) appeared to be much surprised; the latter felt the lappet of my coat, and finding it to hang loose about me, they both looked with new signs of wonder. He stroked my right hand, seeming to admire the softness, and colour; but he squeezed it so hard between his hoof and his pastern, that I was forced to roar; after which they both touched me with all possible tenderness. They were under great perplexity about my shoes and stockings, which they felt very often, neighing to each other, and using various gestures, not unlike those of a philosopher, when he would attempt to solve some new and difficult phænomenon.

Upon the whole, the behaviour of these animals was so orderly and rational, so acute and judicious, that I at last concluded, they must needs be magicians, who had thus metamorphosed themselves upon some design, and seeing a stranger in the way, were resolved to divert themselves with him; or perhaps were really amazed at the sight of a man so very different in habit, feature, and complexion from those who might probably live in so remote a climate. Upon the strength of this reasoning, I ventured to address them in the following manner: Gentlemen, if you be conjurers, as I have good cause to believe, you can understand any language; therefore I make bold to let your Worships know, that I am a poor distressed English man, driven by his misfortunes upon your coast, and I entreat one of you, to let me ride upon his back, as if he were a real horse, to some house or village, where I can be relieved. In return of which favour, I will make you a present of this knife and bracelet (taking them out of my pocket). The two creatures stood silent while I spoke, seeming to listen with great attention; and when I had ended, they neighed frequently towards each other, as if they were engaged in serious conversation. I plainly observed, that their language expressed the passions very well, and the words might with little pains be resolved into an alphabet more easily than the Chinese.

I could frequently distinguish the word *yahoo,* which was repeated by each of them several times; and although it was impossible for me to conjecture what it meant, yet while the two horses were busy in conversation, I endeavoured to practice this word upon my tongue; and as soon as they were silent, I boldly pronounced *yahoo* in a loud voice, imitating, at the same time, as near as I could, the neighing of a horse; at which they were both visibly surprised, and the grey repeated the same word twice, as if he meant to teach me the right accent, wherein I spoke after him as well as I could, and found myself perceivably to improve every time, although very far from any degree of perfection. Then the bay tried me with a second word, much harder to be pronounced; but reducing it to the English orthography, may be spelt thus, *Houyhnhnm.* I did not succeed in this so well as the former, but after two or three farther trials, I had better fortune; and they both appeared amazed at my capacity.

After some farther discourse, which I then conjectured might relate to me, the two friends took their leaves, with the same compliment of striking each other's hoof; and the grey made me signs that I should walk before him, wherein I thought it prudent to comply, till I could find a better director. When I offered to slacken my pace, he would cry *hhuun, hhuun;* I guessed his meaning, and gave him to understand, as well as I could, that I was weary, and not able to walk faster; upon which he would stand a while to let me rest.

CHAPTER II

The author conducted by a Houyhnhnm to his house. The house described. The author's reception. The food of the Houyhnhnms. The author in distress for want of meat, is at last relieved. His manner of feeding in that country.

Having travelled about three miles, we came to a long kind of building, made of timber stuck in the ground, and wattled across; the roof was low, and covered with straw. I now began to be a little comforted, and took out some toys, which travellers usually carry for presents to the savage Indians of America and other parts, in hopes the people of the house would be thereby encouraged to receive me kindly. The horse made me a sign to go

---

Houyhnhnm. Critical tradition pronounces this word "Whinn-um" (after the neighing of a horse).

in first; it was a large room with a smooth clay floor, and a rack and manger extending the whole length on one side. There were three nags, and two mares, not eating, but some of them sitting down upon their hams, which I very much wondered at; but wondered more to see the rest employed in domestic business. They seemed but ordinary cattle; however, this confirmed my first opinion, that a people who could so far civilize brute animals must needs excel in wisdom all the nations of the world. The grey came in just after, and thereby prevented any ill treatment which the others might have given me. He neighed to them several times in a style of authority, and received answers.

Beyond this room there were three others, reaching the length of the house, to which you passed through three doors, opposite to each other, in the manner of a vista; we went through the second room towards the third; here the grey walked in first, beckoning me to attend: I waited in the second room, and got ready my presents for the master and mistress of the house: they were two knives, three bracelets of false pearl, a small looking-glass and a bead necklace. The horse neighed three or four times, and I waited to hear some answers in a human voice, but I heard no other returns than in the same dialect, only one or two a little shriller than his. I began to think that this house must belong to some person of great note among them, because there appeared so much ceremony before I could gain admittance. But that a man of quality should be served all by horses was beyond my comprehension. I feared my brain was disturbed by my sufferings and misfortunes: I roused myself, and looked about me in the room where I was left alone; this was furnished as the first, only after a more elegant manner. I rubbed my eyes often, but the same objects still occurred. I pinched my arms and sides, to awake myself, hoping I might be in a dream. I then absolutely concluded, that all these appearances could be nothing else but necromancy and magic. But I had no time to pursue these reflections; for the grey horse came to the door, and made me a sign to follow him into the third room, where I saw a very comely mare, together with a colt and foal, sitting on their haunches, upon mats of straw, not unartfully made, and perfectly neat and clean.

The mare, soon after my entrance, rose from her mat, and coming up close, after having nicely observed my hands and face, gave me a most contemptuous look; then turning to the horse, I heard the word *yahoo* often repeated betwixt them; the meaning of which word I could not then comprehend, although it were the first I had learned to pronounce; but I was soon better informed, to my everlasting mortification: for the horse beckoning to me with his head, and repeating the word *hhuun, hhuun,* as he did upon the road, which I understood was to attend him, led me out

J. J. Grandville, *Gulliver Compared with the Yahoo,* 1838.

THE BEINECKE RARE BOOK AND MANUSCRIPT LIBRARY, YALE UNIVERSITY.

into a kind of court, where was another building at some distance from the house. Here we entered, and I saw three of those detestable creatures, which I first met after my landing, feeding upon roots, and the flesh of some animals, which I afterwards found to be that of asses and dogs, and now and then a cow dead by accident or disease. They were all tied by the neck with strong withes, fastened to a beam; they held their food between the claws of their forefeet, and tore it with their teeth.

The master horse ordered a sorrel nag, one of his servants, to untie the largest of these animals, and take him into the yard. The beast and I were brought close together, and our countenances diligently compared, both by master and servant, who thereupon repeated several times the word *yahoo*. My horror and astonishment are not to be described, when I observed, in this abominable animal, a perfect human figure; the face of it indeed was flat and broad, the nose depressed, the lips large, and the mouth wide. But these differences are common to all savage nations, where the lineaments of the countenance are distorted by the natives suffering their infants to lie grovelling on the earth, or by carrying them on their backs, nuzzling with their face against the mother's shoulders. The forefeet of the yahoo differed from my hands in nothing else but the length of the nails, the coarseness and brownness of the palms, and the hairiness on the backs. There was the same resemblance between our feet, with the same differences, which I knew very well, although the horses did not, because of my shoes and stockings; the same in every part of our bodies, except as to hairiness and colour, which I have already described.

The great difficulty that seemed to stick with the two horses, was to see the rest of my body so very different from that of a yahoo, for which I was obliged to my clothes, whereof they had no conception: the sorrel nag offered me a root, which he held (after their manner, as we shall describe in its proper place) between his hoof and pastern; I took it in my hand, and having smelt it, returned it to him as civilly as I could. He brought out of the yahoo's kennel a piece of ass's flesh, but it smelt so offensively that I turned from it with loathing: he then threw it to the yahoo, by whom it was greedily devoured. He afterwards showed me a wisp of hay, and a fetlock full of oats; but I shook my head, to signify, that neither of these were food for me. And indeed, I now apprehended, that I must absolutely starve, if I did not get to some of my own species: for as to those filthy yahoos, although there were few greater lovers of mankind, at that time, than myself, yet I confess I never saw any sensitive being so detestable on all accounts; and the more I came near them, the more hateful they grew, while I stayed in that country. This the master horse observed by my behaviour, and therefore sent the yahoo back to his kennel. He then put his fore-hoof to his mouth, at which I was much surprised, although he did it with ease, and with a motion that appeared perfectly natural, and made other signs to know what I would eat; but I could not return him such an answer as he was able to apprehend; and if he had understood me, I did not see how it was possible to contrive any way for finding myself nourishment. While we were thus engaged, I observed a cow passing by, whereupon I pointed to her, and expressed a desire to let me go and milk her. This had its effect; for he led me back into the house, and ordered a mare-servant to open a room, where a good store of milk lay in earthen and wooden vessels, after a very orderly and cleanly manner. She gave me a large bowl full, of which I drank very heartily, and found myself well refreshed.

About noon I saw coming towards the house a kind of vehicle drawn like a sledge by four yahoos. There was in it an old steed, who seemed to be of quality; he alighted with his hind feet forward, having by accident got a hurt in his left forefoot. He came to dine with our horse, who received him with great civility. They dined in the best room, and had oats boiled in milk for the second course, which the old horse eat warm, but the rest cold. Their mangers were placed circular in the middle of the room, and divided into several partitions, round which they sat on their haunches upon bosses of straw. In the middle was a large rack with angles answering to every partition of the manger. So that each horse and mare eat their own hay, and their own mash of oats and milk, with much decency and regularity. The behaviour of the young colt and foal appeared very modest, and that of the master and mistress extremely cheerful and complaisant to their guest. The grey ordered me to stand by him, and much discourse passed between him and his friend concerning me, as I found by the stranger's often looking on me, and the frequent repetition of the word *yahoo.*

I happened to wear my gloves, which the master grey observing, seemed perplexed, discovering signs of wonder what I had done to my forefeet; he put his hoof three or four times to them, as if he would signify, that I should reduce them to their former shape, which I presently did, pulling off both my gloves, and putting them into my pocket. This occasioned farther talk, and I saw the company was pleased with my behaviour, whereof I soon found the good effects. I was ordered to speak the few words I understood, and while they were at dinner, the master taught me the names for oats, milk, fire, water, and some others: which I could readily pronounce after him, having from my youth a great facility in learning languages.

When dinner was done, the master horse took me aside, and by signs and words made me understand the concern he was in, that I had nothing to eat. Oats in their tongue are called *hlunnh.* This word I pronounced two or three times; for although I had refused them at first, yet upon second thoughts, I considered that I could contrive to make of them a kind of bread, which might be sufficient with milk to keep me alive, till I could make my escape to some other country, and to creatures of my own species. The horse immediately ordered a white mare-servant of his family to bring me a good quantity of oats in a sort of wooden tray. These I heated before the fire as well as I could, and rubbed them till the husks came off, which I made a shift to winnow from the grain; I ground and beat them between two stones, then took water, and made them into a paste or cake, which I toasted at the fire, and eat warm with milk. It was at first a very insipid diet, although common enough in many parts of Europe, but grew tolerable by time; and having been often reduced to hard fare in my life, this was not the first experiment I had made how easily nature is satisfied. And I cannot but observe, that I never had one hour's sickness, while I stayed in this island. It is true, I sometimes made a shift to catch a rabbit, or bird, by springes made of yahoos' hairs, and I often gathered wholesome herbs, which I boiled, or eat as salads with my bread, and now and then, for a rarity, I made a little butter, and drank the whey. I was at first at a great loss for salt; but custom soon reconciled the want of it; and I am confident that the frequent use of salt among us is an effect of luxury, and was first introduced only as a provocative to drink; except where it is necessary for preserving of flesh in long voyages, or in places remote from great markets. For we observe no animal to be fond of it but man: and as to myself, when I left this country, it was a great while before I could endure the taste of it in anything that I eat.

This is enough to say upon the subject of my diet, wherewith other travellers fill their books, as if the readers were personally concerned whether we fared well or ill. However, it was necessary to mention this matter, lest the world should think it impossible that I could find sustenance for three years in such a country, and among such inhabitants.

When it grew towards evening, the master horse ordered a place for me to lodge in; it was but six yards from the house, and separated from the stable of the yahoos. Here I got some straw, and covering myself with my own clothes, slept very sound. But I was in a short time better accommodated, as the reader shall know hereafter, when I come to treat more particularly about my way of living.

CHAPTER III

The author studious to learn the language, the Houyhnhnm his master assists in teaching him. The language described. Several Houyhnhnms of quality come out of curiosity to see the author. He gives his master a short account of his voyage.

My principal endeavour was to learn the language, which my master (for so I shall henceforth call him) and his children, and every servant of his house were desirous to teach me. For they looked upon it as a prodigy that a brute animal should discover such marks of a rational creature. I pointed to every thing, and enquired the name of it, which I wrote down in my journal-book when I was alone, and corrected my bad accent, by desiring those of the family to pronounce it often. In this employment, a sorrel nag, one of the under servants, was very ready to assist me.

In speaking, they pronounce through the nose and throat, and their language approaches nearest to the High Dutch or German, of any I know in Europe; but is much more graceful and significant. The Emperor Charles V made almost the same observation, when he said, that if he were to speak to his horse, it should be in High Dutch.

The curiosity and impatience of my master were so great, that he spent many hours of his leisure to instruct me. He was convinced (as he afterwards told me) that I must be a yahoo, but my teachableness, civility and cleanliness astonished him; which were qualities altogether so opposite to those animals. He was most perplexed about my clothes, reasoning sometimes with himself, whether they were a part of my body; for I never pulled them off till the family were asleep, and got them on before they waked in the morning. My master was eager to learn from whence I came, how I acquired those appearances of reason which I discovered in all my actions, and to know my story from my own mouth, which he hoped he should soon do by the great proficiency I made in learning and pronouncing their words and sentences. To help my memory, I formed all I learned into the English alphabet, and writ the words down with the translations. This last, after some time, I ventured to do in my master's presence. It cost me much trouble to explain to him what I was doing; for the inhabitants have not the least idea of books or literature.

In about ten weeks time I was able to understand most of his questions, and in three months could give him some tolerable answers. He was extremely curious to know from what part of the country I came, and how I was taught to imitate a rational creature, because the yahoos (whom he saw I exactly resembled in my head, hands and face, that were only visible), with some appearance of cunning, and the strongest disposition to mischief, were observed to be the most unteachable of all brutes. I answered, that I came over the sea, from a far place, with many others of my own kind, in a great hollow vessel made of the bodies of trees. That my companions forced me to land on this coast, and then left me to shift for myself. It was with some difficulty, and by the help of many signs, that I brought him to understand me. He replied, that I must needs be mistaken, or that I "said the thing which was not." (For they have no words in their language to express lying or falsehood.) He knew it was impossible that there could be a country beyond the sea, or that a parcel of brutes could move a wooden vessel whither they pleased upon water. He was sure no Houyhnhnm alive could make such a vessel, or would trust yahoos to manage it.

The word *Houyhnhnm,* in their tongue, signifies a *horse,* and in its etymology, *the perfection of nature.* I told my master, that I was at a loss for expression, but would improve as fast as I could; and hoped in a short time I should be able to tell him wonders: he was pleased to direct his own mare, his colt and foal, and the servants of the family to take all opportunities of instructing me, and every day for two or three hours he was at the same pains himself: several horses and mares of quality in the neighbourhood came often to our house upon the report spread of a wonderful yahoo, that could speak like a Houyhnhnm, and seemed in his words and actions to discover some glimmerings of reason. These delighted to converse with me; they put many questions, and received such answers as I was able to return. By all which advantages, I made so great a progress, that in five months from my arrival I understood whatever was spoke, and could express myself tolerably well.

The Houyhnhnms who came to visit my master, out of a design of seeing and talking with me, could hardly believe me to be a right yahoo, because my body had a different covering from others of my kind. They were astonished to observe me without the usual hair or skin except on my head, face, and hands; but I discovered that secret to my master, upon an accident, which happened about a fortnight before.

I have already told the reader, that every night, when the family were gone to bed, it was my custom to strip and cover myself with my clothes: it happened one morning early, that my master sent for me, by the sorrel nag, who was his valet; when he came, I was fast asleep, my clothes fallen off on one side, and my shirt above my waist. I awaked at the noise he made, and observed him to deliver his message in some disorder; after which he went to my master, and in a great fright gave him a very confused acount of what he had seen: this I presently discovered; for going, as soon as I was dressed, to pay my attendance upon his Honour, he asked me the meaning of what his servant had reported, that I was not the same thing when I slept as I appeared to be at other times; that his valet assured him, some part of me was white, some yellow, at least not so white, and some brown.

I had hitherto concealed the secret of my dress, in order to distinguish myself as much as possible from that cursed race of yahoos; but now I found it in vain to do so any longer. Besides, I considered that my clothes and shoes would soon wear out, which already were in a declining condition, and must be supplied by some contrivance from the hides of yahoos or other brutes; whereby the whole secret would be known: I therefore told my master, that in the country from whence I came those of my kind always covered their bodies with the hairs of certain animals prepared by art, as well for decency, as to avoid inclemencies of air both hot and cold; of which, as to my own person, I would give him immediate conviction, if he pleased to command me; only desiring his excuse, if I did not expose those parts that nature taught us to conceal. He said my discourse was all very strange, but especially the last part; for he could not understand why nature should teach us to conceal what nature had given. That neither himself nor family were ashamed of any parts of their bodies; but however I might do as I pleased. Whereupon, I first unbuttoned my coat, and pulled it off. I did the same with my waistcoat; I drew off my shoes, stockings, and breeches. I let my shirt down to my waist, and drew up the bottom, fastening it like a girdle about my middle to hide my nakedness.

My master observed the whole performance with great signs of curiosity and admiration. He took up all my clothes in his pastern, one piece after another, and examined them diligently; he then stroked my body very gently and looked round me several times, after which he said, it was plain I must be a perfect yahoo; but that I differed very much from the rest of my species, in the whiteness and smoothness of my skin, my want of hair in several parts of my body, the shape and shortness of my claws behind and before, and my affectation of walking continually on my two hinder feet. He desired to see no more, and gave me leave to put on my clothes again, for I was shuddering with cold.

I expressed my uneasiness at his giving me so often the appellation of *yahoo*, an odious animal, for which I had so utter an hatred and contempt; I begged he would forbear applying that word to me, and take the same order in his family, and among his friends whom he suffered to see me. I requested likewise, that the secret of my having a false covering to my body might be known to none but himself, at least as long as my present clothing should last; for as to what the sorrel nag his valet had observed, his Honour might command him to conceal it.

All this my master very graciously consented to, and thus the secret was kept till my clothes began to wear out, which I was forced to supply by several contrivances, that shall hereafter be mentioned. In the mean time, he desired I would go on with my utmost diligence to learn their language, because he was more astonished at my capacity for speech and reason than at the figure of my body, whether it were covered or no; adding, that he waited with some impatience to hear the wonders which I promised to tell him.

From thenceforward he doubled the pains he had been at to instruct me; he brought me into all company, and made them treat me with civility, because, as he told them privately, this would put me into good humour, and make me more diverting.

Every day when I waited on him, beside the trouble he was at in teaching, he would ask me several questions concerning myself, which I answered as well as I could; and by those means he had already received some general ideas, although very imperfect. It would be tedious to relate the several steps by which I advanced to a more regular conversation: but the first account I gave of myself in any order and length, was to this purpose:

That I came from a very far country, as I already had attempted to tell him, with about fifty more of my own species; that we travelled upon the seas, in a great hollow vessel made of wood, and larger than his Honour's house. I described the ship to him in the best terms I could, and explained by the help of my handkerchief displayed, how it was driven forward by the wind. That upon a quarrel among us, I was set on shore on this coast, where I walked forward without knowing whither, till he delivered me from the persecution of those execrable yahoos. He asked me, who made the ship, and how it was possible that the Houyhnhnms of my country would leave it to the management of brutes? My answer was, that I durst proceed no farther in my relation, unless he would give me his word and honour that he would not be offended, and then I would tell him the wonders I had so often promised. He agreed; and I went on by assuring him, that the ship was made by creatures like myself, who in all the countries I had travelled, as well as in my own, were the only governing, rational animals; and that upon my arrival hither, I was as much astonished to see the Houyhnhnms act like rational beings, as he or his friends could be in finding some marks of reason in a creature he was pleased to call a yahoo, to which I owned my resemblance in every part, but could not account for their degenerate and brutal nature. I said farther, that if good fortune ever restored me to my native country, to relate my travels hither, as I resolved to do, every body would believe that I "said the thing which was not"; that I invented the story out of my own head; and with all possible respect to himself, his family and friends, and under his promise of not being offended, our countrymen would hardly think it probable, that a Houyhnhnm should be the presiding creature of a nation, and a yahoo the brute.

CHAPTER IV

The Houyhnhnms' notion of truth and falsehood. The author's discourse disapproved by his master. The author gives a more particular account of himself, and the accidents of his voyage.

My master heard me with great appearances of uneasiness in his countenance, because *doubting* or *not believing*, are so little known in this country, that the inhabitants cannot tell how to behave themselves under such circumstances. And I remember in frequent discourses with my master concerning the nature of manhood, in other parts of the world, having occasion to talk of *lying* and *false representation*, it was with much difficulty that he comprehended what I meant, although he had otherwise a most acute judgment. For he argued thus; that the use of speech was to make us understand one another, and to receive information of facts; now if any one *said the thing which was not*, these ends were defeated; because I cannot properly be said to understand him, and I am so far from receiving information, that he leaves me worse than in ignorance, for I am led to believe a thing black when it is white, and short when it is long. And these were all the notions he had concerning that faculty of lying, so perfectly well understood, and so universally practised among human creatures.

To return from this digression; when I asserted that the yahoos were the only governing animals in my country, which my master said was altogether past his conception, he desired to know, whether we had Houyhnhnms among us, and what was their employment: I told him, we had great numbers, that in summer they grazed in the fields, and in winter were kept in houses, with hay and oats, where yahoo servants were employed to rub their skins smooth, comb their manes, pick their feet, serve them with food, and make their beds. I understand you well, said my master, it is now very plain, from all you have spoken, that whatever share of reason the yahoos pretend to, the Houyhnhnms are your masters; I heartily wish our yahoos would be so tractable. I begged his Honour would please to excuse me from proceeding any farther, because I was very certain that the account he expected from me would be highly displeasing. But he insisted in commanding me to let him know the best and the worst: I told him, he should be obeyed. I owned, that the Houyhnhnms among us, whom we called horses, were the most generous and comely animal we had, that they excelled in strength and swiftness; and when they belonged to persons of quality, employed in travelling, racing, and drawing chariots, they were treated with much kindness and care, till they fell into diseases, or became foundered in the feet; but then they were sold, and used to all kind of drudgery till they died; after which their skins were stripped and sold for what they were worth, and their bodies left to be devoured by dogs and birds of prey. But the common race of horses had not so good fortune, being kept by farmers and carriers and other mean people, who put them to greater labour, and feed them worse. I described, as well as I could, our way of riding, the shape and use of a bridle, a saddle, a spur, and a whip, of harness and wheels. I added, that we fastened plates of a certain hard substance called "iron" at the bottom of their feet, to preserve their hoofs from being broken by the stony ways on which we often travelled.

My master, after some expressions of great indignation, wondered how we dared to venture upon a Houyhnhnm's back, for he was sure that the weakest servant in his house would be able to shake off the strongest yahoo, or by lying down, and rolling upon his back, squeeze the brute to death. I answered, that our horses were trained up from three or four years old to the several uses we intended them for; that if any of them proved intolerably vicious, they were employed for carriages; that they were severely beaten while they were young, for any mischievous tricks; that the males, designed for the common use of riding or draught, were generally castrated about two years after their birth, to take down their spirits, and make them more tame and gentle; that they were indeed sensible of rewards and punishments; but his Honour would please to consider, that they had not the least tincture of reason any more than the yahoos in this country.

It put me to the pains of many circumlocutions to give my master a right idea of what I spoke; for their language doth not abound in variety of words, because their wants and passions are fewer than among us. But it is impossible to express his noble resentment at our savage treatment of the Houyhnhnm race, particularly after I had explained the manner and use of castrating horses among us, to hinder them from propagating their kind, and to render them more servile. He said, if it were possible there could be any country where yahoos alone were endued with reason, they certainly must be the governing animal, because reason will in time always prevail against brutal strength. But, considering the frame of our bodies, and especially of mine, he thought no creature of equal bulk was so ill contrived for employing that reason in the common offices of life; whereupon he desired to know whether those among whom I lived resembled me or the yahoos of his country. I assured him, that I was as well shaped as most of my age: but the younger and the females were much more soft and tender, and the skins of the latter generally as white as milk. He said, I differed indeed from other yahoos, being much more cleanly, and not altogether so deformed, but in point of real advantage he thought I differed for the worse. That my nails were of no use either to my fore or hinder feet; as to my forefeet, he could not properly call them by that name, for he never observed me to walk upon them; that they were too soft to bear the ground; that I generally went with them uncovered, neither was the covering I sometimes wore on them of the same shape or so strong as that on my feet behind. That I could not walk with any security, for if either of my hinder feet slipped, I must inevitably fall. He then began to find fault with other parts of my body, the flatness of my face, the prominence of my nose, my eyes placed directly in front, so that I could not look on either side without turning my head: that I was not able to feed myself without lifting one of my forefeet to my mouth: and therefore nature had placed those joints to answer that necessity. He knew not what could be the use of those several clefts and divisions in my feet behind; that these were too soft to bear the hardness and sharpness of stones without a covering made from the skin of some other brute; that my whole body wanted a fence against heat and cold, which I was forced to put on and off every day with tediousness and trouble. And lastly, that he observed every animal in this country naturally to abhor the yahoos, whom the weaker avoided, and the stronger drove from them. So that supposing us to have the gift of reason, he could not see how it were possible to cure that natural antipathy which every creature discovered against us; nor consequently, how we could tame and render them serviceable. However, he would (as he said) debate the matter no farther, because he was more desirous to know my own story, the country where I was born, and the several actions and events of my life before I came hither.

I assured him how extremely desirous I was that he should be satisfied in every point; but I doubted much, whether it would be possible for me to explain myself on several subjects whereof his Honour could have no conception, because I saw nothing in his country to which I could resemble them. That however, I would do my best, and strive to express myself by similitudes, humbly desiring his assistance when I wanted proper words; which he was pleased to promise me.

I said, my birth was of honest parents, in an island called England, which was remote from this country as many days' journey as the strongest of his Honour's servants could travel in the annual course of the sun. That I was bred a surgeon, whose trade is to cure wounds and hurts in the body, got by accident or violence; that my country was governed by a female man, whom we called *queen*. That I left it to get riches, whereby I might maintain myself and family when I should return. That in my last voyage I was commander of the ship, and had about fifty yahoos under me, many of which died at sea, and I was forced to supply them by others picked out from several nations. That our ship was twice in danger of being sunk; the first time by a great storm, and the second, by striking against a rock. Here my master interposed, by asking me, how I could persuade strangers out of different countries to venture with me, after the losses I had sustained, and the hazards I had run. I said, they were fellows of desperate fortunes, forced to fly from the places of their birth, on account of their poverty or their crimes. Some were undone by lawsuits; others spent all they had in drinking, whoring, and gaming; others fled for treason; many for murder, theft, poisoning, robbery, perjury, forgery, coining false money, for committing rapes or sodomy, for flying from their colours, or deserting to the enemy, and most of them had broken prison; none of these durst return to their native countries for fear of being hanged, or of starving in a jail; and therefore were under a necessity of seeking a livelihood in other places.

During this discourse, my master was pleased often to interrupt me; I had made use of many circumlocutions in describing to him the nature of the several crimes, for which most of our crew had been forced to fly their country. This labour took up several days' conversation before he was able to comprehend me. He was wholly at a loss to know what could be the use or necessity of practising those vices. To clear up which I endeavoured to give him some ideas of the desire of power and riches, of the terrible effects of lust, intemperance, malice and envy. All this I was forced to define and describe by putting of cases, and making suppositions. After which, like one whose imagination was struck with something never seen or heard of before, he would lift up his eyes with amazement and indignation. Power, government, war, law, punishment, and a thousand other things had no terms wherein that language could express them, which made the difficulty almost insuperable to give my master any conception of what I meant. But being of an excellent understanding, much improved by contemplation and converse, he at last arrived at a competent knowledge of what human nature in our parts of the world is capable to perform, and desired I would give him some particular account of that land which we call Europe, especially of my own country.

CHAPTER V

The author, at his master's commands, informs him of the state of England. The causes of war among the princes of Europe. The author begins to explain the English constitution.

The reader may please to observe, that the following extract of many conversations I had with my master contains a summary of the most material points which were discoursed at several times for above two years;

Flying from their colours. Deserting (Fox, 223).

Land which we call Europe. The specificity of the target here is worth noting.

his Honour often desiring fuller satisfaction as I farther improved in the Houyhnhnm tongue. I laid before him, as well as I could, the whole state of Europe; I discoursed of trade and manufactures, of arts and sciences; and the answers I gave to all the questions he made, as they arose upon several subjects, were a fund of conversation not to be exhausted. But I shall here only set down the substance of what passed between us concerning my own country, reducing it into order as well as I can, without any regard to time or other circumstances, while I strictly adhere to truth. My only concern is, that I shall hardly be able to do justice to my master's arguments and expressions, which must needs suffer by my want of capacity, as well as by a translation into our barbarous English.

In obedience therefore to his Honour's commands, I related to him the Revolution under the Prince of Orange; the long war with France entered into by the said prince, and renewed by his successor the present queen, wherein the greatest powers of Christendom were engaged, and which still continued: I computed, at his request, that about a million of yahoos might have been killed in the whole progress of it, and perhaps a hundred or more cities taken, and five times as many ships burnt or sunk.

He asked me what were the usual causes or motives that made one country go to war with another. I answered they were innumerable, but I should only mention a few of the chief. Sometimes the ambition of princes, who never think they have land or people enough to govern: sometimes the corruption of ministers, who engage their master in a war in order to stifle or divert the clamour of the subjects against their evil administration. Difference in opinions hath cost many millions of lives: for instance, whether flesh be bread, or bread be flesh; whether the juice of a certain berry be blood or wine; whether whistling be a vice or a virtue; whether it be better to kiss a post, or throw it into the fire; what is the best colour for a coat, whether black, white, red, or grey; and whether it should be long or short,

---

Revolution. The *coup d'état* of 1688–90—settled by the Battle of Boyne in Ireland—when the Dutch Calvinist William of Orange replaced the Catholic James II on the English throne, breaking the Stuart succession. William III, inspired by continental imperatives, proceeded to entangle England in continental wars. William funded his wars in part with land confiscated from supporters of James (Jacobites) in Ireland. The war with France to which Gulliver refers is the War of the Grand Alliance. See Israel, 850–53; Cruikshanks, 35–46, 96–102; and Simms, 21–29.

Opinions. As throughout his satire on ecclesiastical history, *A Tale of a Tub* (1704), Swift here mocks conflicts dividing Christendom. Ireland's penal laws against Catholics dwelled on the importance of the doctrinal difference between Anglican and Catholic understandings of the Eucharist. The reference to *whistling* satirizes puritanical excess: Presbyterian bans on organ music. For more on musical worship, see "The Dean to Himself on St. Cecilia's Day" in this volume, pp. 346–47.

narrow or wide, dirty or clean, with many more. Neither are any wars so furious and bloody, or of so long continuance, as those occasioned by difference in opinion, especially if it be in things indifferent.

Sometimes the quarrel between two princes is to decide which of them shall dispossess a third of his dominions, where neither of them pretend to any right. Sometimes one prince quarrelleth with another, for fear the other should quarrel with him. Sometimes a war is entered upon, because the enemy is too strong, and sometimes because he is too weak. Sometimes our neighbours want the things which we have, or have the things which we want; and we both fight, till they take ours or give us theirs. It is a very justifiable cause of war to invade a country after the people have been wasted by famine, destroyed by pestilence, or embroiled by factions amongst themselves. It is justifiable to enter into a war against our nearest ally, when one of his towns lies convenient for us, or a territory of land, that would render our dominions round and compact. If a prince send forces into a nation where the people are poor and ignorant, he may lawfully put half of them to death, and make slaves of the rest, in order to civilize and reduce them from their barbarous way of living. It is a very kingly, honourable, and frequent practice, when one prince desires the assistance of another to secure him against an invasion, that the assistant, when he hath driven out the invader, should seize on the dominions himself, and kill, imprison or banish the prince he came to relieve. Alliance by blood or marriage is a sufficient cause of war between princes, and the nearer the kindred is, the greater is their disposition to quarrel: poor nations are hungry, and rich nations are proud, and pride and hunger will ever be at variance. For these reasons, the trade of a soldier is held the most honourable of all others: because a soldier is a yahoo hired to kill in cold blood as many of his own species, who have never offended him, as possibly he can.

There is likewise a kind of beggarly princes in Europe, not able to make war by themselves, who hire out their troops to richer nations, for so much a day to each man; of which they keep three fourths to themselves, and it is the best part of their maintenance; such are those in Germany and many northern parts of Europe.

What you have told me (said my master) upon the subject of war, does indeed discover most admirably the effects of that reason you pretend to: however, it is happy that the shame is greater than the danger; and that nature hath left you utterly uncapable of doing much mischief. For your mouths lying flat with your faces, you can hardly bite each other to any

---

Richer nations. George I's conspicuous employment of German mercenaries aroused public concern that England's interests were being entangled with those of minor German states.

purpose, unless by consent. Then as to the claws upon your feet before and behind, they are so short and tender, that one of our yahoos would drive a dozen of yours before him. And therefore in recounting the numbers of those who have been killed in battle, I cannot but think that you have *said the thing which is not.*

I could not forbear shaking my head and smiling a little at his ignorance. And being no stranger to the art of war, I gave him a description of cannons, culverins, muskets, carabines, pistols, bullets, powder, swords, bayonets, battles, sieges, retreats, attacks, undermines, countermines, bombardments, sea-fights; ships sunk with a thousand men, twenty thousand killed on each side; dying groans, limbs flying in the air, smoke, noise, confusion, trampling to death under horses' feet; flight, pursuit, victory; fields strewed with carcases left for food to dogs, and wolves, and birds of prey; plundering, stripping, ravishing, burning and destroying. And to set forth the valour of my own dear countrymen, I assured him, that I had seen them blow up a hundred enemies at once in a siege, and as many in a ship, and beheld the dead bodies drop down in pieces from the clouds, to the great diversion of all the spectators.

I was going on to more particulars, when my master commanded me silence. He said, whoever understood the nature of yahoos might easily believe it possible for so vile an animal to be capable of every action I had named, if their strength and cunning equalled their malice. But as my discourse had increased his abhorrence of the whole species, so he found it gave him a disturbance in his mind, to which he was wholly a stranger before. He thought his ears being used to such abominable words, might by degrees admit them with less detestation. That although he hated the yahoos of this country, yet he no more blamed them for their odious qualities, than he did a *gnnayh* (a bird of prey) for its cruelty, or a sharp stone for cutting his hoof. But when a creature pretending to reason could be capable of such enormities, he dreaded lest the corruption of that faculty might be worse than brutality itself. He seemed therefore confident, that instead of reason, we were only possessed of some quality fitted to increase our natural vices; as the reflection from a troubled stream returns the image of an ill-shapen body, not only larger, but more distorted.

He added, that he had heard too much upon the subject of war, both in this and some former discourses. There was another point which a little

---

Culverins. Large cannons.

Carabines. Firearms, shorter than muskets.

Undermines. Excavations under a fortification.

Countermines. Defensive mines placed to fend off invaders.

perplexed him at present. I had said, that some of our crew left their country on account of being ruined by *law;* that I had already explained the meaning of the word; but he was at a loss how it should come to pass, that the *law* which was intended for every man's preservation, should be any man's ruin. Therefore he desired to be farther satisfied what I meant by *law,* and the dispensers thereof according to the present practice in my own country; because he thought nature and reason were sufficient guides for a reasonable animal, as we pretended to be, in showing us what we ought to do, and what to avoid.

I assured his Honour, that law was a science wherein I had not much conversed, further than by employing advocates in vain, upon some injustices that had been done me. However, I would give him all the satisfaction I was able.

I said there was a society of men among us, bred up from their youth in the art of proving by words multiplied for the purpose, that white is black, and black is white, according as they are paid. To this society all the rest of the people are slaves.

For example, if my neighbour hath a mind to my cow, he hires a lawyer to prove that he ought to have my cow from me. I must then hire another to defend my right, it being against all rules of law that any man should be allowed to speak for himself. Now in this case, I who am the true owner lie under two great disadvantages. First, my lawyer, being practiced almost from his cradle in defending falsehood, is quite out of his element when he would be an advocate for justice, which as an office unnatural, he always attempts with great awkwardness, if not with ill will. The second disadvantage is, that my lawyer must proceed with great caution, or else he will be reprimanded by the judges, and abhorred by his brethren, as one who would lessen the practice of the law. And therefore I have but two methods to preserve my cow. The first is to gain over my adversary's lawyer with a double fee, who will then betray his client by insinuating that he hath justice on his side. The second way is for my lawyer to make my cause appear as unjust as he can, by allowing the cow to belong to my adversary; and this if it be skilfully done will certainly bespeak the favour of the bench.

Now, your Honour is to know that these judges are persons appointed to decide all controversies of property, as well as for the trail of criminals, and picked out from the most dextrous lawyers who are grown old or lazy, and having been biassed all their lives against truth and equity, lie under such a fatal necessity of favouring fraud, perjury, and oppression, that I have known several of them refuse a large bribe from the side where justice lay, rather than injure the faculty by doing any thing unbecoming their nature or their office.

It is a maxim among these lawyers, that whatever hath been done before may legally be done again: and therefore they take special care to record all the decisions formerly made against common justice and the general reason of mankind. These, under the name of *precedents,* they produce as authorities, to justify the most iniquitous opinions; and the judges never fail of decreeing accordingly.

In pleading, they studiously avoid entering into the merits of the cause, but are loud, violent, and tedious in dwelling upon all circumstances which are not to the purpose. For instance, in the case already mentioned; they never desire to know what claim or title my adversary hath to my cow, but whether the said cow were red or black, her horns long or short; whether the field I graze her in be round or square, whether she was milked at home or abroad, what diseases she is subject to, and the like; after which they consult precedents, adjourn the cause from time to time, and in ten, twenty, or thirty years come to an issue.

It is likewise to be observed that this society hath a peculiar cant and jargon of their own, that no other mortal can understand, and wherein all their laws are written, which they take special care to multiply; whereby they have wholly confounded the very essence of truth and falsehood, of right and wrong; so that it will take thirty years to decide whether the field left me by my ancestors for six generations belongs to me or to a stranger three hundred miles off.

In the trial of persons accused for crimes against the state the method is much more short and commendable: the judge first sends to sound the disposition of those in power, after which he can easily hang or save the criminal, strictly preserving all due forms of law.

Here my master, interposing, said it was a pity, that creatures endowed with such prodigious abilities of mind as these lawyers, by the description I gave of them, must certainly be, were not rather encouraged to be instructors of others in wisdom and knowledge. In answer to which I assured his Honour, that in all points out of their own trade they were usually the most ignorant and stupid generation among us, the most despicable in common conversation, avowed enemies to all knowledge and learning, and equally disposed to pervert the general reason of mankind in every other subject of discourse, as in that of their own profession.

CHAPTER VI

A continuation of the state of England under Queen Anne. The character of a first minister in the courts of Europe.

My master was yet wholly at a loss to understand what motives could incite this race of lawyers to perplex, disquiet, and weary themselves by engaging in a confederacy of injustice, merely for the sake of injuring their fellow-animals; neither could he comprehend what I meant in saying they did it for hire. Whereupon I was at much pains to describe to him the use of money, the materials it was made of, and the value of the metals; that when a yahoo had got a great store of this precious substance, he was able to purchase whatever he had a mind to, the finest clothing, the noblest houses, great tracts of land, the most costly meats and drinks, and have his choice of the most beautiful females. Therefore since money alone was able to perform all these feats, our yahoos thought they could never have enough of it to spend or to save, as they found themselves inclined from their natural bent either to profusion or avarice. That the rich man enjoyed the fruit of the poor man's labour, and the latter were a thousand to one in proportion to the former. That the bulk of our people were forced to live miserably, by labouring every day for small wages to make a few live plentifully. I enlarged myself much on these and many other particulars to the same purpose: but his Honour was still to seek, for he went upon a supposition that all animals had a title to their share in the productions of the earth, and especially those who presided over the rest. Therefore he desired I would let him know what these costly meats were, and how any of us happened to want them. Whereupon I enumerated as many sorts as came into my head, with the various methods of dressing them, which could not be done without sending vessels by sea to every part of the world, as well for liquors to drink, as for sauces, and innumerable other conveniencies. I assured him, that this whole globe of earth must be at least three times gone round, before one of our better female yahoos could get her breakfast, or a cup to put it in. He said, that must needs be a miserable country which cannot furnish food for its own inhabitants. But what he chiefly wondered at was how such vast tracts of ground as I described should be wholly without fresh water, and the people put to the necessity of sending over the sea for drink. I replied, that England (the dear place of my nativity) was computed to produce three times the quantity of food more than its inhabitants are able to consume, as well as liquors extracted from grain, or pressed out of the fruit of certain trees, which made excellent drink, and the same proportion in every other convenience of life. But in order to feed the luxury and intemperance of the males, and the vanity of the females, we sent away the greatest part of our necessary things to other countries, from whence in return we brought the materials of diseases, folly, and vice, to spend among ourselves. Hence it follows of necessity that vast numbers of our people are compelled to seek their livelihood by begging, robbing, stealing, cheating, pimping, forswearing, flattering, suborning, forging, gaming, lying, fawning, hectoring, voting, scribbling, star-gazing, poisoning, whoring, canting, libelling, free-thinking, and the like occupations: every one of which terms, I was at much pains to make him understand.

That wine was not imported among us from foreign countries to supply the want of water or other drinks, but because it was a sort of liquid which made us merry, by putting us out of our senses; diverted all melancholy thoughts, begat wild extravagant imaginations in the brain, raised our hopes, and banished our fears, suspended every office of reason for a time, and deprived us of the use of our limbs, until we fell into a profound sleep; although it must be confessed, that we always awaked sick and dispirited, and that the use of this liquor filled us with diseases, which made our lives uncomfortable and short.

But beside all this, the bulk of our people supported themselves by furnishing the necessities or conveniencies of life to the rich, and to each other. For instance, when I am at home and dressed as I ought to be, I carry on my body the workmanship of an hundred tradesmen; the building and furniture of my house employ as many more, and five times the number to adorn my wife.

I was going on to tell him of another sort of people, who get their livelihood by attending the sick, having upon some occasions informed his Honour that many of my crew had died of diseases. But here it was with the utmost difficulty that I brought him to apprehend what I meant. He could easily conceive that a Houyhnhnm grew weak and heavy a few days before his death, or by some accident might hurt a limb. But that Nature, who works all things to perfection, should suffer any pains to breed in our bodies, he thought impossible, and desired to know the reason of so unaccountable an evil. I told him, we fed on a thousand things which operated contrary to each other; that we eat when we were not hungry, and drank without the provocation of thirst; that we sat whole nights drinking strong liquors without eating a bit, which disposed us to sloth, enflamed our bodies, and precipitated or prevented digestion. That prostitute female yahoos acquired a certain malady, which bred rotteness in the bones of those who fell into their embraces; that this and many other diseases were propagated from father to son, so that great numbers come into the world with complicated maladies upon them; that it would be endless to give him a catalogue of all diseases incident to human bodies; for they could not be fewer than five or six hundred, spread over every limb and joint; in short, every part, external and intestine, having diseases appropriated to each. To remedy which, there was a sort of people bred up among us, in the profession or pretence of curing the sick. And because I had some skill in the faculty, I would, in gratitude to his Honour, let him know the whole mystery and method by which they proceed.

Their fundamental is, that all diseases arise from repletion, from whence they conclude that a great evacuation of the body is necessary, either through the natural passage, or upwards at the mouth. Their next business is, from herbs, minerals, gums, oils, shells, salts, juices, sea-weed, excrements, barks of trees, serpents, toads, frogs, spiders, dead men's flesh and bones, birds, beasts and fishes, to form a composition for smell and taste the most abominable, nauseous and detestable that they can possibly contrive, which the stomach immediately rejects with loathing; and this they call a vomit; or else from the same storehouse, with some other poisonous additions, they command us to take in at the orifice above or below (just as the physician then happens to be disposed) a medicine equally annoying and disgustful to the bowels, which, relaxing the belly, drives down all before it, and this they call a purge or a clyster. For nature (as the physicians allege) having intended the superior anterior orifice only for the intromission of solids and liquids, and the inferior posterior for ejection, these artists ingeniously considering that in all diseases Nature is forced out of her seat, therefore to replace her in it, the body must be treated in a manner directly contrary, by interchanging the use of each orifice, forcing solids and liquids in at the anus, and making evacuations at the mouth.

But besides real diseases we are subject to many that are only imaginary, for which the physicians have invented imaginary cures; these have their several names, and so have the drugs that are proper for them, and with these our female yahoos are always infested.

One great excellency in this tribe is their skill at prognostics, wherein they seldom fail; their predictions in real diseases, when they rise to any degree of malignity, generally portending death, which is always in their power, when recovery is not: and therefore, upon any unexpected signs of amendment, after they have pronounced their sentence, rather than be accused as false prophets, they know how to approve their sagacity to the world by a seasonable dose.

Clyster. Enema.

They are likewise of special use to husbands and wives who are grown weary of their mates, to eldest sons, to great ministers of state, and often to princes.

I had formerly upon occasion discoursed with my master upon the nature of our government in general, and particularly of our own excellent constitution, deservedly the wonder and envy of the whole world. But having here accidentally mentioned a "minister of state," he commanded me some time after to inform him, what species of yahoo I particularly meant by that appellation.

I told him that a first or chief minister of state, who was the person I intended to describe, was a creature wholly exempt from joy and grief, love and hatred, pity and anger; at least makes use of no other passions but a violent desire of wealth, power, and titles; that he applies his words to all uses, except to the indication of his mind; that he never tells a truth, but with an intent that you should take it for a lie; nor a lie, but with a design that you should take it for a truth; that those he speaks worst of behind their backs are in the surest way to preferment; and whenever he begins to praise you to others or to yourself, you are from that day forlorn. The worst mark you can receive is a promise, especially when it is confirmed with an oath; after which every wise man retires, and gives over all hopes.

There are three methods by which a man may rise to be chief minister: the first is, by knowing how with prudence to dispose of a wife, a daughter, or a sister: the second, by betraying or undermining his predecessor: and the third is, by a furious zeal in public assemblies against the corruptions of the court. But a wise prince would rather choose to employ those who practise the last of these methods; because such zealots prove always the most obsequious and subservient to the will and passions of their master. That these "ministers" having all employments at their disposal, preserve themselves in power by bribing the majority of a senate or great council; and at last, by an expedient called an "act of indemnity" (whereof I de-

---

First or chief minister of state . . . makes use of no other passions but a violent desire of wealth, power, and titles. Another jab at Walpole.

Act of indemnity. A preemptive pardon. Perhaps an allusion to the events of 1660–61, immediately following the restoration of Charles II. So as to soothe the fears of those who had acted against the royalist cause during the Interregnum, an Act of Indemnity and Oblivion was passed. The earl of Clarendon's *History of the Rebellion* (1702–4), approvingly annotated by Swift, makes clear that this amnesty rankled those on the royalist side, especially those whose estates had been plundered by the puritans. See Clarendon, vol. 2, 1–3. A 1708 Act of Indemnity served to place such Whiggish ministers as Robert Walpole, then secretary of war, beyond prosecution. In *Examiner* 38 (April 26, 1711), Swift attacks this law as protecting criminal officials from impeachment.

scribed the nature to him) they secure themselves from after reckonings, and retire from the public, laden with the spoils of the nation.

The palace of a chief minister is a seminary to breed up others in his own trade; the pages, lackeys, and porter, by imitating their master, become ministers of state in their several districts, and learn to excel in the three principal ingredients, of insolence, lying, and bribery. Accordingly, they have a subaltern court paid to them by persons of the best rank, and sometimes by the force of dexterity and impudence arrive through several gradations to be successors to their lord.

He is usually governed by a decayed wench or favourite footman, who are the tunnels through which all graces are conveyed, and may properly be called, in the last resort, the governors of the kingdom.

One day my master, having heard me mention the nobility of my country, was pleased to make me a compliment which I could not pretend to deserve: that he was sure I must have been born of some noble family, because I far exceeded in shape, colour, and cleanliness, all the yahoos of his nation, although I seemed to fail in strength and agility, which must be imputed to my different way of living from those other brutes, and besides, I was not only endowed with the faculty of speech, but likewise with some rudiments of reason, to a degree that with all his acquaintance I passed for a prodigy.

He made me observe, that among the Houyhnhnms, the white, the sorrel, and the iron-grey were not so exactly shaped as the bay, the dapple-grey, and the black; nor born with equal talents of the mind, or a capacity to improve them; and therefore continued always in the condition of servants, without ever aspiring to match out of their own race, which in that country would be reckoned monstrous and unnatural.

I made his Honour my most humble acknowledgments for the good opinion he was pleased to conceive of me; but assured him at the same time that my birth was of the lower sort, having been born of plain honest parents, who were just able to give me a tolerable education: that nobility among us was altogether a different thing from the idea he had of it; that

---

Their own race. The word *race* in this paragraph, as often throughout much of the eighteenth century, refers to *lineage:* a theme of loosely familial or clan distinction rather than a racial one in the more contemporary sense of vast biological subdivisions of the world's population. For the Houyhnhnms, a hereditary caste of black, dapple-gray, and bay horses occupies the highest ranks, while white, sorrel, and iron-gray horses are born to domestic service. Swift may have derived this equine hierarchy from the seventeenth-century authority on horsemanship, Gervase Markham, for whom a horse's complexion signified its dominant "humor" (Nash, 111). On p. 256 the Houyhnhnms as a whole species, in keeping with the early-eighteenth-century fluidity of the term, are described as a "race."

our young noblemen are bred from their childhood in idleness and luxury; that as soon as years will permit, they consume their vigor and contract odious diseases among lewd females; and when their fortunes are almost ruined, they marry some woman of mean birth, disagreeable person, and unsound constitution, merely for the sake of money, whom they hate and despise. That the productions of such marriages are generally scrofulous, ricketty, or deformed children, by which means the family seldom continues above three generations, unless the wife takes care to provide a healthy father among her neighbours or domestics, in order to improve and continue the breed. That a weak diseased body, a meager countenance, and sallow complexion are the true marks of noble blood; and a healthy robust appearance is so disgraceful in a man of quality, that the world concludes his real father to have been a groom, or a coachman. The imperfections of his mind run parallel with those of his body, being a composition of spleen, dulness, ignorance, caprice, sensuality, and pride.

Without the consent of this illustrious body no law can be enacted, repealed, or altered, and these nobles have likewise the decision of all our possessions without appeal.

CHAPTER VII

The author's great love of his native country. His master's observations upon the constitution and administration of England, as described by the author, with parallel cases and comparisons. His master's observations upon human nature.

The reader may be disposed to wonder how I could prevail on myself to give so free a representation of my own species, among a race of mortals who were already too apt to conceive the vilest opinion of human kind from that entire congruity betwixt me and their yahoos. But I must freely confess, that the many virtues of those excellent quadrupeds, placed in opposite view to human corruptions, had so far opened my eyes and enlarged my understanding, that I began to view the actions and passions of man in a very different light, and to think the honour of my own kind not worth managing; which, besides, it was impossible for me to do before a person of so acute a judgment as my master, who daily convinced me of a thousand faults in myself, whereof I had not the least perception before, and which with us would never be numbered even among human infirmities: I had likewise learned from his example an utter detestation of all falsehood or disguise; and truth appeared so amiable to me, that I determined upon sacrificing every thing to it.

Let me deal so candidly with the reader as to confess, that there was yet a much stronger motive for the freedom I took in my representation of things. I had not been a year in this country before I contracted such a love and veneration for the inhabitants, that I entered on a firm resolution never to return to human kind, but to pass the rest of my life among these admirable Houyhnhnms in the contemplation and practice of every virtue; where I could have no example or incitement to vice. But it was decreed by Fortune, my perpetual enemy, that so great a felicity should not fall to my share. However, it is now some comfort to reflect, that in what I said of my countrymen I extenuated their faults as much as I durst before so strict an examiner, and upon every article gave as favourable a turn as the matter would bear. For, indeed, who is there alive that will not be swayed by his bias and partiality to the place of his birth?

I have related the substance of several conversations I had with my master, during the greatest part of the time I had the honour to be in his service, but have indeed for brevity sake omitted much more than is here set down.

When I had answered all his questions, and his curiosity seemed to be fully satisfied, he sent for me one morning early and commanding me to sit down at some distance (an honour which he had never before conferred upon me), he said he had been very seriously considering my whole story, as far as it related both to myself and my country: that he looked upon us as a sort of animals to whose share, by what accident he could not conjecture, some small pittance of reason had fallen, whereof we made no other use than by its assistance to aggravate our natural corruptions, and to acquire new ones which Nature had not given us. That we disarmed ourselves of the few abilities she had bestowed, had been very successful in multiplying our original wants, and seemed to spend our whole lives in vain endeavours to supply them by our own inventions. That as to myself, it was manifest I had neither the strength or agility of a common yahoo, that I walked infirmly on my hinder feet, had found out a contrivance to make my claws of no use or defence, and to remove the hair from my chin, which was intended as a shelter from the sun and the weather. Lastly, that I could neither run with speed, nor climb trees like my brethren (as he called them) the yahoos in this country.

That our institutions of government and law were plainly owing to our gross defects in reason, and by consequence, in virtue; because reason alone is sufficient to govern a rational creature; which was therefore a character we had no pretence to challenge, even from the account I had given of my own people, although he manifestly perceived, that in order to favour them I had concealed many particulars, and often *said the thing which was not.*

He was the more confirmed in this opinion, because he observed, that as I agreed in every feature of my body with other yahoos, except where it was to my real disadvantage in point of strength, speed, and activity, the shortness of my claws, and some other particulars where nature had no part; so from the representation I had given him of our lives, our manners, and our actions, he found as near a resemblance in the disposition of our minds. He said the yahoos were known to hate one another more than they did any different species of animals; and the reason usually assigned was the odiousness of their own shapes, which all could see in the rest, but not in themselves. He had therefore begun to think it not unwise in us to cover our bodies, and, by that invention, conceal many of our deformities from each other, which would else be hardly supportable. But he now found he had been mistaken, and that the dissensions of those brutes in his country were owing to the same cause with ours, as I had described them. For if (said he) you throw among five yahoos as much food as would be sufficient for fifty, they will, instead of eating peaceably, fall together by the ears, each single one impatient to have all to itself, and therefore a servant was usually employed to stand by while they were feeding abroad, and those kept at home were tied at a distance from each other; that if a cow died of age or accident, before a Houyhnhnm could secure it for his own yahoos, those in the neighbourhood would come in herds to seize it, and then would ensue such a battle as I had described, with terrible wounds made by their claws on both sides, although they seldom were able to kill one another, for want of such convenient instruments of death as we had invented. At other times the like battles have been fought between the yahoos of several neighbourhoods without any visible cause; those of one district watching all opportunities to surprise the next before they are prepared. But if they find their project hath miscarried, they return home, and, for want of enemies, engage in what I call a civil war among themselves.

That in some fields of his country there are certain shining stones of several colours, whereof the yahoos are violently fond, and when part of these stones are fixed in the earth, as it sometimes happeneth, they will dig with their claws for whole days to get them out, carry them away, and hide them by heaps in their kennels; but still looking round with great caution, for fear their comrades should find out their treasure. My master said, he could never discover the reason of this unnatural appetite, or how these stones could be of any use to a yahoo; but now he believed it might proceed from the same principle of avarice which I had ascribed to mankind; that he had once, by way of experiment, privately removed a heap of these stones from the place where one of his yahoos had buried it:

whereupon the sordid animal, missing his treasure, by his loud lamenting brought the whole herd to the place, there miserably howled, then fell to biting and tearing the rest, began to pine away, would neither eat, nor sleep, nor work, till he ordered a servant privately to convey the stones into the same hole and hide them as before; which when his yahoo had found, he presently recovered his spirits and good humour, but took care to remove them to a better hiding-place, and hath ever since been a very serviceable brute.

My master farther assured me, which I also observed myself, that in the fields where these shining stones abound, the fiercest and most frequent battles are fought, occasioned by perpetual inroads of the neighbouring yahoos.

He said, it was common, when two yahoos discovered such a stone in a field, and were contending which of them should be the proprietor, a third would take the advantage, and carry it away from them both; which my master would needs contend to have some resemblance with our suits at law; wherein I thought it for our credit not to undeceive him; since the decision he mentioned was much more equitable than many decrees among us: because the plaintiff and defendant there lost nothing beside the stone they contended for, whereas our courts of equity would never have dismissed the cause while either of them had any thing left.

My master, continuing his discourse, said, there was nothing that rendered the yahoos more odious than their undistinguishing appetite to devour every thing that came in their way, whether herbs, roots, berries, corrupted flesh of animals, or all mingled together: and it was peculiar in their temper, that they were fonder of what they could get by rapine or stealth at a greater distance, than much better food provided for them at home. If their prey held out, they would eat till they were ready to burst, after which Nature had pointed out to them a certain root that gave them a general evacuation.

There was also another kind of root very juicy, but somewhat rare and difficult to be found, which the yahoos sought for with much eagerness, and would suck it with great delight; and it produced in them the same effects that wine hath upon us. It would make them sometimes hug, and sometimes tear one another; they would howl and grin, and chatter, and reel, and tumble, and then fall asleep in the mud.

I did indeed observe, that the yahoos were the only animals in this country subject to any diseases; which, however, were much fewer than horses have among us, and contracted not by any ill treatment they meet with, but by the nastiness and greediness of that sordid brute. Neither has their language any more than a general appellation for those maladies, which is borrowed from the name of the beast, and called *hnea-yahoo*, or the *yahoo's-evil*, and the cure prescribed is a mixture of their own dung and urine forcibly put down the yahoo's throat. This I have since often known to have been taken with success, and do here freely recommend it to my countrymen, for the public good, as an admirable specific against all diseases produced by repletion.

As to learning, government, arts, manufactures, and the like, my master confessed he could find little or no resemblance between the yahoos of that country and those in ours. For he only meant to observe what parity there was in our natures. He had heard indeed some curious Houyhnhnms observe, that in most herds there was a sort of ruling yahoo (as among us there is generally some leading or principal stag in a park), who was always more deformed in body, and mischievous in disposition, than any of the rest. That this leader had usually a favourite as like himself as he could get, whose employment was to lick his master's feet and posteriors, and drive the female yahoos to his kennel; for which he was now and then rewarded with a piece of ass's flesh. This favourite is hated by the whole herd, and therefore, to protect himself, keeps always near the person of his leader. He usually continues in office till a worse can be found; but the very moment he is discarded, his successor, at the head of all the yahoos in that district, young and old, male and female, come in a body, and discharge their excrements upon him from head to foot. But how far this might be applicable to our courts and favourites, and ministers of state, my master said I could best determine.

I durst make no return to this malicious insinuation, which debased human understanding below the sagacity of a common hound, who has judgment enough to distinguish and follow the cry of the ablest dog in the pack, without being ever mistaken.

My master told me, there were some qualities remarkable in the yahoos, which he had not observed me to mention, or at least very slightly, in the accounts I had given him of human kind; he said, those animals, like other brutes, had their females in common; but in this they differed, that the she-yahoo would admit the male while she was pregnant, and that the hees would quarrel and fight with the females as fiercely as with each other. Both which practices were such degrees of infamous brutality, that no other sensitive creature ever arrived at.

Another thing he wondered at in the yahoos was their strange disposition to nastiness and dirt, whereas there appears to be a natural love of cleanliness in all other animals. As to the two former accusations, I was glad to let them pass without any reply, because I had not a word to offer upon them in defence of my species, which otherwise I certainly had done from my own inclinations. But I could have easily vindicated human kind from the imputation of singularity upon the last article, if there had been any swine in that country (as unluckily for me there were not), which, although it may be a sweeter quadruped than a yahoo, cannot, I humbly conceive, in justice pretend to more cleanliness; and so his Honour himself must have owned, if he had seen their filthy way of feeding, and their custom of wallowing and sleeping in the mud.

My master likewise mentioned another quality which his servants had discovered in several yahoos, and to him was wholly unaccountable. He said, a fancy would sometimes take a yahoo to retire into a corner, to lie down and howl, and groan, and spurn away all that came near him, although he were young and fat, and wanted neither food nor water; nor did the servants imagine what could possibly ail him. And the only remedy they found was to set him to hard work, after which he would infallibly come to himself. To this I was silent out of partiality to my own kind; yet here I could plainly discover the true seeds of spleen, which only seizeth on the lazy, the luxurious, and the rich; who, if they were forced to undergo the same regimen, I would undertake for the cure.

His Honour had farther observed, that a female yahoo would often stand behind a bank or a bush, to gaze on the young males passing by, and then appear, and hide, using many antic gestures and grimaces, at which time it was observed, that she had a most offensive smell; and when any of the males advanced, would slowly retire, looking often back, and with a counterfeit show of fear, run off into some convenient place where she knew the male would follow her.

At other times if a female stranger came among them, three or four of her own sex would get about her, and stare and chatter, and grin, and smell her all over, and then turn off with gestures that seemed to express contempt and disdain.

Perhaps my master might refine a little in these speculations, which he had drawn from what he observed himself, or had been told him by others: however, I could not reflect without some amazement, and much sorrow, that the rudiments of lewdness, coquetry, censure, and scandal, should have place by instinct in womankind.

I expected every moment that my master would accuse the yahoos of those unnatural appetites in both sexes, so common among us. But Nature, it seems, hath not been so expert a school-mistress; and these politer pleasures are entirely the productions of art and reason, on our side of the globe.

Spleen. The humor-based affliction of melancholia: often lampooned as a fashionable affectation or anxiously noted as the "English malady."

CHAPTER VIII

The author relates several particulars of the yahoos. The great virtues of the Houyhnhnms. The education and exercise of their youth. Their general assembly.

As I ought to have understood human nature much better than I supposed it possible for my master to do, so it was easy to apply the character he gave of the yahoos to myself and my countrymen, and I believed I could yet make farther discoveries from my own observation. I therefore often begged his Honour to let me go among the herds of yahoos in the neighbourhood, to which he always very graciously consented, being perfectly convinced that the hatred I bore those brutes would never suffer me to be corrupted by them; and his Honour ordered one of his servants, a strong sorrel nag, very honest and good-natured, to be my guard, without whose protection I durst not undertake such adventures. For I have already told the reader how much I was pestered by those odious animals upon my first arrival. And I afterwards failed very narrowly three or four times of falling into their clutches, when I happened to stray at any distance without my hanger. And I have reason to believe they had some imagination that I was of their own species, which I often assisted myself, by stripping up my sleeves, and showing my naked arms and breast in their sight, when my protector was with me. At which times they would approach as near as they durst, and imitate my actions after the manner of monkeys, but ever with great signs of hatred, as a tame jackdaw, with cap and stockings, is always persecuted by the wild ones, when he happens to be got among them.

They are prodigiously nimble from their infancy; however, I once caught a young male of three years old, and endeavoured by all marks of tenderness to make it quiet; but the little imp fell a squalling, and scratching, and biting with such violence, that I was forced to let it go, and it was high time, for a whole troop of old ones came about us at the noise, but finding the cub was safe (for away it ran), and my sorrel nag being by, they durst not venture near us. I observed the young animal's flesh to smell very rank, and the stink was somewhat between a weasel and a fox, but much more disagreeable. I forgot another circumstance (and perhaps I might have the reader's pardon if it were wholly omitted) that while I held the odious vermin in my hands, it voided its filthy excrements of a yellow liquid substance all over my clothes; but by good fortune there was a small brook hard by, where I washed myself as clean as I could, although I durst not come into my master's presence, until I were sufficiently aired.

By what I could discover, the yahoos appear to be the most unteachable of all animals, their capacities never reaching higher than to draw or carry burthens. Yet I am of opinion this defect ariseth chiefly from a perverse, restive disposition. For they are cunning, malicious, treacherous and revengeful. They are strong and hardy, but of a cowardly spirit, and by consequence insolent, abject, and cruel. It is observed, that the redhaired of both sexes are more libidinous and mischievous than the rest, whom yet they much exceed in strength and activity.

The Houyhnhnms keep the yahoos for present use in huts not far from the house; but the rest are sent abroad to certain fields, where they dig up roots, eat several kinds of herbs, and search about for carrion, or sometimes catch weasels and *luhimuhs* (a sort of wild rat), which they greedily devour. Nature hath taught them to dig deep holes with their nails on the side of a rising ground, wherein they lie by themselves, only the kennels of the females are larger, sufficient to hold two or three cubs.

They swim from their infancy like frogs, and are able to continue long under water, where they often take fish, which the females carry home to their young. And upon this occasion, I hope the reader will pardon my relating an odd adventure.

Being one day abroad with my protector the sorrel nag, and the weather exceeding hot, I entreated him to let me bathe in a river that was near. He consented, and I immediately stripped myself stark naked, and went down softly into the stream. It happened that a young female yahoo, standing behind a bank, saw the whole proceeding, and inflamed by desire, as the nag and I conjectured, came running with all speed, and leaped into the water within five yards of the place where I bathed. I was never in my life so terribly frighted; the nag was grazing at some distance, not suspecting any harm. She embraced me after a most fulsome manner; I roared as loud as I could, and the nag came galloping towards me, whereupon she quitted her grasp, with the utmost reluctancy, and leaped upon the opposite bank, where she stood gazing and howling all the time I was putting on my clothes.

This was matter of diversion to my master and his family, as well as of mortification to myself. For now I could no longer deny that I was a real yahoo in every limb and feature, since the females had a natural propensity to me as one of their own species: neither was the hair of this brute of a red colour (which might have been some excuse for an appetite a little irregular) but black as a sloe, and her countenance did not make an appearance altogether so hideous as the rest of the kind; for, I think, she could not be above eleven years old.

Having already lived three years in this country, the reader I suppose will expect that I should, like other travellers, give him some account of the

Salomon Gessner, *Gulliver Assaulted by Female Yahoo.* From *Lemuel Gulliver's Sämtliche Reisen* (German edition of *Gulliver's Travels*), 1762.

THE BEINECKE RARE BOOK AND MANUSCRIPT LIBRARY, YALE UNIVERSITY.

manners and customs of its inhabitants, which it was indeed my principal study to learn.

As these noble Houyhnhnms are endowed by nature with a general disposition to all virtues, and have no conceptions or ideas of what is evil in a rational creature, so their grand maxim is, to cultivate reason, and to be wholly governed by it. Neither is reason among them a point problematical as with us, where men can argue with plausibility on both sides of a question; but strikes you with immediate conviction; as it must needs do where it is not mingled, obscured, or discoloured by passion and interest. I remember it was with extreme difficulty that I could bring my master to understand the meaning of the word *opinion,* or how a point could be disputable; because reason taught us to affirm or deny only where we are certain; and beyond our knowledge we cannot do either. So that controversies, wranglings, disputes, and positiveness in false or dubious propositions are evils unknown among the Houyhnhnms. In the like manner, when I used to explain to him our several systems of natural philosophy, he would laugh that a creature pretending to reason should value itself upon the knowledge of other people's conjectures, and in things where that knowledge, if it were certain, could be of no use. Wherein he agreed entirely with the sentiments of Socrates, as Plato delivers them; which I mention as the highest honour I can do that prince of philosophers. I have often since reflected what destruction such a doctrine would make in the libraries of Europe, and how many paths to fame would be then shut up in the learned world.

Friendship and benevolence are the two principal virtues among the Houyhnhnms, and these not confined to particular objects, but universal to the whole race. For a stranger from the remotest part is equally treated with the nearest neighbour, and wherever he goes, looks upon himself as at home. They preserve decency and civility in the highest degrees, but are altogether ignorant of ceremony. They have no fondness for their colts or foals, but the care they take in educating them proceeds entirely from the dictates of reason. And I observed my master to show the same affection to his neighbour's issue that he had for his own. They will have it that nature teaches them to love the whole species, and it is reason only that maketh a distinction of persons, where there is a superior degree of virtue.

When the matron Houyhnhnms have produced one of each sex, they no longer accompany with their consorts, except they lose one of their issue by some casualty, which very seldom happens: but in such a case they meet again, or when the like accident befalls a person whose wife is past bearing, some other couple bestows on him one of their own colts, and then go together a second time till the mother be pregnant. This caution is necessary to prevent the country from being overburthened with numbers. But the race of inferior Houyhnhnms bred up to be servants is not so strictly limited upon this article; these are allowed to produce three of each sex, to be domestics in the noble families.

In their marriages they are exactly careful to choose such colours as will not make any disagreeable mixture in the breed. Strength is chiefly valued in the male, and comeliness in the female, not upon the account of love, but to preserve the race from degenerating; for where a female happens to excel in strength, a consort is chosen with regard to comeliness. Courtship, love, presents, jointures, settlements, have no place in their thoughts, or terms whereby to express them in their language. The young couple meet and are joined, merely because it is the determination of their parents and friends: it is what they see done every day, and they look upon it as one of the necessary actions in a reasonable being. But the violation of marriage, or any other unchastity, was never heard of: and the married pair pass their lives with the same friendship and mutual benevolence that they bear to all others of the same species who come in their way; without jealousy, fondness, quarrelling, or discontent.

In educating the youth of both sexes, their method is admirable, and highly deserves our imitation. These are not suffered to taste a grain of oats, except upon certain days, till eighteen years old; nor milk, but very rarely; and in summer they graze two hours in the morning, and as many in the evening, which their parents likewise observe, but the servants are not allowed above half that time, and a great part of the grass is brought home, which they eat at the most convenient hours, when they can be best spared from work.

Temperance, industry, exercise and cleanliness, are the lessons equally enjoined to the young ones of both sexes: and my master thought it monstrous in us to give the females a different kind of education from the males, except in some articles of domestic management; whereby, as he truly observed, one half of our natives were good for nothing but bringing children into the world: and to trust the care of their children to such useless animals, he said, was yet a greater instance of brutality.

But the Houyhnhnms train up their youth to strength, speed, and hardiness, by exercising them in running races up and down steep hills, or over hard stony grounds, and when they are all in a sweat, they are ordered to leap over head and ears into a pond or a river. Four times a year the youth of certain districts meet to show their proficiency in running and leaping, and other feats of strength or agility, where the victor is rewarded with a song made in his or her praise. On this festival the servants drive a herd of yahoos into the field, laden with hay, and oats, and milk for a repast to the Houyhnhnms; after which these brutes are immediately driven back again, for fear of being noisome to the assembly.

Every fourth year, at the vernal equinox, there is a representative council of the whole nation, which meets in a plain about twenty miles from our house, and continues about five or six days. Here they inquire into the state and condition of the several districts; whether they abound or be deficient in hay or oats, or cows or yahoos. And wherever there is any want (which is but seldom) it is immediately supplied by unanimous consent and contribution. Here likewise the regulation of children is settled: as for instance, if a Houyhnhnm hath two males, he changeth one of them with another who hath two females: and when a child hath been lost by any casualty, where the mother is past breeding, it is determined what family in the district shall breed another to supply the loss.

CHAPTER IX

A grand debate at the general assembly of the Houyhnhnms, and how it was determined. The learning of the Houyhnhnms. Their buildings. Their manner of burials. The defectiveness of their language.

One of these grand assemblies was held in my time, about three months before my departure, whither my master went as the representative of our district. In this council was resumed their old debate, and indeed, the only debate that ever happened in their country; whereof my master after his return gave me a very particular account.

The question to be debated was, whether the yahoos should be exterminated from the face of the earth. One of the members for the affirmative offered several arguments of great strength and weight, alleging, that as the yahoos were the most filthy, noisome, and deformed animal which nature ever produced, so they were the most restive and indocible, mischievous and malicious: they would privately suck the teats of the Houyhnhnms' cows, kill and devour their cats, trample down their oats and grass, if they were not continually watched, and commit a thousand other extravagancies. He took notice of a general tradition, that yahoos had not been always in their country: but that many ages ago two of these brutes appeared together upon a mountain, whether produced by the heat of the sun upon corrupted mud and slime, or from the ooze and froth of the sea, was never known. That these yahoos engendered, and their brood in a short time grew so numerous as to overrun and infest the whole nation. That the Houyhnhnms, to get rid of this evil, made a general hunting, and at last enclosed the whole herd; and destroying the older, every Houyhnhnm kept two young ones in a kennel, and brought them to such a degree of tameness, as an animal so savage by nature can be capable of acquiring; using them for draught and carriage. That there seemed to be much truth in this tradition, and that those creatures could not be *ylnhniamshy* (or *aborigines* of the land) because of the violent hatred the Houyhnhnms, as well as all other animals, bore them; which although their evil disposition sufficiently deserved, could never have arrived at so high a degree, if they had been aborigines, or else they would have long since been rooted out. That the inhabitants taking a fancy to use the service of the yahoos, had very imprudently neglected to cultivate the breed of asses, which were a comely animal, easily kept, more tame and orderly, without any offensive smell, strong enough for labour, although they yield to the other in agility of body; and if their braying be no agreeable sound, it is far preferable to the horrible howlings of the yahoos.

Several others declared their sentiments to the same purpose, when my master proposed an expedient to the assembly, whereof he had indeed borrowed the hint from me. He approved of the tradition, mentioned by the "honourable member" who spoke before, and affirmed, that the two yahoos said to be first seen among them had been driven thither over the sea; that coming to land, and being forsaken by their companions, they retired to the mountains, and degenerating by degrees, became in process of time much more savage than those of their own species in the country from whence these two originals came. The reason of his assertion was, that he had now in his possession a certain wonderful yahoo (meaning myself) which most of them had heard of, and many of them had seen. He then related to them how he first found me; that my body was all covered with an artificial composure of the skins and hairs of other animals: that I spoke in a language of my own, and had thoroughly learned theirs: that I had related to him the accidents which brought me thither: that when he saw me without my covering, I was an exact yahoo in every part, only of a whiter colour, less hairy, and with shorter claws. He added, how I had endeavoured to persuade him, that in my own and other countries the yahoos acted as the governing, rational animal, and held the Houyhnhnms in servitude: that he observed in me all the qualities of a yahoo, only a little more civilized by some tincture of reason, which however was in a degree as far inferior to the Houyhnhnm race as the yahoos of their country were to me: that, among other things, I mentioned a custom we had of castrating Houyhnhnms when they were young, in order to render them tame; that the operation was easy and safe; that it was no shame to learn wisdom from brutes, as industry is taught by the ant, and building by the swallow. (For so I translate the word *lyhannh,* although it be a much larger fowl.)

That this invention might be practised upon the younger yahoos here, which, besides rendering them tractable and fitter for use, would in an age put an end to the whole species without destroying life. That in the mean time the Houyhnhnms should be exhorted to cultivate the breed of asses, which, as they are in all respects more valuable brutes, so they have this advantage, to be fit for service at five years old, which the others are not till twelve.

This was all my master thought fit to tell me at that time of what passed in the grand council. But he was pleased to conceal one particular, which related personally to myself, whereof I soon felt the unhappy effect, as the reader will know in its proper place, and from whence I date all the succeeding misfortunes of my life.

The Houyhnhnms have no letters, and consequently their knowledge is all traditional. But there happening few events of any moment among a people so well united, naturally disposed to every virtue, wholly governed by reason, and cut off from all commerce with other nations, the historical part is easily preserved without burthening their memories. I have already observed, that they are subject to no diseases, and therefore can have no need of physicians. However, they have excellent medicines composed of herbs, to cure accidental bruises and cuts in the pastern or frog of the foot by sharp stones, as well as other maims and hurts in the several parts of the body.

They calculate the year by the revolution of the sun and the moon, but use no subdivisions into weeks. They are well enough acquainted with the motions of those two luminaries, and understand the nature of eclipses; and this is the utmost progress of their astronomy.

In poetry they must be allowed to excel all other mortals; wherein the justness of their similes, and the minuteness, as well as exactness of their descriptions, are indeed inimitable. Their verses abound very much in both of these, and usually contain either some exalted notions of friendship and benevolence, or the praises of those who were victors in races and other bodily exercises. Their buildings, although very rude and simple, are not inconvenient, but well contrived to defend them from all injuries of cold and heat. They have a kind of tree, which at forty years old loosens in the root, and falls with the first storm; it grows very straight, and being pointed like stakes with a sharp stone (for the Houyhnhnms know not the use of iron), they stick them erect in the ground about ten inches asunder, and then weave in oat-straw, or sometimes wattles betwixt them. The roof is made after the same manner, and so are the doors.

The Houyhnhnms use the hollow part between the pastern and the hoof of their forefeet as we do our hands, and this with greater dexterity than I could at first imagine. I have seen a white mare of our family thread a needle (which I lent her on purpose) with that joint. They milk their cows, reap their oats, and do all the work which requires hands, in the same manner. They have a kind of hard flints, which, by grinding against other stones, they form into instruments, that serve instead of wedges, axes, and hammers. With tools made of these flints they likewise cut their hay, and reap their oats, which there groweth naturally in several fields: the yahoos draw home the sheaves in carriages, and the servants tread them in certain covered huts, to get out the grain, which is kept in stores. They make a rude kind of earthen and wooden vessels, and bake the former in the sun.

If they can avoid casualties, they die only of old age, and are buried in the obscurest places that can be found, their friends and relations expressing neither joy nor grief at their departure; nor does the dying person discover the least regret that he is leaving the world, any more than if he were upon returning home from a visit to one of his neighbours; I remember my master having once made an appointment with a friend and his family to come to his house upon some affair of importance; on the day fixed, the mistress and her two children came very late; she made two excuses, first for her husband, who, as she said, happened that very morning to *lhnuwnh.* The word is strongly expressive in their language, but not easily rendered into English; it signifies, "to retire to his first mother." Her excuse for not coming sooner was, that her husband dying late in the morning, she was a good while consulting her servants about a convenient place where his body should be laid; and I observed she behaved herself at our house as cheerfully as the rest: she died about three months after.

They live generally to seventy or seventy-five years, very seldom to fourscore: some weeks before their death they feel a gradual decay, but without pain. During this time they are much visited by their friends, because they cannot go abroad with their usual ease and satisfaction. However, about ten days before their death, which they seldom fail in computing, they return the visits that have been made them by those who are nearest in the neighbourhood, being carried in a convenient sledge drawn by yahoos, which vehicle they use, not only upon this occasion, but when they grow old, upon long journeys, or when they are lamed by any accident. And therefore when the dying Houyhnhnms return those visits, they take a solemn leave of their friends, as if they were going to some remote part of the country, where they designed to pass the rest of their lives.

I know not whether it may be worth observing, that the Houyhnhnms have no word in their language to express any thing that is evil, except what they borrow from the deformities or ill qualities of the yahoos. Thus they denote the folly of a servant, an omission of a child, a stone that cuts their feet, a continuance of foul or unseasonable weather, and the like, by adding to each the epithet of *yahoo.* For instance, *hhnm yahoo, whnaholm yahoo, ynlhnmawihlma yahoo,* and an ill-contrived house *ynholmhnmrohlnw yahoo.*

I could with great pleasure enlarge farther upon the manners and virtues of this excellent people; but intending in a short time to publish a volume by itself expressly upon that subject, I refer the reader thither. And in the mean time, proceed to relate my own sad catastrophe.

CHAPTER X

The author's œconomy and happy life among the Houyhnhnms. His great improvement in virtue, by conversing with them. Their conversations. The author has notice given him by his master that he must depart from the country. He falls into a swoon for grief, but submits. He contrives and finishes a canoe, by the help of a fellow-servant, and puts to sea at a venture.

I had settled my little œconomy to my own heart's content. My master had ordered a room to be made for me after their manner, about six yards from the house, the sides and floors of which I plastered with clay, and covered with rush mats of my own contriving; I had beaten hemp, which there grows wild, and made of it a sort of ticking: this I filled with the feathers of several birds I had taken with springes made of yahoos' hairs, and were excellent food. I had worked two chairs with my knife, the sorrel nag helping me in the grosser and more laborious part. When my clothes were worn to rags, I made myself others with the skins of rabbits, and of a certain beautiful animal about the same size, called *nnuhnoh,* the skin of which is covered with a fine down. Of these I likewise made very tolerable stockings. I soled my shoes with wood which I cut from a tree, and fitted to the upper leather, and when this was worn out, I supplied it with the skins of yahoos dried in the sun. I often got honey out of hollow trees, which I mingled with water, or eat it with my bread. No man could more verify the truth of these two maxims, *That nature is very easily satisfied;* and *That necessity is the mother of invention.* I enjoyed perfect health of body and tranquillity of mind; I did not feel the treachery or inconstancy of a friend, nor the injuries of a secret or open enemy. I had no occasion of bribing, flattering or pimping to procure the favour of any great man or of his minion. I wanted no fence against fraud or oppression; here was neither physician to destroy my body, nor lawyer to ruin my fortune; no informer to watch my words and actions, or forge accusations against me for hire: here were no gibers, censurers, backbiters, pickpockets, highwaymen, housebreakers, attorneys, bawds, buffoons, gamesters, politicians, wits, splenetics, tedious talkers, controvertists, ravishers, murderers, robbers, virtuosos: no leaders or followers of party and faction: no encouragers to vice, by seducement or examples: no dungeon, axes, gibbets, whipping-posts, or pillories: no cheating shopkeepers or mechanics: no pride, vanity, or affectation: no fops, bullies, drunkards, strolling whores, or poxes: no ranting, lewd, expensive wives: no stupid, proud pedants: no importunate, overbearing, quarrelsome, noisy, roaring, empty, conceited, swearing companions: no scoundrels, raised from the dust upon the merit of their vices, or nobility thrown into it on account of their virtues: no lords, fiddlers, judges or dancing-masters.

I had the favour of being admitted to several Houyhnhnms, who came to visit or dine with my master; where his Honour graciously suffered me to wait in the room, and listen to their discourse. Both he and his company would often descend to ask me questions, and receive my answers. I had also sometimes the honour of attending my master in his visits to others. I never presumed to speak, except in answer to a question, and then I did it with inward regret, because it was a loss of so much time for improving myself: but I was infinitely delighted with the station of an humble auditor in such conversations, where nothing passed but what was useful, expressed in the fewest and most significant words: where (as I have already said) the greatest decency was observed, without the least degree of ceremony; where no person spoke without being pleased himself, and pleasing his companions; where there was no interruptions, tediousness, heat, or difference of sentiments. They have a notion, that when people are met together, a short silence doth much improve conversation: this I found to be true; for during those little intermissions of talk, new ideas would arise in their minds, which very much enlivened the discourse. Their subjects are generally on friendship and benevolence, or order and œconomy, sometimes upon the visible operations of nature, or ancient traditions, upon the bounds and limits of virtue, upon the unerring rules of reason, or upon some determinations to be taken at the next great assembly, and often upon the various excellencies of poetry. I may add without vanity, that my presence often gave them sufficient matter for discourse, because it afforded my master an occasion of letting his friends into the history of me and my country, upon which they were all pleased to descant in a manner not very advantageous to human kind; and for that reason I shall not repeat what they said: only I may be allowed to observe, that his Honour, to my great admiration, appeared to understand the nature of yahoos much better than myself. He went through all our vices and follies, and

---

Mechanics. Manual laborers (Fox, 250).

discovered many which I had never mentioned to him, by only supposing what qualities a yahoo of their country, with a small proportion of reason, might be capable of exerting; and concluded, with too much probability, how vile as well as miserable such a creature must be.

I freely confess, that all the little knowledge I have of any value was acquired by the lectures I received from my master, and from hearing the discourses of him and his friends; to which I should be prouder to listen, than to dictate to the greatest and wisest assembly in Europe. I admired the strength, comeliness, and speed of the inhabitants; and such a constellation of virtues in such amiable persons produced in me the highest veneration. At first, indeed, I did not feel that natural awe which the yahoos and all other animals bear towards them; but it grew upon me by degrees, much sooner than I imagined, and was mingled with a respectful love and gratitude, that they would condescend to distinguish me from the rest of my species.

When I thought of my family, my friends, my countrymen, or human race in general, I considered them as they really were, yahoos in shape and disposition, only a little more civilized, and qualified with the gift of speech, but making no other use of reason than to improve and multiply those vices whereof their brethren in this country had only the share that nature allotted them. When I happened to behold the reflection of my own form in a lake or fountain, I turned away my face in horror and detestation of myself, and could better endure the sight of a common yahoo, than of my own person. By conversing with the Houyhnhnms, and looking upon them with delight, I fell to imitate their gait and gesture, which is now grown into a habit, and my friends often tell me in a blunt way that I "trot like a horse"; which, however, I take for a great compliment: neither shall I disown, that in speaking I am apt to fall into the voice and manner of the Houyhnhnms, and hear myself ridiculed on that account without the least mortification.

In the midst of all this happiness, when I looked upon myself to be fully settled for life, my master sent for me one morning a little earlier than his usual hour. I observed by his countenance that he was in some perplexity, and at a loss how to begin what he had to speak. After a short silence, he told me, he did not know how I would take what he was going to say; that in the last general assembly, when the affair of the yahoos was entered upon, the representatives had taken offence at his keeping a yahoo (meaning myself) in his family more like a Houyhnhnm than a brute animal. That he was known frequently to converse with me, as if he could receive some advantage or pleasure in my company: that such a practice was not agreeable to reason or nature, or a thing ever heard of before among them. The assembly did therefore exhort him, either to employ me like the rest of my species, or command me to swim back to the place from whence I came. That the first of these expedients was utterly rejected by all the Houyhnhnms who had ever seen me at his house or their own: for they alleged, that because I had some rudiments of reason, added to the natural pravity of those animals, it was to be feared, I might be able to seduce them into the woody and mountainous parts of the country, and bring them in troops by night to destroy the Houyhnhnms' cattle, as being naturally of the ravenous kind, and averse from labour.

My master added, that he was daily pressed by the Houyhnhnms of the neighbourhood to have the assembly's exhortation executed, which he could not put off much longer. He doubted it would be impossible for me to swim to another country, and therefore wished I would contrive some sort of vehicle resembling those I had described to him, that might carry me on the sea, in which work I should have the assistance of his own servants, as well as those of his neighbours. He concluded, that for his own part he could have been content to keep me in his service as long as I lived, because he found I had cured myself of some bad habits and dispositions, by endeavouring, as far as my inferior nature was capable, to imitate the Houyhnhnms.

I should here observe to the reader, that a decree of the general assembly in this country is expressed by the word *hnhloayn,* which signifies an *exhortation,* as near as I can render it: for they have no conception how a rational creature can be compelled, but only advised or exhorted, because no person can disobey reason, without giving up his claim to be a rational creature.

I was struck with the utmost grief and despair at my master's discourse, and being unable to support the agonies I was under, I fell into a swoon at his feet; when I came to myself he told me that he concluded I had been dead. (For these people are subject to no such imbecilities of nature.) I answered, in a faint voice, that death would have been too great an happiness; that although I could not blame the assembly's exhortation, or the urgency of his friends, yet, in my weak and corrupt judgment, I thought it might consist with reason to have been less rigorous. That I could not swim a league, and probably the nearest land to theirs might be distant above an hundred; that many materials, necessary for making a small vessel to carry me off, were wholly wanting in this country, which, however, I would attempt in obedience and gratitude to his Honour, although I concluded the thing to be impossible, and therefore looked on my self as already devoted to destruction. That the certain prospect of an unnatural death was the least of my evils: for, supposing I should escape with life by some

---

Pravity. Depravity.

strange adventure, how could I think with temper of passing my days among yahoos, and relapsing into my old corruptions, for want of examples to lead and keep me within the paths of virtue? That I knew too well upon what solid reasons all the determinations of the wise Houyhnhnms were founded, not to be shaken by arguments of mine, a miserable yahoo; and therefore, after presenting him with my humble thanks for the offer of his servants' assistance in making a vessel, and desiring a reasonable time for so difficult a work, I told him I would endeavor to preserve a wretched being; and, if ever I returned to England, was not without hopes of being useful to my own species, by celebrating the praises of the renowned Houyhnhnms, and proposing their virtues to the imitation of mankind.

My master in a few words made me a very gracious reply, allowed me the space of two months to finish my boat; and ordered the sorrel nag, my fellow-servant (for so at this distance I may presume to call him) to follow my instructions, because I told my master, that his help would be sufficient, and I knew he had a tenderness for me.

In his company my first business was to go to that part of the coast where my rebellious crew had ordered me to be set on shore. I got upon a height, and looking on every side into the sea, fancied I saw a small island, towards the northeast: I took out my pocket-glass, and could then clearly distinguish it about five leagues off, as I computed; but it appeared to the sorrel nag to be only a blue cloud: for as he had no conception of any country beside his own, so he could not be as expert in distinguishing remote objects at sea as we who so much converse in that element.

After I had discovered this island, I considered no farther; but resolved it should, if possible, be the first place of my banishment, leaving the consequence to fortune.

I returned home, and consulting with the sorrel nag, we went into a copse at some distance, where I with my knife, and he with a sharp flint fastened very artificially after their manner, to a wooden handle, cut down several oak wattles about the thickness of a walking-staff, and some larger pieces. But I shall not trouble the reader with a particular description of my own mechanics; let it suffice to say that in six weeks' time, with the help of the sorrel nag, who performed the parts that required most labour, I finished a sort of Indian canoe, but much larger, covering it with the skins of yahoos well stitched together, with hempen threads of my own making. My sail was likewise composed of the skins of the same animal; but I made use of the youngest I could get, the older being too tough and thick, and I likewise provided myself with four paddles. I laid in a stock of boiled flesh, of rabbits and fowls, and took with me two vessels, one filled with milk, and the other with water.

I tried my canoe in a large pond near my master's house, and then corrected in it what was amiss; stopping all the chinks with yahoos' tallow, till I found it staunch, and able to bear me and my freight. And when it was as complete as I could possibly make it, I had it drawn on a carriage very gently by yahoos to the seaside, under the conduct of the sorrel nag and another servant.

When all was ready, and the day came for my departure, I took leave of my master and lady, and the whole family, my eyes flowing with tears, and my heart quite sunk with grief. But his Honour, out of curiosity, and perhaps (if I may speak it without vanity) partly out of kindness, was determined to see me in my canoe, and got several of his neighbouring friends to accompany him. I was forced to wait above an hour for the tide, and then observing the wind very fortunately bearing towards the island, to which I intended to steer my course, I took a second leave of my master: but as I was going to prostrate myself to kiss his hoof, he did me the honour to raise it gently to my mouth. I am not ignorant how much I have been censured for mentioning this last particular. Detractors are pleased to think it improbable, that so illustrious a person should descend to give so great a mark of distinction to a creature so inferior as I. Neither have I forgot how apt some travellers are to boast of extraordinary favours they have received. But if these censurers were better acquainted with the noble and courteous disposition of the Houyhnhnms, they would soon change their opinion.

I paid my respects to the rest of the Houyhnhnms in his Honour's company; then getting into my canoe, I pushed off from shore.

CHAPTER XI

The author's dangerous voyage. He arrives at New Holland, hoping to settle there. Is wounded with an arrow by one of the natives. Is seized and carried by force into a Portuguese ship. The great civilities of the captain. The author arrives at England.

I began this desperate voyage on February 15, 1714–5, at 9 o'clock in the morning. The wind was very favourable; however, I made use at first only

---

February 15, 1714–1715. The New Year was considered at this time to begin on March 25: hence the ambiguity in dating the year. By our reckoning, as Landa points out, the correct date would be 1715.

Sawrey Gilpin, *Gulliver Taking His Final Leave of the Land of the Houynhnms,* 1769.
COURTESY YALE CENTER FOR BRITISH ART, PAUL MELLON COLLECTION.

of my paddles, but considering I should soon be weary, and that the wind might probably chop about, I ventured to set up my little sail; and thus with the help of the tide I went at the rate of a league and a half an hour, as near as I could guess. My master and his friends continued on the shore till

I was almost out of sight; and I often heard the sorrel nag (who always loved me) crying out, *Hnuy illa nyha maiah yahoo,* Take care of thyself, gentle yahoo.

My design was, if possible, to discover some small island uninhabited, yet sufficient by my labour to furnish me with the necessaries of life, which I would have thought a greater happiness than to be first minister in the politest court of Europe; so horrible was the idea I conceived of returning to live in the society and under the government of yahoos. For in such a solitude as I desired, I could at least enjoy my own thoughts, and reflect with delight on the virtues of those inimitable Houyhnhnms, without any opportunity of degenerating into the vices and corruptions of my own species.

The reader may remember what I related when my crew conspired against me, and confined me to my cabin. How I continued there several weeks, without knowing what course we took, and when I was put ashore in the long-boat, how the sailors told me with oaths, whether true or false, that they knew not in what part of the world we were. However, I did then believe us to be about ten degrees southward of the Cape of Good Hope, or about 45 degrees southern latitude, as I gathered from some general words I overheard among them, being I supposed to the southeast in their intended voyage to Madagascar. And although this were but little better than conjecture, yet I resolved to steer my course eastward, hoping to reach the southwest coast of New Holland, and perhaps some such island as I desired, lying westward of it. The wind was full west, and by six in the evening I computed I had gone eastward at least eighteen leagues, when I spied a very small island about half a league off, which I soon reached. It was nothing but a rock, with one creek, naturally arched by the force of tempests. Here I put in my canoe, and climbing a part of the rock, I could plainly discover land to the east, extending from south to north. I lay all night in my canoe, and repeating my voyage early in the morning, I arrived in seven hours to the southeast point of New Holland. This confirmed me in the opinion I have long entertained, that the maps and charts place this country at least three degrees more to the east than it really is; which thought I communicated many years ago to my worthy friend Mr. Herman Moll, and gave him my reasons for it, although he hath rather chosen to follow other authors.

Herman Moll. Dutch geographer who came to London in 1698 and became the best-known British cartographer of his time. Moll's *New and Correct Map of the Whole World* (1719) is the main source for the coastlines of the maps in *Gulliver's Travels* (Bracher). His *View of the Coasts, Countries and Islands within the Limits of the South Sea Company* appeared in 1711. Moll also published numerous maps of Ireland, including his *New Map of Ireland* (1714).

I saw no inhabitants in the place where I landed, and being unarmed, I was afraid of venturing far into the country. I found some shellfish on the shore, and eat them raw, not daring to kindle a fire, for fear of being discovered by the natives. I continued three days feeding on oysters and limpets, to save my own provisions, and I fortunately found a brook of excellent water, which gave me great relief.

On the fourth day, venturing out early a little too far, I saw twenty or thirty natives upon a height, not above five hundred yards from me. They were stark naked, men, women, and children, round a fire, as I could discover by the smoke. One of them spied me, and gave notice to the rest; five of them advanced towards me, leaving the women and children at the fire. I made what haste I could to the shore, and getting into my canoe, shoved off: the savages observing me retreat, ran after me; and before I could get far enough into the sea, discharged an arrow, which wounded me deeply on the inside of my left knee (I shall carry the mark to my grave). I apprehended the arrow might be poisoned, and paddling out of the reach of their darts (being a calm day), I made a shift to suck the wound, and dress it as well as I could.

I was at a loss what to do, for I durst not return to the same landing-place, but stood to the north, and was forced to paddle; for the wind, although very gentle, was against me, blowing northwest. As I was looking about for a secure landing-place, I saw a sail to the north-northeast, which appearing every minute more visible, I was in some doubt, whether I should wait for them or no; but at last my detestation of the yahoo race prevailed, and turning my canoe, I sailed and paddled together to the south, and got into the same creek from whence I set out in the morning, choosing rather to trust myself among these barbarians, than live with European yahoos. I drew up my canoe as close as I could to the shore, and hid myself behind a stone by the little brook, which, as I have already said, was excellent water.

The ship came within a half a league of this creek, and sent out her long-boat with vessels to take in fresh water (for the place it seems was very well known) but I did not observe it until the boat was almost on shore, and it was too late to seek another hiding-place. The seamen at their landing observed my canoe, and rummaging it all over, easily conjectured that the owner could not be far off. Four of them well armed searched every cranny and lurking-hole, till at last they found me flat on my face behind the stone. They gazed a while in admiration at my strange uncouth dress, my coat made of skins, my wooden-soled shoes, and my furred stockings; from whence, however, they concluded I was not a native of the place, who all go naked. One of the seamen in Portuguese bid me rise, and asked who I was.

I understood that language very well, and getting upon my feet, said, I was a poor yahoo, banished from the Houyhnhnms, and desired they would please to let me depart. They admired to hear me answer them in their own tongue, and saw by my complexion I must be an European; but were at loss to know what I meant by yahoos and Houyhnhnms, and at the same time fell a laughing at my strange tone in speaking, which resembled the neighing of a horse. I trembled all the while betwixt fear and hatred: I again desired leave to depart, and was gently moving to my canoe; but they laid hold on me, desiring to know, what country I was of, whence I came, with many other questions. I told them I was born in England, from whence I came about five years ago, and then their country and ours were at peace. I therefore hoped they would not treat me as an enemy, since I meant them no harm, but was a poor yahoo, seeking some desolate place where to pass the remainder of his unfortunate life.

When they began to talk, I thought I never heard or saw any thing so unnatural; for it appeared to me as monstrous as if a dog or a cow should speak in England, or a yahoo in Houyhnhnmland. The honest Portuguese were equally amazed at my strange dress, and the odd manner of delivering my words, which however they understood very well. They spoke to me with great humanity, and said they were sure their captain would carry me *gratis* to Lisbon, from whence I might return to my own country; that two of the seamen would go back to the ship, inform the captain of what they had seen, and receive his orders; in the mean time, unless I would give my solemn oath not to fly, they would secure me by force. I thought it best to comply with their proposal. They were very curious to know my story, but I gave them very little satisfaction; and they all conjectured that my misfortunes had impaired my reason. In two hours the boat, which went loaden with vessels of water, returned with the captain's commands to fetch me on board. I fell on my knees to preserve my liberty; but all was in vain, and the men having tied me with cords, heaved me into the boat, from whence I was taken into the ship, and from thence into the captain's cabin.

His name was Pedro de Mendez; he was a very courteous and generous person; he entreated me to give some account of my self, and desired to

---

Pedro de Mendez. A much-debated figure, taken by some to affirm normal humanity and discounted by others as minor in the scheme of the *Travels.* Swift may have chosen the particular patronymic *Mendez* in order to suggest that the generous Portuguese captain was a Marrano: a crypto-Jew who concealed his faith to escape religious persecution. See Géracht, 43–47; see also Real and Vienken, 136–40.

know what I would eat or drink; said, I should be used as well as himself, and spoke so many obliging things, that I wondered to find such civilities from a yahoo. However, I remained silent and sullen; I was ready to faint at the very smell of him and his men. At last I desired something to eat out of my own canoe; but he ordered me a chicken and some excellent wine, and then directed that I should be put to bed in a very clean cabin. I would not undress myself, but lay on the bed-clothes, and in half an hour stole out, when I thought the crew was at dinner, and getting to the side of the ship was going to leap into the sea, and swim for my life, rather than continue among yahoos. But one of the seamen prevented me, and having informed the captain, I was chained to my cabin.

After dinner Don Pedro came to me, and desired to know my reason for so desperate an attempt: assured me he only meant to do me all the service he was able, and spoke so very movingly, that at last I descended to treat him like an animal which had some little portion of reason. I gave him a very short relation of my voyage, of the conspiracy against me by my own men, of the country where they set me on shore, and of my three years' residence there. All which he looked upon as if it were a dream or a vision; whereat I took great offence; for I had quite forgot the faculty of lying, so peculiar to yahoos in all countries where they preside, and, consequently, the disposition of suspecting truth in others of their own species. I asked him, whether it were the custom of his country to *say the thing that was not.* I assured him I had almost forgot what he meant by falsehood, and if I had lived a thousand years in Houyhnhnmland, I should never have heard a lie from the meanest servant; that I was altogether indifferent whether he believed me or no; but however, in return for his favours, I would give so much allowance to the corruption of his nature as to answer any objection he would please to make, and he might easily discover the truth.

The captain, a wise man, after many endeavours to catch me tripping in some part of my story, at last began to have a better opinion of my veracity, and the rather because he confessed, he met with a Dutch skipper, who pretended to have landed with five others of his crew upon a certain island or continent south of New-Holland, where they went for fresh water, and observed a horse driving before him several animals exactly resembling those described under the name of *yahoos,* with some other particulars, which the captain said he had forgot; because he then concluded them all to be lies. But he added, that since I professed so inviolable an attachment to truth, I must give him my word of honour to bear him company in this voyage without attempting anything against my life, or else he would continue me a prisoner till we arrived in Lisbon. I gave him the promise he required; but at the same time protested that I would suffer the greatest hardships rather than return to live among yahoos.

Our voyage passed without any considerable accident. In gratitude to the captain I sometimes sat with him at his earnest request, and strove to conceal my antipathy to human kind, although it often broke out, which he suffered to pass without observation. But the greatest part of the day, I confined myself to my cabin, to avoid seeing any of the crew. The captain had often entreated me to strip myself of my savage dress, and offered to lend me the best suit of clothes he had. This I would not be prevailed on to accept, abhorring to cover myself with anything that had been on the back of a yahoo. I only desired he would lend me two clean shirts, which having been washed since he wore them, I believed would not so much defile me. These I changed every second day, and washed them myself.

We arrived at Lisbon, Nov. 5, 1715. At our landing the captain forced me to cover myself with his cloak, to prevent the rabble from crowding about me. I was conveyed to his own house, and, at my earnest request, he led me up to the highest room backwards. I conjured him to conceal from all persons what I had told him of the Houyhnhnms, because the least hint of such a story would not only draw numbers of people to see me, but probably put me in danger of being imprisoned, or burnt by the Inquisition. The captain persuaded me to accept a suit of clothes newly made, but I would not suffer the tailor to take my measure; however, Don Pedro being almost of my size, they fitted me well enough. He accoutred me with other necessaries all new, which I aired for twenty-four hours before I would use them.

The captain had no wife, nor above three servants, none of which were suffered to attend at meals, and his whole deportment was so obliging, added to very good *human* understanding, that I really began to tolerate his company. He gained so far upon me, that I ventured to look out of the back window. By degrees I was brought into another room, from whence I peeped into the street, but drew my head back in a fright. In a week's time he seduced me down to the door. I found my terror gradually lessened, but

---

Nov. 5, 1715. Again, a highly charged date: this time for Gulliver's return to the world of the Yahoos. See note on p. 51 about November 5.

Burnt by the Inquisition. A Roman Catholic tribunal that employed both state and church officials to persecute heretics. It began in 1232, in response to the Albigensian heresy, and was still active in Catholic countries, as Rivero points out, in Swift's own time. The sentences handed down by the Portuguese and Spanish Inquisitions included public burning. The inquisition of Portugal had burned Swift's light-hearted hoax and satire of the astrologer and almanac-maker, John Partridge, *Predictions for the Year 1708.*

my hatred and contempt seemed to increase. I was at last bold enough to walk the street in his company, but kept my nose well stopped with rue, or sometimes with tobacco.

In ten days Don Pedro, to whom I had given some account of my domestic affairs, put it upon me as a point of honour and conscience, that I ought to return to my native country, and live at home with my wife and children. He told me, there was an English ship in the port just ready to sail, and he would furnish me with all things necessary. It would be tedious to repeat his arguments, and my contradictions. He said it was altogether impossible to find such a solitary island as I had desired to live in; but I might command in my own house, and pass my time in a manner as recluse as I pleased.

I complied at last, finding I could not do better. I left Lisbon the 24th day of November, in an English merchantman, but who was the master I never inquired. Don Pedro accompanied me to the ship, and lent me twenty pounds. He took kind leave of me, and embraced me at parting, which I bore as well as I could. During this last voyage I had no commerce with the master or any of his men, but pretending I was sick kept close in my cabin. On the fifth of December, 1715, we cast anchor in the Downs about nine in the morning, and at three in the afternoon I got safe to my house at Redriff.

My wife and family received me with great surprise and joy, because they concluded me certainly dead; but I must freely confess the sight of them filled me only with hatred, disgust and contempt, and the more by reflecting on the near alliance I had to them. For although, since my unfortunate exile from the Houyhnhnm country, I had compelled myself to tolerate the sight of yahoos, and to converse with Don Pedro de Mendez, yet my memory and imaginations were perpetually filled with the virtues and ideas of those exalted Houyhnhnms. And when I began to consider, that by copulating with one of the yahoo species I had become a parent of more, it struck me with the utmost shame, confusion, and horror.

As soon as I entered the house, my wife took me in her arms, and kissed me, at which, having not been used to the touch of that odious animal for so many years, I fell in a swoon for almost an hour. At the time I am writing it is five years since my last return to England: during the first year I could not endure my wife or children in my presence, the very smell of them was 

intolerable, much less could I suffer them to eat in the same room. To this hour they dare not presume to touch my bread, or drink out of the same cup, neither was I ever able to let one of them take me by the hand. The first money I laid out was to buy two young stone-horses, which I keep in a

Stone-horses. Horses not gelded.

good stable, and next to them the groom is my greatest favourite; for I feel my spirits revived by the smell he contracts in the stable. My horses understand me tolerably well; I converse with them at least four hours every day. They are strangers to bridle or saddle; they live in great amity with me, and friendship to each other.

CHAPTER XII

The author's veracity. His design in publishing this work. His censure of those travellers who swerve from the truth. The author clears himself from any sinister ends in writing. An objection answered. The method of planting colonies. His native country commended. The right of the crown to those countries described by the author is justified. The difficulty of conquering them. The author takes his last leave of the reader, proposeth his manner of living for the future, gives good advice, and concludes.

Thus, gentle reader, I have given thee a faithful history of my travels for sixteen years, and above seven months, wherein I have not been so studious of ornament as of truth. I could perhaps like others have astonished thee with strange improbable tales; but I rather chose to relate plain matter of fact in the simplest manner and style, because my principal design was to inform, and not to amuse thee.

It is easy for us who travel into remote countries, which are seldom visited by Englishmen or other Europeans, to form descriptions of wonderful animals both at sea and land. Whereas a traveller's chief aim should be to make men wiser and better, and to improve their minds by the bad as well as good example of what they deliver concerning foreign places.

I could heartily wish a law were enacted, that every traveller, before he were permitted to publish his voyages, should be obliged to make oath before the Lord High Chancellor that all he intended to print was absolutely true to the best of his knowledge; for then the world would no longer be deceived as it usually is, while some writers, to make their works pass the better upon the public, impose the grossest falsities on the unwary reader. I have perused several books of travels with great delight in my younger days; but having since gone over most parts of the globe, and been able to contradict many fabulous accounts from my own observation, it hath given me a great disgust against this part of reading, and some indignation to see the credulity of mankind so impudently abused. Therefore since my acquaintance were pleased to think my poor endeavours might not be unacceptable to my country, I imposed on myself as a maxim, never to be swerved from, that I would *strictly adhere to truth;* neither indeed can I be ever under the least temptation to vary from it, while I retain in my mind the lectures and example of my noble master, and the other illustrious Houyhnhnms, of whom I had so long the honour to be an humble hearer.

> —*Nec si miserum Fortuna Sinonem*
> *Finxit, vanum etiam mendacemque improba finget.*

I know very well how little reputation is to be got by writings which require neither genius nor learning, nor indeed any other talent, except a good memory or an exact journal. I know likewise, that writers of travels, like dictionary-makers, are sunk into oblivion by the weight and bulk of those who come after, and therefore lie uppermost. And it is highly probable, that such travellers who shall hereafter visit the countries described in this work of mine, may, by detecting my errors (if there be any), and adding many new discoveries of their own, jostle me out of vogue, and stand in my place, making the world forget that ever I was an author. This indeed would be too great a mortification if I wrote for fame: but, as my sole intention was the PUBLIC GOOD, I cannot be altogether disappointed. For who can read of the virtues I have mentioned in the glorious Houyhnhnms, without being ashamed of his own vices, when he considers himself as the reasoning, governing animal of his country? I shall say nothing of those remote nations where yahoos preside, amongst which the least corrupted are the Brobdingnagians, whose wise maxims in morality and government it would be our happiness to observe. But I forbear descanting further, and rather leave the judicious reader to his own remarks and applications.

I am not a little pleased that this work of mine can possibly meet with no censurers: for what objections can be made against a writer who relates only plain facts that happened in such distant countries, where we have not

---

Nec si miserum Fortuna Sinonem / Finxit, vanum etiam mendacemque improba finget: A justly famous lie. These false and deceitful words, quoted from the second book of Virgil's *Aeneid,* read as follows in translation: "Nor, if cruel Fortune has made Sinon wretched, should she also make him false and deceitful." The speaker proclaiming his sincerity is Sinon, a Greek warrior who finally pries Troy open to conquest by persuading the Trojans to bring the Trojan Horse inside the fortified walls of Troy. The military stratagem involved—the horse contained Greek warriors—leads to the fall of Troy.

the least interest with respect either to trade or negotiations? I have carefully avoided every fault with which common writers of travels are often too justly charged. Besides, I meddle not the least with any *party*, but write without passion, prejudice, or ill-will against any man or number of men whatsoever. I write for the noblest end, to inform and instruct mankind, over whom I may, without breach of modesty, pretend to some superiority from the advantages I received by conversing so long among the most accomplished Houyhnhnms. I write without any view towards profit or praise. I never suffer a word to pass that may look like reflection, or possibly give the least offence even to those who are most ready to take it. So that I hope I may with justice pronounce myself an author perfectly blameless, against whom the tribe of answerers, considerers, observers, reflecters, detecters, remarkers, will never be able to find matter for exercising their talents.

I confess, it was whispered to me that I was bound in duty, as a subject of England, to have given in a memorial to a secretary of state, at my first coming over; because, whatever lands are discovered by a subject belong to the crown. But I doubt whether our conquests in the countries I treat of would be as easy as those of Ferdinando Cortez over the naked Americans. The Lilliputians, I think, are hardly worth the charge of a fleet and army to reduce them, and I question whether it might be prudent or safe to attempt the Brobdingnagians. Or whether an English army would be much at their ease with the Flying Island over their heads. The Houyhnhnms, indeed, appear not to be so well prepared for war, a science to which they are perfect strangers, and especially against missive weapons. However, supposing myself to be a minister of state, I could never give my advice for invading them. Their prudence, unanimity, unacquaintedness with fear, and their love of their country would amply supply all defects in the military art. Imagine twenty thousand of them breaking into the midst of an European army, confounding the ranks, overturning the carriages, battering the warriors' faces into mummy, by terrible yerks from their hinder hoofs. For they would well deserve the character given to Augustus; *Recalcitrat undique tutus.* But instead of proposals for conquering that magnanimous nation, I rather wish they were in a capacity or disposition to send a sufficient number

---

Meddle not the least with any *party*. A tongue-in-cheek claim to neutrality.

Ferdinando Cortez. Hernán Cortes (1485–1547) led the Spanish destruction of the Aztec empire in 1519–1521.

Mummy. Pulp.

of their inhabitants for civilizing Europe, by teaching us the first principles of honour, justice, truth, temperance, public spirit, fortitude, chastity, friendship, benevolence, and fidelity. The names of all which virtues are still retained among us in most languages, and are to be met with in modern as well as ancient authors; which I am able to assert from my own small reading.

But I had another reason which made me less forward to enlarge his Majesty's dominions by my discoveries. To say the truth, I had conceived a few scruples with relation to the distributive justice of princes upon those occasions. For instance, a crew of pirates are driven by a storm they know not whither, at length a boy discovers land from the topmast, they go on shore to rob and plunder, they see an harmless people, are entertained with kindness, they give the country a new name, they take formal possession of it for the king, they set up a rotten plank or a stone for a memorial, they murder two or three dozen of the natives, bring away a couple more by force for a sample, return home, and get their pardon. Here commences a new dominion acquired with a title by *divine right.* Ships are sent with the first opportunity, the natives driven out or destroyed, their princes tortured to discover their gold, a free license given to all acts of inhumanity and lust, the earth reeking with the blood of its inhabitants: and this execrable crew of butchers employed in so pious an expedition, is a modern colony sent to convert and civilize an idolatrous and barbarous people.

But this description, I confess, doth by no means affect the British nation, who may be an example to the whole world for their wisdom, care, and justice in planting colonies; their liberal endowments for the advancement of religion and learning; their choice of devout and able pastors to propagate Christianity; their caution in stocking their provinces with

---

Crew of butchers . . . is a modern colony sent to convert and civilize an idolatrous and barbarous people. This passage, though condemning the earlier Spanish conquest of America, likewise implicates "modern" British predators. Their piratical violence, though not controlled by the state, was often licensed or pardoned. Some 1,343 vessels were licensed for privateering activities during the War of Spanish Succession (Bowen, 77). See introduction, pp. 27–29.

British nation . . . have no other views than the happiness of the people over whom they preside. One of Swift's better-known stories concerns the bishops appointed by Britain for service in Ireland. The British monarch selected "very good and great men," he said, "but they were murdered by a parcel of highwaymen between London and Chester who slipping on their gowns and cassocks pretend to pass for bishops" (Ehrenpreis, Vol. 3, 168).

people of sober lives and conversations from this the mother kingdom; their strict regard to the distribution of justice, in supplying the civil administration through all their colonies with officers of the greatest abilities, utter strangers to corruption; and to crown all, by sending the most vigilant and virtuous governors, who have no other views than the happiness of the people over whom they preside, and the honour of the king their master.

But as those countries which I have described do not appear to have any desire of being conquered, and enslaved, murdered or driven out by colonies, nor abound either in gold, silver, sugar or tobacco; I did humbly conceive they were by no means proper objects of our zeal, our valour, or our interest. However, if those whom it may concern think fit to be of another opinion, I am ready to depose, when I shall be lawfully called, that no European did ever visit these countries before me. I mean, if the inhabitants ought to be believed; unless a dispute may arise about the two yahoos, said to have been seen many ages ago on a mountain in Houyhnhnmland, from whence the opinion is, that the race of those brutes hath descended; and these, for any thing I know, may have been English, which indeed I was apt to suspect from the lineaments of their posterity's countenances, although very much defaced. But, how far that will go to make out a title, I leave to the learned in colony-law.

But as to the formality of taking possession in my sovereign's name, it never came once into my thoughts; and if it had, yet as my affairs then stood, I should perhaps, in point of prudence and self-preservation, have put it off to a better opportunity.

Having thus answered the *only* objection than can ever be raised against me as a traveller, I here take a final leave of my courteous readers, and return to enjoy my own speculations in my little garden at Redriff, to apply those excellent lessons of virtue which I learned among the Houyhnhnms, to instruct the yahoos of my own family as far as I shall find them docible animals, to behold my figure often in a glass, and thus if possible habituate myself by time to tolerate the sight of a human creature; to lament the

---

People of sober lives. The legal punishment of "transportation" enabled Britain to export substantial numbers of convicted criminals to the colonies in America. It is remarkable that Swift predicted the later use of Australia as a penal colony. In *A Tale of a Tub,* in a specious advertisement about a forthcoming book, in 96 volumes, on *Terra Australis Incognita,* the narrator describes the southern continent as a place where "by a general Doom all transgressors of the law are to be transported" (309).

If the inhabitants ought to be believed. A doubt of Houyhnhm veracity congruent with Don Pedro's account of the Dutch skipper, p. 272.

May have been English. See p. 33.

brutality of Houyhnhnms in my own country, but always treat their persons with respect, for the sake of my noble master, his family, his friends, and the whole Houyhnhnm race, whom these of ours have the honour to resemble in all their lineaments, however their intellectuals came to degenerate.

I began last week to permit my wife to sit at dinner with me, at the farthest end of a long table, and to answer (but with the utmost brevity) the few questions I ask her. Yet the smell of a yahoo continuing very offensive, I always keep my nose well stopped with rue, lavender, or tobacco leaves. And although it be hard for a man late in life to remove old habits, I am not altogether out of hopes in some time to suffer a neighbour yahoo in my company without the apprehensions I am yet under of his teeth or his claws.

My reconcilement to the yahoo-kind in general might not be so difficult if they would be content with those vices and follies only which nature hath entitled them to. I am not in the least provoked at the sight of a lawyer, a pickpocket, a colonel, a fool, a lord, a gamester, a politician, a whoremonger, a physician, an evidence, a suborner, an attorney, a traitor, or the like; this is all according to the due course of things: but when I behold a lump of deformity and diseases both in body and mind, smitten with pride, it immediately breaks all the measures of my patience; neither shall I be ever able to comprehend how such an animal and such a vice could tally together. The wise and virtuous Houyhnhnms, who abound in all excellencies that can adorn a rational creature, have no name for this vice in their language, which hath no terms to express any thing that is evil, except those whereby they describe the detestable qualities of their yahoos, among which they were not able to distinguish this of pride, for want of thoroughly understanding human nature, as it showeth itself in other countries, where that animal presides. But I, who had more experience, could plainly observe some rudiments of it among the wild yahoos.

But the Houyhnhnms, who live under the government of reason, are no more proud of the good qualities they possess, than I should be for not wanting a leg or an arm, which no man in his wits would boast of, although he must be miserable without them. I dwell the longer upon this subject from the desire I have to make the society of an English yahoo by any means not insupportable, and therefore I here entreat those who have any tincture of this absurd vice, that they will not presume to appear in my sight.

FINIS

A Proposal for the Universal Use of Irish *Manufacture, &c*

The Prose Writings of Jonathan Swift, ed. Herbert Davis, 14 vols. (Oxford: Basil Blackwell, 1939–1968).

It is the peculiar Felicity and Prudence of the People in this Kingdom, that whatever Commodities, or Productions, lie under the greatest Discouragements from *England*, those are what they are sure to be most industrious in cultivating and spreading. *Agriculture*, which hath been the principal Care of all wise Nations, and for the Encouragement whereof there are so many Statute-Laws in *England*, we countenance so well, that the Landlords are every where, by *penal Clauses*, absolutely prohibiting their Tenants from Plowing; not satisfied to confine them within certain Limitations, as it is the Practice of the *English;* one Effect of which, is already seen in the prodigious Dearness of Corn, and the Importation of it from *London*, as the cheaper Market: And, because People are the *Riches of a Country*, and that our *Neighbours* have done, and are doing all that in them lie, to make our Wool a Drug to us, and a Monopoly to them; therefore, the politick Gentlemen of *Ireland* have depopulated vast Tracts of the best Land, for the feeding of Sheep.

I could fill a Volume as large as the *History of the wise Men of Goatham*, with a Catalogue only of some *wonderful* Laws and Customs we have observed within thirty Years past. It is true, indeed, our beneficial Traffick of Wool with *France*, hath been our only Support for several Years past; furnishing us all the little Money we have to pay our Rents, and go to Market. But our Merchants assure me, *This Trade hath received a great Damp by the present fluctuating Condition of the Coin in* France; *and that most of their Wine is paid for in Specie, without carrying thither any Commodity from hence.*

However, since we are so universally bent upon enlarging our *Flocks*, it may be worth inquiring, what we shall do with our Wool, in case *Barnstable* should be over-stocked, and our *French* commerce should fail?

I should wish the Parliament had thought fit to have suspended their Regulation of *Church* matters, and Enlargements of the *Prerogative*, until a more convenient Time, because they did not appear very pressing, (at least to the persons *principally concerned*) and, instead of those great

---

By *penal Clauses.* Tenant farmers were prevented by law from changing pasture into cultivated soil, increasing Ireland's dependence on grain imported from England. Mild attempts to modify this "mischievous agricultural regimen" (Ehrenpreis, vol. 3, 119) had been defeated in 1716 and again in 1719.

People are the *Riches of a Country.* A truism dear to mercantile thought. It was scarcely applicable, as Swift often points out, to a population excluded from most forms of economic production.

Wool a Drug to us. As a result of the Woollen Act of 1699. See p. 11.

France. Through illegal smuggling.

Barnstable. A port central to the wool trade

Refinements in *Politicks* and *Divinity*, had *amused* Themselves and their Committees, a little, with the *State of the Nation.* For Example: What if the House of Commons had thought fit to make a Resolution, *Nemine Contradicente*, against wearing any Cloath or Stuff in their Families, which were not of the Growth and Manufacture of this Kingdom? What if they had extended it so far, as utterly to exclude all Silks, Velvets, Calicoes, and the whole *Lexicon* of Female Fopperies; and declared, that whoever acted otherwise, should be deemed and reputed *an Enemy to the Nation?* What if they had sent up such a Resolution to be agreed to by the House of Lords; and by their own Practice and Encouragement, spread the Execution of it in their several Countries? What if we should agree to make *burying in Woollen* a *Fashion*, as our Neighbours have made it a *Law?* What if the Ladies would be content with *Irish* Stuffs for the Furniture of their Houses, for Gowns and Petticoats to themselves and their Daughters? Upon the whole, and to crown all the rest, let a firm Resolution be taken, by *Male* and *Female*, never to appear with one single *Shred* that comes from *England; and let all the People say, AMEN.*

I hope, and believe, nothing could please his Majesty better than to hear that his loyal Subjects, of both Sexes, in this Kingdom, celebrated his *Birth-Day* (now approaching) *universally* clad in their own Manufacture. Is there Vertue enough left in this deluded People to save them from the Brink of Ruin? If the Mens Opinions may be taken, the Ladies will look as handsome in Stuffs as Brocades, and, since all will be equal, there may be room enough to employ their Wit and Fancy in chusing and matching of Patterns and Colours. I heard the late Archbishop of *Tuam* mention a pleasant Observation of some Body's; *that* Ireland *would never be happy 'till a Law were made for* burning *every Thing that came from* England, *except their* People *and their* Coals: I must confess, that as to the former, I should not be sorry if they would stay at home; and for the latter, I hope, in a little Time we shall have no Occasion for them.

Nemine Contradicente. None voting against it.

A *Law.* Passed in the Elizabethan era to boost the English wool trade.

His Majesty. George I, whose sixtieth birthday (May 28, 1720) was greeted with this pamphlet. The later reference to vassals in Germany reflects unfavorably on the origins of the House of Hanover.

Vertue. Civic virtue is a key concept in Swift's "Old Whig" political thought. As it descends from the classical tradition of republican Rome (Tacitus) through Machiavelli and Harrington, the concept denies an easy distinction between ethics and politics: between, for example, "private" consumption and public prosperity. See Pocock, 423–46.

Non tanti mitra est, non tanti Judicis ostrum.

But I should rejoice to see a *Stay-Lace* from *England* be thought *scandalous*, and become a Topick for *Censure* at *Visits* and *Tea Tables*.

If the unthinking Shopkeepers in this Town, had not been *utterly* destitute of common Sense, they would have made some *Proposal to the Parliament*, with a *Petition* to the Purpose I have mentioned; promising to improve the *Cloaths and Stuffs of the Nation, into all possible Degrees of Fineness and Colours, and engaging not to play the Knave, according to their Custom, by exacting and imposing upon the Nobility and Gentry, either as to the Prices or the Goodness.* For I remember, in *London*, upon a general Mourning, the *rascally Mercers* and *Woollen Drapers*, would, in Four and Twenty Hours, raise their *Cloaths* and *Silks* to above a double Price; and if the Mourning continued long, then come whingeing with *Petitions* to the *Court, that they were ready to starve, and their Fineries lay upon their Hands.*

I could wish our Shopkeepers would immediately think on this *Proposal*, addressing it to all Persons of Quality, and others; but first be sure to get some Body who can write Sense, to put it into Form.

I think it needless to exhort the *Clergy* to follow this good Example, because, *in a little Time, those among them who are so unfortunate to have had their Birth and Education in this Country, will think themselves abundantly happy when they can afford* Irish *Crape, and an* Athlone *Hat;* and as to the others, I *shall not presume* to direct them. I have, indeed, seen the present Archbishop of *Dublin* clad from Head to Foot in our own Manufacture; and yet, under the Rose be it spoken, *his Grace deserves as good a Gown, as if he had not been born among us.*

I have not Courage enough to offer *one Syllable* on this Subject to *their Honours* of the Army: Neither have I sufficiently considered the great Importance of *Scarlet* and *Gold Lace.*

The Fable, in *Ovid*, of *Arachne* and *Pallas*, is to this Purpose. The Goddess had heard of one *Arachne* a young Virgin, very famous for *Spinning* and *Weaving:* They both met upon a Tryal of Skill; and *Pallas* finding herself almost equalled in her own Art, stung with Rage and Envy, knockt her *Rival* down, turned her into a *Spyder*, enjoining her to *spin* and *weave* for

---

Non tanti mitra est, non tanti Judicis ostrum. A mitre is not worth so much; the purple robes of a judge are not of so much importance.

An* Athlone *Hat. Irish-born clergy, who are denied patronage even in their own country, will count themselves lucky if they can afford simple clothing and a hat from Athlone (locally well known for hats).

Archbishop of *Dublin.* William King (1650–1729). Strongly opposed the Declaratory Act of 1720 and went on to support Swift during the controversy over Wood's halfpence.

ever, *out of her own Bowels,* and *in a very narrow Compass.* I confess, that from a Boy, I always pitied poor *Arachne,* and could never heartily love the Goddess, on Account of so *cruel and unjust a Sentence;* which, however, is *fully executed* upon *Us* by *England,* with further Additions of *Rigor* and *Severity.* For the greatest Part of *our Bowels and Vitals* is extracted, without allowing us the Liberty of *spinning* and *weaving* them.

The Scripture tells us, that *Oppression makes a wise Man mad;* therefore, consequently speaking, the Reason why some Men are not *mad,* is because they are not *wise:* However, it were to be wished that *Oppression* would, in Time, teach a little *Wisdom* to *Fools.*

I was much delighted with a Person, who hath a great Estate in this Kingdom, upon his Complaints to me, *how grievously POOR* England *suffers by Impositions from* Ireland. *That we convey our own Wool to* France, *in Spight of all the* Harpies *at the Custom-House. That Mr.* Shutleworth, *and others on the* Cheshire *Coasts, are such Fools to sell us their* Bark *at a good Price, for tanning* our own Hydes *into Leather; with other Enormities of the like Weight and Kind.* To which I will venture to add more: *That the* Mayorality *of this City is always executed by an* Inhabitant, *and often by a* Native, *which might as well be done by a* Deputy, *with a moderate Salary, whereby POOR* England *loseth, at least, one thousand Pounds a Year upon the Ballance. That the Governing of this Kingdom costs the Lord Lieutenant three Thousand six Hundred Pounds a Year, so much* net *Loss to POOR* England. *That the People of* Ireland *presume to dig for Coals* in their own Grounds; *and the Farmers in the Country of* Wicklow *send their Turf to the very Market of* Dublin, *to the great Discouragement of the Coal Trade at* Mostyn *and* White-haven. *That the Revenues of the* Post-Office *here, so righteously belonging to the* English *Treasury, as arising chiefly from our own Commerce with each other, should be remitted to* London, *clogged with that grievous Burthen of Exchange, and the Pensions paid out of the* Irish *Revenues to* English Favourites, *should lie under the same Disadvantage, to the great Loss of the Grantees. When a* Divine *is sent over to a* Bishoprick *here, with the Hopes of Five and Twenty Hundred Pounds a Year; upon his Arrival, he finds, alas! a dreadful Discount of Ten or Twelve* per Cent. *A* Judge, *or a* Commissioner *of the Revenue, has the same Cause of Complaint.* Lastly, *The Ballad upon* Cotter *is vehemently suspected to be* Irish *Manufacture; and yet is allowed to be sung in our open Streets, under the very* Nose *of the* Government.

Discount. Due to the relative strength of British and Irish currency.

***Ballad upon* Cotter.** Ballad about a prominent local trial, and so locally "manufactured." The trial was that of Sir James Cotter, as Carpenter notes, convicted of rape and executed.

These are a *few* among the many Hardships we put upon that *POOR* Kingdom of *England;* for which, I am confident, every *honest* Man wisheth a *Remedy:* And, I hear, there is a Project *on Foot* for transporting our best Wheaten *Straw*, by Sea and Land Carriage, to *Dunstable;* and *obliging us by a Law*, to take off yearly so many *Tun of Straw-Hats*, for the Use of our Women; which will be a *great Encouragement* to the Manufacture of that industrious Town.

I would be glad to learn among the Divines, whether a Law *to bind Men without their own Consent*, be obligatory *in foro Conscientiae;* because, I find *Scripture, Sanderson* and *Suarez*, are wholly silent in the Matter. The Oracle of *Reason*, the great *Law of Nature*, and general Opinion of *Civilians*, wherever they treat of *limited Governments*, are, indeed, decisive enough.

It is wonderful to observe the Biass among our People in favour of *Things, Persons*, and *Wares* of all Kinds that come from *England.* The *Printer* tells his *Hawkers*, that *he has got an excellent new Song just brought from* London. I have somewhat of a Tendency that way my self; and upon hearing a *Coxcomb* from thence displaying himself, with great Volubility, upon the *Park*, the *Play-House*, the *Opera*, the *Gaming Ordinaries*, it was apt to beget in me a Kind of Veneration for his Parts and Accomplishments. It is not many Years, since I remember a *Person* who, by his Style and Literature, seems to have been *Corrector* of a Hedge-Press, in some *Blind-Alley* about *Little-Britain*, proceed *gradually* to be an *Author*, at least a **Translator* of a lower Rate, although somewhat of a larger Bulk, than any that now *flourishes* in *Grub-street;* and, upon the Strength of this Foundation, came over *here; erect* himself up into an *Orator* and *Politician*, and lead a *Kingdom* after him. This, I am told, was the *very Motive* that prevailed on the † *Author* of a Play called, *Love in a Hollow-Tree*, to do us the *Honour* of a Visit; presuming, with very good Reason, *that he was a Writer of a superior Class.* I know *another*, who, for thirty Years past, hath been the *common Standard of Stupidity in England*, where he was never heard a Minute in any *Assembly*, or by any *Party*, with *common Christian Treatment;* yet, upon his Arrival hither, could put on a *Face of Importance and Authority*, talked more than Six, without either *Gracefulness, Propriety*, or *Meaning;* and, at the same Time, be admired and followed as the Pattern of *Eloquence* and *Wisdom.*

In foro Conscientiae. Before the tribunal of conscience.

* Supposed to be *Caesar's* Commentaries, dedicated to the d[uke] of *Marlborough* [original publisher].

† L. *G*[*ri*]*mst*[*o*]*n* [original publisher].

Nothing hath humbled me so much, or shewn a greater Disposition to a *contemptuous* Treatment of *Ireland* in some chief *Governors*, than that high Style of several Speeches from the *Throne*, delivered, as usual, after the *Royal Assent*, in *some Periods* of the two last *Reigns*. Such Exaggerations of the prodigious *Condescensions* in the Prince, to pass *those good Laws*, would have but an odd Sound at *Westminster:* Neither do I apprehend, how any *good Law* can pass, wherein the *King's* Interest is not as much concerned as that of the *People*. I remember, after a Speech on the like Occasion, delivered by my Lord *Wharton*, (I think it was his last) he desired Mr. *Addison to ask my Opinion of it:* My Answer was, *That his Excellency had very honestly forfeited his Head, on Account of one Paragraph; wherein he asserted, by plain Consequence, a* dispensing Power *in the Queen*. His Lordship owned *it was true*, but *swore* the Words were *put into his Mouth* by direct Orders from Court. From whence it is clear, that some *Ministers* in those Times, were apt, from their *high* Elevation, to look *down* upon this Kingdom, as if it had been one of their *Colonies* of *Out-casts* in *America*. And I observed a little of the same Turn of Spirit in *some great Men*, from whom I expected better; although, to do them Justice, it proved no Point of Difficulty to make them *correct their Idea*, whereof the *whole Nation* quickly found the Benefit.—But that is *forgotten*. How the Style hath since run, I am wholly a Stranger; having never seen a Speech since the last of the Queen.

I would now expostulate a little with our Country Landlords; who, by unmeasurable *screwing* and *racking* their Tenants all over the Kingdom, have already reduced the miserable *People* to a *worse Condition* than the *Peasants* in *France*, or the *Vassals* in *Germany* and *Poland;* so that the whole *Species* of what we call *Substantial Farmers*, will, in a very few Years, be utterly at an End. It was pleasant to observe these Gentlemen, *labouring* with all their *Might*, for preventing the *Bishops* from letting their Revenues at a moderate half Value, (whereby the whole *Order* would, in an Age, have been reduced to manifest Beggary) at the very Instant, when they were every where *canting* their own Lands upon short Leases, and sacrificing their *oldest Tenants for a Penny an Acre advance*. I know not how it comes to pass, (and yet, perhaps, I know well enough) that *Slaves* have a natural Disposition to be *Tyrants;* and that when my *Betters* give me a Kick, I am apt to revenge it with six upon my *Footman;* although, perhaps, he may be an honest and diligent Fellow. I have heard *great* Divines affirm, that *nothing is so likely to call down an universal Judgment from Heaven upon a Nation, as universal Oppression;* and whether this be not already verified in

---

***Colonies* of *Out-casts* in *America*.** Many convicted criminals were transported to the American colonies.

Part, *their Worships* the Landlords are *now* at full Leisure to consider. Whoever travels this Country, and observes the *Face* of Nature, or the *Faces*, and Habits, and Dwellings of the *Natives*, will hardly think himself in a Land where either *Law, Religion*, or *common Humanity* is professed.

I cannot forbear saying one Word upon a *Thing* they call a *Bank*, which, I hear, is projecting in this Town. I never saw the *Proposals*, nor understand any one Particular of their Scheme: What I wish for, at present, is only a sufficient Provision of *Hemp*, and *Caps*, and *Bells*, to distribute according to the several Degrees of *Honesty* and *Prudence* in *some Persons*. I *hear* only of a monstrous Sum already named; and, if Others do not soon hear of it too, and *hear* it with a *Vengeance*, then am I a Gentleman of less Sagacity than my self, and very few besides, take me to be. And the Jest will be still the better, if it be true, as judicious Persons have assured me, that one Half of this Money will be *real*, and the other Half altogether imaginary. The Matter will be likewise much mended, if the Merchants continue to carry off our Gold, and our Goldsmiths to melt down our heavy Silver.

Bank. See note, pp. 10–11.

The Drapier's First Letter

To the Shopkeepers, Tradesmen, Farmers, and Common People of Ireland

Concerning the Brass Halfpence Coined by one William Wood, Hardwareman, with a Design to Have Them Pass in This Kingdom,

Wherein is shown the power of his Patent, the value of the Halfpence, and how far every person may be obliged to take the same in payments, and how to behave himself, in case such an attempt should be made by Wood, or any other person.

(very proper to be kept in every family)

—*By M. B. Drapier.*

Gulliver's Travels and Other Writings, ed. Louis Landa (Boston: Houghton Mifflin, 1960).

Brethren, Friends, Countrymen, and Fellow-Subjects.

What I intend now to say to you, is, next to your duty to God, and the care of your salvation, of the greatest concern to your selves and your children; your bread and clothing, and every common necessary of life entirely depend upon it. Therefore I do most earnestly exhort you as men, as Christians, as parents, and as lovers of your country, to read this paper with the utmost attention, or get it read to you by others; which that you may do at the less expense, I have ordered the printer to sell it at the lowest rate.

It is a great fault among you, that when a person writes with no other intention than to do you good, you will not be at the pains to read his advices: one copy of this paper may serve a dozen of you, which will be less than a farthing apiece. It is your folly that you have no common or general interest in your view, not even the wisest among you, neither do you know or inquire, or care who are your friends, or who are your enemies.

About four years ago a little book was written, to advise all people to wear the manufactures of this our own dear country. It had no other design, said nothing against the king or parliament, or any person whatsoever; yet the poor printer was prosecuted two years with the utmost violence, and even some weavers themselves, for whose sake it was written, being upon the jury, found him guilty. This would be enough to discourage any man from endeavoring to do you good, when you will either neglect him, or fly in his face for his pains; and when he must expect only danger to himself, and to be fined and imprisoned, perhaps to his ruin.

However, I cannot but warn you once more of the manifest destruction before your eyes, if you do not behave yourselves as you ought.

I will therefore first tell you the plain story of the fact; and then I will lay before you how you ought to act in common prudence, and according to the laws of your country.

The fact is thus, it having been many years since copper halfpence or farthings were last coined in this kingdom, they have been for some time very scarce, and many counterfeits passed about under the name of raps: several applications were made to England, that we might have liberty to coin new ones, as in former times we did; but they did not succeed. At last one Mr. Wood, a mean ordinary man, a hardware dealer, procured a patent under his Majesty's broad seal to coin £ 108,000 in copper for this kingdom; which patent, however, did not oblige anyone here to take them,

---

At the lowest rate. As Carpenter points out, the price was indeed exceedingly cheap. Swift bore the cost of the printer, John Harding.

Poor printer. Edward Waters, prosecuted for sedition by Chief Justice William Whitshed. See p. 370.

unless they pleased. Now you must know, that the halfpence and farthings in England pass for very little more than they are worth; and if you should beat them to pieces, and sell them to the brazier, you would not lose much above a penny in a shilling. But Mr. Wood made his halfpence of such base metal, and so much smaller than the English ones, that the brazier would not give you above a penny of good money for a shilling of his; so that this sum of £ 108,000 in good gold and silver, must be given for trash, that will not be worth above eight or nine thousand pounds real value. But this is not the worst; for Mr. Wood, when he pleases, may by stealth send over another £ 108,000 and buy all our goods for eleven parts in twelve under the value. For example, if a hatter sells a dozen of hats for five shillings apiece, which amounts to three pounds, and receives the payment in Mr. Wood's coin, he really receives only the value of five shillings.

Perhaps you will wonder how such an ordinary fellow as this Mr. Wood could have so much interest as to get his Majesty's broad seal for so great a sum of bad money to be sent to this poor country; and that all the nobility and gentry here could not obtain the same favour, and let us make our own halfpence, as we used to do. Now I will make that matter very plain. We are at a great distance from the king's court, and have nobody there to solicit for us, although a great number of lords and squires, whose estates are here, and are our countrymen, spend all their lives and fortunes there. But this same Mr. Wood was able to attend constantly for his own interest; he is an Englishman, and had great friends; and it seems knew very well where to give money to those that would speak to others that could speak to the king, and would tell a fair story. And his Majesty, and perhaps the great lord or lords who advised him, might think it was for our country's good; and so, as the lawyers express it, the king was deceived in his grant, which often happens in all reigns. And I am sure if his Majesty knew that such a patent, if it should take effect according to the desire of Mr. Wood, would utterly ruin this kingdom, which hath given such great proofs of its loyalty, he would immediately recall it, and perhaps show his displeasure to somebody or other: but a word to the wise is enough. Most of you must have heard with what anger our honorable House of Commons received an

---

Spend all their lives and fortunes there. As absentee landlords.

Where to give money. The Drapier alludes to a common story, as McMinn points out, that Wood had obtained his private patent through a bribe to the king's mistress (the duchess of Kendal).

Somebody or other. Sir Robert Walpole, the prime minister of Great Britain.

account of this Wood's patent. There were several fine speeches made upon it, and plain proofs, that it was all a wicked cheat from the bottom to the top; and several smart votes were printed, which that same Wood had the assurance to answer likewise in print; and in so confident a way, as if he were a better man than our whole parliament put together.

This Wood, as soon as his patent was passed, or soon after, sends over a great many barrels of those halfpence to Cork and other seaport towns; and to get them off, offered a hundred pounds in his coin for seventy or eighty in silver: but the collectors of the king's customs very honestly refused to take them, and so did almost everybody else. And since the parliament hath condemned them, and desired the king that they might be stopped, all the kingdom do abominate them.

But Wood is still working underhand to force his halfpence upon us; and if he can by help of his friends in England prevail so far as to get an order that the commissioners and collectors of the king's money shall receive them, and that the army is to be paid with them, then he thinks his work shall be done. And this is the difficulty you will be under in such a case; for the common soldier, when he goes to the market or alehouse, will offer this money; and if it be refused, perhaps he will swagger and hector, and threaten to beat the butcher or alewife, or take the goods by force and throw them the bad halfpence. In this and the like cases, the shopkeeper or victualer, or any other tradesman, has no more to do, than to demand ten times the price of his goods, if it is to be paid in Wood's money: for example, twenty pence of that money for a quart of ale, and so in all things else, and not part with his goods till he gets the money.

For suppose you go to an alehouse with that base money, and the landlord gives you a quart for four of these halfpence, what must the victualer do? His brewer will not be paid in that coin, or, if the brewer should be such a fool, the farmers will not take it from them for their bere, because they are bound, by their leases, to pay their rents in good and lawful money of England, which this is not, nor of Ireland neither; and the squire, their landlord, will never be so bewitched to take such trash for his land; so that it must certainly stop somewhere or other; and wherever it stops it is the same thing, and we are all undone.

The common weight of these halfpence is between four and five to an ounce; suppose five, then three shillings and fourpence will weigh a pound, and consequently twenty shillings will weigh six pounds butter weight. Now there are many hundred farmers, who pay two hundred pounds a year rent; therefore when one of these farmers comes with his half-year's rent, which is one hundred pounds, it will be at least six hundred pounds weight, which is three horses' load.

If a squire has a mind to come to town to buy clothes and wine and spices for himself and family, or perhaps to pass the winter here, he must bring with him five or six horses loaden with sacks as the farmers bring their corn; and when his lady comes in her coach to our shops, it must be followed by a car loaded with Mr. Wood's money. And I hope we shall have the grace to take it for no more than it is worth.

They say Squire Conolly has sixteen thousand pounds a year; now if he sends for his rent to town, as it is likely he does, he must have two hundred and fifty horses to bring up his half-year's rent, and two or three great cellars in his house for stowage. But what the bankers will do I cannot tell. For I am assured, that some great bankers keep by them forty thousand pounds in ready cash, to answer all payments; which sum in Mr. Wood's money would require twelve hundred horses to carry it.

For my own part, I am already resolved what to do; I have a pretty good shop of Irish stuffs and silks, and instead of taking Mr. Wood's bad copper, I intend to truck with my neighbors the butchers and bakers and brewers, and the rest, goods for goods; and the little gold and silver I have, I will keep by me like my heart's blood till better times, or until I am just ready to starve, and then I will buy Mr. Wood's money, as my father did the brass money in King James's time, who could buy ten pounds of it with a guinea, and I hope to get as much for a pistole, and so purchase bread from those who will be such fools as to sell it me.

These halfpence, if they once pass, will soon be counterfeited, because it may be cheaply done, the stuff is so base. The Dutch likewise will probably do the same thing, and send them over to us to pay for our goods; and Mr. Wood will never be at rest, but coin on: so that in some years we shall have at least five times £ 108,000 of this lumber. Now the current money of this kingdom is not reckoned to be above four hundred thousand pounds in all; and while there is a silver sixpence left, these blood-suckers will never be quiet.

When once the kingdom is reduced to such a condition, I will tell you what must be the end: the gentlemen of estates will all turn off their tenants

---

A car loaded with Mr. Wood's money. See illustration, p. 12.

Squire Conolly. William Conolly (1662–1729). Speaker of the Irish House of Commons (1715–29). Reputedly one of the richest commoners in Ireland, he was an *arriviste* who owned both a castle and a mansion. Conolly was a local power broker (or "undertaker") who served the interests of successive English ministries. As such, he supported Wood's patent to mint halfpence in Ireland.

The brass money in King James's time. Recalling another coinage fiasco due to the devalued brass and copper coinage minted in Ireland by James II to pay his troops during the tumult of 1689–90.

for want of payment; because, as I told you before, the tenants are obliged by their leases to pay sterling, which is lawful current money of England; then they will turn their own farmers, as too many of them do already; run all into sheep where they can, keeping only such other cattle as are necessary; then they will be their own merchants, and send their wool, and butter, and hides, and linen beyond sea for ready money, and wine, and spices, and silks. They will keep only a few miserable cottagers. The farmers must rob or beg, or leave their country. The shopkeepers in this and every other town must break and starve; for it is the landed man that maintains the merchant, and shopkeeper, and handicraftsman.

But when the squire turns farmer and merchant himself, all the good money he gets from abroad, he will hoard up to send for England, and keep some poor tailor or weaver, and the like, in his own house, who will be glad to get bread at any rate.

I should never have done, if I were to tell you all the miseries that we shall undergo, if we be so foolish and wicked as to take this cursed coin. It would be very hard, if all Ireland should be put into one scale, and this sorry fellow Wood into the other; that Mr. Wood should weigh down this whole kingdom, by which England gets above a million of good money every year clear into their pockets: and that is more than the English do by all the world besides.

But your great comfort is, that as his Majesty's patent does not oblige you to take this money, so the laws have not given the Crown a power of forcing the subject to take what money the king pleases; for then by the same reason we might be bound to take pebblestones, or cockleshells, or stamped leather for current coin, if ever we should happen to live under an ill prince; who might likewise by the same power make a guinea pass for ten pounds, a shilling for twenty shillings, and so on; by which he would in a short time get all the silver and gold of the kingdom into his own hands, and leave us nothing but brass or leather, or what he pleased. Neither is anything reckoned more cruel or oppressive in the French government, than their common practice of calling in all their money after they have sunk it very low, and then coining it anew at a much higher

---

Run all into sheep. A reference to the changing use of land in Ireland to anti-social grazier farming, which did not produce food for human beings. See "Ireland," pp. 344–46.

But your great comfort. This technical legal argument—a dispute about the king's prerogative—pervades the *Drapier's Letters.* The Drapier asserts the legal liberty not to accept, as legal tender, anything other than gold or silver. Since the brass coin in question would be stamped with the king's image, the Drapier has to dissociate refusal of the coin from any semblance of defying royal authority.

value; which however is not the thousandth part so wicked as this abominable project of Mr. Wood. For the French give their subjects silver for silver, and gold for gold; but this fellow will not so much as give us good brass or copper for our gold and silver, nor even a twelfth part of their worth.

Having said thus much, I will now go on to tell you the judgments of some great lawyers in this matter, whom I fee'd on purpose for your sakes, and got their opinions under their hands, that I might be sure I went upon good grounds.

A famous lawbook, called *The Mirror of Justice*, discoursing of the charters (or laws) ordained by our ancient kings, declares the law to be as follows: "It was ordained that no king of this realm should change or impair the money, or make any other money than of gold or silver, without the assent of all the counties"; that is, as my Lord Coke says, without the assent of parliament.

This book is very ancient, and of great authority for the time in which it was wrote, and with that character is often quoted by that great lawyer my Lord Coke. By the laws of England the several metals are divided into lawful or true metal, and unlawful or false metal: the former comprehends silver or gold, the latter all baser metals. That the former is only to pass in payments, appears by an act of parliament made the twentieth year of Edward the First, called the *Statute Concerning the Passing of Pence;* which I give you here as I got it translated into English; for some of our laws at that time were, as I am told, written in Latin: "Whoever in buying or selling presumeth to refuse a half-penny or farthing of lawful money, bearing the stamp which it ought to have, let him be seized on as a contemner of the king's majesty, and cast into prison."

By this statute, no person is to be reckoned a contemner of the king's Majesty, and for that crime to be committed to prison, but he who refuseth to accept the king's coin made of lawful metal; by which as I observed before, silver and gold only are intended.

That this is the true construction of the act, appears not only from the plain meaning of the words, but from my Lord Coke's observation upon it. By this act (says he) it appears, that no subject can be forced to take, in buying or selling or other payments, any money made but of lawful metal; that is, of silver or gold.

The Mirror of Justice. A Latin compendium of common-law cases. Used by Coke to argue that Anglo-Saxon liberties had been subverted by the Normans.

My Lord Coke. Sir Edward Coke (1552–1634). Famous jurist during the reign of James I and author of the legally influential *Institutes.* Coke ruled against the royal right to make law by proclamation (1610) and generally sought to limit the royal prerogative.

The law of England gives the king all mines of gold and silver; but not the mines of other metals: the reason of which prerogative or power, as it is given by my Lord Coke, is because money can be made of gold and silver; but not of other metals.

Pursuant to this opinion, halfpence and farthings were anciently made of silver, which is evident from the act of parliament of Henry the Fourth, chap. 4, whereby it is enacted as follows: "Item, for the great scarcity that is at present within the realm of England of halfpence and farthings of silver, it is ordained and established, that the third part of all the money of silver plate which shall be brought to the bullion, shall be made in halfpence and farthings." This shows that by the words "halfpenny and farthing of lawful money," in that statute concerning the passing of pence, is meant a small coin in halfpence and farthings of silver.

This is farther manifest from the statute of the ninth year of Edward the Third, chap. 3, which enacts "that no sterling halfpenny or farthing be molten for to make vessels, or any other thing, by the goldsmiths, nor others, upon forfeiture of the money so molten" (or melted).

By another act in this king's reign, black money was not to be current in England. And by an act made in the eleventh year of his reign, chap. 5, galley halfpence were not to pass. What kind of coin these were I do not know; but I presume they were made of base metal. And these acts were no new laws, but further declarations of the old laws relating to the coin.

Thus the law stands in relation to coin. Nor is there any example to the contrary, except one in Davis's Reports, who tells us that in the time of Tyrone's rebellion, Queen Elizabeth ordered money of mixed metal to be coined in the Tower of London, and sent over hither for the payment of the army, obliging all people to receive it; and commanding that all silver money should be taken only as bullion; that is, for as much as it weighed. Davis tells us several particulars in this matter too long here to trouble you with, and that the privy council of this kingdom obliged a merchant in England to receive this mixed money for goods transmitted hither.

But this proceeding is rejected by all the best lawyers, as contrary to law, the privy council here having no such legal power. And besides it is to be

---

Davis's Reports. Sir John Davies (1569–1626). Author of *Discovery of the True Causes why Ireland has never been subdued to the English Crown* (1612). During the era of Ulster plantations, Queen Elizabeth had flooded Ireland with debased coinage in order to raise revenue.

Tyrone's rebellion. The uprising between 1598 and 1603 led by Hugh O'Neill (c. 1550–1616), the earl of Tyrone, which involved coordination with an invading force from Spain.

considered, that the queen was then under great difficulties by a rebellion in this kingdom assisted from Spain. And whatever is done in great exigencies and dangerous times, should never be an example to proceed by in seasons of peace and quietness.

I will now, my dear friends, to save you the trouble, set before you, in short, what the law obliges you to do; and what it does not oblige you to.

First, you are obliged to take all money in payments which is coined by the king, and is of the English standard or weight, provided it be of gold or silver.

Secondly, you are not obliged to take any money which is not of gold or silver; not only the halfpence or farthings of England, but of any other country. And it is merely for convenience, or ease, that you are content to take them; because the custom of coining silver halfpence and farthings hath long been left off; I suppose on account of their being subject to be lost.

Thirdly, much less are we obliged to take those vile halfpence of that same Wood, by which you must lose almost eleven pence in every shilling.

Therefore, my friends, stand to it one and all: refuse this filthy trash. It is no treason to rebel against Mr. Wood. His Majesty in his patent obliges nobody to take these halfpence: our gracious prince hath no such ill advisers about him; or if he had, yet you see the laws have not left it in the king's power to force us to take any coin but what is lawful, of right standard, gold and silver. Therefore you have nothing to fear.

And let me in the next place apply myself particularly to you who are the poorer sort of tradesmen; perhaps you may think you will not be so great losers as the rich, if these halfpence should pass, because you seldom see any silver, and your customers come to your shops or stalls with nothing but brass, which you likewise find hard to be got. But you may take my word, whenever this money gains footing among you, you will be utterly undone. If you carry these halfpence to a shop for tobacco or brandy, or any other thing that you want, the shopkeeper will advance his goods accordingly, or else he must break, and leave the key under the door. Do you think I will sell you a yard of tenpenny stuff for twenty of Mr. Wood's halfpence? No, not under two hundred at least; neither will I be at the trouble of counting, but weigh them in a lump. I will tell you one thing further, that if Mr. Wood's project should take, it will ruin even our beggars; for when I give a beggar a halfpenny, it will quench his thirst, or go a good way to fill his belly; but the twelfth part of a halfpenny will do him no more service than if I should give him three pins out of my sleeve.

In short, these halfpence are like the accursed thing, which as the Scripture tells us, the children of Israel were forbidden to touch. They will run about like the plague and destroy everyone who lays his hands upon them. I have heard scholars talk of a man who told the king that he had invented a way to torment people by putting them into a bull of brass with fire under it, but the prince put the projector first into his own brazen bull to make the experiment. This very much resembles the project of Mr. Wood; and the like of this may possibly be Mr. Wood's fate; that the brass he contrived to torment this kingdom with, may prove his own torment, and his destruction at last.

N.B. The author of this paper is informed by persons, who have made it their business to be exact in their observations on the true value of these halfpence, that any person may expect to get a quart of twopenny ale for thirty-six of them.

I desire that all families may keep this paper carefully by them, to refresh their memories whenever they shall have farther notice of Mr. Wood's halfpence, or any other the like imposture.

Accursed thing. Gold, silver, brass, and iron plundered from the city of Jericho. See Josh. 7:18.

Letter IV. To the Whole People of Ireland

N.B. This was the Letter against which the Lord Lieutenant (Carteret) *and Council, issued a Proclamation, offering three Hundred Pounds to discover the Author; and for which,* Harding *the Printer was tried before one* Whitshed, *then Chief Justice: But the noble Jury would not find the Bill; nor would any Person discover the Author.*

The Prose Writings of Jonathan Swift, ed. Herbert Davis, 14 vols. (Oxford: Basil Blackwell, 1939–1968).

My dear Countrymen,

Having already written three *Letters,* upon so disagreeable a Subject as Mr. *Wood* and his *Half-pence;* I conceived my Task was at an End: But, I find that Cordials must be frequently applied to weak Constitutions, *Political* as well as *Natural.* A People long used to Hardships, lose by Degrees the very Notions of *Liberty;* they look upon themselves as Creatures at Mercy; and that all Impositions laid on them by a stronger Hand, are, in the Phrase of the *Report, legal* and *obligatory.* Hence proceed that *Poverty* and *Lowness of Spirit,* to which a *Kingdom* may be subject, as well as a *particular Person.* And when *Esau* came fainting from the Field, at the Point to die, it is no Wonder that he sold his *Birth-Right for a Mess of Pottage.*

I thought I had sufficiently shewn to all who could want Instruction, by what Methods they might safely proceed, whenever this *Coin* should be offered to them: And, I believe, there hath not been, for many Ages, an Example of any Kingdom so firmly united in a Point of great Importance, as this of ours is at present, against that detestable Fraud. But, however, it so happens, that some weak People begin to be alarmed a-new, by Rumours industriously spread. *Wood* prescribes to the News-Mongers in *London,* what they are to write. In one of their Papers published here by some obscure Printer, (and certainly with a bad Design) we are told, that the *Papists in* Ireland *have entered into an Association against his Coin;* although it be notoriously known, that they never once offered to stir in the Matter: So that the two Houses of Parliament, the Privy-Council, the great Number of Corporations, the Lord-Mayor and Aldermen of *Dublin,* the Grand-Juries, and principal Gentlemen of several Counties, are stigmatized in a Lump, under the Name of *Papists.*

This Impostor and his Crew, do likewise give out, that, by refusing to receive his Dross for Sterling, we *dispute the King's Prerogative; are grown ripe for Rebellion, and ready to shake off the Dependency of* Ireland *upon the Crown of* England. To Countenance which Reports, he hath published a Paragraph in another News-Paper, to let us know, that *the Lord Lieutenant is ordered to come over immediately to settle his Half-pence.*

I intreat you, my dear Countrymen, not to be under the least Concern upon these and the like Rumours; which are no more than the last Howls of a Dog dissected alive, as I hope he hath sufficiently been. These

---

To settle his Half-pence. The lord lieutenant whose impending arrival seemed menacing was John Cartaret. Though Cartaret and Swift were friends, Cartaret accepted the awkward assignment of attempting to resolve the controversy to London's satisfaction. See pp. 351, 377.

Calumnies are the only Reserve that is left him. For surely, our continued and (almost) unexampled Loyalty, will never be called in Question, for not suffering our selves to be robbed of all that we have, by one obscure *Ironmonger*.

As to disputing the King's *Prerogative*, give me Leave to explain to those who are ignorant, what the Meaning of that Word *Prerogative* is.

The Kings of these Realms enjoy several Powers, wherein the Laws have not interposed: So, they can make War and Peace without the Consent of Parliament; and this is a very great *Prerogative*. But if the Parliament doth not approve of the War, the King must bear the Charge of it out of his own Purse; and this is as great a Check on the Crown. So the King hath a *Prerogative* to coin Money, without Consent of Parliament: But he cannot compel the Subject to take that Money, except it be Sterling, Gold or Silver; because, herein he is limited by Law. Some Princes have, indeed, extended their *Prerogative* further than the Law allowed them: Wherein, however, the Lawyers of succeeding Ages, as fond as they are of *Precedents*, have never dared to justify them. But, to say the Truth, it is only of late Times that *Prerogative* hath been fixed and ascertained. For, whoever reads the Histories of *England*, will find that some former Kings, and those none of the worst, have, upon several Occasions, ventured to controul the Laws, with very little Ceremony or Scruple, even later than the Days of Queen *Elizabeth*. In her Reign, that pernicious Counsel of sending *base Money* hither, very narrowly failed of losing the Kingdom; being complained of by the Lord Deputy, the Council, and the whole Body of the *English* here: So that soon after her Death, it was recalled by her Successor, and lawful Money paid in Exchange.

Having thus given you some Notion of what is meant by the King's *Prerogative*, as far as a *Tradesman* can be thought capable of explaining it, I will only add the Opinion of the great Lord *Bacon*, that, *as God governs the World by the settled Laws of Nature, which he hath made, and never transcends those Laws, but upon high important Occasions: So, among earthly Princes, those are the Wisest and the Best, who govern by the known Laws of the Country, and seldomest make Use of their* Prerogative.

Now, here you may see that the vile Accusation of *Wood* and his Accomplices, charging us with *disputing the King's Prerogative*, by refusing his Brass, can have no Place; because compelling the Subject to take any Coin, which is not Sterling, is no Part of the King's *Prerogative;* and I am very

---

The Opinion of the great Lord *Bacon*. As McMinn points out, this does not seem to be a direct quotation from Bacon. Bacon is one of the mediators of the Florentine tradition of political thought upon which Swift drew for his conception of republican virtue (Pocock, 357). Bacon did make analogies between rules of policy and those of nature.

confident, if it were so, we should be the last of his People to dispute it; as well from that inviolable Loyalty we have always paid to his Majesty, as from the Treatment we might in such a Case justly expect from some, who seem to think, we have neither *common Sense*, nor *common Senses.* But, God be thanked, the best of them are only our *Fellow-Subjects*, and not our *Masters.* One great Merit I am sure we have, which those of *English* Birth can have no Pretence to; that our Ancestors reduced this Kingdom to the Obedience of England; for which we have been rewarded with a worse Climate, the Privilege of being governed by Laws to which we do not consent; a ruined Trade, a House of *Peers* without *Jurisdiction;* almost an Incapacity for all Employments, and the Dread of *Wood*'s Half-pence.

But we are so far from disputing the King's *Prerogative* in coining, that we own he hath Power to give a Patent to any Man, for setting his Royal Image and Superscription upon whatever Materials he pleases; and Liberty to the Patentee to offer them in any Country from *England* to *Japan;* only attended with one small Limitation, that *no body alive is obliged to take them.*

Upon these Considerations, I was ever against all Recourse to *England* for a Remedy against the present impending Evil; especially, when I observed, that the Addresses of both Houses, after long Expectance, produced nothing but a report altogether in Favour of *Wood;* upon which, I made some Observations in a former Letter; and might at least have made as many more: For, it is a Paper of as singular a Nature as I ever beheld.

But I mistake; for before this *Report* was made, his Majesty's *most gracious Answer* to the House of Lords was sent over, and printed; wherein there are these Words, *granting the Patent for coining Half-pence and Farthings*, agreeable to the Practice of his Royal Predecessors, *&c.* That King *Charles* II, and King *James* II, (and they only) did grant Patents for this Purpose, is indisputable, and I have shewn it at large. Their Patents were passed under the great Seal of *Ireland*, by References to *Ireland;* the Copper to be coined in *Ireland*, the Patentee was bound, on Demand, to receive his Coin back in *Ireland*, and pay Silver and Gold in Return. *Wood's* Patent was made under the great Seal of *England*, the Brass coined in *England*, not the least Reference made to *Ireland;* the Sum immense, and the Patentee under no Obligation to receive it again, and give good Money for it: This I only

Our Ancestors. While highlighting the "Anglo" side of Swift's Irishness, this passage is not so immediately sectarian as may first appear. The Drapier's legal theory harks back to events long prior to the Reformation, involving negotiations between the Gaelic rulers of Ireland and the English crown. The conquering "Old English" ancestors, though not Gaelic, were of course Catholic.

A former Letter. The third part of the *Drapier's Letters, Some Observations upon a Report.*

mention, because, in my private Thoughts, I have sometimes made a Query, whether the *Penner* of those Words in his Majesty's *most gracious Answer,* agreeable to the Practice of his Royal Predecessors, had maturely considered the several Circumstances; which, in my poor Opinion, seem to make a Difference.

Let me now say something concerning the other great Cause of some People's Fear; as *Wood* has taught the *London* News-Writer to express it: That *his Excellency the Lord Lieutenant is coming over to settle* Wood's *Half-pence.*

We know very well, that the Lords Lieutenants, for several Years past, have not thought this Kingdom *worthy the Honour of their Residence,* longer than was absolutely necessary for the King's Business; which consequently *wanted no Speed in the Dispatch.* And therefore, it naturally fell into most Mens Thoughts, that a new Governor coming at an *unusual* Time, must portend some *unusual* Business to be done; especially, if the common Report be true; that the Parliament prorogued to I know not when, is, by a new Summons (revoking that Prorogation) to assemble soon after his Arrival: For which extraordinary Proceeding, the Lawyers on t'other Side the Water, have, by great good Fortune, found two *Precedents.*

All this being granted, it can never enter into my Head, that so *little a Creature as Wood* could find Credit enough with the King and his Ministers, to have the Lord Lieutenant of *Ireland* sent hither in a Hurry, upon his Errand.

For, let us take the whole Matter nakedly, as it lies before us, without the Refinements of some People, with which we have nothing to do. Here is a Patent granted under the great Seal of *England,* upon false Suggestions, to one *William Wood,* for coining Copper Half-pence for *Ireland:* The Parliament here, upon Apprehensions of the worst Consequences from the said Patent, address the King to have it recalled: This is refused, and a Committee of the Privy-Council *report* to his Majesty, that *Wood* has performed the Conditions of his Patent. He then is left to do the best he can with his Half-pence; no Man being obliged to receive them; the People here, being likewise left to themselves, unite as one Man; resolving they will have nothing to do with his Ware. By this plain Account of the Fact, it is manifest, that the King and his Ministry are wholly out of the Case; and the Matter is left to be disputed between him and us. Will any Man therefore attempt to persuade me, that a Lord Lieutenant is to be dispatched over in great Haste, before the ordinary Time, and a Parliament summoned, by anticipating a Prorogation; merely to put an Hundred Thousand Pounds into the Pocket of a *Sharper,* by the Ruin of a most loyal Kingdom?

But supposing all this to be true. By what Arguments could a Lord Lieutenant prevail on the same Parliament, which addressed with so much Zeal and Earnestness against this Evil; to pass it into a Law? I am sure their Opinion of *Wood* and his Project is not mended since their last Prorogation: And supposing those *Methods* should be used, which, *Detractors* tell us, have been sometimes put in Practice for *gaining Votes;* it is well known, that in this Kingdom there are few Employments to be given; and if there were more; it is *as well known* to whose Share they must fall.

But, because great Numbers of you are altogether ignorant in the Affairs of your Country, I will tell you some Reasons, why there are so few Employments to be disposed of in this Kingdom. All considerable Offices for Life here, are possessed by those, to whom the Reversions were granted; and these have been generally Followers of the Chief Governors, or Persons who had Interest in the Court of *England.* So the Lord *Berkely* of *Stratton,* holds that great Office of *Master of the Rolls;* the Lord *Palmerstown* is *First Remembrancer,* worth near 2000 *l. per Ann.* One *Dodington,* Secretary to the Earl of *Pembroke,* begged the Reversion of *Clerk of the Pells,* worth 2500 *l.* a Year, which he now enjoys by the Death of the Lord *Newtown.* Mr. *Southwell* is Secretary of State, and the Earl of *Burlington* Lord High Treasurer of *Ireland* by Inheritance. These are only a few among many others, which I have been told of, but cannot remember. Nay the Reversion of several Employments during Pleasure are granted the same Way. This among many others, is a Circumstance whereby the Kingdom of *Ireland* is distinguished from all other Nations upon Earth; and makes it so difficult an Affair to get into a Civil Employ, that Mr. *Addison* was forced to purchase an old obscure Place, called *Keeper of the Records in* Bermingham's *Tower,* of Ten Pounds a Year, and to get a Salary of 400 *l.* annexed to it, though all the Records there are not worth Half a Crown, either for Curiosity or Use. And we lately saw a **Favourite Secretary,* descend to be *Master of the Revels,* which by his *Credit and Extortion* he hath made *Pretty Considerable.* I say nothing of the Under-Treasurership worth about 9000 *l.* a Year; nor the Commissioners of the Revenue, Four of whom generally live in *England:* For I think none of these are granted in Reversion. But the Jest is, that I have known upon Occasion, some of these absent Officers as *Keen* against the Interest of *Ireland,* as if they had never been indebted to Her for a *Single Groat.*

I confess, I have been sometimes tempted to wish that this Project of *Wood* might succeed; because I reflected with some Pleasure what a *Jolly Crew* it would bring over among us of *Lords* and *Squires,* and *Pensioners* of

---

So few Employments. The issue is government patronage in Ireland, which was almost entirely doled out to Englishmen. See p. 377.

* *Mr.* Hopkins, *Secretary to the Duke of Grafton* [original publisher].

Both Sexes, and Officers *Civil* and *Military;* where we should live together as merry and sociable as Beggars; only with this one Abatement, that we should neither have *Meat* to feed, nor *Manufactures* to Cloath us; unless we could be content to *Prance* about in *Coats of Mail;* or eat Brass as Ostritches do Iron.

I return from this Digression, to that which gave me the Occasion of making it: And I believe you are now convinced, that if the Parliament of *Ireland* were as *Temptable* as any *other* Assembly, *within a Mile of* Christendom (which God forbid) yet the *Managers* must of Necessity fail for want of *Tools* to work with. But I will yet go one Step further, by Supposing that a Hundred new Employments were erected on Purpose to gratify *Compliers:* Yet still an insuperable Difficulty would remain. For it happens, I know not how, that *Money* is neither *Whig* nor *Tory*, neither of *Town* nor *Country Party;* and it is not improbable, that a Gentleman would rather chuse to live upon his *own Estate*, which brings him *Gold* and *Silver*, than with the Addition of an *Employment;* when his *Rents* and *Sallary* must both be paid in *Wood*'s Brass, at above Eighty *per Cent.* Discount.

For these, and many other Reasons, I am confident you need not be under the least Apprehensions, from the sudden Expectation of the *Lord Lieutenant*, while we continue in our present hearty Disposition; to alter which, there is no suitable Temptation can possibly be offered: And if, as I have often asserted from the best Authority, the *Law* hath not left a *Power* in the *Crown* to force any Money, except Sterling, upon the Subject; much less can the Crown *devolve* such a *Power* upon *another.*

This I speak with the utmost Respect to the *Person* and *Dignity* of his Excellency the Lord *Carteret;* whose Character was lately given me, by a Gentleman that hath known him from his first Appearance in the World: That Gentleman describes him as a young Man of great Accomplishments, excellent Learning, Regular in his Life, and of much Spirit and Vivacity. He hath since, as I have heard, been employed abroad; was principal Secretary of State; and is now about the 37th Year of his Age appointed Lord Lieutenant of *Ireland.* From such a Governour this Kingdom may reasonably hope for as much Prosperity, as *under so many Discouragements* it can be capable of receiving.

It is true indeed, that within the Memory of Man, there have been Governors of so much Dexterity, as to carry Points of terrible Consequence to this Kingdom, by their Power with *those who were in Office;* and by their Arts in managing or deluding others with *Oaths, Affability*, and even with *Dinners.* If *Wood*'s Brass had, in those Times, been upon the *Anvil*, it is obvious enough to conceive what Methods would have been taken. *Depending* Persons would have been told in plain Terms, that it was a

Service expected from them, under Pain of the publick Business being put into more complying Hands. Others would be allured by *Promises.* To the *Country Gentlemen,* besides *good Words, Burgundy* and *Closeting;* it might, perhaps, have been hinted, how *kindly it would be taken to comply with a Royal Patent, although it were not compulsory.* That if any Inconveniences ensued, it might be made up with other *Graces or Favours hereafter:* That *Gentlemen ought to consider, whether it were prudent or safe to disgust* England: They would be desired to *think of some good Bills for encouraging of Trade, and setting the Poor to work: Some further Acts against Popery, and for uniting Protestants.* There would be solemn Engagements, that we should *never be troubled with above Forty Thousand Pounds in his Coin, and all of the best and weightiest Sort; for which we should only give our Manufactures in Exchange, and keep our Gold and Silver at home.* Perhaps, *a seasonable Report of some Invasion would have been spread in the most proper Juncture;* which is a great Smoother of Rubs in publick Proceedings: And we should have been told, that *this was no Time to create Differences, when the Kingdom was in Danger.*

These, I say, and the like Methods, would, in corrupt Times, have been taken to let in this Deluge of Brass among us: and, I am confident, would even then have not succeeded; much less under the Administration of so excellent a Person as the Lord *Carteret;* and in a Country, where the People of all Ranks, Parties, and Denominations, are convinced to a Man, that the utter undoing of themselves and their Posterity for ever, will be dated from the Admission of that execrable Coin: That if it once enters, it can be no more confined to a small or moderate Quantity, than the *Plague* can be confined to a few Families; and that no *Equivalent* can be given by any earthly Power, any more than a dead Carcass can be recovered to Life by a Cordial.

There is one comfortable Circumstance in this universal Opposition to Mr. *Wood,* that the People sent over hither from *England,* to *fill up our Vacancies, Ecclesiastical, Civil and Military,* are all on our Side: *Money,* the great *Divider* of the World, hath, by a strange Revolution, been the great *Uniter* of a most *divided* People. Who would leave a Hundred Pounds a Year in *England, (a Country of Freedom)* to be paid a Thousand in *Ireland* out of *Wood*'s Exchequer? The *Gentleman They* have lately made *Primate,* would never quit his Seat in an *English* House of Lords, and his Preferments

---

Some further Acts against Popery. A hint that bashing Catholics, in the vein of the endless penal laws, was a cynical ruse wheeled out when necessary to distract Irish Protestants from *British* domination.

The *Gentleman They* have lately made *Primate.* Hugh Boulter (1671–1742), formerly bishop of Bristol. He had been deliberately appointed archbishop of Armagh, in the wake of the Wood's halfpence controversy, to tighten England's control over Irish affairs.

at *Oxford* and *Bristol*, worth Twelve Hundred Pounds a Year, for four Times the Denomination here, but not half the Value: Therefore, I expect to hear he will be as good an *Irishman*, at least, upon *this one Article*, as any of his Brethren; or even of *Us*, who have had the *Misfortune* to be born in this Island. For those who, in the common Phrase, do not *come hither to learn the Language*, would never change a better Country for a worse, to receive *Brass* instead of *Gold*.

Another Slander spread by *Wood* and his Emissaries is, that, by opposing him, we discover an Inclination to *shake off our Dependance upon the Crown of* England. Pray observe, how important a Person is this same *William Wood;* and how the publick Weal of two Kingdoms, is involved in his private Interest. First, all those who refuse to take his Coin *are Papists;* for he tells us, that *none but Papists are associated against him*. Secondly, they *dispute the King's Prerogative*. Thirdly, they *are ripe for Rebellion*. And Fourthly, they are going to *shake off their Dependance upon the Crown of* England; that is to say, *they are going to chuse another King:* For there can be no other Meaning in this Expression, however some may pretend to strain it.

And this gives me an Opportunity of explaining, to those who are ignorant, another Point, which hath often *swelled in my Breast*. Those who come over hither to us from *England*, and some *weak* People among ourselves, whenever, in Discourse, we make mention of *Liberty* and *Property*, shake their Heads, and tell us, that *Ireland* is a *depending Kingdom;* as if they would seem, by this Phrase, to intend, that the People of *Ireland* is in some State of Slavery or Dependance, different from those of *England:* Whereas, a *depending Kingdom* is a *modern Term of Art;* unknown, as I have heard, to all antient *Civilians*, and *Writers upon Government*, and *Ireland* is, on the contrary, called in some Statutes an *Imperial Crown*, as held only from God; which is as high a Style, as any Kingdom is capable of receiving. Therefore by this Expression, a *depending Kingdom*, there is no more understood, than that by a Statute made here, in the 33d Year of *Henry* VIII, *The King and his Successors, are to be Kings Imperial of this Realm, as united and knit to the Imperial Crown of* England. I have looked over all the *English* and *Irish* Statutes, without finding any Law that makes *Ireland depend* upon *England;* any more than *England* doth upon *Ireland*. We have, indeed, obliged ourselves to have *the same King with them;* and consequently they are obliged to have the *same King with us*. For the Law was made by *our own Parliament;* and our Ancestors then were not such *Fools (whatever they*

Writers upon Government. As McMinn points out, Swift here deliberately ignores the Declaratory Act of 1720, reprinted in this volume on pp. 416–17.

were in the preceding Reign) to bring themselves under I know not what *Dependance*, which is now talked of, without any Ground of *Law, Reason*, or *common Sense*.

Let whoever think otherwise, I *M. B. Drapier*, desire to be excepted. For I declare, next under God, I *depend* only on the King my Sovereign, and on the Laws of my own Country, And I am so far from *depending* upon the People of *England*, that, if they should ever *rebel* against my Sovereign, (which God forbid) I would be ready at the first Command from his Majesty to take Arms against them; as some of *my* Countrymen did against *theirs* at *Preston*. And, if such a Rebellion should prove so successful as to fix the *Pretender* on the Throne of *England;* I would venture to transgress that *Statute* so far, as to lose every Drop of my Blood, to hinder him from being *King* of *Ireland*.

It is true, indeed, that within the Memory of Man, the Parliaments of *England* have *sometimes* assumed the Power of binding this Kingdom, by Laws enacted there; wherein they were, at first, openly opposed (as far as *Truth, Reason*, and *Justice* are capable of *opposing*) by the famous Mr. *Molineaux*, an *English* Gentleman born here; as well as by several of the greatest Patriots, and *best Whigs* in *England;* but the *Love and Torrent* of Power prevailed. Indeed, the Arguments on both Sides were invincible. For in *Reason*, all *Government* without the Consent of the *Governed*, is the *very Definition of Slavery:* But in *Fact, Eleven Men well armed, will certainly subdue one single Man in his Shirt*. But I have done. For those who have used *Power* to cramp *Liberty*, have gone so far as to resent even the *Liberty* of *Complaining;* although a Man upon the Rack, was never known to be refused the Liberty of *roaring* as loud as he thought fit.

And, as we are apt to *sink* too *much* under *unreasonable* Fears, so we are too soon inclined to be *raised* by groundless Hopes, (according to the

---

M. B. Drapier. The Drapier's initials conjure up the ghost of Marcus Brutus, who represented for Swift a classical model of political virtue. As a reluctant assassin of Julius Caesar, he placed resistance to tyranny above private friendship. This incendiary paragraph, flirting with regicidal fantasies, brought the charge of sedition down upon the Drapier. See pp. 178, 198.

Mr. *Molineaux.* William Molyneux (1656–98). Scientist (optics and mathematics); friend of John Locke; member of Parliament for Trinity College, Dublin. Responding to preliminary proposals for the Woollen Act, Molyneux first articulated the case, according both to constitutional history and a "natural rights" theory, for the independence of Ireland from the English Parliament. Declared seditious at the time, his pamphlet *The Case of Ireland's Being Bound by Acts of Parliament in England, Stated* (1698) gained new life as a reference point for the *Drapier's Letters* controversy.

One single Man in his Shirt. The Drapier equates the legal double standard in Britain and Ireland with the illegitimate use of force by outlaws.

Nature of all *consumptive* Bodies like ours.) Thus, it hath been given about for several Days past, that *Somebody in England,* empowered a second *Somebody* to write to a third *Somebody* here, to assure us, that we *should no more be troubled with those Half-pence.* And this is reported to have been done by the* *same Person,* who was said to have sworn some Months ago, that he would *ram them down our Throats,* (though I doubt they would *stick in our Stomachs*). But which ever of these Reports is true or false, it is no Concern of ours. For, *in this Point,* we have nothing to do with *English Ministers:* And I should be sorry to leave it in their Power to *redress* this Grievance, or to *enforce* it: For the *Report of the Committee* hath given me a *Surfeit.* The Remedy is wholly in your own Hands; and therefore I have digressed a little, in order to refresh and continue that *Spirit* so seasonably raised amongst you; and to let you see, that by the Laws of God, of Nature, of Nations, and of your own Country, you are and ought to be as free a People as your Brethren in *England.*

If the Pamphlets published at *London* by *Wood* and his *Journeymen,* in Defence of his Cause, were Re-printed here, and that our Countrymen could be persuaded to read them, they would convince you of his wicked Design, more than all I shall ever be able to say. In short, I make him a perfect *Saint,* in Comparison of what he appears to be, from the Writings of those whom he *Hires* to justify his *Project.* But he is so far *Master of the Field (let others guess the Reason)* that no *London* Printer dare publish any Paper written in Favour of *Ireland:* And here no Body hath yet been so *bold,* as to publish any Thing in *Favour* of *him.*

There was a few Days ago a Pamphlet sent me of near 50 Pages, written in Favour of Mr. *Wood* and his Coinage; printed in *London:* It is not worth answering, because probably it will never be published here: But it gave me an Occasion, to reflect upon an Unhappiness we lie under, that the People of *England* are utterly ignorant of our Case; Which, however, is no Wonder; since it is a Point they do not in the least concern themselves about; farther than, perhaps, as a Subject of Discourse in a Coffee-House, when they have nothing else to talk of. For I have Reason to believe, that no Minister ever gave himself the Trouble of reading any Papers written in our Defence; because I suppose *their Opinions are already determined,* and are formed wholly upon the Reports of *Wood* and his Accomplices; else it would be impossible, that any Man could have the Impudence, to write such a Pamphlet, as I have mentioned.

Our *Neighbours, whose Understandings are just upon a Level with Ours* (which perhaps are none of the *Brightest*) have a strong Contempt for most

---

* *Mr.* Walpole, *now Sir* Robert [original publisher].

Nations, but especially for *Ireland:* They look upon us as a Sort of *Savage Irish,* whom our Ancestors conquered several Hundred Years ago: And if I should describe the *Britons* to you, as they were in *Cæsar's* Time, when they *painted their Bodies, or cloathed themselves with the Skins of Beasts,* I should act full as reasonably as they do. However, they are so far to be excused, in relation to the present Subject, that, hearing only *one Side of the Cause,* and having neither Opportunity nor Curiosity to examine the *other,* they *believe a Lye,* merely for their Ease; and conclude, because Mr. *Wood* pretends to have *Power,* he hath also *Reason* on his Side.

Therefore, to let you see how this Case is represented in *England* by *Wood* and his Adherents, I have thought it proper to extract out of that Pamphlet, a few of those notorious Falshoods, in Point of *Fact* and *Reasoning,* contained therein; the Knowledge whereof, will confirm my Countrymen in their *Own* Right Sentiments, when they will see by comparing both, how much their *Enemies are in the Wrong.*

First, The Writer positively asserts, *That* Wood's *Halfpence were current among us for several Months, with the universal Approbation of all People, without one single Gain-sayer; and we all to a Man thought our selves Happy in having them.*

Secondly, He affirms, *That we were drawn into a Dislike of them, only by some Cunning Evil-designing Men among us, who opposed this Patent of* Wood, *to get another for themselves.*

Thirdly, That *those who most declared at first against* Wood's *Patent, were the very Men who intended to get another for their own Advantage.*

Fourthly, That *our Parliament and Privy-Council, the Lord Mayor and Aldermen of* Dublin, *the Grand-Juries and Merchants, and in short the whole Kingdom; nay, the very Dogs* (as he expresseth it) *were fond of those Half-pence, till they were inflamed by those few designing Persons aforesaid.*

Fifthly, He says directly, That *all those who opposed the Half-pence, were Papists, and Enemies to King* George.

Thus far I am confident the most ignorant among you can safely swear from your own Knowledge, that the Author is a most notorious Lyar in every Article; the direct contrary being so manifest to the whole Kingdom, that if Occasion required, we might get it confirmed *under Five hundred thousand Hands.*

Sixthly, He would persuade us, That *if we sell Five Shillings worth of our Goods or Manufactures for Two Shillings and Four-pence worth of Copper, although the Copper were melted down, and that we could get Five Shillings*

They look upon us as a Sort of *Savage Irish.* See p. 471.

in Gold or Silver for the said Goods; yet to take the said Two Shillings and Four-pence in Copper, would be greatly for our Advantage.

And Lastly, He makes us a very fair Offer, as empowered by *Wood*, That *if we will take off Two hundred thousand Pounds in his Half-pence for our Goods, and likewise pay him Three* per Cent. *Interest for Thirty Years, for an hundred and Twenty thousand Pounds (at which he computes the Coinage above the intrinsick Value of the Copper) for the Loan of his Coin, he will after that Time give us good Money for what Half-pence will be then left.*

Let me place this Offer in as clear a Light as I can, to shew the unsupportable Villainy and Impudence of that incorrigible Wretch. First (says he) *I will send Two hundred thousand Pounds of my Coin into your Country: The Copper I compute to be in real Value Eighty thousand Pounds, and I charge you with an hundred and twenty thousand Pounds for the Coinage; so that you see, I lend you an Hundred and twenty thousand Pounds for Thirty Years; for which you shall pay me Three* per Cent. *That is to say, Three thousand Six hundred Pounds,* per Ann. *which in Thirty Years will amount to an Hundred and eight thousand Pounds. And when these Thirty Years are expired, return me my Copper, and I will give you Good Money for it.*

This is the Proposal made to us by *Wood* in that Pamphlet, written by one of his *Commissioners:* And the Author is supposed to be the same Infamous *Coleby* one of his *Under-Swearers* at the *Committee of Council*, who was tryed for *Robbing the Treasury here*, where he was an Under-Clerk.

By this Proposal he will first receive Two hundred thousand Pounds, in Goods or Sterling, for as much Copper as he values at Eighty thousand Pounds; but in Reality not worth Thirty thousand Pounds. Secondly, He will receive for Interest an Hundred and Eight thousand Pounds: And when our Children come Thirty Years hence, to return his Half-pence upon his Executors (for before that Time he will be probably gone *to his own Place*) those Executors will very reasonably reject them as Raps and Counterfeits; which they will be, and Millions of them of his own Coinage.

Methinks, I am fond of such a *Dealer* as this, who mends every Day upon our Hands, like a *Dutch* Reckoning; where, if you dispute the Unreasonableness and Exorbitance of the Bill, the Landlord shall bring it up every Time with new Additions.

Although these and the like Pamphlets, published by *Wood* in *London*, be altogether unknown here, where no body could read them, without as much *Indignation as Contempt* would allow; yet I thought it proper to give you a Specimen how the *Man* employs his Time; where he Rides alone without any Creature to contradict him; while our few Friends there wonder at our Silence: And the *English* in general, if they think of this Matter at all, impute our Refusal to *Wilfulness* or *Disaffection*, just as *Wood* and his *Hirelings* are pleased to represent.

But although our Arguments are not suffered to be printed in *England*, yet the Consequence will be of little Moment. Let *Wood* endeavour to *persuade* the People *There*, that we ought to *Receive* his Coin; and let Me *Convince* our People *Here*, that they ought to *Reject* it under Pain of our utter Undoing. And then let him do his *Best* and his *Worst*.

Before I conclude, I must beg Leave, in all Humility to tell Mr. *Wood*, that he is guilty of great *Indiscretion*, by causing so Honourable a Name as that of Mr. *Walpole* to be mentioned so often, and in such a Manner, upon his Occasion. A short Paper, printed at *Bristol*, and re-printed here, reports Mr. *Wood* to say, that he *wonders at the Impudence and Insolence of the* Irish, *in refusing his Coin*, and *what he will do when Mr.* Walpole *comes* to *Town*. Where, by the Way, he is mistaken; for it is the *True English People* of *Ireland*, who refuse it; although we take it for granted, that the *Irish* will do so too, whenever they are asked. In another printed Paper of his contriving, it is roundly expressed, that Mr. *Walpole will cram his Brass down our Throats*. Sometimes it is given out, that we must *either take these Half-pence or eat our Brogues*. And, in another News-Letter but of Yesterday, we read, that the same great Man *hath sworn to make us swallow his Coin in Fire-Balls*.

This brings to my Mind the known Story of a *Scotch* Man, who receiving Sentence of Death, with all the Circumstances of *Hanging, Beheading, Quartering, Embowelling*, and the like; cried out, *What need all this* Cookery? And I think we have Reason to ask the same Question: For if we believe *Wood*, here is a *Dinner* getting ready for us, and you see the *Bill of Fare;* and I am sorry the *Drink* was forgot, which might easily be supplied with *Melted Lead* and *Flaming Pitch*.

What vile Words are these to put into the Mouth of a great Counsellor, in high Trust with his Majesty, and looked upon as a prime Minister? If Mr. *Wood* hath no better a Manner of representing his Patrons; when I come to be a *Great Man*, he shall never be suffered to attend at my *Levee*. This is not the Style of a Great Minister; it savours too much of the *Kettle* and the *Furnace;* and came entirely out of *Wood's Forge*.

As for the Threat of making us *eat our Brogues*, we need not be in Pain; for if his Coin should pass, that *Unpolite Covering for the Feet*, would no longer be a *National Reproach;* because, then we should have neither *Shoe* nor *Brogue* left in the Kingdom. But here the Falshood of Mr. *Wood* is fairly detected; for I am confident Mr. *Walpole* never heard of a *Brogue* in his whole Life.

As to *Swallowing these Half-pence in Fire-balls*, it is a Story equally improbable. For, to execute this *Operation*, the whole Stock of Mr. *Wood's* Coin and Metal must be melted down, and molded into hollow *Balls* with *Wild-fire*, no bigger than a *reasonable* Throat can be able to swallow. Now, the Metal he hath prepared, and already coined, will amount to at least Fifty Millions of Half-pence to be *Swallowed* by a Million and a Half of People; so that allowing Two Half-pence to each *Ball*, there will be about Seventeen *Balls* of *Wild-fire* a-piece, to be swallowed by every Person in the Kingdom: And to administer this Dose, there cannot be conveniently fewer than Fifty thousand *Operators*, allowing one *Operator* to every Thirty; which, considering the *Squeamishness* of some Stomachs, and the *Peevishness* of *Young Children*, is but reasonable. Now, under Correction of better Judgments, I think the Trouble and Charge of such an Experiment, would exceed the Profit; and therefore I take this *Report* to be *spurious;* or, at least, only a new *Scheme* of Mr. *Wood* himself; which, to make it pass the better in *Ireland*, he would Father upon a *Minister of State.*

But I will now demonstrate, beyond all Contradiction, that Mr. *Walpole* is against this Project of Mr. *Wood;* and is an entire Friend to *Ireland;* only by this one invincible Argument, That he has the Universal Opinion of being a wise Man, an able Minister, and in all his Proceedings, pursuing the *True Interest* of the *King his Master:* And that, as his *Integrity* is above all *Corruption*, so is his *Fortune* above all *Temptation.* I reckon therefore, we are perfectly safe from that *Corner;* and shall never be under the Necessity of Contending with so *Formidable a Power;* but be left to possess our *Brogues* and *Potatoes* in *Peace*, as * *Remote from Thunder as we are from Jupiter.*

I *am, My dear Countrymen, your Loving Fellow-Subject, Fellow-Sufferer, and Humble Servant,*

Oct. 13, 1724 M. B.

A Million and a Half of People. A foretaste, as McMinn observes, of the mock quantitative language of *A Modest Proposal.*

* *Procul à Jove, procul à fulmine* [original publisher].

A Short View of the State of Ireland

Written in the Year 1727

The Prose Writings of Jonathan Swift, ed. Herbert Davis, 14 vols. (Oxford: Basil Blackwell, 1939–1968).

I am assured, that it hath, for some Time, been practised as a Method of making Men's Court, when they are asked about the Rate of Lands, the Abilities of Tenants, the State of Trade and Manufacture in this Kingdom, and how their Rents are paid; to answer, that in their Neighbourhood, all Things are in a flourishing Condition, the Rent and Purchase of Land every Day encreasing. And if a Gentleman happen to be a little more sincere in his Representations; besides being looked on as not well affected, he is sure to have a Dozen Contradictors at his Elbow. I think it is no Manner of Secret why these Questions are so *cordially* asked, or so *obligingly* answered.

But since, with regard to the Affairs of this Kingdom, I have been using all Endeavours to subdue my Indignation; to which, indeed, I am not provoked by any personal Interest, being not the Owner of one Spot of Ground in the whole *Island;* I shall only enumerate by Rules generally known, and never contradicted, what are the true Causes of any Countries flourishing and growing rich; and then examine what Effects arise from those Causes in the Kingdom of *Ireland.*

The first Cause of a Kingdom's thriving, is the Fruitfulness of the Soil, to produce the Necessaries and Conveniences of Life; not only sufficient for the Inhabitants, but for Exportation into other Countries.

The Second, is the Industry of the People, in working up all their native Commodities, to the last Degree of Manufacture.

The Third, is the Conveniency of safe Ports and Havens, to carry out their own Goods, as much manufactured, and bring in those of others, as little manufactured, as the Nature of mutual Commerce will allow.

The Fourth is, that the Natives should, as much as possible, export and import their Goods in Vessels of their own Timber, made in their own Country.

The Fifth, is the Priviledge of a free Trade in all foreign Countries, which will permit them; except to those who are in War with their own Prince or State.

The Sixth, is, by being governed only by Laws made with their own Consent; for otherwise they are not a free People. And therefore, all Appeals for Justice, or Applications for Favour or Preferment, to another Country, are so many grievous Impoverishments.

Vessels of their own Timber, made in their own Country. A series of Navigation Acts in the 1650s and 1660s established England as a major maritime power. The protectionist laws provoked a series of minor wars with the Dutch, at whom they were originally aimed. They also prohibited Irish competition with English trade and specifically mandated, in order to build up an English merchant fleet, that English-made ships must be used for goods imported to or exported from the colonies.

The Seventh is, by Improvement of Land, Encouragement of Agriculture, and thereby encreasing the Number of their People; without which, any Country, however blessed by Nature, must continue poor.

The Eighth, is the Residence of the Prince, or chief Administrator of the Civil Power.

The Ninth, is the Concourse of Foreigners for Education, Curiosity, or Pleasure; or as to a general Mart of Trade.

The Tenth, is by disposing all Offices of Honour, Profit, or Trust, only to the Natives, or at least with very few Exceptions; where Strangers have long inhabited the Country, and are supposed to understand, and regard the Interest of it as their own.

The Eleventh, is when the Rents of Lands, and Profits of Employments, are spent in the Country which produced them, and not in another; the former of which will certainly happen, where the Love of our native Country prevails.

The Twelfth, is by the publick Revenues being all spent and employed at home; except on the Occasions of a foreign War.

The Thirteenth is, where the People are not obliged, unless they find it for their own Interest or Conveniency, to receive any Monies, except of their own Coinage by a publick Mint, after the Manner of all civilized Nations.

The Fourteenth, is a Disposition of the People of a Country to wear their own Manufactures, and import as few Incitements to Luxury, either in Cloaths, Furniture, Food, or Drink, as they possibly can live conveniently without.

There are many other Causes of a Nation's thriving, which I cannot at present recollect; but without Advantage from at least some of these, after turning my Thoughts a long Time, I am not able to discover from whence our Wealth proceeds, and therefore would gladly be better informed. In the mean Time, I will here examine what Share falls to *Ireland* of these Causes, or of the Effects and Consequences.

It is not my Intention to complain, but barely to relate Facts; and the Matter is not of small Importance. For it is allowed, that a Man who lives in a solitary House, far from Help, is not wise in endeavouring to acquire, in the Neighbourhood, the Reputation of being rich; because those who come for Gold, will go off with Pewter and Brass, rather than return empty: And in the common Practice of the World, those who possess most Wealth, make the least Parade; which they leave to others, who have nothing else to bear them out, in shewing their Faces on the *Exchange*.

As to the first Cause of a Nation's Riches, being the Fertility of the Soil, as well as Temperature of Climate, we have no Reason to complain; for, although the Quantity of unprofitable Land in this Kingdom, reckoning

Bogg, and Rock, and barren Mountain, be double in Proportion to what it is in *England;* yet the native Productions which both Kingdoms deal in, are very near on Equality in Point of Goodness; and might, with the same Encouragement, be as well manufactured. I except Mines and Minerals; in some of which, however, we are only defective in Point of Skill and Industry.

In the Second, which is the Industry of the People; our Misfortune is not altogether owing to our own Fault, but to a Million of Discouragements.

The Conveniency of Ports and Havens, which Nature hath bestowed so liberally on this Kingdom, is of no more Use to us, than a beautiful Prospect to a Man shut up in a Dungeon.

As to Shipping of its own, *Ireland* is so utterly unprovided, that of all the excellent Timber cut down within these Fifty or Sixty Years, it can hardly be said, that the Nation hath received the Benefit of one valuable House to dwell in, or one Ship to trade with.

IRELAND is the only Kingdom I ever heard or read of, either in ancient or modern Story, which was denied the Liberty of exporting their native Commodities and Manufactures, wherever they pleased; except to Countries at War with their own Prince or State: Yet this Privilege, by the Superiority of meer Power, is refused us, in the most momentous Parts of Commerce; besides an Act of Navigation, to which we never consented, pinned down upon us, and rigorously executed; and a Thousand other unexampled Circumstances, as grievous, as they are invidious to mention. To go on to the rest.

It is too well known, that we are forced to obey some Laws we never consented to; which is a Condition I must not call by its true uncontroverted Name, for fear of Lord Chief Justice *Whitshed's* Ghost, with his **Libertas & natale Solum*, written as a Motto on his Coach, as it stood at the Door of the Court, while he was perjuring himself to betray both. Thus, we are in the Condition of Patients, who have Physick sent them by Doctors at a Distance, Strangers to their Constitution, and the Nature of their Disease: And thus, we are forced to pay five Hundred *per Cent.* to decide our Properties; in all which, we have likewise the Honour to be distinguished from the whole Race of Mankind.

As to Improvement of Land; those few who attempt that, or Planting, through Covetousness, or Want of Skill, generally leave Things worse than they were; neither succeeding in Trees nor Hedges; and by running into the

---

Lord Chief Justice *Whitshed.* See "Whitshed's Motto on His Coach" (pp. 341–42).

*Liberty and my native country [original publisher].

Fancy of Grazing, after the Manner of the *Scythians*, are every Day depopulating the Country.

We are so far from having a King to reside among us, that even the Viceroy is generally absent four Fifths of his Time in the Government.

No strangers from other Countries, make this a Part of their Travels; where they can expect to see nothing, but Scenes of Misery and Desolation.

Those who have the Misfortune to be born here, have the least Title to any considerable Employment; to which they are seldom preferred, but upon a political Consideration.

One third Part of the Rents of *Ireland*, is spent in *England;* which, with the Profit of Employments, Pensions, Appeals, Journeys of Pleasure or Health, Education at the *Inns* of Court, and both Universities, Remittances at Pleasure, the Pay of all Superior Officers in the Army, and other Incidents, will amount to a full half of the Income of the whole Kingdom, all clear Profit to *England*.

We are denied the Liberty of Coining Gold, Silver, or even Copper. In the Isle of *Man*, they coin their own *Silver;* every petty Prince, Vassal to the *Emperor*, can coin what Money he pleaseth. And in this, as in most of the Articles already mentioned, we are an Exception to all other States or Monarchies that were ever known in the World.

As to the last, or Fourteenth Article, we take special Care to act diametrically contrary to it in the whole Course of our Lives. Both Sexes, but especially the Women, despise and abhor to wear any of their own Manufactures, even those which are better made than in other Countries; particularly a Sort of Silk Plad, through which the Workmen are forced to run a Sort of Gold Thread that it may pass for *Indian*. Even Ale and Potatoes are imported from *England*, as well as Corn: And our foreign Trade is little more than Importation of *French* Wine; for which I am told we pay ready Money.

Now, if all this be true, upon which I could easily enlarge; I would be glad to know by what secret Method, it is, that we grow a rich and flourishing People, without *Liberty, Trade, Manufactures, Inhabitants, Money*, or the *Privilege of Coining;* without *Industry, Labour*, or *Improvement of Lands*, and with more than half the Rent and Profits of the whole *Kingdom*,

---

Scythians. A nomadic tribe from an area north of the Black Sea. Believed by Edmund Spenser and others to have settled in the north of Ireland.

Pass for *Indian*. Textiles from India, regarded as superior, were in great demand. In 1720 Daniel Defoe claimed that the East India trade was engrossing all the bullion of Europe, thereby enriching "Heathens," and so proposed legislation forbidding the "Use and Wearing of printed Callicoes and Linnens" (vol. 7, 101).

annually exported; for which we receive not a single Farthing: And to make up all this, nothing worth mentioning, except the Linnen of the *North*, a Trade casual, corrupted, and at Mercy; and some Butter from *Cork*. If we do flourish, it must be against every Law of Nature and Reason; like the Thorn at *Glassenbury*, that blossoms in the Midst of Winter.

Let the worthy *Commissioners* who come from *England*, ride round the Kingdom, and observe the Face of Nature, or the Faces of the Natives; the Improvement of the Land; the thriving numerous Plantations; the noble Woods; the Abundance and Vicinity of Country-Seats; the commodious Farmers Houses and Barns; the Towns and Villages, where every Body is busy, and thriving with all Kind of Manufactures; the Shops full of Goods, wrought to Perfection, and filled with Customers; the comfortable Diet and Dress, and Dwellings of the People; the vast Numbers of Ships in our Harbours and Docks, and Ship-wrights in our Seaport-Towns; the Roads crouded with Carriers, laden with rich Manufactures; the perpetual Concourse to and fro of pompous Equipages.

With what Envy, and Admiration, would those Gentlemen return from so delightful a Progress? What glorious Reports would they make, when they went back to *England?*

But my Heart is too heavy to continue this Irony longer; for it is manifest, that whatever Stranger took such a Journey, would be apt to think himself travelling in *Lapland*, or *Ysland*, rather than in a Country so favoured by Nature as ours, both in Fruitfulness of Soil, and Temperature of Climate. The miserable Dress, and Dyet, and Dwelling of the People. The general Desolation in most Parts of the Kingdom. The old Seats of the Nobility and Gentry all in Ruins, and no new ones in their Stead. The Families of Farmers, who pay great Rents, living in Filth and Nastiness upon Butter-milk and Potatoes, without a Shoe or Stocking to their Feet; or a House so convenient as an *English* Hog-sty, to receive them. These, indeed, may be comfortable Sights to an *English* Spectator; who comes for a short Time, only *to learn the Language*, and returns back to his own Country, whither he finds all our Wealth transmitted.

Nostrâ miserià magnus es.

There is not one Argument used to prove the Riches of *Ireland*, which is not a logical Demonstration of its Poverty. The Rise of our Rents is

---

Glassenbury. Refers to the legend of the "Glastonbury Thorn" in the Somerset town of Glastonbury, which explains the phenomenon of the December rose (supposedly budding on Christmas day) as a miraculous celebration of the birth of Christ.

Nostrâ miserià magnus es. Our misery is great.

squeezed out of the very Blood, and Vitals, and Cloaths, and Dwellings of the Tenants; who live worse than *English* Beggars. The Lowness of Interest, in all other Countries a Sign of Wealth, is in us a Proof of Misery; there being no Trade to employ any Borrower. Hence, alone, comes the Dearness of Land, since the Savers have no other Way to lay out their Money. Hence the Dearness of Necessaries for Life; because the Tenants cannot afford to pay such extravagant Rates for Land, (which they must take, or go a-begging) without raising the Price of Cattle, and of Corn, although themselves should live upon Chaff. Hence our encrease of Buildings in this City; because Workmen have nothing to do, but employ one another; and one Half of them are infallibly undone. Hence the daily Encrease of *Bankers*, who may be a necessary Evil in a trading Country, but so ruinous in ours; who, for their private Advantage, have sent away all our Silver, and one Third of our Gold; so that within three Years past, the running Cash of the Nation, which was about five Hundred Thousand Pounds, is now less than two; and must daily diminish, unless we have Liberty to coin, as well as that important Kingdom the Isle of *Man;* and the meanest Prince in the *German* Empire, as I before observed.

I have sometimes thought, that this Paradox of the Kingdom growing rich, is chiefly owing to those worthy Gentlemen the BANKERS; who, except some Custom-house Officers, Birds of Passage, oppressive thrifty 'Squires, and a few others who shall be nameless, are the only thriving People among us: And I have often wished, that a Law were enacted to hang up half a Dozen *Bankers* every Year; and thereby interpose at least some short Delay, to the further Ruin of *Ireland.*

Ye are idle, ye are idle, answered *Pharoah* to the *Israelites*, when they complained to *his Majesty*, that they were forced to make Bricks without Straw.

England enjoys every one of those Advantages for enriching a Nation, which I have above enumerated; and, into the Bargain, a good Million returned to them every Year, without Labour or Hazard, or one Farthing Value received on our Side. But how long we shall be able to continue the Payment, I am not under the least Concern. One Thing I know, that *when the Hen is starved to Death, there will be no more Golden Eggs.*

I think it a little unhospitable, and others may call it a subtil Piece of Malice; that, because there may be a Dozen Families in this Town, able to

---

Daily Encrease of *Bankers*. Given Ireland's fundamental lack of economic autonomy, Swift opposed the creation of a (supposedly) Irish bank (Ehrenpreis, vol. 3, 162–165). For motives in general behind his doubts about bankers, see pp. 8–9.

Bricks without Straw. Exod. 5:17.

entertain their *English* Friends in a generous Manner at their Tables; their Guests, upon their Return to *England*, shall report, that we wallow in Riches and Luxury.

Yet, I confess, I have known an Hospital, where all the Household-Officers grew rich; while the Poor, for whose Sake it was built, were almost starving for want of Food and Raiment.

To conclude. If *Ireland* be a rich and flourishing Kingdom; its Wealth and Prosperity must be owing to certain Causes, that are yet concealed from the whole Race of Mankind; and the Effects are equally invisible. We need not wonder at Strangers, when they deliver such Paradoxes; but a Native and Inhabitant of this Kingdom, who gives the same Verdict, must be either ignorant to Stupidity; or a Man-pleaser, at the Expence of all Honour, Conscience, and Truth.

A Modest Proposal

for

Preventing the Children of Poor People in Ireland from Being a Burden to Their Parents or Country, and for Making Them Beneficial to the Public

---

Gulliver's Travels and Other Writings, ed. Louis Landa (Boston: Houghton Mifflin, 1960).

It is a melancholy object to those who walk through this great town, or travel in the country, when they see the streets, the roads and cabin-doors crowded with beggars of the female sex, followed by three, four, or six children, all in rags, and importuning every passenger for an alms. These mothers, instead of being able to work for their honest livelihood, are forced to employ all their time in strolling, to beg sustenance for their helpless infants, who, as they grow up, either turn thieves for want of work, or leave their dear native country to fight for the Pretender in Spain, or sell themselves to the Barbadoes.

I think it is agreed by all parties that this prodigious number of children, in the arms, or on the backs, or at the heels of their mothers, and frequently of their fathers, is in the present deplorable state of the kingdom a very great additional grievance; and therefore whoever could find out a fair, cheap, and easy method of making these children sound and useful members of the commonwealth would deserve so well of the public as to have his statue set up for a preserver of the nation.

But my intention is very far from being confined to provide only for the children of professed beggars; it is of a much greater extent, and shall take in the whole number of infants at a certain age who are born of parents in effect as little able to support them as those who demand our charity in the streets.

As to my own part, having turned my thoughts for many years upon this important subject, and maturely weighed the several schemes of other projectors, I have always found them grossly mistaken in their computation. It is true a child just dropped from its dam may be supported by her milk for a solar year with little other nourishment, at most not above the value of two shillings, which the mother may certainly get, or the value in scraps, by her lawful occupation of begging, and it is exactly at one year old that I propose to provide for them, in such a manner as, instead of being a charge upon their parents, or the parish, or wanting food and raiment for the rest of their lives, they shall, on the contrary, contribute to the feeding and partly to the clothing of many thousands.

There is likewise another great advantage in my scheme, that it will prevent those voluntary abortions, and that horrid practice of women

---

This great town. Dublin.

To fight for the Pretender in Spain. That is, James Edward Stuart (the "Old Pretender"), son of the deposed James II. The Catholic peasantry, predominantly Jacobites, are the main object of the Proposer's project.

Sell themselves to the Barbadoes. Here looms the shadow of a broader system that was commodifying vast numbers of human beings both as indentured laborers and as slaves. Prevailing discourse about the Atlantic slave trade—a controversy between free traders and defenders of the Royal African Company's monopoly—followed an economic logic much like the proposal here (see Richardson). In the 1650s, Cromwell had directly linked Ireland to the West Indies by transporting several thousand Irish prisoners to servitude there. Desperate Irish laborers continued to sell themselves into indentured servitude.

murdering their bastard children, alas, too frequent among us, sacrificing the poor innocent babes, I doubt, more to avoid the expense than the shame, which would move tears and pity in the most savage and inhuman breast.

The number of souls in Ireland being usually reckoned one million and a half, of these I calculate there may be about two hundred thousand couples whose wives are breeders, from which number I subtract thirty thousand couples who are able to maintain their own children, although I apprehend there cannot be so many under the present distresses of the kingdom, but this being granted, there will remain an hundred and seventy thousand breeders. I again subtract fifty thousand for those women who miscarry, or whose children die by accident or disease within the year. There only remain an hundred and twenty thousand children of poor parents annually born: the question therefore is, how this number shall be reared, and provided for, which, as I have already said, under the present situation of affairs is utterly impossible by all the methods hitherto proposed, for we can neither employ them in handicraft or agriculture; we neither build houses (I mean in the country), nor cultivate land: they can very seldom pick up a livelihood by stealing until they arrive at six years old, except where they are of towardly parts, although I confess they learn the rudiments much earlier, during which time they can however be properly looked upon only as probationers, as I have been informed by a principal gentleman in the Country of Cavan, who protested to me that he never knew above one or two instances under the age of six, even in a part of the kingdom so renowned for the quickest proficiency in that art.

I am assured by our merchants that a boy or a girl before twelve years old, is no saleable commodity, and even when they come to this age, they will not yield above three pounds, or three pounds and half-a-crown at most on the Exchange, which cannot turn to account either to the parents or the kingdom, the charge of nutriment and rags having been at least four times that value.

A principal gentleman of the County of Cavan. Probably an inside joke on Swift's friend Thomas Sheridan, whom he often visited in County Cavan.

A very knowing American. The term *American* has invited various readings. It may recall the visit to London, in 1710, of four Iroquois leaders courted as military allies against the French (Macpherson, 109–12). It may refer to emigrants from Ireland, many of whom were Ulster Presbyterians, reporting back on their fortunes as new American settlers (McMinn, 145). It may refer to colonial officials in the West Indies (Richardson, 407). The blurriness of the term emerges from its implication in colonial history.

I shall now therefore humbly propose my own thoughts, which I hope will not be liable to the least objection.

I have been assured by a very knowing American of my acquaintance in London, that a young healthy child well nursed is at a year old a most delicious, nourishing and wholesome food, whether stewed, roasted, baked, or boiled, and I make no doubt that it will equally serve in a fricassee, or a ragout.

I do therefore humbly offer it to public consideration, that of the hundred and twenty thousand children already computed, twenty thousand may be reserved for breed, whereof only one fourth part to be males, which is more than we allow to sheep, black-cattle, or swine, and my reason is that these children are seldom the fruits of marriage, a circumstance not much regarded by our savages, therefore one male will be sufficient to serve four females. That the remaining hundred thousand may at a year old be offered in sale to the persons of quality, and fortune, through the kingdom, always advising the mother to let them suck plentifully in the last month, so as to render them plump, and fat for a good table. A child will make two dishes at an entertainment for friends, and when the family dines alone, the fore or hind quarter will make a reasonable dish, and seasoned with a little pepper or salt will be very good boiled on the fourth day, especially in winter.

I have reckoned upon a medium, that a child just born will weigh twelve pounds, and in a solar year if tolerably nursed increaseth to twenty-eight pounds.

I grant this food will be somewhat dear, and therefore very proper for landlords, who, as they have already devoured most of the parents, seem to have the best title to the children.

Infant's flesh will be in season throughout the year, but more plentiful in March, and a little before and after, for we are told by a grave* author, an eminent French physician, that fish being a prolific diet, there are more children born in Roman Catholic countries about nine months after Lent than at any other season; therefore reckoning a year after Lent, the markets will be more glutted than usual, because the number of Popish infants is at least three to one in this kingdom, and therefore it will have one other collateral advantage by lessening the number of Papists among us.

Upon a medium. On average.

Landlords. Mostly Anglo-Irish and Protestant.

Lessening the number of Papists among us. A "collateral advantage" for those needing a sectarian rationale to clinch their embrace of the proposal.

*Rabelais [original publisher].

I have already computed the charge of nursing a beggar's child (in which list I reckon all cottagers, labourers, and four-fifths of the farmers) to be about two shillings *per annum*, rags included, and I believe no gentleman would repine to give ten shillings for the carcass of a good fat child, which, as I have said, will make four dishes of excellent nutritive meat, when he hath only some particular friend or his own family to dine with him. Thus the Squire will learn to be a good landlord and grow popular among his tenants, the mother will have eight shillings net profit, and be fit for work until she produces another child.

Those who are more thrifty (as I must confess the times require) may flay the carcass; the skin of which artificially dressed, will make admirable gloves for ladies, and summer boots for fine gentlemen.

As to our city of Dublin, shambles may be appointed for this purpose, in the most convenient parts of it, and butchers we may be assured will not be wanting, although I rather recommend buying the children alive, and dressing them hot from the knife, as we do roasting pigs.

A very worthy person, a true lover of his country, and whose virtues I highly esteem, was lately pleased, in discoursing on this matter to offer a refinement upon my scheme. He said that many gentlemen of this kingdom, having of late destroyed their deer, he conceived that the want of venison might be well supplied by the bodies of young lads and maidens, not exceeding fourteen years of age, nor under twelve, so great a number of both sexes in every county being now ready to starve, for want of work and service: and these to be disposed of by their parents if alive, or otherwise by their nearest relations. But with due deference to so excellent a friend, and so deserving a patriot, I cannot be altogether in his sentiments. For as to the males, my American acquaintance assured me from frequent experience that their flesh was generally tough and lean, like that of our schoolboys, by continual exercise, and their taste disagreeable, and to fatten them would not answer the charge. Then as to the females, it would, I think with humble submission, be a loss to the public, because they soon would become breeders themselves: and besides, it is not improbable that some scrupulous people might be apt to censure such a practice (although indeed very unjustly) as a little bordering upon cruelty, which I confess, hath always been with me the strongest objection against any project, howsoever well intended.

Four-fifths of the farmers. A comment, as Carpenter points out (388), on changing land-use in Ireland. Landlords were perceived as displacing tenant-farmers and switching to grazing cattle and sheep.

Shambles. Slaughter-house.

But in order to justify my friend, he confessed that this expedient was put into his head by the famous Psalmanazar, a native of the island Formosa, who came from thence to London, above twenty years ago, and in conversation told my friend that in his country when any young person happened to be put to death, the executioner sold the carcass to persons of quality, as a prime dainty, and that, in his time, the body of a plump girl of fifteen, who was crucified for an attempt to poison the emperor, was sold to his Imperial Majesty's Prime Minister of State, and other great Mandarins of the Court, in joints from the gibbet, at four hundred crowns. Neither indeed can I deny that if the same use were made of several plump young girls in this town who, without one single groat to their fortunes, cannot stir abroad without a chair, and appear at the playhouse and assemblies in foreign fineries, which they never will pay for, the kingdom would not be the worse.

Some persons of a desponding spirit are in great concern about that vast number of poor people, who are aged, diseased, or maimed, and I have been desired to employ my thoughts what course may be taken to ease the nation of so grievous an encumbrance. But I am not in the least pain upon that matter, because it is very well known that they are every day dying, and rotting, by cold, and famine, and filth, and vermin, as fast as can be reasonably expected. And as to the younger labourers they are now in almost as hopeful a condition. They cannot get work, and consequently pine away from want of nourishment, to a degree that if at any time they are accidentally hired to common labour, they have not strength to perform it; and thus the country and themselves are in a fair way of being soon delivered from the evils to come.

I have too long digressed, and therefore shall return to my subject. I think the advantages by the proposal which I have made are obvious and many, as well as of the highest importance.

For first, as I have already observed, it would greatly lessen the number of Papists, with whom we are yearly over-run, being the principal breeders of the nation, as well as our most dangerous enemies, and who stay at home on purpose with a design to deliver the kingdom to the Pretender, hoping to take their advantage by the absence of so many good Protestants, who have chosen rather to leave their country than stay at

---

Psalmanazar. George Psalmanazar. Ethnic impersonator. Pretending to be a Formosan, he ascribed child-sacrifice to the Formosans. See p. 21.

Stay at home on purpose. Mocks anti-Jacobite paranoia. Also acknowledges that Ireland is "home" for Catholics.

Absence of so many good Protestants. Jabbing at absentee landlords, who mostly lived in England.

home and pay tithes against their conscience to an idolatrous Episcopal curate.

Secondly, the poorer tenants will have something valuable of their own, which by law may be made liable to distress, and help to pay their landlord's rent, their corn and cattle being already seized, and money a thing unknown.

Thirdly, whereas the maintenance of an hundred thousand children, from two years old, and upwards, cannot be computed at less than ten shillings a piece *per annum*, the nation's stock will be thereby increased fifty thousand pounds *per annum*, besides the profit of a new dish, introduced to the tables of all gentlemen of fortune in the kingdom, who have any refinement in taste, and the money will circulate among ourselves, the goods being entirely of our own growth and manufacture.

Fourthly, the constant breeders, besides the gain of eight shillings sterling *per annum*, by the sale of their children, will be rid of the charge of maintaining them after the first year.

Fifthly, this food would likewise bring great custom to taverns, where the vintners will certainly be so prudent as to procure the best receipts for dressing it to perfection, and consequently have their houses frequented by all the fine gentlemen, who justly value themselves upon their knowledge in good eating; and a skilful cook, who understands how to oblige his guests, will contrive to make it as expensive as they please.

Sixthly, this would be a great inducement to marriage, which all wise nations have either encouraged by rewards, or enforced by laws and penalties. It would increase the care and tenderness of mothers towards their children, when they were sure of a settlement for life, to the poor babes, provided in some sort by the public to their annual profit instead of expense. We should soon see an honest emulation among the married women, which of them could bring the fattest child to the market. Men would become as fond of their wives, during the time of their pregnancy, as they are now of their mares in foal, their cows in calf, or sows when they are ready to farrow, nor offer to beat or kick them (as it is too frequent a practice) for fear of a miscarriage.

Many other advantages might be enumerated. For instance, the addition of some thousand carcasses in our exportation of barrelled beef; the

---

Tithes. A ten percent tax on every property owner and tenant in Ireland, paid (regardless of religious affiliation) to the Church of Ireland. As Carpenter points out, tithes in Swift's day were still levied in corn as well as money.

Liable to distress. To be seized because of unpaid rent (Carpenter, 389).

Money a thing unknown. Refers to a shortage of actual coins, a shortage that had led to Britain's attempt to introduce Wood's halfpence.

propagation of swine's flesh, and improvement in the art of making good bacon, so much wanted among us by the great destruction of pigs, too frequent at our tables, are no way comparable in taste or magnificence to a well-grown, fat yearling child, which roasted whole will make a considerable figure at a Lord Mayor's feast, or any other public entertainment. But this and many others I omit, being studious of brevity.

Supposing that one thousand families in this city would be constant customers for infants flesh, besides others who might have it at merry meetings, particularly weddings and christenings; I compute that Dublin would take off annually about twenty thousand carcasses, and the rest of the kingdom (where probably they will be sold somewhat cheaper) the remaining eighty thousand.

I can think of no one objection that will possibly be raised against this proposal, unless it should be urged that the number of people will be thereby much lessened in the kingdom. This I freely own, and it was indeed one principal design in offering it to the world. I desire the reader will observe, that I calculate my remedy *for this one individual Kingdom of* Ireland, *and for no other that ever was, is, or, I think, ever can be upon earth.* Therefore let no man talk to me of other expedients: *Of taxing our absentees at five shillings a pound: Of using neither clothes, nor household furniture, except what is of our own growth and manufacture. Of utterly rejecting the materials and instruments that promote foreign luxury: Of curing the expensiveness of pride, vanity, idleness, and gaming in our women: Of introducing a vein of parsimony, prudence, and temperance: Of learning to love our country, wherein we differ even from* Laplanders, *and the inhabitants of* Topinamboo: *Of quitting our animosities and factions, nor act any longer like the* Jews, *who were murdering one another at the very moment their city was taken: Of being a little cautious not to sell our country and consciences for nothing: Of teaching landlords to have at least one degree of mercy towards their tenants.* Lastly, *of putting a spirit of honesty, industry, and skill into our shopkeepers, who, if a resolution could now be taken to buy only our native goods, would immediately unite to cheat and exact upon us in the price, the measure, and the goodness, nor could ever yet be brought to make one fair proposal of just dealing, though often and earnestly invited to it.*

Other expedients. A catalogue of Swift's previously published (serious) proposals.

Our own growth and manufacture. A grimly hilarious parody of Swift's own preoccupation with the economic self-reliance of Ireland, as in his *Proposal* of 1720.

Topinamboo. Brazilian region made famous as the homeland of the cannibals discussed in Michel de Montaigne's "On Cannibals" (1580). A tip of Swift's hat to an earlier critic of European barbarities, including colonial oppression of indigenes.

Therefore I repeat, let no man talk to me of these and the like expedients, till he hath at least a glimpse of hope that there will ever be some hearty and sincere attempt to put them in practice.

But as to myself, having been wearied out for many years with offering vain, idle, visionary thoughts, and at length utterly despairing of success, I fortunately fell upon this proposal, which as it is wholly new, so it hath something solid and real, of no expense and little trouble, full in our own power, and whereby we can incur no danger in disobliging England. For this kind of commodity will not bear exportation, the flesh being of too tender a consistence to admit a long continuance in salt, *although perhaps I could name a country which would be glad to eat up our whole nation without it.*

After all I am not so violently bent upon my own opinion as to reject any offer, proposed by wise men, which shall be found equally innocent, cheap, easy and effectual. But before some thing of that kind shall be advanced in contradiction to my scheme, and offering a better, I desire the author, or authors, will be pleased maturely to consider two points. First, as things now stand, how they will be able to find food and raiment for a hundred thousand useless mouths and backs? And secondly, there being a round million of creatures in human figure, throughout this kingdom, whose whole subsistence put into a common stock would leave them in debt two millions of pounds sterling; adding those who are beggars by profession, to the bulk of farmers, cottagers, and labourers with their wives and children, who are beggars in effect; I desire those politicians who dislike my overture, and may perhaps be so bold to attempt an answer, that they will first ask the parents of these mortals whether they would not at this day think it a great happiness to have been sold for food at a year old, in the manner I prescribe, and thereby have avoided such a perpetual scene of misfortunes as they have since gone through, by the oppression of landlords, the impossibility of paying rent without money or trade, the want of common sustenance, with neither house nor clothes to cover them from the inclemencies of weather, and the most inevitable prospect of entailing the like, or greater miseries upon their breed for ever.

I profess in the sincerity of my heart that I have not the least personal interest in endeavouring to promote this necessary work, having no other motive than the *public good of my country, by advancing our trade, providing for infants, relieving the poor, and giving some pleasure to the rich.* I have no children by which I can propose to get a single penny; the youngest being nine years old, and my wife past child-bearing.

Disobliging England. Which restricted Irish exports.

I could name a country. England: the country largely responsible for Ireland's "cannibal economy."

SWIFT'S POEMS

An Excellent new SONG on a seditious Pamphlet

To the Tune of Packington's Pound

Written in the Year 1720

Brocado's, and Damasks, and Tabbies, and Gawses,
  Are by *Robert Ballentine* lately brought over;
With Forty Things more: Now hear what the Law says,
  Whoe'er will not were them, is not the King's Lover.
5   Tho' a Printer and Dean
      Seditiously mean
  Our true *Irish* Hearts from old *England* to wean;
We'll buy *English* Silks for our Wives and our Daughters,
In Spight of his Deanship and Journeyman *Waters.*

II

10 In *England* the Dead in Woollen are clad,
  The Dean and his Printer then let us cry Fye on;
To be cloath'd like a Carcass would make a Teague mad,
  Since a living Dog better is than a dead Lyon,
      Our Wives they grow sullen
15   At wearing of Woollen,

The Poems of Jonathan Swift, 3 vols., ed. Harold Williams, 2nd ed. (Oxford: Clarendon Press, 1958).

Title. The pamphlet is Swift's call for a boycott of English goods: *A Proposal for the Universal Use of Irish Manufacture* (1720), pp. 281–88.

Journeyman *Waters.* Swift's printer, Edward Waters, who was legally harassed for printing the pamphlet. See the relevant selections from Swift's correspondence, pp. 370, 373–74.

The Dead in Woollen are clad. By law, since the reign of Charles II, in order to encourage the English wool trade.

Teague. Stock pejorative name for an Irishman (Anglicized from the Irish name *Tadhg*).

And all we poor Shopkeepers must our Horns pull in.
Then we'll buy *English* Silks, &c.

III

Whoever our Trading with *England* would hinder,
To *inflame* both the Nations do plainly conspire;
20 Because *Irish* Linen will soon turn to Tinder;
And Wool it is greasy, and quickly takes Fire.
Therefore I assure ye,
Our noble Grand Jury,
When they saw the Dean's Book they were in a great Fury:
25 They would buy *English* Silks for their Wives, &c.

IV

This wicked Rogue *Waters*, who always is sinning,
And before *Corum Nobus* so oft has been call'd,
Henceforward shall print neither Pamphlets nor Linnen,
And, if Swearing can do't, shall be swingingly mawl'd:
30 And as for the Dean,
You know whom I mean,
If the Printer will peach him, he'll scarce come off clean.
Then we'll buy *English* Silks for our Wives and our Daughters,
In Spight of his Deanship and Journeyman *Waters*.

The Bubble

[p. 1] Ye wise Philosophers explain
What Magick makes our Money rise
When dropt into the Southern Main,
Or do these Juglers cheat our Eyes?

5 Put in Your Money fairly told;
Presto be gone—Tis here ag'en,
Ladyes, and Gentlemen, behold,
Here's ev'ry Piece as big as ten.

If the Printer will peach him. That is, testify against him.

Scarce come off clean. A jest about the state of one's underwear after hanging: a punishment known to induce involuntary purges of the bladder and bowels.

Title. Also known as "Upon the South Sea Project."

As big as ten. Multiplied tenfold.

Thus in a Basin drop a Shilling,
10 Then fill the Vessel to the Brim,
You shall observe as you are filling
The pond'rous Metal seems to swim;

It rises both in Bulk and Height,
Behold it mounting to the Top,
15 The liquid Medium cheats your Sight,
Behold it swelling like a Sop.

In Stock three hundred thousand Pounds;
I have in view a Lord's Estate,
My Mannors all contig'ous round,
20 A Coach and Six, and serv'd in Plate:

Thus the deluded Bankrupt raves,
Puts all upon a desp'rate Bett,
Then plunges in the *Southern* Waves,
Dipt over head and Ears—in Debt.

25 So, by a Calenture misled,
The Mariner with Rapture sees
On the smooth Ocean's azure Bed
Enamell'd Fields, and verdant Trees;

With eager Hast he longs to rove
30 In that fantastick Scene, and thinks
It must be some enchanted Grove,
And in he leaps, and down he sinks.

Rais'd up on Hope's aspiring Plumes,
The young Advent'rer o'er the Deep
35 An Eagle's Flight and State assumes,
And scorns the middle Way to keep:

On *Paper* Wings he takes his Flight,
With *Wax* the *Father* bound them fast,
The *Wax* is melted by the Height,
40 And down the towring Boy is cast:

A Moralist might here explain
The Rashness of the *Cretan* Youth,

Calenture. Tropical fever that often afflicted South Sea sailors.

***Paper* Wings.** Refers to paper credit and paper money: bank notes, bills of exchange, and so on.

***Cretan* Youth.** Icarus, of Greek myth, who flew too near the sun.

Describe his Fall into the Main,
And from a Fable form a Truth:

45 [col. 2] His *Wings* are his *Paternall Rent,*
He melts his *Wax* at ev'ry Flame,
His Credit sunk, his Money spent,
In Southern *Seas he leaves his Name.*

Inform us, You that best can tell,
50 Why in yon dang'rous Gulph profound
Where hundreds and where thousands fell,
Fools chiefly float, the *Wise* are drown'd.

So have I seen from *Severn*'s Brink
A Flock of *Geese* jump down together,
55 Swim where the Bir[d] of Jove would sink,
And swimming ne[ver] wet a Feather.

But I affirm, 'tis false in Fact,
Directors better know their Tools,
We see the Nation['s] Credit crackt,
60 Each Knave hath [ma]de a thousand Fools.

One Fool may f[r]om another win,
And then get off with Money stor'd,
But if a *Sharper* once comes in,
He throws at all, and sweeps the Board.

65 As Fishes on each other prey
The great ones swall'wing up the small
So fares it in the *Southern* Sea
But Whale *Directors* eat up all.

When *Stock* is high they come between,
70 Making by second hand their Offers,
Then cunningly retire unseen,
With each a Million in his Coffers.

So when upon a Moon-shine Night
An Ass was drinking at a Stream,
75 A Cloud arose and stopt the Light,
By intercepting e[v]'ry Beam;

The Day of Judgment will be soon,
Cryes out a Sage among the Croud,

Directors. Of the South Sea Company, now the objects of public fury.

An Ass hath swallow'd up the Moon,
80 The Moon lay safe behind the Cloud.

Each poor *Subscriber* to the Sea
Sinks down at once, and there he lyes,
Directors fall as well as they,
Their Fall is but a Trick to rise:

85 So Fishes rising from the Main
Can soar with moistned Wings on high,
The Moysture dry'd they sink again,
And dip their Fins again to fly.

[p. 2] Undone at Play, the Femal[e] Troops
90 Come here their Losses to retrieve,
Ride o'er the Waves in spacious Hoops,
Like *Lapland* Witches in a Sieve:

Thus *Venus* to the Sea descends
As Poets fein; but where's the Moral?
95 It shews the Queen of Love intends
To search the Deep for Pearl and Coral.

The Sea is richer than the Land,
I heard it from my Grannam's Mouth,
Which now I clearly understand,
100 For by the Sea she meant the *South.*

Thus by *Directors* we are told,
Pray Gentlemen, believe your Eyes,
Our Ocean's cover[d o]'er with Gold,
Look round about [h]ow thick it lyes:

105 We, Gentlemen, a[re] Your Assisters,
We'll come and hol[d] you by the Chin,
Alas! all is not Go[l]d that glisters;
Ten thousand sunk by leaping in.

Oh! would these Patriots be so kind
110 Here in the Deep to *wash their Hands,*
Then like *Pactolus* we should find
The Sea indeed had *golden Sands.*

***Lapland* Witches.** Wizards.

Pactolus. King Midas, to rid himself of his "golden touch," washed his hands in the Pactolus.

A Shilling in the *Bath* You fling,
The Silver takes a nobler Hue,
115 By Magick Virtue in the Spring,
And seems a Guinnea to your View:

But as a Guinnea will not pass
At Market for a Farthing more
120 Shewn through a multiplying Glass
Than what it allways did before;

So cast it in the *Southern* Seas,
And view it through a *Jobber's* Bill,
Put on what Spectacles You please,
125 Your Guinnea's but a Guinnea still.

One Night a Fool into a Brook
Thus from a Hillock looking down,
The *Golden* Stars for Guinneas took,
And *Silver Cynthia* for a Crown;

130 The Point he could no longer doubt,
He ran, he leapt into the Flood,
There sprawl'd a while, at last got out,
All cover'd o'er with Slime and Mud.

[col. 2] Upon the Water cast thy Bread
135 And after many Days thou'lt find it,
But Gold upon this Ocean spred
Shall sink, and leave no mark behind it.

There is a Gulph where thousands fell,
Here all the bold Advent'rers came,
140 A narrow Sound, though deep as Hell,
CHANGE-ALLY is the dreadfull Name;

Nine times a day it ebbs and flows,
Yet He that on the Surface lyes
Without a Pilot seldom knows
145 The Time it falls, or when 'twill rise.

***Jobber's* Bill.** Stockjobbers were speculative manipulators of the price of stocks. See the description in *Gulliver's Travels*, p. 194, of men who plot "to sink or raise the opinion of public credit, as either shall best answer their private advantage." Swift's attacks on the "monied men" were directed at such financiers rather than at merchants as a whole.

CHANGE-ALLY. Across from the Royal Exchange, and so a center of stockjobbing.

Subscribers here by thousands float,
And justle one another down,
Each padling in his leaky Boat,
And here they fish for Gold and drown:

150 *Now bury'd in the Depth below,*
Now mounted up to Heav'n again,
They reel and stagger too and fro,
At their Wits end like drunken Men.

Mean time secure on GARR'WAY Clifts
155 A savage Race by Shipwrecks fed,
Ly waiting for the foundred Skiffs,
And strip the Bodyes of the Dead.

But these, you say, are factious Lyes
From some malicious Tory's Brain,
160 For, where Directors get a Prize,
The *Swiss* and *Dutch* whole Millions drain.

Thus when by Rooks a Lord is ply'd,
Some Cully often wins a Bett
By vent'ring on the cheating Side,
165 Tho not into the Secret let.

While some build Castles in the Air,
Directors build 'em in the Seas;
Subscribers plainly see 'um there,
For Fools will see as Wise men please.

170 Thus oft by Mariners are shown,
Unless the Men of *Kent* are Ly'rs,
Earld Godwin's Castles overflown,
And Castle roofs, and Steeple Spires.

Mark where the Sly *Directors* creep,
175 Nor to the Shore approach too nigh,
The Monsters nestle in the Deep
To seise you in your passing by:

[p. 3] Then, like the Dogs of *Nile* be wise,
Who taught by Instinct how to shun

GARR'WAY Clifts. Garroway's was a popular coffee house and deal-making venue.
***Earld Godwin*'s castles.** Refers to a legend in Kent about a submerged castle.

180 The Crocodile that lurking lyes,
Run as they drink and drink and run.

Antaeus could by Magick Charms
Recover Strength whene'er he fell,
Alcides held him in his Arms,
185 And sent him *up in Air* to Hell.

Directors thrown into the Sea
Recover Strength and Vigor there,
But may be tam'd another way,
Suspended for a while in Air.

190 *Directors;* for tis you I warn,
By long Experience we have found
What Planet rul'd when you were born;
We see you never can be drown'd:

Beware, nor over-bulky grow,
195 Nor come within your Cullyes Reach,
For if the Sea should sink so low
To leave you dry upon the Beach,

You'll ow Your Ruin to your Bulk;
Your Foes already waiting stand
200 To tear you like a foundred Hulk
While you ly helpless on the Sand:

[col. 2] Thus when a Whale hath lost the Tide
The Coasters crowd to seise the Spoyl,
The Monster into Parts divide,
205 And strip the Bones, and melt the Oyl.

Oh, may some *Western* Tempest sweep
These *Locusts* whom our Fruits have fed,
That Plague, *Directors,* to the Deep,
Driv'n from the *South*-Sea to the *Red.*

210 May He whom Nature's Laws obey,
Who *lifts* the Poor, and *sinks* the Proud,
Quiet the Raging of the Sea,
And *Still the Madness of the Crowd.*

Antaeus. A gigantic wrestler from Greek myth who drew strength from touching the earth.

Alcides. Hercules, who defeated Antaeus by lifting him and squeezing him in midair.

Suspended. With overtones of hanging.

But never sh[all our is]le have Rest
215 Till those devour[ing] *Swine* run down,
(*The Devils leavi[ng] the Possess't*)
And *headlong i[n] the Waters drown.*

The Nation t[oo] too late will find
Computing all th[eir] Cost and Trouble,
210 *Directors* Promi[ses] but Wind,
South-Sea at best [a m]ighty Bubble.

Prometheus, a Poem

When first the '*Squire*, and *Tinker Wood*
Gravely consulting *Ireland*'s Good,
Together mingl'd in a Mass
Smith's *Dust*, and *Copper, Lead* and *Brass*,
5 The Mixture thus by Chymick Art,
United close in ev'ry Part.
In Fillets roll'd, or cut in Pieces,
Appear'd like one continu'd Spec'es,
And by the forming Engine struck,
10 On all the same IMPRESSION stuck.

So to confound, this *hated Coin*
All *Parties* and *Religions* joyn;
Whigs, Tories, Trimmers, Hannoverians,
Quakers, Conformists, Presbyterians,
15 *Scotch, Irish, English, French* unite
With *equal Int'rest, equal Spight,*
Together mingled in a Lump,
Do all in *One Opinion* jump;
And ev'ry one begins to find,
20 The same IMPRESSION on his Mind;
A strange Event! whom *Gold* incites,
To Blood and Quarrels, *Brass* unites:

Devour[ing] *Swine.* Refers to the scriptural story of the Gadarene swine (Mark 5:11–13), in which "possessed" swine, the victims of diabolical spirits, destroy themselves by running into the sea.

Tinker Wood. Wood's status as a commoner reinforced the *national* insult to Ireland inherent in the Wood's halfpence affair.

So Goldsmiths say, the coursest Stuff,
Will serve for *Sodder* well enuff.
25 So, by the *Kettles* loud Allarm,
The *Bees* are gather'd to a *Swarm*:
So by the *Brazen* Trumpets Bluster,
Troops of all Tongues and Nations Muster:
And so the *Harp* of *Ireland* brings,
30 Whole Crouds about its *Brazen* Strings.

There is a *Chain* let down from *Jove*,
But fasten'd to his Throne above;
So strong, that from the lower End,
They say, all human Things depend:
35 This *Chain*, as Antient Poets hold,
When *Jove* was Young, was made of *Gold*.
Prometheus once this *Chain* purloin'd,
Dissolv'd, and into *Money* Coin'd;
Then whips me on a *Chain* of *Brass*,
40 (*Venus* was Brib'd to let it pass.)

Now while this *Brazen Chain* prevail'd,
Jove saw that all *Devotion* fail'd;
No *Temple*, to his *Godship* rais'd,
No *Sacrifice* on *Altars* blaz'd;
45 In short such *dire Confusions* follow'd,
Earth must have been in *Chaos* swallow'd.
Jove stood amaz'd, but looking round,
With much ado, the *Cheat* he found;
'Twas plain he cou'd no longer hold
50 The *World* in any *Chain* but *Gold*;
And to the *God of Wealth* his *Brother*,
Sent *Mercury* to get another.

Prometheus on a Rock is laid,
Ty'd with the *Chain* himself had made;
55 On Icy *Caucasus* to shiver,
While *Vultures* eat his growing Liver:

Prometheus. A Titan of Greek myth who stole fire from heaven and was punished as described in the poem.

***Venus* was Brib'd.** Alluding to the Duchess of Kendal. See note, p. 291.

Whips me. That is, "whips for me" (*me* is an ethical dative).

Sent *Mercury*. Probably alluding to John Cartaret, dispatched by the English ministry as lord lieutenant of Ireland, to resolve the crisis. See pp. 6, 351.

Ye Pow'rs of *Grub-street* make me able,
Discreetly to apply this *Fable.*
Say, who is to be understood,
60 By that old Thief *Prometheus?* WOOD
For *Jove*, it is not hard to guess him,
I mean *His M[ajesty], God bless him.*
This *Thief* and *Black-Smith* was so bold,
He strove to steal that *Chain* of *Gold*,
65 Which links the *Subject* to the *King*:
And change it for a *Brazen String.*
But sure if nothing else must pass,
Between the *K[ing]* and US but *Brass*,
Altho' the *Chain* will never crack,
70 Yet *Our Devotion* may *Grow Slack.*

But *Jove* will soon convert I hope,
This *Brazen Chain* into a *Rope*;
With which *Prometheus* shall be ty'd,
And high in Air for ever ride;
75 Where, if we find his *Liver* grows,
For want of *Vultures*, we have *Crows.*

Whitshed's Motto on His Coach

Libertas & natale Solum

Liberty and my native Country

Written in the Year 1724

Libertas & natale Solum;
Fine Words; I wonder where you stole 'um.

Rope. The popular protests against Wood's halfpence included ceremonies in which he was destroyed in effigy. The rope here implies hanging.

Title. William Whitshed (1679–1727) infuriated Swift by presiding unfairly over two court cases involving his printers in Dublin: first for his 1720 *Proposal* (printed by Edward Waters) and then for the Drapier's *Letter to the Whole People of Ireland* (printed by John Harding). Whitshed flagrantly intimidated the jurors, sending them back nine times in the case of Waters, until he got a special verdict. The grand jury in Harding's case, influenced by a pamphlet Swift addressed directly to them, refused to indict him. Waters was released, due to Swift's string-pulling, after a year in prison. See Swift's letters, p. 370.

Libertas & natale Solum. "Liberty and my native Country."

Could nothing but thy chief Reproach,
Serve for a Motto on thy Coach?
5 But, let me now the Words translate:
Natale Solum: My Estate:
My dear Estate, how well I love it;
My Tenants, if you doubt, will prove it:
They swear I am so kind and good,
10 I hug them till I squeeze their Blood.

Libertas bears a large Import;
First; how to swagger in a Court;
And, secondly, to shew my Fury
Against an uncomplying Jury:
15 And, Thirdly; 'tis a new Invention
To favour *Wood* and keep my Pension:
And, Fourthly; 'tis to play an odd Trick,
Get the Great Seal, and turn out *Brod'rick.*
And, Fifthly; you know whom I mean,
20 To humble that vexatious Dean.
And, Sixthly; for my Soul, to barter it
For Fifty Times its Worth, to *Carteret.*

Now, since your Motto thus you construe,
I must confess you've spoken once true.
25 *Libertas & natale Solum*;
You had good Reason when you stole 'um.

Holyhead. Sept. 25. 1727

Lo here I sit at holy head
With muddy ale and mouldy bread
All Christian vittals stink of fish
I'm where my enemyes would wish
5 Convict of lyes is every sign,

Wood. William Wood, the patentee of Wood's halfpence.

Great Seal. Of the lord chancellor of Ireland.

Brod'rick. Alan Brodrick, Viscount Midleton (c. 1660–1728): a distinguished legal and political figure in Ireland. He was lord chancellor of Ireland when this poem was written, and Swift gibes here at Whitshed's ambition to occupy that post.

Carteret. The lord lieutenant of Ireland. See pp. 6, 93, and 351.

The Inn has not one drop of wine
I'm fasnd both by wind and tide
I see the ship at anchor ride
The Captain swears the sea's too rough
10 He has not passengers enough.
And thus the Dean is forc't to stay
Till others come to help the pay
In Dublin they'd be glad to see
A packet though it brings in me.
15 They cannot say the winds are cross
Your Politicians at a loss
For want of matter swears and fretts,
Are forced to read the old gazettes.
I never was in hast before
20 To reach that slavish hateful shore
Before, I always found the wind
To me was most malicious kind
But now, the danger of a friend
On whom my fears and hopes depend
25 Absent from whom all Clymes are curst
With whom I'm happy in the worst
With rage impatient makes me wait
A passage to the land I hate.
Else, rather on this bleaky shore
30 Where loudest winds incessant roar
Where neither herb nor tree will thrive,
Where nature hardly seems alive.
I'd go in freedom to my grave,
Than Rule yon Isle and be a Slave.

Packet. A regular service boat carrying mail and passengers (Rogers, 772).

Danger of a friend. That is, Swift's "most valuable friend," Esther Johnson ("Stella"), whose health was fading rapidly. This poem belongs to a fretful journal kept by Swift while he was delayed for a week at Holy Head, impatient, for once, to return to Ireland. Stella died, about four months later, on January 28, 1728. Swift and Stella, now buried side by side in St. Patrick's Cathedral, have attracted endless speculation as a mystery couple. Never legally married, theirs was an intense union, at any rate, of minds. Stella was considerably younger, and both she and Swift must have expected her to outlive him. In her poem "To Dr Swift on His Birth-Day, November 30, 1721," she expresses the hope that she will outlive him by one day only (see Carpenter, 1998, 159).

Irel[an]^{d}

Remove me from this land of slaves
Where all are fools, and all are knaves
Where every knave & fool is bought
Yet kindly sells himself for nought
5 Where Whig and Tory fiercely fight
Who's in the wrong, who in the right
And when their country lyse at stake
They only fight for fighting sake,
While English sharpers take the pay,
10 And then stand by to see fair play,
Mean time the whig is always winner
And for his courage gets—a dinner.
His Excellency too perhaps
Spits in his mouth and stroaks his Chaps
15 The humble whelp gives ev'ry vote.
To put the question strains his throat.
His Excellency's condescension
Will serve instead of place or pension
When to the window he's trepan'd
20 When my L^{d} shakes him by the hand
Or in the presence of beholders,
His arms upon the booby's shoulders
You quickly see the gudgeon bite,
He tells his broth^{r} fools at night
25 How well the Governor's inclind.
So just, so gentle and so kind
He heard I kept a pack of hounds,
And longd to hunt upon my grounds
He sd our Ladyes were so fair
30 The Court had nothing to compair.
But that indeed which pleasd me most
He calld my Dol a perfect toast.
He whisprd publick things at last,
Askt me how our elections past.

Whig and Tory. See note, p. 123 and p. 372. Swift implicates both Irish parties here in neglecting their country for the sake of partisan advantage. See pp. 305, 339.

His Excellency. The lord lieutenant, accused here of reserving patronage for the English and bestowing only condescension on the Anglo-Irish.

35 Some augmentation Sr You know
Would make at least a handsom show
New Kings a compliment expect
I shall not offer to direct
There are some prating folks in town,
40 But Sr we must support the Crown.
Our Letters say a Jesuite boasts
Of some Invasion on your coasts
The King is ready when you will
To pass another Pop-ry bill
45 And for dissenters he intends
To use them as his truest friends
I think they justly ought to share
In all employmts we can spare.
Next for encouragemt of spinning,
50 A duty might be layd on linnen
An act for laying down the Plough,
England will send you corn enough.
Anothr act that absentees
For licences shall pay no fees.
55 If Englands friendship you would keep
Feed nothing in your lands but sheep
But make an act secure and full
To hang up all who smuggle wool.
And then he kindly give me hints
60 That all our wives should go in Chints.

New Kings. George II had just acceded.

Another Pop-ry bill. Seen by Swift as a cynical distraction to the Anglo-Irish, who ought to put *national* concerns above the religious overkill of yet more penal legislation against Catholics in both England and Ireland. The aftermath of the Atterbury trial for Jacobitism (see note, p. 194) had led to further legislation in this vein.

Dissenters. Protestants who refused to conform to the established Church of Ireland, the sister branch of the Anglican Church. Swift's greatest antipathy is reserved for these dissenters, especially the powerful Presbyterian community in Ulster. As a staunch High Churchman, Swift strongly opposed their efforts to repeal the Sacramental Test Act, which excluded them from official posts. In the same vein, he opposed the frequent overtures to Irish Dissenters from the Hanoverian regime. See p. 372.

Feed nothing in your lands but sheep. Refers to the conversion of crop-based farming to grazing. The previous seven lines refer to Swift's familiar complaints about laws that restricted the export of Irish textiles, prohibited tilling pasturage (to protect England's grain exports), and allowed absentee landlords to avoid Irish taxation.

Chints. An imported luxury fabric.

To morrow I shall tell you more,
For I'm to dine with him at four
 This was the Speech, and here's the jest
His arguments convinc't the rest.
65 Away he runs with zealous hotness
Exceeding all the fools of Totness.
To move that all the Nation round
Should pay a guinnea in the pound
Yet should this Blockhead beg a Place
70 Either from Excellence or grace
Tis pre-eng[a]ged and in his room
Townshends cast Page or Walpole's groom

The Dean to himself on St. Cecilia's day

Grave D. of St P— ho[w] comes it to pass
That y[ou] who know musick no more than an ass
That you [who] was found writing of Drapiers
Should lend your cathedrall to players and scrapers
5 To act such an opera once in a year
Is offensive to every true Protestant ear
With trumpets and fiddles and organs and singing
Will sure the Pretendr and Popery bring in.
No Protestant Prelate, His Ldshp or Grace
10 Durst there show his right or most revnd face
How would it pollute their Crosiers and Rochets
To listen to minimms and quavers and Crochets

The fools of Totness. Townfolk of Totness in Devon, recently satirized, according to Rogers, for expressing in print their fulsome loyalty to the king.

Townshend. Charles Townshend (1674–1738). A powerful lieutenant in Walpole's administration and leader in the heavily politicized trial of Atterbury. "Turnip Townshend," as he came to be known after his rural retirement, was Walpole's brother-in-law.

St. Cecilia's Day. St. Cecilia is the patron saint of music, and the occasion for this poem was probably a musical festival held by the Dublin Musical Society on November 23, 1730.

A Libel on D[r.] D[elany] and a Certain Great Lord

Deluded Mortals, whom the *Great*
Chuse for Companions *tete à tete*,
Who at their Dinners, *en famille*
Get Leave to sit whene'er you will;
5 Then, boasting tell us where you din'd,
And, how his *Lordship* was so kind;
How many pleasant Things he spoke,
And, how you *laugh'd* at every *Joke:*
Swear, he's a most facetious Man,
10 That you and he are *Cup* and *Cann.*
You Travel with a heavy Load,
And quite mistake *Preferment's* Road.
Suppose my *Lord* and you alone;
Hint the least Int'rest of your own;
15 His Visage drops, he knits his Brow,
He cannot talk of Bus'ness now:
Or, mention but a vacant *Post,*
He'll turn it off with; *Name your Toast.*
Nor could the nicest Artist Paint,
20 A Countenance with more Constraint.
For, as their Appetites to quench,
Lords keep a Pimp to bring a Wench;
So, Men of Wit are but a kind
Of Pandars to a vicious Mind,

Crosiers. The staffs symbolizing the offices of bishop or archbishop.

Rochets. Linen surplices worn by bishops (Rogers, 1983, 822).

Crochets. Quarter notes.

D[r.] D[elany]. Patrick Delany (c. 1685–1768), Swift's close friend since 1718, was part of the literary coterie that sustained him in Ireland. The immediate occasion for this "libel" was Delany's flattering poem to the lord lieutenant of Ireland. Delany's poem, "An Epistle to His Excellency Lord Cartaret," was also—and quite directly—a request for additional preferment. Swift's poem suggests an alternative ending for Delany's. Swift's poem is a mode of "gentle ridicule" (Carpenter, 1988, 166) toward Delany, though striking indeed in its irreverence toward British authority, the monarch included.

***Preferment's* Road.** Patronage: the evils and failures of which are the poem's topic.

My *Lord.* John Cartaret, lord lieutenant of Ireland, and so the English viceroy. The poem expresses both Swift's personal friendship and immense political frustration with Cartaret.

25 Who proper Objects must provide
To gratify their Lust of Pride,
When weary'd with Intrigues of State,
They find an idle Hour to Prate.
Then, shou'd you dare to ask a *Place*,
30 You Forfeit all your *Patron*'s Grace,
And disappoint the sole Design,
For which he summon'd you to *Dine*.
Thus, *Congreve* spent, in writing Plays,
And one poor Office, half his Days;
35 While *Montague*, who claim'd the Station
To be *Mæcenas* of the Nation,
For *Poets* open Table kept,
But ne'er consider'd where they Slept.
Himself, as rich as fifty *Jews*,
40 Was easy, though they wanted Shoes;
And, crazy *Congreve* scarce cou'd spare
A Shilling to discharge his Chair,
Till Prudence taught him to appeal
From *Pæan*'s Fire to *Party* Zeal;
45 Not owing to his happy Vein
The Fortunes of his latter Scene,
Took proper *Principles* to thrive;
And so might ev'ry *Dunce* alive.
Thus, *Steel* who own'd what others writ,
50 And flourish'd by imputed Wit,
From Lodging in a hundred Jayls,

Congreve. Swift's friend William Congreve (1670–1729). Famous dramatist, best known for *The Way of the World.* In 1700 Congreve retired from the theater, cutting short his brilliant career as a playwright to accept various government sinecures. He had died shortly before Swift wrote this poem.

Montague. Charles Montagu, the earl of Halifax (1661–1715). A patron, less than adequate on Swift's account, both of Congreve and Addison. He was involved in establishing the national debt and founding the Bank of England. See pp. 7, 27.

Maecenas. Patron made immortal by Horace, the Roman poet.

Chair. A hired vehicle (a sedan chair).

Steel. Richard Steele (1672–1729). Known both for his career in the theater and for his collaboration with Joseph Addison on *The Spectator.* Swift's amiable relations with Steele had been unable to sustain the partisan pamphleteering in which both became engaged during the Tory administration of 1710–14.

Was left to starve, and dye in *Wales.*
Thus *Gay*, the *Hare* with many Friends,
Twice sev'n long Years the *Court* attends,
55 Who, under Tales conveying Truth,
To Virtue form'd a *Princely* Youth,
Who pay'd his Courtship with the Croud,
As far as *Modest Pride* allow'd,
Rejects a servile *Usher's* Place,
60 And leaves *St. James's* in Disgrace.
Thus *Addison* by Lords Carest,
Was left in Foreign Lands distrest,
Forgot at Home, became for Hire,
A trav'lling Tutor to a *Squire*;
65 But, wisely left the *Muses* Hill,
To Bus'ness shap'd the *Poet's* Quil,
Let all his barren Lawrel's fade
Took up himself the *Courtier's* Trade,
And grown a *Minister of State*,
70 Saw Poets at his Levee wait.
Hail! happy *Pope*, whose gen'rous Mind,
Detesting all the Statesmen kind,
Contemning *Courts*, at *Courts* unseen,
Refus'd the Visits of a Queen;
75 A Soul with ev'ry Virtue fraught
By *Sages, Priests*, or *Poets* taught;
Whose filial Piety excels

Gay, the Hare. John Gay (1685–1732), Swift's close friend and fellow member of the Scriblerus Club. Poet and dramatist. Gay had glancingly compared himself to a hare in one of his fables, "The Hare and Many Friends." Walpole had insulted Gay by offering him the humble post of "gentleman usher" to one of the queen's infant daughters (Ehrenpreis, vol. 3, 555–56). Gay, best known for *The Beggar's Opera* (1728)—a withering satire on Walpole—was fortunate to be patronized in defiance of the court by the duke and duchess of Queensbury.

Addison. Joseph Addison (1672–1719). Writer and politician best known for his collaboration with Richard Steele on *The Spectator* (1711–12). Addison was secretary of state from 1717 to 1718 and held other official posts as well. Despite their political differences, Addison and Swift remained on cordial terms.

Pope. Alexander Pope (1688–1744). Leading poet of the age and Swift's close comrade, fellow Scriblerian, and active correspondent. Pope had dedicated his *Dunciad* to Swift in 1728, and this passage returns the favor. Pope was especially proud of his financial independence as an author. He seems to have been slightly discomfited, however, by the line suggesting he had refused the visit of Queen Caroline.

Whatever *Grecian* Story tells:
A Genius for all Stations fit,
80 Whose *meanest Talent* is his *Wit:*
His Heart too Great, though Fortune little,
To lick a *Rascal Statesman*'s Spittle.
Appealing to the Nation's Taste,
Above the Reach of Want is plac't:
85 By *Homer* dead was taught to thrive,
Which *Homer* never cou'd alive.
And, sits aloft on *Pindus* Head,
Despising *Slaves* that *cringe* for Bread.
True *Politicians* only Pay
90 For solid Work, but not for Play;
Nor ever chuse to Work with Tools
Forg'd up in *Colleges* and *Schools.*
Consider how much more is due
To all their *Journey-Men*, than you,
95 At Table you can *Horace* quote;
They at a Pinch can bribe a Vote:
You shew your Skill in *Grecian* Story,
But, they can manage *Whig* and *Tory:*
You, as a *Critick*, are so curious
100 To find a Verse in *Virgil* Spurious;
But, they can *smoak* the deep Designs,
When *Bolingbroke* with *Pult'ney* Dines.
Besides; your Patron may upbraid ye,
That you have got a Place already,
105 An Office for your Talents fit,
To Flatter, Carve, and shew your Wit;
To snuff the Lights, and stir the Fire,
And get a *Dinner* for your Hire,
What Claim have you to *Place*, or *Pension*?
110 He overpays in Condescension.
But, Rev'rend *Doctor*, you, we know,

By *Homer* dead. Refers to Pope's translation of Homer's *Iliad* (1715–20), which made him a professionally self-supporting poet.

***Bolingbroke* with *Pult'ney* Dines.** Leaders of the Tory opposition to Walpole, whose journal *The Craftsman* became the organ of Bolingbroke's political thought in 1726. Book 1 of *Gulliver's Travels*, especially the "urinary fireman" episode (see pp. 81–82), apparently alludes to the earlier phase of Bolingbroke's career as the architect of foreign policy in Queen Anne's Tory cabinet.

Cou'd never Condescend so low;
The *Vice-Roy,* whom you now attend,
Wou'd, if he durst, be more your Friend;
115 Nor will in you those Gifts despise,
By which himself was taught to rise:
When he has Virtue to retire,
He'll Grieve he did not raise you higher,
And place you in a better Station,
120 Although it might have pleas'd the Nation.
This may be true—submitting still
To W[alpole]'s more than R[oyal] Will.
And what Condition can be worse?
He comes to *drain* a *Beggar's Purse:*
125 He comes to tye our Chains on faster,
And shew us, *E[ngland]* is our Master:
Caressing Knaves and Dunces wooing,
To make them work their own undoing.
What has he else to bait his Traps,
130 Or bring his *Vermin* in, but *Scraps*?
The Offals of a *Church* distress't,
A hungry *Vicarage* at best;
Or, some remote inferior *Post,*
With forty Pounds a Year at most.
135 But, here again you interpose;
Your favourite *Lord* is none of those,
Who owe their Virtues to their Stations,
And Characters to Dedications:
For keep him in, or turn him out,
140 His *Learning* none will call in doubt;
His *Learning,* though a *Poet* said it,
Before a Play, wou'd lose no Credit:
Nor Pope wou'd dare deny him Wit,
Although to Praise it Philips Writ.
145 I own, he hates an Action base,
His *Virtues* battling with his *Place*;
Nor wants a nice discerning Spirit,
Betwixt a true and spurious Merit;

The *Vice-Roy.* Cartaret.

Philips. Ambrose Philips (1674–1749). Poet in Addison's circle; author of pastorals that created rivalry between him and Pope. After holding a series of government posts through Walpole's patronage, he became a government placeman in Ireland.

Can sometimes drop a *Voter's* Claim,
150 And give up Party to his Fame.
I do the most that *Friendship* can;
I hate the *Vice-Roy*, love the Man.
But, You, who till your Fortune's made
Must be a Sweet'ner by your Trade,
155 Shou'd swear he never meant us ill;
We suffer sore against his Will;
That, if we could but see his Heart,
He wou'd have chose a milder part;
We rather should Lament his Case
160 Who must Obey, or lose his *Place.*
Since this Reflection slipt your Pen,
Insert it when you write agen:
And, to Illustrate it, produce
This *Simile* for his Excuse.
165 "So, to destroy a guilty Land,
"An *Angel* sent by *Heav'n*'s Command,
"While he obeys *Almighty* Will,
"Perhaps, may feel *Compassion* still,
"And wish the Task had been assign'd
170 "To *Spirits* of less gentle kind.
But I, in *Politicks* grown old,
Whose Thoughts are of a diff'rent Mold,
Who, from my Soul, sincerely hate
Both [Kings] and *Ministers* of *State,*
175 Who look on *Courts* with stricter Eyes,
To see the Seeds of *Vice* arise,
Can lend you an Allusion fitter,
Though *flatt'ring Knaves* may call it *bitter.*
Which, if you durst but give it place,
180 Would shew you many a *Statesman*'s Face.
Fresh from the *Tripod* of Apollo,
I had it in the Words that follow.
(Take Notice, to avoid Offence
I here except *His Excellence.*)
185 So, to effect his *M[onarc]h's* ends,
From *Hell* a *V[iceroy]* dev'l ascends,
His *Budget* with *Corruptions* cramm'd,
The Contributions of the *damn'd*;
Which with unsparing Hand, he strows
190 Through *Courts* and *Senates* as he goes;

And then at *Beelzebub's Black-Hall,*
Complains his *Budget* was too small.
Your *Simile* may better shine
In Verse; but there is *Truth* in mine.
195 For, no imaginable things
Can differ more than God and [kings]
And, *Statesmen* by ten thousand odds
Are Angels, just as [kings] are Gods.

Verses on the Death of Dr. *Swift*, D.S.P.D.

Occasioned

By reading a Maxim in *Rochefoulcault*

Dans l'adversité de nos meilleurs amis nous trouvons quelque chose, qui ne nous deplaist pas.
In the Adversity of our best Friends, we find something that doth not displease us.

As *Rochefoucault* his Maxims drew
From Nature, I believe 'em true:
They argue no corrupted Mind
In him; the Fault is in Mankind.

5 This Maxim more than all the rest
Is thought too base for human Breast;
"In all Distresses of our Friends
"We first consult our private Ends,
"While Nature kindly bent to ease us,
10 "Points out some Circumstance to please us.

If this perhaps your Patience move
Let Reason and Experience prove.

Black-Hall. Parodying Whitehall (Rogers, 1983, 810).

[La] Rochefoucault. Rochefoucault. (1613–80). The French aphorist whose theme is self-love (*amour-propre*). The maxim in question asserts, "In the adversity of our best friends, we find something that doth not displease us." The title "D. S. P. D." refers to "Dean of St. Patrick's, Dublin."

We all behold with envious Eyes,
Our *Equal* rais'd above our *Size;*
15 Who wou'd not at a crowded Show,
Stand high himself, keep others low?
I love my Friend as well as you,
But would not have him stop my View;
Then let him have the higher Post;
20 I ask but for an Inch at most.

If in a Battle you should find,
One, whom you love of all Mankind,
Had some heroick Action done,
A Champion kill'd, or Trophy won;
25 Rather than thus be over-topt,
Would you not wish his Lawrels cropt?

Dear honest *Ned* is in the Gout,
Lies rackt with Pain, and you without:
How patiently you hear him groan!
30 How glad the Case is not your own!

What Poet would not grieve to see,
His Brethren write as well as he?
But rather than they should excel,
He'd wish his Rivals all in Hell.

35 Her End when Emulation misses,
She turns to Envy, Stings and Hisses:
The strongest Friendship yields to Pride,
Unless the Odds be on our Side.

Vain human Kind! Fantastick Race!
40 Thy various Follies, who can trace?
Self-love, Ambition, Envy, Pride,
Their Empire in our Hearts divide:
Give others Riches, Power, and Station,
'Tis all on me an Usurpation.
45 I have no Title to aspire;
Yet, when you sink, I seem the higher.
In Pope, I cannot read a Line,
But with a Sigh, I wish it mine:
When he can in one Couplet fix
50 More Sense than I can do in Six:
It gives me such a jealous Fit,
I cry, Pox take him, and his Wit.

Why must I be outdone by Gay,
In my own hum'rous biting Way?

55 Arbuthnot is no more my Friend,
Who dares to Irony pretend;
Which I was born to introduce,
Refin'd it first, and shew'd its Use.

St. John, as well as Pultney knows,
60 That I had some repute for Prose;
And till they drove me out of Date,
Could maul a Minister of State:
If they have mortify'd my Pride,
And made me throw my Pen aside;
65 If with such Talents Heav'n hath blest 'em
Have I not Reason to detest 'em?

To all my Foes, dear Fortune, send
Thy Gifts, but never to my Friend:
I tamely can endure the first,
70 But, this with Envy makes me burst.

Thus much may serve by way of Proem,
Proceed we therefore to our Poem.

The Time is not remote, when I
Must by the Course of Nature dye:
75 When I foresee my special Friends,
Will try to find their private Ends:
Tho' it is hardly understood,
Which way my Death can do them good;
Yet, thus methinks, I hear 'em speak;
80 See, how the Dean begins to break:
Poor Gentleman, he droops apace,
You plainly find it in his Face:
That old Vertigo in his Head,

St. John. Henry St. John (pronounced "Sanjun"), Viscount Bolingbroke. Like those listed before him—Alexander Pope, John Gay, and John Arbuthnot—a long-time member of Swift's Scriblerian circle. Bolingbroke was secretary of state during Queen Anne's Tory ministry, 1710–14.

Pultney. Sir William Pultney (1684–1764). Collaborator, with Bolingbroke, on the opposition journal *The Craftsman.*

That old Vertigo. Throughout much of his life, Swift suffered from Ménière's syndrome, a disorder of the inner ear, which caused him to have periodic episodes of giddiness linked with deafness.

Will never leave him, till he's dead:
85 Besides, his Memory decays,
He recollects not what he says;
He cannot call his Friends to Mind;
Forgets the Place where last he din'd:
Plyes you with Stories o'er and o'er,
90 He told them fifty Times before.
How does he fancy we can sit,
To hear his out-of-fashion'd Wit?
But he takes up with younger Fokes,
Who for his Wine will bear his Jokes:
95 Faith, he must make his Stories shorter,
Or change his Comrades once a Quarter:
In half the Time, he talks them round;
There must another Sett be found.

For Poetry, he's past his Prime,
100 He takes an Hour to find a Rhime:
His Fire is out, his Wit decay'd,
His Fancy sunk, his Muse a Jade.
I'd have him throw away his Pen;
But there's no talking to some Men.

105 And, then their Tenderness appears,
By adding largely to my Years:
"He's older than he would be reckon'd,
"And well remembers *Charles* the Second.

"He hardly drinks a Pint of Wine;
110 "And that, I doubt, is no good Sign.
"His Stomach too begins to fail:
"Last Year we thought him strong and hale;
"But now, he's quite another Thing;
"I wish he may hold out till Spring.

115 Then hug themselves, and reason thus;
"It is not yet so bad with us."

In such a Case they talk in Tropes,
And, by their Fears express their Hopes:
Some great Misfortune to portend,
120 No Enemy can match a Friend;

Well remembers *Charles* the Second. Swift, born in 1667, would have been a very young man when Charles II died in 1685.

With all the Kindness they profess,
The Merit of a lucky Guess,
(When daily Howd'y's come of Course,
And Servants answer; *Worse and Worse*)
125 Wou'd please 'em better than to tell,
That, God be prais'd, the Dean is well.
Then he who prophecy'd the best,
Approves his Foresight to the rest:
"You know, I always fear'd the worst,
130 "And often told you so at first:"
He'd rather chuse that I should dye,
Than his Prediction prove a Lye.
Not one foretels I shall recover;
But, all agree, to give me over.

135 Yet shou'd some Neighbour feel a Pain,
Just in the Parts, where I complain;
How many a Message would he send?
What hearty Prayers that I should mend?
Enquire what Regimen I kept;
140 What gave me Ease, and how I slept?
And more lament, when I was dead,
Than all the Sniv'llers round my Bed.

My good Companions, never fear,
For though you may mistake a Year;
145 Though your Prognosticks run too fast,
They must be verify'd at last.

"Behold the fatal Day arrive!
"How is the Dean? He's just alive.
"Now the departing Prayer is read:
150 "He hardly breathes. The Dean is dead.
"Before the Passing-Bell begun,
"The News thro' half the Town has run.
"O, may we all for Death prepare!
"What has he left? And who's his Heir?
155 "I know no more than what the News is,
"'Tis all bequeath'd to publick Uses.
"To publick Use! A perfect Whim!
"What had the Publick done for him!
"Meer Envy, Avarice, and Pride!
160 "He gave it all:—But first he dy'd.
"And had the Dean, in all the Nation,

"No worthy Friend, no poor Relation?
"So ready to do Strangers good,
"Forgetting his own Flesh and Blood?

165 Now Grub-Street Wits are all employ'd;
With Elegies, the Town is cloy'd:
Some Paragraph in ev'ry Paper,
To *curse* the *Dean*, or *bless* the *Drapier*.[1]

The Doctors tender of their Fame,
170 Wisely on me lay all the Blame:
"We must confess his Case was nice;
"But he would never take Advice:
"Had he been rul'd, for ought appears,
"He might have liv'd these Twenty Years:
175 "For when we open'd him we found,
"That all his vital Parts were sound.

From *Dublin* soon to *London* spread,
'Tis told at Court, the Dean is dead.[2]

Kind Lady *Suffolk* in the Spleen,[3]
180 Runs laughing up to tell the Queen.
The Queen, so Gracious, Mild, and Good,
Cries, "Is he gone? 'Tis time he shou'd.
"He's dead you say; why let him rot;
"I'm glad the Medals were forgot.[4]

---

[1]The Author imagines, that the Scriblers of the prevailing Party, which he always opposed, will libel him after his Death; but that others will remember him with Gratitude [original publisher].

[2]The Dean supposeth himself to dye in *Ireland* [original publisher].

[3]Mrs. *Howard*, afterwards Countess of *Suffolk*, then of the Bed-chamber to the Queen, professed much Friendship for the Dean. The Queen then Princess, sent a dozen times to the Dean (then in *London*) with her Command to attend her; which at last he did, by Advice of all his Friends. She often sent for him afterwards, and always treated him very Graciously. He taxed her with a Present worth Ten Pounds, which she promised before he should return to *Ireland*, but on his taking Leave, the Medals were not ready [original publisher].

[4]The Medals were to be sent to the Dean in four Months, but she forgot them, or thought them too dear. The Dean, being in *Ireland*, sent Mrs. *Howard* a Piece of *Indian* Plad made in that Kingdom: which the Queen seeing took from her, and wore it herself, and sent to the Dean for as much as would cloath herself and Children, desiring he would send the Charge of it. He did the former. It cost thirty-five Pounds, but he said he would have nothing except the Medals. He was the Summer following in *England*, was treated as usual, and she being then Queen, the Dean was promised a Settlement in England, but returned as he went, and, instead of Favour or Medals, hath been ever since under her Majesty's Displeasure [original publisher].

185 "I promis'd them, I own; but when?
"I only was the Princess then;
"But now as Consort of the King,
"You know 'tis quite a different Thing.

Now, *Chartres* at Sir *Robert*'s Levee,
190 Tells, with a Sneer, the Tidings heavy:
"Why, is he dead without his Shoes?
(Cries *Bob*) "I'm Sorry for the News;
Oh, were the Wretch but living still,
And in his Place my good Friend *Will*;
195 Or, had a Mitre on his Head
Provided *Bolingbroke* were dead.

Now *Curl* his Shop from Rubbish drains;
Three genuine Tomes of *Swift*'s Remains.
And then to make them pass the glibber,
200 Revis'd by *Tibbalds, Moore, and Cibber.*
He'll treat me as he does my Betters.
Publish my Will, my Life, my Letters.
Revive the Libels born to dye;
Which Pope must bear, as well as I.

205 Here shift the Scene, to represent
How those I love, my Death lament.
Poor Pope will grieve a Month; and Gay
A Week; and Arbuthnott a Day.

St. John himself will scarce forbear,
210 To bite his Pen, and drop a Tear.
The rest will give a Shrug and cry,
I'm sorry; but we all must dye.
Indifference clad in Wisdom's Guise,
All Fortitude of Mind supplies:
215 For how can stony Bowels melt,
In those who never Pity felt;
When *We* are lash'd, *They* kiss the Rod;
Resigning to the Will of God.

The Fools, my Juniors by a Year,
220 Are tortur'd with Suspence and Fear.
Who wisely thought my Age a Screen,
When Death approach'd, to stand between:
The Screen remov'd, their Hearts are trembling,
They mourn for me without dissembling.

225 My female Friends, whose tender Hearts
Have better learn'd to act their Parts.
Receive the News in *doleful Dumps*,
"The Dean is dead, (*and what is Trumps*?)
"Then Lord have Mercy on his Soul.
230 "(Ladies I'll venture for the *Vole.*)
"Six Deans they say must bear the Pall.
"(I wish I knew what *King* to call.)
"Madam, your Husband will attend
"The Funeral of so good a Friend.
235 "No Madam, 'tis a shocking Sight,
"And he's engag'd To-morrow Night!
"My Lady *Club* wou'd take it ill,
"If he shou'd fail her at *Quadrill.*
"He lov'd the Dean. (*I lead a Heart.*)
240 "But dearest Friends, they say, must part.
"His Time was come, he ran his Race;
"We hope he's in a better Place.

Why do we grieve that Friends should dye?
No Loss more easy to supply.
245 One Year is past; a different Scene;
No further mention of the Dean;
Who now, alas, no more is mist,
Than if he never did exist.
Where's now this Fav'rite of *Apollo*?
250 Departed; *and his Works must follow:*
Must undergo the common Fate;
His Kind of Wit is out of Date.
Some Country Squire to *Lintot* goes,[5]
Enquires for Swift in Verse and Prose:
255 Says *Lintot*, "I have heard the Name:
"He dy'd a Year ago." The same.
He searcheth all his Shop in vain;
"Sir you may find them in *Duck-lane:*[6]
"I sent them with a Load of Books,
260 "Last *Monday* to the Pastry-cooks.

Vole. In quadrille, the feat of taking all thirteen tricks.
Quadrill. Popular card game.

[5] *Bernard Lintot*, a Bookseller in *London*. Vide Mr. *Pope's* Dunciad [original publisher].
[6] A Place in *London* where old Books are sold [original publisher].

"To fancy they cou'd live a Year!
"I find you're but a Stranger here.
"The Dean was famous in his Time;
"And had a Kind of Knack at Rhyme:
265 "His way of Writing now is past;
"The Town hath got a better Taste:
"I keep no antiquated Stuff;
"But, spick and span I have enough.
"Pray, do but give me leave to shew 'em;
270 "Here's *Colley Cibber*'s Birth-day Poem.
"This Ode you never yet have seen,
"By *Stephen Duck*, upon the Queen.
"Then, here's a Letter finely penn'd
"Against the *Craftsman* and his Friend;
275 "It clearly shews that all Reflection
"On Ministers, is disaffection.
"Next, here's Sir *Robert*'s Vindication,[7]
"And Mr. *Henly*'s last Oration:[8]
"The Hawkers have not got 'em yet,
280 "Your Honour please to buy a Set?

"Here's *Wolston*'s Tracts, the twelfth Edition;
"'Tis read by ev'ry Politician:
"The Country Members, when in Town,
"To all their Boroughs send them down:
285 "You never met a Thing so smart;
"The Courtiers have them all by Heart:
"Those Maids of Honour (who can read)
"Are taught to use them for their Creed.
"The Rev'rend Author's good Intention,
290 "Hath been rewarded with a Pension:
"He doth an Honour to his Gown,

***Colley Cibber's* Birth-day Poem.** Cibber, though a figure of real importance in the theater, was a mediocre poet. He had been made poet laureate in 1730.

Stephen Duck. The self-educated "Thresher Poet" (1705–56), patronized by Queen Caroline and others. Duck's educational deficits, somewhat exaggerated by his patrons, began to be sentimentally celebrated as an instance of "natural," or "untutored," genius. His signature piece is "The Thresher's Labour" (1730).

[7] *Walpole* hires a Set of Party Scriblers, who do nothing else but write in his Defence [original publisher].

[8] *Henly* is a Clergyman who wanting both Merit and Luck to get Preferment [original publisher].

"By bravely running *Priest-craft* down:
"He shews, as sure as God's in *Gloc'ster*,
"That *Jesus* was a Grand Impostor:
295 "That all his Miracles were Cheats,
"Perform'd as Juglers do their Feats:
"The Church had never such a Writer:
"A Shame, he hath not got a Mitre!

Suppose me dead; and then suppose
300 A Club assembled at the *Rose;*
Where from Discourse of this and that,
I grow the Subject of their Chat:
And, while they toss my Name about,
With Favour some, and some without;
305 One quite indiff'rent in the Cause,
My Character impartial draws:

"The Dean, if we believe Report,
"Was never ill receiv'd at Court:
"As for his Works in Verse and Prose,
310 "I own my self no Judge of those:
"Nor, can I tell what Criticks thought 'em;
"But, this I know, all People bought 'em;
"As with a moral View design'd
"To cure the Vices of Mankind:
315 "His Vein, ironically grave,
"Expos'd the Fool, and lash'd the Knave:
"To steal a Hint was never known,
"But what he writ was all his own.

"He never thought an Honour done him,
320 "Because a Duke was proud to own him:
"Would rather slip aside, and chuse
"To talk with Wits in dirty Shoes:
"Despis'd the Fools with Stars and Garters,
"So often seen caressing *Chartres*:
325 "He never courted Men in Station,
"*Nor Persons had in Admiration;*
"Of no Man's Greatness was afraid,
"Because he sought for no Man's Aid.
"Though trusted long in great Affairs,

The *Rose*. A fashionable London tavern.

All People bought 'em. An interesting appeal to the credentials of popularity.

330 "He gave himself no haughty Airs:
"Without regarding private Ends,
"Spent all his Credit for his Friends:
"And only chose the Wise and Good;
"No Flatt'rers; no Allies in Blood;
335 "But succour'd Virtue in Distress,
"And seldom fail'd of good Success;
"As Numbers in their Hearts must own,
"Who, but for him, had been unknown.

"With Princes kept a due Decorum,
340 "But never stood in Awe before 'em:
"He follow'd *David*'s Lesson just,
"*In Princes never put thy Trust.*
"And, would you make him truly sower;
"Provoke him with *a slave in Power:*
345 "The *Irish* Senate, if you nam'd,
"With what Impatience he declaim'd!
"Fair LIBERTY was all his Cry;
"For her he stood prepar'd to die;
"For her he boldly stood alone;
350 "For her he oft expos'd his own.
"Two Kingdoms, just as Faction led,[9]
"Had set a Price upon his Head;
"But, not a Traytor cou'd be found,
"To sell him for Six Hundred Pound.

355 "Had he but spar'd his Tongue and Pen,
"He might have rose like other Men:
"But, Power was never in his Thought;
"And, Wealth he valu'd not a Groat:
"Ingratitude he often found,
360 "And pity'd those who meant the Wound:
"But, kept the Tenor of his Mind,
"To merit well of human Kind:

---

[9] In the Year 1713, the late Queen was prevailed with by an Address of the House of Lords in *England*, to publish a Proclamation, promising Three Hundred Pounds to whatever Person would discover the Author of a Pamphlet called, *The Publick Spirit of the Whiggs*; and in *Ireland*, in the Year 1724, my Lord *Carteret* at his first coming into the Government, was prevailed on to issue a Proclamation for promising the like Reward of Three Hundred Pounds, to any Person who could discover the Author of a Pamphlet called, *The Drapier's Fourth Letter*, &c. writ against that destructive Project of coining Halfpence for *Ireland*; but in neither Kingdoms was the Dean discovered [original publisher].

"Nor made a Sacrifice of those
"Who still were true, to please his Foes.
365 "He labour'd many a fruitless Hour[10]
"To reconcile his Friends in Power;
"Saw Mischief by a Faction brewing,
"While they pursu'd each others Ruin.
"But, finding vain was all his Care,
370 "He left the Court in meer Despair.

"And, oh! how short are human Schemes!
"Here ended all our golden Dreams.
"What St. John's Skill in State Affairs,
"What Ormond's *Valour*, Oxford's Cares.
375 "To save their sinking Country lent,
"Was all destroy'd by one Event.
"Too soon that precious Life was ended,[11]
"On which alone, our Weal depended.
"When up a dangerous Faction starts,[12]
380 "With Wrath and Vengeance in their Hearts:
"*By solemn League and Cov'nant bound,*
"To ruin, slaughter, and confound;
"To turn Religion to a Fable,

By solemn League and Cov'nant bound. The language here recalls the language by which the Long Parliament—engaged in civil war against Charles I—agreed in 1643 to demands in Scotland for legal reforms of the national Church of Scotland along Presbyterian lines: a setback for the Anglican establishment. The phrase links eighteenth-century Whigs to double-dealing "covenanters."

[10] Queen *ANNE*'s Ministry fell to Variance from the first Year after their Ministry began: *Harcourt* the Chancellor, and Lord *Bolingbroke* the Secretary, were discontented with the Treasurer *Oxford*, for his too much Mildness to the Whig Party; this Quarrel grew higher every Day till the Queen's Death: The Dean, who was the only Person that endeavoured to reconcile them, found it impossible; and thereupon retired to the Country about ten Weeks before that fatal Event: Upon which he returned to his Deanry in *Dublin*, where for many Years he was worryed by the new People in Power, and had Hundreds of Libels writ against him in *England* [original publisher].

[11] In the Height of the Quarrel between the Ministers, the Queen died [original publisher].

[12] Upon Queen *ANNE*'s Death the Whig Faction was restored to Power, which they exercised with the utmost Rage and Revenge; impeached and banished the Chief Leaders of the Church Party, and stripped all their Adherents of what Employments they had, after which *England* was never known to make so mean a Figure in *Europe*. The greatest Preferments in the Church in both Kingdoms were given to the most ignorant Men, Fanaticks were publickly caressed, *Ireland* utterly ruined and enslaved, only great Ministers heaping up Millions, and so Affairs continue until this present third Day of May, 1732, and are likely to go on in the same Manner [original publisher].

"And make the Government a *Babel:*
385 "Pervert the Law, disgrace the Gown,
"Corrupt the Senate, rob the Crown;
"To sacrifice old *England*'s Glory,
"And make her infamous in Story.
"When such a Tempest shook the Land,
390 "How could unguarded Virtue stand?

"With Horror, Grief, Despair the Dean
"Beheld the dire destructive Scene:
"His Friends in Exile, or the Tower,
"Himself within the Frown of Power;[13]
395 "Pursu'd by base envenom'd Pens,
"Far to the Land of Slaves and Fens;[14]
"A servile Race in Folly nurs'd,
"Who truckle most, when treated worst.

"By Innocence and Resolution,
400 "He bore continual Persecution;
"While Numbers to Preferment rose;
"Whose Merits were, to be his Foes.
"When, *ev'n his own familiar Friends*
"Intent upon their private Ends;
405 "Like Renegadoes now he feels,
"*Against him lifting up their Heels.*

"The Dean did by his Pen defeat
"An infamous destructive Cheat.[15]
"Taught Fools their Int'rest how to know;
410 "And gave them Arms to ward the Blow.
"Envy hath own'd it was his doing,
"To save that helpless Land from Ruin,
"While they who at the Steerage stood,
"And reapt the Profit, sought his Blood.

415 "To save them from their evil Fate,
"In him was held a Crime of State.

---

[13] Upon the Queen's Death, the Dean returned to live in *Dublin*, at his Deanry-House: Numberless Libels were writ against him in *England*, as a Jacobite; he was insulted in the Street, and at Nights was forced to be attended by his Servants armed [original publisher].

[14] The Land of Slaves and Fens, is *Ireland* [original publisher].

[15] One *Wood*, a Hardware-man from *England*, had a Patent for coining Copper Half-pence in *Ireland*, to the Sum of 108,000 l. which in the Consequence, must leave that Kingdom without Gold or Silver (See *Drapier's* Letters.) [Original publisher.]

"A wicked Monster on the Bench,[16]
"Whose Fury Blood could never quench;
"As vile and profligate a Villain,
420 "As modern *Scroggs*,[17] or old *Tressilian*;
"Who long all Justice had discarded,
"*Nor fear'd he GOD, nor Man regarded*;
"Vow'd on the Dean his Rage to vent,
"And make him of his Zeal repent;
425 "But Heav'n his Innocence defends,
"The grateful People stand his Friends:
"Not Strains of Law, nor Judges Frown,
"Nor Topicks brought to please the Crown,
"Nor Witness hir'd, nor Jury pick'd,
430 "Prevail to bring him in convict.

"In Exile with a steady Heart,[18]
"He spent his Life's declining Part;
"Where, Folly, Pride, and Faction sway,
"Remote from St. John, Pope, and Gay.[19]
435 "His Friendship there to few confin'd,[20]
"Were always of the midling Kind:

Modern *Scroggs*, or old *Tressilian*. Sir William Scroggs (1623?–83), unleashed legal severity on the victims of Titus Oates's perjury during the Popish Plot. Sir Robert Tresilian, Chief Justice of the King's Bench during the peasants' revolt of 1381, likewise notorious for judicial severity. Both men were eventually impeached, and Tresilian was hanged.

[16] One *Whitshed* was then Chief Justice: He had some Years before prosecuted a Printer for a Pamphlet writ by the Dean, to perswade the People of *Ireland* to wear their own Manufactures. *Whitshed* sent the Jury down eleven Times, and kept them nine Hours, until they were forced to bring in a special Verdict. He sat as Judge afterwards on the Tryal of the Printer of the *Drapier*'s Fourth Letter; but the Jury, against all he could say or swear, threw out the Bill: All the Kingdom took the *Drapier*'s Part, except the Courtiers, or those who expected Places. The *Drapier* was celebrated in many Poems and Pamphlets: His Sign was set up in most Streets of *Dublin* (where many of them still continue) and in several Country Towns [original publisher].

[17] *Scroggs* was Chief Justice under King *Charles* the Second: His Judgment always varied in State Tryals, according to Directions from Court. *Tressilian* was a wicked Judge, hanged above three hundred Years ago [original publisher].

[18] In *Ireland*, which he had Reason to call a Place of Exile; to which Country nothing could have driven him, but the Queen's Death, who had determined to fix him in *England*, in Spight of the Dutchess of *Somerset*, &c [original publisher].

[19] *Henry St. John*, Lord Viscount *Bolingbroke*, mentioned before [original publisher].

[20] In *Ireland* the Dean was not acquainted with one single Lord Spiritual or Temporal. He only conversed with private Gentlemen of the Clergy or Laity, and but a small Number of either [original publisher].

"No Fools of Rank, a mungril Breed,
"Who fain would pass for Lords indeed:
"Where Titles give no Right or Power,[21]
440 "And Peerage is a wither'd Flower,
"He would have held it a Disgrace,
"If such a Wretch had known his Face.
"On Rural Squires, that Kingdom's Bane,
"He vented oft his Wrath in vain:
445 "Biennial Squires, to Market brought;[22]
"Who sell their Souls and Votes for Naught;
"The Nation stript go joyful back,
"To rob the Church, their Tenants rack,
"Go Snacks with Thieves and Rapparees,[23]
450 "And, keep the Peace, to pick up Fees:
"In every Jobb to have a Share,
"A Jayl or Barrack[24] to repair;
"And turn the Tax for publick Roads
"Commodious to their own Abodes.

455 "Perhaps I may allow, the Dean
"Had too much Satyr in his Vein;
"And seem'd determin'd not to starve it,
"Because no Age could more deserve it.
"Yet, Malice never was his Aim;
460 "He lash'd the Vice but spar'd the Name.
"No Individual could resent,

Peerage is a wither'd Flower. The Declaratory Act (1720) subordinated the Irish Parliament to the British Parliament, reducing the former's jurisdiction to matters of local taxation. See pp. 416–17.

[21] The Peers of *Ireland* lost a great Part of their Jurisdiction by one single Act, and tamely submitted to this infamous Mark of Slavery without the least Resentment, or Remonstrance [original publisher].

[22] The Parliament (as they call it) in *Ireland* meet but once in two Years; and, after giving five Times more than they can afford, return Home to reimburse themselves by all Country Jobs and Oppressions, of which some few only are here mentioned [original publisher].

[23] The Highway-Men in *Ireland* are, since the late Wars there, usually called Rapparees, which was a Name given to those *Irish* Soldiers who in small Parties used, at that Time, to plunder the Protestants [original publisher].

[24] The Army in *Ireland* is lodged in Barracks, the building and repairing whereof, and other Charges, have cost a prodigious Sum to that unhappy Kingdom [original publisher].

"Where Thousands equally were meant.
"His Satyr points at no Defect,
"But what all Mortals may correct;
465 "For he abhorr'd that senseless Tribe,
"Who call it Humour when they jibe:
"He spar'd a Hump or crooked Nose,
"Whose Owners set not up for Beaux.
"True genuine Dulness mov'd his Pity,
470 "Unless it offer'd to be witty.
"Those, who their Ignorance confess'd,
"He ne'er offended with a Jest;
"But laugh'd to hear an Idiot quote,
"A Verse from *Horace*, learn'd by Rote.

475 "He knew an hundred pleasant Stories,
"With all the Turns of *Whigs* and *Tories:*
"Was chearful to his dying Day,
"And Friends would let him have his Way.

"He gave the little Wealth he had,
480 "To build a House for Fools and Mad:
"And shew'd by one satyric Touch,
"No Nation wanted it so much:
"That Kingdom he hath left his Debtor,[25]
"I wish it soon may have a Better.

House for Fools and Mad. Swift's will bequeathed most of his fortune to the founding of St. Patrick's Hospital in Dublin, still flourishing as a leading psychiatric hospital.

[25]Meaning *Ireland*, where he now lives, and probably may dye [original publisher].

CORRESPONDENCE

Swift to Charles Ford

Declaratory Act and South Sea Bubble

Dublin Apr. 4th 1720

I had your former Letter with the inclosed from our Mississipi Friend, I can make no excuse for my not acknowledging it than my perpetuall ill Health. I should not scrupule going abroad to mend it, if it were not for a foolish importunate Ailment that quite disspirits me; I am hardly a Month free from a Deafness which continues another month on me, and dejects me so, that I can not bear the thoughts of stirring out, or suffering any one to see me, and this is the most mortal Impediment to all Thoughts of travelling, and I should dy with Spleen to be in such a Condition in strange Places; so that I must wait till I grow better, or sink under it if I am worse. You healthy People cannot judge of the sickly. Since I had your last of Mar. 10th I have not been able to write; and three Days ago having invited severall Gentlemen to dinner, I was so attacked with a fitt of Giddyness for 5 Hours, that I was forced to constitute a Grattan to be my Deputy and do the Honors of the House while I lay miserable on my Bed. Your friendly Expostulations force me upon this old Woman's Talk, but I can bring all my few Friends to witness that you have heard more of it, than ever I troubled them with. I cannot understand the South-Sea Mystery, perhaps the Frolick may go round, and every Nation (except this which is no Nation) have it's Mississippi. I believe my self not guilty of too much veneration for the Irish H. of Lds, but I differ from you in Politicks, the Question is whether People ought to be Slaves or no.

The Correspondence of Jonathan Swift, 5 vols., ed. Harold Williams (Oxford: Clarendon Press, 1963–65).

Mississipi Friend. Bolingbroke, who had invested in the French equivalent of the South Sea Bubble: John Law's Mississippi scheme of 1719.

Deafness. Swift's labyrinthine vertigo, a disorder of the inner ear linked to the giddiness of which he also complains.

South-Sea Mystery. The inflationary phase of the Bubble. See pp. 8–9.

People ought to be Slaves or no. Refers to the subordination of the Irish Parliament by the Declaratory Act. See p. 416.

Swift to Sir Thomas Hanmer

Printer Prosecuted

Dublin. Oc^{tbr} 1st 1720

S^{r}

There is a little Affair that I engaged some Friends of mine to trouble You about, but am not perfectly informed what Progress they have made. Last Term one Waters a Printer was accused and tryed for printing a Pamphlet persuading the People here to wear their own Manufactures exclusive of any from Engld with some Complaints of the Hardships they lye under. There was nothing in the Pamphlet either of Whig or Tory or reflecting upon any Person whatever. But the Chanceller afraid of losing his Office, and the Chief Justice desirous to come into it, were both vying who should shew their Zeal most to discountenance the Pamphlet; the Printer was tryed with a Jury of the most Violent Party men, who yet brought him in not guilty, but were sent back nine times, and at last brought in a Speciall Verdict, so that the Man is to be tryed again next Term. The Whigs in generall were for the Pamphlet tho it be a weak hasty Scribble, and generally abominated the Proceeding of the Justice, particularly all the Bishops except the late ones from Engld, the Duke of Wharton Lord Molesworth and many others. Now if the Chief Justice continues his Keeness, the Man may be severely punished: but the Business may be inconvenient, because I am looked on as the Author. And my Desire to you is that you would please to prevayl on the Duke of Grafton to write to the Chief Justice to let the Matter drop, which I believe his Grace would easily do on Your Application if he knew that I truly representd the Matter, for which I appeal both to the Duke of Wharton and Lord Molesworth . . .

Chanceller. Lord Midleton.

Chief Justice. William Whitshed. See pp. 341–42.

Duke of Grafton. The lord lieutenant of Ireland.

Swift to Alexander Pope

Political Principles

Dublin. Jan. 10, 1721.

I have written in this kingdom, a discourse to persuade the wretched people to wear their own Manufactures instead of those from England: This Treatise soon spread very fast, being agreeable to the sentiments of the whole nation, except of those gentlemen who had Employments, or were Expectants. Upon which a person in great office here immediately took the alarm; he sent in hast for the Chief Justice, and inform'd him of a seditious, factious and virulent Pamphlet, lately publish'd with a design of setting the two kingdoms at variance, directing at the same time that the printer should be prosecuted with the utmost rigour of Law. The Chief Justice had so quick an understanding, that he resolved if possible to out-do his orders. The Grand-Juries of the county and city were practised effectually with to represent the said Pamphlet with all aggravating Epithets, for which they had thanks sent them from England, and their Presentments publish'd for several weeks in all the news-papers. The Printer was seized, and forced to give great bail: After his tryal the Jury brought him in Not Guilty, although they had been culled with the utmost industry; the Chief Justice sent them back nine times, and kept them eleven hours, until being perfectly tired out, they were forced to leave the matter to the mercy of the Judge, by what they call a special Verdict. During the tryal, the Chief Justice among other singularities, laid his hand on his breast, and protested solemnly that the Author's design was to bring in the Pretender; although there was not a single syllable of party in the whole Treatise, and although it was known that the most eminent of those who professed his own principles, publickly disallowed his proceedings. But the cause being so very odious and impopular, the tryal of the Verdict was deferred from one Term to another, until upon the Duke of G-ft-n the Lord Lieutenant's arrival his Grace after mature advice, and permission from England, was pleased to grant a *noli prosequi.*

A person in great office. The chancellor, Lord Midleton.

Bring in the Pretender. That is, the "Old Pretender": James Edward Stuart (1688–1766), son of James II, who represented the delegitimated claims of the Stuart dynasty to the throne. To accuse someone of Jacobitism, especially after the failed uprising of 1715, was to smear them as a traitor to the Hanoverian occupants of the throne.

This is the more remarkable, because it is said that the man is no ill decider in common cases of property, where Party is out of the question; but when that intervenes, with ambition at heels to push it forward, it must needs confound any man of little spirit, and low birth, who hath no other endowment than that sort of Knowledge, which, however possessed in the highest degree, can possibly give no one good quality to the mind.

. . .

I ought to let you know, that the Thing we called a Whig in England is a creature altogether different from those of the same denomination here, at least it was so during the reign of Her late Majesty. Whether those on your side have changed or no, it hath not been my business to inquire. I remember my excellent friend Mr. Addison, when he first came over hither Secretary to the Earl of Wharton, then Lord Lieutenant, was extremely offended at the conduct and discourse of the Chief Managers here: He told me they were a sort of people who seemed to think, that the principles of a Whig consisted in nothing else but damning the Church, reviling the Clergy, abetting Dissenters, and speaking contemptibly of revealed Religion.

I was discoursing some years ago with a certain Minister about that whiggish or fanatical Genius so prevalent among the English of this kingdom: his Lordship accounted for it by that number of Cromwell's soldiers, adventurers establish'd here, who were all of the sourest Leven, and the meanest birth, and whose posterity are now in possession of their lands and their principles.

Now in possession of their lands and their principles. A hostile reference to the land confiscation under Cromwell, which in part served as pay for his invading troops. Swift's antipathy to Ulster Presbyterians—the major element of the Dissenters mentioned here—was determined by several factors: (1) the Scots Presbyterian role in the English Civil War; (2) the present antagonism of such Dissenters to the established Church of Ireland; (3) the consequences for Ireland of the Act of Union in 1707, which included Scotland in Great Britain but excluded Ireland; and (4) Swift's earlier experiences in the northern county of Antrim (as prebend of Kilroot), where his Anglican congregants were outnumbered by Presbyterians.

. . .

First, I always declared my self against a Popish Successor to the Crown, whatever Title he might have by the proximity of blood: Neither did I ever regard the right line except upon two accounts, first as it was establish'd by law; and secondly, as it hath much weight in the opinions of the people. For necessity may abolish any Law, but cannot alter the sentiments of the vulgar; Right of inheritance being perhaps the most popular of all topicks; and therefore in great Changes, when that is broke, there will remain much heart burning and discontent among the meaner people; which (under a weak Prince and corrupt Administration) may have the worst consequences upon the peace of any state.

As to what is called a Revolution-principle, my opinion was this; That whenever those evils which usually attend and follow a violent change of government, were not in probability so pernicious as the grievances we suffer under a present power, then the publick good will justify such a Revolution; and this I took to have been the Case in the Prince of Orange's expedition, although in the consequences it produced some very bad effects, which are likely to stick long enough by us.

I had likewise in those days a mortal antipathy against Standing Armies in times of Peace. Because I always took Standing Armies to be only servants hired by the master of the family, for keeping his own children in slavery: And because, I conceived that a Prince who could not think himself secure without Mercenary Troops, must needs have a separate interest from that of his subjects. Although I am not ignorant of those artificial Necessities which a corrupted Ministry can create, for keeping up forces to support a Faction against the publick Interest.

Swift to Charles Ford

Printer Prosecuted

Dublin. Apr. 15th 1721

I have been employing my Credit by Ld Arran and other Means to get the D. of Gr— to order putting off the Affair of the Printer till He comes over,

---

Against a Popish Successor to the Crown. A clear statement, perhaps self-protective, that Swift was no Jacobite. The "Old Whig" principles he articulates explain his acceptance of the principles of the Glorious Revolution (1688–90)—note its bad effects in Ireland—and express his disdain for Whigs in the present, whom he regarded as corrupt.

D[uke] of Gr[afton]. The lord lieutenant of Ireland, who came from England to Ireland at the end of August 1721.

but my Sollicitor M[r] Charleton meets no Success; Surely tis a small Favor, and I desired S[r] Th. Hanmer might use his Credit the same way: But I find there is less trusting in Friends than ever our Grandmothers warn us again[st]; and the Term begins in ten days, and the Matter will be resumed afresh, to great Expence and more Vexation neither of which I am well capable of bearing either by my Health or Fortune, and this hinders me from going to England as I intended.—The letter of Brutus to Cicero should have been better translated; Your Ministry seems to me to want Credit in suffering so many Libells published against them; and here there is a worse Matter; for many of the violent Whigs profess themselves perfect Jacobites, and plead for it the Miseryes and Contempt they suffer by the Treatment of England. We abound in Papers as well as you, and I have observed it to be one of the Consequences of wretched Times, and it seems naturall enough, that when People are reduced to Rags they should turn them to the onely Use that Rags are proper for.—

Swift to Alexander Pope

Security of Mind

Dublin Septemb. 20th 1723

Your happiness is greater than your Merit in chusing your Favorites so Indifferently among either party, this you owe partly to your Education and partly to your Genius, employing you in an Art where Faction has nothing to do. For I suppose Virgil, and Horace are equally read by Whigs and Toryes you have no more to do with the Constitution of Church and State than a Christian at Constantinople, and you are so much the wiser, and the happier because both partyes will approve your Poetry as long as you are known to be of neither. But I who am sunk under the prejudices of another Education, and am every day perswading my self that a Dagger is at my Throat, a halter about my Neck, or Chains at my Feet, all prepared by those in Power, can never arrive at the Security of Mind you possess.

We abound in Papers. Including, as Williams notes, the *Dublin Gazette*, the *Dublin Courant*, the *Post-Man*, *Whalley's News-Letter*, *Harding's Weekly Newsletter*, *Pue's Occurences*, and *Dublin Intelligence.*

Swift to Charles Ford

The Name of a Drapier

Dublin Apr. 2d 1724

I came just now from a Commission with the Chancellor. ArchB[p] Dublin &c. I spoke very severely to the knaves about the Farthings. I told them the Baseness and pusilanimity when they and others were sent for by the L[t] upon that Subject they all talked as much against the Thing as I. but People are more in fear than ever. I do not know whether I told you that I sent out a small Pamphlet under the Name of a Draper, laying the whole Vilany open, and advising People what to do; about 2000 of them have been dispersd by Gentlemen in severall Parts of the Country, but one can promise nothing from such Wretches as the Irish People.

Swift to the Earl of Oxford

Important to Themselves

27 November 1724

My unconversable Disorder hath hindred me from seeing my old Friend the Lord Lieutenant, from whom I never received since his Arrival, any more than one day Message. He hath half frighten[d] the People here out of their Understandings. There is a Fellow in London, one Wood, who got a Patent for coyning Halfpence for this Kingdom, which hath so terrifyed us, that if it were not for some Pamphlets against these Halfpence, we must have submitted. Against these Pamphlets the Lieutenant hath put out a Proclamation: and is acting the most unpopular Part I ever knew, though I warned him against it, by a Letter before he came over;

Chancellor. Viscount Midleton.

Lt. The lord lieutenant of Ireland, the duke of Grafton.

Draper. Refers to the first of *The Drapier's Letters*, reprinted in this volume.

Unconversable Disorder. That is, Ménière's syndrome, which caused episodes of deafness.

My old Friend the Lord Lieutenant. John Cartaret, who reached Dublin on October 22, 1724, with the thankless charge to settle the Wood's halfpence controversy. He and Swift had become acquainted in London, and their mutual regard survived even the strain of being on the opposite side of the Wood's halfpence controversy. See Ehrenpreis, vol. 3, 224–26.

and thought by his Answer, that he would have taken my Opinions. This is just of as much Consequence to your Lordship, as the news of a Skirmish between two petty States in Greece was to Alexander while he was conquering Persia, But even a Knot of Beggars, are of Importance among themselves.

Swift to Charles Ford

Teazed at Whitehall

Dublin. Mar. 11th 1724–25

I have been resolving for some time past to go to England about the End of this month, and have lately communicated my Intention to five or six Friends, who are all dissuading me with the greatest Violence, and desire that I would at least defer it till next Year. Their Reasons I do not all approve; because I know very well how apt the People of Ireland are to think that their little Affairs are regarded in England. They would have it that what has been lately written about the Drapier has given great Offence on your side, that the private Malice of the Projector and those who were examined in his Behalf might tempt them to some violent Action of Revenge, and that Mr W— thinks himself personally offended, and that somebody for whose Advantage that Project was contrived would use all means to prosecute whoever has opposed it, which may end in Messengers heads, Accusations, Imprisonments &c. Now in my own Mind I am quite of another Opinion. I do not think the thing is of Weight enough for a Ministry to trouble themselves about, and as for the Malice of mean paltry Rascals it may be avoyded by common Care. There was a Time when in England some great Friends looked on me as in Danger, and used to warn me against Night walking &c.; but I thought it was a shame to be afraid of such Accidents and looked as if a man affected to be thought of Importance. Neither do I find that Assassinations are things in fashion at present; and in my Opinion a Secretary of State is a much more terrible animal, when he has a mind to be malicious.

Even a Knot of Beggars, are of Importance among themselves. A mode of identification, against English arrogance, with Ireland and its national interests. See Fabricant, 1995, 253–54.

Mr. W. Walpole.

Somebody for whose Advantage. The duchess of Kendal, suspected of taking a bribe from William Wood to procure the patent to mint halfpence in Ireland.

Our Friend in Grafton Street swears it is a Fatality upon me. In order to their Satisfaction I desire to know your Opinion, whether I may be in any Danger of being teazed at Whitehall, or have Searches for Papers &c. for as to private malice, I very little apprehend it. Pray write me your Thoughts as soon as you can, that I may take my Measures.

Swift to Lord Carteret

Patronage

3 July 1725

Since your Excellency hath had an opportunity so early in your Government of gratifying your *English* Dependents by a Bishoprick and the best Deanery in the Kingdom, I cannot but hope that the Clergy of *Ireland* will have their Share in your Patronage.

...

The Misfortune of having Bishops perpetually from *England*, as it must needs quench the Spirit of Emulation among us to excel in Learning and the Study of Divinity, so it produces another Great Discouragement, that those Prelates usually draw after them Colonies of Sons, Nephews, Cousins, or old College-Companions, to whom they bestow the best Preferments in their Gift; and thus the young Men sent into the Church from the University here, have no better prospect than to be Curates, or small Country-Vicars, for Life.

It will become so excellent a Governor as you, a little to moderate this great Partiality; wherein as you will act with Justice and Reason, so you will gain the Thanks and Prayers of the whole Nation, and take away one great Cause of universal Discontent: For I believe your Excellency will agree, that there is not another Kingdom in *Europe*, where the Natives (even those descended from the Conquerors) have been treated as if they were almost unqualify'd for any Employment either in Church of State.

Friend in Grafton Street. Not certain. Possibly Stella.

Swift to Alexander Pope

Vexing the World

Sep. 29. 1725

I have employd my time (besides ditching) in finishing correcting, amending, and Transcribing my Travells, in four parts Compleat newly Augmented, and intended for the press when the world shall deserve them, or rather when a Printer shall be found brave enough to venture his Eares, I like your Schemes of our meeting after Distresses and dispertions but the chief end I propose to my self in all my labors is to vex the world rather then divert it, and if I could compass that designe without hurting my own person or Fortune I would be the most Indefatigable writer you have ever seen without reading I am exceedingly pleased that you have done with Translations Lord Treasurer Oxford often lamented that a rascaly World should lay you under a Necessity of Misemploying your Genius for so long a time. But since you will now be so much better employd when you think of the World give it one lash the more at my Request. I have ever hated all Nations professions and Communityes and all my love is towards individualls for instance I hate the tribe of Lawyers, but I love Councellor such a one, Judge such a one for so with Physicians (I will not Speak of my own Trade) Soldiers, English, Scotch, French; and the rest but principally I hate and detest that animal called man, although I hartily love John, Peter, Thomas and so forth. this is the system upon which I have governed my self many years (but do not tell) and so I shall go on till I have done with them I have got Materials Towards a Treatis proving the falsity of that Definition *animal rationale;* and to show it should be only *rationis capax.* Upon this great foundation of Misanthropy (though not Timons manner) The whole building of my Travells is erected: And I never will have peace of mind till all honest men are of my Opinion: by Consequence you are to embrace it immediatly and procure that all who deserve my Esteem may do so too. The matter is so clear that it will admit little dispute. nay I will hold a hundred pounds that you and I agree in the Point.

Rationis capax. Capable of reason.

Timons manner. Timon was a famous misanthrope, perhaps legendary, from classical times. An Athenian, Timon became misanthropic due to the ingratitude of his friends.

Swift to Alexander Pope

It Is *Vous Autres*

Dublin Novr 26, 1725

I tell you after all that I do not hate Mankind, it is vous autres who hate them because you would have them reasonable Animals, and are Angry for being disappointed. I have always rejected that Definition and made another of my own. I am no more angry with——. Then I was with the Kite that last week flew away with one of my Chickins and yet I was pleas'd when one of my Servants Shot him two days after.

Swift to the Earl of Peterborough

Meeting with Walpole

April 28, 1726

My Lord,

Your Lordship having, at my request, obtained for me an hour from Sir *Robert Walpole*, I accordingly attended him yesterday at eight o'clock in the morning, and had somewhat more than an hour's conversation with him. Your Lordship was this day pleased to inquire what passed between that great Minister and me, to which I gave you some general answers, from whence you said you could comprehend little or nothing.

I had no other design in desiring to see Sir *Robert Walpole*, than to represent the affairs of *Ireland* to him in a true light, not only without any view to myself, but to any party whatsoever: and, because I understood the affairs of that kingdom tolerably well, and observed the representations he had received were such as I could not agree to, my principal design was to set him right, not only for the service of *Ireland*, but likewise of *England*, and of his own administration.

I failed very much in my design; for, I saw, he had conceived opinions from the examples and practices of the present and some former governors, which I could not reconcile to the notions I had of liberty, a possession always understood by the *British* nation to be the inheritance of a human creature.

Vous Autres. You others.

Angry with ______. Walpole.

Sir *Robert Walpole* was pleased to enlarge very much upon the subject of Ireland, in a manner so alien from what I conceived to be rights and privileges of a subject of *England*, that I did not think proper to debate the matter with him so much as I otherwise might, because I found it would be in vain. I shall, therefore, without entering into dispute, make bold to mention to your Lordship some few grievances of that kingdom, as it consisteth of a people, who, beside a natural right of enjoying the privileges of subjects, have also a claim of merit from their extraordinary loyalty to the present King and his Family.

First, That all persons born in *Ireland* are called and treated as *Irishmen*, although their fathers and grandfathers were born in *England;* and their predecessors having been conquerors of *Ireland*, it is humbly conceived they ought to be on as good a foot as any subjects of *Britain*, according to the practice of all other nations, and particularly of the *Greeks* and *Romans.*

Secondly, That they are denied the natural liberty of exporting their manufactures to any country which is not engaged in a war with *England.*

Thirdly, That whereas there is a University in *Ireland*, founded by Queen *Elizabeth*, where youth are instructed with a much stricter discipline than either in *Oxford* or *Cambridge*, it lieth under the greatest discouragements, by filling all the principal employments, civil and ecclesiastical, with persons from *England*, who have neither interest, property, acquaintance, nor alliance, in that kingdom; contrary to the practice of all other States in *Europe* which are governed by viceroys, at least what hath never been used without the utmost discontents of the people.

Fourthly, That several of the bishops sent over to *Ireland*, having been clergymen of obscure condition, and without other distinction than that of chaplains to the governors, do frequently invite over their old acquaintance or kindred, to whom they bestow the best preferments in their gift. The like may be said of the judges, who take with them one or two dependents, to whom they give their countenance, and who, consequently, without other merit, grow immediately into the chief business of their courts. The same practice is followed by all others in civil employments, if they have a cousin, a valet, or footman, in their family, born in *England.*

Fifthly, That all civil employments, grantable in reversion, are given to persons who reside in *England.*

. . .

I think it manifest, that whatever circumstances can possibly contribute to make a country poor and despicable, are all united with respect to *Ireland.* The nation controled by laws to which they do not consent, disowned by their brethren and countrymen, refused the liberty not only of trading with their own manufactures but even their native commodities, forced to seek for justice many hundred miles by sea and land, rendered in a manner incapable of serving their King and country in any employment of honour, trust, or profit; and all this without the least demerit: while the governors sent over thither can possibly have no affection to the people, further than what is instilled into them by their own justice and love of mankind (which do not always operate); and whatever they please to represent hither is never called in question.

. . .

What part of these grievances may be thought proper to be redressed by so wise and great a minister as Sir *Robert Walpole,* he perhaps will please to consider; especially because they have been all brought upon that kingdom since the Revolution, which, however, is a blessing annually celebrated there with the greatest zeal and sincerity.

I most humbly entreat your Lordship to give this paper to Sir *Robert Walpole,* and desire him to read it, which he may do in a few minutes. I am, with the greatest respect, my Lord, | Your Lordship's, | Most obedient humble servant | Jon. Swift.

Swift to Mrs. Howard

Wearing Irish Wool

[October 1726]

Madam
Being perpetually teazed with the Remembrance of you by the sight of Your Ring on my Finger my patience at last is at an End, and in order to be revenged I here send you a Piece of Irish Plad made in Imitation of the Indian, wherein our Workmen here are grown so expert, that in this kind of Stuff they are said to excel that which comes from the Indies and because our Ladyes are too proud to wear what is made at home, the Workman is forced to run a gold Thread through the middle, and sell it as Indian. But I ordered him to leave out that Circumstance, that you may be clad in Irish

Stuff, and in my Livery. But I beg you will not tell any Parliem[t] man from whence you had this Plad, otherwise out of Malice they will make a Law to cut off all our Weavers Fingers. I must likewise tell you, to prevent Your Pride, my Intention is to use you very scurvily; for my reall Design is that when the Princess asks you where you got that fine Night-gown, you are to say, that it is an Irish Plad sent you by the Dean of St Patrick's, who with his most humble Duty to Her Royal Highness is ready to make her another such Present, at the terrible Expence of eight shillings and three pence a Yard, if she will descend to honor Ireland with receiving and wearing it. And in Recompence, I who govern the Vulgar will take Care to have Her Royal Highness's health drank by five hundred Weavers as an Encourager of the Irish Manufactury. And I command you to, add that I am no Courtier, nor have any Thing to ask.

Swift to Mrs. Howard

Mercenary Yahoo

[Dublin Nov[r] 27th 1726]

Madam.

When I received your Letter I thought it the most unaccountable one I ever saw in my Life, and was not able to comprehend three words of it together. The Perverseness of your Lines astonished me, which tended downwards to the right on one Page, and upward in the two others. This I thought impossible to be done by any Person who did not squint with both Eyes; an Infirmity I never observed in you. However, one thing I was pleased with, that after you had writ me *down*, you repented, and writ me *up*. But I continued four days at a loss for your meaning, till a Bookseller sent me the Travells of one Cap[tn] Gulliver, who proved a very good Explainer, although at the same time, I thought it hard to be forced to read a Book of seven hundred Pages in order to understand a Letter of fifty lines; especially since those of our Faculty are already but too much pestered with Commentators. The Stuffs you require are making, because the Weaver piques himself upon having them in perfection, but he has read Gulliver's Book, and has no Conception of what you mean by returning Money, for he is become a Proselyte of the Houyhnhnms, whose great Principle (if I rightly remember) is Benevolence. And as to my self, I am rightly affronted with such a base Proposall, that I am determined to complain of you to her Royal Highness, that you are a mercenary Yahoo fond of shining Pebbles. What have I to do with you or your Court further than to show the Esteem I have for your Person, because you happen to deserve it, and my Gratitude to Her Royall Highness, who was pleased, a little to distinguish me; which, by the way is the greatest Compliment I ever made, and may probably be the last. For I am not such a prostitute Flatterer as Gulliver; whose chief Study is to extenuate the Vices, and magnify the Virtues, of Mankind, and perpetually dins our Ears with the Praises of his Country, in the midst of Corruptions, and for that Reason alone, hath found so many readers; and probably will have a Pension, which, I suppose, was his chief design in writing: As for his Compliments to the Ladyes, I can easily forgive him as a naturall Effect of that Devotion which our Sex always ought to pay to Yours.

Swift to Alexander Pope

Improbable Lies

Dublin, Nov. [27] 1726

I am just come from answering a Letter of Mrs. Howard's writ in such mystical terms, that I should never have found out the meaning, if a Book had not been sent me called *Gulliver's Travellers*, of which you say so much in yours. I read the Book over, and in the second volume observe several passages which appear to be patched and altered, and the style of a different sort (unless I am much mistaken) Dr. Arbuthnot likes the Projectors least, others you tell me, the Flying island; some think it wrong to be so hard upon whole Bodies or Corporations, yet the general opinion is, that reflections on particular persons are most to be blamed: so that in these cases, I think the best method is to let censure and opinion take their course. A Bishop here said, that Book was full of improbable lies, and for his part, he hardly believed a word of it; and so much for Gulliver.

"The Prince of Lilliput" to "Stella"

[11 March 1726–7]

†**‡*
In *European* characters and *English* thus;

The high and mighty prince Egroego born to the most puissant empire of the *East*,

Unto Stella, the most resplendent glory of the *Western* hemisphere, sendeth health and happiness.

Brightest Princess,

That invincible heroe, the Man Mountain, fortunately arriving at our coasts some years ago, delivered us from ruin by conquering the fleets and armies of our enemies, and gave us hopes of a durable peace and happiness. But now the martial people of *Blefuscu*, encouraged from his absence, have renewed the war, to revenge upon us the loss and disgrace they suffered by our valiant champion.

The fame of your superexcellent person and virtue, and the huge esteem which that great general has for you, urged as in this our second distress to sue for your favour. In order to which we have sent our able and trusty Nardac Koorbnilob, requesting, That if our general does yet tread upon the terrestrial globe, you, in compassion for us, would prevail upon him to take another voyage for our deliverance.

And, lest any apprehensions of famine amongst us, should render Nardac mountain averse to the undertaking, we signify to you, that we have stored our folds, our coops, our granaries and cellars with plenty of provision for a long supply of the wastes to be made by his capacious stomach.

And furthermore, because as we hear you are not so well as we could wish, we beg you would compleat our happiness by venturing your most valuable person along with him into our country; where, by the salubrity of our finer air and diet, you will soon recover your health and stomach.

In full assurance of your complying goodness, we have sent you some provision for your voyage, and we shall with impatience wait for your safe arrival in our kingdom. Most illustrious lady, farewel. | Prince Egroego.

Dated the 11th day of the 6th Moon, in the 2001 year of the *Lilliputian* aera.

Swift to John Wheldon

Longitude

Holy. Sept. 27, 1727

I understand not Mathematicks, but have been formerly troubled too much with Projectors of the Longitude to my great Mortification and some

---

Koorbnilob. Anagram for Bolingbroke.

John Wheldon. Either a "crackpot speculator" or, as McMinn suggests (1994, pp. 113–14), a "prankster" using a pseudonym. Swift wrote this letter during his nightmarish week stranded at the port of Holyhead, during which he also wrote "Holyhead. September 25, 1727" and "Ireland." For more about the large prize offered by Parliament in 1714 to anyone who could solve the navigational problem of determining longitude at sea, see the note on p. 209.

Charges by encouraging them. It is only to Mathematicians you must apply. Newton, Halley, and Keil have all told me they doubted the Thing was impossible. If you can demonstrate that you have found it, there is, I hear, a course taken that you may discover it in London without being defrauded of your Invention. One of my Projectors cut his Throat, and the other was found an Imposter. This is all I can say; but am confident you would deceive others, or are deceived yourself.

Swift to Alexander Pope

Stranger in a Strange Land

Aug. 11, 1729.

As to this country, there have been three terrible years dearth of corn, and every place strowed with beggars, but dearths are common in better climates, and our evils here lie much deeper. Imagine a nation the two-thirds of whose revenues are spent out of it, and who are not permitted to trade with the other third, and where the pride of the women will not suffer them to wear their own manufactures even where they excel what come from abroad: This is the true state of Ireland in a very few words. These evils operate more every day and the kingdom is absolutely undone, as I have been telling it often in print these ten years past.

What I have said requires your forgiveness; but I had a mind for once to let you know the state of our affairs, and my reason for being more moved than perhaps becomes a Clergyman, and a piece of a philosopher: and perhaps the increase of years and disorders may hope for some allowance to complaints, especially when I may call my self a stranger in a strange land.

Swift to Alexander Pope

Dublin's Anti-Catholicism

Dublin May 2d. 1730.

I must tell you that the Mortal Sin of your painter was praising a *Papist*, for we have no other zeal or merit than what arises from the utter detestation of your Religion. *Ludlow* in his Memoirs mentions one Lord Fitzwilliam with this Character, that he was a civil Person, *though a Papist*.

Swift to the Countess of Suffolk

A Dose to the Dead

[26 October 1731]

If any State-scribble writ here should happen to reach London, I entreat your Ladyship would continue to do me the justice of beleiving my innocence. Because I lately assured the D. of Dorset, that I would never have a hand in any such thing: and I gave him my reason before his Secretary; that, looking upon this Kingdom's condition as absolutely desperate, I would not prescribe a dose to the dead.

Swift to Mary Pendarves [Delany]

Sociable Evenings

[6 August 1733]

Madam, I have had one great, and not very usual, misfortune in my life, which was to come to a kingdom where I was utterly a stranger, when it was too late to make new friendships; every body worth knowing being already bespoke. As to the *many* friends I left in England when I first came over, they are either banished or dead, or by a tacit agreement we have dropt correspondence; and the *few* remaining, my ill health hath condemned me never to see again. Another ill circumstance is, that years have not hardened me; and therefore, when I lament my absence from those I love and esteem, I fly for a remedy to ill-nature: I recollect whatever I found amiss in them; one was positive, another was a bad listener; a third talked too much, and a fourth was too silent, and so on. For these reasons, I would give half my goods that I had known you five times more than I did; and had the forecast to watch all your behaviour till I could have found something that was wrong, though it was in the least significant part of your conduct; and upon that one point I would have forced my memory and observation to dwell, as some little cure for the vexation of despairing ever to see you again. Pray, Madam, will you be pleased, in mere mercy, to send me the

---

Philological Quarterly 74:4 (1995): 428–30.

names and places of abode of your enemies and censurers (for God forbid you should want either): after which, I will desire a commerce of letters with them, whereof you shall be the subject; and then I shall be able to talk ill of you to myself, as well as to other people, without being believed by either.

...

Dr. Delany is absolutely a country squire; he hath given up his town-house; I have not seen or heard of him these five weeks; we all think he hath acted exceedingly wrong. He hath a fortune sufficient to live as he pleases in this cheap kingdom, and grow rich besides. Neither he nor his lady are naturally inclined to solitude, which however in the winter season he must be condemned to, and in evenings the whole year. I extremely disapprove of this monkish way of living. The great and only happiness of Dublin is the sociable evening meetings, in which it much exceeds London, especially (with submission to your Whiggism) since the Queen's death. And indeed out of mere poverty we are dropping them here. There is but one family in all Dublin where I can get a dinner; and that is with Dr. Helsham, which I compass once or twice a month. All other days I eat my chicken alone like a king, or carry my bread, meat, and wine, to some country parson 4 or 5 miles off. But if you come over, I will give you a dinner once a week, whereof your share will cost me eighteen pence, and six pence for your chair. I am now going to dine, chicken 6d. pint of Fr. wine 8d. bread 1/2, butter for sauce 1d.; total 1s. 3 1/2 d. dressing 0 0 0. In London the bill would be, a chicken 1s.6d. wine 2s.6d. butter 3d. bread 1d. dressing 3d.; total 4s.7d. And would I live in London? And will not you live in Ireland, with so fair an invitation? Well, I hear all you say, but am not convinced. The apology you make in the postscript is, in few words, a compound of falsehood and affectation. You are ashamed, you say, of your blunders: and I cannot observe one. I suppose it is a civil way of reproaching mine; for my ill head makes me always mistake syllables, letters, words, and sometimes half sentences; you may see how often I am forced to interline. Pray God preserve you! I am, with the truest respect and great esteem, Madam, your most obedient and humble servant,

J. Swift

Dr. Delany. Swift's friend, Patrick Delany, whom Mary Pendarves would go on to marry in 1743. See pp. 347–353.

Part Two

EIGHTEENTH-CENTURY CONTEXTS

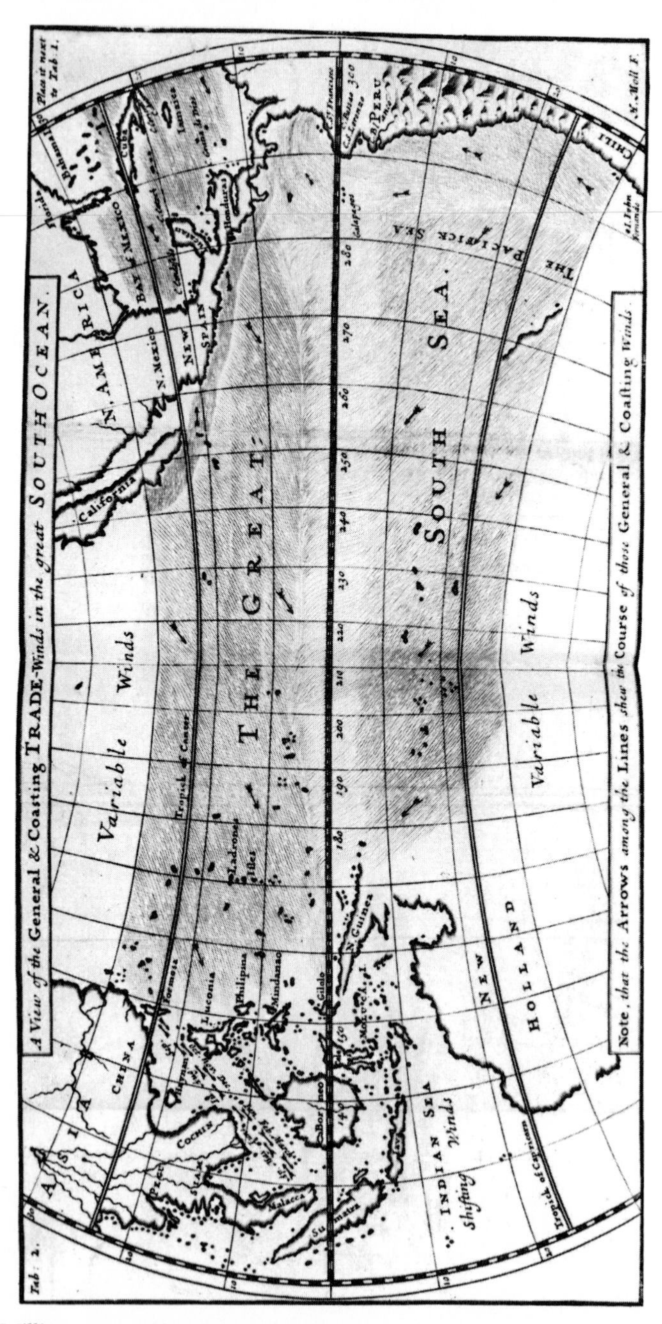

William Dampier's *Discourse on Winds* (1699), his most respected work, featured his cartographic work in the South Sea. The map reproduced here comes from a 1729 reprint, *Mr. Dampier's Voyages to the Bay of Campeachy,* in volume II of a four-volume compilation entitled *A Collection of Voyages* (1729).

WILLIAM DAMPIER (1652–1715)

William Dampier, a buccaneer-scientist, circumnavigated the globe several times in the late seventeenth and early eighteenth centuries. His greatest success, upon publishing his unvarnished accounts of these voyages, came as an author. For more about his influential roles in the histories of travel-narration, science, literature, and piracy, see pp. 21–22, 26.

DUNG-HURLING MONKEYS ON THE ISLE OF TRIST, 1676

The first excerpt from his writings included here describes an incident of 1676, when Dampier was in Campeachy (now Campeche, Mexico), in an island in the bay off the northern coast of the Yucatan. Dampier was there harvesting logwood, a tropical tree useful in the making of dye. His companions in this enterprise were pirates, and Dampier's career continued to involve buccaneering as well as mapmaking, scientific observation, and journal keeping. This account of dung-hurling monkeys on the Isle of Triste first appeared in his Voyages and Descriptions *(London, 1699). This volume also contained his well-known* "Discourse on Winds"*—a respected contribution to hydrography—and the map of the South Sea reprinted on p. 390. Like all of his writings, Dampier's account of Campeachy was reprinted many times thereafter.*

The Monkeys that are in these Parts are the ugliest I ever saw. They are much bigger than a Hare, and have great Tails about Two foot and a half long. The underside of their tails is all bare, with a black hard skin; but the upper-side, and all the Body is covered with coarse, long, black star[t]ing Hair. These Creatures keep together 20 or 30 in a Company, and ramble over the Woods; leaping from Tree to Tree. If they meet with a single

From *A Collection of Voyages*, Vol. 2, *Mr. Dampier's Voyages to the Bay of Campeachy* (London, 1729), 59–60.

Person they will threaten to devour him. When I have been alone I have been afraid to shoot them, especially the first Time I met them. They were a great Company dancing from Tree to Tree over my Head; chattering and making a terrible Noise; and a great many grim Faces, and Shewing antick Gestures. Some broke down dry Sticks and threw at me; others scattered their Urine and Dung about my Ears; at last one bigger than the rest, came to a small Limb just over my Head; and leaping directly at me, made me start back; but the Monkey caught hold of the Bough with the tip of his Tail; and there continued swinging to and fro, and making Mouths at me. ——— At last I past on, they still keeping me Company, with the like menacing Postures, till I came to our Huts.

JEOLY, THE "PAINTED PRINCE"

The second series of excerpts all come from Dampier's most well-known work, A New Voyage Round the World *(1697). The excerpts focus on Dampier's laconic account of Jeoly, an enslaved South Sea island native whom he acquired in 1690. This account moves geographically from the Philippines and Spice Islands of Indonesia, to India (where Dampier obtains Jeoly), and then back to England. As a sample of exotica, Jeoly's elaborately tattooed body constituted the particular commodity he represented. The public appetite in England for human spectacles absorbed Jeoly into its circuit of raree shows, where he was advertised on handbills and displayed as the "Painted Prince." A few months after this routine began, Jeoly died in Oxford of smallpox. The term* Pagally, *used below in the plural, refers to a custom in Mindanao, as Dampier has explained earlier: a* Pagally *is "an innocent Platonick friend of the other sex."*

•

For the Islands *Meangis*, which I mentioned in the beginning of this Chapter, lye within twenty Leagues of *Mindanao*. These are three small Islands that abound with Gold and Cloves, if I may credit my Author Prince *Jeoly*, who was born on one of them, and was at that time a Slave in the City of *Mindanao*. He might have been purchased by us of his Master for a small matter, as he was afterwards by Mr. *Moody*, (who came hither to trade, and laded a Ship with Clove-Bark) and by transporting him home to his own Country, we might have gotten a Trade there. But of Prince *Jeoly* I shall speak more hereafter. These Islands are as yet probably unknown to the

---

A New Voyage Round the World (Argonaut Press #2: New York: Da Capo Press, 1970). A facsimile of the 1927 Argonaut edition ed. Sir Albert Gray.

J. Savage, *Prince Giolo*, ca. 1700. From *Memoirs of John Evelyn*, 1824. Apparently based on Dampier's description, and perhaps as well on the advertising poster circulated by Jeoly/Giolo's exhibitor in 1692.

Dutch, who as I said before, indeavour to ingross all the Spice into their own Hands.

The other Passage I shall speak of, that occurred during this Interval of the Tour I made from *Achin*, is with Relation to the painted Prince, whom I brought with me into *England*, and who died at *Oxford*. For while I was at *Fort St. George*, about *April* 1690, there arrived a Ship called the *Mindanao*-Merchant, laden with Clove-bark from *Mindanao*.

By this time I was very intimately acquainted with Mr. *Moody*, and was importun'd by him to go with him, and to be Gunner of the Fort there. I always told him I had a great desire to go to the Bay of *Bengal*, and that I had now an offer to go thither with Captain *Metcalf*, who wanted a Mate, and had already spoke to me. Mr. *Moody*, to encourage me to go with him, told me, that if I would go with him to *Indrapore*, he would buy a small Vessel there, and send me to the Island *Meangis*, Commander of her; and that I should carry Prince *Jeoly* and his Mother with me, (that being their Country) by which means I might gain a Commerce with his People for Cloves.

Thus it was that I came to have this painted Prince, whose Name was *Jeoly*, and his Mother. They were born on a small Island called *Meangis*, which is once or twice mentioned in *Chap*. XIII. I saw the Island twice, and two more close by it: Each of the three seemed to be about four or five Leagues round, and of a good heighth. *Jeoly* himself told me, that they all three abounded with Gold, Cloves and Nutmegs: For I shewed him some of each sort several times, and he told me in the *Malayan* Language, which he spake indifferent well, *Meangis Hadda Madochala se Bullawan:* That is, there is abundance of Gold at *Meangis*. *Bullawan*, I have observed to be the common Word for Gold at *Mindanao*; but whether the proper *Malayan* Word I know not, for I found much difference between the *Malayan* Language as it was spoken at *Mindanao*, and the Language on the Coast of *Malacca* and *Achin*. When I shewed him Spice, he would not only tell me that there was *Madochala*, that is, abundance; but to make it appear more plain, he would also show me the Hair of his Head, a thing frequent among all the *Indians* that I have met with, to show their Hair, when they would express more than they can number. He told me also, that his Father was *Raja* of the Island where they lived: That there were not above Thirty Men on the Island, and about one Hundred Women: That he himself had five Wives and eight Children, and that one of his Wives painted him.

He was painted all down the Breast, between his Shoulders behind; on his Thighs (mostly) before; and in the Form of several broad Rings, or Bracelets round his Arms and Legs. I cannot liken the Drawings to any Figure of Animals, or the like; but they were very curious, full of great variety of Lines, Flourishes, Chequered-Work, &c. keeping a very graceful Proportion, and appearing very artificial, even to Wonder, especially that upon and between his Shoulder-blades. By the Account he gave me of the manner of doing it, I understood that the Painting was done in the same manner, as the *Jerusalem* Cross is made in Mens Arms, by pricking the Skin, and rubbing in a Pigment. But whereas Powder is used in making the *Jerusalem* Cross, they at *Meangis* use the Gum of a Tree beaten to Powder, called by the *English*, Dammer, which is used instead of Pitch in many parts of *India*. He told me, that most of the Men and Women on the Island were thus painted: And also that they had all Ear-rings made of Gold, and Gold Shackles about their Legs and Arms: That their common Food, of the Produce of the Land, was Potatoes and Yams: That they had plenty of Cocks and Hens; but no other tame Fowl. He said, that Fish (of which he was a great Lover, as wild *Indians* generally are) was very plentiful about the Island; and that they had Canoas, and went a fishing frequently in them; and that they often visited the other two small Islands, whose Inhabitants spake the same Language as they did; which was so unlike the *Malayan*, which he had learnt while he was a Slave at *Mindanao*, that when his Mother and he were talking together in their *Meangian* Tongue, I could not understand one Word they said. And indeed all the *Indians* who spake *Malayan*, who are the trading and politer sort, lookt on these *Meangians* as a kind of *Barbarians;* and upon any occasion of dislike, would call them *Bobby*, that is, Hogs; the greatest Expression of Contempt that can be, especially from the Mouth of *Malayans*, who are generally *Mahometans;* and yet the *Malayans* every where call a Woman *Babby*, by a Name not much different, and *Mamma* signifies a Man; tho' these two last Words properly denote Male and Female: And as *Ejam* signifies a Fowl, so *Ejam Mamma* is a Cock, and *Ejam Babbi* is a Hen. But this by the way.

He said also that the Customs of those other Isles, and their manner of living, was like theirs, and that they were the only People with whom they had any Converse: And that one time as he, with his Father, Mother and Brother, with two or three Men more were going to one of these other Islands, they were driven by a strong Wind on the Coast of *Mindanao*, where they were taken by the Fishermen of that Island, and carried ashore, and sold as Slaves; they being first stript of their Gold Ornaments. I did not see any of the Gold that they wore, but there were great Holes in their Ears, by which it was manifest that they had worn some Ornaments in them.

Jeoly was sold to one *Michael* a *Mindanayan*, that spoke good *Spanish*, and commonly waited on *Raja Laut*, serving him as our Interpreter, where the *Raja* was at a loss in any word, for *Michael* understood it better. He did often beat and abuse his painted Servant, to make him work, but all in vain; for neither fair means, threats nor blows, would make him work as he would have him. Yet he was very timerous, and could not endure to see any sort of Weapons; and he often told me that they had no Arms at *Meangis*, they having no Enemies to fight with.

I knew this *Michael* very well while we were at *Mindanao:* I suppose that Name was given him by the *Spaniards*, who baptized many of them at the time when they had footing at that Island: But at the departure of the *Spaniards*, they were *Mahometans* again as before. Some of our People lay at this *Michael*'s House, whose Wife and Daughter were *Pagallies* to some of them. I often saw *Jeoly* at his Master *Michael*'s House, and when I came to have him so long after, he remembered me again. I did never see his Father nor Brother, nor any of the others that were taken with them; but *Jeoly* came several times aboard our Ship when we lay at *Mindanao*, and gladly accepted of such Victuals as we gave him; for his Master kept him at very short Commons.

Prince *Jeoly* lived thus a Slave at *Mindanao* four or five Years, till at last Mr. *Moody* bought him and his Mother for 60 Dollars, and as is before related, carried him to *Fort St. George*, and from thence along with me to *Bencouli*. Mr. *Moody* stayed at *Bencouli* about three Weeks, and then went back with Captain *Howel*, to *Indrapore*, leaving *Jeoly* and his Mother with me. They lived in a House by themselves without the Fort. I had no Employment for them; but they both employed themselves. She used to make and mend their own Cloaths, at which she was not very expert, for they wear no Cloaths at *Meangis*, but only a Cloath about their Wastes: And he busied himself in making a Chest with four Boards, and a few Nails that he begged of me. It was but an ill-shaped odd Thing, yet he was as proud of it as if it had been the rarest Piece in the World. After some time they were both taken sick, and though I took as much care of them as if they had been my Brother and Sister, yet she died. I did what I could to comfort *Jeoly;* but he took on extremely, insomuch that I feared him also. Therefore I caused a Grave to be made presently, to hide her out of his sight. I had her shrouded decently in a piece of new Callico; but *Jeoly* was not so satisfied, for he wrapt all her Cloaths about her, and two new pieces of Chints that Mr. *Moody* gave her, saying that they were his Mother's , and she must have 'em. I would not disoblige him for fear of endangering his Life; and I used all possible means to recover his Health; but I found little Amendment while we stay'd here.

In the little printed Relation that was made of him when he was shown for a Sight in *England*, there was a romantick Story of a beautiful Sister of his a Slave with them at *Mindanao;* and of the Sultan's falling in Love with her; but these were Stories indeed. They reported also that this Paint was of such Virtue, that Serpents, and venomous Creatures would flee from him, for which reason, I suppose, they represented so many Serpents scampering about in the printed Picture that was made of him. But I never knew any Paint of such Virtue: and as for *Jeoly*, I have seen him as much afraid of Snakes, Scorpions, or Centapees, as my self.

Having given this account of the Ship that left me at *Nicobar*, and of my painted Prince whom I brought with me to *Bencouli*, I shall now proceed on with the Relation of my Voyage thence to *England*, after I have given this short Account of the occasion of it, and the manner of my getting away.

My stay ashore here was but two Days, to get Refreshments for my self and *Jeoly*, whom I carried ashore with me: and he was very diligent to pick up such things as the Islands afforded, carrying ashore with him a Bag, which the People of the Isle filled with Roots for him. They flock'd about him, and seemed to admire him much. This was the last place where I had him at my own disposal, for the Mate of the Ship, who had Mr. *Moody*'s share in him, left him entirely to my management, I being to bring him to *England*. But I was no sooner arrived in the *Thames*, but he was sent ashore to be seen by some eminent Persons; and I being in want of Money, was prevailed upon to sell first, part of my share in him, and by degrees all of it. After this I heard he was carried about to be shown as a Sight, and that he died of the Small-pox at *Oxford*.

SIR WILLIAM PETTY (1623–87)

William Petty, like Lemuel Gulliver, was trained as a physician in Leiden, where he may also have acquired an interest in the making of maps. Petty eventually abandoned medicine in favor of demography and cartography. In addition to producing the first general atlas of Ireland, Petty is among the inventors of "political arithmetic." Petty's friend, the diarist John Evelyn, thought him unequalled in the entire world in his grasp of the related arts of improving trade and governing a plantation. The two excerpts reprinted here come from *The Political Anatomy of Ireland* (1691). The first excerpt is the preface to this book; the second, a brief passage in which Petty defends absentee landlords in Ireland. Although Petty is famous for statistic-laden discourse about aggregate production and consumption, these excerpts give the lie to the effect of neutrality that quantitative arguments often achieve. For more on Petty's roles in intellectual history and in Irish history, see pp. 15–17.

FROM *THE POLITICAL ANATOMY OF IRELAND*

I. The Author's Preface

Sir Francis Bacon, *in his* Advancement of Learning, *hath made a judicious* Parallel *in many particulars, between the* Body Natural, *and* Body Politick, *and between the Arts of preserving both in Health and Strength: And it is as reasonable, that as* Anatomy *is the best foundation of one, so also of the other; and that to practice upon the Politick, without knowing the* Symmetry, Fabrick, *and* Proportion *of it, is as* casual *as the practice of Old-women and Empyricks.*

Now, because Anatomy *is not only necessary in Physicians, but laudable in every Philosophical person whatsoever; I therefore, who profess no Politicks, have, for my curiosity, at large attempted* the first Essay of Political Anatomy.

Furthermore, as Students in Medicine, practice their inquiries upon cheap and common Animals, *and such whose actions they are best acquainted with, and where there is the least confusion and perplexure o[f] Parts; I have chosen* Ireland *as such a* Political Animal, *who is scarce Twenty years old; where the* Intrigue *of* State *is not very complicate and with which I have been conversant from an* Embrion; *and in which, if I have done amiss, the fault may be easily mended by another.*

'Tis true, that curious Diffections *cannot be made without variety of proper Instruments; whereas I have had only a commin* Knife *and a* Clout, *instead of the many more helps which such a Work requires: However, my rude approaches being enough to find whereabout the Liver and Spleen, and Lungs lye, tho' not to discern the Lymphatick Vessels, the* Plexus, Choroidus, *the* Volvuli *of vessels within the Testicles; yet not knowing, that even what I have here readily done, was much considered, or indeed thought useful by others, I have ventur'd to* begin a new *Work, which, when Corrected and Enlarged by better Hands and Helps, I believe will tend to the Peace and Plenty of my Country; besides which, I have no other end.*

II. [Absentee Landlords]

Lastly, Many think that *Ireland* is much impoverished, or at least the money thereof much exhausted, by reason of Absentees, who are such as having Lands in *Ireland*, do live out of the Kingdom, and do therefore think it just that such, according to former Statutes, should lose their said Estates.

Which Opinion I oppose, as both unjust, inconvenient, and frivolous. For 1st. If a man carry Money or other Effects out of *England* to purchase Lands in *Ireland*, why should not the Rents, Issues and Profits of the same

---

The Political Anatomy of Ireland (Shannon: Irish University Press, 1970).

Land return into *England*, with the same Reason that the Money of *England* was diminished to buy it?

2. I suppose ¼ of the Land of *Ireland* did belong to the Inhabitants of *England*, and that the same lay all in one place together; why may not the said quarter of the whole Land be cut off from the other three sent into *England*, were it possible so to do? and if so, why may not the Rents of the same be actually sent, without prejudice to the other three parts of the Interessors thereof?

3. If all men were bound to spend the Proceed of their Lands upon the Land itself; then as all the Proceed of *Ireland*, ought to be spent in *Ireland;* so all the Proceed of one County of *Ireland*, ought to be spent in the fame; of one Barony, in the same Barony; and so Parish and Mannor; and at length it would follow, that every eater ought to avoid what he hath eaten upon the same Turf where the same grew. Moreover, this equal spreading of Wealth would destroy all Splendor and Ornament; for if it were not fit that one place should be more splendid than another, so also that no one man should be greater or richer than another; for if so, then the Wealth, suppose of *Ireland*, being perhaps 11 Millions, being divided among 1,100 M. people, then no one man having above 10 l. he could Probably build no House worth above 3 l. which would be to leave the face of Beggery upon the whole Nation: And withal such Parity would beget Anarchy and Confusion.

REASONS HUMBLY OFFER'D . . .

Unlikely to edify, this pamphlet is included here for its historical interest only. Crude propaganda supporting the notion of castrating "lascivious Jesuits" had already surfaced during the Thirty Years War of the previous century. A 1620 broadside from Germany, illustrated with a clumsy woodcut, made its parallel argument that "The good fathers now/Must give up their Fraterculos*" (that is, "little brothers"; Beller, Plate 3). The first version of the pamphlet was printed by A. Baldwin in London in 1700. When* Reasons Humbly offer'd *was anonymously reprinted in Dublin in 1710, minimal changes were made.* England *was changed to* Ireland, *and the reigning monarch (Queen Anne) was updated. One infers from this easy continuity an axis of anti-Catholic sentiment running from Westminster to Dublin Castle. As I have noted in the introduction (pp. 28–30),* Reasons Humbly offer'd *anticipated policy discussions in 1719 that involved the Irish Privy Council, the Irish Parliament, and the English Privy Council.*

REASONS
Humbly offer'd to both Houses of
PARLIAMENT,
For a Law to Enact the
CASTRATION,
OR
GELDING
OF
Popish Eccelesiastics,
In this KINGDOM
As the best way to prevent the Growth of Popery

Dryden's *EPILOGUE to the Spanish Fryar.*

Un-Man the Fryar, your Wives and Daughters soon will leave their Cells.
When they have lost the sound of *Aran's* Bells[1]
LONDON Printed, And Re-Printed in Dublin, 1710.
Reasons Humbly offer'd for a Law to Enact the Castration or Gelding of Popish Eccelesiastics, &c.
The Honourable House of Commons having been Pleased to take into their Consideration the unaccountable growth of Popery amongst us: It is thought fit for that end, to publish what follows.

We may, without intrenching upon the Province of Divines, make bold to assert, That when the Church of *Rome* is call'd in the Sacred Scriptures,[2] *The Mother of Harlots, and of the Abominations of the Earth;* there's something else meant by it than a mere Religious Impurity, or going a whoring after false Gods, as their Saints and Angels, and multitudes of Mediators

---

[1]The passage actually reads

> Unman the Friar, and leave the holy drone
> To hum in his forsaken hive alone;
> He'll work no honey when his sting is gone.
> Your wives and daughters soon will leave the cells,
> When they have lost the sound of Aaron's bells (*Epilogue,* 41–45).

The brother of Moses and the first high priest of Israel, Aaron had a special robe with bells and pomegranates hanging down from its hem.

[2]No such identification exists in scripture. Protestant glosses on the Book of Revelation, however, going back to the Geneva Bible of the sixteenth century, made this equation a Protestant commonplace.

Reasons Humbly offer'd. . . (Dublin, 1710). Reprinted here from copy in Trinity College Dublin Library (shelfmark P. gg. 9. no. 7). Edited by volume editor with assistance from Lori Molinari.

between God and Men, undoubtedly are. We need but cast our Eye upon *Platina's* Lives of the Popes,[3] and turn over a few leaves of the Histories of most Nations of *Europe*, to be convinc'd that the *Romish* Clergy have ever since the Pope's Usurpation been branded with Uncleanness. The wanton Observation made by *Henry* the 4th of *France*, as he passed one day betwixt a Friary and a Nunnery. *That the latter was the Barn, and the former were the Thrashers*, was found to have too much of truth in it, in all those Countreys where Monasteries were overturn'd or search'd upon the Reformation. The vast heaps of Childrens Bones that were found in Draw wells, and other places about them, were speaking, tho not living Monuments of the horrid Impurity, as well as barbarous Cruelty of those pretended Religious Communities. To insist any more upon this, were to accuse the Age of inexcusable Ignorance in History, and therefore we shall conclude this Introduction with an Observation from *Fox's Acts and Monuments*.[4] That before the Reformation the Priests alone were computed to have 100000 Whores in *ENGLAND;* which must be understood of what the Dialect of those times call'd *Lemmans*, from the French, *L'Amante*, that is, in the modern Phrase, *kept Misses;* besides their promiscuous Whoredoms with the Women, they confessed, &c.

This horrid Uncleanness of the *Romish* Clergy cannot appear incredible to those who consider, that besides their being judicially given up of God to work all manner of Uncleaness with greediness, their Vow of Chastity, and being forbidden to Marry, lays them under a temptation peculiar to their Order.

It will yet appear less strange, if we consider their way of living, and opportunity: They eat and drink of the best, are Caressed in all Families of their Way; have an Advantage of knowing the Inclinations, and private converse with Women by their Auricular Confession, and by their pretended Power to give Pardon; have a Door open to perswade the Committing of one Sin for expiating another, and accordingly improve it.

This is so far from being a Calumny, that the Popish Laity themselves in all Ages and Countreys have been sensible of it; and therefore most of the

---

[3] *Platina's* Lives of the Popes. Bartolomeo Sacchi Platina was a fifteenth-century Italian humanist who wrote on a wide variety of subjects, including history, politics, philosophy, and rhetoric. His *Liber de vita Christi ac omnium pontificum* (1st ed., Venice, 1479) was dedicated to Sixtus IV.

[4] *Fox's Acts and Monuments.* John Foxe was an English Puritan preacher and author of *Actes and monuments of these latter and perilous dayes.* Popularly known as *The Book of Martyrs* (English translation 1563), this widely read book graphically described the ways various Protestants had suffered for their faith, and it thereby fueled English animosity toward Roman Catholicism.

Popish Kingdoms sollicited the Council of *Trent* to allow Priests marriage. But the Pope, for Reasons we shall touch anon, did not think fit to grant it; tho' *Aeneas Silvius* himself, afterwards Pope,[5] was so fully convinc'd of the necessity of it, that he said, *Tho' Priests were forbidden to marry for very good Reasons, yet there were better Reasons to allow it.*

They that have Travel'd in Popish Countrey's, and observ'd their Priests and Monks, know, that generally speaking, they carry about them no marks of that Austerity and Mortification which they pretend to. They look as fat and generally fatter than other Men; which is an infallible Token that they fare as well, if not better, than others do. You shall see as white and plump a hand under a Monks Hood, as in any Family of Quality; and a Foot as clean and neat many times in a Sandal, as is to be found under a Spanish Leather Shoe and Silk Stocking: Nor is it any Secret, that in the Neighborhood of Convents there's as good Diet prepar'd for the use of Monks and Nuns, as comes to Gentlemens Tables. Nay, those very places of Retirement, with their large Gardens, adorn'd with Walks and Shades, and many times water'd by pleasant Fountains or murmuring Streams, together with their Idle way of living, seem to be accommodated to inspire them with amorous Sentiments, against which their Vows of Chastity, and the Rules of their Order, are so far from being Preservatives, that they only add Fewel to their Flames, and make them commit Sin with the higher relish. So that when they go abroad from their Monasterys, they are like so many fed Horses neighing, as the Scripture expresses it of the lustful *Jews*, after every Woman they see; and if they have not opportunity of giving vent to their Lusts that way, they many times do it by other methods, which Nature, as well as Religion forbids to name. This we may justly suppose to have been the Motive that induc'd *Emanuel de Saa*[6] in his Aphorisms to maintain that *Fornication, Adultery* and *Sodomy* did not make a Priest irregular, whereas *Marriage* did.

If besides their being forbidden to marry, we consider that they are provided for by the sweat of other Men's Faces, have not Families to take care

---

[5] *Aeneas Silvius* himself, afterwards Pope. Pius II, who served as Pope from 1458 to 1464, was born Enea Silvio Piccolomini. Remembered as a humanist, poet, and orator, he became increasingly concerned with organizing a crusade against the Turks following the fall of Constantinople (1453).

[6] *Emanuel de Saa.* Manoel de Sa (Saa) was a Portuguese Jesuit theologian of the sixteenth century. Among his works was *Aphorismi Confessariorum ex Doctorum sententiis collecti* (Venice, 1595). Forty years in the making, this theological treatise was censured in 1603. After some corrections, it was eventually removed from the Roman index of prohibited books in 1900.

of, have no hard Labour to mortify and keep them low, and are under no Obligation to study hard, we shall find that there's no reason to wonder if they be more inclinable to Venery than any other Men whatsoever: and since by Experience it is found to be so, forbidding them Marriages may well be call'd *a Doctrine of Devils*, both as to its Original and Effects. That it comes from the Devil, the Father of Lies, and by consequence the Anchor of every false Doctrine, is not to be controverted, since the Law of God and Nature commands us to increase and multiply, and fits us for it; and that it might be in a regular way, God himself instituted Marriage in Paradise, and the Apostle tells us, *that Marriage is honourable in all:* and that this Doctrine is Devilish in its effects, is evident from the horrid impurity of the *Romish* Clergy abovementioned [*sic*], and the mischiefs they do by it to particular Persons, Families, Kingdoms, and Common-wealths.

We come next to take a view of the Cause, why the Court of *Rome* does so stiffly insist on the Celibacy of their Clergy, which will further demonstrate the reasonableness of Guelding[7] them to prevent their infesting this Nation.

Tho' *Rome* pretends to have changed her Religion, and hath actually changed her form of Government, by taking an Ecclesiastical instead of a Temporal Head; yet it's visible she hath abated nothing of her Ambition, to be Mistress of the Universe, and did in a great measure effect it by her Papacy, to which so great a part of those called Christian Nations submitted before the Reformation. So as *Cataline*,[8] when *Rome* was Heathen, thought it necessary to debauch the Women, and then to carry on his Conspiracy against the Government by their Interest, because of the influence leud Women had upon the loose Rabble, and that they could either murder their Husbands, or bring them over to his Party. *Rome* since it became Antichristian, hath enjoin'd Celebacy [*sic*] upon her Clergy, that they might be rendered the more apt to debauch Women, and to make use of their Interest in order to deprive the Civil Magistrates of their Right, and to usurp the Temporal, as well as the Spiritual Sword.

1. Because they know that Nature having inclin'd all Men to propagate their Species, their Priests so and so Circumstantiated, as beforementioned, could nat [*sic*] possibly refrain from the Act, tho' they were not allow'd to do it in a regular way: and therefore so many Women as they de-

[7] Guelding. Obsolete form of gelding (*OED*).

[8] *Cataline.* Lucius Sergius Catilina (c. 108 B.C.–62 B.C.) is famous for having organized a major conspiracy that would have had implications throughout Italy. Marcus Tullius Cicero was instrumental in proving the guilt of Catiline, who was killed in a battle shortly thereafter.

bauch, which they knew by their Circumstances and Opportunity, must needs be innumerable, so many Proselytes they were sure of.

2. Because they knew that their Clergy being pamper'd and restrain'd from the use of the Marriage Bed, must needs be more inclinable to Venery than other Men, and consequently more pleasing Companions to insatiable Women, and therefore the better fitted for the practice of *creeping into Houses, and leading captive silly Women, laden with divers Lusts,*[9] as the Apostle expresses it.

3. Because they knew that their Clergy by this means having an Opportunity of bringing to their Lure a Buxom Wife, who perhaps has a sickly, weak, or absent Husband, a Green-Sickness Daughter, or a wanton Maid; they would by the same means become Masters in a manner of all that belong'd to the Family, have the command of their Purses, know all their Secrets, and improve all to the advantage of the See of *Rome,* which indulg'd them thus with a *Mahomet's* Paradise.[10]

4. By restraining their Clergy from Marriage, they knew it would make them the more impetuous to satisfy their desires; and that they might have the better Opportunity of doing it, they are enjoyn'd by their Directory in confessing Women, to examine them most as to the Sins of the Flesh, which they tell'em they must discover on pain of Damnation. This being a ready method to inflame them mutually, attended with Secrecy, and the Priests pretended Power of giving a Pardon, they knew it could not miss of the design'd Effect; they knew also that so many of those silly Women as they captivated, so many Champions and Advocates for their Religion they should have in Families, Courts, or elsewhere; for they might assure themselves that such Women would not easily part with a Religion that did so much gratify their depraved Appetites, by allowing them as many Men, tho' not Husbands, as they have Priests or Confessors: And therefore many of the wise Popish Laicks have been of Opinion themselves, that no Man ought to confess a Wife but her Husband and that a Daughter ought to be confessed by none but her Father.

5. Another, and that none of the least Reasons why they forbid Marriage to their Ecclesiastics, is, That if they had Wives or Families, they could not so easily be sent on Missions, and encompass Sea and Land to make

---

[9] *Creeping into Houses, and leading captive silly Women, laden with divers Lusts*—a quotation from 2 Tim. 4.6.

[10] Possibly a reference to the following passage from the Koran: "Those who work righteousness will enjoy Paradise at [*sic*] their Lord, with flowing streams. Forever they abide therein, with pure spouses, and blessings from God" (3:15; see also 2:25).

Proselytes. They would not be so ready, nor so fit to engage in Assassinations, Conspiracies, and Rebellions against Princes and States, at the Commands of their Superior: Nor could they by their Whoredoms so much propagate the Interest of the great Harlot; for then their Wives would be so many checks and spies upon them.

From all which it seems reasonable to infer, that the best way to rid this Kingdom of Popish Priests, and to prevent the growth of Popery, is to make a Law, that all of them who shall be discover'd in *Ireland*, shall be Gelded, as they are in *Sweden*[11]; where, since the same was Enacted into a Law, and practis'd upon a few of them, that Kingdom hath never been infested with Popish Clergy, or Plots, nor their Women reproach'd with want of Chastity.

This will appear the more reasonable, if we consider that the Havock they are allow'd to make of Womens Chastity, is one of the principal things that induces lustful Fellows to take *Romish* Orders upon them, and to engage in desperate Designs to promote the Interest of that Church. This any man may easily be convinc'd of, that will give himself leave to consider what dangers other men of better Principles, and who may have opportunities of satisfying Nature by lawful Marriage, do many times expose themselves to, for the Satisfaction of their bruitish Passions, and how they frequently sacrifice Honour, Interest, and Estate, with the Peace of their Families and Consciences, to their irregular Appetites of that sort.

The Case then being thus, let's consider what a deluge of Uncleanness may be pour'd out upon this Nation by 1000 or 2000, supposing there were no more of those Popish Ecclesiasticks in *Ireland* at a time; especially since they look upon it to be their interest to debauch the Nation, as one of the best Expedients to advance Popery, as was evident from the Practice of the late Reigns: and therefore it seems to be the natural way of obviating the growth of Popery, to make the Romish Ecclesiaticks uncapable of promoting it by that Method which they like best, and find most successful.

It will still appear to be more reasonable, because they have vow'd Chastity and by their own Confession have no occasion for those Seminary Vessels; therefore if they resolve to live as they have Sworn to do, they

[11] Various seventeenth-century English sources demonstrate the belief that such a law, directed specifically against the Jesuits, was on the books in Sweden around this time. See John Dryden, *The Spanish Friar* (*Epilogue*, 1.40); John Oldham, *Satyrs Upon the Jesuits*, "Satyr II" (ll. 252–53); see also the poem, attributed simply to W. M., titled "*A satirical poem on the most horrid and execrable Jesuitish Plot . . .*" (1679). There does not appear to be any evidence to corroborate this belief.

would willingly unman themselves as *Origen*[12] did; so far would they be from having any reason to complain, if others should do it for them.

It can no ways be reckon'd cruel, since it may be done without hazard of Life, as common experience shews both in Man and Beast, and by consequence less to be complain'd of, than those Laws which condemn them to the Gallows. There have been more Priests put to death in *England*, than ever were gelded in *Sweden;* yet Experience teaches us it hath not had near so good an Effect. This is demonstrable from the many Conspiracies against our Princes and Nation, that the Priests have form'd since the enacting of those Laws, and from the great Progress their Idolatry makes among us at this very day; whereas *Sweden*, since the enacting of that Law, hath been liable to none of these misfortunes. This Law of *Castration* occasion'd a pleasant Railery upon the Jesuits at *Brussels* by Queen *Christina of Sweden.*[13] When those Fathers came to Congratulate her there upon her Conversion, they entertain'd her, among other things with the wonderful Effects of their Missions in the *Indies*, and other remote parts: That Princess applauded their Zeal, but at the same time rebuk'd their Indifference for her Countrey of *Sweden*, where their endeavours were so much needed: She pleasantly told them, That tho' the Law of *Castration* was a Bar in their way, they ought not to prefer the keeping of those things of which they stood in no need, and of which she hop'd they made no use to the advancement of the Catholick Faith. But this, tho' the severest Reproof in the World, has never been able to bring the Romish Clergy to so much sense of their Duty, as to renew their Attempts of converting *Sweden.* This may serve to confirm the story told us of an old Capuchin in the *Menagiana*, the Works of the Abbot *Manage*[14], that he rejected the Advice of his Physicians to be out of the Stone, for fear it should make him Impotent, tho' he was then 80 Years of Age.

[12] *Origen.* (b. 184 or 185, d. 253 or 254) The principal theologian and biblical scholar of the early Greek church. Origen is also remembered for having emasculated himself in accordance with a very literal reading of Matth. 19:12 and 5:28–30.

[13] Queen *Christina of Sweden.* Kristina (or Christina Alexander), who reigned from 1644 to 1654, was the child of Gustav II Adolf (Gustavus Adolphus II), a military innovator who has often been viewed as the Protestant hero of the Thirty Years' War. Considered one of the wittiest and most learned women of her day, Kristina abdicated the throne approximately ten years after her accession, and she secretly converted to Roman Catholicism, a religion outlawed in Sweden.

[14] Abbot *Manage.* Gilles Ménage (1613–92) was a French philologist and man of letters who eventually became prior of Montdidier. After his death, his friends assembled and published the *Menagiana*, a compilation of his thoughts and witticisms.

Namque ad Vivendum castrari valde recusat,
Et propter vitam vivendi perdere causam.[15]

The Romish Clergy have so much accustom'd themselves to those impure Pleasures, that they will be sure to avoid those Countreys where they must be render'd uncapable of enjoying them.

If it be thought that the Laws already made, will be more effectual against them, there's no need of repealing them, tho' a new one of *Castration* be added. Since that hath had so good an Effect in *Sweden*, we have no reason to despair of the like here. It's generally concluded, that our *Irish* Women are as tempting as any in *Europe*, and are therefore as likely to prevail on a Romish Priest to venture hanging to enjoy their Favours as any others: But if they be rendered uncapable of it, the temptation will have no force; and so the Priests will save their Lives, our Women will preserve their Chastity, and our Religion and Liberty will be freed from their Attacques.

The only Objection of weight that can be made against it is, that it may provoke our Popish Allies, and other Popish Princes, to treat Protestant Ministers in the like manner. To which we answer, That, admitting it should be so, it is not half so bad as to have them broke on the Wheel, Hang'd, or sent to the Gallies. In the next place, there's not the like Reason for treating Protestant Ministers in that manner, for they generally marry; or if they be guilty of Uncleanness, are thrust from the Ministry. And in the last place, there's no reason why we should have any more regard to our Allies, or other Popish Princes, than they have to us. We hear every day of the cruel Persecution in *France* and *Germany*, notwithstanding our mildness to the Papists here; so that our enacting a Law of *Castration*, cannot possibly make them persecute the Protestants more severely than they do, but may rather put a stop to it.

And indeed it is to be wondred [*sic*] at, that the Protestants should be so much wanting in their Zeal, and so little sensible of their own Interest, when we have so Warlike and Zealous a *Protestant Princes*[*s*], upon the Throne of *Great Britain*, as not to agree on Methods for obliging the Papists to forbear that barbarous Persecution of their Brethren. Endeavours of that Nature were us'd in some of those Reigns when Popery had so much Interest at Court, that it seem'd to have a share of the Throne; therefore it's strange if nothing should be attempted towards it in this Reign. To effect this would, humanly speaking, seem to be no difficult work, since the Naval Strength of *Europe* is in the hands of the Protestants; and that the

[15] "For he strongly objects to being castrated for life/And on account of life to lose the reason for living."

strength of *Great Britain* and *Holland* is now under the Command of one Princes, who is the *Hero* of her Age.[16]

This our own Safety seems to require, and charity and compassion to our Brethren beyond Sea does loudly call for; but if for reasons of State, or otherwise, it be found impracticable for us to impose in behalf of persecuted Protestants abroad, there's nothing can hinder us, if we be willing to secure our selves against Popery at home, by putting the old Laws in Execution, or Enacting new ones.

This seems to be absolutely necessary, if we consider, either the State of the Protestants beyond Sea, or our own Condition at home.

If we look abroad, we shall find the Protestant Interest, which was once so considerable in *France*, quite ruin'd; and one of the chief Causes of its being so, was the neglect of our *English* Governments since Queen *Elizabeth's* time: we have done nothing effectual for them since then, which was a mighty oversight, both in respect of Duty and Interest; That it was our duty, will scarcely be deny'd by any Man that has any true Impressions of the Protestant Religion. That it was our Interest is demonstrable, because, had the Protestants of *France* been supported by our Meditation and Assistance, they would never have concurr'd in any ambitious design of their Monarchs against the Protestant Interest of this Nation: and perhaps the fears of that Court, that they might be a Curb on their Designs of that Nature, was none of the least causes of their having ruin'd them by the most ungrateful, as well as the most barbarous Persecution that ever was known. From all which it will naturally result that it is the Interest of *Ireland* to save, if possible, the Remnant of the Protestants in *France*, by some Effectual Interposition.

If we look a little further into the State of the Protestants of the Valleys of *Piedmont*, we shall find that Ancient Church almost totally ruin'd and disperst. If we turn our Eye towards *Hungary, Transilvania* [*sic*], and *Poland*, the Reformed Interest is almost quite exterminated in those Countreys, as it is totally ruin'd in *Bohemia:* What danger it is liable to in the Neighboring Countrey of *Saxony*, is known to every one, since that

---

[16] A reference to Queen Anne (r. 1702–14), the second daughter of James II. Although her father was a Catholic, Anne was a staunch Anglican who accepted the revolutionary settlement of 1688. Sympathetic to the High Church Tories, Anne disliked both Catholics and Dissenters. During the War of the Spanish Succession (1701–13), Britain was the senior partner in the Grand Alliance, which also included Austria and the Netherlands. These allied forces were under the leadership of Prince Eugene of Savoy and John Churchill, the duke of Marlborough, whose wife was at that point a close friend of Anne.

Countrey, whose Prince was the first that embrac'd the Reformation, is now under a Popish Government; and if we come nearer home to the *Palatinate,*[17] there we shall also find a Protestant Church, once the most flourishing, and best reformed in all *Germany*, under an unreasonable and cruel Persecution. If we consider the Treaty of *Reswick*, by that we shall find the *German* Protestants despoil'd of eight or nine hundred Churches: The once famous Protestant City of *Strasburgh* deliver'd in Prey to the Church of *Rome*; and the Protestants in *Alsace*, and the Neighboring Principalities on each side, as the Dutchy of *Montbelliard*, Country of *Veldents*, &c. subject to Popish Incroachments. In a word, if we look throughout the whole *Empire*, and take a view of the Diet at *Ratisbon,*[18] we shall find the Popish Interest everywhere rampant, and Incroaching upon the Reformation, contrary to the Fundamental Laws, and most solemn Treaties of the *Empire*. If we cast an Eye upon *Swisserland*, the little Republick of *Geneva*, and the Principality of *Neufchatel*, there also we shall find the Protestant Interest threatned [*sic*], and languishing.

If we look Northward, there we find the Protestant Kingdoms of *Sweden* and *Denmark* ready to ingage in a War with one another, and that the Quarrels betwixt them are fomented by those who carry on an Interest which is destructive both to the Protestant Religion, and the Civil Liberties of *Europe*. This is sufficient to discover the bad State of the Protestant Interest abroad.

If we consider the Posture of Affairs at home, it's evident from a late printed Letter, said to be wrote by a worthy Bishop, and Dedicated to a Member of Parliament, that Popery comes in upon us like a Flood. It is not to be denied that there's a Party in the three Nations,[19] who favour the Title

---

[17] *Palatinate.* The region controlled by the elector palatine, the leading secular prince of the Holy Roman Empire. Two major parts made up this territory. Located around the middle Rhine River, the Rhenish, or Lower, Palatine had its capital in Heidelberg until the eighteenth century. The Upper Palatine, around the Naab River, was in northern Bavaria. Under Elector Frederick III, the Palatinate became Calvinist in the 1560s. An important region for the Protestant cause in seventeenth-century Germany, the Rhenish Palatinate was devastated by Catholic soldiers during the Thirty Years' War and again by the French king Louis XIV's troops during the War of the Grand Alliance (1689–97).

[18] Diet at *Ratisbon.* At the diet of Ratisbon in February 1623, the Catholic Holy Roman emperor Ferdinand II transferred the Palatine Electorate to the Catholic Wittelsbach family of Bavaria. This act was widely viewed as an unconstitutional abuse of his prerogative. Now called Regensburg, Ratisbon is a city in southeastern Germany on the Danube River.

[19] Three Nations. England, Scotland, and Ireland.

of an Abdicated Popish Prince[20] and his pretended Succession, against the present Government, and the Succession establish'd by Law. It is not to be forgot, that their Interest was so strong as to advance a Popish King to our Throne; and tho' they could not keep him there, because he dismounted himself by a furious Career, yet they have endanger'd us since by repeated Plots against his late Majesty's Life, and endeavouring to bring in a French Invasion upon us. It is also known, that there are mighty discontents fomented and nourish'd in all the three Nations, in relation to Trade, Parties, and different Pretensions; and that this gives the Popish Clergy an opportunity of adding fewel to our Flames, which makes it likewise evident that the Protestant Interest is in danger abroad.

This is further demonstrable from the Trouble the Papists have from time to time given, and continue to give to our Government and Parliaments; what's the meaning else of those Proclamations formerly and lately ommitted, commanding Papists to retire from *London, &c.* What else is the meaning of those Bills brought in to prevent their disinheriting their Protestant Heirs. [*sic*] and to hinder their sending Children abroad to foreign Seminaries, to be bred up in Idolatry, or made Priests, Monks and Nuns? This, besides the danger that accrues thereby to our Religion and Liberties, takes vast Summs of Money out of the Kingdom Yearly. They likewise give trouble to our Parliaments, by bringing in Bills for discovering Estates[21] and Money given to superstitious Uses, which is every way mighty prejudicial to the Kingdom, and enables the Papists to breed Vipers in our Bowels, in order to rend us in pieces.

Then since it is undeniable that we are in danger from the Papists, whether we consider the State of Affairs at home or abroad, and that the

---

[20] A party . . . who favour . . . an Abdicated Popish Prince. The Jacobites continued to support the heirs of James II in their claim to the throne. The Catholic James II was forced to flee during the Glorious Revolution of 1688–9. To this settlement, Jacobite resistance (loyalty to the Stuart dynasty) persisted for approximately sixty years. At the time that this pamphlet was written, the Jacobites would have been supporting James II's son, James Edward Stuart (1688–1766), the "Old Pretender," who had unsuccessfully attempted to invade Scotland with French troops in 1708.

[21] Discovering Estates. Political struggles over land ownership, legally conducted by searches for land with defective titles, had snarled up Ireland's legal system throughout the seventeenth century. The eighteenth-century penal laws placed legal restrictions on the ability of Catholics to lease, sell, and inherit land. In practice, however, bills "discovering" such transactions were frequently filed by legal agents of the Catholic party itself in order to preempt an unfriendly discovery and expropriation. A legal procedure established under an Irish act of 1709 reinforced these spiraling legal snarls by stipulating that Protestants who filed bills with the chancery to "discover" such transactions became entitled to the Catholic party's interest in it.

Laws hitherto enacted have not been able to prevent the recourse of Popish Priests, &c. nor the growth of Popery in this Kingdom; what should hinder us from trying new Methods, and particularly this Law of *Castration*?

It would certainly be a punishment very proper for them, and might make them read their Sin in their Judgment; since it's evident that by their own personal Villainy, and their loose Doctrine of Pardons, &c. which incourages People in Licentiousness, they make more Proselytes than by any other method.

Those, who perhaps would scruple to be any ways Instrumental in taking these Priests, when the Penalty inflicted upon them by Law is Death, would not have reason to be so scrupulous to take and discover them when the punishment is only *Castration*, and therefore would be more diligent to put the Laws in execution upon them.

It must also be reckon'd a deserv'd Punishment, since under the Seal of Confession they commit Uncleanness with those they have the Trust of as Ghostly Fathers,[22] so that it is a sort of Spiritual Incest, and a destroying People with Arms that make no Report; both which Crimes are Capital in all well-governed States, and therefore the punishment of *Castration* in such a Case must needs be accounted mild.

If it be objected that tho' some of the *Romish* Clergy be guilty of Incontinence, yet all of them are not so: and therefore such only are to be punish'd in that manner as are convicted of the Crime: It's easy to answer, That it is equally true that all of them are not guilty of Conspiring against the Government, nor is it possible to convict all of 'em of perverting the Subjects; yet the 27th of *Eliz.*[23] makes it Treason for any Popish Priest, bred up beyond Sea, to be here, or to return into *Ireland*, without submitting to the Government, and taking the Oath of Supremacy. And indeed it is but reasonable it should be so, for their being here supposes their Design; and therefore there's as much reason to punish them, tho' we cannot prove the Overt Acts upon them, as there is to punish Thieves for coming into our Houses in an illegal manner, tho' we cannot prove that they have robb'd us, or stole any thing. If we find a Wolfe or other Beast of Prey among

---

[22] Ghostly Fathers—father confessors (i.e., priests); *ghostly* here means "pertaining to the spirit or soul," as opposed to the body or flesh (*OED*, "ghostly," 1 and 1c).

[23] 27th of *Eliz.*—The 27 Elizabeth, c. 2, "An Act againste Jesuites Semynarie Priestes and such other like disobedient Persons" (1584), commanded that these clerics leave England and all of the queen's other "Realmes and Dominions" for fear that they would "withdraw her Highnesse Subjects from their due obedience to her Majestie" and "stire up and move Sedition Rebellion and open Hostilitie" among them. Clause VIII included a proviso declaring that those priests who took the Oath of Supremacy were exempt from this declaration.

our Flocks, we take their design of destroying them for granted, and treat them accordingly, tho' we don't see the Limbs of our Cattle in their Mouths. And therefore since the Practices and Principles of the *Romish* Clergy are so well known, their being found in the Nation ought to have sufficient Conviction.

It still remains a Question, how they shall be discovered? But the Answer is at hand: Let a competent and certain Reward be propos'd for such as shall do it, and the like Reward, and a Pardon to any of their own Number that shall discover the rest; or let provision be made for some of every English Seminary beyond Sea that turn Protestants, plant some of them in the several Ports of the Kingdom; and let some of each of those Seminaries be likewise constantly in *Dublin* to assist in Searches, and view those that are taken upon suspition: And at the same time, let provision be made for such as will inform of all the Popish Clergy that haunt the great Families of that Opinion in *Ireland*, and we need not doubt of an effectual discovery in a little time: for besides the influence that the hopes of a Reward will have, those Goatish Fellows, the *Romish* Clergy, do many times disoblige Families of their own way, by attempting to debauch their Wives, Children, or Servants, some of whom have so much Virtue as to reject the Temptation, and to hate the Tempters; and many times their blind Zeal occasions them likewise to take indescreet Methods to pervert Protestant Servants, who would not be wanting, in case of such provision as above-mention'd to discover those dangerous Fellows.

To inflict this punishment of *Castration* upon them, is so much the less to be thought cruel or unreasonable, since it is so ordinary in *Italy*, and other Popish Countries, for the meaner sort of People to Geld their own Sons, that they may make the better market of them for singing Boys, and Musitians, or to be Catamites to Cardinals, and other Dignitaries of the Romish Church. In those hot Countries the Romish Clergy are much addicted to that damnable and unnatural Crime: and such of them as are not, keep lewd Women almost avowedly; they are in-deed more upon the Reserve, and live according to the Maxim of *Cauté* tho not *Casté*[24], in such Countreys where the Government is Reformed; or where the Protestants are numerous; but then they are under the greater temptation to perpetrate their Villanies, on the pretext of Confessing women: therefore there's the more Reason to Enact a Law of *Castration* against them in this Kingdom.

We have the more ground to think that such a Law duly executed, would have a good Effect, because the Lust of the Flesh is so bewitching, and natural to the greatest part of mankind, and continues to have a predominancy in them for so great a part of their lives, that it hath occasion'd, and

---

[24] *Cauté . . . Casté.* "Carefully, though not Chastely."

does occasion more disorders, and is apter to engage Men, over whom it obtains the ascendant, in more desperate undertakings than any other passion whatever. Histories are full of Examples of Princes and great Men, that have ruin'd themselves and their Countreys in pursuit of their irregular Amours. We have no need to turn over foreign Stories, or to go out of our own Nation for proofs of this. It is not so long ago as to be forgot, since we had the chief Affairs of State manag'd, and Parliaments dissolv'd, &c. at the beck of *Courtisans.* The Interest of *Popery* and *Tyranny* in the late Reigns was chiefly advanc'd by such.

Do we not find, even in private persons of all Ranks, that where that passion is not kept in due bounds, or cur'd by the proper Remedies of a suitable Match, that Honour, Health, and Estates, nay Life it self, is many times sacrific'd to the pleasure of the Flesh; and therefore the Apostle had Reason as well as Revelation on his side, when he rank'd all that is in the World under the three Heads of *the Lust of the Flesh, the Lust of the Eye,* and *the Pride of Life;* and gave that of the Flesh the preference. It is plain from Experience, that the other two are made generally subservient to it, as is visibly every day from that excess in Jewels, Apparel and Houshold Furniture, and the vast expence which the Gallants of both Sexes put themselves to in one or all of these, in order to obtain the Favour of their *Paramours.*

From all which we may make this Inference, that if the *Romish* Clergy were made uncapable by a Law of enjoying that which they account the greatest pleasure of Life, they would avoid those Countreys where such Laws are put in execution, as they would avoid the Plague. 'Twould be happy if by this means we could deliver our Posterity from those Conspiracies, Civil Wars, Dreadful Fires, Massacrees, Assassinations of Princes, and other mischiefs which these Kingdoms have been liable to from the Papists; and against which all our other Laws have hitherto signified but little to preserve us.

We have also found, by sad Experience, that they have had so much influence as to get the Ascendant over some of our Princes, by tempting them, as they have done the *French* King, with the hopes of an absolute Sway, and we know not what Visionary Empires. By this means they prevail'd with them to overthrow our Laws, the recovery of which hath cost the Nation so much Blood and Treasure, that after Ages are like to feel the smart of it: Tho' they have run one of our Princes[25] off the Stage, and have

---

[25] One of our Princes . . . great Champion beyond [the] Sea. The prince run off the stage is probably a reference to James II of England, who was forced to abdicate because of his Catholicism. His pro-Catholic policies and absolutist tendencies alarmed many English Protestants. "Their great Champion beyond [the] Sea" possibly refers to the pretender James Edward Stuart, who was taken to France as a boy upon his father's abdication in 1688.

well-nigh ruin'd their great Champion beyond [the] Sea, as they did formerly the *Spanish* Monarchy, by spurring on those Princes to persecute Protestants, and establish Despotical Government. They will never give over that Game, but inspire all Princes to whom they can have access, either by themselves or others, with one or both of those Designs; and therefore it is the Interest of *Ireland*[26] to use all possible means to secure the Nation against those *Romish* Clergymen, for which *Castration* is humbly conceiv'd to be the properest Method, and is so far from being cruelty, that it may well be reckon'd as a great piece of Clemency to *Romish* Priests, as Transportation[27] is instead of the Gallows to other Condemned Criminals.

In short, it will be so far from being a real diskindness to the Popish Laics of this Nation, that it will be the greatest piece of Friendship to them imaginable: this we hope they will be the more readily convinc'd of, if their Wives, Daughters, and Maid-Servants, cry out against this Law, for then to be sure they have some particular concern in the matter.

We hope that our Popish Laics in *Ireland*[28] are Men of as good Observation as those in other Countreys, and particularly in *France* and *Italy*, where their very Proverbs are sufficient to demonstrate, that they have no great Opinion of their Clergymens Chastity. It is not possible to expose those goatish Fellows with more severity and contempt, than the *Italians* do by saying *fate Lui Corunna*,[29] by way of sarcasm[,] of a Stallion that they don't think performs his part; alluding to the Prists [*sic*] shaven Crowns as if that sacerdotal Character were sufficient even to invigorate a Horse. Their other Proverb of *fate lo Prete*[30] let's make him a Priest, when they have any ungovernable Wanton in a Family, that over runs all their Females, is kin to the other; and their covering their Stone Horses with a Monk's Frock when they find them indifferent for a Mare in season, is a scandalous Reproof of those bruitish [*sic*] Clergymen. Answerable to these is the *French* Proverb:

---

[26] The version of this pamphlet published in 1700 reads *England* here.

[27] Transportation. An alternative to execution, transportation was a punishment by which convicted felons were deported (either for a term of years or for life) to penal colonies outside of Britain. At the time of this publication, it most commonly involved sending convicts to the Americas. Although transportation had been used since the seventeenth century, it would become much more common following legislation in 1718. Transportation to Australia was not used until the British landed there in 1788, after having lost the American colonies.

[28] Here again, the 1700 version of the pamphlet reads *England*.

[29] *fate Lui Corunna*. "Make him a crown."

[30] *fate lo Prete*. "Make him a priest."

Qui veut tenir nette Maison
Qui'll n'y souffre ni Petri ni Moin ni Pigeon[31]

Comparing the Popish Clergy to the Pigeons for their Venerious Inclinations; and may be Englished thus,

They that would keep their Houses Chast [*sic*] and Neat
From thence must Priests, Monks, Nuns; and Pigeons beat

As all Proverbs of that sort are founded upon something universally known or conceiv'd to be true, it is not at all for the Honour of the Popish Clergy, that their Chastity should be thus Reflected upon in Countries where they are the sole Directors of Conscience, and have their Religion establish'd by Law.

But that which fixes yet more upon them, is that in the Pop[e]'s Chancery the Tax for eating *Eggs* in *Lent*, is greater than that for Sodomy; and the penalty upon a Priest that Marries, is greater than upon those that commit that monstrous and unnatural Villainy just now mention'd. From all which it is manifest, that they did not speak at random who inform'd us that the Celibacy of such an innumerable multitude of Popish Ecclesiastics, is the *maximum Arcanum dominationis Papalis*,[32] and *that the Priests Testicles are the greatest Promoters of the Pop[e]'s Empire.* This will appear yet more plain, that it is of the highest Importance to them, since the Church of *Rome* maintains, that Marriage is a sacrament, and that all Sacraments confer Grace; and yet deny's it to her Clergy; a manifest Indication that they have their graceless Designs to promote by it, especially since at the same time the want of those parts which they will not allow them to make use of in a Regular way, renders them uncapable of being Priests according to their Canons; but yet they are so kind to their Gelded Martyrs, as to allow it to be Sufficient if they have them about them, in Powder or any other way.

These things confirm, in a literal sense, the odious Characters given the Church of *Rome* in the *Revelations*, Chap. 17, 18, &c. As, *the great Whore, with whom the Kings and Inhabitants of the Earth have committed Fornication; the Mother of Harlots, and Ambominations* [*sic*] *of the Earth, having a Golden Cup in her hand full of Abominations, and of the Filthiness of her Fornications, &c.* Then since by the testimony of God and Man, the *Romish*

[31] *Qui veut . . . Pigeon.* "Whoever wants to keep a clean house/Let him not put up with a priest, or a monk, or a pigeon."

[32] *maximum . . . Papalis.* "the greatest Secret of Papal domination."

Clergy is such an impure and lascivious Crew, it makes a Law of *Castration* a just and adequate Punishment for them.

To conclude; since our Queen and Parliament have both testify'd their Zeal and Forwardness to suppress Immorallity [*sic*] and Profaneness, it follows naturally that such a Law as this deserves their serious Thoughts; for it is impossible to suppress this Reigning Vice, so long as those Goatish Fellows are suffered to swarm among us. They not only corrupt the Morrals of People themselves by such Practices and Principles as above mention'd, but bring over, and encourage others to do it; [parti]cularly those *Italians*, &c. who sell and Print *Aretin's Postures*[33], and in order to Debauch the minds of Women, and to make them Guilty of unnatural Crimes, invent and sell 'em such things as Modesty forbids to name. 'Tis evident that as Popery advanc'd upon us in the late Reigns, Debauchery gain'd Ground at the same time, for they naturally make way for one another; and therefore we can never suppress Immorrality, without securing our selves effectually against Popery. If this should be attempted by a Law of *Castration* against *Romish* Priests, it must be own'd that it would be more Charitable and Humane to save our selves from Popish Superstition, and all its mischievous Consequences, by that method alone, than to Practice it, together with other Punishments, upon such of those Wretches as come to the Gibbet for Treason; the cutting off their Privities in such Cases, and throwing 'em in the Fire, just before they be Totally bereft of Life, can be of no manner of use, whereas *Castration* alone before hand might have sav'd us from the Danger of their Plots, and prevented themselves from coming to the Gallows.

THE DECLARATORY ACT

This act, passed in 1720, asserted the binding legislative authority of the British Parliament over Irish affairs. In effect, it rendered the Irish Parliament impotent and denied appellate jurisdiction to the

---

From *The Statutes* at large from Magna Charta, to the end of the eleventh Parliament of Great Britain, anno 1761. Anno sexto Georgii I. c. 5.

[33] *Aretin's Postures.* An Italian poet, satirist, and dramatist, Pietro Aretino (1492–1556) was the notorious author of the *Sonetti lussuriosi* (*Lewd Sonnets,* also referred to as *I modi,* or *The Ways*). Known in English as *The Sixteen Postures* (or *The Sixteen Pleasures*), this collection of sonnets accompanied illustrations of sixteen sexual positions drawn by Giuliano Romano, a student of Raphael.

Irish House of Lords. The Declaratory Act was not repealed until the Renunciation Act of 1783.

An act for the better securing the dependency of the kingdom of Ireland upon the crown of Great Britain

Whereas *the house of lords of* Ireland *have of late, against law, assumed to themselves a power and jurisdiction to examine, correct and amend the judgments and decrees of the courts of justice in the kingdom of* Ireland: therefore for the better securing of the dependency of *Ireland* upon the crown of *Great Britain,* may it please your most excellent Majesty that it may be declared, and be it declared by the King's most excellent majesty, by and with the advice and consent of the lords temporal and spiritual and commons, in this present parliament assembled, and by the authority of the same, That the said kingdom of *Ireland* hath been, is, and of right ought to be subordinate unto and dependent upon the imperial crown of *Great Britain,* as being inseparably united and annexed thereunto; and that the King's majesty, by and with the consent of the lords spiritual and temporal and commons of *Great Britain* in parliament assembled, had, hath, and of right ought to have full power and authority to make laws and statutes of sufficient force and validity, to bind the kingdom and people of *Ireland.*

II. And be it further declared and enacted by the authority aforesaid, That the house of lords of *Ireland* have not, nor of right ought to have any jurisdiction to judge of, affirm or reverse any judgment, sentence, or decree, given or made in any court within the said kingdom, and that all proceedings before the said house of lords upon any such judgment, sentence, or decree, are, and are hereby declared to be utterly null and void to all intents and purposes whatsoever.

To bind the kingdom. Compare Swift's phrasing on pp. 286, 308.

Part Three

CRITICISM

Swift as Intellectual

Edward W. Said

For reasons having to do both with contemporary critics and with what the great Augustan writers present to them, the early eighteenth century in England has not been particularly responded to by the major contemporary literary theorists. If we compare the kind of use made by the modern critical sensibility of figures like Dr. Johnson, Sterne, Gibbon, and Richardson with what has been made of Pope and Swift, the contrast will be stark. Another way of understanding what I mean is to note the extent to which the study of Gibbon and Johnson, say, is felt to be of interest to non-specialists in the eighteenth century. Walter Jackson Bate's Johnson biography or the 1976 *Dedalus* symposium on Gibbon have a way of attracting general attention, as much for their subjects' intrinsic merit as for the interest a literate reader might take in the way they are approached. Such an interest has simply not been the case with recent work on Swift. There have been works by well-known critics such as Irvin Ehrenpreis and Denis Donoghue, and there remains the formidable fact of Swift's untarnished, undiminished reputation as a classic. Why then this vacancy, this ominous gap between Swift's potential as an author of extraordinary power for modern critics and the disappointing critical performance outside the professional guild of eighteenth-century scholarship?

It is perfectly possible that what we might call advanced contemporary criticism has not come round to Swift as the result of simple accident. After all, it is true that Norman O. Brown did study Swift very appreciatively twenty-odd years ago, and since his *Life Against Death* was a vanguard work then, there is a good possibility that Swift will again become the exemplary author for vanguard contemporary criticism. In other words we might stipulate that the time has not yet occurred, but it will.

Yet this is an argument that refuses to take seriously the intellectual and cultural circumstances that, throughout human history, have made the avoidance of or the attention to certain texts matters of deliberate will and conscious choice, not of raw accident. As for Swift's threadbare case before

---

From *The World, the Text, and the Critic* (Cambridge, Mass.: Harvard University Press, 1983).

the contemporary critical jury, there are ample grounds for judging that case to be the result of certain very concrete determinations.

In the first place I think it must be said that Swift, along with contemporaries of his like Dryden and Pope, to say nothing of Steele, Addison and Bolingbroke, has been the beneficiary in the main of a certain kind of scholarship. I do not mean to be sarcastic when I say that so formidable are the scholars who maintain the Swift canon, who uphold his textual orthodoxy—a very important thing, after all—that approaching him has become a daunting prospect. In Swift's case there are such facts to be reckoned with as the great Harold Williams and Herbert Davis editions. So high is the standard of work that such labors have upheld, so focused and so scrupulous their attention to strict factuality (which is what one must have from good editors), that Swift seems even more like the rather dry and abrasive Anglican divine he must have been at least some of the time in real life. It is not that Swift scholarship has restricted Swift's appeal, but that with so many of the textual problems having been so spendidly solved, scholars seem to have felt a certain unwillingness to venture beyond that realm. And indeed that realm has come to resemble the ambiance of a club, which is not so surprising perhaps if we remember that Swift's circle during his London days was called a club.

An important aspect of the club for modern readers seems to have been determined by what, some years ago, Louis Bredvold called the gloom of the Tory satirists. This view of Swift, Pope, and Arbuthnot is, I believe, a natural intellectual concomitant of the textual scholarship I spoke of a moment ago. It is a view with which most readers of Swift and Pope must concur because it is true and it is persuasive. So far as human nature was concerned, Swift was a pessimist, and whether in the final analysis we belong to the "hard" or "soft" school of interpreters of *Gulliver's Travels* we must say that taken in isolation the Yahoos represent an idea of human nature that is uncomfortably close to being misanthropic. That this view further corresponds to Swift's own is something that most readers are prepared to allow, so ingrained in the cultural consciousness is the idea of Swift's generalized *saeva indignatio.*

The trouble with these readings of Swift is that their currency and authority have confined him either to a circle of like-minded associates ("the Tory satirists") or to a set of beliefs that is not at all difficult to ferret out from his writing. With the possible exception of *A Tale of a Tub*, whose unrestrained exuberance seems to have amazed its own author later in life, all of Swift's work does in fact support a fairly strict, not to say uninteresting, conservative philosophy. Man is either unimprovable or predisposed to nastiness, corruption, or pettiness; the body is naturally disgusting; enthusiasm, like schemes of conquest or of pseudo-scientific projection, is dangerous and threatens the polity; the Church of England, the classics, and the monarch (those three institutions Swift believed were fully comprised in the right-minded sentiments of a Church of England man) together formed the pillars and the legacy of moral and physical health—this is not an unfair summary of Swift's doctrine. There are several other regretably pathological traits that, when they are put next to the barely controlled violence of Swift's imagination, present us with a man whose outlook is narrow, constricted, even sadistic.

No one would argue then that Swift is a canonical or classic author because, like Johnson for example, he offers the reader vitality of mind in alliance with sanity of perspective. He is *not* like Johnson, the movement of whose writing is to open things out; Swift's shuts things down. Even if we agree with Herbert Read, that Swift is the greatest prose stylist in English, we are likely to feel his effects as essentially unyielding, hard, tight. He belongs to an important and select group—the Shakespeare of *Troilus and Cressida*, Milton at times, Gerard Manley Hopkins—for whom language can scarcely bear the weight of some urgency or other and thereby becomes at once, and with equal force, afflicted and afflicting. In Swift's intense and yet highly polished fury of language, there is little room for what Wordsworth called the still sad music of humanity. We find ourselves dealing with contortions of the mind, acrobatics of spirit that intrigue and debate with us but that tend to refuse us in the end, since so often Swift impersonates people we would not like to resemble. The questions we ask when we read Swift are usually of the "what is going on" or "how does it work" sort. Not illogically such questions arise precisely because of Swift's incredible economy of line, which is the essence of Swift's description of the style, "proper words in proper places," a description to which we might only add "with a vengeance."

It is worth going a bit further in stressing the limitations that seem to have removed Swift as a candidate for interesting critical attention. One of the most consistent themes in Swift's work is loss, and even above its lithe power his writing frequently sets about to communicate a literal sense of loss. Therefore one misses in Swift the very dimension of amplitude and sanity which, in the course of his writing, we can see being pushed out of sight. The human body, for example, is exhibited (as in the *Tale* or *Gulliver*) only to be flayed or abused with so intense a microscopic attention as to transmute it into a disgusting object. The poignancy of such deliberate impoverishments is that the writer seems to know this, and even to record the loss with self-mocking revelry in technique that has the uniquely coruscating accuracy we call "Swiftian." The objects of Swift's attention—ideas, people, events—are stripped of real power or life and left, in his prose, as remnants, exhibits that shock, amuse, or fascinate. When we think of the human "content" of Swift's work, and think of it suspended in the plain style, we realize with some discomfort that we have before us a show of freaks and horrors: a mad writer, an astrologer being murdered, an absurd and impossible war, a disjointed political writer (Steele), a gallery of raving freethinkers, men burrowing in dung, and so on. The violent images of war, disease, madness, and depravity, to say nothing of the consequences of dwarfism and giantism offered us by *Gulliver's Travels*, are of a piece with the general loss of normality he seems attracted to. We would not be wrong in saying that a significant aspect of Swift's coherence as a writer is the intellectual and spiritual feat that sustained such a style as his, performing so drastic a transmutation of reality with such forceful negativity for such regrettably narrow ends.

I would not have succeeded in describing the case for Swift the limited, deeply flawed writer if I do not clinch it now with some reference to George Orwell's essay "Politics vs. Literature: An Examination of *Gulliver's Travels*," which was originally published in a late 1946 issue of *Polemic*. Again, my reason for doing so is that I take seriously the fact that Swift has not had his due from contemporary criticism, a failure I ascribe in large measure to certain influential aspects of the general kind of critical attention that Swift *has* had. My point, of course, is that even though Swift must be admitted to be a problematic and in many ways a limited and humanly unattractive figure, these admissions need not prevent him from becoming the object of really fruitful contemporary criticism—but more about that later.

Orwell's essay belongs to the period of his growing disenchantment with modern politics. He tells us that Swift has meant a great deal to him ever since his eighth birthday, when he was given a copy of *Gulliver's Travels*. Orwell's argument is familiar enough and, so far as it goes, one we can recognize from reading Lukacs on Balzac or, more recently, Fredric Jameson on Wyndham Lewis (in *Fables of Aggression*). The general line is that, despite a writer's expressed ideological commitment to right-wing views, his great literary gifts give him special value. Unlike Lukacs and Jameson, Orwell does not try to prove that by virtue of style or technique the author is really progressive. Quite the contrary, Orwell insists that "in a political and moral sense" he is against Swift even though "curiously enough he is one of the writers I admire with least reserve." Thus Orwell's liking for Swift is built around an attempt at finding a great deal to admire in Swift even though he was reactionary, nihilistic, and diseased, words that Orwell uses more than once in this context. In addition he suggests that Swift is one of those writers whose enjoyment can, for his reader, overwhelm disapproval. According to Orwell, "In his endless harping on disease, dirt and deformity, Swift is not actually inventing anything, he is merely leaving something out. Human behaviour, too, especially politics, is as he describes it, although it contains other more important factors which he refuses to admit . . . Swift did not possess ordinary wisdom, but he did possess a terrible intensity of vision, capable of picking out a single hidden truth and then magnifying and distorting it. The durability of *Gulliver's Travels* goes to show that, if the force of belief is behind it, a world-view which only just passes the test of sanity is sufficient to produce a great work of art."[1]

This is a fair summary of Orwell's judgment on Swift, except that it leaves out a very interesting observation, which I shall come back to later, on what he calls Swift's "irresponsible violence of the powerless." In the meantime, we can safely say that like most scholarly authorities Orwell finds Swift to be admirable over and above whatever he says about life, politics, and mankind. In other words, Swift's views are so compellingly unpleasant in their anarchism, in their illiberal attacks on all society and the human race, as to leave the modern reader with very little either to approve or to respect.

Let me state my own position at last. Orwell, to begin with, is not so much wrong as characteristically partial, insufficient, not really political enough in his verdict. Reading his assessment of Swift one would not know that *Gulliver's Travels* is a late book, or that during most of his earlier life Swift was an active, perhaps even an opportunistic political pamphleteer and polemicist. It is perfectly fair for Orwell to read *Gulliver's Travels* alone and then derive Swift's political views from that isolated reading; it is distorted, however, to make *Gulliver* stand for everything about Swift. Orwell's analogies between Swift and Alan Herbert, G. M. Young, and Ronald Knox, "the innumerable silly-clever Conservatives of our own day," are silly-clever analogies themselves, and rigidly close-minded to boot. To say of Swift that "he did not like democracy" is to say something of great irrelevance to the context of the time, since not even Swift's enemies of the "progressive party," to which Orwell alludes quickly in passing, could be described as believers in democracy. Can one seriously believe that Godolphin or the Duke of Marlborough, both of whom are Whigs that Swift attacked mercilessly, believed in democracy? When Orwell gives Swift credit for being astonishingly prescient about "what would now be called totalitarianism"—spy trials, informers, police plots, and so on—he does so only to be able to damn him in the next breath for not thinking "better of the common people than of their rulers, or to be in favour of increased social equality, or to be enthusiastic about representative institutions." Orwell seems unable to realize that one can be steadfastly opposed to tyranny, as Swift was all his life, and not have a well-developed position on "representative institutions."

What Orwell takes no account of then is ideological consciousness, that aspect of an individual's thought which is ultimately linked to sociopolitical and economic realities. Swift is very much a part of his time: there is no point therefore in expecting him to think and act like a prototype of George Orwell since the cultural options, the social possibilities, the political activities offered Swift in his time were more likely to produce a Swift than an Orwell.

As for the canonical view of Swift as a Tory satirist, it too diminishes Swift the activist and promotes Swift the producer of teleological images. My impression is that too many claims are made for Swift as a moralist and thinker who peddled one or another final view of human nature, whereas not enough claims are made for Swift as a kind of local activist, a columnist, a pamphleteer, a caricaturist. Even the useful analyses of Swift's satiric methods, his use or personae for example, are sometimes vitiated by this prejudice. It is as if critics assume that Swift really wanted to be a John Locke or a Thomas Hobbes, but somehow couldn't: therefore it becomes a critic's job to help Swift fulfill his ambition, turning him from a kind of marginal, sporty political fighter into a pipesmoking armchair philosopher.

Swift is, I think, preeminently a *reactive* writer. Nearly everything he wrote was occasional, and we must quickly add that he responded to, but did not create, the occasions. There are doubtless evident economic reasons for this: Swift, after all, was a minor cleric most of his life and needed the opportunities given him by wealthier patrons, from Temple to Harley to, finally, the Irish polity, on whose behalf he spoke in *The Drapier's Letters.* His originality therefore was in answering, reacting to situations he tried to influence or change. Something he says in the Apology to *A Tale of a Tub* gives a very marked emphasis to his self-consciousness about this: "to answer a Book effectively, requires more Pain and Skill, more Wit, Learning, and Judgement than were employed in creating the situations in the first place." His contribution almost always overturned whatever he discussed by creating new situations, persons, or books in his writing. Hence the new creation, which his polemical methods invariably engendered, and with that a release of energy far in excess of the amount presented to him at the outset, plus a great deal of irony.

Orwell is absolutely correct to say that in *Gulliver's Travels* Swift attacks that aspect of totalitarianism which makes people "less conscious" in general. I would go further and put the matter in positive terms. Swift's aim is to make people more conscious than they would otherwise be of what is being put before them. As Wilde said, "no class is ever really conscious of its own suffering. They have to be told of it by other people, and they often entirely disbelieve them . . . Agitators are a set of interfering, meddling people, who come down to some perfectly contented class of the community and sow the seeds of discontent among them. That is the reason why agitators are so completely necessary.[2] Swift's interfering and meddling agitational method is always to blow up or draw out the implications of a book, a position, or a situation, all of which are otherwise likely to be digested mindlessly by people. Thus he induces consciousness and awareness, he activates recognition. But what has made his later readers (and perhaps even his contemporaries) uncomfortable about his writing is that it has seemed so parasitic on what it responds to. In other words, Swift's impersonations have either seemed too close to what they caricature or too unforgiving about what they propose as an alternative: his portrait of the deranged hack in *A Tale* is an instance of the former, the Yahoos and Houyhnhnms examples of the latter. Swift's severity has then had to be tempered with references to a Tory ethos, to which he belonged, or to some derangement or misanthropic craziness that gave him no choice. No wonder that Coleridge spoke about Swift as the spirit of Rabelais in a dry place—*anima Rabelaisii in sicco.*

I should like to suggest, however, that if we restrict ourselves to seeing Swift not as a philosopher or as a madman or even as a canonically "creative" writer, but rather as an intellectual, his dryness, severity, and intensity will seem a great deal more systematic and modern. No doubt Swift wanted more out of life than to be Dean of St. Patrick's, or that he hoped Harley and St. John would some day make him a minister, or that he would acquire more wealth and position than his modest station allowed him initially. But these ambitions, however much their frustration angered him, did not prevent him from being energetic, powerful, and effective when he did his writing. In other words there is enough going on, and more than enough to engage the contemporary critic's attention, in Swift's actual, his *local,* performances.

It is probable that the notion of an *intellectual* is not usually associated with any period before the late nineteenth century, just as the role of intellectuals in society is not often studied in periods that antedate the French Revolution. Lewis Coser's *Men of Ideas,* which is one of the best historical surveys of the modern Occidental intellectual, confines its account of eighteenth-century England to half a dozen pages on the London coffeehouses, for which it relies on Harold Rossitt's chapter on Addison and Steele in the 1912 *Cambridge History of English Literature.* Coser is right to say that the coffeehouses leveled class ranks, "bred a new respect and tolerance for the idea of others," encouraged "sociability," and led to "new forms of integration" based on conversational exchange.[3] But he is quite wrong to exclude from investigation the spirited intellectual activity carried on in print during the period. Still Coser's two conditions for "the intellectual vocation to become socially feasible and socially recognized" can usefully be mentioned here:

> First, intellectuals need an audience, a circle of people to whom they can address themselves and who can bestow recognition. Such an audience will also, as a rule, provide economic rewards, but the prestige or esteem accorded to the intellectual by his public, his psychic income, may often be more important to him than his economic return. Second, intellectuals require regular contact with their fellow intellectuals, for only through such communication can they evolve common standards of method and excellence, common norms to guide their conduct. Despite popular myth to the contrary, most intellectuals cannot produce their work in solitude, but need the give and take of debate and discussion with their peers in order to develop their ideas. Not all intellectuals are gregarious, but most of them need to test their own ideas in exchange with those they deem their equals.[4]

This is roughly true of Swift, except that it needs to be qualified on one or two points. Swift needed the approbation of his peers, it is true, but it is also the case that he aimed for and generally got a wider audience beyond them. *The Conduct of the Allies* was by any standard a best-selling pamphlet not because it accidentally became one, but because Swift himself deliberately wrote it for a very large audience. Similarly, Swift wrote for *The Examiner* in a remarkably adroit and canny way, even to the extent of using journalistic tricks to encourage the paper's extensive distribution. But, after all is said and done, we should probably not underestimate the importance Swift attached to the good opinion his peers had of him. This is as true during his London days with Arbuthnot and Gay as it is of later Dublin friends like Delaney and Sheridan.

Intellectuals traffic in ideas: this is a minimum kind of definition. In modern times, intellectuals are thought of as playing the important role of gaining legitimacy and currency for ideas. In addition, there is a long tradition of intellectuals being the propagators of useful knowledge and values, and in doing that they are sometimes thought of as functioning as a sort of conscience, as keepers of values, for the society in which they work. This is clearly the idea of an intellectual that Julien Benda had in mind when he published *La Trahison des clercs* in 1928. Benda's definition of the intellectual is doubtless too narrow and idealistic, but his argument on behalf of the intellectual's obligation to adhere to absolute values and to tell the truth regardless of material consequences is powerfully appealing. The duty of intellectuals, he says, "is precisely to set up a corporation whose sole cult is that of justice and of truth, in opposition to the peoples and the injustice to which they are condemned by their religions of this earth."[5] There are echoes of Benda's indictment of intellectuals who have sold out to the ruling passions of state, class, and race in what Noam Chomsky has been writing for the past decade.[6]

In addition to the thesis that the intellectual's models are to be found among such people as Voltaire, Zola, and Socrates, there is another tradition, which begins in Marx's and Engels' *The German Ideology*, where the intellectual is depicted as playing a crucial role in both the change and the preservation of civil society. To a certain extent I think it is true to say of Swift that he was an intellectual in Benda's sense of the word. He certainly thought of himself as a champion of conscience and as an enemy of oppression. Most of his earlier life, however, he was a man engaged in sociopolitical issues, and it is in this more or less partisan role that he needs to be discussed. For this role, we are in need of the critical vocabulary that derives from the broad Marxist and neo-Marxist tradition, which happens also to include a paradoxically anti-Marxist strain.

The authors of *The German Ideology* demonstrate that, far from having an autonomous and sheltered life of its own, philosophy is part of material reality. Consciousness itself is determined by economic conditions they say, and even if we wish to argue, along with Marxists like Lukacs, that Marx and Engels did not mean that consciousness was simply the result of economic conditions, it is certainly the case that *The German Ideology* argues that even such rarefied things as ideas, consciousness, and metaphysics cannot be fully understood without taking stock of politics, sociology, and economics. In any event, what concerns us here is that the intellectual—who is not named as such by Marx and Engels—is either anyone involved in propagating ideas that seem to be independent of social reality or someone (like the two of them) whose main purpose is to show the connections between ideas and social reality. The former kind is obviously a conservative, the latter a revolutionary, since, they argue, anyone who strips ideas of their transcendental aloofness is really urging a revolutionary change in the intellectual and hence the sociopolitical status quo. The struggle between the two types of intellectual is, in Marxist terms, described as taking place not only in consciousness and in society, but in a realm called the *ideological*, a realm of discourse that falsely pretends to be made up of ideas but in reality veils its complicity with and its dependence on material institutions. Thus when Bruno Bauer speaks about self-consciousness, Marx and Engels say, he is disguising the fact that self-consciousness is made possible as a subject for discussion not because it is real but because traditional philosophy, which is an ally of the church, the university, and the state, enables philosophers to speak that way and to create subjects for discussion.

None of what Marx and Engels say as revolutionary intellectuals using what Marx calls "the weapons of criticism" would have been unacceptable to nonrevolutionary intellectuals in the later nineteenth century. This may seem a paradox, but it is not when we think, say, of Matthew Arnold and Ernest Renan, whom no one ever accused of being socialists let alone Marxists. When Arnold writes *Culture and Anarchy* he, like the authors of *The German Ideology*, asserts the social function of culture and ideas; the same is just as true of Renan in his *L'Avenir de la science.* For the nineteenth-century intellectual, being an intellectual includes the ideas of a central social role in addition to furnishing the public with what we might call a critical self-consciousness; this is one reason why a celebrated study of intellectuals (Karl Mannheim's *Ideology and Utopia*) ascribes to the intellectual the role of unmasking ideas.

I want to mention only two further items of recent thinking on intellectuals, both of whom shed useful light on Swift. The first of these items comes from Antonio Gramsci, who was the first—and in my opinion the most acute—modern Marxist to make the intellectual the central point of his sociopolitical analyses. Gramsci says that intellectuals are usually of two kinds: organic intellectuals, those who appear in connection with an emergent social class and who prepare the way for that class's conquest of civil society by preparing it ideologically; and traditional intellectuals, those who seem to be unconnected with social change and who occupy positions in society designed to conserve the traditional processes by which ideas are produced—teachers, writers, artists, priests, and the like. Gramsci's thesis is that all intellectuals are really organic intellectuals to some extent; even when they seem completely disconnected with a political cause, schoolteachers, for instance, play a social role to the extent that they unconsciously legitimate the status quo they serve. Throughout his life Gramsci spent time studying Croce, whom he described in one of his prison letters as a sort of lay pope because of the philosophic hegemony he exercised over the liberal Italian society that, Gramsci believed, directly produced fascism.

Since Gramsci the discussion of intellectuals has taken center stage in analyses of the modern postindustrial state, certainly a far cry from Swift's England. But there are interesting analogies. In 1979 Alvin Gouldner wrote his *Future of the Intellectuals and the Rise of the New Class*, where he sees the new class of intellectuals as challenging the old monied class for power. Leaving aside the questionable aspects of Gouldner's thesis, he is worth soliciting on the question of what he calls the intellectual's *capital.* Earlier I said that many of Swift's critics pay too much attention to his ideas and not enough to the deployment and disposition of his energies, his local performances I called them. What such assertions do is to ally Swift too closely with the real holders of those basically reactionary values, the great landed aristocracy, the established church, the imperial monarchy. Translated into ideology this class is represented by these Tory values ascribed to Swift. Swift himself was not a propertyowner, and it is perfectly evident from his work that he had a low opinion of conquering armies, of colonial oppression, and of scientific schemes for manipulating people and opinion. In Gouldner's terminology, Swift's capital was that of the intellectual: rhetorical skill as a writer on the ideological field of battle. By the same token, then, we must look at Swift as an intellectual engaged in particular struggles of a very limited sort, not as a man who formulated, defended and owned a consistent set of ideological values, which were not his class prerogative to begin with since they quite literally belonged to the class he sometimes served.

During his lifetime Swift could fairly be described as an outsider. He was not well-born, his high-placed patrons invariably disappointed him, and he regularly angered and alienated authorities he was supposed to be serving. There is an ironic reminder of this in Gulliver's voyage to Lilliput, when in putting out the fire by urinating on it Gulliver also succeeds in offending the Queen. So far as I know, Swift had no alternative to social advancement outside the church, except through patronage, intellectual activity on behalf of partisan causes (most but not all of the time), and sheer wit (as a conversationalist and writer). He never amassed anything resembling a fortune, and he died as alienated from Ireland as he had been, over twenty years before, from England. From a class standpoint, then, Swift was a traditional intellectual—a cleric—but what makes him unique is that unlike almost any other major writer in the whole of English literature (except possibly for Steele) he was also an extraordinarily important organic intellectual because of his closeness to real political power. At certain stages in their careers Defoe and Johnson were pamphleteers and, in Johnson's case, public figures; neither of them, however, was visibly affiliated with a political formation in ascendancy as Swift was with the Tory government between 1711 and 1713. For then it was Swift's job to legitimize Harley's admittedly opportunistic politics of peace (culminating in the Peace of Utrecht) and to delegitimize the Whig politics of war. It must also be said of his later intellectual work that it was organically linked to a very different kind of nascent political power, the Irish colonial community, which Swift himself played a significant part in creating. Who except Swift could say as simply and as truthfully as he does in *The Drapier's Letters:* "By engaging in the Trade of a Writer I have drawn upon myself the Displeasure of the Government."[7]

What are the major issues—barring such teleological questions as the nature of man and the forms of civil or ecclesiastical authority—that Swift's work defined? Principally I would say anything connected with human aggression or organized human violence. Under this heading Swift was able to place such disparate things as war itself (about which he never had a good word to say: a remarkable fact), conquest, colonial oppression, religious factionalism, the manipulation of minds and bodies, schemes for projecting power on nature, on human beings, and on history, the tyranny of the majority, monetary profit for its own sake, the victimization of the poor by a privileged oligarchy. Each of these things can be easily documented in at least one of Swift's works, and it should be remembered that there are very few authors before the late nineteenth century—Blake and Shelley being among the few—whose position on these matters diverges so sharply from the reigning majority view. There is nothing that so consciously and so deliberately reveals both the sheer horror of war and the even more horrible delight and pride that men take in it than this passage from *Gulliver:*

> To confirm what I have now said, and further to shew the miserable Effects of a *confined Education;* I shall here insert a Passage which will hardly obtain Belief. In hopes to ingratiate myself farther into his Majesty's Favour, I told him of an Invention discovered between three and four hundred Years ago, to make a certain Powder; into an heap of which the smallest Spark of Fire falling, would kindle the whole in a Moment, although it were as big as a Mountain; and make it all fly up in the Air together, with a Noise and Agitation greater than Thunder. That, a proper Quantity of this Powder rammed into an hollow Tube of Brass or Iron or Lead with such Violence and Speed, as nothing was able to sustain its Force. That, the largest Balls thus discharged, would not only Destroy whole Ranks of an Army at once; but batter the strongest Walls to the Ground; sink down Ships with a Thousand Men in each, to the Bottom of the Sea; and when linked together by a Chain, would cut through Masts and Rigging; divide Hundreds of Bodies in the Middle, and lay all Waste before them. That we often put this Powder into large hollow Balls of Iron, and discharged them by an Engine into some City we were besieging; which would rip up the Pavement, tear the Houses to Pieces, burst and throw Splinters on every Side, dashing out the Brains of all who came near . . . .
>
> The King was struck with Horror at the Description I had given of those terrible Engines, and the Proposal I had made. He was amazed how so impotent and groveling an Insect as I (these were his Expressions) could entertain such inhuman Ideas, and in so familiar a Manner as to appear wholly unmoved at all the Scenes of Blood and Desolation, which I had painted as the common Effects of those destructive Machines; whereof he said, some evil Genius, Enemy to Mankind, must have been the first Contriver. As for himself, he protested, that although few Things delighted him so much as new Discoveries in Art or in Na-

> ture; yet he would rather lost Half his Kingdom than be privy to such a Secret; which he commanded me, as I valued my Life, never to mention any more.[8]

Or there is this devastating analysis of the war of Spanish succession in *The Conduct of the Allies:*

> whether this War were prudently begun or not, it is plain, that the true Spring or Motive of it, was the aggrandizing a particular Family, and in Short, a War of the General and the Ministry, and not of the Prince or People; since those very Persons were against it, when they knew the Power, and consequently the Profit, would be in other Hands.[9]

Here Swift speaks the truth simply; he tries neither to dress it up nor to conceal the secrecy or greed with which profitable wars are planned. Hence the anger Swift feels on behalf of future generations: "it will no doubt be a mighty Comfort to our Grandchildren when they see a few Rags hung up in Westminster Hall, which cost an hundred Millions, whereof they are paying the Arrears, and boasting, as Beggars do, that their Grandfathers were Rich and Great."[10] And there is no more relevant description than Swift's of the way great powers tie themselves to allies who are supposed to be their surrogates, but become their masters (one thinks of Generals Thieu and Ky during the Vietnamese war):

> By two other Articles (beside the honour of being Convoys and Guards in ordinary to the Portugese Ships and Coasts) we are to guess the Enemies Thoughts, and to take the King of Portugal's Word, whenever he has a Fancy that he shall be invaded: We are also to furnish him with a Strength superior to what the Enemy intends to invade any of his Dominions with, let that be what it will: And, till we know what the Enemy's forces are, his Portugese Majesty is sole Judge what Strength is superior, and what will be able to prevent an invasion; and may send our Fleets, whenever he pleases, upon his Errands, to some of the Furthest Parts of the World, or keep them attending upon his own Coasts till he thinks fit to dismiss them. These Fleets must likewise be subject, in all things, not only to the King, but to his Viceroys, Admirals and Governours, in any of his foreign Dominions, when he is in a humour to apprehend an Invasion; which, I believe, is an indignity that was never offered before, except to a Conquered Nation.[11]

When it was assumed by his countrymen that they knew everything important about their Irish colony, it was Swift who in his letter to Lord Chancellor Middleton on October 26, 1724, described the stereotype that made it possible for England to mistreat Ireland so cavalierly (similar caricatures of African and Asian peoples exist even today):

> There is a Vein of Industry and Parsimony, that runs through the whole people of England; which, added to the Easiness of their Rents, makes them rich and sturdy. As to Ireland, they know little more than they do of Mexico; further than that it is a Country subject to the King of England, full of Boggs, inhabited by wild Irish Papists; who are kept in Awe by mercenary Troops sent from thence: And their general Opinion is, that it were better for England if this whole Island were sunk into the Sea: For, they have a tradition, that every Forty Years there must be a Rebellion in Ireland. I have seen the grossest suppositions pass upon them; that the wild Irish were taken in Toyls; but that, in some time, they would grow so tame, as to eat out of your hands.[12]

We can see the unmistakable connection between this sort of thinking and the logic that gave rise to *A Modest Proposal*, for once you dehumanize people into a mere bundle of unchanging attributes it is a very short step to turning them into articles of consumption.

Despite all this, it would not be fair to Swift simply to characterize him as a courageous intellectual. What we must also be able to understand about him is that everything he did as an intellectual heightened and affected consciousness, even to the extent that he brought out his own self-conscious position in his writing. This immediately gets us to the canonical question of Swift's satire, his irony, and the use of personae.

Let me do so first by returning to what I said at the outset about modern criticism. I had made it seem then that Swift has not been favored with avant-garde critical attention because he has seemed the exclusive property of a circle of scholars, and because there is general agreement that Swift's values are, in Orwell's words, clearly reactionary. In general, contemporary criticism has been concerned with authors and texts whose formal characteristics exist in some disjunctive relationship with their ideological or thematic surface: thus the critic's job is to illuminate the disjunction by exposing, or deconstructing, the contradictions woven into the text's formal being. Moreover, the critic's position about the texts he analyzes is a marginal one; that is, the text is important whereas the critic's role is a secondary one, limited to revealing the text's conditions of being. This procedure is true, I think, of the Derridean school, the school of Marxist readers, of Foucault's disciples, the semioticians, of the so-called Yale school.

Swift resists this approach and, as I said earlier, it is his resistance that makes him so interesting and challenging a figure. My argument is that the main avenue to understanding Swift is that we take seriously the way in which he resists any kind of critical approach that does not make his existence, his functioning, and above all his self-consciousness as an intellectual—albeit an intellectual in the special historical circumstances of his cultural moment—the main avenue to approaching him.

Consider therefore three theses I want to propose. (1) Swift has no reserve capital: his writing brings to the surface all he has to say. His fictions, his personae, his self-irony turn around the scandal, first announced in *A Tale of a Tub*, that what is being said is being said at that moment, for that moment, by a creature of that moment. This is always literally true—what we can know about Swift or Gulliver or the Drapier is what is before us, and only that. The irony completes itself in the reading; there is nothing to check it against (who would consider appealing from the "modest proposal" to a real person who doesn't think that people should be eaten?) since what it says is what it means. (2) Swift is invariably attacking what he impersonates. In other words, his technique is to become the thing he attacks, which is normally not a message or a political doctrine but a style or a manner of discourse. Note how many of Swift's works are about iterative performances, activities, styles of behavior: proposal, tale, conduct, conversation, voyage, letter, argument, examination, sermon. The space between satirist and object satirized disappears, as for instance in a digression concerning digression or madness. (3) Ahead of his critics, Swift is always aware—and troubles the reader with the awareness—that what he is doing above all is *writing* in a world of power. Swift is the realist par excellence and can make, indeed embody in what he writes, distinctions between idle language and the language of authority, the language of institutions and the language of alienated or marginal individuals, the language of reason and what he called polite conversation. Thus Swift is among the most worldly of writers—perhaps the most worldly. Yet these distinctions have a habit of collapsing into one another. He will, for example, seriously propose a scheme for ascertaining, establishing, and correcting the language, then a few years later parody the scheme by writing *The Polite Conversation*, which is nothing if not a centralized, socially agreed upon scheme for all language in society.

This habit of turning something into its opposite is a corollary of Swift's vocation as a reactive writer. It is also the consequence of Swift's realization that what he is doing is merely writing, albeit on behalf of one or another cause. Yet more than anything else Swift's activity as intellectual, that is, his mission to make his reader more conscious of what a given political or moral position entails, seems always to have infected his own self-consciousness. The worm of consciousness, to borrow from Nicola Chiaromonte, infects Swift the writer. This is the source of his extraordinary self-irony. I am reminded of an observation about Wittgenstein made by Erich Heller: such self-consciousness as Wittgenstein's arrives at "the stage where every act of creation is inseparable from the critique of its medium, and every work, intensely reflecting upon itself, looks like the embodied doubt of its own possibility."[13] Surely this is the ironic consequence of *A Tale of a Tub*, which in attacking enthusiasts of all sorts turns and incriminates the author of the writing himself. Or as a wonderfully suggestive series of images seems to be saying, isn't all writing by someone like Swift just as vulnerable to criticism, irony, and answering as the things he attacks? I am thinking of Swift's images in *A Tale* for the ridiculous and shaky opportunities available if one wishes to intervene verbally into reality—the pulpit, the stage itinerant, or the ladder—and how these things, like a tract, a tale, a digression, or a pamphlet, are subject to other sorts of more worldly power, which a writer or an intellectual without really solid capital does not possess. Intellectual writing protrudes into space and time, but its occasions are in the end controlled by real power. Beyond its immediately serviceable qualities (which are in thrall to a monied or political class), all such writing has its internal ironies, which concern and delight the intellectual. Or consider the occasion in the *Travels* when Gulliver creates a space on his spread-out handkerchief for the Lilliputian cavalry and how we realize that, if the giant Gulliver withdraws, they will collapse. The power he possesses as a giant works against him in turn when as a dwarf in Brobdingnag he performs on small tables for the audience.

The greatest intellectual irony, or the greatest irony of an intellectual, is to be found in the fourth voyage, that one episode in Swift's work that has haunted all his readers. We cannot easily exhaust its power or its devastating imaginative originality, nor should we try. But we can see in the Houyhnhnms and the Yahoos—with Gulliver between them—a measure of Swift's general intellectual disenchantment with society, a disenchantment that in the end presents us with minimal options for a satisfactory life. The crucial thing about the Houyhnhnms is not whether they are supposed to be an ideal, but that they are animals; as for the Yahoos, they are humans who act more like animals than men. This state of affairs is perhaps an instance of what Orwell calls "the irresponsible violence of the powerless": nothing of human life is left for Swift to take pleasure in, so he attacks it all. But what has always impressed me in the fourth voyage is that over and above its genuine disillusionment there still remains, as impressive as anything else in the tale, Gulliver himself, recording his recognitions and discoveries, still making sense, still—even in Houyhnhnmland—finding out where the occasions might exist for him to do something. That each of the voyages ends with Gulliver's banishment or escape reflects, I think, the ultimately tragic restlessness of Swift's intellectual energy, just as Gulliver's voyages to fully imagined places, where he must respond to the minute pressures of each situation, testify to Swift's energetic desire to look for concrete things in order to "answer" them.

I think finally that in a passage from *The Drapier's Letters* we can hear the accents of Swift's general intellectual alertness, and his sense of the healthy cynicism, the fragility, the marginality, but also the mastered irony of the intellectual's true situation:

> I am now resolved to follow (after the usual Proceeding of Mankind, because it is too late) the Advice given me by a certain Dean. He shewed the mistake I was in, of trusting to the general good Will of the people; that I had succeeded hitherto, better than could be expected; but that some unfortunate circumstantial Lapse, would probably bring me within the reach of Power: that my good intentions would be no Security against those who watched every Motion of my Pen, in the Bitterness of my Soul.[14]

Endnotes

1. George Orwell, *In Front of Your Nose, 1945–1950,* ed. Sonia Orwell and Ian Angus, vol. 4 of *The Collected Essays, Journalism and Letters of George Orwell* (New York: Harcourt Brace Jovanovich, 1968), pp. 222–223. See also the comments on Swift's reactionary versus progressive political positions in (for the former) Perry Anderson, *Arguments Within English Marxism* (London: New Left Books, 1980), pp. 83–88, and (for the latter) E. P. Thompson, *The Poverty of Theory and Other Essays* (London: Merlin Press, 1978), p. 234.

2. Oscar Wilde, "The Soul of Man Under Socialism," in *The Artist as Critic: Critical Writings of Oscar Wilde,* ed. Richard Ellmann (1969; rprt. New York: Vintage, 1970), p. 259.

3. Lewis Coser, *Men of Ideas: A Sociologist's View* (New York: Free Press, 1970), pp. 20–21.

4. Ibid., p. 3.

5. Julien Benda, *The Treason of the Intellectuals,* trans. Richard Aldington (1928; rprt. New York: Norton, 1969), p. 57.

6. See, most recently, Noam Chomsky, "Intellectuals and the State," in *Towards A New Cold War: Essays on the Current Crisis and How We Got There* (New York: Pantheon, 1982).

7. Jonathan Swift, *The Drapier's Letters,* in *Prose Works,* ed. Herbert Davis (1939; rprt. Oxford: Basil Blackwell, 1964–1968), X, 81.

8. Swift, *Gulliver's Travels,* in *Prose Works,* XI, 134.

9. Swift, *The Conduct of the Allies,* in *Prose Works,* VI, 41.

10. Ibid., 55–56.

11. Ibid., 25.

12. Ibid., 103.

13. Erich Heller, *The Artist's Journey into the Interior and Other Essays* (New York: Random House, 1965).

14. Swift, *Drapier's Letters*, p. 89.

Three Times Round the Globe: Gulliver and Colonial Discourse

Clement Hawes

I assured him, that this whole globe of earth must be at least three times gone round before one of our better female yahoos could get her breakfast, or a cup to put it in.

—*Gulliver's Travels*, p. 242

A cluster of related questions haunts the commentary on *Gulliver's Travels*. There has been frequent debate about whether or not Gulliver is a genuine character, a personality who undergoes conflict and change. Gulliver has many of the trappings of "character"[1]—a proper name, an obtrusively present physique, a family of middling status with its own burying ground, a particularized education, a profession in which he advances (from surgeon to captain), national pride, traits of curiosity and wanderlust, an idiosyncratic and unfailing gift for languages—and yet his outlook is disturbingly unstable. Challengers of Gulliver's personhood thus argue that "Gulliver" is nothing more than an inconsistently used vehicle for satire, a mere mask to be dropped and reassumed at the whim of the author.[2] A significant domain of interpretation is at stake, for if Gulliver is not seen to some extent as a "character"—and if Gulliver is thus not read both with and against the conventions of the nascent novel—then the entire dimension of the narrative that shows his sequential shifts and changes is rendered meaningless.

Critics likewise debate the extent to which a full reading of *Gulliver* requires recourse to the supposed failings, such as misanthropy or neurosis, of Swift. This tradition of reading Swift, still influential, produces, by way of historical interpretation, only an individual case history. The moral and

Cultural Critique 18 (Spring 1991): 187–214.

psychological terms of this debate, precisely to the extent that they condemn or pathologize Swift, tend to depoliticize interpretation of *Gulliver's Travels* and, especially, to domesticate its insights into colonial practice and discourse. While gross abuses of psychoanalysis are now mercifully scarce, a less clinical emphasis on Swift's psychology remains common.

A third reiterated critical debate attempts to say just how "historical" *Gulliver* is. It inquires, more specifically: does or does not Swift's mode of satire require us to seek particular historical parallels for every event in *Gulliver*—for instance, in the maneuvering of the Tory cabinet ministers Oxford and Bolingbroke? Is the book a continuous political allegory of long-past events (Case, 69–80)? Opponents of such minutely historicized allegories, dismayed by a daunting pedantry, often retreat altogether from history into notions of universality (*Gulliver* as a parable of the human predicament) or of the ludic spirit (*Gulliver* as the playful enactment of such childhood fantasies). The parties to such a debate seem to assume history to be little more than the driest of chronicles. Full weight must be given, as I argue in the introduction to this volume, to the colonial resonance of early eighteenth-century history, especially in Ireland (pp. 7–10). The contributions in this vein of an impressive cadre of critics—Carol Fabricant, Andrew Carpenter, Joseph McMinn, Robert Mahony, Thomas McLoughlin, Ann Cline Kelly, and Declan Kiberd, among others—need to be systematically digested and traced through the rhetorical texture of *Gulliver's Travels.*

As Britain emerged as the leading maritime power in the early eighteenth century, institutionalized languages—a fabric of repeated commonplaces—emerged to legitimate colonial expansion. This colonial discourse reconfigured a matrix of older genres: travel literature, ethnography, cartography, and natural history. The expansionist ethos of these reshaped genres, more than the minutiae of Queen Anne's reign, resonates now with a collectively significant history. *Gulliver*, responding to an ongoing and supercharged colonial history, is indeed "historical"—but in a less dull and more urgent sense than is sometimes recognized.

Each of these apparently "formal" problems can be reframed by raising a political and ideological issue that links them. My reading, which takes up, as a problematic of form, the cultural representation of "history" in a strong sense—as European colonialism—also offers a possible explanation for the reception of *Gulliver's Travels.*

In the long view, the reception of *Gulliver's Travels* has reflected a defensive tendency to foreclose the colonial dialectic on which the full satiric effect of the book depends. The satiric effect of *Gulliver's Travels* depends on Swift's ironizing, literalizing, and, above all, reversing of the commonplaces of seventeenth- and eighteenth-century British colonial discourse. This appropriation of colonial discourse, very typical of Swift's satirical strategies, turns it, through excessive zeal, against the "wrong" object: the Englishman. And though it would be wrong to argue that Swift could have avoided implication in the systems he inhabited,[3] his particular satirical strategies in fact led to a withering critique of colonialism. *Gulliver's* plot, indeed—drawing, as it does, on genres with obvious ties to the political institutions of trade, fiscal policy, ethnography, and South Sea exploration—consists of a narrative in which Gulliver, the English narrator, is himself colonized. Since readers are so positioned by the conventions of first-person narrative as to identify more or less closely with Gulliver, they likewise undergo an increasingly painful confrontation with the experience of the colonized. By the end it is not merely mercantile values, but the very identity of the colonizing subject, that has been dismantled.

Alternative literary sources for *Gulliver* can certainly be adduced. Ancient travel literature is full of monstrous ethnic "Others," from doglike men who bark rather than speak to cyclopean beings, from men with eyes in their shoulders to hermaphroditic or pygmy communities. Such discourses about fantastic alterity have a superficial similarity that can seem timeless. In Swift's time, however, such discourses were increasingly drawn into the orbit of a historically specific project: colonial expansion, based on a combination of commercial and military power, from northwest Europe. *Gulliver* thus responds less to classical or medieval models than to the emerging discourses specific to eighteenth-century colonialism. In order to grasp the dialectic of Swift's satire, then, it is necessary to specify further some of the chief topoi and narrative strategies of these early colonial discourses.[4] I offer the following topoi as a somewhat desultory inventory of the rhetorical resources used to legitimate the colonial project. Alterity is a theme with many variations: cannibalism, abasement, display, exotic-pet status, filthiness, pendulous breasts (a misogynist inflection of ethnic defamation), and kinship with apes. Absence is likewise a richly elaborated theme: the colonized, it seems, *lack* so very many things. Mimicry and the denial of coevalness round out the repertoire.

The theme of alterity, as a great deal of recent work demonstrates, serves to justify aggression and violence toward a group designated as "Other." Thence comes, to take one crucial example, the theme of cannibalism, a term so freighted with colonial ethnography that some, like Peter Hulme, question whether the concept ever applied "outside the discourse of European colonialism" (Hulme, 1986, 84). Such skepticism may be met with this or that counterexample of "real" cannibalism. But the more important question remains, in Hulme's words, why Europeans were "so desirous of finding confirmation of their suspicions of cannibalism." (Hulme, 1998, 4). At any rate, the rhetorical function of the cannibalism topos is clear. The hack writer and editor John Dunton opined in 1691 that cannibalism, because it was worse than slavery, justified the latter: "[Africans] must either be *killed* or *eaten*, or both, by their barbarous conquering enemy" (cited in Dabydeen, 28). Cannibalism is of course the key motif in *Robinson Crusoe* (1719) establishing at the most visceral level a frozen opposition between Christian civilization and its nauseatingly imagined inversion. Cannibalism appears as well in earlier "voyage" books, including some books owned by Swift.[5] For instance, Sir Thomas Herbert, author of *Some Years Travels into Divers Parts of Asia and Afrique* (1638), describes the African people of Loango as "divels incarnate" who butcher their neighbors and friends with a "vultures appetite" and even proffer themselves, when "worne by age," to be "joynted" and "set to sell upon the stalls" (11).[6] As Robert Mahony shows in an essay reprinted here, fears of being "devoured" by the Catholic majority were central to the siege mentality of Anglo-Irish Protestants. The ideological uses of cannibalism explain why Swift uses the topos of cannibalism in *A Modest Proposal* (1729) to represent, in an ironic reversal, the exploitation of the Irish poor both by Britain and by Anglo-Irish landlords. In his marginalia to his own copy of Herbert's travels, Swift writes, "If this book were stripped of its Impertinence, Conceitedness and tedious Digressions, it would almost be worth reading, and would then be two thirds smaller than it is." He also refers to a later edition as even more "insufferable" (Davis, vol. 5, 243).

A hyperbolic depiction of the "Other" is evident also in the many topoi of abasement generated in colonial discourse. Hence, for example, the grateful yielding—a highly convenient and guilt-reducing self-enslavement—of the Caribbean Amerindian Friday to English Crusoe, symbolized in colonial sign-language by his placing Crusoe's foot above his head (Hulme, 1986, 204–206; see also the illustration on p. 24). Defoe, writing about seven years before the publication of *Gulliver*, renders this scene of native groveling twice in the space of a few pages. It signifies not only Friday's personal debt to Crusoe, but also, along with the scenes of cannibals and shootings thereof, the emblematic colonial encounter when the relationship between European and native must be settled (Hulme, 1986, 201).

Yet another discursive construction of colonial alterity derives primarily from combined impulses of voyeurism and exploitation. Based on the actual practice of exhibiting "unusual" human beings,[7] it could be termed the topos of display. In *The Tempest*, Trinculo's first thought upon sighting Caliban is to exhibit him as a freak in England: "Not a holiday fool there but would give a piece of silver . . . When they will not give a doit to relieve a lame beggar, they will lay out ten to see a dead Indian" (II. ii. 29–33). And the colonized were in fact displayed like zoo animals in "ethnological" exhibitions throughout the capitals of Europe from the sixteenth century well into the early twentieth century (Altick, 266–87; Gilman, 76–108; Gould,

291–305). It is perhaps too seldom noted that Montaigne's justly famous essay "Des Cannibales" was fashioned out of conversations he had with Tupinamba Indians then exhibited in Europe (Stam and Spence, 17). In Swift's time, between 1704 and 1709, a West Indian "midget" was similarly displayed at Leeds and in Lincoln's Inn Fields (Stallybrass and White, 40). In the winter of 1711–12, while Swift still lived in London, this same midget and his pregnant wife were displayed (as the vastly popular and well-advertised "Little Family") at Charing Cross by a showman who exulted in print about the prospect of "breeding" them (Taylor, 65–66). Although similar popular spectacles of the period included Swiss and German dwarves, an infant acrobat, a rope-dancing monkey, a trained marmoset, a baboon, seven-year-old Siamese twins, and a "wonderful Femal[e] Creature having a head like a Hog" (Taylor, 30–31, 57–64), the display of colonized people went beyond such exoticism. Unlike, say, the exhibition of a German dwarf, the exhibition of West Indian midgets constituted a specifically colonial mode of voyeurism: a gaze mediated by the violent domination of one group by another. In "dramatizing the psychology of monster-viewing" (Todd, 155), Swift emphasizes the colonial mentality that reconstructed traditional freak-shows along new lines.

The sheer fact of such exhibitions, that someone dared to conceive and build the brutalizing booths, boxes, and cages, seemed to confirm that the spectacle contained nothing human. The phenomenon demonstrates, chillingly, how colonial discourse authorizes the reduction of human beings to exotic curiosities. For our purposes, it is also important that the nonreciprocal ethnological gaze provides a generic source, in colonial discourse, for that fascination with the lower body, that morbid dwelling on what R. W. Frantz terms "man's ugliness, lecherousness, and loathsome natural functions" (53), for which Swift is notorious. As so often, "thinking the body" became in colonial discourse a means of "thinking social topography" (Stallybrass and White, 192). I have no wish to deny that Swift's temperament played a role in his choice of topics. But such choices are always determined by multiple factors, and they oblige us to avoid reductive explanations. Moreover, only by evading the actual content of colonial rhetoric and practice—its voyeurism and coprophilia—can we dismiss Swift's use of such passages as mere individual pathology. We deplore Swift's "misanthropy," we shake our heads at his "pathology," in short, to deflect the intolerable implications of a specific colonial history. The public register of Swift's famously excremental vision, his literary scatology, partly derives from the colonial discourse of his era.

It helps to recall here the suggestive conclusion reached by Stallybrass and White, that strong social differentiation, such as colonial conquest demands, depends on disgust (191). It then becomes comprehensible that, as

Frantz points out, nauseating descriptions of naked, filthy, flat-nosed, fat-lipped, and depraved "natives" appeared in print "with striking frequency throughout the seventeenth and early eighteenth centuries" (53). To be sure, no coherent racial ideology in the modern sense yet existed (Malik; Wheeler). Africa as a whole was often seen as teeming with diverse ethnicities and kingdoms. Both English and Dutch travelers, however, expressed a negative fascination with the obstinate alterity of the so-called Hottentots (now known as the Khoikhoi peoples, inhabiting southern Africa). The Hottentots, as Linda Merians demonstrates, became a favorite travelogue example of humanity at its lowest. Take the following passages from several authors of travel literature likely known to Swift. The Hottentots (now known as the Khoikhoi peoples) were, according to Sir Thomas Herbert, "an accursed Progeny of *Cham*, who differ in nothing from bruit beasts save forme" (Frantz, 53). Or again, as Frantz paraphrases Captain Cowley, author of *Voyage round the Globe* (1699): "It was their habit to dance about the *Hollanders* shaking their Privy Parts, with an offer. . . . that they should lye with their Wives for a bit of rolled Tobacco" (Frantz, 53). Moreover, according to Cowley, they "are a People that will eat anything that is foul: If the *Hollanders* kill a Beast, they will get the Guts and squeez [*sic*] the Excrements out, and then without washing or scraping, lay them upon the Coals, and before they are well hot through, will take them and eat them" (cited in Frantz, 53).

Swift's "excremental vision" is idiosyncratic only in that he extends it to European bodily functions and folkways: a political repudiation both of the colonizers and their ethnographic slanders.

Descriptions of native women, moreover, focused with intense misogyny on their terrible smell, their nether parts, and their pendulous breasts. Herbert, capping an inventory of the "infernal postures" of Angolan natives, seems to out-Swift Swift with the claim that "the female sex each new Moone [defy] pale fac't *Cynthia* by turning up their bummes, imagining her the cause of their distempers" (10). And the following is only one of several possible examples cited by Frantz, taken from Daniel Beeckman's *A Voyage to and from the Island of Borneo* (1718):

> "The women are generally short squat creatures, but built strong, altogether as ugly in their kind as the men, having long flabby breasts, odiously dangling down to their waist; which they can toss over their shoulders for their children to suck, whom they generally carry on their backs. . . ." (55)

Jennifer L, Morgan's analysis of many similar reports, most by early modern travelers in the Americas and Africa, makes clear the extent to which the theme of pendulous breasts had served to inspire fascinated disgust in one European traveler after another. In the earlier eighteenth century, adult female breasts had not yet been subjected to the sentimental discourse of motherhood. Maternal discourse, revolving around the ideal of a nuclearized family, emphasized personal (rather than delegated) breast-feeding of infants (Perry). Pendulous breasts, considered bovine, provided an aesthetic rationale for domination: a laboriously cultivated, and yet still ambivalent disgust. Rawson recounts several examples from the nineteenth and twentieth centuries as well (2001, 98–108).

The final degradation of "natives" involves innumerable comparisons between them and sundry anthropoid primates found in the same area. Sometimes there are allegations of a kind of interspecies "miscegenation." Herbert, for instance, remarks that the Hottentot language "is apishly sounded (with whom tis thought they mixe unnaturally) . . ." (18). Beeckman draws the conclusion that obviously lurked behind this allegation:

> They are not really unlike monkeys or baboons in their gestures, especially when they sit sunning themselves, as they often do in great numbers. (cited in Frantz, 56)

In his *A Voyage to Surat* (1696) John Ovington makes a common application of this logic to the Great Chain of Being: ". . . if there's any medium between a Rational Animal and a Beast, the *Hottentot* lays fairest Claim to that Species" (cited in Frantz, 56). The lethal consequences of such a subhuman status are clear enough.

The theme of *absence* often appears in colonial representations in order to render unthinkable the inconvenient facts of extant native culture (Stam and Spence, 7). The colonial representation of the Khoikhoi language as "a farrago of bestial sounds resembling the chatter of apes or the clucking of hens" (Frantz, 55) suggests a determination to see lack rather than an engaged response to novel linguistic registers. Similarly made invisible are native thought ("superstitious") and native self-reflexivity (fettered by "tradition"). Native history is shown to be static: neither essentially disrupted by external invasion nor progressive in its own right. Conventions of characterization and point of view similarly produce invisibility by depicting named and individuated white "characters" in depth while assigning natives, often seen in crowds or "hordes," the depersonalizing and nameless "mark of the plural" (Memmi, 85). Consider the following passage about names from William Dampier's *New Voyage Round the World* (1697), a book owned by Swift:

> The Natural Inhabitants of the Cape are the *Hodmadods,* as they are commonly called, which is a corruption of the word *Hottantot;* for this is the Name by which they call to one another, either in their Dances, or on any occasion, as if every one of them had this for his name. The word

> probably hath some signification or other in their language, whatever it is. (536–37)

Dampier's refusal to differentiate is thus projected onto the natives themselves as a "lack." Above all, there is native territory, often shown as previously "unoccupied," like Crusoe's island (Hulme, 1986, 185–186), in a consciously emblematic moment of colonial origins. J. M. Coetzee points out that the landscape poetry and "official historiography" of South Africa have often converged in seeing the African landscape as silent, unpeopled, and empty, a vacuum waiting to be filled by white settlers (177). The material stakes of the colonial project involve land, and this recurrent myth of "a land without people" softens the process of displacement and expropriation.

Another colonial distortion, the exact obverse of the construction of the savage "Other," involves variations on the theme of "sameness." The genealogy of this image is lengthy. From its earliest phases, European colonialism has tended to divide the colonized into "good" and "bad" natives such as the "bad" Caribs and the "good," but regrettably annihilated, Arawaks (Hulme, 1986, 43–67). In the more culturally intrusive and advanced phase of colonial domination, when the native's internalization of foreign values is required, various topoi of assimilation mark the adaptation of a "good" (useful, tractable) native to the hegemonic culture. Thus Dampier concludes a description of some "good natives," the Moskito Indians, as follows:

> They have no form of Government among them, but acknowledge the King of *England* for their Sovereign: They learn our Language, and they take the Governor of *Jamaica* to be one of the greatest Princes in the World. (10–11)

The Moskitos are also described as being, in matters of religion, "ready to imitate us in whatsoever they saw us do at any time" (8–9). As Homi Bhabha's work has made clear, *successful* assimilation, fully acknowledged, would in fact have constituted a subversive redistribution of cultural identifications: an emotionally charged encounter, on a leveled playing field, disrupting the dependence of the colonizer on recognition of his superiority. Such a hybrid phenomenon, as happened around the world, threatened to deconstruct the biological and essentialist identities maintaining the hierarchical difference on which the colonial system depended. "Mimicry" was ambivalent: both reassuring and threatening. So it is that the native attempt to assimilate is often rendered as only marginally successful, an amusingly superficial bit of mimicry. This derisive treatment of the Other's mimicry of civilization manifests, through the topos of "failed assimilation," both the need of the native for European culture and his or her implacable inferiority to it: his being almost the same, in Bhabha's formulation, but not quite. It consolidates the sense that, as Stallybrass and White put it, "the civilized is always-already-given" (41).

One cannot conclude this dismal catalogue of colonial distortions without remarking on the colonial representation of time. Nineteenth- and twentieth-century schemes of social evolution, as much recent work has shown, divided the human race according to a criterion of development. This "denial of coevalness" (Fabian, 32) marks the state of the native culture as belonging, in its self-contained local time-warp, to some other historical moment. Early modern ethnography, moreover, even before the nineteenth-century development of professional anthropology, had tentatively begun to map geographical territory through categories of temporal difference. Such topoi serve as a temporal distancing mechanism, most often insinuating that the colonized people, as a cultural phenomenon, are degenerate or child-like. They mask the fact that, in Fabian's words, "What are opposed, in conflict, in fact, locked in antagonistic struggle, are not the same societies at different stages of development, but different societies facing each other at the same Time" (155). The blame for casualties in the present can be shifted to the sad but inexorable workings of history itself.

Gulliver is huge; the Lilliputians are tiny. Even if they have successfully tied him up, Gulliver's apparent omnipotence promises to enact, all too literally, the dynamics of European encounters with indigenous peoples as the Europe has imagined them. Manipulation of scale, then, is a hyperbolic figuration of British colonial power. In this context, we expect to find, and quickly do, evidence of English technological superiority. In a classic colonial topos, Gulliver dazzles the Lilliputians with the awesome sound of his pistol:

> The astonishment here was much greater than at the sight of my scymiter. Hundreds fell down as if they had been struck dead; and even the emperor, although he stood his ground, could not recover himself in some time. (p. 64)

So Robinson Crusoe, having astonished Friday by shooting a parrot, remarks of Friday, "I believe, if I would have let him, he would have worshipp'd me and my Gun" (Defoe, 212). The almost godlike power of one superior European individual over "lesser" non-European beings is perfectly traditional. If Gulliver is a bit vainglorious, the vanity belongs to his position as an omnipotent colonial subject. His omnipotence, however, is short-lived. For we soon encounter, in reversed form, another familiar colonial topos. As in *Robinson Crusoe*, this topos generally has something to do with kissing, or otherwise groveling near, the feet of the European master. In this case however, it is the English-speaking European who is thus made abject:

> The emperor himself in person, did me the honour to be by at the whole ceremony. I made my acknowledgments by prostrating myself at his majesty's feet. (70–71)

It does nothing for Gulliver's dignity, of course, that the emperor is all of six inches tall. And, indeed, no fate could be further from Gulliver's than that of the all-conquering European individual. He is, as the illustrations included in this volume remind us, constantly groveling.

Gulliver, mighty as he seems to be, is essentially enslaved and used as a one-man mercenary army by the Lilliputians. Moreover, we encounter all too soon the colonial topos of exhibition, focusing, as often, on the enlarged private parts of the "native." The Lilliputian Emperor orders Gulliver to stand "like a *Colossus*" with his legs apart. He then orders Lilliputian troops to march between his legs. Unfortunately, as Gulliver confesses, "my breeches were at that time in so ill a condition, that they afforded some opportunities for laughter and admiration" (p. 68). This topos recurs throughout *Gulliver's Travels*, as, indeed, it does throughout colonial discourse; it reappears soon enough in its most objectifying form. After Gulliver has tactlessly extinguished a fire in the queen's palace by urinating on it, the Lilliputians ponder his punishment. Eventually they decide on the "lenient" course of merely blinding him. However, the Lilliputians reveal to Gulliver that they had also considered starving him by degrees, cutting his flesh from his bones, and "leaving the skeleton as a monument of admiration to posterity" (p. 94). Gulliver's bones, awaiting the attention of a physical anthropologist, in a Lilliputian museum: no greater contrast could be imagined between colonial subject and anatomized object.

What most marks the voyage to Lilliput as an ironic appropriation of colonial discourse, however, is the topos of assimilation. Gulliver quickly begins to discard his own culture and to adopt the Lilliputian view of everything. The sharp discontinuities in Gulliver's character thus do not stem merely from the generic sacrifice of character development in satire. They are, rather, a satiric appropriation, turned against the English, of colonial topoi of comic or painless assimilation. Gulliver simply cannot be understood without some minimal concept of an evolving "character," but he exists in a surrealistic historical dimension that cannot be adequately represented within the conventions of formal realism. As he changes societies, the malleability of his character comes to seem like so much soft clay. In this presentation, moreover, Swift's satire does indeed engage with the conventions of the emerging novel. In foregrounding an intimate relation between the novel as a genre and nation-building through print culture,[8] Benedict Anderson hits upon the constellation of identifications that Swift seeks to critique in *Gulliver's Travels.* As a genre, the novel confirms, in Anderson's words, "the solidarity of a single community, embracing characters, authors and readers, moving onward through calendrical time" (33). "Characters" as we know them belong to a world of citizens: they balance a healthy measure of autonomy, once they have come of age, with the solidarity of belonging, usually both to a nuclear family and to a national community (no less real for being "imagined", often with chauvinistic pride). The plot of Gulliver's "failed assimilation" works with and against this standard narrative, revealing it to be dependent upon the exclusion and oppression of others.

The satisfying trajectory of the realistic novel—the achievement of "ethical autonomy" (Lloyd, 21)—has of course been a far from universal experience. Those denied autonomy, as second-class citizens or inhabitants of a territory denied self-determination, lack full access to it. Moreover, as Deidre Lynch reminds us, the British eighteenth century as a whole was quite different in this regard from what came later. "Individuated meaning", she writes, "did not come naturally to British writers and readers in the long eighteenth century" (Lynch, 9). Lemuel Gulliver (1726), for good historical reasons, is less finely individuated than, say, Jane Austen's Elinor Dashwood (1811). A more telling comparison might invoke the inner life of Defoe's Robinson Crusoe (1719), inflected as the novel is with the introspective accents of puritan journal-keeping. Crusoe, wracked with guilt for disobeying his father, is a sympathetic character. Finding a mysterious footprint on his island—among the most evocative scenes in Anglophone literature—Crusoe is a paranoid character. Surviving his own experience of domestic slavery unchanged, Crusoe seems invulnerable. Selling his companion Xury into indentured servitude, Crusoe is a cold customer. Severely deficient in the key eighteenth-century value of sociability, Crusoe is, above all, a self-maximizing character: an exceptionally hardened "individual." Naming Friday, Crusoe is both a character and a colonial subject. To Crusoe Friday must assimilate. Friday's lack of autonomy and the erasure of his past disrupt his access to ethical subjectivity.

In *Gulliver's Travels,* however, it is Gulliver who assimilates. Change is abrupt, mysterious, and far-reaching. So it is that Gulliver suddenly takes such pathetic pride in being—as opposed to Flimnap, his hated rival in Lilliputian court intrigue and a mere "Clumglum"—a lofty "Nardac" (p. 90). And indeed, so labile is Gulliver's identity that he even feels compelled to make an absurdly solemn defense of the honor of a Lilliputian lady supposedly seen in his chambers. Although the supposedly conjoined parts "differ in volume in the ratio of 1728 to 1" (Traugott, 130), Gulliver expends a lengthy paragraph vindicating her honor (pp. 89–90). It is a bawdy joke, of course, in the first degree, one that again calls attention to Gulliver's relatively enormous genitals. But it is likewise a sign that Gulliver, entrapped in an increasingly dehumanizing colonial plot, has lost his own perspective. The assaults on the coherence of his identity merely intensify as the book goes on.

Book 2 is in a rather trivial sense the mirror-image of book 1. The big man becomes the little man. But it is more deeply a reversal of positions between colonizer and colonized. Book 1 features the aestheticizing and disarming charms of miniaturization, but book 2, by politicizing the prettified "games" of colonial domination, reveals the perspective of the dominated. The experience of public exhibition, for instance, now truly painful, becomes the "controlling idea of the Voyage" (Taylor, 56):

> My master, to avoid a crowd, would suffer only thirty people at a time to see me. . . . I turned about several times to the company, paid my humble respects, said they were welcome; and used some other speeches I had been taught. . . . I drew out my hanger, and flourished with it after the manner of fencers in England. . . . I was that day shewn to twelve sets of company; and as often forced to go over again with the same fopperies, till I was half-dead with weariness and vexation. (p. 115)

Despite precautions, moreover, an "unlucky school-boy" almost brains Gulliver with a well-aimed Brobdingnagian hazelnut (p. 115). This traveling show—much like what befalls Jeoly, the "Painted Prince" brought from the South Sea islands to England by Dampier (p. 393)—goes on for some ten weeks. Gulliver performs in eighteen large towns, in many villages, for some private families, and, finally, in the metropolis of Lorbrulgrud. His death seems imminent, just as Jeoly died in Oxford of smallpox. And even after Gulliver is rescued by the queen, who buys him, he graduates only to the status of a pet, a sort of humanoid lapdog or canary. Pets were increasingly anthropomorphized during the Enlightenment, as Keith Thomas points out (117), and, conversely, as Srinivas Aravamudan observes, certain select favorites among the colonized were elevated to petlike status: a choice of private playmate over public commodity (38).

The Brobdingnagians see Gulliver as merely a clever animal, and the queen's maids of honor use him as a sexual toy. But the reversal goes deeper still. What usually passes in the more grotesque descriptions for Swift's neurotic aversion to "the flesh"—note the assumption of universality—is in reality an exemplary demystification of white skin. The magnified view of the "monstrous Breast" of a Brobdingnagian woman is thus described in terms worthy of the most hyperbolic European voyager:

> It stood prominent six foot, and could not be less than sixteen in circumference. The nipple was about half the bigness of my head, and

> the hue both of that and the dug so varified with spots, pimples, and freckles, that nothing could appear more nauseous. . . . This made me reflect upon the fair skins of our English ladies, who appear so beautiful to us, only because they are of our own size, and their defects not to be seen but through a magnifying glass. . . . (p. 110)

Although it is tempting to ascribe this merely to misogyny, we are quickly reminded of its application to Gulliver. Reminiscing about his discussion of "complexions" in Lilliput, Gulliver recalls an intimate friend who said

> He could discover great holes in my skin; that the stumps of my beard were ten times stronger than the bristles of a boar; and my complexion made up of several colours altogether disagreeable. . . . (p. 110)

This is not so much an assault on "the flesh" as on a quite specifically color-conscious theme: a topos that justifies colonialism by way of the supposed aesthetic superiority of white skin, hair, and breasts. Even Gulliver himself, in this case, draws the tolerant lesson of cultural relativity.

Among the innumerable "ridiculous and troublesome accidents" that befall Gulliver in the land of Brobdingnag is an adventure with a "frolick-some" monkey. The adventure is both dangerous and humiliating, insinuating as it does a kinship between Gulliver and a "lower" primate. The monkey holds Gulliver as if to suckle him. "I have good reason to believe," Gulliver concludes, "that he took me for a young one of his own species, by his often stroaking my face very gently with his other paw" (p. 135). Precisely that insinuation, as we have seen, is the common currency of colonial voyage literature.

As if this were not sufficient humiliation, Gulliver is also revealed to be morally inferior. Gulliver could be said, in some sense, to enjoy a technological superiority to the Brobdingnagians: he knows how to concoct gunpowder. His knowledge, indeed, of gunpowder, cannons, and their military capacities, is expert and detailed, as he informs the king. It is a secret, as the ingratiating Gulliver sees it, that would make the king "absolute master of the lives, the liberties, and the fortunes of his people" (p. 146). In this replay of the earlier topos, however, the king—far from being dazzled—is merely horrified. Gulliver is shown to be morally lacking, himself a product (as he says of the king) of "narrow principles and short views" (p. 146). He is himself a parrotlike mouthpiece, uncritically parroting the coarse mentality of his militaristic culture. The sheer passivity of Gulliver's absorption of English culture—the term *brainwashing* comes to mind (Donoghue, 1998, 171)—disturbs the easy assumption that individual characters can reliably "think for themselves." Because Gulliver has conformed so unreflectively to the ethos his own culture, moreover, he turns out to be defenseless against an external critique of its failings.

In Brobdingnag, Gulliver speaks of England in automatic and sanctimonious formulas like the ingenious clockwork toy he appears to be. He spews out the party line. As Clive T. Probyn suggests, Gulliver's "crass complacency" and "smug insularity" are most likely a parody of the scene near the beginning of *Robinson Crusoe*, where the elder Crusoe's advice to his son, equally scripted in its tone, becomes a "paean to middle-class values" (184). One of the most famous instances of Swift's supposed misanthropy occurs in this book, during Gulliver's searching conversations with the king of Brobdingnag about the history and social institutions of England. Having interrogated Gulliver's fatuous, cliché-ridden, and yet ultimately damning account of English culture, the king makes the following pronouncement: "But, by what I have gathered from your own relation, and the answers I have with much pains wringed and extorted from you; I cannot but conclude the bulk of your natives, to be the most pernicious race of little odious vermin that nature ever suffered to crawl upon the surface of the earth" (p. 144). To be sure, the English chauvinist is meant to feel the force of this withering judgment. But the real twist in Swift's satire here comes a few pages later, as Gulliver escapes from Brobdingnag aboard an English ship. Of the English sailors, who first appeared to him as pygmies, Gulliver informs the captain, "I thought they were the most little contemptible creatures I had ever beheld" (p. 156). The echo of the king's judgment here makes this more than a clever relativistic manipulation of scale. Gulliver has again adopted the perspective of an alien culture. Self-contempt is the predictable consequence: "For, indeed, while I was in that prince's country, I could never endure to look in a glass after my eyes had been accustomed to such prodigious objects; because the comparison gave me so despicable a conceit of my self" (p. 156). Unless we assume Gulliver to be at least a rudimentary character, the force of this passage is lost. Not painlessly, but in direct conflict with himself and his own kind, Gulliver assimilates. He is indeed a character, but one who redefines himself through the eyes of another.

Although the personal colonizing process of which Gulliver is victim is largely suspended in book 3, the theme of colonial rule is not. What Swift presents instead is a narrative about the collective subjects of colonial antagonisms, nations, and peoples. One episode in particular emphasizes the antagonisms that colonial rule inevitably generates. In the Voyage to Laputa, Swift depicts a magnetically powered "flying island" that reigns over, and exacts tribute from, the various dominions on the continent below. When gentler and safer methods of ensuring obedience to colonial administration fail, the flying island literally presses down—suppresses—the cities below, making "a universal destruction both of houses and men" (p. 176). As Thomas Metscher observes in an article on the Irish perspective in *Gulliver*, Swift makes clear by implication that in such a situation of colonial suppression, "resistance and insurrections are normal" (14). One episode in particular, censored out in the first and all subsequent editions until 1899, deserves more notice than it has previously received. It contains, as Metscher correctly emphasizes, "the parable of a successful Irish revolution" (14). Some three years prior to Gulliver's visit, it seems, the king of Laputa (generally decoded as "The Whore," that is, England) declared war on the "proud people" of Lindalino (= two Lins = double-Lin = Dublin). Gradually escalating his military tactics against their rebellion, the king first caused the island to hover over Lindalino to deprive it of sunshine and rain (p. 177). When this and harsher tactics were met with defiance, he ordered that preparations be made for his "last remedy" of "letting the island drop directly on their heads" (p. 176). This tactic, however, which risked cracking the "adamantine bottom" of the island, likewise failed. After an experiment demonstrated that a magnetic force was indeed pulling the island violently toward the towers of Lindalino, the king "was forced to give the town their own conditions" (p. 178). Moreover, as Gulliver was assured by a high official, "if the island had descended so near the town, as not to be able to raise it self, the citizens were determined to fix it forever, to kill the king and all his servants, and entirely change the government (p. 178)." Almost all critics see an allusion here to Ireland's campaign against the debasing currency of Wood's halfpence, led by Swift's *Drapier's Letters* (1724). Metscher correctly insists that the parable is also *anticipatory*, a fantasy of "complete national freedom" (14). Both readings make it unmistakably clear that Swift's sympathies, as Metscher says, "are with the 'proud people' of Lindalino" (14).

The full implications of Gulliver's links with the oppression of Ireland, and with Swift's tracts protesting that oppression, are beginning to be fleshed out. Metscher, now joined by a chorus of critics, claims that "the Irish point of view in *Gulliver's Travels* constitutes the *fundamental satiric perspective* of the book" (15). Gulliver must indeed be read as of a piece with Swift's Irish tracts. Ireland was, as David Nokes says," a colony in all but name," and, thus, "it was a colonial system which the *Drapier's Letters* were written to challenge" (286). The "Irish perspective," however, is not a provincial limitation. As becomes fully clear in book 4, Britain's colonial system extended far beyond the borders of Ireland. This voyage also brings to a gruesome climax the cumulative effects, on Gulliver, of his Friday-like sequence of assimilations and renamings.

If the voyage to Lilliput is the most popular of the four travels, the most controversial is book 4. The reason lies in its relentless and merciless completion of the colonial dialectic. The depiction of the flat-nosed and droopy-breasted yahoos, as Frantz demonstrates, is indebted precisely to the colonial voyage literature. But the yahoos are in fact a hybrid creation, a representation also, as in the description of their violent scramble after *shining Stones*, their drunkenness, and their sycophantic foot- and arse-licking, of European greed, hypocrisy, and brutality (pp. 250–51). The merging of Gulliver with that image of supposed otherness is inexorable. But the final twist is of course Gulliver's desperate identification with the Houyhnhnms, as an "exceptional" yahoo, and his violent repudiation of humankind. Gulliver fails to belong at the end, fails to fit in, fails to conform to the norms of character-development that constitute the realistic novel. Not quite a Houyhnhnm, Gulliver comes close to losing his humanity as well.

Gulliver initially takes the intelligent horses, the Houyhnhnms, for magicians (p. 224). And though he tries to win favor with the Houyhnhnms by presenting them with bracelets and other such trinkets (p. 222), he is already in the mystified position of the colonized culture, awestruck by the wonders he sees. That reversal, however, is little compared with his ultimate degradation into a yahoo "taught to imitate a rational creature" (p. 229) and endowed with "some small pittance of reason" (p. 248). That reversal, of course, is the meaning of the episode in which the lusty black-haired female yahoo tries to mate with Gulliver as he is bathing (pp. 254–55): "For now," says the mortified Gulliver, "I could no longer deny, that I was a real yahoo" (p. 254).

It is a key turning point, not only of book 4, but of the entire book, when Gulliver adopts the self-hating term *yahoos* to describe his own kind. It occurs as he recounts his own adventures to the "master" Houyhnhnm:

> I said, my birth was of honest parents, in an island called England, which was remote from this country, as many days journey as the strongest of his honour's servants could travel in the annual course of the sun. . . . That in my last voyage, I was commander of the ship and had about fifty yahoos under me, many of which died at sea. . . . (p. 235)

The word *yahoos* insinuates itself almost unnoticed into Gulliver's language. Yet is it among the Houyhnhnms the byword for all that is evil or badly made (p. 261). Its use represents nothing less than the cultural dispossession of Gulliver, his alienation from his own history and origins. Gulliver is becoming more and more the object rather than the subject of his own story and speech.

It is a crucial point, and far more than a mere "limitation" of the Houyhnhnms, that they display "equine chauvinism" (Elliott, 52) in discussion of Gulliver's anatomy. The master Houyhnhnm, in fact, is as complacently ethnocentric as the average smug colonist. He sees only what Gulliver *lacks*, in comparison with a Houyhnhnm:

> He said, I differed indeed from other yahoos, being much more cleanly and not altogether so deformed; but in point of real advantage, he thought I differed for the worse. That my nails were of no use either to my fore or hinder feet: As to my fore feet, he could not properly call them by that name, for he never observed me to walk upon them. . . . He then began to find fault with other parts of my body; the flatness of my face, the prominence of my nose, mine eyes placed directly in front, so that I could not look on either side without turning my head. . . . (pp. 234–35)

Absurd as this is, it is even more absurd, and more painful, of course, that "flat-faced" Gulliver, under the pressure of such horse-centered scrutiny, agrees.

As the process of colonization intensifies, Gulliver begins to ape the mannerisms of the Houyhnhnms. Moreover, as in the voyage to Brobdingnag, his assimilation to the Houyhnhnms is accompanied by extreme self-hatred and self-abasement:

> When I happened to behold the reflection of my own form in a lake or fountain, I turned away from my face in horror and detestation of my self; and could better endure the sight of a common yahoo, than of my own person. By conversing with the houyhnhnms, and looking upon them with delight, I fell to imitate their gait and gesture, which is now grown into a habit; and my friends often tell me in a blunt way, that I trot like a horse; which, however, I take for a great compliment. . . . (p. 264)

Still more violently than before, Gulliver defines himself through the eyes of another. We cannot be surprised, then, that Gulliver is likewise "apt to fall into the voice and manner of the Houyhnhnms, and hear my self ridiculed on that account without the least mortification" (p. 264). Not only has he assimilated, but his assimilation is painfully idiotic and outlandish, confirmation that he is indeed a perfect yahoo. It makes all the more pathetic his dream that the Houyhnhnms "would condescend to distinguish me from the rest of my species" (p. 264). No wonder that Linda Colley had suggested that one way of reading *Gulliver's Travels* is as "a narrative of multiple overseas captivities in which the hero finally discards his identity and crosses over to the Houyhnhnms" (Colley, 174). The cumulative effects of Gulliver's four voyages here produce a conversion—a snapping, an alienation—that completes the colonial dialectic. England makes Gulliver, but the lands across the sea remake him.

Just as Gulliver has achieved the bliss of a conversion that breaks every tie with his past, however, disquiet intrudes into his well-ordered utopia. The Houyhnhnms hold one of their parleys about the sole controversy in their country, the question of "whether the yahoos should be exterminated from the face of the earth" (p. 258). The spokesman for genocide, as Gulliver's "master" recounts the debate, produced a lengthy catalogue of the vices of that "most filthy, noisome, and deformed animal," the yahoo (p. 258). The spokesman also reproduced a classic colonial topos, the denial that the yahoos have any claim as original inhabitants of the land:

> He took notice of a general tradition, that yahoos had not always been in their country: But, that many ages ago, two of these brutes appeared together upon a mountain. . . . That these yahoos engendered, and their brood in a short time grew so numerous as to over-run and infest the whole nation. . . . that those creatures could not be ylnhniamshy (or aborigines of the land) because of the violent hatred the houyhnhnms as well as all other animals, bore them; which although their evil disposition sufficiently deserved, could never have arrived at so high a degree if they had been aborigines, or else they would have long since been rooted out. (pp. 258–59)

This argument is, despite the Houyhnhnms' claim to perfect rationality, a tautology. The yahoos deserve to be exterminated because they cannot be aborigines; they cannot be aborigines because they deserve to be exterminated. The tautology indeed, is similar to the vicious circle involving the very etymology of the word Houyhnhnm, "the Perfection of Nature." Such a derivation claims that they are rational, by nature, and so identical with the static perfection they attribute to the natural. The sinister closure of their seeming utopia—their "boring life of certitude" (Donoghue, 1998, 184)—emerges just at the moment of their discussion of exterminating the group *against* which they define themselves.

We ought not to be surprised that the Houyhnhnms resort to a version of history that discredits the claims of the yahoos to have been there first. The dubious "tradition" they invoke, like Sir Thomas Herbert's pseudo-scriptural view of the Khoi-San as "accursed progeny of *Cham*," has every feature of colonial mythology. Unmistakably an allusion to the account in Genesis of human creation and "degeneration" prior to the Flood (Anderson, 160–163), it is a self-serving use, whether the Houyhnhnms know it or not, of that sort of sacred myth. Precisely through the "denial of coevalness," it seeks to place the degenerate yahoos in an *other* time. The Houyhnhnms are thus spared the full responsibility for their part in a violent conflict in the same time and place in which the yahoos exist. Thus, like the "modest proposer" of Anglo-Irish cannibalism, the spokesman for the extermination of yahoos is willing, in the most suave tone imaginable, to appoint himself chief executor of mass death. And though the Houyhnhnm Grand Assembly did not implement this proposal, they did, as Gulliver is informed, consider the master's own alternative: an incrementally genocidal program, modeled after the human gelding of horses, of castration (p. 259). Later Gulliver himself goes so far as to use yahoos' skin and tallow to make the canoe in which he leaves the country (pp. 266–67).

Citing the biblical flood as an authoritative precedent for sanctioned scenarios of mass extermination, Claude Rawson takes the Houyhnhnms straight. He disputes the idea that Swift, in order to discredit the Houyhnhnms, is putting obviously ghastly ideas into their mouths. Rawson has dwelled at some length on the twentieth-century resonance of book 4 of *Gulliver's Travels:* flayed skin, the Houyhnhnms' plans to exterminate or at least castrate the yahoos, the Wannsee Conference, and so on. He describes Swift unflinchingly as "radically hostile to extermination projects and murderous behaviour, but simultaneously capable of strongly charged exterminationist velleities of his own" (Rawson, 2001, 35). He suggests that Swift plays riskily along a slippery spectrum of aggressions that reaches from flirtations with the scenario killing all the yahoos to scriptural "drown-the-world" jokes. The result, in his most nuanced formulation, creates a "volatile combination of 'meaning it', not meaning it, and not *not* meaning it . . ." (2001, 12). He prefers to understand such sudden and violent shifts in the text's perspectives as quasi-volcanic "eruptions"—a psychological notion—that mark Swift's simultaneous contempt and compassion for the oppressed. This reading brilliantly captures Swift's genius for unsparing self-implication. It deflects attention, however, from the specificity, beyond universal human wickedness, of Swift's particular eighteenth-century targets.

Along with the evidence presented thus far, the conclusion of Gulliver strongly militates against such a literal reading of Houyhnh. In the closing and most emphatic narrative position comes a passage often attributed to the voice of Swift rather than to the character of Gulliver. It is a justly famous denunciation of the colonial process:

> A crew of pyrates are driven by a storm they know not whither; at length a boy discovers land from the top-mast; they go on shore to rob and plunder; they see an harmless people, are entertained with kindness, they give the country a new name, they take formal possession of it for the king, they set up a rotton [*sic*] plank or a stone for a memorial, they murder two or three dozen of the natives, bring away a couple more by force for a sample, return home, and get their pardon. Here commences a new dominion acquired with a title by divine right. Ships are sent with the first opportunity; the natives driven out or destroyed, their princes

> tortured to discover their gold; a free license given to all acts of inhumanity and lust; the earth reeking with the blood of its inhabitants: And this execrable crew of butchers employed in so pious an expedition, is a modern colony sent to convert and civilize an idolatrous and barbarous people. (p. 278)

This outburst is certainly Swift's in some sense, and it bears comparison with the end of "A Modest Proposal," where, as Ehrenpreis points out (36), we find similar direct and bitter diatribes about, for instance, the ready willingness of England to devour the whole Irish nation. It is preceded by an apologetic account of why Gulliver failed to claim Brobdingnag and the rest for the crown (p. 277), and it is followed by one disclaiming, with bitter irony, any possible connection between such "butchers" and the British nation (pp. 278–79).

Such disillusioned irony is in fact also consistent with Gulliver's character at this point—or, rather, with Swift's anticolonial plot against "Gulliver" and against that bourgeois genre, the realistic novel, which often tries to organize reality around a centered and privileged subject or character. Gulliver is himself now the victimized, radically misanthropic—and, indeed, quite insane—product of repeated colonization. The puzzles of Gulliver's disintegrating character and decentered voice thus belong neither to Swift's compartmentalized feelings nor to the genre of Menippean satire, but rather to Gulliver's narrative enactment of that violent colonial process which it so consistently and lucidly condemns. For not only is Gulliver *not* a heroic and conquering European individual, but he so patently lacks true autonomy of voice and thought that he can just barely be said to be an "individual" at all. *Gulliver's Travels* is, as Terry Eagleton says, "a work which, tempting the reader into its space with the bait of the 'coherent subject' Gulliver, does so only to reveal Gulliver as an area traversed and devastated by intolerable contradiction" (18). Gulliver, ruthlessly dispersed among "mutually incompatible discourses" (Eagleton, 18), is the deliberate antithesis of the superbly self-sufficient Robinson Crusoe, a hero whose proud individuality is ruthlessly defined over and against an inferior "Other."

Near the very end of the book, Gulliver is exiled from the land of the Houyhnhnms for fear he will lead an uprising of the enslaved yahoos. Upon departing he again abases himself in good native fashion (see the illustration on p. 25):

> Then . . . I took a second leave of my master; But as I was going to prostrate myself to kiss his hoof, he did me the honour to raise it gently to my mouth . . . (p. 267)

Moreover, Gulliver's defensiveness about this incident involves his veracity rather than his dignity. "Detractors," he notes, "are pleased to think it improbable, that so illustrious a person should descend to give so great a mark of distinction to a creature so inferior as I" (p. 267). This sense of inferiority Gulliver carries home to England, where it translates into a hatred of his own kind. Gulliver, for instance, cannot bear the smell, another colonial topos, of even his own wife and children. Even five years after his return he is so incompletely adjusted to English "yahoos" that his wife and children, to this hour, "dare not presume to touch my bread, or drink out of the same cup" (p. 274). Gulliver is hopelessly alienated. As the prefatory "Letter to his Cousin Sympson" asserts, Gulliver, ensconced in the inhuman and false utopia of his own stable, now claims to prefer the neighing of two "degenerate Houyhnhnms" to "the united praise of the whole race" (p. 42).

In this powerfully ironic conclusion we register the full force of Swift's critique of the notion of "character" articulated primarily in the intimate life of the private nuclear family. Swift objects to a cozy politics that constitutes "private" individuals, through the political quarantine of domestic life and economic behavior, as truly distinct from the larger public life where public decisions occur. Consumption, to take an example central to Swift's advocacy of boycotts, has public consequences. At the same time, of course, Gulliver seems to be barking mad—the victim of one voyage too many. Gulliver's final misanthropy, as Howard Erskine-Hill argues (81), is contrasted with the exceptional humanity of Don Pedro de Mendez, the Portuguese captain who rescues Gulliver.

Gulliver's loathing of humanity, enforced by his inability to return home, is Swift's last satirical target. Swift laughs at Gulliver's absurd misanthropy. To be sure, Swift also intends to flout the "family values" assiduously promoted by puritan elements in English culture: values that tended to insulate and privatize domestic life. But we are meant to laugh as well at Gulliver, supposedly conversing with ordinary horses. Among early examples of Gulliveriana—spinoffs from Swift's generative fiction—is a serious marriage manual in 1745 printed under the pseudonym of Lemuel Gulliver's name: *The Pleasures and Felicity of Marriage*. The anonymous author plays amusingly upon our sense that marriage is a topic about which Gulliver's competence seems especially doubtful. And indeed, jokes about Gulliver's domestic failings began with Swift's immediate circle. Alexander Pope greeted the appearance of the *Travels* with a bawdy verse epistle, "Mary Gulliver to Captain Gulliver," in which Gulliver's neglected wife voices her dissatisfaction with his residence, after returning from his last voyage, in their stable. Colonization by the Houyhnhnms has wrecked the ostensibly private space of Gulliver's life at home. Swift refuses Voltaire's homey solution for Candide: to cultivate one's garden.

Do we laugh at Lemuel or Mary Gulliver? Some have felt that Gulliver's repudiation of domesticity confirms his—and perhaps Swift's—loathing of women. Alison Fell's novel, *The Mistress of Lilliput* (1999) revises the story, no doubt intending a certain correction of its perceived "misogyny." *The Mistress of Lilliput* resumes the story of Gulliver subsequent to the scene of his alienated homecoming, after he has again absconded to the South Sea. The novel, however, fleshes out the happily sensual story of Mary Gulliver. In Fell's version, Mary dutifully pursues her wandering husband. In the book's wittiest scenes, she experiences a carnal awakening with Lilliputian libertines. Eventually she finds Gulliver deluded in a foreign madhouse; bids him a last farewell; and takes up in France with the far more human Antoine Duchesne, a French naturalist preoccupied with grafting strawberries. The novel swerves away from *Gulliver's Travels* by affirming both domesticity and desire. In this recuperation of domesticity, however, the constellation of norms enabled by an imperial society is reinstated. As felicitous domesticity swims into the foreground, so the issue of imperialism disappears into the inert background. Swift's eighteenth-century satirical fiction, which vexes our grasp of Gulliver's individual character, remains far more critical than its late twentieth-century reinvention as a novel about one English woman's sexual awakening. The ethos of revisionism predominant in our climate of thought, self-congratulatory in its political acumen, often manages to dodge issues concerning the global distribution of wealth. To laugh at Gulliver's self-righteousness is healthy; to dismiss Swift's critique of the colonial process is self-serving.

Alison Fell's imaginative retelling nevertheless offers a useful clue to the history of *Gulliver's* reception more generally. There has been a long-standing urge, in various senses, to "domesticate" *Gulliver.* Swift is too good to be ignored, but he must be house-broken. And so *Gulliver* has often been reduced to a nursery classic, bowdlerized as a Disney animated cartoon, rewritten as a children's book about cute little people hanging out in Gulliver's hair. The charming spell of domesticity serves to eclipse the broader horizons of imperial antagonisms. Like the popular reception of *Huckleberry Finn* as a boyhood idyll, and like two centuries of reading *Robinson Crusoe*, set in the cradle of European slavery, as almost anything but a Caribbean book,[9] the ahistorical reception of *Gulliver* bespeaks the operation of a collective amnesia. Family values serve to eclipse the cosmopolitan perspectives that might make Europe's project of colonial domination seem anything but natural or inevitable. *Gulliver's Travels* was in its own time a riposte to the propagandists for expansion, who have so far ended up speaking for the "winners of history." Coming to terms with this colonial and neocolonial history, for both the British and then the American superpower, has evidently been considerably more difficult than reconstituting *Gulliver* as a case study in psychopathology, or as a nursery classic, or as an esoteric and remote political allegory, or as a gloomy fable about the human condition.

Endnotes

1. Orwell argues that "whenever Gulliver is not acting as a stooge, there is a sort of continuity in his character, which comes out especially in his resourcefulness and his observation of physical detail" (192–93). Lawlor argues that Swift's characterization of Gulliver is the "masterstroke in the design of *Gulliver's Travels*" (320).

2. The *locus classicus* of this view has been expressed by Ehrenpreis: "In the creation of Gulliver, Swift cannot be recommended for consistency either of character or of fact. Again and again the veneer of probability is broken" (34). Similarly, according to Elliot, "Swift pays little regard to psychological consistency; Gulliver's can hardly be said to develop; it simply changes" (45). But what "in novels would be considered inconsistency in characterization can be found in nearly all Menippean satires" (45). Donaghue asserts that "Gulliver is not, strictly speaking, a character at all" (1969, 19). Finally, according to Rawson in 1983, "Intelligent readers. . . . do not regard Gulliver as a 'character' or *Gulliver's Travels* as a novel. What they witness is a tactical shift in the manner of Swift's irony, while the *matter* remains constant (168). . . ."

3. Swift had invested in the South Sea Company, brainchild of his patron Sir Robert Harley. Moreover, the Treaty of Utrecht (1713) for which the Tory ministry pushed included the *Asiento* clause, giving Britain the right (exclusive, but undermined by smugglers) to supply an annual quota of slaves to the Spanish colonial possessions. See Richardson.

4. The hallmark of such colonial discourses is the production of a reductive difference—a "manichean allegory," as Abdul R. JanMohamed has said—that transforms racial difference into moral and metaphysical opposition between "good and evil, superiority and inferiority, civilization and savagery . . ." (JanMohamed, 63). The kinds of "difference" so allegorically produced are wildly inconsistent, impossible to synthesize into a coherent portrait of the subjugated group (Memmi, 83). But, though colonial stereotypes vary according to the given ideological needs of the moment, the very flexibility of colonial discourse preserves its power. What really matters, as Edward Said has written of "Orientalism," is a "flexible *positional* superiority, which puts the Westerner in a whole series of possible relationships with the Orient without ever losing him the relative upper hand" (Said, 7). The colonized, as Stam and Spence argue, "were ridiculed

as lacking in culture and history *because* colonialism, in the name of profit, was destroying the basis of that culture and the memory of that history" (Stam and Spence, 4).

5. Swift's personal copy of Herbert's travels is still extant (Frantz, 50). Dampier's *A New Voyage Round the World* is also known to have been in Swift's library.

6. Herbert hedges this description with a qualifying admission that it is true "if Gonsalvo soza [*sic*] say true" (11). To his credit, another early global voyager, William Dampier, flies in the face of "common opinion of *Anthropophagi*, or Man-Eaters" by averring that he "never did meet with any such people" (Dampier, 485).

7. The early nineteenth-century saga of Saartje Baartman, the "Hottentot Venus," perfectly exemplifies this colonial phenomenon. Viewed only as "a collection of sexual parts" (Gilman, 87–88), Baartman was displayed in a cage for some five years in London, the provinces, and Paris in the early nineteenth century, until her death in 1815, arranged so as to emphasize her steatopygia. "Her rear end," as Gould writes, "*was* the show" (Gould, 297). She was examined while alive by leading anatomists, painted in the nude for scientific paintings at the Jardin du Roi, and dissected after death (Gould, 294–95); her genitalia and buttocks were on display until recently at the Musée de l'Homme in Paris (Gilman, 88; Gould, 292). Claude Rawson provides many relevant illustrations of this episode in *God, Gulliver, and Genocide.*

8. Benedict Anderson, *Imagined Communities: Reflections on the Origins and Spread of Nationalism* (London: verso, 1983).

9. Prior to the last twenty years, *Robinson Crusoe* has traditionally been seen as "a Puritan 'fable', the first true work of 'realism', the novel of 'economic individualism' or, most importantly, the story quite simply of a man on an island—the location of that island being of, at best, subsidiary importance" (Hulme, 1986, 176).

Works Cited

Altick, Richard. *The Shows of London.* Cambridge: Belknap, 1978.

Anderson, Benedict. *Imagined Communities: Reflections on the Origin and Spread of Nationalism.* London: Verso, 1983.

Anderson, William S. "Paradise Gained by Horace, Lost by Gulliver." In *English Satire and the Satiric Tradition*, edited by Claude Rawson, 151–66. Oxford: Basil Blackwell, 1984.

Aravamudan, Srinivas Aravamudan. *Tropicopolitans: Colonialism and Agency, 1688–1804.* Durham: Duke University Press, 1999.

Brantlinger, Patrick. *Rule of Darkness: British Literature and Imperialism, 1830–1914.* Ithaca: Cornell University Press, 1988.

Case, Arthur. *Four Essays on Gulliver's Travels.* Gloucester, Mass.: Peter Smith, 1958.

Coetzee, J. M. *White Writing: On the Culture of Letters in South Africa.* New Haven: Yale University Press, 1988.

Colley, Linda. "Going Native, Telling Tales: Collaboration, Captivity, and Empire." *Past and Present* 168 (2000): 170–93.

Dabydeen, David. Eighteenth-Century English Literature on Commerce and Slavery." In *The Black Presence in English Literature,* edited by David Dabydeen, 26–49. Manchester: Manchester University Press, 1985.

Dampier, William S. *A New Voyage Round the World.* London, 1697.

Davis, Herbert, ed. *The Prose Works of Jonathan Swift.* 14 vols. Oxford: Basil Blackwell, 1965–68.

Defoe, Daniel. *The Life and Strange Surprizing Adventures of Robinson Crusoe of York, Mariner,* edited by J. Donald Crowley. Oxford: Oxford University Press, 1972.

Donoghue, Denis. *Jonathan Swift: A Critical Introduction.* London: Cambridge University Press, 1969.

———. *The Practice of Reading.* New Haven: Yale University Press, 1998.

Eagleton, Terry. *Walter Benjamin: Or Towards a Revolutionary Criticism.* London: Verso, 1981.

Ehrenpreis, Irvin. "Personae." In *Restoration and Eighteenth-Century Literature: Essays in Honor of Alan Dugald McKillop,* edited by Carroll Camden, 25–38. Chicago: University of Chicago Press, 1963.

Elliot, Robert C. "The Satirist Satirized." In *Twentieth Century Interpretations of Gulliver's Travels: A Collection of Critical Essays,* edited by Frank Brady, 41–53. Englewood Cliffs: Prentice, 1968.

Erskine-Hill, Howard. *Swift: Gulliver's Travels.* Cambridge: Cambridge University Press, 1993.

Fabian, Johannes. *Time and the Other: How Anthropology Makes Its Object.* New York: Columbia University Press, 1983.

Frantz, R. W. "Swift's Yahoos and the Voyagers." *Modern Philology* 29 (1931): 49–57.

Gilman, Sander. *Difference and Pathology: Stereotypes of Sexuality, Race, and Madness.* Ithaca: Cornell University Press, 1985.

Gould, Stephen Jay. *The Flamingo's Smile.* New York: Norton, 1985.

Herbert, Sir Thomas. *Some Yeares Travels into Divers Parts of Asia and Afrique.* London, 1638.

Hulme, Peter. *Colonial Encounters: Europe and the Native Caribbean 1492–1797.* London: Methuen, 1986.

———. "The Cannibal Scene." In *Cannibalism and the Colonial World,* edited by Francis Barker, Peter Hulme, and Margaret Iversen, 1–38. Cambridge: Cambridge University Press, 1998.

JanMohamed, Abdul R. "The Economy of Manichean Allegory: The Function of Racial Difference in Colonialist Literature." *Critical Inquiry* 12, no. 1 (1985): 59–87.

Lawlor, John. "The Evolution of Gulliver's Character." In *Essays and Studies,* 69–73. Reprinted in *Gulliver's Travels,* edited by Robert A. Greenberg, 320–24. New York: Norton, 1961.

Leavis. F. R. "The Irony of Swift." *Swift: Modern Judgments,* edited by A. Norman Jeffares, 121–34. London: Aurora, 1969.

Lloyd, David. *Nationalism and Minor Literature: James Clarence Mangan and the Emergence of Irish Cultural Nationalism: Berkeley:* University of California Press, 1987.

Lynch, Deidre. *The Economy of Character: Novels, Market Culture, and the Business of Inner Meaning.* Chicago: University of Chicago Press, 1998.

Malik, Kenan. *The Meaning of Race: Race, History, and Culture in Western Society.* New York: New York University Press, 1996.

Memmi, Albert. *The Colonizer and the Colonized.* New York: Orion, 1965.

Metscher, Thomas. "The Radicalism of Swift: Gulliver's Travels and the Irish Point of View." In *Studies in Anglo-Irish Literature,* edited by Heinz Kosok, 13–22. Bonn: Bouvier Verlag Herbert Greundmann, 1982.

Monk, Samuel H. "The Pride of Lemuel Gulliver." In *Twentieth Century Interpretations of* Gulliver's Travels: *A Collection of Critical Essays,* edited by Frank Brady, 70–79. Englewood Cliffs: Prentice Hall, 1968.

Moore-Gilbert, Bart. "Spivak and Bhabha." *A Companion to Postcolonial Studies,* edited by Henry Schwarz and Sangeeta Ray, 451–66. Oxford: Blackwell, 2000.

Morgan, Jennifer. L. "'Some Could Suckle over Their Shoulder': Male Traveler, Female Bodies, and the Gendering of Racial Ideology." *The William and Mary Quarterly*, 3rd series, 54, no. 1 (1997): 167–92.

Nokes, David. *Jonathan Swift: A Hypocrite Reversed: A Critical Biography*. Oxford: Oxford University Press, 1985.

Orwell, George. "Politics *vs.* Literature." *Swift: Modern Judgments*, edited by A. Norman Jeffares, 192–209. London: Aurora, 1969.

Perry, Ruth. "Colonizing the Breast: Sexuality and Maternity in Eighteenth-Century England." *Eighteenth-Century Life* 16 (1992): 185–213.

Probyn, Clive T. *Jonathan Swift: The Contemporary Background*. Manchester: Manchester University Press, 1978.

Rawson, Claude. "Gulliver, Marlow, and the Flat-Nosed People: Colonial Oppression in Satire and Fiction." *Dutch Quarterly Review of Anglo-American Letters* 13, nos. 3–4 (1983): 162–78, 282–99.

———. *God, Gulliver, and Genocide: Barbarism and the European Imagination, 1492–1945*. Oxford. Oxford University Press, 2001.

Richardson, John. "Swift, *A Modest Proposal*, and Slavery," *Essays in Criticism* 51, no. 4 (2001): 404–23.

Said, Edward. *Orientalism*. New York: Vintage, 1979.

Stallybrass, Peter, and Allon White. *The Politics and Poetics of Transgression*. Ithaca: Cornell University Press, 1986.

Stam, Robert, and Louise Spence. "Colonialism, Racism, and Representation: An Introduction." *Screen* 24, no. 2 (1983): 2–20.

Taylor, Aline Mackenzie. "Sights and Monsters and Gulliver's Voyage to Brobdingnag." *Tulane Studies in English* 7 (1957): 29–82.

Thomas, Keith. *Man and the Natural World: Changing Attitudes in England, 1500–1800*. New York: Oxford University Press.

Todd, Dennis. *Imagining Monsters: Miscreations of the Self in Eighteenth-Century England*. Chicago: University of Chicago Press, 1995.

Traugott, John. "The Yahoo in the Doll's House: *Gulliver's Travels*, the Children's Classic." In *English Satire and the Satiric Tradition*, edited by Claude Rawson, 127–50. Oxford: Basil Blackwell, 1984.

Wheeler, Roxann. *The Complexion of Race: Categories of Difference in Eighteenth-Century British Culture*. Philadelphia: University of Pennsylvania Press, 2000.

Speaking for the Irish Nation: The Drapier, the Bishop, and the Problems of Colonial Representation

Carole Fabricant

When Swift, as M. B. Drapier, addresses "the Whole People of Ireland" in his famous Fourth Letter, written to bring about defeat of William Wood's coinage scheme, whom exactly is he speaking to?[1] And, more germane to my concerns here, whom is he speaking *for?* The general consensus has been that "the Whole People" refers only to the small circle of the Anglo-Irish elite and the established church to which Swift belonged—a position reflected in R. F. Foster's contention that the "restricted and exclusive views of Swift" typified "Ascendancy attitudes."[2] I read the Drapier's Fourth Letter very differently, as a document that articulates the interests of a broad spectrum of Irish society and that invokes a conception of nationhood considerably more comprehensive than these sectarian constructions would indicate. I will be offering evidence for this reading later in my discussion; however, my primary aim here is not to offer an interpretation of a particular text but rather, to examine a number of interrelated theoretical and historical issues that underpin the questions I pose at the outset. In the absence of such examination, it is impossible to adequately address questions of the Drapier's viewpoint, audience, and representative, or non-representative, status. More broadly, I want to explore the contradictions, and in the process weigh the meaning, of Protestant attempts to speak for the Irish nation in the first half of the eighteenth century. To this end I will be focusing primarily on Swift, but also considering texts by George Berkeley and (more briefly) Thomas Sheridan.[3]

I

The example of Swift, one of many instances in which a member of a privileged minority purports to represent an oppressed majority through the figure of "the whole nation," points up the relevance of current theoretical

ELH 66: 2 (1999): 337–72.

investigations into the question of who can legitimately speak for whom in situations where a clear power differential exists: in the case of Ireland, where the nationalist spokespersons, on the strength of their membership in their country's social and religious elite, can be considered at least partially complicit with the colonizers even if treated by them as subordinates. In such circumstances, do Anglo-Irish acts of speaking as the nation silence the colonized Catholic majority (by subsuming the latter's voice into their own) or do they, on the contrary, enable the colonized to be heard by giving them a voice they would otherwise lack? One of the assumptions underlying this essay is that there is no simple, or single, answer to this question—that the answer varies according to a number of specific factors while at the same time limited by the political and historical constraints operating on both speaker and spoken for. My aim here is to establish some grounds for distinguishing those circumstances in which such representation can function constructively, to minimize hierarchically-based exclusions and expand the field of expression, from those circumstances in which this mode of representation shows its "violent" side, functioning to suppress differences and to impose a monolithic structure of order.

The whole problematic of "speaking for" has considerable resonance given recent poststructuralist critiques of both identity and representation, which challenge the very grounds upon which one individual or group can speak for another. Gayatri Chakravorty Spivak's highly influential essay "Can the Subaltern Speak?" has helped to crystallize the theoretical and ideological stakes in this line of questioning, as have various recent formulations of a feminist epistemology.[4] Donna Haraway, for example, rejects "a politics of semiotic representation" for a "politics of articulation" in analyzing the speciousness of certain advocacy claims by Western environmentalists "speaking for" endangered species in distant lands and by anti-abortion activists "speaking for" the fetus.[5] Linda Alcoff agrees about the dangers in such acts of representation but nevertheless reminds us that these acts are not in all cases detrimental since there are times when we do need someone "to advocate for our needs."[6] Bringing this whole question closer to home (that is, Ireland), Vincent Cheng considers this problematic both in terms of the endeavors by English and American scholars to represent Irish literature through their "attempts to fashion a hegemonic reading of a native son like Joyce," and in terms of a newly politicized Joyce made to represent all of postcolonial Irish literature, thereby in effect functioning to silence less canonical, more marginalized Irish writers. Noting several examples in which white "first world" males have undertaken to write books purporting to recount the lives of first-person female and/or "third world" narrators (for example, the English vicar Toby Forward's publication, under the name Rahila Khan, of what claimed to be an Indian feminist's true experiences struggling to survive in Margaret Thatcher's Britain), Cheng observes, "From [such examples] one might conclude that it is better not to speak for others at all, not to intervene so as not to act like Haines (in the 'Telemachus' episode of *Ulysses*). On the other hand, such a retreat from 'representation' and 'speaking for' is frequently politically detrimental or even suicidal."[7]

Joyce himself directly addressed this question in his most explicitly anticolonialist piece of writing, "Ireland, Island of Saints and Sages," which lists a number of Irish "patriots" from the late eighteenth century onward whom he judged to be legitimate spokesmen for the cause of Ireland despite the fact that many were Protestant and unable to claim "even a drop of Celtic blood"; after all, he reminds us, "to deny the name of patriot to all those who are not of Irish stock would be to deny it to almost all the heroes of the modern movement."[8] Undoubtedly foremost among the "heroes" he had in mind here was Charles Parnell, whom Joyce revered (and mourned) as a leader who, "like another Moses, led a turbulent and unstable people from the house of shame to the verge of the Promised Land."[9] Joyce's view here, if overly romanticized, is nevertheless understandable given Parnell's prominent role in Ireland's nationalist struggles for land reform and Home Rule in the late nineteenth century. But what about the Irish proto-nationalists of the first half of the eighteenth century, whose notion of an independent Ireland was of a nation enjoying political and legal parity with England, similarly ruled by an established church and by a religiously defined class (enjoying a power bolstered by both the Penal Laws against the Catholics and the Test Act against the Dissenters) that seemed to evidence little concern for the rights of the Catholic majority, or even of other Protestant denominations that were not Anglican?[10]

In this situation, acts of representation—specifically, of speaking for the oppressed or the colonized—become particularly fraught (if not indeed, on the face of it, a blatant contradiction in terms), and seem inconceivable without postulating a bad faith or false consciousness of mammoth proportions. Such acts seem to provide powerful justification for Gilles Deleuze's insistence on "the indignity of speaking for others" and his assertion that "only those directly concerned can speak in a practical way on their own behalf."[11] And yet, Spivak too has a point (even though she chooses to overlook the compelling circumstances, namely the *événements* of May 1968, motivating his protest) when she challenges Deleuze on this matter, deriding the idea that we, as intellectuals (or relatively privileged members of society) should simply back off in silence and let the oppressed speak for themselves: an act which conveniently absolves us from the responsibility of intervening in intolerable situations and which assumes the possibility of transparency, of an end to the need for all representation. But as Spivak succinctly reminds us, "representation has not withered away."[12] Certainly it showed little sign of withering away in eighteenth-century Ireland, where, when the oppressed *did* speak for themselves, it was often both literally and figuratively in another language, one that required translation into the idiom of power to have any effect within the governing structures of society.

Once again we can look to Joyce for a pertinent comment on this state of affairs—specifically, in his essay, "Ireland at the Bar," which describes the celebrated trial in Galway of one Myles Joyce, accused (with several others) of murdering a family in the town. Because he spoke only Irish and "seemed stupefied by all the judicial ceremony," he was forced to depend on the services of an interpreter, who would listen to his lengthy and involved explanations, punctuated by wild gesticulations and imprecations to the heavens, and then succinctly translate to the judge, "'He says no, your worship.'" Not surprisingly, he was found guilty and executed. James Joyce transforms this episode into a comprehensive metaphor for Ireland's untenable situation as a silenced and subjugated country: "The figure of this dumbfounded old man, a remnant of a civilization not ours, deaf and dumb before his judge, is a symbol of the Irish nation at the bar of public opinion."[13] The essay is most obviously a scathing exposure of colonialism's corrupting effects on a society's legal institutions, but it is also an extended reflection on the problematic of representation within a colonial context. One may well be tempted to interpret the parabolic account as a call for an end to all representational modes of expression so that the native would be able to state his case directly to a jury of his peers, without having to negotiate the system of inherently falsifying mediations that accompany colonialist rule. However, even if Ireland were independent of Britain, an exclusively Irish-speaking denizen from the wilds of Connemara would be likely to encounter formidable difficulties in trying to communicate to his fellow countrymen in a nation divided (even without a colonial presence) along linguistic, cultural, class, and regional lines. (How much more difficult would he find the task of stating Ireland's case to the world at large!) In this sense effective representation may be seen as a necessary (if insufficient) condition for creating a free and equitable society. And indeed, one might argue that it is precisely this kind of representation that is embodied in Joyce's essay, which was originally written in Italian while he was staying in Trieste, and which in effect sets its author up to be the successful translator and advocate so conspicuously missing in the courtroom that condemned Myles Joyce.

Among the many things that "Ireland at the Bar" exposes is the well-meaning but flawed assumption that all we need do is let the oppressed speak for themselves and all social inequities will be righted. Myles Joyce *did* speak for himself, and he was summarily executed for his pains. We might recall in this connection that Spivak answers the question in her essay's title by concluding that "the subaltern cannot speak"—which I take to mean, not a literal incapacity for speech, but an inability to speak to *effect* in the face of the recalcitrant structures of established power: an inability to express oneself in a way that will be clearly understood and correctly interpreted by the dominant culture.[14] The ill-fated Bhuvaneswari Bhaduri expresses herself (however negatively and self-destructively) by carefully staging her suicide so as to prevent certain misinterpretations of the act; yet it is precisely these misinterpretations that subsequently shape the official view of what happened. Myles Joyce also expresses himself only to find his words and gestures misconstrued. The real problem, then, is not that the marginalized cannot speak, but that the powerful cannot (or do not want to) rightly hear and interpret what is being said. Until the latter circumstance changes, and barring actual revolutionary conditions, the act of the oppressed speaking on their own behalf does not, in and of itself, promise to bring about any significant improvement in society. It is primarily for this reason that I situate myself in opposition to those who hold up the ideal of transparency as a way of short-circuiting the whole problem of representation—of pretending that it can be done away with altogether.

At the same time, I am very far from wishing to argue that the oppressed can never speak effectively without outside help—that their position always and necessarily forces them into a state of dependency on others, along the lines of Marx's small peasant proprietors, who "cannot represent themselves; they must be represented."[15] On the contrary, this essay proceeds on the assumption that the oppressed in eighteenth-century Ireland—or, to be more accurate, the *most* oppressed among the various groups *unevenly* victimized by British colonialism, the Catholics—were not simply silent and passive recipients of help from above but did in fact speak for themselves on a number of occasions and in a variety of ways, in words as well as in deeds. Notwithstanding C.D.A. Leighton's contention that "the Catholics, as a whole, were very quiet" about their subjection to the Penal Laws, they made their dissatisfactions known in other ways: through the versified expressions of violation and loss by Gaelic poets such as Dáibhí Ó Bruadair and Aodhagán Ó Rathaille (Egan O'Rahilly); through the accounts of native historians intent upon correcting misrepresentations of the Irish perpetuated by their British and Anglo-Irish counterparts (for example, Hugh Reilly, a lawyer as well as historian, whose *Ireland's Case Briefly Stated* anticipates Joyce's perceived need to advocate for "Ireland at the Bar"); through regular Jacobite gatherings at St. Stephen's Green in Dublin to celebrate the Pretender's birthday (June 10); and through acts of rebellion and social unrest, such as the Hougher disturbances in 1711–12 in the west of Ireland and the Dublin riots of the 1720s.[16]

And by the same token, just as I decline to treat the Catholics in terms of an undifferentiated mass of docile, mute oppression, I eschew treating the Anglo-Irish as a monolithic class of active, vocal oppressors, all of whose speech acts (conceived in the broadest terms) were modes of colonialist repression and/or appropriation, which would lead to the argument that taking seriously the nationalist sentiments expressed by a member of their class is tantamount to "allow[ing] the colonizer to speak for the colonized" because it "perniciously renders invisible the indigenous Irish themselves."[17] My disagreement with this view is based on several considerations. For one thing, to dismiss the Anglo-Irish class as a whole as automatically repressive prevents us from making some important distinctions among the different parties, sub-classes, and individuals who constituted its membership: between Whigs and Tories, between the English and the Irish interest, between Hanoverians and Jacobites—as well as between those who walked the meaner streets of Dublin, mingling with the tradesmen, the homeless, and the unemployed, and those who confined their movements to the fashionable sections of Georgian Dublin, relying on carriages to whisk them from one elegant townhouse to another in order to prevent contaminating contact with "the rabble"; between those who fostered connections with the native Irish culture (including Swift's friends the antiquarian Anthony Raymond, rector of Trim, who embarked on an English translation of Geoffrey Keating's classic history of Ireland, *Foras Feasa ar Éirinn*, and Patrick Delany, chancellor of St. Patrick's Cathedral, later dean of Down, who was patron to the last of the great Irish harpist-bards, Toirdhealbhach Ó Cearbhallain [Turlough Carolan]), and those who rejected all aspects of Irish culture as expressions of a barbarism inimical to the putative height of civilization embodied in their "mother" country, England. Swift's poem, *The Description of an Irish Feast*, based on the Irish verses *Pléaráca na Ruarcach*, attributed to Hugh MacGauran and set to music by Carolan, exemplifies Swift's own interest in Irish popular culture. In each of these cases, the act of speaking for Ireland necessarily conveyed its own distinct set of nuances and implications. The challenge is to acknowledge individual differences in this regard without (as has been the case with many recent revisionist histories) losing the forest for the trees—without becoming so fixated on specific examples that the larger outlines of Ireland's colonial subordination to Britain virtually disappear from view, leaving what appears to be a level playing field, unencumbered by the lop-sided power relationships that perforce deeply influenced all forms of representation and limited what individual acts of "speaking for" could mean and do.

II

Another problem with viewing the Anglo-Irish as a monolithic class of oppressors is that such a view ignores the contradictions of their hyphenated identity and their complex history, which positioned them as both colonizers and colonized: as members of a group subordinated and exploited by England even as they functioned as the agents of British colonial rule in Ireland. These contradictions may be glimpsed, for example, in the "migrating pronouns" of Swift's Irish tracts, where "we" and "our" slip in and out of contexts in which they refer, sometimes alternately, sometimes simultaneously, to the original English settlers, to the Irish-born Protestants, and to the "whole people" of Ireland, including (at least in theory and potential) the Catholics. The following passage from the Drapier's Fourth Letter points to the porous line that exists between "us Irish" conceived as a general, national group, and "us Irish" conceived as a more specific, sectarian group laying claims to a privileged English heritage; it shows how "our" can at one and the same time conflate and sharply differentiate the two: "Our *Neighbours, whose Understandings are just upon a Level with Ours* (which perhaps are none of the *Brightest*) have a strong Contempt for most Nations, but especially for *Ireland:* They look upon us as a sort of *Savage Irish,* whom our Ancestors conquered several Hundred Years ago" (*D*, 10:64). What these words at once reveal and try to deny is that the "us" who are considered "a sort of *Savage Irish*" include *both* the "old Irish" *and* the subsequent waves of English settlers (including members of Swift's own family), who were viewed as being contaminated by their new surroundings and as eventually merging with the Irish "natives." The speaker's immediate recoil from this recognition and rush to identify with "our [not the expected *their*] Ancestors," who "conquered [the *Savage Irish*] several Hundred Years ago," rather than establishing the grounds of his separation from the latter, serve mainly to underscore the ambiguity of his position and his awareness that, from the perspective of the English observers—which is to say, the observers who *matter* in the larger political scheme of things—he will always be lumped together with them.

The shift here from the initial "our" and "ours," which situates Swift as an Irish denizen distinct from his "neighbours," the English, to the final "our," which reconfigures him as an Englishman, no longer merely a "neighbour" but now a blood brother and fellow conqueror, undergoes yet another reversal in the sentence immediately following, which once again establishes a clear distinction between, on the one hand, "I" and "you" (the speaker and his Irish audience) and on the other, "they" (the deluded and supercilious beings across the Channel): "And if I should describe the *Britons* to you, as they were in *Caesar's* Time, when they *painted their*

Bodies, or Cloathed themselves with the Skins of Beasts, I should act full as reasonably as they do" (*D*, 10:64). Here the reversal is not only of pronouns and referents but also of modes of perception. The Englishman's gaze, which regularly reduces the Anglo-Irish as well as the native Catholics to "savages," is thrown back at him as the Irish are invited to step through the looking glass and see the English themselves as primitives—a procedure aided by the use of the same pronoun ("they") to refer both to the "savage" Britons of Caesar's time and to the putatively "civilized" Britons of Swift's own day. While this invitation is, strictly speaking, being extended specifically to other members of his own class, the reversal mechanism Swift recommends offers an even more suitable and effective strategy for the native Irish Catholics, in whose hands it promises to be a far more subversive tool for relativizing established hierarchies of value and status—for calling the very construct of "savage" into question.

In this brief passage two very different solutions to Swift's identity crisis (so to speak) are presented: to reject as erroneous the identification with Ireland's native population and reaffirm ties to the "master race"; or to accept this identification but use it to turn the tables on those who have made it a sign of innate inferiority. Swift's inability to make a definitive choice between one or the other of these alternatives produced fissured texts marked by continual shifts in tone and perspective: texts whose speakers at times embrace the collective category of "us" (even on occasion expanding it to include Africans, American Indians, and others), while in other instances strenuously attempting to wrest a more limited "us," defined by its "purer" English roots, from the undifferentiated "us" of the "native Irish." From this confusion of pronouns and signifiers we can derive no small insight into why the question of whom Swift is speaking for in his writings is so problematic.

That these confusions had broad historical roots is evident from their presence in texts produced by other Anglo-Irish writers contemporaneous with Swift—George Berkeley's tract, *A Word to the Wise; or An Exhortation to the Roman Catholic Clergy of Ireland* being a case in point. Addressing his Catholic counterparts in his role as Bishop of Cloyne, Berkeley begins and ends his exhortation with affirmations of solidarity with them. At the outset he asks rhetorically, "Do we not inhabit the same spot of ground, breathe the same air, and live under the same government? why, then, should we not conspire in one and the same design, to promote the common good of our country?"; and he closes by assuring his audience, "I consider you as my countrymen, as fellow-subjects, as professing belief in the same Christ."[18] In between these two assertions of a communal and seemingly all-inclusive "we," however, the first-person pronouns signify two more restrictively defined groups: the body of church officials (Anglican and Catholic alike, including the pope himself, lauded for his "endeavor[s] to put new life into the trade and manufactures of his country" [*W*, 247]), who have the responsibility of setting a moral example for the slothful Irish natives; and the privileged Protestant class, whose domestic economy depends on the labor of native Catholic servants and who (at least indirectly, through their political and psychological ties to the British) own colonies—and slaves—abroad. In *A Word to the Wise* Berkeley moves ideologically and linguistically between these distinct groups, in the process offering up three very different models for conceptualizing who constitutes "the Irish nation," and what the act of speaking on its behalf means.

One passage in particular sheds revealing light on this ambivalence of identification, inviting interesting comparisons with the passage from the Drapier's Fourth Letter previously considered. Describing a "kitchen-wench" in his household who refused to carry cinders because she felt it was beneath someone "descended from an old Irish stock," Berkeley declares:

> Never was there a more monstrous conjunction than that of pride with beggary; and yet this prodigy is seen every day in almost every part of this kingdom. At the same time these proud people are more destitute than savages, and more abject than negroes. The negroes in our plantations have a saying, If negro was not negro, Irishman would be negro. (*W*, 237)

Having put forward an expansive view of an Ireland where national definition transcends sectarian (if not class) divisions, Berkeley is suddenly pulled back into the vortex of his immediate surroundings: a world of pronounced social and cultural differences governed in no small part by racial classifications. It is as though Berkeley's more liberal and visionary tendencies must give way under the enormous pressure exerted by the inescapable stigma attached to the category of "Irishman"—the latter's proverbial resemblance to the "savage" as well as his status as "negro"—and by the recognition that he (Berkeley), too, is perceived to belong to this category. That the equation of "Irishman" and "negro" is being made here, not by the colonial class across the channel but by the black slaves themselves, adds a level of irony, and a further layer of humiliation, to Berkeley's equivocal status. Although the plantation negroes are presumably referring in this comparison to the native Irish—the "poor white trash" of Britain's nearby colony—even the merest threat that through some perceptual or taxonomic slippage the category of "Irishman" (through the eyes or on the lips of slaves no less!) could include those of Berkeley's own class creates a source of unbearable tension that is only just contained by the detached, magisterial tone of *A Word to the Wise*. What we see here is a movement common to many Anglo-Irish texts of the period: as they approach the "heart of darkness," the savage or the negro at the center of their most obsessive and terrified apprehensions, they reveal not only the schizophrenia generated by their hyphenated status but also the phobic strategies designed to put these fears to rest. For Berkeley this means falling back on prevailing stereotypes by labeling the native Irish "a lazy, destitute, and degenerate race" who are "wedded to dirt on principle" (*W*, 238, 242)—a people whose tainted Scythian blood has produced "innate hereditary sloth" (*W*, 235).[19]

For a man so open to enlightened ideas of national and religious unity, Berkeley gets racially ugly very quickly—a circumstance perhaps not all that surprising given his untroubled acceptance of slavery as biblically defensible. Having set aside the sectarian grounds for distinguishing the Anglo-Irish from the 'native' Irish ("Why should disputes about faith interrupt the duties of civil life? or the different roads we take to heaven prevent our taking the same steps on earth?" [*W*, 235]), but loth to jettison the system of hierarchies that ensures his own privileged position in society, Berkeley has little option but to play the race card as a way of affirming radical difference—and, by implication, vindicating his own sense of entitlement. This is a card Swift too can play, though in his case a sense of complicity in the "degenerate race" he excoriates functions to destabilize the clear-cut racial hierarchy we discern in Berkeley's texts, which lack the kind of complex satiric and ironic mechanisms capable of revealing speaker and savage as mirror images of one another or opposite sides of the same coin rather than as simple antitheses (think of Gulliver's horrified recognition of his own close resemblance to the Yahoos).

And yet, for all of the ways in which *A Word to the Wise* speaks for the most conservative and elitist elements in contemporary Irish society, it also gives voice to a quite different perspective, which in part helps to explain the highly favorable response it received from the Roman Catholic clergy of the Diocese of Dublin, who, in a letter first appearing in the *Dublin Journal* of November 18, 1749, "return[ed] their sincere and hearty thanks" to "that great and good man," Berkeley, and expressed their determination "to comply with every particular recommended in [the exhortation] to the utmost of their power."[20] Although this response was obviously motivated by a number of highly pragmatic and self-interested concerns, and might strike us today as a perfect example of what we now commonly refer to as colonial mimicry, it attests at the same time to a genuinely liberal dimension of Berkeley's tract, which in spite of the at times insufferably condescending tone adopted toward the Catholic clergy ("You are known to have great influence on the minds of your people, be so good as to use this influence for their benefit" [*W*, 235]), created a forum in which the latter could carry on a dialogue with a Protestant Bishop, the very symbol of Ascendancy power, about "the nation"—invoking references to "the public good" and "the true patriot" generally reserved for the lips (and pens) of only those within the inner circles of power. Thus in *A Word to the Wise* and other tracts dealing with Ireland (such as *The Querist*), Berkeley—without abandoning the ideology, and consequently the prejudices, of his class—does more than speak for the narrow interests of a small elite. In this sense he, like Swift, though in a less subversive and destabilizing way, highlights the contradictions of colonial representation in eighteenth-century Ireland.

III

The whole issue of representation, in all of its perplexing dimensions, occupies a prominent place in the Swiftian canon, constituting both text and subtext for much of his writing. On the most basic level, his works highlight the difficulties surrounding the act of speaking *per se*, for oneself as well as for others, within the contemporary state of affairs. It is not surprising that Swift should have been so preoccupied with this issue, given his continuing battles with government censorship, which resulted in surveillance of his mail, confiscation of his papers, and prosecutions against (as well as jailings of) his printers. As he explained in a letter addressed to Pope, "I dare not publish [my sentiments on publick affairs]: For however orthodox they may be while I am now writing, they may become criminal enough to bring me into trouble before midsummer."[21] The letter goes on to describe the furtiveness with which he was forced to work on his history of Queen Anne's reign, "digesting [the documents] into order by one sheet at a time, for I dare not venture any further, lest the humour of searching and seizing papers should revive" (*SP*, 9:26).

And suggestively anticipating the (albeit far more severe) problems of Myles Joyce in the colonial courtroom, Swift dramatizes his own judicial victimization at the hands of Lord Chief Justice William Whitshed, who was determined to punish Swift to the full extent of the law (and beyond) for his authorship of *A Proposal for the Universal Use of Irish Manufacture* (as well as, several years later, for the Drapier's Fourth Letter), "protest[ing] solemnly that the Author's design was to bring in the Pretender," and angrily sending the jury back nine times to reconsider their verdict after they had found the printer of the pamphlet not guilty (*SP*, 9:27). Swift questions the efficacy of all judicial appeals, since "[the gentlemen of the Long-robe and those in Furs] will just give themselves time to libel and accuse me, but cannot spare a minute to hear my defence" (*SP*, 9:33). He presents his inability to defend himself against false accusations in court as part and parcel of the same problem as his difficulties in writing and publishing his thoughts without government intervention: both result in blatant *mis*representations, of both the individual and the nation at large. Hence, along with the personal slander he continually complains of, Swift regularly protests against the "[false] Rumours industriously spread" about Ireland in English newspapers (*D*, 10:53) and the fact that "no Minister ever gave himself the Trouble of reading any Papers written in our defence" (*D*, 10:64). Note the shift in pronouns, from "*my* defence" to "*our* defence," which underscores the close link Swift saw between personal and national persecution at the hands of England.

It is true, of course, that Swift's circumstances were far more favorable than many others among his countrymen; thus, when confronted by a biased and overzealous judge resolved at all costs to punish him (through his surrogate, the printer Edward Waters), he was able to prevail upon higher authorities to issue a *nolle prosequi*, which won Waters his freedom and ended his own legal liability.[22] Hence to view Swift as the quintessential victim of British colonialism in Ireland (as certain of his writings encourage us to do) would be in effect to occlude the vast body of Irishmen who were far more egregiously victimized, not only by Britain's economic policies but also by Irish legislation that defined them as second-class citizens in their own place of birth. There is no question but that Swift's tendency to offer up his own experiences (just as elsewhere he offers up his own body, described in terms of the painful and debilitating effects of his Ménière's syndrome) as a symbol of Ireland's colonial afflictions skirts the danger of becoming an appropriative gesture of the kind discussed earlier. At the same time, his generalizing formulations often provide access to the experiences of less privileged members of Irish society, articulating grievances suffered even (at times especially) by the lower ranks in society and thereby enabling the latter's voices to be heard along with his own. Thus, for example, Swift's personal complaint about the refusal of those in power to hear his defense is immediately followed by the more sweeping observation: "So in a plot-discovering age, I have often known an innocent man seized and imprisoned, and forced to lie several months in chains, while the Ministers were not at leisure to hear his petition, until they had prosecuted and hanged the number they proposed" (*SP*, 9:33). Since in eighteenth-century Ireland, persons of Swift's class and position were least likely to be among those imprisoned and hanged (as, indeed, his poem *An Excellent New Ballad; or, the True English Dean to be Hang'd for a Rape* makes clear in its sardonic treatment of Thomas Sawbridge, Dean of Ferns, who escaped punishment despite having raped a young woman), the innocent victims evoked in this passage function as vivid reminders of those

Irishmen whose anonymous identities or lowly status in society rendered their sufferings unworthy of official consideration.

My point here is simply this: As long as we view Swift's situation in an appropriately critical way, not as exemplary of all the afflictions imposed on Ireland by British colonialism, but instead as emblematic of a whole range of such afflictions as they *variously* and *unevenly* affected different groups within Irish society, we can fruitfully talk about Swift's "representation" of Ireland without falling into the trap of letting his enormous symbolic presence and rhetorical power silence, or render invisible, the rest of his aggrieved countrymen. To use a present-day analogy, we might think of the way that the putative sufferings of the (seemingly ubiquitous) middle class are regularly invoked nowadays to protest against various inequities in the system and to support a variety of proposed reforms. The main effect of this invocation is an almost total displacement, a consignment to near-invisibility, of those groups in society—the working poor, the unemployed, the homeless—who bear the real brunt of the current economic crisis. Too often the difficulties that professional couples who earn six-figure salaries face in buying a house in a fashionable suburb or in sending their children to private schools come to stand in for the severe deprivations suffered by an underclass without access to the most basic necessities of life. Nevertheless, I would argue that their act of speaking for the economically afflicted can, *under certain circumstances*, function in more enlightened ways as well, offering access to a clearer understanding of those developments in the domestic and world economy that have significantly affected not only their lives but also the lives of the less privileged, and providing the grounds for a *meaningful, non-appropriative* sense of identification with the truly deprived, based on recognition of the widening gap between the (obscenely) rich and the rest of society (middle class and poor alike) and the consequent need for a redistribution of society's resources. Whether in terms of eighteenth-century Ireland or late twentieth-century United States, representational acts embody the conflicting impulses, and contradictory political potential, inherent in all endeavors to speak simultaneously for oneself and others within a framework defined by pronounced social and political inequalities.

Consider, for example, Swift's protestation against Englishmen being given the chief employments in Ireland that should by rights go to native-born Anglo-Irishmen, where he argues that these (very recent and often temporary) English transplants "had no common ligament to bind them with us; they suffered not with our Sufferings, and if it were possible for us to have any Cause of Rejoycing, they could not rejoyce with us."[23] On one level this protest has a rather narrow focus: the misfortunes of those within Ireland's privileged class who have in effect been cheated out of better jobs by carpetbaggers from across the channel. Even if this situation were to change for the better, no Catholic or Dissenter was likely to benefit (directly) from the expanded access to these sorts of positions. And yet, on another level, Swift's outcry may be said to articulate the grievances of a much broader spectrum of the population. In class terms, it speaks for the many Protestants who (despite the assumptions fostered by the term "Ascendancy") were far from prosperous—those referred to in Thomas Sheridan's acid observation: "This is the Modern way of Planting Colonies. . . . When those who are so unfortunate to be born here, are excluded from the meanest Preferments, and deem'd incapable of being entertain'd, even as common Soldiers, whose poor stipend is but Four pence a Day."[24]

Going even beyond this expanded conception, Swift's protest may be said to speak for the Irish nation as a whole in other crucial ways. For one thing, it focuses attention on the presence of suffering as an inescapable consequence of British policies toward Ireland—*suffering*, not mere discomfort or annoyance. For another, it insists on the validity of a peculiarly Irish body of experiences, wholly alien to an English sensibility and mode of valuation ("[they] had no common ligament to bind them with us"). Finally, it underscores the fundamental inequity of a situation in which people are denied participation in the very institutions and political mechanisms that govern their lives. Texts such as this one support Joep Leerssen's conclusion that "Swift seemed to regard the division between Protestants and Catholics as less important than the one between Irish interest and English interest," a position he considers "Swift's most important contribution to the development of Irish Patriotism."[25] Advocacy of this Irish interest meant that the deprivations endured by thwarted Anglo-Irish place-seekers, in themselves hardly indicative of Ireland's worst hardships, could be transformed into a vantage point from which the nation's severest problems were able to be seen more clearly, and understood within the broader context of a system (Sheridan's "Modern way of Planting Colonies") in which the sufferings of relatively well-off Protestants were merely (so to speak) the tip of the iceberg—a point, indeed, explicitly acknowledged by the Swiftian persona "A. North" (modelled on Sir Arthur Acheson) upon noting the severity of his own economic problems: "But the Sufferings of me, and those of my Rank, are Trifles in Comparison of what the meaner Sort [Shopkeepers, Farmers, Pedlars, common Labourers] undergo."[26]

IV

The story of how the problematic of representation profoundly shaped Swift's outlook and writings would not be complete without considering the very basic and literal level of political representation: specifically, the failure of the Irish legislature to effectively speak for the interests of its constituents. Obviously its most blatant shortcoming was its failure to represent the majority of the population; but even within the limited parameters of a colonial Protestant institution it failed to meaningfully function as a representative body for a number of reasons, most dramatically because it effectively ceased having any independent existence after 1720, when the so-called Declaratory Act, insisting on the full rigors of Poynings's Law, asserted the right of the Westminster Parliament to pass laws binding on Ireland and to act as the final court of appeal in all Irish cases, the explicit aim being to "better secur[e] the Dependence of the Kingdom of Ireland upon the Crown of Great Britain."[27] The Drapier's scornful rejection of the very term "*depending Kingdom*" on the grounds that it is "a *modern Term* of *Art;* unknown, . . . to all antient *Civilians,* and *Writers upon Government*" (*D,* 10:62) is an obvious response to this Act, as was Swift's publication (in the same year the Act was passed) of *A Proposal for the Universal Use of Irish Manufacture,* which declares the invalidity of laws that "*bind Men without their Consent.*"[28] The Act's humiliating subjection of Ireland was still fresh in Swift's mind over a decade later, when he came to write *Verses on the Death of Dr Swift.* The poem's speaker observes that Swift's circle of friends in Ireland included "No Fools of Rank, a mungril Breed, / Who fain would pass for Lords indeed"; in a note to Faulkner's edition, Swift glosses these lines in the following way: "The Peers of *Ireland* lost a great Part of their jurisdiction by one single Act [the Declaratory Act of 1720], and tamely submitted to this infamous Mark of Slavery without the least Resentment, or Remonstrance."[29]

The Declaratory Act obviously produced a major political crisis in Ireland; but also, and more to the point of my specific concerns here, it produced a major crisis in representation, making it in certain crucial ways impossible for *any* group in Ireland to speak for the Irish, since the official channels and structures of representation had been removed from Irish soil and transferred to London. This circumstance haunts all of Swift's political writings throughout the 1720s, many of which at one and the same time insist on the necessity for acts of representation and dramatize the futility of attempting them. These writings depict the Act's debilitating effects in terms of Ireland's reduction to little more than a puppet, mechanically uttering words put into its mouth by those pulling the strings (either the English themselves or their flunkeys in Ireland); as Swift wryly observes to Pope, "I have often wished. . . . that a political Catechism might be published by authority four times a year, in order to instruct us how we are to speak and write, and act during the current quarter" (*SP,* 9:33). The implied image governing this statement gives a whole new, indeed *opposite,* meaning to the construction of "speaking for," since when the puppet speaks for the ventriloquist, the act signifies mechanical obedience and dependency, not domination or appropriation. The puppet imagery is made explicit in a poem such as *Mad Mullinix and Timothy*, where the titular Mullinix, a stand-in for a half-crazed beggar known as Molyneux who roamed the streets of Dublin during Swift's time spouting Tory sentiments, engages in alternately abusive and comical dialogue with Timothy: namely, Richard Tighe, a staunch Whig and Walpole supporter who was a member of both the Irish Parliament and the Irish Privy Council.[30] In a lengthy passage (comprising a full sixty lines), Mullinix describes the state of Irish affairs through an extended analogy to a Punch show, invoking a putatively universal definition—"Thus *Tim*, Philosophers suppose, / *The World consists of Puppet-shows*" (*MM*, 123–24)—to delineate Ireland's very specific situation:

> So at this Booth, which we call *Dublin*,
> *Tim* thou'rt the *Punch* to stir up trouble in;
> You Wrigle, Fidge, and make a Rout
> Put all your Brother Puppets out,
> Run on in one perpetual Round,
> To Teize, Perplex, Disturb, Confound, . . . (*MM*, 127–32)

Tighe would have seemed to Swift perfect material for a Punchinello given his slavish exertions on behalf of the English interest in Ireland, which included informing on Swift's friend Sheridan to the authorities in Dublin Castle after Sheridan delivered a provocatively-titled sermon, "Sufficient unto the Day is the Evil thereof," on the anniversary of King George's accession.[31] Swift's lifelong hatred of informers can be gauged by his characterization of them as "the most accursed, and prostitute, and abandoned race, that God ever permitted to plague mankind" (SP, 9:32–33). Tighe's example conflates the roles of informer and puppet, revealing both as stooges that mouth the words and perform the gestures demanded of them by those pulling the strings behind the scene. Neither is capable of independent thought, speech, or action; thus Timothy, having been convinced that his image needs a complete overhaul, pleads for guidance in learning how to become just like Mullinix. The latter is only too happy to comply, readily seizing the reins of control: "Be studious well to imitate / My portly Motion, Mien, and Gate. / Mark my Address, and learn my Style, / When to look Scornful, when to Smile" (*MM*, 223–26). Timothy's eagerness to join the ranks of Dublin's madmen foreshadows the depiction of Ireland's new Parliament House in *A Character, Panegyric, and Description of the Legion Club*, as a lunatic asylum whose members "sit a picking Straws" and "dabble in their Dung," manifesting behavior typical of Bedlamites while they "Sell the Nation for a Pin."[32] But even more than madness, it is abject submissiveness and slavish imitation that constitute the basic traits of Timothy's character; and it is not coincidental that these are the very same traits Swift regularly attributed to the Irish as a whole, in what he saw as their self-destructive willingness to accept their state of subjection by becoming (among other things) mere mouthpieces for the ventriloquists and puppet masters across the channel.

If we were to think of this situation in rhetorical terms, we might describe the impact of the Declaratory Act as a reduction of Ireland to the status of England's persona: a figure lacking an independent existence, set up to mouth the words decreed by an authorizing power, in much the same way that the fictive speakers in Swift's works utter the words written by their author (though note that in both cases the inability to exert total control from above, combined with bursts of anarchic energy from below, creates political and rhetorical situations of marked subversive potential). Obviously Ireland was a real place peopled by flesh-and-blood inhabitants, which would have existed with or without British intervention; but we can think of it as a "creation" of England in the sense that Declan Kiberd suggests when he observes, "If Ireland had never existed, the English would have invented it; and since it never existed in English eyes as anything more than a patchwork-quilt of warring fiefdoms, their leaders occupied the neighbouring island and called it Ireland."[33] Within this conceptual framework it is possible to understand Swift's utilization of personae in his political writings (after 1720 in particular) as a means of turning the tables on England: of wresting back control and voice from the self-proclaimed master ventriloquist and asserting Ireland's right to speak for itself. To be sure, this strategy is based on mechanisms of repression and displacement in that the goal of *Catholic* Ireland's independence and *its* right to speak for itself, no longer subordinated to the laws and institutions of both British- and Protestant-dominated Ireland, is what can never be expressly articulated in Swift's writings—what must be displaced onto Protestant Ireland's struggle against British rule. The symbolism of the master ventriloquist-puppet relationship had to be carefully controlled, limited to the England-Ireland connection, even though it could as readily be analogized to the relationship between Irish Protestants and Irish Catholics.

Yet here again, as in earlier-noted instances, the basic paradigm Swift offers, in this case through his persona strategy, is capable of being appropriated for considerably more subversive ends. And indeed, Swift himself, in his tract, *Reasons Humbly Offered to the Parliament of* Ireland *For Repealing the Sacramental Test, in Favour of the Catholicks*, goes a long way toward demonstrating the possibilities of such appropriation by creating a (pro-)Catholic speaker who powerfully refutes the official Protestant interpretation of the Rebellion of 1641, replacing it with a view consistent with that of Catholic historians at the time.[34] That the tract was intended as an ironic piece, part of Swift's polemical works in support of the Test Act, does not negate the fact that many of its positive constructions of Irish Catholics and their role in their country's history occur also in Swift's non-ironic texts.[35] Nor does it negate the subversive force of the way in which Swift uses a persona in this instance to turn the tables on not only the English but also the Irish Protestant "ventriloquists" by presenting a political and historical perspective that belies the official "scripts" of both dominant groups: "It is well known, that the first Conquerors of this Kingdom were *English Catholicks*, subject to *English Catholick* Kings. . . . It is confessed, that the Posterity of those first victorious *Catholicks* were often forced to rise in their own Defence, against new Colonies from *England*, who treated them like mere native *Irish*, with innumerable Oppressions."[36] Here the speaker deftly turns on its head the argument based on conquest that was commonly adduced by *Protestants* to rationalize their domination of Ireland; he underscores the impossibility of locating an originary or foundational moment in Irish history capable of justifying Protestant claims to be the rightful rulers of the country. Moreover, the protest against being treated "like mere native *Irish*," usually voiced by the Protestants in Ireland (on occasion, by Swift himself) miffed at English *hauteur* towards them, here takes on a rather satirical tone through its being uttered by a Catholic. The shift in voice and perspective exposes both the absurdity of the Anglo-Irish complaint and the injustice of the English stance of superiority toward Ireland. Among Swift's post-1720 tracts, *Reasons Humbly Offered* might well demonstrate the most subversive potential of his rhetorical strategy of wresting voice away from the master ventriloquist (in this case Irish Protestants as well as English), which is no doubt one of the reasons why it was never published in his lifetime.

The Drapier's affair provided Swift with a set of circumstances ideally suited to this political and rhetorical use of personae. The seeming anomaly of having a (mere) tradesman represent all of Ireland pales in comparison with the infinitely greater anomaly of having William Wood—"a *Single, Rapacious, Obscure, Ignominious* PROJECTOR" (D, 10:35)—and the corrupt, hibernophobic Robert Walpole determine what is best for Ireland and her monetary system. Compared with the "fraudulent representations of Wood" (*D*, 10:47), the Drapier's acts of representation seem almost unproblematic. The fact that there was so broad a consensus opposed to the coinage scheme meant that the Drapier could plausibly claim to speak for the whole nation without having to deal with pesky questions about how this claim could be reconciled with the obvious social and religious divisions in Irish society.[37]

Although partly inspired by William Molyneux's *The Case of Ireland . . . Stated*, the Drapier's Fourth Letter diverges from the earlier tract by shifting the emphasis of the case for Ireland's legislative independence from the historical precedents and common law argument spotlighted by Molyneux to the assertion of natural rights: "by the Laws of GOD, of NATURE, of NATIONS, and of your own Country, you ARE and OUGHT to be as FREE a People as your Brethren in *England*" (*D*, 10:63). The subsequent *Letter to Molesworth* extends this thread of argumentation, citing the influence of "dangerous Authors, who talk of *Liberty as a Blessing, to which the whole Race of Mankind hath an Original Title*" (*D*, 10:86), and declaring, "I ever thought it the most uncontrolled and universally agreed Maxim, that *Freedom consists in a People being governed by Laws made with their own Consent; and Slavery in the Contrary*" (*D*, 10:87). The Drapier's assertion of natural rights necessarily (whether consciously intended or not) extends their application to all of Ireland's inhabitants, without exception; it is what Thomas Bartlett terms "the Achilles' heel of the whole Protestant position," since "natural rights could not be restricted to Englishmen, nor to Englishmen born in Ireland, nor to Irish Protestants: they were inherent in all mankind."[38]

There is another telling difference between *The Case of Ireland . . . Stated* and the Drapier's Fourth Letter. Molyneux makes a point of defining "the people of Ireland" for whom he speaks as the Protestants of English origin. He claims, for example, that "it was only the *Antient Race* of the *Irish*, that could suffer by [Henry II's] Subjugation," while "the *English* and *Britains*, that came over and Conquered with him, retain'd all the Freedoms and Immunities of *Free-born* Subjects," as do necessarily their descendants, and he offers highly sectarian accounts of particularly polarizing events in Irish history, such as rebellions in which "*The Irish Papists* [rose] against the *King* and *Protestants* of *Ireland*," and the year 1689, "when most of the Protestant Nobility, Gentry, and Clergy of *Ireland*, were driven out of that Kingdom by the Insolencies and Barbarities of the *Irish Papists*."[39] Swift, on the contrary, exploits the specific occasion—the need to present a united front against Wood and his English backers—to convey a picture of Irish society that transcends the sectarian conflicts foregrounded in Molyneux's tract, stressing instead his citizenship in "a Country, where the People of all Ranks, Parties, and Denominations, are convinced to a Man, that the undoing of themselves and their Posterity for ever, will be dated from the Admission of [Wood's halfpence]" (D, 10:60). Of course, given that the Letter (not to mention the entire campaign to defeat Wood's patent) depended for its credibility and effectiveness on refuting the false reports widely circulating that the anti-Wood opposition was in essence a Catholic plot against British Protestant interests, the

Fourth Letter does affirm the specifically Protestant character of the opposition.[40] Thus at the outset the Drapier enumerates the ruling-class institutions and groups that have declared themselves against the coinage—"the two Houses of Parliament, the Privy-Council, the great Number of Corporations, the Lord-Mayor and Aldermen of Dublin, the Grand-Juries, and principal Gentlemen of several Counties" (D, 10:54)—and he later states, "it is the *True English People of Ireland*, who refuse [Wood's halfpence]; although we take it for granted, that the *Irish* will do so too, whenever they are asked" (D, 10:67). This statement reflects something of the same patronizing tone noted earlier in Berkeley's exhortation to the Catholic clergy. At the same time, it reveals Swift's awareness that, having asserted the natural right of all mankind to liberty and government by consent, it was no longer possible to simply leave the Catholics out of the picture, nor to ignore the importance of their support.

Under the circumstances, the surprise is not that Swift in this Letter distinguishes between the Protestant people of Ireland and the Catholic natives, but that he gives this distinction so little emphasis, subordinating it instead to a vision of solidarity among all groups in Irish society. The internal logic of the Fourth Letter demands that "the Whole People of Ireland" include the Catholic population, even though existing political conditions demanded that the latter be excluded. The Drapier deals with this impasse by in effect acknowledging that the Catholics must be part of the opposition, but only on terms consistent with Ascendancy rule. The central contradiction governing *The Drapier's Letters* lies in their need to avoid undermining this rule while at the same time expanding the oppositional base against Wood to include groups in society ordinarily ignored when advocating for the people of Ireland. The Drapier cannot explicitly incorporate the Catholics into this expanded conception of nationhood, but in a sense he does sneak them in through a series of displacements in which religious divisions are replaced by class differences that are at least somewhat more assimilable into a national ideal. Thus in an earlier letter, the Drapier asserts his credentials by telling us, "I am no inconsiderable Shopkeeper in this Town. I have discoursed with several of my own, and other Trades; with many Gentlemen both of City and Country; and also, with great Numbers of Farmers, Cottagers, and Labourers" (D, 10:16). He deliberately presents a list of the humblest groups in Irish society (several of which were composed largely of Catholics), whose opinions about Wood's proposed coinage are accorded as much attention as the views of "the two Houses of Parliament, [and] the Privy-Council" invoked in the subsequent letter. The Drapier's Fourth Letter is the one that most explicitly asserts his role as speaker for "the Whole People of Ireland," but it is only when we consider all of the Letters together that we can fully appreciate the extent to which Swift manages to accomplish that aim—even while he avoids taking the final step that would pull the rug from under his own feet by negating the grounds of his own and his class's privileged position in Irish society.[41]

V

Swift's activities as M. B. Drapier proved to be highly successful, of course, culminating in the revocation of Wood's patent in August, 1725. I want to conclude this discussion, however, not with an example of Swift's success in representing the Irish nation but with a consideration of his frustrated attempts in this regard: of writings of his that dramatize the profound difficulties, at times even impossibility, of such representation. One such example is the *Letter to the Archbishop of Dublin concerning the Weavers*, which not only failed to achieve its ostensible purpose but was never even published in Swift's lifetime, despite his assertion that he was writing to "offer my notions to the publick."[42] Herbert Davis, referring to this and several other tracts written in 1729, comments that "the real problem is to explain why they were not printed," and concludes that the reason must have been "that mood of despondency to which [Swift] often gives expression in these unpublished pieces."[43] I want to consider this "despondency" further, not only as despair over Ireland's deteriorating economic conditions (which included a serious famine during the course of that year), but also in terms of Swift's deepening sense of the futility of all forms of representation designed to make this situation known to others and thereby bring about relief.

The opening to the *Letter to the Archbishop* immediately foregrounds the act of representation as one of the tract's central preoccupations by having Swift describe a meeting the previous week with the corporation of weavers in the woollen manufacture, "when he who spoke for the rest and in the name of his absent brethren" delivered what he said was "the opinion of the whole body"—namely, that Swift write something to "persuade the People of the Kingdom to wear their own woollen Manufactures" (L, 12:65). Apart from the fact that this request by its very nature functions as a sign of futility, underscoring as it does the failure of earlier Swift interventions (such as his *Proposal for the Universal Use of Irish Manufacture*) to achieve their goal, the detail of the account presented in this *Letter* serves to highlight the conditions and hence the limitations of the representational act. Swift's acceptance of an advocacy role for the corporation would place him at not one, but two removes from those he is supposed to speak for; the absent body first represented by one of their own would now be re-represented by someone completely outside of their group. This problem of the gap created by standing in for what is absent takes on another dimension through Swift's subsequent suggestion that the weavers "apply themselves to the Parliament in their next Session" with a view toward "prevail[ing] in the House of Commons to grant one very reasonable request" (L, 12:71)—namely, vote to wear clothing made only of Irish manufacture. Elsewhere in Swift's writings, the distance between the formally constituted representative bodies of society and those seeking representation is satirically magnified through the use of speakers who are at the very bottom of the social hierarchy, as in the poem, *The Petition of Frances Harris*, and *The Humble Petition of the Footmen in and about the City of Dublin*, where lowly members of the Irish servant class farcically present their cases to the most powerful officials in the nation.[44] Swift's advice to the weavers to petition Parliament with their grievance, if not similarly satirical, nevertheless conveys a hint of absurdity given the Irish Parliament's record of caving in to English pressures and doing nothing to oppose the restrictions on Ireland's trade. It also underscores the inextricable links between the two kinds of representation (rhetorical and political) and restores the colonial context to the weavers' predicament. The point is clear: Even if Swift were to devote the rest of his life to representing the weavers in his writings, they would still not be meaningfully represented—no more than Ireland itself could ever be under the prevailing circumstances.

Almost every existing problem with regard to representational acts within the Irish context is touched upon in the *Letter to the Archbishop*, including political reprisals against protest ("if God Almighty for our sins would most justly send us a Pestilence, whoever should dare to discover his grief in publick for such a visitation, would certainly be censured for disaffection to the Government" [*L*, 12:65]), the frustration of the advocate (whose previous advice has repeatedly been ignored), and the unreliability of those seeking to be represented ("This Corporation of Weavers in Woollen and Silks . . . are the hottest and coldest generation of Men that I have known" [*L*, 12:68]). But what is perhaps the most interesting feature of the *Letter* with respect to this theme is Swift's suggestion that there is something about the Irish situation so peculiar and aberrant that it falls outside the scope of representation altogether: "For, I will not deny to your Grace, that I cannot reflect on the singular condition of this Country, different from all others upon the face of the Earth, without some Emotion" (L, 12:65). The same point is made even more dramatically in his tract, *Maxims Controlled in Ireland*, where Ireland's radical otherness is conveyed through a series of conditional clauses suggesting monstrosity: "For, if we could conceive a nation where each of the inhabitants had but one eye, one leg, and one hand, it is plain that, before you could institute them into a republic, an allowance must be made for those material defects, wherein they differed from other mortals."[45] Indeed, this entire tract is based on the premise of Ireland's irreducible singularity as the only place in the world where otherwise universal maxims do not apply—where political and economic principles taken for granted everywhere else are "controlled" (that is, refuted). It is this grotesque and unenviable uniqueness that makes Ireland's problems impervious to the recommendations of projectors "who are every day publishing their thoughts . . . for improving the trade of Ireland, and referring us to the practice and example of England, Holland, France, or other nations" (M, 12:131).

It is possible to argue that Swift speaks most powerfully for the Irish nation, not when he is clearly articulating the interests of his countrymen in works like *The Drapier's Letters*, but when he is indicating Ireland's resistance to normal modes of representation due to the "unspeakable" nature of its conditions. The claims of unrepresentability that pervade Swift's post-1720 political writings function, among other things, as an ironic counterpart to the overabundance and violence of representation that England inflicted on its "dependencies." Looking at a later period in Irish history, Seamus Deane points to "the generation of a narrative of strangeness, the story or stories of a country that is in a condition that cannot be represented at all or that still has to be represented."[46] Swift's distinctive twist on this narrative, and very possibly his strongest claim to being an Irish patriot, was his transformation of the (to him) inherent strangeness of Ireland, as a country with an alien language and culture, into the artificially produced strangeness of a country deformed and rendered unrecognizable by colonialism. We can see a microcosm of this transformation in Swift's letter of June 30, 1732 addressed to Dean Brandreth:

> I think I was once in your county, Tipperary, which is like the rest of the whole kingdom, a bare face of nature, without house or plantations; filthy cabins, miserable, tattered, half-starved creatures, scarce in human shape . . . a parish church to be found only in a summer-day's journey, in comparison of which, an English farmer's barn is a cathedral; a bog of fifteen miles round; every meadow a slough, and every hill a mixture of rock, heath, and marsh. . . . There is not an acre of land in Ireland turned to half its advantage; yet it is better improved than the people; and all these evils are the effects of English tyranny: so your sons and grandchildren will find it to their sorrow.[47]

This passage begins with a speaker indistinguishable from an Englishman confronting the dreaded heart of darkness on an expedition into deepest Africa, or an Anglo-Irishman railing in disgust against the native savagery of the land to which a malevolent fate has condemned him; it ends with the forceful, angry voice of an Irish nationalist, exposing the almost indescribable wretchedness of Ireland as a manifestation of the barbarism not within but without: the barbarism emanating from, and created in the name of, English "civilization." A half-century ago George Orwell argued that Swift spoke (if only partially and contradictorily) for the forces of anarchy; several decades later, Norman O. Brown noted the ways in which Swift spoke for the id, not for civilization but for its discontents.[48] In the spirit of these interpretations, I want to suggest that Swift also spoke for those extreme aspects of eighteenth-century Irish society that resisted all forms of rational explanation and verbal closure. The exposure of the mechanisms of sexual sublimation (as in *A Tale of a Tub's* "Digression on Madness") that prompted Brown to view Swift as a kind of pre-Freudian psychoanalyst also allows us to understand Swift as one who adamantly rejected those mechanisms of political and linguistic repression which enable the supposedly civilizing processes of rationalization and normalization to take place on a historical level: which conceal from view the unassimilable vis-à-vis the established institutions of polite society.

In a different time and place, Aimé Césaire powerfully protested against similar forces of sublimation, also within a colonial context, by exposing the savagery at the very core of refined European culture, the "unctuous and sanctimonious cannibalism" regularly staged as normal political operations in the French National Assembly. His observations, based chiefly on the twentieth-century experience of Martinique, have their own peculiar applicability to eighteenth-century Ireland: "Colonization: bridgehead in a campaign to civilize barbarism, from which there may emerge at any moment the negation of civilization, pure and simple."[49] To offer a detailed, even eloquent description of this civilizing campaign is not remarkably difficult given a sufficient level of education and socialization. But how—with what language and mode of address—does one record the "negation" of civilization: those moments that can erupt suddenly, at any time, and tear apart the smooth fabric of social and rhetorical sublimations? For Césaire the answer is an impassioned outcry that sets up, but then quickly subverts, expectations of a sober philosophic discourse: that consists in sentence fragments, fierce ejaculations, and a generic olio of historical reportage, diatribe, satire, and theatrical dramatizations. For Swift, the answer is a body of writings with built-in satiric mechanisms enabling them to self-destruct at the same time that they give voice to the madman, the cannibal, the excrementalist, and others functioning outside of the sublimation machine; writings that on occasion cast doubts on their own powers of communication and persuasion by remaining fragmentary and/or unpublished despite their intended appeal to the public; writings that insist on the absolute, monstrous singularity of the Irish condition, which no established modes of explanation or analysis can adequately describe.

The enormities of twentieth-century history have foregrounded the problem of trying to speak the unspeakable, to represent that which falls outside the boundaries of normal human experience; they have forced us to ask (in George Steiner's words) "whether language itself can justly communicate, express, give rational or metaphoric constructs to the realities of modern torture and extermination."[50] But what about eighteenth-century Ireland? Could its conditions really have been so horrible that they defied the signifying powers of language as well as the conventions of rational discourse? On the face of it this seems to be a gross exaggeration of the facts—as do Swift's impassioned diatribes on the existing situation. Sooner or later most of us are probably moved to ask ourselves, What was this guy's problem anyway? Why the constant negativity, the repeated outcries against the circumstances of his existence, given a mode of life more privileged than desperate and a position in society many would have considered enviable? I think that Swift on some level realized the inevitability of such questions, and that this realization made him even more strident in his denunciations as well as more overwhelmed by a sense of the sheer hopelessness of trying to get his point across, given the power of sublimating mechanisms to turn shit into the products of high culture and to replace aberration or pervasive disease with the varied forms of normalcy. In the years since his death we can see the effect of these mechanisms in the way that his most disturbing and obscene works have been, when not dismissed as morally loathsome orignored altogether, converted into models of ironic prose or satiric dexterity deserving of literary canonization; alternatively, in the way in which his extreme diagnoses of the Irish condition have been turned on himself, normalizing the depicted situation while pathologizing the author.

Moving beyond the specific case of Swift, we find many other examples where these forces have worked to normalize aspects of Irish history. With the addition of a generous dose of historical relativism, what we might term the "civilized barbarism" of the genial, philosophically detached Bishop Berkeley—his defense of slavery in the name of religion and his urging that planters baptize "those who belong to them" since "their Slaves would only become better Slaves by becoming Christians" and since "it would be of Advantage to their Affairs, to have Slaves who should *obey in all Things their Masters according to the Flesh, . . . in Singleness of Heart as fearing God*"—has been converted by a subsequent scholarly commentator into a stage in the upward march of human progress: "While to a later age it may seem no great service to blacks to argue that they could lawfully be both Christians and slaves at the same time, the case is otherwise. . . . Berkeley took a step, however tentative and tiny, when he argued for greater intensity and responsibility in trying to Christianize blacks."[51]

(We might recall here Césaire's discovery of "howling savagery" in the writings of "the Western *humanist*, the 'idealist' philosopher," as well as his scathingly sarcastic look at various French "scientific" and philosophic texts that blithely normalize slavery—for example, Lapouge's "*it must not be forgotten that* [slavery] *is no more abnormal than the domestication of the horse or the ox.*")[52]

And leaving behind individual cases altogether, we might think of the way that some recent historians have employed rationalizing and normalizing techniques to re-present aspects of the Irish past in a putatively dispassionate, objective manner, devoid of the ideologically engaged tone of nationalist historiography.[53] With regard to the Great Famine, this has meant (once again) invoking historical relativism in order to examine the events of 1845–52 in a detached, clinical fashion. Thus Mary Daly, for one, having warned her readers against "adopting a late-twentieth-century attitude of moral superiority," turns the catastrophic events of that period into a less than remarkable (because part of a recurring) scenario that called forth government relief measures which, though undoubtedly inadequate, are not subject to second-guessing and undeserving of condemnation by later historians.[54] The transformation, in Daly's study, of millions of starved and displaced bodies into a largely administrative problem immune to moral judgments is the very opposite of the mercilessly desublimating strategy of Césaire as he reconverts European industrial growth and economic prosperity into "the highest heap of corpses in history."[55] It is equally inimical to Swift's desublimations of what passed for civilization in his day, which also entailed recovering heaps of dead bodies from underneath layers of abstraction and repressed material realities: for example, the Irishman lured to the American colonies under false pretenses, to be used as colonial foot soldiers, "as a Screen [for the English settlers] against the Assaults of the *Savages*," and afterwards to "fill up Trenches with their dead Bodies."[56]

With regard to eighteenth-century Ireland, the rationalizing and normalizing procedures of many revisionist histories have taken the form of assimilating Ireland into contemporary European models of governance, thereby effectively eliminating colonialism altogether from the picture. Thus Jacqueline Hill, noting that in Ireland "politics was mainly the preserve of an aristocracy . . . claiming rights that derived, in part at least, from conquest," insists that "there was nothing unusual, by contemporary standards, about that. Aristocratic pre-eminence was to be observed all over Europe, and it was frequently explained in terms of conquest."[57] In a similar vein, S. J. Connolly, acknowledging Ireland's "many-sided subordination" but seeing it as no different from that of Southern Italy, Norway, or Poland during this period, argues that "*Ancien régime* Europe offers many examples of territories or historic nations under the domination of foreign rulers. . . . Yet none of [these nations] is normally described as a case of colonial rule. Why then should Ireland, alone in Western Europe, be considered for that status?"[58]

Why indeed? Clearly there were many in Swift's own day who asked that very same question (or a variant thereof) and who answered it with unequivocal assurances of Ireland's normalcy in this regard: with descriptions of the country that ignored its anomalous, unassimilable features and instead emphasized the array of familiar benefits it offered both its own and England's ruling class (the only ones deemed worth considering in this matter). It was these kinds of descriptions that drove Swift to distraction, provoking his most mordant sarcasm and eliciting some of his most vehement denunciations. Much of the exceedingly bleak commentary in *A Short View of the State of Ireland* was designed to counter the reassuringly rosy reports made about the country by contemporary pamphleteers, such as John Browne in his *Seasonable Remarks on Trade* (1728), who promoted Ireland's alleged wealth as a source of growing profit for England, portraying the colony as "a milch Cow [which], if we let it run into good Pasture . . . will overflow our Pails."[59] The same deluded and/or deluding attitude is attributed in the *Short View* to those who come to Dublin for brief visits, frequenting the homes of the privileged few and then returning to England to spread the word that Ireland's inhabitants "wallow in Riches and Luxury."[60] Swift tells us that "with regard to the Affairs of this Kingdom, I have been using all Endeavors to subdue my Indignation" (SV, 12:5), but the body of the pamphlet shows that even his most vaunted satiric and rhetorical skills fail him in the attempt to transmute this "Indignation" into something more restrained, more socially acceptable, more literary ("But my heart is too Heavy to continue this Irony longer" [SV, 12:10]). As a response to the complacent, normalizing reports of English visitors to the country (and the Irish "Man-pleaser[s]" eager to curry favor with them [SV, 12:12]), Swift again insists on the appalling singularity of Ireland's situation, which removes it from any possible comparison with other countries—even, one must assume, those of the *ancien régime.* Having enumerated a series of disastrous circumstances besetting Ireland, he concludes, "And in this, as in most of the Articles already mentioned, we are an Exception to all other States or Monarchies that were ever known in the World" (SV, 12:9).

The language of the *Short View* is extreme and uncompromising; it moves between the starkest of concrete, factual details ("The Families of Farmers, who pay great Rents, living in Filth and Nastiness upon Buttermilk and Potatoes, without a Shoe or Stocking to their Feet" [SV, 12:10]) and tropes whose very banality is used for shock effect ("One Thing I know, that *when the Hen is starved to Death, there will be no more Golden Eggs*" [SV, 12:12]). Should we be inclined to interpret this (and similar tracts) as a distortion of the actual state of affairs through vituperative exaggeration, we must at the same time be prepared to entertain the possibility that the comforting, familiarizing descriptions of all those, whether in the eighteenth century or today, who reject Swift's diagnoses distort reality in another way—and perhaps with far more pernicious results in the sense that, unlike exaggeration, the latter practice does away with reality altogether, removing the problem from view and making disappear those who stand witness to its appalling results. Thomas Sheridan's version of the *Short View*, his own graphic account of a journey he took from Dublin to Dundalk, published in the *Intelligencer* Number 6, which emphatically endorses the picture of wretchedness offered by Swift ("As to Trade, I met nine Carrs loaden with old musty shrivel'd Hydes, one Carload of Butter. Four Jockeys driving eight Horses, all out of Case. One Cow and Calf, driven by a Man and his Wife. Six tattered Families flitting to be shipped off to the *West-Indies*. A Colony of a hundred and fifty Beggars, all repairing to people our Metropolis"), explicitly addresses the possible challenges to his (and Swift's) perception of the Irish condition:

> It may be objected, What use it is of to display the Poverty of the Nation in the manner I have done. In answer, I desire to know for what Ends, and by what Persons, This new Opinion of our flourishing State has of late been so Industriously advanced. One thing is certain, that the Advancers have either already found their own Account, or have been heartily promised, or at least have been entertained with hopes, by seeing such an Opinion pleasing to those who have it in their power to reward.[61]

Sheridan's point here is as relevant to our own interpretations of eighteenth-century Irish history as it was to his contemporary detractors. Mere avoidance of the impassioned criticism pervading his own and Swift's accounts of Ireland in favor of serene testimonies to the nation's normal development or flourishing state does not equate to a detached, objective viewpoint. On the contrary, it can just as readily be an expression of flagrant partiality, of the most blatant form of self-interest and narrow vision. Sheridan does not make any claim here for the objective truth of his own position. He does, however, invite us to consider what there is to gain, in the personal and political terms suggested above, from the relentless exposure of Ireland's singularly miserable conditions; and if we conclude that the answer is nothing, to wonder why we should reject the testimony of people like himself and Swift for the complacent reports of a well-functioning society provided by those who stand to profit from reassuring the ruling powers about the status quo in which they have so great an investment.

It is perhaps in the *Intelligencer* Number 6 that Sheridan comes closest to approximating Swift's perspective and mode of expression; yet even in this piece the emotional and linguistic extremity of the *Short View* can only be hinted at. Verbal excess is one of the signs under which Swift (like Césaire) attested to the outrages of his time; and while excess by definition can never be consonant with an exact representation of historical reality, its operations *can* bring to the level of consciousness, and thus help render discernible, those elements in an extreme situation that refuse accommodation to official historical narratives rooted in standardized explanatory models and closure. Another sign under which Swift offered witness to the times was the very opposite of verbal excess: spareness, starkness, silence—the terse recognition that mere words cannot communicate the enormities that the writer or speaker wishes to, indeed *must*, convey. Faced with the absurdities of Ireland's economic situation as regulated by English interests, Swift is moved to note that "there is something so monstrous . . . there is, I say, something so softish, that it wants a Name, in our Language, to express it by."[62] This awareness did not of course prevent Swift from producing a very substantial number of words in the course of a long life devoted to commenting on, satirizing, and urging measures to improve the state of affairs in Ireland. Nevertheless, I want to conclude by suggesting that Swift's contribution to Irish history rests not only on what he said but also on what he did *not* say—or, to be more precise, on what he kept insisting he *could not* say: rests in no small measure on his demonstration that the struggle to represent Ireland's situation, and through that the struggle to underscore its unrepresentability due to man-made (politically-inflicted) deformation, was a task not to be evaded even by an Anglican churchman in relatively cushy circumstances who could, if he chose, have spoken in the confident, magisterial tones of the Ascendancy.

University of California, Riverside

Endnotes

1. Swift, *The Drapier's Letters* (1724), in the *Prose Works of Jonathan Swift,* ed. Herbert Davis, 14 vols. (Oxford: Basil Blackwell, 1939–1968), 10:53–68. Hereafter abbreviated *D* and cited parenthetically in the text by volume and page number.

2. R.F. Foster, *Modern Ireland, 1600–1972* (London: Penguin, 1988), 175. Technically the term "Protestant Ascendancy" is anachronistic when applied to Swift since it did not come into use until the 1780s. However, it

is possible to argue, along with Jacqueline Hill, that the term nevertheless "serves to describe the political reality in Ireland from the mid-seventeenth to the nineteenth century." See Hill, *From Patriots to Unionists: Dublin Civic Politics and Irish Protestant Patriotism, 1660–1840* (Oxford: Clarendon Press, 1997), 9. For additional insight into the historical background and meaning of the term, see Kevin Whelan, *The Tree of Liberty: Radicalism, Catholicism and the Construction of Irish Identity* (Notre Dame: Univ. of Notre Dame Press, 1996), 107–10.

3. Although all three of these "speakers for the Irish nation" were Anglican—indeed, officials of the Church of Ireland for at least some period in their lives—a distinction needs to be made between the Anglo-Irish background of Swift and Berkeley on the one hand, and on the other, the Irish Protestantism of Sheridan, who came from a native Gaelic-speaking family, the O Sioradains (or O'Sheridans) of county Cavan, that converted in the first half of the seventeenth century, forging relationships with high-ranking members of the Protestant Church (such as William Bedell, Bishop of Kilmore) while retaining its ties to Irish culture. For details of this family history, see Fintan O'Toole, *A Traitor's Kiss: The Life of Richard Brinsley Sheridan, 1715–1816* (New York: Farrar, Straus, and Giroux, 1998), 3–10.

4. See Spivak, "Can the Subaltern Speak?" in *Marxism and the Interpretation of Culture*, ed. Cary Nelson and Lawrence Grossberg (Urbana: Univ. of Illinois Press, 1988), 271–313.

5. Haraway, "The Promises of Monsters: A Regenerative Politics for Inappropriate/d Others," in *Cultural Studies*, ed. Lawrence Grossberg, Cary Nelson, and Paula A. Treichler (New York: Routledge, 1992), 311–12.

6. Alcoff, "The Problem of Speaking for Others," in *Who Can Speak? Authority and Critical Identity*, ed. Judith Roof and Robyn Weigman (Urbana: Univ. of Illinois Press, 1995), 116.

7. Cheng, "Of Canons, Colonies, and Critics: The Ethics and Politics of Postcolonial Joyce Studies," *Cultural Critique* 35 (1996–97): 89. I use the terms "first world" and "third world" as a convenient and familiar shorthand reference, but the quotation marks placed around them indicate my agreement with such critics as Arif Dirlik and Aijaz Ahmad, who argue that "the transnationalization of production calls into question earlier divisions of the world into First, Second, and Third Worlds" (Dirlik, "The Postcolonial Aura: Third World Criticism in the Age of Global Capitalization," *Critical Inquiry* 20 [1994]: 350) and that under present global conditions "we live not in three worlds but in one" (Ahmad, *In Theory: Classes, Nations, Literatures* [London: Verso, 1994], 103).

8. "Ireland, Island of Saints and Sages" (1907), in *The Critical Writings of James Joyce,* ed. Ellsworth Mason and Richard Ellmann (Ithaca: Cornell Univ. Press, 1959), 162.

9. "The Shade of Parnell" (1912), in *The Critical Writings,* 225.

10. The views of Anglo-Irish nationalists in the early part of the eighteenth century are commonly termed "colonial nationalism," implying their strict containment within an imperial framework and their supposed difference from "real" nationalism; see, for example, the Introduction to J. G. Simms, *War and Politics in Ireland, 1649–1730,* ed. D. W. Hayton and Gerard O'Brien (London and Ronceverte, W. Va: The Hambledon Press, 1986), xiii-xiv. Often the term is used in an overtly pejorative way, as when Foster declares that "many of [Swift's] arguments carry the authentic exclusiveness and brutality of colonial nationalism" (181). But see D. George Boyce's cogent counter-argument that "it is misleading . . . to refer to Protestants' sentiment as 'colonial nationalism,' as if it were in some way to be distinguished from the mainstream of the Irish nationalist tradition." Boyce, *Nationalism in Ireland,* 3rd ed. (London: Routledge, 1995 [1982]), 107.

11. See "Intellectuals and Power" (1972), in *Language, Counter-Memory, Practice: Selected Essays and Interviews by Michel Foucault,* ed. Donald F. Bouchard (Ithaca: Cornell Univ. Press, 1977), 209.

12. Spivak, 308.

13. "Ireland at the Bar" (1907), in *The Critical Writings,* 198.

14. Spivak, 308.

15. In *The Eighteenth Brumaire of Louis Bonaparte,* Marx attributes this need for outside representation to the small peasants' lack of unity and class consciousness. See *Marx: Later Political Writings,* ed. and trans. Terrell Carver (Cambridge: Cambridge Univ. Press, 1996), 117.

16. Leighton, *Catholicism in a Protestant Kingdom: A Study of the Irish 'Ancien Régime'* (Dublin: Gill and Macmillan, 1994), 10 ("Catholics, as a whole"). On Catholic discontent, see, for example, Archbishop Hugh Boulter's account, in a letter to the Duke of Newcastle, of "the popish rabble coming down to fight the whig mob" on the Pretender's birthday in 1726, and in the process "assault[ing the Lord Mayor, Sheriffs, and some aldermen, attended with a number of constables] with stones, bricks, and dirt" (Hugh Boulter to the Duke of Newcastle, June 11, 1726, in *Letters Written by His Excellency Hugh Boulter to Several Ministers of State in England, and Some Others,* Vol. One [Dublin, 1770], 65–66). For a general overview of

Catholic activism and political protest during this period, see S. J. Connolly, *Religion, Law and Power: The Making of Protestant Ireland, 1660–1760* (Oxford: Clarendon Press, 1992), 233–49.

17. This argument appears in Warren Montag's "Forum Response" to my review of his book in *Eighteenth-Century Fiction* 9 (1996): 102. The Forum exchange between Montag and myself continued over the next several issues of *ECF*.

18. *A Word to the Wise; or An Exhortation to the Roman Catholic Clergy of Ireland* (1749), in *The Works of George Berkeley*, ed. A. A. Luce and T. E. Jessop, 9 vols. (Edinburgh: Thomas Nelson and Sons, 1948–57), 6:235, 248. Hereafter abbreviated W and cited parenthetically in the text by page number.

19. A fascinating reversal of this phobic response to the "savage" may be seen in the *literal* journey into the "heart of darkness" undertaken in 1903 by the Anglo-Irishman Roger Casement, sent as a British consul into the Congo's interior to investigate reports of the barbarous treatment of the natives by the rubber traders in King Leopold's employ, which resulted in his psychic and political identification with the brutalized blacks along with his discovery, and full acceptance, of his Irish identity ("In those lonely Congo forests where I found Leopold . . . I also found myself, the incorrigible Irishman"). In the years immediately following, Casement devoted himself to the cause of eradicating slave labor in the Congo, becoming a prominent figure in the first international human rights movement of the twentieth century; later, as a committed Irish nationalist, he fought to liberate his own country from British rule. Casement was hung for treason by the British on August 3, 1916, to the end affirming what he saw as the inextricable links between his role as Irish patriot and his exertions on behalf of the enslaved Africans. See Adam Hochschild, *King Leopold's Ghost* (Boston: Houghton Mifflin, 1998), 195–208; 267 ("lonely Congo forests"); 267–68, 285–87.

20. The letter of reply from the Roman Catholic clergy was appended to *A Word to the Wise* in the Dublin edition of 1750 and in most editions thereafter, including Berkeley's *Miscellany* (1752). It is reprinted immediately following *A Word in Works of Berkeley*, 6:248–49. The passages quoted appear on 248.

21. *A Letter from Dr Swift to Mr Pope*, January 10, 1721, in *Prose Works*, 9:33. Hereafter abbreviated *SP* and cited parenthetically in the text by volume and page number.

22. See Introduction, *Prose Works*, 9:xvi.

23. *Advice to the Freemen of Dublin* (1733), in *Prose Works,* 13:82.

24. This comment appears in Number 6 of the *Intelligencer,* a periodical put out by Swift and Sheridan in 1728–29. See *The Intelligencer,* ed. James Woolley (Oxford: Clarendon Press, 1992), 86–87.

25. Leerssen, *Mere Irish and Fíor-Ghael: Studies in the Idea of Irish Nationality . . . prior to the Nineteenth Century* (Cork: Cork Univ. Press, 1996), 311.

26. *Intelligencer* 19 (1728), in *Prose Works,* 12:54.

27. See Introduction, *Prose Works,* 9:x.

28. *A Proposal for the Universal Use of Irish Manufacture,* in *Prose Works,* 9:19.

29. *Verses on the Death of Dr Swift,* 437–38, in *The Poems of Jonathan Swift,* ed. Harold Williams, 2nd ed., 3 vols. (Oxford: Clarendon Press, 1958), 2:570, n. 4 ("The Peers of *Ireland*"). Subsequent quotations of Swift's poetry are taken from this edition.

30. This poem was originally published in Number 8 of the *Intelligencer.* See Woolley's edition (which includes Sheridan's Introduction to the poem), 103–14. Hereafter abbreviated *MM* and cited parenthetically in the text by line number. For additional background information on Tighe, see Woolley's prefatory comments, 101–3.

31. See Swift's account of the incident in *A Vindication of His Excellency John, Lord Carteret* (1730), in *Prose Works,* 12:163.

32. Swift, *A Character, Panegyric, and Description of the Legion Club,* 49, 52, 48.

33. Kiberd, *Inventing Ireland: The Literature of the Modern Nation* (Cambridge: Harvard Univ. Press, 1995), 9.

34. For a more extended discussion of this tract, see my essay, "Swift as Irish Historian," in *Walking Naboth's Vineyard: New Studies of Swift,* ed. Christopher Fox and Brenda Tooley (Notre Dame: Univ. of Notre Dame Press, 1995), 64–66.

35. Swift defended the Irish Catholics' basic loyalty to the British Crown on a number of occasions, asserting, for example, that they had not "the least Design to depose or murder their King, much less to abolish Kingly Government" (*Queries Relating to the Sacramental Test* [1732], in *Prose Works,* 12:257). He also firmly rejected the notion that the Catholics continued to pose a military threat to Protestant rule, declaring it "a gross

imposition upon common Reason, to terrify us with their Strength" (*Queries*, 12:258), and insisting that the Catholics had been "put out of all visible Possibility of hurting us" (*On Brotherly Love*, sermon preached in St. Patrick's Cathedral on December 1, 1717, in *Prose Works*, 9:172).

36. *Reasons Humbly Offered . . .*, in *Prose Works*, 12:287.

37. The Drapier's assertion that "the People here . . . unite as one Man: resolving they will have nothing to do with [Wood's] Ware" (*D*, 10:57) was confirmed even by those opposed to his agitation against the coinage scheme. Archbishop Boulter, for example, was forced to admit to an English correspondent, the Duke of Newcastle, in a letter dated January 19, 1724 that "the people of every religion, country, and party here, are alike set against *Wood's* halfpence" (*Letters to Several Ministers of State in England*, 7).

38. Bartlett, *The Fall and Rise of the Irish Nation: The Catholic Question, 1690–1830* (Dublin: Gill and Macmillan, 1992), 35–36.

39. Molyneux, *The Case of Ireland's being bound by acts of parliament in England, stated* (Dublin, 1698), 19, 146, 106.

40. The Drapier attributes this specious view to "Rumours industriously spread" by "News-Mongers in *London*" that "the *Papists* in Ireland *have entered into an Association against* [Wood's] *coin*" (*D*, 10:53). However, that these "Rumours" were also "home-grown" products is evident from Archbishop Boulter's comment to the Duke of Newcastle: "That there has been a great deal of art used to spread this infection [the agitation against Wood's patent], and that the Papists and jacobites have been very industrious in this affair for very bad ends, I find most of the men of sense here [in Ireland] will allow" (*Letters to Several Ministers of State in England*, 7-8).

41. That Swift, in his role as the Drapier, was deemed by contemporaries to be a unifier of a divided nation is suggested by verses written shortly after the affair—appropriately entitled *A Poem To the whole People of Ireland, Relating to M. B. Drapier* and signed "A. R. Hosier" (Dublin, 1726)—which counter criticisms of the Drapier by observing: "But let those consider, how firmly united, / Were *Whigs, Tories, Trimmers*, and the *H*[anoveria]*ns;* / And with what Delight [the Drapier] all others invited, / Even *Quakers, Conformists*, and the *Presbyterians*."

42. *Letter to the Archbishop of Dublin concerning the Weavers* (written in 1729; first published in 1765), in *Prose Works*, 12:71. Hereafter abbreviated *L* and cited parenthetically in the text by volume and page number.

43. See Introduction, *Prose Works*, 12:xvi–xvii.

44. See *The Humble Petition of the Footmen . . .* (1732), in *Prose Works,* 12:235–37.

45. *Maxims Controlled in Ireland* (1729), in *Prose Works,* 12:131. Hereafter abbreviated *M* and cited parenthetically in the text by volume and page number. This is but one of many instances in which Swift figures the debilitating effects of colonialism through images of bodily deformity and mutilation. Addressing a member of the English House of Commons, for example, Swift's persona declares, "If your little Finger be sore, and you think a Poultice made out of our [Ireland's] *Vitals* will give it any Ease, speak the Word, and it shall be done" (*A Letter . . . Concerning the Sacramental Test* [1709], in *Prose Works,* 2:114); fifteen years later, the Drapier, while acknowledging the scarcity of money in Ireland, asserts that "Mr. *Wood's* Remedy, would be, to cure a Scratch on the Finger by cutting off the Arm" (*D,* 10:16). Swift's insistence on dramatizing how England's actions register in very concrete (at times graphic) terms on the Irishman's body anticipates the colonial analyses of Frantz Fanon, who describes the profound dislocations resulting from being "battered down" by racial stereotypes—including, as in the case of the Irish, cannibalism—by asking, "What else could it be for me but an amputation, an excision, a hemorrhage that spattered my whole body with black blood?" Fanon also relates that "the crippled veteran of the Pacific war says to my brother, 'Resign yourself to your color the way I got used to my stump; we're both victims.'" *Black Skin, White Masks,* trans. Charles Lam Markmann (1952; New York: Grove Press, 1967), 112; 140.

46. Deane, *Strange Country: Modernity and Nationhood in Irish Writing since 1790* (Oxford: Clarendon Press, 1997), 146. From a somewhat different perspective David Lloyd discusses the "unrepresentable" (and "unrepresentative") in Irish history in terms of popular oral culture such as street balladry as well as, more generally, those counter-hegemonic forces "resistant to the unifying drive of the ethical state." See *Anomalous States: Irish Writing and the Post-Colonial Moment* (Durham: Duke Univ. Press, 1993), 9 ("the generation of").

47. Swift to Dean Brandreth, 30 June 1732, in *The Correspondence of Jonathan Swift,* ed. Harold Williams, 5 vols. (Oxford: Clarendon Press, 1963–65), 4:34.

48. See Orwell, "Politics vs. Literature: An Examination of *Gulliver's Travels,*" in *Shooting An Elephant and Other Essays* (New York: Harcourt, Brace & World, 1950, 1945), 53–76; and Brown, "The Excremental Vision," in *Life Against Death: The Psychoanalytical Meaning of History* (Middletown: Wesleyan Univ. Press, 1959), 179–201.

49. Césaire, *Discourse on Colonialism* (1955), trans. Joan Pinkham (New York: Monthly Review Press, 1972), 27, 18.

50. See the Introduction to *George Steiner: A Reader* (New York: Oxford Univ. Press, 1984), 14.

51. These Berkeley quotations are taken from *A Proposal for the better supplying of Churches in our Foreign Plantations* (1725), in *The Works of George Berkeley*, 7:346. Also relevant in this regard is Berkeley's *Anniversary Sermon before the Society for the Propagation of the Gospel* (1731), which rejects as "an erroneous Notion" the idea that "being baptized is inconsistent with a State of Slavery" (in *Works*, 7:122). See Edwin S. Gaustad, *George Berkeley in America* (New Haven: Yale Univ. Press, 1979), 91 ("Berkeley took a step"). David Berman makes some relevant comments in this connection in *George Berkeley: Idealism and the Man* (Oxford: Clarendon Press, 1994), 131–32.

52. Césaire, 15, 29. Cesaire is referring in his first remark to Renan's *La Réforme intellectuelle et morale.*

53. For a good introduction to the issues involved in the historical revisionist controversy regarding Irish history, as well as for some of the seminal essays in this controversy, see *Interpreting Irish History: The Debate on Historical Revisionism*, ed. Ciaran Brady (Dublin: Irish Academic Press, 1994). See also the argument against revisionism (particularly as exemplified by S. J. Connolly) in Emer Nolan, "Swift: The Patriot Game," *British Journal of Eighteenth-Century Studies* 21 (Spring 1998): 50–53.

54. Daly, "The Operations of Famine Relief, 1845–47," in *The Great Irish Famine*, ed. Cathal Póirtéir (Dublin: Mercier Press, 1995), 123. Swift's own response to an earlier famine (the one of 1729) belies Daly's implication that the value judgments of later nationalist historians would have been alien to the way people looked at things back then. Swift tells a naïve proposal writer that "if our *Brethren* in England would contribute, upon this Emergency, out of the Million they gain from us every Year, they would do a Piece of *Justice* as well as *Charity*," admonishing the proposer and his neighboring squires that if they do not act responsibly to prevent crop shortages they will "die with the Guilt of having driven away half the Inhabitants, and starving the rest" (*An Answer to a Paper Called a Memorial* [1728], in *Prose Works*, 12:22).

55. Césaire, 24.

56. *Intelligencer* 19 (1728), in *Prose Works*, 12:60.

57. Hill, 8.

58. Connolly, 110.

59. Browne, *Seasonable Remarks.* See Woolley, *The Intelligencer*, 170.

60. *A Short View of the State of Ireland* (1728), in *Prose Works*, 12:12. Hereafter abbreviated SV and cited parenthetically in the text by volume and page number.

61. *The Intelligencer*, 90, 89. It is worth keeping in mind that Swift's *A Short View of the State of Ireland* was itself reprinted in the *Intelligencer* Number 15, with an Introduction by Sheridan; see 173–81.

62. *An Answer to a Paper Called a Memorial*, in *Prose Works*, 12:18–19.

Protestant Dependence and Consumption in Swift's Irish Writings

Robert Mahony

I

An old Irish nationalist witticism holds that unionists are loyal not so much to the Crown as to the half-crown, the largest silver coin commonly circulating before decimalization in 1971. Unfairly as the joke elides the political principles of Irish Protestants, it yet highlights the link between allegiance and economics among their traditional concerns. That connection was of utmost significance to Jonathan Swift, who though hardly the first commentator on Irish affairs to look at money and trade—Richard Lawrence and Sir William Petty, to name only two, preceded him by a generation—became the best-known writer in eighteenth-century Ireland to give patriotic advocacy and protest an economic footing. In Swift's consideration of economics, indeed, what matters most is his rhetoric: Petty was a more thorough economist, but a dull writer; Swift, an amateur in economics, was a surpassing rhetorician. That Swift's contribution to Irish political thought was primarily rhetorical, however, should not detract from its genuine importance. For rhetorical formulations clear the path that popular political expression follows; a shift in popular articulation is predicated upon altering the rhetorical pathways. Measured in terms of practical effect, Swift did not succeed in making that alteration during his lifetime, which he found very disappointing, though he was gratified by the

---

From Political Ideas in Eighteenth-Century Ireland, ed. S. J. Connolly (Dublin: Four Courts Press, 2000).

popular reputation as a patriotic hero his efforts had gained him. Only over time did it became evident that he had indeed inspired a shift in Irish popular political expression.[1]

Swift's rhetorical achievement, however partial, can be discerned even from a very brief comparison with that of Richard Lawrence. Lawrence's *The Interest of Ireland in its Trade and Wealth, Stated* (1682) anticipates Swift by some forty years in identifying as serious economic defects the prevalence of idleness in the countryside, absenteeism among landlords, the bestowal of public offices mainly on those not born in Ireland, and notably the 'excessive consumption of foreign growth and manufacturies.[2] Nevertheless, the impact of Lawrence's work was fleeting; not only was his style far from memorable, but his rhetorical anti-Catholicism clouds his diagnosis. Addressing mainly an Irish Protestant audience, he attributed these and other Irish ills to the influence of the Catholic clergy, manifesting a reflexive anti-Catholicism at once personal and altogether conventional in his day.[3] When difficulties arose in Ireland, one would not have to seek far for their cause. The Catholic clergy were of course more evident and comfortable in the early 1680s than they had been in the 1650s, but their numbers were inadequate to affect the Irish economy very substantially. The Catholic landed class of the 1660s–70s, moreover, whose economic proclivities the clergy would most have reflected and influenced, had been prostrated economically during the Cromwellian era, their holdings usually reduced and often displaced from Munster or Leinster to the poorer land of Connacht. By the early 1680s they had made little progress in recovering their economic position despite prolonged litigation, nor would they. They might live away from their now less productive estates (though few were based in England or further abroad), or indulge themselves with imports; their tenants might have seemed idler than those on better land who, frequently settlers themselves, served the more recently-established Protestant gentry. But for more than a generation before Lawrence's *Interest of Ireland*, Catholics had not dominated the Irish economy, and they were certainly not among the non-Irish granted public office. What would appear to have exercised Lawrence's rhetorical reflexes was the palpable presence of Catholic clergy and gentry, obscuring for him their loss of economic power and influence.

---

[1] For a fuller discussion of this phenomenon, see Robert Mahony, *Jonathan Swift: The Irish Identity* (New Haven 1995).

[2] Richard Lawrence, *The Interest of Ireland in its Trade and Wealth, Stated* (Dublin 1682), p. [ii].

[3] For Lawrence's background, see T. C. Barnard, 'Crises of identity among Irish Protestants, 1641–1685,' *Past and Present* 127 (1990), 39–83, esp. 59–68.

Forty years later, when Swift in his *Proposal for the Universal Use of Irish Manufacture* (1720) addressed the now mostly Protestant Irish gentry and merchant classes, he was no more effective than Lawrence in countering their taste for imports, nor in inspiring them to attend to the other ills of Ireland that Lawrence had indicated. But Swift was luckier in his circumstances and capitalized upon that with a more accurate, as well as stylistically more appealing, rhetoric. In the first place, he was subtly questioning the economic value of Ireland's political dependence upon Britain, by arguing for economic self-reliance at a time when there was widespread Irish Protestant resentment at British restrictions upon Irish trade and political autonomy. Although his audience ignored his prescriptions, Swift's pamphlet quickly gained him a popularity Lawrence never had. Swift's rhetoric also, however, offered a means of discussing and analysing the British-Irish relationship by concentrating upon its economic features, without resorting to the longstanding convention of anti-Catholicism. That rhetorical convention, though stale, was often populist; Swift's perception that the ways Britain and Ireland interacted in the 1720s were in everyday respects economic led him to employ a ramblingly down-to earth, hence equally populist, style for his alternative rhetoric, which avoided rehearsing Irish religious differences. Neither Swift nor Lawrence was, then, effective in a purely practical sense; but Swift's breaking with rhetorical convention enabled his becoming in time, if not so obviously in his own day, a 'leader of public opinion in Ireland', to adopt the title of W.E.H. Lecky's 1861 study.

Pleased as Swift was by his popularity, his intention in writing on Irish affairs from 1720 was to change the way his audience, in the main Irish Protestants like himself, thought about themselves in relation both to Britain, their ethnic and his preferred homeland, and, more indirectly, to the Catholic majority in Ireland. Hence his practical objective was intertwined with his rhetorical method. Swift's consideration of Irish affairs is nowhere comprehensive and systematic, since he commonly addressed particular circumstances, so that the overall diagnosis to be gathered from his numerous pamphlets and briefer comments must in part be inferred. But the conclusion is nonetheless clear. Irish Protestants, though dominant in Ireland, were a minority in the country and therefore depended for their ultimate security upon Britain. The British government took that dependence as affording it multiple opportunities to restrict Irish trade and otherwise foster the British consumption of the Irish economy. Resent though they did such British oppression, Irish Protestants nonetheless had no recourse but to seek their prosperity by oppressing their tenantry in turn. This was to Swift's mind ultimately self-destructive: their own economy consumed by Britain, they exacerbated that consumption at the expense of the poor, breeding poverty, idleness, duplicity and thievery.

In outlining the relationships between Britain and Ireland, and within Ireland, as primarily economic Swift sidesteps the religious issue, the factor that conventionally, in his time and earlier, had framed understanding of these relationships. Most of the gentry and indeed the rich were Protestants of British stock, while most of the poor were native Irish Catholics, a situation resulting largely from the success of England's planting of Protestant settlers in Ireland during the sixteenth and seventeenth centuries, together with its (and their) victories over Ireland's Catholic leadership in that period. But religion in this sense obscured rather than clarified the economic issues that Swift saw at stake, because it encouraged the Irish Protestant dependence upon Britain that enabled Britain's exploitation of Ireland. Swift's articulating the pressures upon and within Ireland as economic does correspond to his calling as a Christian minister: that alone would justify his attacking oppression. Yet, while he bridled at oppression and personally practised numerous charities, he was not opposed to riches and manifested little sympathy for the poor, despising their propensity for lying and theft. More than his Christian vocation, what informs his rhetoric is a fairly rudimentary political economy: Britain's self-interest accounts for its economic and political oppression of Ireland, provoking in turn the exploitation of the poor within Ireland. The remedy is for those better off in Ireland to awaken to its self-interest, and thus the necessity for economic selfreliance. This would break the vice of oppression, foster industriousness among the poor and, though implicitly, relax the psychological grip of Irish Protestant dependence upon Britain.

Indeed, Swift realized full well the hold of anti-Catholicism upon Irish Protestant self-understanding, for this informed that crippling sense of dependence. His economic rhetoric is not airily dismissive of the issue, but instead brings into play the disastrous nature of the connection he perceived between dependence and consumption in the Irish Protestant mentality that throughout his Irish writings he mainly addresses. The rhetoric of Swift's Irish writings is largely informed by this connection between dependence and consumption. That he regarded dependence as degrading is apparent throughout his writing career: Martin and Jack are ridiculous in their slavish imitation of Peter before they break with him in *A Tale of a Tub;* Gulliver's obsequiousness toward the Lilliputians is patently risible; and in 'A Beautiful Young Nymph going to Bed', the cosmetic and prosthetic evidences of the prostitute Corinna's attempts to remain enticing render her pathetic instead. Irish Protestants are degraded as well by their dependence upon Britain; it corrupts them psychologically and economically. All the same, satirical as Swift occasionally becomes in his Irish writings, they are usually not satires *tout court;* Irish Protestants might well exhibit the human perversity that his satires often target, but in his earlier

Irish writings he is more committed to arguing for an effectual remedy. Embracing it would entail a profound psychological shift in his audience, which therefore he attempts to encourage indirectly in these earlier Irish works, the *Irish Manufacture* pamphlet and the *Drapier's Letters.* In particular, while religion was an inescapable factor in the nexus of external and internal oppression besetting Ireland, Swift considers both sorts of oppression overtly in economic terms, as varieties of consumption. After the mid 1720s, he alters his method, generally becoming more direct about the link between consumption and dependence (though treating them, and especially consumption, satirically indeed in *A Modest Proposal*), and, while continuing to eschew anti-Catholic rhetoric, manifesting his disappointment that his Irish Protestant audience would not heed his recommendation of self-reliance.

II

Consumption and dependence are multiply linked in Swift's understanding of the Irish condition: they mark the country's relationship with England (as he usually termed Britain) as well as its internal political, religious and economic relationships. Their history in the former relationship dates to its earliest years. After Pope Adrian IV in 1155–6 assigned the governance of Ireland to the English crown, and King Henry II allowed his restless lords to invade the country at the request of a claimant to an Irish throne late in the next decade, he insisted upon their renewing their fealty to him once they had succeeded, effectively taking title to the country that the pope had privileged him to govern. To insure their dependence upon him, that is, he consumed what his lords had conquered. Thereafter, the country's status as a dependency of the English crown was explicit in its inclusion among the kingly dignities, initially 'Lord of Ireland,' a title granted to Henry's son, John, who kept it upon succeeding to the crown, and 'King of Ireland' from 1540, under Henry VIII. But the Anglo-Norman colonization of Ireland was never comprehensive, and the English government embarked upon a more ambitious colonial project in the later sixteenth century and throughout the seventeenth. To buttress the security of England from continental Catholic aggression, the 'Old English' descendants of the earlier settlers, who remained Catholic despite the Reformation, were gradually displaced from political power and social position by English and Scottish Protestant settlers. This Protestant colonization encountered considerable sporadic opposition for a century after the 1590s, but was at length a very successful project in consumption, for by 1700 the great bulk of Irish territory was in the hands of loyal Protestants. By planting Protestants in Ireland, then, by removing Old English Catholic officials and expropriating land from Catholic occupiers for newer settlers who professed the reformed religion, by, in other words, consuming Catholic Ireland, England forestalled her own consumption by Catholic Europe.

But England's consumption of Ireland was not limited by the demands of security from external aggression. As Swift saw the matter, after England colonized the country with Protestants, it yet restricted the economic benefits they could gain as colonists. To protect English mercantile interests from Irish competition, free trade was denied to Ireland; to satisfy English political interests, major posts in the Irish administration and established church were staffed by Englishmen, restricting opportunities for the younger sons of the Protestant gentry. Their dependence upon England kept Protestants from resisting this perpetuated English consumption of Ireland, much though they resented it. Protestant landowners instead pursued their own prosperity by rackrenting their tenant farmers, which produced widespread rural poverty, a result we would now term economically counter-productive. Swift oversimplifies this account of Ireland's condition in a letter of 1726 to Lord Peterborough, to emphasize his perception that the intertwining of consumption and dependence was destroying the possibility that Ireland as a whole might prosper. England had ultimate responsibility for this catastrophe, and it would have been forestalled, he implies, if the government in London had considered his own people, the descendants of those who completed the conquest of Ireland in the seventeenth century, 'to be on as good a foot as any subjects of Britain, according to the practice of all other nations, and particularly of the Greeks and Romans'.[4]

What he seems to mean, at least with respect to Greek colonization, we may elucidate by recalling a passage from Thucydides' history of the Peloponnesian War. Corcyra was at war with Epidamnus, and Corinth had joined the war on the side of the Epidamnians, even though Corcyra had originally been colonized from Corinth. Both Corcyra and Corinth had sent representatives to Athens, which had a defensive treaty with Corinth: the Corcyrans to dissuade the Athenians from joining the fight, the Corinthians to persuade them to do just that. The Corinthian representatives contended that their treaty bound the Athenians to come in on their side, and argued further that Corcyra, having been colonized from Corinth, did not have the standing to make a case for Athenian neutrality. The Corcyrans replied to the latter contention: 'If they object in justice, in that you receive their colony, henceforth let them learn, that all colonies, so long as they receive no wrong from their mother City, so long they honour

---

[4] Swift to Peterborough, 28 April 1726 (*Swift Corr.* vol. 3, p. 132).

her; but when they suffer injury from her, they then become alienate: for they are not sent out to be the slaves of them that stay, but to be their equals.[5] Though from a late twentieth-century perspective, ancient Greek colonization encompassed more oppressiveness than this classic description suggests, especially if native peoples were involved, this was long the standard statement of the case. It provided the classical foundation for any such argument as Swift's that Ireland deserved to be treated as England's equal, since those dominant in Ireland were not sent there as colonists 'to be the slaves of them that stay' in England, 'but to be their equals'. As Henry Maxwell noted in 1703, this holds all the more in a case like that of Ireland, whether the country be considered a conquest or an 'annexed government':

> The design of maintaining conquests or annexed government by colonies, is to avoid the great expense and hazard that attends their being maintained by a standing force. From which design it plainly follows, that after colonies are once settled, and have a constitution given to them agreeable to that of their mother country; they must afterwards be indulged the liberty of making their own laws, provided they be not repugnant to the laws of their mother country.

This was the precedent established by Roman as well as Greek practice, and Maxwell added, 'The Romans gave them [colonies] another privilege, and that was to be governed by their own magistrates, and for these reasons the Romans were always most faithfully served by their colonies.'[6]

In his letter to Peterborough, Swift was not basing his case for Irish equality upon its character as a kingdom *per se*, an area of longstanding debate which most Englishmen considered as having been settled by the declaratory act of 1720, which determined that Ireland was a 'depending kingdom' bound by statutes of the Westminster parliament. Rather he asserts that a sense of equity ought, by universal but especially classical practice, to govern the relationship of colonists with their mother-country. Throughout the letter, Swift complains that England has refused to observe such equity, that Thucydidean idea of fairness. Obviously this idea can be related to that of Ireland's distinctness as a kingdom: the country became a kingdom, after all, during the reign of Henry VIII, long after it had come

---

[5]Thucydides, *Eight Bookes of the Peloponnesian Warre*, translated by Thomas Hobbes (London 1629), p. 20. Swift's executor, the Revd John Lyons, recorded his abstracting Hobbes's Thucydides at Moor Park in early 1698, cf. *The Battle of the Books*, ed. Hermann J. Real (Berlin 1978), p. 129. My thanks to Hermann Real for acquainting me with this reference.

[6]Maxwell, *An Essay towards an Union of Ireland with England* (London 1703), p. 5. I am indebted to Sean Connolly for bringing this reference to my attention.

under English political dominion. But the argument for distinctness—with its implications of autonomy—he tends to press in works meant primarily for Irish readers, sympathetic to the notion that the declaratory act was bad law (a procedure he adopts in the *Drapier's Letters*); Swift seems to have considered that the point to make to his noble British friend (really intending the letter to be read by Walpole, the prime minister) was that the people the government was oppressing were the descendants of those British Protestants 'sent out' to colonize Ireland in the seventeenth century, who in fact bore the brunt of conquering Jacobite Ireland within, in 1726, living memory. They should have the rights long since conceded to the British people whence they had sprung, rather than be denied such rights like the native Irish their forbears had defeated.

But if England was ultimately responsible for distorting the Irish economy, Swift also saw the connection between dependence and consumption in the self-awareness of Irish Protestants as inducing them to compensate themselves irresponsibly for English restrictions. Not only did they behave as though they had no choice but to accept, albeit resentfully, England's economic interference, but they seemed to Swift not to have discerned sufficiently that their sense of dependence underlay their own internal consumption of Ireland. When addressing his Irish Protestant audience, then, his rhetorical methods included capitalizing upon their resentment at English economic interference even to the point of exaggerating its extent; showing them that accepting such interference had led them in turn to distort their own economic behaviour with consumptionist practices detrimental to their long-term economic interest; and insisting that self-sufficiency offered an alternative to their both accepting English interference and adopting compensatory economic distortions. Swift's prescription of self-reliance involves more than Irish Protestants' cultivating 'moral self-discipline and frugality';[7] rather, it is the only means of halting their self-destructive complicity—of which they were inadequately aware— in England's ongoing consumption of Ireland.

Hence, while Swift argued in his letter of 1726 to Peterborough, and often elsewhere, that England should allow free trade to Ireland and more often appoint Irish Protestants to official positions, he also pressed those Protestants, whom he termed 'the people of Ireland,' to become self-

[7] Patrick Kelly, '"Conclusions by no means calculated for the circumstances and condition of Ireland": Swift, Berkeley and the solution to Ireland's economic problems' in Aileen Douglas, Patrick Kelly and Ian Campbell Ross (eds.), *Locating Swift: Essays from Dublin on the 250th Anniversary of the Death of Jonathan Swift, 1667–1745* (Dublin 1998), p. 59.

sufficient. At the least, as Swift argued in the anonymous *Proposal for the Universal Use of Irish Manufacture* of 1720, his first published work addressing Irish affairs since becoming dean of St. Patrick's Cathedral in 1713, Irish landlords should cease rackrenting their tenantry so as to afford imported English and foreign goods. This practice diverts to other countries, particularly England, the proceeds from Irish rents. Instead, the gentry and merchants should support Irish domestic industries, especially the production of wool. The self-reliance he advocated had patriotism in its favour, as well as justice of the sort a Christian minister should press for, since it would diminish the fact of dependence and its oppressive effects. But adopting it meant forwarding the self-interest of individuals in the long rather than the short term, what we might describe as delayed gratification, never a welcome proposition. Inasmuch, further, as this would entail a different, more just relationship between landlord and tenant, it also ran counter to the ideological inclination of colonialism in Ireland. Given that the colonists were Protestant, and those they dominated mainly Catholic, this inclination may be seen as equating Protestant dominance or supremacy in Ireland with the subordination or oppression (or, indeed, consumption) of Irish Catholics.

The roots of that ideologically-privileged equation ran deep. Catholics had rebelled in 1641 and massacred thousands of Protestant settlers; the number of victims probably totalled between three and four thousand, but was massively inflated at the time, rising into the hundreds of thousands: by 1647, it was officially alleged, 154,000 had died by rebel hands, and the poet John Milton in 1649 gave an estimate of 'more than 200,000'.[8] The massacres renewed legendary characterizations of the native Irish as barbarians, and since their inspiration was attributed to Catholic clergy, old barbarism could be linked to the old religion. Popularized in such accounts as Sir John Temple's *Irish Rebellion* (1646), the massacres of 1641 assumed an enormous significance in Protestant self-understanding as a people at risk. Vengeance might be the Lord's, but the Scriptures could also encourage them to inflict it themselves.[9] Catholic blood-thirstiness justified the retributive zeal of Oliver Cromwell in suppressing the rebellion, and lay behind an Irish parliamentary statute of 1662 fixing 23 October, the date the rebellion began in 1641, for annual commemoration in every Church of

[8] Jane Ohlmeyer, *Ireland from Independence to Occupation: 1641–1660* (Cambridge 1995), p. xx; Milton, *Observations upon the Articles of Peace . . .* (London 1649), p. 49.

[9] See *That Great Expedition for Ireland by way of Underwriting Proposed* (London 1642), p. 14, quoted in Raymond Gillespie, *Devoted People: Belief and Religion in Early Modern Ireland* (Manchester 1997), p. 75.

Ireland parish. The service rubric for that commemoration recalled the extent of the massacres and gave thanks that God had seen fit to avert a complete annihilation of the Protestants of Ireland by sparing a remnant.[10] It was no great leap from this rhetorical fixture in Protestant self-awareness to the idea that Providence had appointed that remnant to rule over the Catholic natives. This notion may be gathered from the tenor of the published commemorative sermons for 23 October that have survived, especially after James II's Irish regime of 1689–91, which caused Protestants to fear a reprise of the 1641 massacres, was defeated by King William III.[11] In the ensuring years, the sermons mix gratitude for providential deliverance with an increasingly positive consciousness of Protestantism as a minority faith, even the faith of an elect. And they hail the Irish parliament's enactment of a penal code to defend that faith by curbing Catholic landownership and ecclesiastical organization. From the perspective these sermons generate, by holding Catholicism at bay the penal laws represent the Protestant mission—obviously endorsed by Providence—to consume Catholic Ireland.

This is not to say that the tenor of the 23 October sermons in their aggregate reflects accurately Protestant perceptions of Catholics in Ireland, or indeed, the actual operation of the penal laws. For, though mandated by statute for delivery in every Church of Ireland parish annually, only a few such sermons appeared in print, delivered to congregations of Irish Protestant notables in Dublin and London. Comprising insufficient evidence from which to generalize about Protestant attitudes in the country at large toward Catholics or the penal laws, they form instead a homilitic genre, with a commemorative purpose tied to events on a specific date long past. But as that date had become symbolic, these surviving sermons do evidence a privileged rhetoric, an official liturgy of sorts, for remembering the historical event and learning the lesson it teaches. In this rhetorical context the penal laws figure metaphorically as an embodiment of Protestant Ireland's having learned that lesson, a bulwark against the repetition of that event. That rhetoric was consumptionist: its terms presented the consumption of Catholic Ireland, metaphorically facilitated by the penal laws, as the means of preventing the Catholics from consuming Protestant Ireland as they had attempted in 1641. By privileging consumpton as defence, this rhetoric also valorized the demographic status of Protestants as an

---

[10] E.g. 'For it was thy goodness alone that we were not delivered over for a prey unto their teeth,' [Second Collect], 'A form of Divine Service to be used October 23,' *The Book of Common Prayer . . . According to the Use of the Church of Ireland* (Dublin 1680), n. p.

[11] See T.C. Barnard, 'The uses of 23 October 1641 and Irish Protestant celebrations,' *English Historical Review* 106 (1991), 889–920.

Irish minority. Whatever the actual attitudes of Protestants toward Catholics, or the varied inconsistencies of the practical application of the penal laws, the rhetorical formulation that so promoted consumption by an elite had so strong an appeal to the self-interest of that elite that a departure from such rhetoric—even if this posed no challenge to Protestant supremacy—was likely to prove ineffectual in practice. The rhetoric of the sermons, that is, acquired by virtue of its nearly-liturgical repetition and its appeal at once to religious solidarity, the historical favour of Providence, and the human pleasure in consumption an ideological sturdiness that continued for much of the eighteenth century; the metaphorical value of the penal laws, among various other reasons, kept them on the statute books well after they were compromised by inconsistent application. But so promoting Protestant consumption also, as Swift saw it, confirmed Protestant dependence upon England.

While it was the link between consumption and dependence that energized Swift to challenge and displace them by advocating economic self-reliance, he was not the first to find fault with the rhetoric of consumption as religious defence. Even as the penal laws were initially being formulated in their eighteenth-century shape in the aftermath of the Jacobite collapse—and so before they came into metaphorical play within the rhetoric of consumption—Bishop Wetenhall of Cork and Ross, in a 23 October sermon of 1692, questioned the religious and indeed practical value of the Protestant preference for consumption over a serious effort to convert the Catholic natives:

> had we Protestants been as industrious, first, ourselves to have lived according to the truth and power of the reformed religion, and then to have instructed the Irish therein, as we were to secure ourselves the Irish lands; had we been as careful to make them knowing good Christians, as ourselves rich and great; we had, in all probability, never seen the rebellion of forty one *nor* the tyranny of the late eighty-eight, and following years.[12]

No large-scale project for converting the Catholic natives, such as Wetenhall seems to insinuate would optimally have defended and advanced Protestantism, ever took place. To be sure, as S.J. Connolly has summarized in *Religion, Law and Power*, there were stirrings in this direction as the penal laws made headway, offsetting somewhat their coerciveness as an instrument of conversion.[13] Both houses of Convocation in the Church of

[12]Wetenhall, *A Sermon Preached Octob. 23, 1692 . . .* (Dublin 1692), p. 17.

[13]See S.J. Connolly, *Religion, Law and Power: The Making of Protestant Ireland* (Oxford 1992), pp. 294–307.

Ireland, bishops as well as parish clergy, approved resolutions in 1703–4 and again in 1709 supporting evangelization among the Catholics at large, through preaching and other forms of instruction in the Irish language. In addition, John Richardson, a County Cavan clergyman, attracted significant support in 1711 for a project of printing religious materials in Irish and establishing charter schools to advance literacy and religious instruction in English. But concerns lest the Irish language be thereby encouraged, and fear that the Church of Ireland lacked the resources necessary for effecting such proposals, foredoomed their coming into practice, though similar schemes surfaced from time to time afterwards. As Connolly notes, 'it is clear that many Protestants were indifferent, to say the least, to the conversionist schemes of men like Richardson'.[14] Even the charter school movement, fostering the education of Catholic children in basic skills and Protestant doctrine, had only a limited and faltering effect. Thus, though whatever might forward spiritual motives for conversion was officially welcomed and certainly made some progress, the penal laws became over the years a prominent metaphor for the advancement of Protestantism, not least for their practical effect of converting Catholic landowners to the established church.[15] And that is to say that in the rhetoric of colonialist ideology, consumptionism remained dominant for generations after Wetenhall cautioned against it.

Indeed, as Connolly has noted, both Archbishop Edward Synge of Tuam and Archbishop William King of Dublin compained in 1719 that a great many Protestant landowners would, in Synge's words, 'rather keep the Papists as they are, in an almost slavish subjection', for thus they were more tractable.[16] The penal laws might have little actually to do with the Catholic poor, but the consumptionist ideology they represented had become so entrenched that Arch-bishop Synge's son, Bishop Edward Synge of Clonfert, in a 23 October sermon of 1731, was deeply concerned by the unwillingness of most Catholics to follow their self-interest, embrace that ideology and convert. From this he perceived an ideological defect: in fact the penal code gave Catholics in his time greater reason to hate Protestants than their forefathers had in 1641, even while their loyalty to the Jacobite pretender, and a natural barbarity as bloodthirsty as their ancestors', made them a formidable threat to Protestantism. Yet the remedy he proposed—

[14] Connolly, *Religion, Law and Power*, p. 306.

[15] Connolly notes (*Religion, Law and Power*, p. 309) that conversions during the penal era could account for the transfer of about ten percent of Irish land from Catholic to Protestant hands.

[16] Quoted in *Religion, Law and Power*, p. 309.

though Synge was himself not at all the most rabidly anti-Catholic among Church of Ireland bishops—was all the greater stringency in the penal laws, since 'the great law of self-preservation directs and empowers us to use proper means to secure ourselves against' that threat.[17] The true reformed religion, that is, was best defended by penal laws enabling the consumption of Catholic Ireland, even though (or, by Synge's logic, *because*) such legislation perpetuated and deepened the Catholic hatred of Protestants that latently threatened the security of the reformed religion. Synge's exercise in circular logic evinces neatly the rhetoric of Protestant self-perception, as a people simultaneously empowered and endangered, which made the ideology of consumption so formidable despite its contradictory ramifications. Historical victimhood, as a condition of Protestant identity, meant victimizing the historic aggressor. And the primary arena for the exercise of that ideological imperative was economic.

Swift himself believed in Protestant supremacy, but considered the penal laws adequate to protect it. He was palpably reserved about some of the implications of the ideology of consumption, however, as actually or potentially subverting that supremacy. He was certainly suspicious of the anti-Catholic rhetorical gloss customary in articulating such ideology, for not only was it superfluous but it also distracted attention from the real economic and political underpinnings of Protestant supremacy. The sermon of 1731 by the younger Synge, for instance—who, Swift told Laetitia Pilkington in the 1730s, 'I knew was not an honest man[18]— ascribed the barbarous poverty of most Catholics to an inveterately perverse hatred of Protestants, which blinded them to the economic advantages of converting. With a clearer sense of economic motivations, Swift complained repeatedly that peasants were brutalized by their landlords' rackrenting, which had so curtailed economic activity in the countryside as to promote idleness, begging and thievery. And their landlords rackrented because English prohibitions upon Irish exports left them no quicker avenue to prosperity, however self-destructive this was in the long run. Swift actually had little sympathy for Catholics as such or for their faith and he railed against the poor as liars and thieves. But he nevertheless regarded their condition as resulting from poverty rather than from their religion. The security of Protestant Ireland hardly demanded the utter impoverishment of the Catholic natives, and was indeed ultimately endangered by it.

If Protestant supremacy be taken narrowly, moreover—as Swift thought proper—to embrace members of the established church rather

---

[17] Edward Synge, *A Sermon Preached . . . the 23rd of October, 1731* (Dublin 1731), p. 13.

[18] Laetitia Pilkington, *Memoirs*, ed. A.C. Elias (Athens, Ga. 1997), vol. I, p. 282.

than dissenters, privileging anti-Catholic rhetoric to defend it posed another danger. Unsympathetic to Catholicism, Swift was fiercely bigotted against Presbyterians, the largest body of dissenters, who outnumbered episcopal Protestants in the north of Ireland. Regarding them as religious fanatics and political republicans whose forebears had torn England asunder in the seventeenth century, he favoured the continuance of political sanctions against them and little lamented the emigration of many of them to the American colonies. He feared their numbers in Ireland as a greater threat to the established church than Catholicism posed, since the penal laws precluded a Catholic political resurgence. In 1732, disdaining to indulge in anti-Catholic rhetoric, he voiced the suspicion that the 'dreaders of Popery' who did so had as their real object weakening or dismantling the establishment he stoutly defended.[19] Exaggerating the popish menace could persuade members of the Church of Ireland to make common cause with the Presbyterian interest, blurring distinctions between the two main Protestant churches that he was determined should be maintained. His poem of 1733 'On the Words "Brother Protestants and Fellow Christians"' satirized this phrase, favoured by Presbyterians referring to the Anglican establishment, likening it to what might be spoken by detritus caught up with the farmyard apples in a rural flash flood:

> A Ball of new-dropt Horse's Dung,
> Mingling with Apples in the Throng,
> Said to the Pippin, plump, and prim,
> *See, Brother, how we Apples swim.* (11–14)[20]

Swift's loathing of Presbyterianism is a constant in his career from the early *Tale of a Tub* (1704). In his Irish writings from the period before the 1730s, however, it is most apparent in some of his sermons, and muted in the pamphleteering of the 1720s. There was in fact little occasion to articulate this antipathy more openly until the Presbyterians in 1731 mounted a campaign for the repeal of the test act which barred them from public office. And in the earlier years of his deanship, when he was widely suspected in government circles of Jacobite sympathies, it would have been imprudent to suggest that Protestant supremacy was more in danger from Presbyterians than from Catholics. Economic issues prompted his writings on Irish

---

[19] Swift, 'Queries Relating to the Sacramental Test' (1732) in Swift, *Prose Works*, vol. 12, p. 259.

[20] *Poems of Jonathan Swift*, ed. Harold Williams, 3rd edn (Oxford 1958), vol. 3, p. 811.

affairs in the 1720s, and for his challenge to prevalent habits of consumption to evince a sanguine attitude toward the ancient Catholic threat would have revived suspicions of his Jacobitism, rendering his argument ineffective. That argument would instead have to focus upon the economic implications of the ideology of consumption without recourse to its religious dimensions.

III

What enabled Swift to intervene in Irish politics with this approach, after six years as Dean of St Patrick's spent 'in the greatest privacy'[21] and professed ignorance of the political world, was an outburst of Irish Protestant resentment at their dependence upon England. A controversy over Irish parliamentary prerogatives had prompted the British ministry to enact the declaratory act in 1720, defining Ireland's subordination to the London parliament. In the *Proposal for the Universal Use of Irish Manufacture* Swift did not address forthrightly the furore continuing in Ireland around the notion of Ireland's dependency; rather, he invoked such patriotic resentment indirectly while echoing a chorus of contemporary exhortations to the Irish to support their own industries by purchasing Irish goods only. In fact he hints broadly enough that resorting to self-reliance, which would enable them to take their economy into their own hands, was tantamount to rejecting their dependence upon England. With calculated offhandedness, for instance, he makes the circumspectly inflammatory comment that he had heard 'the late Archbishop of *Tuam* mention a pleasant observation of some body's' recommending burning everything English except their people and their coal.[22] The advice is not his; its source is dead or forgotten, and he doesn't himself actually espouse it, but the point is made, the more by his adding that he would not be sorry to see the people stay at home, and hoping soon to do without the coal. The clarity of such apparent indirection harnesses the resentment of Irish Protestants to his implicating them, by their dependence upon England, in the ruin of their own economy.

But the response to his pamphlet was hardly what he had recommended. The Irish administration condemned the work as seditious and apprehended the printer, who refused to betray the anonymous author (widely known to be Swift), and whom a jury refused to convict. This was

---

[21] Swift to Alexander Pope, 10 January 1721 (Swift, *Prose Works*, vol. 9, pp. 25–26).

[22] Swift, *Prose Works*, vol. 9, p. 17.

a victory for the freedom of the press, yet popular acclaim for Swift's defiance of English authority over Ireland's economy, and protest at the surrogate prosecution of his printer, did not translate into any alteration in the preference of the Irish gentry and merchants for imported goods. Happy to criticize England, they were averse to disciplining their own consumption. By advocating patriotic self-sufficiency as the counter to indiscipline, Swift had attempted to strike the chords both of consumption and resentment at dependence in Protestant self-awareness as he perceived it; but only one sounded, however loudly. This may have cautioned him against focussing again on the excesses of Irish Protestant consumption when writing the *Drapier's Letters* some years later. The occasion itself called for a different approach, however, a forthright emphasis upon the English consumption of Ireland that Irish Protestant dependence emboldened. Hence, without mentioning dependence as Irish Protestants' historical bulwark against Catholicism, Swift implicates it instead as the avenue the ministry in London takes to insult them and threaten their economic security. Implicitly again, as in the *Irish Manufacture* pamphlet but without the concomitant of sacrifice or deferred gratification for the common good, self-reliance is the means of defying that insult.

To supply an apparent need for small coins in Ireland, the Walpole government, through the king, had awarded a patent to an English fabricator, William Wood, for a very substantial minting order. Fearing that the free exchange of Wood's copper coins would displace gold and silver in current circulation, major Irish authorities, including parliament, decried the project as destructive to Ireland's economy. These protests had all been couched in assertions of loyalty to the king, concurring with which Swift entered the controversy. Disguising himself for a series of open letters as a trader in woollens, to underscore the ostensible simplicity of his advice, he held that Ireland could at once demonstrate loyalty to the king himself and refuse to accept the coins the king had licensed Wood to mint. For coppers were a convenience rather than legal tender: it was not obligatory in law to accept them in payment for any debt or goods. The Irish need not injure their own commerce by taking coins that would drive out gold and silver; moreover, Wood's solicitations for the patent were untoward, and in issuing it the king was badly advised by the ministry. Nonacceptance is presented as an altogether loyal refusal to innovate—though in fact it is a form of self-reliance and thus strikes at the psychology of dependence.

The second and third letters lay greatest stress upon the insult—to the Irish generally in the second and to the Irish parliament in the third—offered by Wood (and, by no great extension, by the ministry that arranged his patent). Wood expresses his contempt for the Irish in the very phrasing even of efforts to conciliate them; they ought to resent such an insult, which bespeaks his low birth—and, implicitly, the obtuseness of the government in empowering a man of such humble origins to threaten the economic ruin of Ireland. Of course, the Drapier is also implying that the Irish Protestant psychology of dependence invites such behaviour even from the tools of the English ministry. The fourth letter, much celebrated in Swift's day and by generations of nationalists later, continues in this vein, if far more eloquently. And here the inference that Ireland ought not to be dependent is carried more clearly than before. The Drapier describes Ireland and England as obliged to share the same king, but denies any basis except English power for the dependence of Ireland upon England or its subjection to the parliament in London. Thereby he affirms Ireland's loyalty to the king, while running counter to the declaratory act of 1720. Swift's insistence upon that loyalty implies its reciprocation by right, which means that the king must not abandon a loyal people. As the Protestant sense of dependence upon England derived from fear of the consequences if England abandoned them, his implication confutes the possibility of any such abandonment. That understanding of reciprocal loyalty, of course, takes monarchy literally, ignoring the supremacy of parliament, recently manifested in the Declaratory Act, in constructing national policy for Ireland.

The prominence of loyalty as a concept in the fourth letter problematizes the tendency in the Irish nationalist tradition to take literally its being addressed 'To the Whole People of Ireland'. To maintain that here Swift simply becomes a patriot comprehensively Irish, transcending religious antagonisms by speaking to the whole body of Catholics as well as Protestants, contradicts the tenor common to his Irish writings, in which 'the people' are most distinctly the Protestants of Ireland. Yet his insistence particularly in this letter that the people of Ireland have been outstandingly loyal to the present king and his family, which most Protestants would think contestable if Catholics were included, could indeed be understood as recognizing that Catholic Ireland, for all its covert Jacobitism, was overtly quiescent in the face of the Hanoverian succession. Such loyalty, of course, however outward, is hardly what the nationalist tradition would celebrate. Swift could, alternatively, be inserting an ironic note with his insistence upon the loyalty of the 'Whole People,' but this would compromise his hailing in this and the other letters the real loyalty of Irish Protestants to the English connection through the crown. A sounder alternative is to find Swift shifting the import of the 'Whole People' between the Protestants of Ireland and the entire population, rather as the speaker in *A Tale of a Tub* shifts between the 'Tale-teller' and other voices, subtly to satirize here the English tendency to continue perceiving the people of Ireland as disloyal, whereas the kingdom is in fact now in the hands of a loyal Protestant population indeed.[23]

In the face of the popular agitation to which Swift had contributed, the London ministry eventually conceded defeat and withdrew Wood's patent. Swift was lionized by the people, hailed as the 'Hibernian patriot,' and it was with this wind in his sails that he completed *Gulliver's Travels* early in 1726. Ireland is prominent in Part III, the last of four parts to be written (probably after the Wood's coinage affair), as Balnibarbi, a land oppressed by the floating island of Laputa, or England. Less specific to Ireland, Gulliver's degradingly ingratiating dependence can be taken as satirizing a distortion typifying colonial self-awareness, while in the Lilliput episode, at least, the burden of his consumption has a distorting effect on the local economy as well. But though Gulliver exhibits insufficient self-reliance, he does not demonstrably resort to irresponsible consumption, the link Swift had implied in the *Irish Manufacture* pamphlet of 1720. That link emerges clearly again, however, in Swift's letter to Lord Peterborough in April 1726, when he was visiting London, which gives an account of his meeting with the prime minister.

What brings the conection of dependence and consumption to light with such explicitness in this letter is, in part, the fact that it was written for an English reader, but more because whatever hopes Swift might have had from his interview with Walpole were obviously and very precipitously dashed. The meeting had barely begun before Walpole 'enlarge[d] very much upon the subject of Ireland, in a manner so alien from what I conceived to be rights and privileges of a subject of England, that I did not think proper to debate the matter with him so much as I otherwise might, because I found it would be in vain'.[24] Thus the letter to Peterborough, which it was intended that Walpole should read, lays out the grievances of Ireland as Swift had not done in the meeting. That these are Protestant grievances is clear from the prefatory assertion of the people's 'extraordinary loyalty' and the initial complaint that they are despised, as if all Irishmen, though they are descendants of the British conquerors of Ireland. Beyond this the recital emphasizes the denial to Irish Protestants of free trade and access to office in church and state, while England gains

---

[23] For a more sophisticated and compelling elaboration of the traditional nationalist understanding of Swift's addressing the 'Whole People of Ireland', however, see Carole Fabricant, 'Speaking for the Irish nation: The Drapier, the bishop, and the problems of colonial representation,' *ELH,* 66 (1999), 337–92. [Reprinted in this volume, pp. 465–501.]

[24] Swift to Peterborough, 28 April 1726 (*Swift Corr.* vol. 3, p. 132).

hugely from commerce and rents paid to absentees. More than simply misgoverned, Ireland is being consumed by England, which forces 'the whole body of the gentry' to follow suit within Ireland:

> All they have left is . . . to rack their tenants . . . to such a degree, that there is not one farmer in a hundred throughout the kingdom who can afford shoes or stockings to his children, or to eat flesh, or drink anything better than sour milk or water, twice in a year, so that the whole country, except the Scotch plantation in the north, is a scene of misery and desolation.[25]

Writing for the eyes of the king's chief minister, Swift asserts the direct relation of English to Irish Protestant consumption within the context of dependence. His clarity is the product of despair, however: rather than consider any form of palliation, England, he now knows for certain, is intent to continue consuming Ireland.

IV

The tone of despair itself continues in Swift writings over the next three years, between his interview with Walpole and *A Modest Proposal* (1729). With a directness he had formerly avoided in addressing his local, Protestant audience, he elaborates the thesis he had laid out for Peterborough. The admonitory tone of the earlier writings is absent, nor, though dependence remains a central issue in *A Short View of the State of Ireland* (1727–28) and *Maxims Controlled in Ireland* (1729), where he certainly points to English responsibility for the condition of the country, does he evoke resentment overtly at England's interference. A degree of hopelessness pervades both works, probably because of the onset of agricultural depression and famine, and perhaps traceable as well to the ill-success of his meeting with Walpole. But it is hopelessness controlled by an expository tone, as he adjusts his criticism of dependence and consumption to demonstrate that Irish conditions are uniquely perverse. The *Short View* lists the generally-accepted reasons for any country's prosperity, some the gifts of nature, others the result of a rational political and economic system. In Ireland, that system is so distorted that even the gifts of nature are of no avail: 'The conveniency of ports and havens, which nature hath bestowed so liberally upon this kingdom, is of no more use to us, than a beautiful prospect to a man in a dungeon.'[26] The diagnosis is familiar, but here Swift

---

[25] Ibid., p. 133.

[26] Swift, *Prose Works*, vol. 12, p. 8.

advocates no remedy; his irony runs simply, too, to stress the country's literal perverseness: 'There is no one argument used to prove the riches of Ireland, which is not a logical demonstration of its poverty.'[27] Despair in such a situation becomes itself logical. He does not complain that the self-sufficiency he formerly promoted has gone unheeded by his audience; it is as though the perverseness imposed upon and distorting the country makes good advice itself irrational.

Despair is even more muted in *Maxims Controlled.* Swift notes at length the common wisdom guiding economic thought: it is a sign of wealth in a country if the necessities of life are expensive; low interest rates signify an abundance of money; increasing urban construction indicates that the country flourishes; people are the riches of a nation. But the facts of Ireland's economy confute each of these. Prices of life's necessities have been driven up as an effect of rackrenting; interest is low because the country lacks sufficient currency, and trade in general is depressed; construction in Dublin has been impelled mainly by speculation; and the population of Ireland, far from contributing to the nation's wealth, is so frequently beset by idleness that half the people live by begging and thievery. Here, indeed, remedies like selling the unnecessary population into slavery, or transporting them, can be dreamt of. But these are only dreams; the speaker is left to confess that when he learns of the death of some country wretch, he finds himself pleased. The bitterness of *Maxims Controlled* is nonetheless restrained; it would seem from the 'Verses on the Death of Dr. Swift,' begun around this period, that he might already be taking some compensatory solace from his reputation as 'the Hibernian patriot', even if his audience was demonstrating no likelihood of taking his advice to rely upon themselves.

Bitterness and fantasy, though, colour *A Modest Proposal,* written and published in 1729. Swift's most famous short satire, its very success can tempt literary commentators to regard it as transcending Ireland altogether. It becomes a satire upon inhumanity, or more specifically upon the 'projecting' mentality that is so fixated upon the remedy proposed for a given defect that morality is (almost comically) overridden. But the *Proposal* does in fact as well as ostensibly deal with Ireland, and reflects at once his sense of despair at its condition and his bitterness at the irresponsibility producing that desperate state. For here, quite directly, Swift takes up the theme of consumption, whose perverse results he had explicated in the *Short View* and *Maxims Controlled.* The portrayal of poverty with which he

[27] Swift, *Prose Works,* vol. 12, p. 11.

opens the *Proposal* is more intensely drawn than in the earlier works, and focusses, as Swift hasn't before, on children. The excess of appetite, in the begetting of children and more immediately in respect to their wanting (in both senses) sustenance, points to the theme of consumption, but it is that of the poor themselves to which the Proposer draws our attention. Only by an inversion as yet unprompted in the reader could that reader understand who is to blame for the state of the poor as described; we have no reference to rackrenting, for instance. Only when the Proposer gives his recommendation that the rich could consume the poor directly, by literally feeding upon the offspring of the poor, is that inversion of blame triggered, and then—odd though it may seem—subtly. For the Proposer's focus now is on the good of the commonwealth: he seems intent on realizing the maxim that people are the wealth of the nation. The trope of cannibalism, however, represents the apogee of consumption: 'I grant this food will be somewhat dear, and therefore very *proper for landlords;* who, as they have already devoured most of the parents, seem to have the best title to the children.'[28]

What is proposed, therefore, literalizes Protestant consumption of the Catholic poor; no simple cause-and-effect explication, as in the letter to Peterborough or the *Short View*, showing how rackrenting impoverishes rural Ireland, has the effect of this consumptionist fantasy. But the trope of cannibalism has a deeper resonance, reaching to the justification of Protestant consumption in the ideology of Protestant supremacy. That ideology has as its basis the fear that, left unprotected as in 1641, Protestant Ireland would be consumed by the Catholics, for they are barbarous, bloodthirsty and filled with hatred for Protestants. The cannibal, of course, is the very type of the barbarian, and legendary descriptions of the native Irish, as well as the polemics and sermons of the sixteenth and seventeenth century, often present them as cannibals. Allowed free rein, Catholics would literally or figuratively consume the Protestants. It is the mordancy, the 'toothiness', of this rhetoric of fear, fundamental to the defensive ideology of Protestant consumption, to which Swift's trope of cannibalism most specifically responds. That trope is one of Swift's best-known examples of satiric imagery, and working even beyond ridiculing the ideology of Protestant consumption, it functions also to *invert*, as Swift's satire does so often. We can understand that the whole of the *Proposal* rests upon thematic inversion—Swift is not the Proposer, the remedy proposed is not his, and, toward the end of the piece, the Proposer echoes various remedies

[28] Swift, *Prose Works*, vol. 12, p. 112.

Swift *had* proposed in earlier works, all of them aiming at self-sufficiency, simply to discard them as nowhere at all so efficacious as his recommendation of cannibalism. The inversion suits, in fact, the perverseness Swift has ascribed to Ireland in the *Short View* and *Maxims Controlled.* Finally, however, since the whole work pivots on the technique of inversion, inverting the objects of ideologically-imputed cannibalism—that is, proposing that Protestants become the cannibals—evokes its very opposite. For Catholics now become the objects of cannibalism *because* they are barbarously less than human: they can be eaten because prospectively, in the supremacist ideology that underlies the consumptionism mocked here, they are man-eaters themselves. So invertedly, the threat of Catholic consumption is itself invoked; and even justified, as Protestants are placed on the same plane as those they fear.

The *Modest Proposal,* Swift's bitterest comment on the Irish economy, is also one of the greatest and best-known satiric works in any language, a literary monument at the intersection of Swift's advocacy of reforms and his despair at gaining their adoption. It is rather fortuitous than the product of thematic development and aesthetic precision, that such an artistic achievement should come at the end of a decade more devoted to Irish affairs than any other period in Swift's writing career; but it is also true that nothing he wrote about Ireland before or after it meets the same literary standard. And by modern moral standards, the last of such works noticed here, the sermon 'Causes of the Wretched Condition of Ireland,' probably dating from the early 1730s, seems to degenerate into peevishness. Swift begins by indicating England's general culpability for Ireland's economic distortions, to be sure, and that more specifically of absentee landlords, yet hopeless that such factors can be altered, after touching quickly upon the preference for imports and luxuries among the gentry, he devotes himself at length to the character of the poor. Though hating oppression, Swift never considered that its victims were by that token more virtuous than their oppressors, an attitude discernible even in the *Modest Proposal.* On the contrary, the disposition of the poor to laziness, begging and thievery, and the dishonesty of servants, are themes that recur through his lesser-known Irish writings. But here, since he can expect no remedy for this issuing from landlords' treating tenants more justly, his proposals that education in charity schools be restricted to the children of the deserving poor, and that rural beggars be forced to stay in their own parishes lest they migrate to the city, seem by comparison niggardly, almost trivial. They hardly invoke the themes of consumption and dependence in the grander forms of *Irish Manufacture* or the *Drapier's Letters.* Yet these themes are very much sounded. English and Irish Protestant economic distortions are seen as the ultimate source of the defects of the poor, while even among them the fact is seen to operate that dependence causes distorted consumption. There is an implicit analogy, indeed, to the relation between England and Ireland, and between Irish Protestants and Catholic tenants, in the recognition that the dependence of the poor upon society at large accounts for their consuming from it, as beggars and thieves, disproportionately to their contributing to it. Here, however, the effect of economic distortions among the poor—which is to say, their own self-indulgence—can be somewhat corrected by selective education and by equalizing the burden of charity upon society. And here, too, Swift's recommendations—since it is a sermon, they are undisguisedly his own—seek to adjust Irish Protestant self-awareness. Only this time they look to the manner in which the practice of charity might be altered to increase its efficacy. For undifferentiated kindness merely blunts the edge of conscience, without relieving the weight of oppression.

But even these suggestions went unheeded. There is an element of the counterintuitive in Swift's efforts on behalf of Ireland for over a decade. Though he left his most memorable formulation of the human inclination to perverse thinking and action to 'On Poetry: A Rapsody', written in 1732:

> But *Man* we find the only Creature,
> Who, led by *Folly*, fights with *Nature;*
> Who, when *she* loudly cries, *Forbear,*
> With Obstinacy fixes there. (19–22)[29]

his satires had targeted human perversity well before he began to give public, albeit anonymous advice to Protestant Ireland in 1720. But the force of that obstinacy he recognized as a satirist and moralist he appears to have hesitated for some time to acknowledge as a writer on Irish economic affairs. We might say that he should have foreseen that his efforts were doomed; or we could echo the Whig literary tradition and consider that Swift's writings on Ireland were prompted mainly by hatred of the Whig government that had displaced his Tory friends and foreshortened his influence on English high politics. Perhaps, however, it is the case instead that, having gained public standing with the *Irish Manufacture* pamphlet, and increased it with the *Drapier's Letters,* he was tempted to equate his celebrity with formative influence on the Irish Protestant self-concept, and even Whig policy. Why else would he have sought an interview with Walpole in 1726? If such was the case, he came at length to his unhappy senses.

---

[29] Swift, *Poems,* vol. 2, p. 641.

By 1731 he could concede in a letter to the countess of Suffolk, 'I shall not attempt to convince England of any thing that relates to this kingdom. The Drapier . . . could not do it in relation to the halfpence . . . looking upon this kingdom's condition as absolutely desperate, I would not prescribe a dose to the dead.'[30] And perhaps in that latter comment he realised his inability to alter the self-awareness of Irish Protestants, an emblem of the very perversity he had satirized for years.

---

[30] Swift to the countess of Suffolk, 26 October 1731 (*Swift Corr.* vol. 3, pp. 500–1).

WORKS CITED

Adams, Percy G. *Travel Literature and the Evolution of the Novel.* Lexington: University Press of Kentucky, 1983.

Beier, A. L., David Cannadine, and James M. Rosenheim, eds. *The First Modern Society: Essays in Honour of Lawrence Stone.* Cambridge: Cambridge University Press, 1989.

Beller, Elmer A. *Propaganda in Germany during the Thirty Years War.* Princeton: Princeton University Press, 1940.

Bertelsen, Lance. "Ireland, Temple, and the Origins of the Drapier." *Papers on Language and Literature* 13 (1977): 413–19.

Bonner, W. H. *Captain William Dampier, Buccaneer-Author.* Stanford: Stanford University Press, 1934.

Bowen, H. V. *War and British Society, 1688–1815.* Cambridge: Cambridge University Press, 1998.

Bracher, Frederick. "The Maps in Gulliver's Travels." *Huntington Library Quarterly* 8 (1944–45): 59–74.

Brantlinger, Patrick. *Fictions of State: Culture and Credit in Britain, 1694–1994.* Ithaca: Cornell University Press, 1996.

Braudel, Fernand. *Civilization and Capitalism.* 2 vols. Translated by Siân Reynolds. New York: Harper & Row, 1979.

Butterfield, Herbert. *The Englishman and His History.* Cambridge: Cambridge University Press, 1944.

———. *The Whig Interpretation of History.* New York: Norton, 1965.

Cain, P. J., and A. G. Hopkins. *British Imperialism.* 2 vols. London: Longman, 1993.

Carpenter, Andrew, ed. "Jonathan Swift." In *The Field Day Anthology of Irish Writing.* 3 vols. Derry: Field Day Publications, 1991, I vol. 1, 327–94.

———, ed. *Verses in English from Eighteenth-Century Ireland.* Cork: Cork University Press, 1998.

Carswell, John. *The South Sea Bubble.* Stanford: Stanford University Press, 1960.

Case, Arthur E. *Four Essays on* Gulliver's Travels. Princeton: Princeton University Press, 1945.

Cordingly, David. *Under the Black Flag: The Romance and Reality of Life Among the Pirates.* San Diego: Harcourt Brace & Co., 1995.

Coughlin, Patricia. "'Cheap and Common Animals': The English Anatomy of Ireland in the Seventeenth Century." In *Literature and the English Civil War,* edited by Thomas Healy and Jonathan Sawday, 205–26. Cambridge: Cambridge University Press, 1990.

Clarendon, Edward Hyde, Earl of. *The Life of Edward Earl of Clarendon . . . in Which Is Included a Continuation of His History of the Grand Rebellion.* 3 vols. Oxford: Clarendon Press, 1827.

Connolly, S. J. "Eighteenth-Century Ireland: Colony or Ancien Régime?" In *The Making of Modern Irish History: Revisionism and the Revisionist Controversy,* 15–33. Edited by D. George Boyce and Alan O'Day. London: Routledge, 1996.

Cruickshanks, Eveline. *The Glorious Revolution.* London: Macmillian, 2000.

Curry, Patrick. *Prophecy and Power: Astrology in Early Modern England.* Princeton: Princeton University Press, 1989.

Dampier, William. *A Supplement to the Voyage Round the World.* Volume 2 of *A Collection of Voyages,* compiled by William Dampier. 4 vols. London, 1729.

Davis, Herbert, ed. *The Prose Works of Jonathan Swift.* 14 vols. Oxford: Basil Blackwell, 1939–68.

De Beer, G. R. *Sir Hans Sloane and the British Museum.* London: Oxford University Press, 1953.

Defoe, Daniel. "An Essay upon Projects." In *Political and Economic Writings of Daniel Defoe,* edited by W. R. Owens and P. N. Furbank. Vol. 8, *Social Reform,* 27–142. London: Pickering and Chatto, 2000.

———. "The Trade to India Critically and Calmly Consider'd." In vol. 17, *Trade,* of *Political and Economic Writings of Daniel Defoe.* 8 vols., edited by W. R. Owens and P. N. Furbank, 85–104. London: Pickering and Chatto, 2000.

———. "A New Voyage Round the World." In *Romances and Narratives by Daniel Defoe*, edited by George A. Aitken. Vol. 14. New York: AMS Press, 1974.

Dickson, P. G. M. *The Financial Revolution in England: A Study in the Development of Public Credit, 1688–1756.* New York: Macmillan, 1967.

Dodd, Nigel. *The Sociology of Money: Economics, Reason and Contemporary Society.* New York: Continuum Press, 1994.

Downie, J. A. *Robert Harley and the Press.* Cambridge: Cambridge University Press, 1979.

———. *Jonathan Swift: Political Writer.* London: Routledge, 1984.

Edwards, Philip. *The Story of the Voyage: Sea-Narratives in Eighteenth-Century England.* Cambridge: Cambridge University Press, 1994.

Ehrenpreis, Irvin. *Swift: The Man, His Works, and the Age.* 3 vols. Cambridge, MA: Harvard University Press, 1962–83.

Erskine-Hill, Howard. *Jonathan Swift: Gulliver's Travels.* Cambridge: Cambridge University Press, 1993.

Evelyn, John. *The Diary of John Evelyn.* 2 vols. Edited by William Bray. Akron: St. Dunstan Society, 1901.

Exquemelin, Alexander. *The Buccaneers of America.* New York: Dover Press, 1967.

Fabricant, Carole. *Swift's Landscape.* Notre Dame: Notre Dame Press, 1995.

Fitzgerald, Robert P. "Ancients and Moderns in Swift's Brobdingnag." *Journal of English and Germanic Philology* 87, no. 1 (1968): 89–100.

Flynn, Carol Houlihan. *The Body in Swift and Defoe.* Cambridge: Cambridge University Press, 1990.

Foster, Roy. *Modern Ireland, 1600–1972.* London: Penguin, 1989.

Fox, Christopher, ed. *Gulliver's Travels.* Boston: Bedford Books of St. Martin's Press, 1995.

Gandhi, Mohandas K. Letter to Maganlal Gandhi, May 18, 1911. In *The Collected Works of Mahatma Gandhi.* 90 vols. Delhi: Publications Division, Ministry of Information and Broadcasting, Govt. of India, 1958, vol. 11, letter no. 63.

Gardiner, Anne Barbeau. "Licking the Dust in Luggnagg: Swift's Reflections on the Legacy of King William's Conquest of Ireland." *Swift Studies* 8 (1993): 35–44.

Geneva, Ann. *Astrology and the Seventeenth Century Mind: William Lilly and the Language of the Stars.* Manchester: Manchester University Press, 1995.

Géracht, Maurice A. "Pedro de Mendez: Marrano Jew and Good Samaritan in Swift's Voyages." *Swift Studies* 5 (1990): 39–52.

Glacken, Clarence J. *Traces on the Rhodian Shore.* Berkeley: University of California Press, 1967.

Hill, B. W. *The Growth of Parliamentary Parties, 1689–1742.* London: Allen and Unwin Ltd., 1976.

Hubbard, Lucius L. *Contributions Towards a Bibliography of Gulliver's Travels.* Chicago: Walter M. Hill, 1922.

Israel, Jonathan. *The Dutch Republic: Its Rise, Greatness, and Fall, 1477–1806.* Oxford: Clarendon Press, 1995.

Jansen, Marius B. *The Making of Modern Japan.* Cambridge, MA: Harvard University Press, 2000.

Johnson, Samuel. *Life of Swift. Lives of the English Poets.* 3 vols. Edited by G. B. Hill. Oxford: Clarendon Press, 1905.

Kearney, Richard. *Postnationalist Ireland: Politics, Culture, Philosophy.* London: Routledge, 1997.

Kelly, Ann Cline. "Swift's Explorations of Slavery in Houyhnhnmland and Ireland." *Publications of the Modern Language Association* 91 (1976): 846–55.

———. *Jonathan Swift and Popular Culture: Myth, Media, and the Man.* New York: Palgrave, 2002.

Kiberd, Declan. *Irish Classics.* Cambridge, Mass.: Harvard University, 2001.

Kiernan, V. G. *The Lords of Human Kind: Black Man, Yellow Man, and White Man in an Age of Empire.* Boston: Little, Brown, & Co., 1969.

Lamb, Jonathan. *Preserving the Self in the South Seas, 1680–1840.* Chicago: University of Chicago Press, 2001.

Landa, Louis, ed. *Gulliver's Travels and Other Writings.* Boston: Houghton Mifflin, 1960.

Lecky, W. E. H. *A History of Ireland in the Eighteenth Century.* 5 vols. London: Longmans, Green, and Co., 1913.

Lock, F. P. "The Text of Gulliver's Travels." *Modern Language Review* 76 (1981): 513–33.

Mahony, Robert. *Jonathan Swift: The Irish Identity.* New Haven: Yale University Press, 1995.

Markley, Robert. "'Credit Exhausted': Satire and Scarcity in the 1690s." In *Cutting Edges: Postmodern Critical Essays on Eighteenth-Century Satire,* edited by James Gill, 110–26. Knoxville: University of Tennessee Press, 1995.

MacGregor, Arthur. *Sir Hans Sloane: Collector, Scientist, Antiquary, Founding Father of the British Museum.* London: British Museum Press, 1994.

Macpherson, Jay. "Swift's Very Knowing American." In *Lumen,* edited by Donald W. Nichol and Margarete Smith, vol. 13, 109–116. Edmonton: Academic Printing and Publishing, 1994.

McLoughlin, Thomas. *Contesting Ireland: Irish Voices against England in the Eighteenth Century.* Dublin: Four Courts Press, 1999.

McMinn, Joseph, ed. *Swift's Irish Pamphlets: An Introductory Selection.* Gerrards Cross: Colin Smythe, 1991.

———. *Jonathan's Travels.* Belfast: Appletree Press, 1994.

Merians, Linda E. *Envisioning the Worst: Representations of "Hottentots" in Early-Modern England.* Newark: University of Delaware Press, 2001.

Moll, Herman. *Atlas Geographus: or, A Compleat System of Geography, Ancient and Modern.* London, 1711–1717.

Montag, Warren. *The Unthinkable Swift: The Spontaneous Philosophy of a Church of England Man.* London: Verso, 1994.

Montagu, Charles. *An Epistle to the Right Honorable Earl of Dorsett and Middlesex, Lord Chamberlain of His Majesties Household.* London, 1690. Reprinted in *Poems of the Reign of William III,* edited by Earl Miner. Los Angeles: University of California Press, 1974. Pub. 166 of the Augustan Reprint Society, Clark Memorial Library.

Morris, James. *Pax Britannica: The Climax of an Empire.* San Diego: Harcourt Brace Jovanovich, 1968.

Nash, Richard Nash. "Of Sorrels, Bays, and Dapple Greys." *Swift Studies* 15 (2000): 110–115.

Needham, Joseph. *Science and Civilization in China.* Vol. 5, part 7, *Military Technology: The Gunpowder Epic.* Cambridge: Cambridge University Press, 1986.

Ovington, John. *A Voyage to Suratt in the Year 1689*. London, 1696.

Phillips, Richard. *Mapping Men and Empire*. London: Routledge, 1997.

Pocock, J. G. A. *The Machiavellian Moment*. Princeton: Princeton University Press, 1975.

Poovey, Mary. *A History of the Modern Fact: Problems of Knowledge in the Sciences of Wealth and Society*. Chicago: University of Chicago Press, 1998.

Purchas, Samuel. *Purchas His Pilgrimage*. 4 vols. London, 1617.

Rawson, Claude. *God, Gulliver, and Genocide: Barbarism and the European Imagination, 1492–1945*. Oxford: Oxford University Press, 2001.

Real, Hermann J. "Voyages to Nowhere: More's Utopia and Swift's Gulliver's Travels. In *Eighteenth-Century Contexts*, edited by Howard D. Weinbrot, Peter J. Schakel, and Stephen E. Karian, 96–113. Madison: Wisconsin University Press, 2001.

Real, Hermann J., and Heinz J. Vienken. "What's in a Name: Pedro de Mendez Again." *American Notes and Queries* 24, nos. 9–10 (May–June 1986): 136–40.

Richardson, John. "Swift, A Modest Proposal, and Slavery." *Essays in Criticism* 51, no. 4 (2001): 404–23.

Rivero, Albert J., ed. *Gulliver's Travels*. New York: Norton, 2002.

Rodino, Richard H. "'Splendide Mendax': Authors, Characters, and Readers in Gulliver's Travels." *Publications of the Modern Language Association PMLA* 106, no. 5 (1991): 1054–70.

Roberts, Lissa. "Going Dutch: Situating Science in the Dutch Enlightenment." In *The Sciences in Enlightened Europe*, edited by William Clark, Jan Golinski, and Simon Schaffer, 350–88. Chicago: University of Chicago Press, 1999.

Rogers, Pat. "Gulliver's Glasses." In *The Art of Jonathan Swift*, edited by Clive T. Probyn, 179–88. London: Clarke, Doble & Brendon, 1978.

———, ed. *Jonathan Swift: The Complete Poems*. New York: Penguin, 1983.

Ross, Angus. *Swift: Gulliver's Travels*. London: Edward Arnold, 1968.

Rothschild, Emma. "Globalization and the Return to History." *Foreign Policy* 115 (1999): 106–116.

Rusnock, Andrea. "Biopolitics: Political Arithmetic in the Enlightenment." In *The Sciences in Enlightened Europe*, edited by William Clark, Jan

Golinski, and Simon Schaffer, 49–68 Chicago: University of Chicago Press, 1999.

Said, Edward W. *The World, the Text, and the Critic.* Cambridge, Mass.: Harvard University Press, 1983.

Schama, Simon. *A History of Britain.* 2 vols. New York: Hyperion, 2001.

Schmidt, Johann M. "Swift's Uses of Facts and Fiction: *The Drapier's Letters.*" In *Proceedings of the First Münster Symposium on Jonathan Swift,* edited by Hermann J. Real and Heinz J. Vienken, 247–256. München: Wilhelm Fink Verlag, 1985.

Sherbo, Arthur. "Swift and Travel Literature." *Modern Language Studies* 9, no. 3 (1979): 114–27.

Sherman, Stuart. *Telling Time: Clocks, Diaries, and English Diurnal Form, 1660–1785.* Chicago: University of Chicago Press, 1996.

Shimada, Takau. "Xamosi Where Gulliver Landed." *Notes and Queries* 228, no. 1 (February 30, 1998): 33.

Simms, J. G. *The Williamite Confiscation in Ireland, 1690–1703.* London: Faber and Faber, 1956.

Sobel, Dava, and William J. H. Andrewes. *The Illustrated Longitude.* London: Fourth Estate, 1995.

Spivak, Gayatri Chakravorty. "Can the Subaltern Speak?" In *Marxism and the Interpretation of Culture,* edited by Cary Nelson and Lawrence Grossberg, 271–313. Urbana: University of Illinois Press, 1988.

Stafford, Barbara M. *Voyage into Substance: Art, Science, Nature, and the Illustrated Travel Account, 1760–1840.* Cambridge, Mass.: MIT Press, 1984.

Stone, Lawrence. *The Past and the Present Revisited.* London: Routledge, 1987.

Swift, Jonathan. *Conduct of the Allies. Prose Works of Jonathan Swift,* Vol. 4: *Political Tracts, 1711–1713,* edited by Herbert Davis et al., 5–65. 14 vols. Oxford: Basil Blackwell, 1939–68.

———. *The Correspondence of Jonathan Swift.* Edited by Harold Williams. 4 vols. Oxford: Clarendon Press, 1963.

———. *A Tale of a Tub.* Edited by A. C. Guthkelch and D. Nichol Smith, 2nd ed. Oxford: Clarendon Press, 1958.

Tanner, Marcus. *Ireland's Holy Wars: The Struggles for a Nation's Soul, 1500–2000.* New Haven: Yale University Press, 2001.

Thomson, Janice E. *Mercenaries, Pirates, and Sovereigns.* Princeton: Princeton University Press, 1994.

Treadwell, Michael. "Benjamin Motte, Andrew Tooke and *Gulliver's Travels.*" In *Proceedings of the First Munster Symposium on Jonathan Swift,* edited by Hermann J. Real and Heinz J. Vienken, 277–304. Munich: Wilhelm Fink Verlag, 1985.

———. "The Text of *Gulliver's Travels,* Again." *Swift Studies* 10 (1995): 62–79.

Wagner, Peter. *Reading Iconotexts: From Swift to the French Revolution.* London: Reaktion Books, 1995.

Wallis, Helen. "The Patagonian Giants." In *Byron's Journal of His Circumnavigation, 1764–1766,* edited by Robert E. Gallagher, 185–96. Cambridge: Cambridge University Press, 1962.

Welcher, Jeanne K. *Gulliveriana.* Vol. 7, *Visual Imitations of Gulliver's Travels, 1726–1830.* Delmar, New York: Scholar's Facsimiles and Reprints, 1999.

White, Michael. *Isaac Newton: The Last Sorcerer.* Reading, Mass.: Addison-Wesley, 1997.

Williams, Harold, ed. *Gulliver's Travels.* London: First Edition Club, 1926.

FOR FURTHER READING

Note: The Works Cited constitutes a thorough bibliography of useful works on the period as well as on Swift's life and career. Below we recommend a few texts not cited in this volume and therefore not listed there.

Barnett, Louise K. *Swift's Poetic Worlds.* Newark: University of Delaware Press, 1981.

Douglas, Aileen, Patrick Kelly, and Ian Campbell Ross, eds. *Locating Swift: Essays From Dublin on the 250th Anniversary of the Death of Jonathan Swift, 1667–1745.* Dublin, Four Courts Press, 1998.

Downie, J. A. "The Political Significance of *Gulliver's Travels.*" In *Swift and His Contexts,* edited by John Irwin Fischer, Hermann J., Real, and James Woolley, 1–19. New York: AMS Press, 1989.

Elias, A. C. *Swift at Moor Park: Problems in Biography and Criticism.* Philadelphia: University of Pennsylvania Press, 1982.

Ellis, Frank, ed. *Swift vs. Mainwaring:* The Examiner *and* The Medley. Oxford: Clarendon Press, 1985.

Ferguson, Oliver W. *Jonathan Swift and Ireland.* Urbana: University of Illinois Press, 1962.

Fischer, John Irwin, and Donald C. Mell, Jr. *Contemporary Studies of Swift's Poetry.* Newark: University of Delaware Press, 1981.

Fox, Christopher, and Tooley, Brenda. *Walking Naboth's Vineyard: New Studies of Swift.* Notre Dame: University of Notre Dame Press, 1995.

———. "A Critical History of *Gulliver's Travels.*" In *Gulliver's Travels,* edited by Christopher Fox, 269–304. New York: St. Martin's, 1995.

Ginzburg, Carlo. "Making Things Strange: The Prehistory of a Literary Device." In *Representations* 56 (1996): 8–28.

Goldgar, Bertrand A. *Walpole and the Wits: The Relation of Politics to Literature, 1722–1742.* Lincoln: University of Nebraska Press, 1976.

Harth, Philip. "The Problem of Political Allegory in Gulliver's Travels." *Modern Philology* 73 (1976): 40–47.

———. *Swift and Anglican Rationalism: The Religious Background of* A Tale of a Tub. Chicago: University of Chicago Press, 1961.

Karian, Stephen. "Problems and Paratexts in Eighteenth-Century Collections of Swift." *Studies in the Literary Imagination* 32, no. 1 (1999), 59–80.

McMinn, Joseph. *Jonathan Swift: A Literary Life.* London: Macmillan, 1991.

Nokes, David. *Jonathan Swift, A Hypocrite Reversed: A Critical Biography.* Oxford: Oxford University Press, 1985.

Parker, Todd. "Swift's 'A Description of a City Shower': The Epistemological Force of Filth." In *1650–1850: Ideas, Aesthetics, and Inquiries in the Early Modern Era,* 4(1998), 285–304.

Rawson, Claude. "The Injured Lady and the Drapier: A Reading of Swift's Irish Tracts." *Prose Studies* 3, no. 1 (1980): 15–43.

———, ed. *The Character of Swift's Satire: A Revised Focus.* Newark: University of Delaware Press, 1983.

———, ed. *English Satire and the Satirical Tradition.* Oxford: Basil Blackwell, 1984.

Real, Hermann J., and Richard H. Rodino, eds. *Reading Swift: Papers from the Second Münster Symposium on Swift.* München: Wilhelm Fink Verlag, 1993.

Real, Hermann J., and Helgard Stöver-Leidig, eds. *Reading Swift: Papers from the Third Münster Symposium on Swift.* München: Wilhelm Fink Verlag, 1998.

———. *Reading Swift: Papers from the Fourth Münster Symposium on Swift.* München: Wilhelm Fink Verlag, 2003.

Ross, Angus, and David Woolley, eds. *Jonathan Swift: Major Works.* Revised edition. Oxford University Press, 2003.

Stewart, Susan. *On Longing: Narratives of the Miniature, the Gigantic, the Souvenir, the Collection.* Durham: Duke University Press, 1993.

Sussman, Charlotte. *Consumer Protest, Gender, and British Slavery, 1713–1833.* Stanford: Stanford University Press, 2000.

Swift, Jonathan. *Journal to Stella.* Edited by Herbert Williams. 2 vols. Oxford: Clarendon Press, 1948.

Woolley, James. *Swift's Later Poems: Studies in Circumstances and Texts.* New York: Garland, 1988.

———, ed. *Jonathan Swift and Thomas Sheridan: The Intelligencer.* Oxford: Clarendon Press, 1992.

Irish and Colonial History

Armitage, David. *The Ideological Origins of the British Empire.* Cambridge: Cambridge University Press, 2000.

Beckett, J. C. *Confrontations: Studies in Irish History.* Totowa: Rowman and Littlefield, 1972.

———. *The Anglo-Irish Tradition.* Ithaca: Cornell University Press, 1976.

Canny, Nicholas. "The Marginal Kingdom: Ireland as a Problem in the First British Empire," *In Strangers Within the Realm: Cultural Margins of the First British Empire* edited by Bernard Bailyn and Philip D. Morgan, 35–66. Chapel Hill: University of North Carolina Press, 1991.

———, and Anthony Pagden. *Colonial Identity in the Atlantic World, 1500–1800.* Princeton: Princeton University Press, 1987.

Connolly, S. J. ed. *Political Ideas in Eighteenth-Century Ireland.* Dublin: Four Courts Press, 2000.

———, ed. *The Oxford Companion to Irish History.* Oxford: Clarendon Press, 1998.

Hechter, Michael. *Internal Colonialism: The Celtic Fringe in British National Development, 1536–1966.* Berkeley: University of California Press, 1975.

Marshall, P. J., ed. *The Eighteenth Century,* edited by William Roger Louis Vol. 2, *The Oxford History of the British Empire.* Oxford: Oxford University Press, 1998–99.

Marshall, P. J. and Glyndwr Williams. *The Great Map of Mankind: Perceptions of New Worlds in the Age of Enlightenment.* Cambridge, Mass.: Harvard University Press, 1982.

Neill, Anna. "Buccaneer Ethnography: Nature, Culture, and Nation in the Journals of William Dampier." *Eighteenth-Century Studies* 33, no. 2 (2000): 165–80.

CHRONOLOGY

Year	*Swift's Life and Major Works*	*Irish History*
1641		Sir Phelim O'Neill leads Catholic uprising against "New English" Settlers
1642		
1643		
1646		Sir John Temple's lurid atrocity stories promote Protestant backlash
1649	Thomas Swift, grandfather of JS, moves to Ireland; he remains passionately loyal to Charles I	Cromwell massacres garrisons at Wexford and Drogheda; Ireland truly conquered by English
1650		Beginning in this decade, the power of Catholic "Old English" overthrown
1652		Cromwellian legislation for settling of Ireland targets resistant landowners (Act of Settlement)
1653		Land stripped from Cromwell's opponents; priests deported to Barbados
1654		William Petty begins Down Survey: a mapping operation to facilitate land confiscation
1655		
1660		Stuarts restored (Charles II to Anne); Charles II restores some land to Catholic "innocents" in Ireland

English/British History	*Pertinent Cultural Events*	*Fictional Events in* Gulliver's Travels
Charles I's policies spawn insurrection in Ulster; English Parliament enumerates grievances against him in hostile petition (The Grand Remonstrance)	Authorities in Japan restrict Dutch traders to a small island in the harbor of Nagasaki: isolationist policy maintains a tightly controlled contact with Europe	
English Civil War begins as armies of Charles I and Parliament clash	Puritans close theaters; Isaac Newton born; Abel Tasman sails to Van Dieman's Land	
The Solemn League and Covenant: by conceding Anglican reforms, Parliament makes alliance with Presbyterian Scots		
Civil War tips in favor of Cromwell and Parliament; King Charles tries to escape	Sir John Temple publishes *History of the Irish Rebellion*	In this year or the following one, the Academy of Projectors in Lagado is founded
Charles I is beheaded; Puritan Interregnum begins; Cromwell suppresses Levellers, invades Ireland	The "Ranters" emerge: an enthusiastic movement challenging Cromwell and mainstream Puritans	
Navigation Act, directed against Dutch "middlemen," aims at monopoly on foreign trade	Emergence of more enthusiastic sects such as Quakers and Fifth Monarchists; Dutch South Africa founded	
First Anglo-Dutch War (over Navigation Act)	Birth of William Dampier	
Cromwell established as Lord Protector	James Naylor (1618–1660) recognized by some Quakers as the new Messiah	
Confiscated Irish land used as spoils of war, to pay Cromwell's soldiers		
Cromwell captures Jamaica from Spain		
Restoration to throne of Charles II, a Stuart, who returns from exile in France; Act of Indemnity and Oblivion preemptively pardons most opponents of Charles I	Royal Society founded; includes William Petty; theaters open; Daniel Defoe born; Hans Sloane born; Samuel Pepys begins diary	

Year	*Swift's Life and Major Works*	*Irish History*
1661		
1663		Cattle Act restricts export of cattle from Ireland through prohibitive duty
1666	Death of Swift's father some seven months before the birth of his son	
1667	JS born in Dublin to Abigail Swift (after death of his father)	Cattle exports to England prohibited
1675		
1676		
1678		
1680		
1681	Birth of "Stella" (Esther Johnson)	
1682	JS admitted to Trinity College, Dublin	
1685		James II elevates Tyrconnell, who pursues pro-Catholic policy in Ireland
1686	JS receives B.A. degree from Trinity College, Dublin ("by special grace")	Law and army begin to be Catholicized

English/British History	*Pertinent Cultural Events*	*Fictional Events in* Gulliver's Travels
Fifth Monarchists attempt armed revolt against Charles II	Brilliant age of English drama begins	Gulliver born (either this year or in 1660)
Navigation Act passed; restricts exports to colonies to goods shipped from England	Drury Lane Theatre built; Samuel Butler publishes *Hudibras,* Part I	
Great Fire in London; Museum-like "repository" established by Royal Society	Isaac Newton discovers law of gravity	
Treaty ends naval wars between English and Dutch	John Milton publishes *Paradise Lost*	
Money from French monarch Louis XIV enables Charles II some independence from Parliament	Royal Observatory founded at Greenwich	Gulliver enters Emanuel College at age fourteen
Robert Walpole born	Dampier in Bay of Campeachy with buccaneer logwood cutters	
Political panic about "Popish Plot" leads to unjust trials and executions		Gulliver bound as apprentice to Mr. Bates
Buccaneers Sharp and Ringrose leave Will, a Muskito Indian, at Juan Fernandez	Dampier involved in sacking Panama; Lionel Wafer sojourns with Cuna Indians there	
Defeat of Duke of Monmouth's conspiracy to claim throne	John Dryden publishes *Absalom and Achitophel;* Dampier begins South Sea voyages	
Exclusion Crisis, conflict over succession of James, reaches boiling point	Edmund Halley investigating appearance of comet that bears his name	Gulliver goes to Leiden to study medicine
Death of Charles II; James II, a Catholic, succeeds; Monmouth executed after second rebellion	Dampier at Juan Fernandez, rescues Will; birth of John Gay	
James II appoints Catholics to high positions		

Year	*Swift's Life and Major Works*	*Irish History*
1687		Tyrconnell sworn in as Lord Deputy; he threatens to restore ancestral estates to Catholics
1688–89	JS leaves Ireland for England as a result of turmoil in Ireland; tutors young Stella at Moor Park, home of Sir William Temple	Jacobite parliament in Ireland; James II "abdicates" throne, flees to France after William of Orange arrives with large fleet; Marlborough defects from James II to William
1690	First symptoms of Ménière's syndrome; JS returns to Ireland on medical advice; dizziness and deafness will afflict him intermittently throughout his life	Battle of Boyne in Ireland marks triumph of Williamite forces over Jacobites (supporters of James II); it is Ireland's misfortune to be theater of European war
1691	JS returns to England; serves as secretary to Sir William Temple at Moor Park	Treaty of Limerick offers decent terms to defeated Catholics
1692	JS receives M.A. at Oxford (a step to ordination)	
1693		
1694	JS returns to Ireland; takes orders in the Irish branch of the Anglican Church	
1695	JS appointed rector of Kilroot; his congregation greatly outnumbered by dissenting Presbyterians	Penal laws (contrary to Treaty of Limerick) begin to impose legal disabilities on Catholics; Catholic education restricted
1696	JS returns to Moor Park; works on *A Tale of a Tub*	

English / British History	*Pertinent Cultural Events*	*Fictional Events in* Gulliver's Travels
James II declares general tolerance: liberty of conscience to Papists and non-conformists	Newton publishes *Principia mathematica;* Sloane in Jamaica as physician to governor; death of Sir William Petty	
Birth of a potential Catholic royal heir alarms English Protestants; Parliament invites Dutch Protestant, William of Orange, to assume throne; War of the Grand Alliance begins; Parliament issues Declaration of Rights	Still in Dutch exile, John Locke publishes *Letter Concerning Toleration* and anti-absolutist *Two Treatises on Government;* Aphra Behn publishes *Oroonoko;* birth of Alexander Pope; Dampier marooned at Nicobar	Gulliver resumes medical practice in London
Joint rule of William and Mary begins: a unique phenomenon in English history; they remain guarded by Dutch troops; Newton becomes Warden of the Royal Mint	Dampier observes Australian aborigines; also acquires Jeoly, the "Painted Prince"	
	Sir William Petty's *The Political Anatomy of Ireland* is published after his death; Dampier back in England	
	Atlantic and Indian Oceans become infested with pirates	
English monarch's private debt becomes a *national* debt	Meeting of diarists: Dampier dines with John Evelyn and Samuel Pepys	
"Financial Revolution": Bank of England is established		
Pirate Henry Every plunders ship of Mughal Emperor, causing fury at English in Surat	Lapse of Licensing Act unleashes press. Age of "Grub Street" begins	
	John Ovington publishes *A Voyage to Suratt;* Captain Kidd, mandated to hunt pirates, reaches Madagascar in the *Adventure Galley*	

Year	*Swift's Life and Major Works*	*Irish History*
1697		Catholic clergy banished by act of Parliament
1698		Book by Molyneux disputes legislative supremacy of English parliament
1699	Death of Sir William Temple; JS domestic chaplain to Lord Berkeley in Dublin; JS publishes first political pamphlet	Woollen Act ends export of woollen manufactures from Ireland to any place other than England (which had prohibitive duties)
1700		
1701	Stella (Esther Johnson) moves to Dublin	Archbishop Marsh's library built in Dublin; Williamite land confiscations enrich Dutch favorites
1702	JS receives doctor of divinity degree from Trinity College, Dublin	
1703		William King made archbishop of Dublin; opposes most of the penal laws
1704	*A Tale of a Tub* and *Battle of the Books* and *The Mechanical Operation of the Spirit* published anonymously	Catholics barred from public office, from voting, from education, from the military, and from inheriting land
1706		

English/British History	*Pertinent Cultural Events*	*Fictional Events in* Gulliver's Travels
	Dampier publishes *New Voyage Round the World,* with maps by Herman Moll; Captain Kidd attacks Moorish ship	
Westminster Parliament condemns Molyneux's pamphlet	William Molyneux publishes *The Case of Ireland's Being Bound*	
Question of succession to the throne of Spain heats up European politics	Dampier sails to East Indies, Australia, and New Guinea (1699–1701); publishes his *Discourse of Winds;* meets *Antelope*	Gulliver sails to Lilliput, southwest of Sumatra, in *Antelope* (1699–1702)
Carlos II names grandson of Louis XIV as heir to Spanish throne	Anonymous pamphlet published in London calls for a law to enact the castration of "Popish Ecclesiastics"	
War of the Spanish Succession begins. Land forces in hands of the earl of Marlborough	Much attention to hanging of Captain Kidd, a supposed pirate-hunter accused of turning pirate	Gulliver leaves Blefuscu
Queen Anne succeeds William III; Marlborough family dominates ministry until 1710; buccaneers enlist as legal privateers in war against France	Dampier courtmartialed for excessively harsh discipline aboard his ship	Gulliver returns to England; departs for Surat
John Churchill, now duke of Marlborough, captures Bonn and Limburg	Dampier publishes *A Voyage to New Holland;* Newton made President of Royal Society	Gulliver sails to Brobdingnag (northwest coast of North America)
Marlborough triumphant in Battle of Blenheim; French soundly defeated; the power of Louis XIV is checked	Dampier sails around the world (1703–1707); George Psalmanazar, impersonating a native of Formosa, publishes spurious description of that island	
Marlborough routs French at Battle of Ramillies	Halley predicts return of comet	Gulliver departs again; will end up near Japan (1706–1710)

Year	*Swift's Life and Major Works*	*Irish History*
1707	JS writes *The Story of the Injur'd Lady* (not published until 1746); back in England, JS seeking remission of tax on Irish clergy; moving in Whig circles of Addison and Steele	Ireland is excluded from the Act of Union—a turning point in Irish history; Swift depicts Ireland as a discarded mistress
1708	JS meets Esther Vanhomrigh in London; writes against the repeal of Test Act for Presbyterians (an item on the Whig agenda); publishes *Bickerstaff* papers	
1709	JS, as emissary of Church of Ireland, still seeking remission of a clerical tax (First Fruits)	Copyright Act does not extend to Dublin, so book trade there thrives on reprints
1710	Death of JS's mother; JS writes the *Journal to Stella* to Esther Johnson; he is recruited as writer for Tory *Examiner;* accuses Whigs of waging war for private gain	Peaceful transfer of power as Whig ministry falls and Tories, led by Harley and Bolingbroke, take power
1711	JS publishes *An Argument Against Abolishing Christianity* and *The Conduct of the Allies*	Tories, aided by Swift's pen, maneuver to topple Marlborough
1712	JS meets John Arbuthnot	
1713	JS installed as dean of St. Patrick's Cathedral in Dublin; forms Scriblerus Club with circle of leading English literati	
1714	JS returns to Ireland after fall of Tory ministry; Hester Vanhomrigh ("Vanessa") follows him to Ireland; *Public Spirit of the Whigs*	

English/British History	*Pertinent Cultural Events*	*Fictional Events in Gulliver's Travels*
Act of Union unites England and Scotland as Great Britain; Union Jack adopted as national flag	Sir Hans Sloane begins serial publication of *Natural History of Jamaica;* William Funnell's *Voyage Round the World*	Gulliver arrives at Fort St. George (Madras), and then Laputa (between Japan and California)
Robert Walpole assumes first major post as secretary of war; Marlborough defeats French at Oudenarde	Dampier sails to the South Sea and around the world as pilot for Woodes Rogers (1708–1711)	Gulliver leaves Laputa
Marlborough wins a pyrrhic victory at Malplaquet; Copyright Act passed	Dampier and Woodes Rogers rescue Alexander Selkirk from the Juan Fernandez island cluster	Gulliver in Luggnagg and Japan
Tory ministry, led by Oxford and Bolingbroke, initiates peace policy against wishes of Dutch allies	Anonymous Dublin reprint of 1700 pamphlet calling for a law to enact the castration of Catholic priests	After a brief return home, Gulliver sails as captain of *Adventure.* He ends up in Land of the Houyhnhnms (1711–1715), somewhere southwest of Madagascar
Marlborough dismissed by Tory cabinet; South Sea Company founded; Occasional Conformity Bill passed	Herman Moll's *Atlas Geographus,* a periodical. begins to appear (1711–1717); Handel's opera *Rinaldo* success in London; Psalmanazar widely recognized as a fraud	
Marlborough in exile; Walpole in London Tower on charges of corruption in arranging military contracts	Woodes Rogers, *A Cruising Voyage Around the World;* Hans Sloane becomes physician to Queen Anne	
Tory-brokered Treaty of Utrecht ends War of Spanish Succession, leaves Britain dominant in America; buccaneers return to piracy as usual	Scriblerus Club founded; includes Jonathan Swift, Alexander Pope, John Arbuthnot, and John Gay; Pope publishes *Windsor Forest*	
Queen Anne dies; George I succeeds; Whigs assume control of government; Walpole becomes paymaster-General	Longitude Act establishes huge prize for method of determining longitude at sea; Pope publishes final version of *Rape of the Lock*	

Year	*Swift's Life and Major Works*	*Irish History*
1715	Ministerial friends in the Tower (Oxford) or exile (Bolingbroke)	
1716		
1719		Spanish troops land in Scotland in support of "Old Pretender"; Toleration Act for Protestant Dissenters
1720	JS publishes "The Bubble"; first important Irish tract, *A Proposal for the Universal Use of Irish Manufacture*	British Parliament passes Declaratory Act, which subordinates Irish Parliament
1721	JS begins working on *Gulliver's Travels*	
1722		Wood's halfpence controversy begins
1724	*Drapier's Letters* campaign in Dublin raises question of Ireland's subordination to English Parliament	Lord Cartaret sent to Ireland to deal with Wood's halfpence crisis
1726	*Gulliver's Travels* published under "Gulliver" pseudonym in London; JS returns to Dublin	Crop failures and potato shortage
1727	On JS's final visit to England, he longs to return to Ireland because Stella is seriously ill; he writes "Ireland" and "Holyhead. September 25, 1727"	
1728	Death of Stella; JS publishes *A Short View of the State of Ireland* two months later	
1729	JS publishes *A Modest Proposal*	Famine continues
1730	JS publishes "A Libel on Doctor Delaney, and a Certain Great Lord"	

English/British History	Pertinent Cultural Events	Fictional Events in Gulliver's Travels
Unsuccessful Jacobite uprising in Scotland around "Old Pretender"	Death of Dampier in London; spurious voyage to East Indies published by William Symson	Gulliver, age fifty-four, returns to England by way of Lisbon
Walpole devises "sinking fund" to pay off national debt over time		
Hans Sloane becomes president of Royal College of Physicians	Daniel Defoe publishes *Robinson Crusoe* (taking off from stories of Selkirk and Will)	
Scandal and turmoil from South Sea Bubble in England and Mississippi Bubble in France	Japanese scholars permitted a window into the world through Dutch books on medicine and other sciences	Gulliver begins to write up his travels
Sir Robert Walpole rises to power by containing Bubble crisis		
Atterbury conspiracy on behalf of "Old Pretender"	Defoe publishes *Moll Flanders*	
Walpole sees Irish boycott of coin as subversive desire for independence	*A General History of the Pyrates* published, possibly by Defoe (the attribution is disputed)	
	First issue of *The Craftsman* (opposition journal attacking "crafty" Walpole)	
Death of George I; George II succeeds; Walpole, who has cultivated friendship with Queen Caroline, stays in power	Death of Newton; Sir Hans Sloane becomes President of Royal Society	"Letter to Cousin Sympson" has date, probably fictitious, of April 2, 1727, making Gulliver sixty-six years old
	Pope publishes *The Dunciad* in three books; Gay's *The Beggar's Opera* produced	
Beginning of nine years of military conflict with Maroons in Jamaica	Colley Cibber made Poet Laureate; Methodist Society at Oxford	

Year	*Swift's Life and Major Works*	*Irish History*
1735	Faulkner edition of *The Works of Jonathan Swift*, with corrected version of *Gulliver's Travels*, published in Dublin	
1739	"Verses on the Death of Dr. Swift" is published	Duties on woollen exports to Britain lifted
1742	Health of JS declines	Handel's *Messiah* first performed in Dublin
1745	Death of JS after three years of mental decline and aphasia	

English/British History	*Pertinent Cultural Events*	*Fictional Events in* Gulliver's Travels
	Pope publishes "Epistle to Dr. Arbuthnot"; death of Arbuthnot	
War of Jenkin's Ear against Spain		
	Death of Pope	
Jacobite rebellion (1745–46) leads to crushing of Jacobites; last dynastic war in British history	London College of Surgeons founded	

CREDITS

From Harold Williams, ed., *The Poems of Jonathan Swift,* Volume I, Second Edition. England, Oxford University Press. Copyright © 1937.

Excerpts from William Dampier, *A New Voyage Round the World.* Copyright © 1968. Reprinted by permission of Dover Publications, Inc.

Edward W. Said, "Swift as Intellectual," from *The World, the Text, and the Critic,* pp. 72–87. Cambridge, Mass: Harvard University Press. Reprinted by permission of the publisher. Copyright © 1983 by Edward W. Said.

Clement Hawes, "Three Times Round the Globe: Gulliver and Colonial Discourse," *Cultural Critique* 18 (Spring 1991): 187–214. Reprinted by permission of the publisher, the University of Minnesota Press.

Carole Fabricant, "Speaking for the Irish Nation: The Drapier, the Bishop, and the Problems of Colonial Representation," *ELH* 66:2 (1999): 337–372. © the Johns Hopkins University Press. Reprinted with permission of the Johns Hopkins University Press.

Robert Mahony, "Protestant Dependence and Consumption in Swift's Irish Writings," from *Political Ideas in 18th-Century Ireland* (Four Courts Press, Dublin, 2000), is reproduced with the kind permission of Robert Mahony and Four Courts Press.